CURRENT ISSUES IN PUBLIC ADMINISTRATION

Sixth Edition

Frederick S. Lane

Baruch College, CUNY

Bedford/St. Martin's
Boston • New York

In memory of
J. Peter Altgeld Adler
February 5, 1969 – May 30, 1995
They give birth astride a grave. The light gleams
for an instant, and then it is night once more.
—Samuel Beckett in *Waiting for Godot*

Executive Editor: James R. Headley
Manager, Publishing Services: Emily Berleth
Project Management: Dewey Publishing Services
Cover Design: Evelyn Horovicz
Cover Art: Copyright © Rebecca Ruegger/SIS

Library of Congress Catalog Card Number: 97-65192

Manufactured in the United States of America.

4 3 2 1 0 9
f e d c b a

For information, write:
Bedford/St. Martin's
75 Arlington Street
Boston, MA 02116
(617-426-7440)

ISBN: 0-312-15249-3

Acknowledgments

Acknowledgments and copyrights appear at the back of the book on pages 428-429,
which constitute an extension of the copyright page.

It is a violation of the law to reproduce these selections by any means whatsoever
without the written permission of the copyright holder.

Contents

●●

PREFACE

●●●

ABOUT THE BOOK

There are 20 million civilian public employees in some 86,000 units of government in the United States today. Governmental expenditures add up to about one-third of the nation's total of goods and services. It is hard to imagine any aspect of contemporary life in which government and especially its administrative agencies are not involved. Public bureaucracies deliver most of our educational and health care services, fight fires and crime, protect the air and water, and regulate business practices—just to list a few public functions. No matter what the contemporary challenge—AIDS, drugs, homelessness, political change in Eastern Europe—public administration is central to the response.

As important as public bureaucracies are, Americans have shown concern about the bureaucratization of modern society. Many claim that government is too big and tries to do too much, that bureaucracy only means red tape and inefficiency, and that public administrators are too powerful in American life. Yet there are others who claim that government needs to provide even more services, especially for the poor and disadvantaged; these Americans often view public organizations more favorably, although they are still interested in making government work better. These concerns are as current as today's newspaper headlines or TV news stories. And the background for much of this discussion can be found in this volume, *Current Issues in Public Administration.*

This sixth edition of *Current Issues* has five main objectives:

1. *To introduce and survey* the workings of public organizations and public administrators to students without any previous coursework in this field.

2. *To present articles that are interesting, readable, and thought-provoking,* involving and challenging the student to learn how these bureaucracies actually work.

3. *To provide a comprehensive set of readings,* blending material about the political environment in which public agencies operate, the organizational and managerial aspects of work inside bureaucracies, and analytical approaches to improving public administration.

4. *To focus on state, local, and intergovernmental aspects* of modern public administration in addition to the national scene, even when it is the federal government that sets the tone for much public administrative activity in our country.

5. In all this, *to emphasize the current dimensions* of the many important issues facing governmental administrative agencies at the beginning of the twenty-first century.

All of these have been carefully placed into the thirty-one articles in this volume. In terms of student reading, this means two or three articles a week during a typical academic term.

NEW TO THE SIXTH EDITION

Of the thirty-one articles presented here, sixteen are new to this edition. *Current Issues* continues to attempt to balance historical, political, organizational, managerial, analytical, and policy perspectives on Public Administration, and it asks the classic questions in this field as they appear in the contemporary context.

However, there have been two important alterations in this edition:

1. Perhaps inevitably, *this edition focuses on American public administration at the dawn of the new century;* the emphasis throughout is on a new environment, including the topics of information technology and a global society.

2. *Four public administration cases have been added* at the end of the volume for instructors who like to include real-life, contemporary, and richly illustrative case studies in their survey course in this field.

ACKNOWLEDGMENTS

In preparing the sixth edition, I have sought the advice of faculty members throughout the nation who regularly teach the introductory graduate and undergraduate courses in public administration. Their advice was most helpful, and their contributions are hereby acknowledged:

Ruth Hoogland DeHoog, University of North Carolina at Greensboro; Jeffrey D. Greene, University of Montana; Mark W. Huddleston, University of Delaware; Susan Hunter, West Virginia University; Robert LaPorte Jr., The Pennsylvania State University; Douglas Shumavon, Miami University (Ohio); Khi V. Thai, Florida Atlantic University; and Lou Weschler, Arizona State University.

In this revision, three academic libraries provided valuable assistance: the Anita and William Newman Library at Bernard M. Baruch College of the City University of New York, the Mina Rees Library at the Graduate School and University Center of the City University of New York, and the Francis Harvey Green Library at West Chester University of Pennsylvania. In connection with library research for this edition, I would also like to acknowledge the efforts of my graduate assistant, Fengping Guo.

I would also like to acknowledge others who tirelessly support my activities, especially Lila Siller, Gail Haney, Becky Hook, and Grace Kelly.

For their patience and diligence, I especially appreciate having the assistance of Scott Hitchcock, Susan Cottenden, and the entire staff at Bedford/St. Martin's.

In this and in all things, I am deeply indebted to my wife, Madeleine Wing Adler, and my sons, Cary and Rand Lane, for their love, support, and advice.

On May 30, 1995, I lost a dear friend, and stepson, at the age of 26. J. Peter Adler enjoyed government and politics, but he loved the theater even more. Through no fault of his own, for an instant he happened to be at the wrong place at the wrong time. Each day he is sorely missed—his brilliance, his energy, and his caring—and this book is dedicated, with love, to J. Peter.

INTRODUCTION

Public administration is an ancient activity common to just about all countries and all levels of government.[1] But public administrative traditions, structures, and processes vary widely from one country to another. This volume concerns public administration in the United States.

The term *public administration* combines two words. *Administration* is easier to define: organizing and maintaining human and fiscal resources to attain a group's goals. The group might be a small social club or a large automobile manufacturer. It might also be your local police department or the U.S. Department of Health and Human Services.

Public is harder to define. Public has to do with people, a community, or a society. Most of us went to public schools. We play in public parks. Your state's governor and others hold public office.

Public has another meaning. It also suggests that public administration is open to general knowledge, scrutiny, and review.

A variety of other terms are closely associated with the field of public administration. Higher education for public administration takes place in a wide range of settings: political science departments; schools and programs called public affairs, public policy, public service, government, or public administration; and schools of business and public administration, where public administration is sometimes called public management. Closely related courses can also be found in programs dealing with criminal justice, health care, social work, education, and recreation administration. All of these terms and activities are closely related. The traditional, most widely accepted, and most meaningful label, however, remains *public administration*.

THE PUBLIC POLICY SYSTEM

For the introductory student, it is particularly important to understand the relationships between government, politics, public policy, and public administration. To begin with, government is the mechanism that a human community employs to protect its members from internal and external threats and to establish the policies that will provide the most favorable conditions for pursuing individuals' lives.[2] Government then, is the formal mechanism created and used to guide a society. Democratic government is influenced and, in the end, controlled by the participants in the political system through the process of politics.

As indicated in the foregoing definition, public policies are the results of government. The nation's political system is also its policy system. Social and economic factors are important to policy making but influence public policies only as they affect the political system.

Figure 1 depicts the national policy system, eight principal participants in the national policy system:

1. Citizens
2. Congress
3. The president
4. The U.S. Supreme Court and federal court system
5. The federal bureaucracy
6. Interest groups
7. Political parties
8. The media

The lines in Figure 1 represent the relationships and interactions among the actors in the policy system. Depending on the issues at any particular time and the specific actors involved, these relations range from direct and continuous and intense to indirect and intermittent.

In the United States, state and local levels of government have their own policy systems, which are connected through our federal form of government. Federalism and intergovernmental relations raise some of the most important current issues regarding the formulation of public policy and its implementation.

Governmental administrative agencies make up the overwhelming majority of the apparatus of government. These public agencies are often called bureaucracies. The field of public administration is the study of the activities and impact of governmental bureaucracies.

Figure 1. The National Policy System

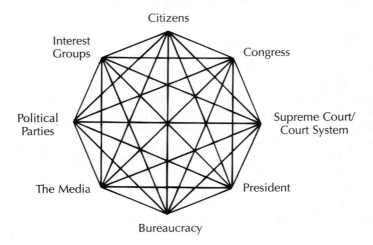

Adapted from a pictorial scheme developed by the late Professor Roscoe C. Martin.

THE STAGES OF THE PUBLIC POLICY-MAKING PROCESS

We think of public policy as occurring in five stages:

1. Policy initiation
2. Policy formulation, articulation, and consideration
3. Policy legitimation (formal approval)
4. Policy implementation
5. Policy evaluation

These stages are shown in Figure 2.

Public bureaucracies are most often associated with policy implementation. This has a long tradition in the public administration literature. A century ago, in 1887, a then young scholar, Woodrow Wilson, published an essay titled "The Study of Administration."[3] In this article, Wilson advocated a distinction between the first three stages of the policy-making process—initiation, formulation, and legitimation—and the fourth stage, implementation. This is sometimes referred to as the policy-administration dichotomy.

Wilson's essay came out of a legally oriented tradition in political science, where elected legislators, "lawmakers," were expected to make public policy, and administrators were expected to carry out these policies. Wilson's essay also appeared after a century of the "spoils" approach to governmental employment, and Wilson sought to increase the competence and ethics expected of public employees.

From the beginning, Wilson's dichotomy greatly oversimplified reality. And if it was ever true, the policy-administration dichotomy is certainly not valid today. As shown in Figure 2, public administrative agencies are engaged in all stages of public policy making, in addition to implementation. Some examples: Public executives often initiate ideas for new or improved public policies. Public administrators regularly interact with their agency's clients and other interested groups as well as with legislative committees, their members, and their staffs in the formulation of new public policies. Public executives testify regularly at legislative hearings considering proposals for different public policies. And administrative agencies increasingly evaluate the effectiveness and impact of public policies by surveying citizens and otherwise employing systematic research methods.

Figure 2. Public Administration in Terms of the Public Policy-Making Process

Stages in the
  Policy-Making Process   *Relative Contribution of Public Administrative Agencies*

Policy initiation

Policy formulation/articulation/
  consideration

Policy legitimation

Policy implementation

Policy evaluation

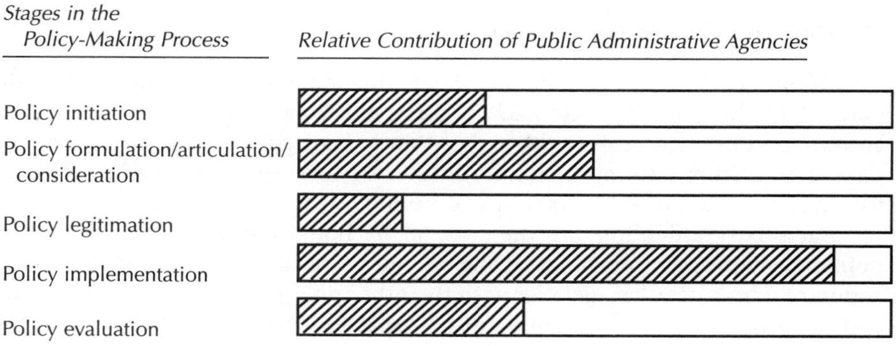

PUBLIC ADMINISTRATION AND POWER

Much is said these days about the power of public bureaucracies. It is a topic we will begin to address in the first chapter and continue to consider throughout this book. The basic reason public administrative agencies have power is because of their expertise—to build dams, fight fires, even just process the paperwork so that an elderly relative receives a social security check on time. But power and public administration are far more complicated than that.

How can we understand why bureaucracies have power within the policy system and even why some bureaucracies are more powerful than others? To begin with, the power of public agencies derives from two main sources: the influence of the agency's clients and constituents and the character and priority of the agency's activities.[4] If an agency's clients are organized and powerful—business groups, for example—the agency has relatively greater authority and influence. In addition, if a public agency is concerned with broad-based matters of importance—like national defense or economic development—it is more powerful. The relative importance of an agency can change over time, as in the example of public policy toward the energy issue and the federal Department of Energy.

There are other sources of agency power as well. The technical nature of the organization's work (if its activities are hard for the average person to understand, much less perform) and the agency's record of accomplishment also influence an agency's power.

The quality of organizational leadership may also be important. The skill, style, experience, personality, and ability to communicate of the top agency executives are naturally related to the power of an agency.

Similarly, organizational morale and commitment by employees can influence an agency's power. There is a big difference between an organization where everyone leaves at 5 P.M. and another organization where staff members remain after 5 P.M. if there is work to be completed, even if they are not paid to do so.

Finally, an agency's sheer size also affects its power. The number of employees, size of budget, scope of functions, and even geographic distribution of an agency's activities often influence an organization's power in the policy system.

All of these factors influence the power of a public agency—the power available in the policy-making process.

ORGANIZATION OF THIS BOOK

The main text of this volume has been divided into four parts, generally parallel to the current textbooks in this field. Part One introduces public administration as a real-world activity and distinguishes administration in government from administration in business. Moreover, Chapter 1 highlights the challenges and the satisfactions of public service as a career.

Parts Two and Three are the core of the book. Part Two focuses on the political environment in which public bureaucracies operate. It treats the interaction of administrative agencies with the other policy makers, both in the federal government and throughout our intergovernmental system. Chapter 4 gives special attention to the fit between bureaucracy and democracy in modern America.

Part Three focuses on the internal, organizational dynamics basic to understanding bureaucracies and making them work better. This section stresses the management of resources, especially people and money.

Part Four begins by surveying relations among all three sectors of American society: government, business, and nonprofit organizations. Public-private partnerships, regulation, and privatization are all considered. Chapter 10 examines the challenges to American public administration at the beginning of the twenty-first century: reinvention and renewal, and a global society.

The Appendix augments this edition with four, carefully written case studies about public administration in action—one case about the federal government and three cases about local government. These current cases may be used at different points throughout the course or toward its end.

As we enter a new century, this sixth edition of *Current Issues in Public Administration* is designed to provide the solid background needed to understand how the management of government works. In a period of increasing distrust of many societal institutions, *Current Issues* analyzes how the administrative branch of government actually functions and how it *could* function.

Notes

1. See Frederick C. Mosher, "Public Administration," *Encyclopedia Britannica,* 15th ed. (1974).
2. Adapted from Max J. Skidmore and Marshall Carter Tripp, *American Government: A Brief Introduction,* 4th ed. (New York: St. Martin's Press, 1985), p. 1.
3. Woodrow Wilson, "The Study of Administration," *Political Science Quarterly* 2 (June 1887): 197-222.
4. This section is drawn from Francis E. Rourke, *Bureaucracy, Politics, and Public Policy* (Boston: Little, Brown, 1969).

PART ONE

What Is Public Administration?

• •

1 Introduction to Public Administration

Most of us were born in public hospitals, graduated from public schools, and brush our teeth with water from a public water supply system. We ride public transportation or drive on public roads in automobiles whose safety features are regulated by another public agency.

Public *bureaucracy* is a key characteristic of modern society. Public organizations, large and small, are needed to provide these types of services or implement these kinds of regulations to promote the well-being of citizens.

The term *bureaucracy* has a negative connotation these days. As a result, some authors prefer the terms *public organizations* or *administrative agencies.* These try to get around the negative tone often encountered in everyday language or in the media when "bureaucracy"—governmental or business—is mentioned.

There is another reason why the term *bureaucracy* is misleading. It suggests that there actually is a single, large, monolithic organizational entity somewhere, like in Washington, D.C., or Sacramento. Such an entity does not exist. Studies of public agencies indicate that, in actuality, there are many administrative agencies rather than a single government bureaucracy, and these organizations often have difficulty coordinating activities and sometimes even compete with each other.

At the federal level, there are three different kinds of administrative agencies: cabinet-level departments, independent agencies, and boards and commissions. These are shown, with examples, in Table 1-1.

In the first article in this chapter, sociologists Peter M. Blau and Marshall W. Meyer introduce us to the study of bureaucracy in society, what the term means, and why bureaucracy is so important. Blau and Meyer also explain the classic formulation of bureaucracy by the great German sociologist Max Weber.

Written by Graham T. Allison Jr., the second article helps the reader to understand the differences between business administration and public administration. Allison makes clear that the most important difference is in the context in which administration takes place: public management occurs primarily in a political environment, while business takes place primarily in a market situation. As it turns out, this key difference in the environment for administration also has a great deal to do with internal organizational activities.

1

Table 1-1 Three Types of Federal Agencies	
Departments	Agriculture
	Commerce
	Defense
	Education
	Energy
	Health and Human Services
	Housing and Urban Development
	Interior
	Justice
	Labor
	State
	Transportation
	Treasury
	Veterans Affairs
Independent agencies (examples only)	Environmental Protection Agency
	General Services Administration
	National Aeronautics and Space Administration
	National Science Foundation
	Small Business Administration
Boards and commissions (examples only)	Consumer Product Safety Commission
	Equal Employment Opportunity Commission
	Federal Communications Commission
	Federal Reserve Board
	Nuclear Regulatory Commission
	Securities and Exchange Commission

Based on "Major Organizational Units of the Executive Branch," in Lawrence C. Dodd and Richard L. Schott, *Congress and the Administrative State* (New York: John Wiley & Sons, Inc., 1979)

The third article in Chapter 1 is a signal to twenty-somethings and to all of us: Working for government can be interesting, important, and rewarding. The key questions in this chapter for the student of public administration are:

- What does "bureaucracy" mean?
- Why is it important to study public bureaucracy in today's society?
- Is there something inherently bad about bureaucracy?
- How is public administration different from business administration? Is this significant to public executives? To citizens?
- Since we often hear about how bad government is, what's so good about working in the federal government or in a unit of state or local government?

Why Study Bureaucracy?

PETER M. BLAU
MARSHALL W. MEYER

"That stupid bureaucrat!" "That dumb bureaucracy!" Who has not felt this way at one time or another? When we are sent from one office to the next without getting the information we want; when forms are returned to us because of some inconsequential omission; when rules are of such complexity that no two people understand them alike—these are the times when we think of bureaucracy. "Bureaucracy" is often used as an epithet connoting inefficiency and confusion in government or elsewhere, such as in universities. But this is not its only meaning, and it is not the way the word will be used in this article.

If you alone had the job of collecting the dues in a small fraternity, you could proceed at your own discretion. However, if five persons had this job in a large club, they would find it necessary to organize their work, lest some members were asked for dues repeatedly and others never. If hundreds of persons had the assignment of collecting taxes from the citizens of a city or state, their work would have to be organized systematically to prevent chaos. A hundred years ago, there was little coordination of tax collecting in most U.S. municipalities. Tax "farmers" had license to collect from whomever they could persuade to pay. Chaos and corruption resulted. Through the efforts of reformers, modern bureaus responsible for collecting taxes systematically and fairly from everyone were put in place. The type of organization designed to accomplish large-scale administrative tasks by coordinating the work of many people systematically is called a bureaucracy. *The concept of bureaucracy, then, applies to organizing principles that are intended to achieve control and coordination of work in large organizations.* Since control and coordination are required in most large organizations nowadays, bureaucracy is not confined to government but is found in businesses, voluntary organizations, and wherever administrative tasks are undertaken.

Control and coordination are not, of course, ends in themselves. They are means toward the end of administrative efficiency, of completing successfully large and complicated tasks that no individual person could accomplish alone. The organizing principles of bureaucracy thus have the purpose of creating efficient organizations, not inefficient ones. But simply because bureaucracy is intended as an efficient form of organization does not mean that it always achieves efficiency. Critics of bureaucracy claim that its principles are inherently inefficient, and many citizens who are irritated by unresponsive and sometimes inept government agencies tend to agree.

Interestingly, while the term "bureaucratic" is often used as a synonym for "inefficient," at other times it is used to imply ruthless efficiency. The German sociologist Max Weber, whose analysis of bureaucratic structures will be discussed presently, held bureaucracy to be so efficient that its power was "overtowering." Weber's American contemporaries, such as Woodrow Wilson, also worried considerably that the power of a large civil service organized according to bureaucratic principles would be inconsistent with democratic governance. Contemporary critics of both the political left and right also fear the power of bureaucracy. The left blames bureaucratic institutions for many of the evils of the world—the domination of weak nations by imperialist powers, the oppression of poor people, the uncertainties facing today's youth. The right blames bureaucracy for inflation, high taxes, and the sapping of individual initiative by excessive regulation. There is some truth to all these allegations, but there is also much exaggeration.

The criticisms of bureaucracy leveled by the political right and left can be understood as a result of its ethical neutrality. Bureaucratic administration can be used as an instrument of economic domination, or it can be used to curb inequities that would arise were economic forces permitted to operate without restraint. Bureaucratic administration is necessarily employed to administer health and social service programs, whether governmental or private, whose purpose is to sustain the ill and needy. Bureaucracies have also been responsible for evils unimaginable in the prebureaucratic era. Hannah Arendt's *Eichmann in Jerusalem* portrays Adolph Eichmann as the consummate bureaucrat meticulously carrying out Hitler's orders to implement the "final solution" by exterminating all the Jews of Europe. The abolition of bureaucracies, to be sure, would limit the possibility of evils such as the Holocaust. But it would also eliminate their positive accomplishments. The challenge for democratic societies is to gain and maintain control over their bureaucracies so that they function for the benefit of the commonweal rather than for that of bureaucrats themselves or of special interests. . . .

THE RATIONALIZATION OF MODERN LIFE

Much of the magic and mystery that used to pervade human life and lend it enchantment has disappeared from the modern world.[1] This is largely the price of rationalization. In olden times, nature was full of mysteries, and humanity's most serious intellectual endeavors were directed toward discovering the ultimate meaning of existence. Today, nature holds fewer secrets for us. Scientific advances, however, have not only made it possible to explain many natural phenomena but have also channeled human thinking. In modern times, people are less concerned than they were, say, in the medieval era with ultimate values and symbolic meanings, with those aspects of mental life that are not subject to scientific inquiry, such as religious truth and artistic creation. This remains an age of science, not of philosophy or of religion, even though there is now greater interest in philosophy and religious belief than there was twenty years ago.

The secularization of the world that spells its disenchantment is indicated by the large amount of time we spend in making a living and getting ahead and the little time we spend in contemplation and religious activities. Compare the low prestige of moneylenders—lending at interest was once considered sinful—and the high prestige of priests in former eras with the very different position of bankers and preachers today. Preoccupied with perfecting efficient means for achieving objectives, we tend to forget why we want to reach these goals. Since we neglect to clarify the basic values that determine why some objectives are preferable to others, objectives lose their significance, and their pursuit becomes an end in itself. This tendency is portrayed in Budd Shulberg's novel *What Makes Sammy Run?* The answer to the question in the title is that only running makes him run, because he is so busy trying to get ahead that he has no time to find out where he is going. Continuous striving for success is not Sammy's means for the attainment of certain ends but the very goal of his life.

These consequences of rationalization have often been deplored, and some observers have even suggested that it is not worth the price.[2] There is no conclusive evidence, however, that alienation from profound values is the inevitable and permanent by-product of rationalization; it may be merely an expression of its growing pains. The beneficial results of rationalization—notably the higher standard of living and greater amount of leisure it makes possible, and the raising of the level of popular education it makes necessary—permit an increased proportion of the population, not just a privileged elite, to participate actively in the cultural life of a society.

Our high standard of living is usually attributed to the spectacular technological developments that have occurred since the Industrial Revolution, but this explanation ignores two related facts. First, the living conditions of most people during the early stages of industrialization, after they had moved from the land into the cities with their sweatshops, were probably much worse than they had been before. Dickens depicts these terrible conditions in certain novels, and Marx describes them in his biting critique of the capitalistic economy.[3] Second, major improvements in the standard of living did not take place until administrative procedures as well as material technology had been revolutionized. Modern machines could not be utilized without the complex administrative machinery needed for running industries employing thousands of people. For example, it was not so much the invention of railroad technology as the invention of management that permitted railroads to traverse long distances. Early railroads had no managers supervising operations and no printed timetables. At fixed times—say 9 A.M., noon, and 4 P.M.—trains would start at both ends of the line. The first to reach the midpoint, where there was a passing siding, would simply wait for the other. And each train had to reach the end of the line before another could begin its journey in the opposite direction. This system worked well so long as rail lines were short: thirty to forty miles. Once railroads were extended beyond this distance, however, trains could no longer wait for one another at the midpoint of a line. Many accidents resulted; to guarantee safety, therefore, the management of railroads was bureaucratized. Managers responsible for coordinating train movements were hired and timetables printed.[4] Rationalization of railroad administration, in other words, was necessary to take advantage of technological changes.

Let us examine some of the administrative principles on which the productive efficiency of modern organizations—whether railroads, factories, or government offices—depends. If a person were responsible for all the different tasks at a given place of work, he or she would have to have many years of education and would still not be able to perform the job well. Imagine, for example, an automobile factory where every car was planned and assembled by a single worker. That worker would have to be at once a designer, a mechanical engineer, and a skilled craftsman. Not only would there be a shortage of people with these qualifications, but those workers who had the necessary skills would probably produce cars of low quality, since none of them would have the time or experience to perfect the manufacture or assembly of any particular part. Specialization, whereby only a small number of tasks are assigned to each worker, permits the hiring of less qualified employees, and, moreover, workers with superior qualifications for the most difficult jobs; it also permits workers to become experienced at their jobs.

What has been taken apart through specialization must be put back together again. A high degree of specialization creates a need for a complex system of coordination. Formal coordination is not needed in a small workplace where tasks are less specialized, all workers have direct contact with one another, and the boss can supervise everyone's performance directly. But the president of a large company cannot possibly discharge his responsibilities through direct supervision of each of several thousand workers. Managerial responsibility is therefore exercised through a hierarchy of authority, which furnishes lines of communication between top management and every employee for obtaining information on operations and transmitting operating directives. (Sometimes, these lines of communication become blocked, and this is a major source of inefficiency in administration.)

Effective coordination requires disciplined performance, which cannot be achieved by supervision alone but must pervade the work process. This is a function of rules and regulations that govern operations, whether they specify the dimensions of nuts and bolts or the criteria to be used in promoting subordinates. Even in the ideal case, where every employee is a highly intelligent and skilled expert, there is a need for disciplined adherence to regulations. Imagine that one worker had discovered that he could produce bolts of superior quality by making them $1/8$ inch larger and another worker had found that she could increase her efficiency by making nuts $1/8$ inch smaller. Although each made the most rational decision in terms of the given task, the nuts and bolts would be useless because they would not match. How one's work fits with that of others is usually far less obvious than in this illustration. If the operations of hundreds of employees are to be coordinated, each must conform to prescribed standards even in situations where a different course of action appears to the individual to be most reasonable. This is a requirement of all teamwork, although in genuine teamwork the rules are based on common agreement rather than being imposed from above.

Efficiency also suffers when emotions or personal considerations influence administrative decisions. If the owner of a small grocery expands her business and opens a second store, she may put her son in charge even though another employee is more qualified for the job. She acts on the basis of her personal attachment rather than in the interest of business efficiency. Similarly, an official in a large company might not promote the best qualified worker to supervisor if one of the candidates were his brother. Indeed, his personal feelings could prevent him from recognizing that his brother's qualifications were inferior. Since the subtle effects of strong emotions cannot easily be suppressed, the best way to check their interference with efficiency is to exclude from the administrative hierarchy those interpersonal relationships that are characterized by emotional attachments. While relatives sometimes work for the same company, they are generally not put in charge of one another. Impersonal relationships assure the detachment necessary if efficiency alone is to govern administrative decisions. However, relationships between employees who have frequent social contacts do not remain impersonal, as we shall see.

These four factors—specialization, a hierarchy of authority, a system of rules, and impersonality—are the basic characteristics of bureaucratic organization. Factories are bureaucratically organized, as are government offices; if this were not the case, they could not operate on a large scale....

THE VALUE OF STUDYING BUREAUCRACY

Learning to understand bureaucracies is more important today than it ever was. It has, moreover, special significance in a democracy. In addition, the study of bureaucratic organization makes a particular contribution to the advancement of sociological knowledge.

Today

Bureaucracy is not a new phenomenon. It existed in relatively simple forms thousands of years ago in Egypt and Rome. But the trend toward bureaucratization has greatly accelerated since the beginning of this century. In contemporary society, bureaucracy has become a dominant institution—indeed, the institution that epitomizes modernity. Unless we understand this form, we cannot understand the social life of today.

The enormous size of modern nations and the organizations within them is one reason for the spread of bureaucracy. In earlier periods, most countries were small, even large ones had only a loose central administration, and there were few formal organizations except the government.[5] Modern nations have many millions of citizens, vast armies, giant corporations, huge unions, and numerous voluntary associations.[6] To be sure, large size does not necessarily compel bureaucratic organization. However, the problems posed by administration on a large scale tend to lead to bureaucratization. Put somewhat differently, in the absence of bureaucratization, large-scale centralized administration has been very difficult to maintain.

In the United States, employment statistics illustrate the trend toward large, bureaucratized organizations. The federal government employed some eight thousand civilian personnel in 1820, a quarter million at the beginning of this century, and almost 3 million now. The largest private firms, such as General Motors and Exxon, have upward of half a million employees apiece. Self-employment, which was once the norm, has become rare. In 1800, 57 percent of the U.S. working population were self-employed; in 1970, however, only 10 percent were.[7] Moreover, within organizations of all kinds, the proportion of employees with supervisory or administrative duties has increased dramatically, especially in recent years. In 1900, the ratio of administrative to production employees in U.S. manufacturing industry was about 1:10; it was approximately 2:10 in 1950.[8] This A/P ratio, as it is known to sociologists, now exceeds $4^1/_2:10$ in manufacturing. Perhaps of greater importance, supervisory or administrative ratios have increased in other industries—for example, mining, finance and insurance, retailing, service—just as rapidly as in manufacturing.[9]

A large and increasing proportion of the American people, then, spend their working lives in large organizations, and these organizations are increasingly bureaucratized in the sense that a greater proportion of work is of a supervisory or administrative character. To be sure, the average size of workplaces (or what the U.S. Census calls establishments) has decreased slightly since World War II,[10] but individual workplaces are increasingly linked together in bureaucratic hierarchies.[11] Outside of work, the organizations we deal with are themselves becoming more bureaucratic. The corner hamburger stand has been largely displaced by the franchised outlet that is part of a national chain. The independent physician is increasingly rare as medical care becomes organized into group practices and health maintenance organizations, the latter often owned by giant corporations.[12] Bureaucratization of our institutions has become so ubiquitous that it is now difficult to imagine alternatives to the bureaucratic form. But alternatives to bureaucracy are essential, as we shall point out below, to preserve individual autonomy and innovativeness in organizations.

In a Democracy

Bureaucracy, as [German sociologist] Max Weber pointed out, "is a power instrument of the first order—for the one who controls the bureaucratic apparatus."[13]

> Under normal conditions, the power position of the fully developed bureaucracy is always overtowering. The "political master" finds himself in the position of the "dilettante" who stands opposite the "expert," facing the trained official who stands within the management of administration. This holds whether the "master" whom the bureaucracy serves is a "people," equipped with the weapons of "legislative initiative," the "referendum," and the right to remove officials, or a parliament, elected on a ... "democratic" basis and equipped with the right to vote a lack of confidence, or with the actual authority to vote it.[14]

Totalitarianism is the polar case of such concentration of bureaucratic power that destroys democratic processes, but it is not the only example. The same antidemocratic tendencies can be observed in political machines that allow political bosses to assume power legally belonging to voters, in business corporations that enable managers to take power rightfully belonging to stockholders, and in unions that let union leaders exercise the power rightfully belonging to rank-and-file members. The use of bureaucratic administration by totalitarian regimes has led some writers to contend that the present trend toward bureaucratization spells the doom of democratic institutions.[15] This may well be too pessimistic a viewpoint, but there can be little doubt that this problem constitutes a challenge. To protect ourselves against the threat of bureaucratic domination while continuing to take advantage of the efficiencies of bureaucracy, we must first learn fully to understand how bureaucracies function. Knowledge alone is not power, but ignorance surely facilitates subjugation. This is one reason why the study of bureaucratic organization has such great significance in a democracy.

Another and perhaps more subtle threat posed by bureaucratization is erosion of public confidence in democratic institutions. The taxpayers' revolt evident in California's Proposition 13 is but one expression of the discontent with government that has become widespread in recent years. Discontent with large organizations is also exemplified by the dramatic increase in both antigovernment and antibusiness sentiments found in opinion surveys of the American public. From the late 1950s through the present, increasing numbers of people have expressed doubts about government and business, although negative sentiments about government have risen much more rapidly than negative attitudes toward business.[16] Antigovernment attitudes may be attributed partly to the Watergate scandal and the failure of U.S. policy in Vietnam. But there is evidence also that the large size of government and business organizations has contributed to declining confidence in them. Large institutions, the federal government and large corporations particularly, are suspect." Whether aversion to large size is due to the perception of "fat" or inefficiency in big government and big business, the perception that power is misused by both, or the substantial rewards that accrue to executives, cannot be determined from opinion data. It is clear, however, that considerable distrust of large, bureaucratized organizations has accumulated. An understanding of the sources of perceived inefficiency and misuse of power in both public and private bureaucracies could possibly suggest correctives that would help rebuild confidence in our institutions....

THE CONCEPT OF BUREAUCRACY

The main characteristics of a bureaucratic structure (in the "ideal-typical" case,[18] according to Weber) are the following:

1. "The regular activities required for the purposes of the organization are distributed in a fixed way as official duties."[19] The clear-cut division of labor makes it possible to employ only specialized experts in each particular position and to make every one of them responsible for the effective performance of his duties. This high degree of specialization has become so much part of our life that we tend to forget that it did not prevail in former eras but is a relatively recent bureaucratic invention.

2. "The organization of offices follows the principle of hierarchy; that is, each lower office is under the control and supervision of a higher one."[20] Every official in this administrative hierarchy is accountable to her superior for her subordinates' decisions and actions as well as her own. To be able to discharge the responsibility for the work of subordinates, the superior has authority over them, which means that she has the right to issue directives and they have the duty to obey them. This authority is strictly circumscribed and confined to those directives that are relevant to official operations. The use of status prerogatives to extend the power of control over subordinates beyond these limits does not constitute the legitimate exercise of bureaucratic authority.

3. Operations are governed "by a consistent system of abstract rules ... [and] consist of the application of these rules to particular cases."[21] This system of standards is designed to assure uniformity in the performance of every task, regardless of the number of persons engaged in it, and the coordination of different tasks. Explicit rules and regulations define the responsibility of each member of the organization and relationships among them. This does not imply that bureaucratic duties are necessarily simple or routine. It must be remembered that strict adherence to general standards in deciding specific cases characterizes not only the job of the file clerk but also that of the Supreme Court justice. For the former, it may involve merely filing alphabetically; for the

latter, it involves interpreting the law of the land in order to settle the most complicated legal issues. Bureaucratic duties range in complexity from one of these extremes to the other.

4. "The ideal official conducts his office ... [in] a spirit of formalistic impersonality, *'Sine ira ac studio,'* without hatred or passion, and hence without affection or enthusiasm."[22] For rational standards to govern operations without interference from personal considerations, a detached approach must prevail within the organization and especially toward clients. If an official develops strong feelings about subordinates or clients, she can hardly keep letting those feelings influence her official decisions. As a result, and often without being aware of it herself, she might be particularly lenient in evaluating the work of one of her subordinates or might discriminate against some clients and in favor of others. The exclusion of personal considerations from official business is a prerequisite for impartiality as well as for efficiency. The very factors that make a government bureaucrat unpopular with his clients, an aloof attitude and lack of genuine concern with them as human beings, usually benefits these clients. Disinterestedness and lack of personal interest go together. The official who does not maintain social distance and becomes personally interested in the cases of his clients tends to be partial in his treatment of them, favoring those he likes over others. Impersonal detachment engenders equitable treatment of all persons and thus equal justice in administration.

5. Employment in the bureaucratic organization is based on technical qualifications and is protected against arbitrary dismissal. "It constitutes a career. There is a system of 'promotions' according to seniority or to achievement, or both."[23] These personnel policies, which are found not only in civil service but also in many private companies, encourage the development of loyalty to the organization and esprit de corps among its members. The consequent identification of employees with the organization motivates them to exert greater efforts in advancing its interest. It may also give rise to a tendency among civil servants or employees to think of themselves as a class apart from and superior to the rest of society. This tendency has been especially pronounced among European civil servants, but it may be found in the United States too.

6. "Experience tends universally to show that the purely bureaucratic type of administrative organization ... is, from a purely technical point of view, capable of attaining the highest degree of efficiency...."[24]

The fully developed bureaucratic mechanism compares with other organizations exactly as does the machine with nonmechanical modes of production. Precision, speed, unambiguity, knowledge of the files, continuity, discretion, unity, strict subordination, reduction of friction and of material and personal costs—these are raised to the optimum point in the strictly bureaucratic administration, and especially in its monocratic form. As compared with all collegiate, honorific, and avocational forms of administration, trained bureaucracy is superior on all these points. And as far as complicated tasks are concerned, paid bureaucratic work is not only more precise but, in the last analysis, it is often cheaper than formally unremunerated honorific service.[25]

Bureaucracy, then, solves the distinctive organizational problem of maximizing coordination and control and thereby organizational efficiency, not only the productive efficiency of individual employees.

The superior effectiveness of bureaucracy—its capacity to coordinate large-scale administrative tasks—and superior efficiency are the expected results of its various characteristics as outlined by Weber. An individual who is to work effectively must have the necessary skills and apply them rationally and energetically; but more is required of an organization that is to operate effectively and efficiently. Every one of its members must have the expert skills needed for the performance of her tasks. This is the purpose of specialization and employment on the basis of technical qualifications, often ascertained by objective tests. Even experts, however, may be prevented by personal bias from making rational decisions. The emphasis on impersonal detachment is needed to eliminate this source of nonrational action. But individual rationality is not enough. As noted above, if members of the organization were to make rational decisions independently, their work would not be coordinated and the efficiency of the organization would suffer. Hence there is need for discipline to limit the scope of rational discretion, which is met by the system of rules and regulations and the hierarchy of supervision. Moreover, there are personnel policies that permit employees to feel secure in their jobs and to anticipate advancements for faithful performance of duties, and these policies discourage attempts to impress superiors by inducing clever innovations, which may endanger coordination. Lest this stress on disciplined obedience to rules and regulations undermine the employee's motivation to devote his energies to his job, incentives for exerting effort must be furnished. Personnel policies that cultivate organizational loyalties and that provide for promotion on the basis of merit serve this function. In other words, bureaucracy's characteristics are intended to create social conditions constraining each member of the organization to act in ways that, whether they appear rational or otherwise from the individual's standpoint, further the rational pursuit of organizational objectives.

So far, Weber's analysis of bureaucratic structures emphasizes mainly their positive functions. The division of labor and specialization promotes expertise, but the work of specialists must be coordinated through organizational hierarchies. Rules and the norm of impersonality contribute further to coordination by removing individual biases from decisions. And career incentives motivate employees to perform their duties diligently. But Weber also identified some potentially negative consequences of bureaucracy. Among these are the following:

1. Bureaucracies tend to monopolize information, rendering outsiders unable to determine the basis on which decisions are made. "Every bureaucracy seeks to increase the superiority of the professionally informed by keeping their knowledge and intentions secret....The concept of the 'official secret' is the specific invention of bureaucracy, and nothing is defended so fanatically by the bureaucracy as this attitude."[26]

2. "Once it is fully established, bureaucracy is among those social structures which are the hardest to destroy....The idea of eliminating these organizations becomes more and more utopian."[27] The very specialization and expertise of bureaucracies makes it almost impossible to

administer large nation-states or private enterprises without them. To be sure, individual officials can be replaced should they leave, voluntarily or otherwise. But the overall pattern of administration consistent with the bureaucratic model is not easily changed. This occurs not simply because people are reluctant to change but especially because they rightly fear that the elimination of existing procedures may well lead to disorganization or return to the "spoils system" dominated by favoritism and corrupt practices.

3. Established bureaucracies are, at best, ambivalent toward democracy. On the one hand, bureaucratization tends to accompany mass democracy. "This results from the characteristic principle of bureaucracy: the abstract regularity of the execution of authority, which is a result of the demand for 'equality before the law' in the personal and functional sense—hence of the horror of 'privilege,' and of the principled rejection of doing business 'from case to case.'"28 On the other hand, bureaucracies tend not to be responsive to public opinion.

> Democracy inevitably comes into conflict with the bureaucratic tendencies which,by its fight against notable rule, democracy has produced. . . .The most decisive thing there—indeed it is rather exclusively so—is *the leveling of the governed* in opposition to the ruling and bureaucratically articulated group, which in its turn may occupy a quite autocratic position. . . .29

Weber's analysis of bureaucracy leads thereby to paradoxical conclusions. Due to the effectiveness and efficiency it imparts to large-scale administration, bureaucracy has many positive functions. But its tendencies toward monopolizing information, resisting change, and acting autocratically (even if in compliance with rules) are usually not viewed positively; they were not so regarded at the time Weber wrote, nor are they today. Both the positive and negative effects of bureaucracy can be understood as outcomes of organizing principles intended to achieve coordination and control. Effectiveness and efficiency are attained because bureaucracy concentrates technical expertise and acts predictably. But the same predictable action based on expertise makes bureaucracies extremely powerful institutions, which have the capacity to resist external forces pressing for change. In the language of sociological theory, Weber's analysis suggests both positive *functions* as well as negative *dysfunctions* of the bureaucratic form.30 The fact that bureaucratic organizations (as well as most other social institutions) have both functions that contribute to and dysfunctions that detract from adaptation and adjustment is not always understood, but it is important to a complete and scientific understanding of bureaucracy. Weber's penetrating analysis has become the prototype of bureaucracy—it is the basic concept we use in comparing organizations. . . .

Notes

1. The disenchantment of the world is one of the main themes running through the work of Max Weber.
2. See Pitirim Sorokin, *Cultural and Social Dynamics* (New York: American Book Company, 1937-1941). The author traces fluctuations in cultural emphasis on science and rationality, on the one hand, and faith and supernatural phenomena, on the other, from the earliest times to the present trend toward rationalization.

3. Karl Marx, *Capital* (New York: International Publishers, 1967), vol. I, chaps. 26–31.
4. The bureaucratization of railroads is described fully by Alfred D. Chandler, Jr., in *The Visible Hand* (Cambridge, Mass.: Harvard University Press, 1977), chaps. 3–6.
5. See Robert LaPolombara, *Bureaucracy and Political Development* (Princeton, N.J.: Princeton University Press, 1963).
6. See Kenneth Boulding, *The Organizational Revolution* (New York: Harper & Row, 1953).
7. Lynne G. Zucker, "Organizations as Institutions," *Research in the Sociology of Organizations* 2(1983):14–17.
8. Reinhard Bendix, *Work and Authority in Industry* (Berkeley, Calif.: University of California Press, 1956), chap. 5.
9. Marshall W. Meyer, William Stevenson, and Stephen Webster, *Limits to Bureaucratic Growth* (New York: de Gruyter, 1985), chap. 2.
10. Mark Granovetter, "Small is Beautiful: Labor Markets and Establishment Size," *American Sociological Review* 49(1984):323–334.
11. Meyer, Stevenson, and Webster, loc. cit.
12. See Paul Starr, *The Social Transformation of American Medicine* (New York: Basic Books, 1982).
13. H. H. Gerth and C. W. Mills, eds., *From Max Weber: Essays in Sociology* (New York: Oxford University Press, 1946), p. 228.
14. Ibid., p. 232.
15. See Ludwig von Mises, *Bureaucracy* (New Haven, Conn.: Yale University Press, 1944), and Karl Mannheim, *Man and Society in an Age of Reconstruction* (London: Routledge & Kegan Paul, 1951).
16. Seymour Martin Lipset and William Schneider, *The Confidence Gap* (New York: Free Press, 1983), chap. 1.
17. Ibid., pp. 81–83.
18. The "ideal type" is discussed in Peter M. Blau and Marshall W. Meyer, *Bureaucracy in Modern Society*, 3rd ed. (New York: Random House, 1987), pp. 25–44.
19. Gerth and Mills, op. cit., p. 196.
20. Max Weber, *The Theory of Social and Economic Organization*, trans. A. M. Henderson and Talcott Parsons (New York: Oxford University Press, 1947), p. 331.
21. Ibid., p. 330.
22. Ibid., p. 340.
23. Ibid., p. 334.
24. Ibid., p. 337.
25. Gerth and Mills, op. cit., p. 214.
26. Ibid., p. 233.
27. Ibid., pp. 228–229.
28. Ibid., p. 224.
29. Ibid., p. 226.
30. See Robert K. Merton's discussion of functional analysis in *Social Theory and Social Structure*, 3rd ed. (New York: Free Press, 1968), pp. 73–138.

Public and Private Management: Are They Fundamentally Alike in All Unimportant Respects?

GRAHAM T. ALLISON JR.

My subtitle puts Wallace Sayre's oft quoted "law" as a question. Sayre had spent some years in Ithaca helping plan Cornell's new School of Business and Public Administration. He left for Columbia with this aphorism: public and private management are fundamentally alike in all unimportant respects.

Sayre based his conclusion on years of personal observation of governments, a keen ear for what his colleagues at Cornell (and earlier at OPA) said about business, and a careful review of the literature and data comparing public and private management. Of the latter there was virtually none. Hence, Sayre's provocative "law" was actually an open invitation to research.

Unfortunately, in the 50 years since Sayre's pronouncement, the data base for systematic comparison of public and private management has improved little.... I would, in effect, like to take up Sayre's invitation to *speculate* about similarities and differences among public and private management in ways that suggest significant opportunities for systematic investigation....[1]

FRAMING THE ISSUE: WHAT IS PUBLIC MANAGEMENT?

What is the meaning of the term *management* as it appears in *Office of Management and Budget* or *Office of Personnel Management*? Is "management" different from, broader, or narrower than "administration"? Should we distinguish between management, leadership, entrepreneurship, administration, policy making, and implementation?

Who are "public managers"? Mayors, governors, and presidents? City managers, secretaries, and commissioners? Bureau chiefs? Office directors? Legislators? Judges?

Recent studies of OPM and OMB shed some light on these questions. OPM's major study of the "current status of public management research" completed in May 1978 by Selma Mushkin and colleagues of Georgetown's Public Service Laboratory starts with this question. The Mushkin report notes the definition of *public administration* employed by the Interagency Study Committee on Policy Management Assistance in its 1975 report to OMB. That study identified the following core elements:

1. *Policy Management.* The identification of needs, analysis of options, selection of programs, and allocation of resources on a jurisdiction-wide basis.
2. *Resource Management.* The establishment of basic administrative support systems, such as budgeting, financial management, procurement and supply, and personnel management.

3. *Program Management.* The implementation of policy or daily operation of agencies carrying out policy along functional lines (education,
law enforcement, etc.).[2]

The Mushkin report rejects this definition in favor of an "alternative list
of public management elements." These elements are:

- Personnel management (other than work force planning and collective
  bargaining and labor-management relations)
- Work force planning
- Collective bargaining and labor-management relations
- Productivity and performance measurement
- Organization/reorganization
- Financial management (including the management of intergovern-
  mental relations)
- Evaluation research, and program and management audit.[3]

Such terminological tangles seriously hamper the development of public
management as a field of knowledge. In our efforts to discuss the public management curriculum at Harvard, I have been struck by how differently people
use these terms, how strongly many individuals feel about some distinction
they believe is marked by a difference between one word and another, and
consequently, how large a barrier terminology is to convergent discussion.
These verbal obstacles virtually prohibit conversation that is both brief and
constructive among individuals who have not developed a common language
or a mutual understanding of each other's use of terms.

This terminological thicket reflects a more fundamental conceptual confusion. There exists no overarching framework that orders the domain. In an
effort to get a grip on the phenomena—the buzzing, blooming confusion of
people in jobs performing tasks that produce results—both practitioners and
observers have strained to find distinctions that facilitate their work. The
attempts in the early decades of this century to draw a sharp line between
"policy" and "administration," like more recent efforts to mark a similar
divide between "policy-making" and "implementation," reflect a common
search for a simplification that allows one to put the value-laden issues of
politics to one side (who gets what, when, and how), and focus on the more
limited issue of how to perform tasks more efficiently.[4] But can anyone really deny that the "how" substantially affects the "who," the "what," and the
"when"? The basic categories now prevalent in discussions of public management—strategy, personnel management, financial management, and control—
are mostly derived from a business context in which executives manage hierarchies. The fit of these concepts to the problems that confront public managers
is not clear.

Finally, there exist no ready data on what public managers do. Instead,
the academic literature, such as it is, mostly consists of speculation tied to bits
and pieces of evidence about the tail or the trunk or other manifestation of
the proverbial elephant.[5] In contrast to the literally thousands of cases
describing problems faced by private managers and their practice in solving

these problems, case research from the perspective of a public manager is just beginning. . . .[6] The paucity of data on the phenomena inhibits systematic empirical research on similarities and differences between public and private management, leaving the field to a mixture of reflection on personal experience and speculation.

For the purpose of this presentation, I will follow Webster and use the term *management* to mean the organization and direction of resources to achieve a desired result. I will focus on *general managers*, that is, individuals charged with managing a whole organization or multifunctional subunit. I will be interested in the general manager's full responsibilities, both *inside* his organization in integrating the diverse contributions of specialized subunits of the organization to achieve results, and *outside* his organization in relating his organization and its product to external constituencies. I will begin with the simplifying assumption that managers of traditional government organizations are public managers, and managers of traditional private businesses [are] private managers. Lest the discussion fall victim to the fallacy of misplaced abstraction, I will take the Director of EPA and the Chief Executive Officer of American Motors as, respectively, public and private managers. Thus, our central question can be put concretely: in what ways are the jobs and responsibilities of Doug Costle as Director of EPA similar to and different from those of Roy Chapin as Chief Executive Officer of American Motors?

SIMILARITIES: HOW ARE PUBLIC AND PRIVATE MANAGEMENT ALIKE?

At one level of abstraction, it is possible to identify a set of general management functions. The most famous such list appeared in Gulick and Urwick's classic *Papers in the Science of Administration.*[7] [They] summarized the work of the chief executive in the acronym POSDCORB. The letters stand for:

- Planning
- Organizing
- Staffing
- Directing
- Coordinating
- Reporting
- Budgeting

With various additions, amendments, and refinements, similar lists of general management functions can be found through the management literature from Barnard to Drucker.[8]

I shall resist here my natural academic instinct to join the intramural debate among proponents of various lists and distinctions. Instead, I simply offer one composite list (see Table 1-2) that attempts to incorporate the major functions that have been identified for general managers, whether public or private.

These common functions of management are not isolated and discrete, but rather integral components separated here for purposes of analysis. The character and relative significance of the various functions differ from one

---

Table 1-2
Functions of General Management

Strategy

1. *Establishing objectives and priorities* for the organization (on the basis of forecasts of the external environment and the organization's capacities).
2. *Devising operational plans* to achieve these objectives.

Managing Internal Components

3. *Organizing and staffing.* In organizing the manager establishes structure (units and positions with assigned authority and responsibilities) and procedures for coordinating activity and taking action. In staffing he tries to fit the right persons in the key jobs.*
4. *Directing personnel and the personnel management system.* The capacity of the organization is embodied primarily in its members and their skills and knowledge, the personnel management system recruits, selects, socializes, trains, rewards, punishes, and exits the organization's human capital, which constitutes the organization's capacity to act to achieve its goals and to respond to specific directions from management.
5. *Controlling performance.* Various management information systems—including operating and capital budgets, accounts, reports, and statistical systems, performance appraisals, and product evaluation—assist management in making decisions and in measuring progress towards objectives.

Managing External Constituencies

6. *Dealing with "external" units* of the organization subject to some common authority: Most general managers must deal with general managers of other units within the larger organization—above, laterally, and below—to achieve their unit's objectives.
7. *Dealing with independent organizations.* Agencies from other branches or levels of government, interest groups, and private enterprises that can importantly affect the organization's ability to achieve its objectives.
8. *Dealing with the press and the public* whose action or approval or acquiescence is required.

---

* Organization and staffing are frequency separated in such lists, but because of the interaction between the two, they are combined here. See Graham Allison and Peter Szanton, *Remaking Foreign Policy* (New York: Basic Books, 1976), p. 14.

time to another in the history of any organization, and between one organization and another. But whether in a public or private setting, the challenge for the general manager is to integrate all these elements so as to achieve results.

DIFFERENCES: HOW ARE PUBLIC
AND PRIVATE MANAGEMENT DIFFERENT?

While there is a level of generality at which management is management, whether public or private, functions that bear identical labels take on rather different meanings in public and private settings. As Larry Lynn has pointed out, one powerful piece of evidence in the debate between those who emphasize "similarities" and those who underline "differences" is the nearly unanimous conclusion of individuals who have been general managers in both business and government. Consider the reflections of George Shultz (Secretary of State; former Director of OMB, Secretary of Labor, Secretary of the Treasury, President of Bechtel), Donald Rumsfeld (former congressman, Director of OEO, Director of the Cost of Living Council, White House Chief of Staff, and Secretary of Defense; now President of G. D. Searle and Company), Michael Blumenthal (former Chairman and Chief Executive Officer of Bendix, Secretary of the Treasury, and now Vice Chairman of Burroughs), Roy Ash (former President of Litton Industries, Director of OMB; later President of Addressograph), Lyman Hamilton (former Budget Officer in BOB, High Commissioner of Okinawa, Division Chief in the World Bank and President of ITT), and George Romney (former President of American Motors, Governor of Michigan, and Secretary of Housing and Urban Development).[9] All judge public management different from private management—and harder!

Orthogonal Lists of Differences

My review of these recollections, as well as the thoughts of academics, has identified [two] interesting, orthogonal lists that summarize the current state of the field: one by John Dunlop . . . and one by Richard E. Neustadt, prepared for the National Academy of Public Administration's Panel on Presidential Management.

John T. Dunlop's "impressionistic comparison of government management and private business" yields the following contrasts.[10]

1. *Time Perspective.* Government managers tend to have relatively short time horizons dictated by political necessities and the political calendar, while private managers appear to take a longer time perspective oriented toward market developments, technological innovation and investment, and organization building.

2. *Duration.* The length of service of politically appointed top government managers is relatively short, averaging no more than 18 months recently for assistant secretaries, while private managers have a longer tenure both in the same position and in the same enterprise. A recognized element of private business management is the responsibility to train a successor or several possible candidates, [whereas] the concept is largely alien to public management, since fostering a successor is perceived to be dangerous.

3. *Measurement of Performance.* There is little if any agreement on the standards and measurement of performance to appraise a government manager, while various tests of performance—financial return, market share, performance measures for executive compensation— are well established in private business and often made explicit for a particular managerial position during a specific period ahead.

4. *Personnel Constraints.* In government there are two layers of managerial officials that are at times hostile to one another: the civil service (or now the executive system) and the political appointees. Unionization of government employees exists among relatively high-level personnel in the hierarchy and includes a number of

supervisory personnel. Civil service, union contract provisions, and other regulations complicate the recruitment, hiring, transfer, and layoff or discharge of personnel to achieve managerial objectives or preferences. By comparison, private business managements have considerably greater latitude, even under collective bargaining, in the management of subordinates. They have much more authority to direct the employees of their organization. Government personnel policy and administration are more under the control of staff (including civil service staff outside an agency) compared to the private sector in which personnel are much more subject to line responsibility.

5. *Equity and Efficiency.* In governmental management great emphasis tends to be placed on providing equity among different constituencies, while in private business management relatively greater stress is placed upon efficiency and competitive performance.

6. *Public Processes versus Private Processes.* Governmental management tends to be exposed to public scrutiny and to be more open, while private business management is more private and its processes more internal and less exposed to public review.

7. *Role of Press and Media.* Governmental management must contend regularly with the press and media; its decisions are often anticipated by the press. Private decisions are less often reported in the press, and the press has a much smaller impact on the substance and timing of decisions.

8. *Persuasion and Direction.* In government, managers often seek to mediate decisions in response to a wide variety of pressures and must often put together a coalition of inside and outside groups to survive. By contrast, private management proceeds much more by direction or the issuance of orders to subordinates by superior managers with little risk of contradiction. Governmental managers tend to regard themselves as responsive to many superiors, while private managers look more to one higher authority.

9. *Legislative and Judicial Impact.* Governmental managers are often subject to close scrutiny by legislative oversight groups or even judicial orders in ways that are quite uncommon in private business management. Such scrutiny often materially constrains executive and administrative freedom to act.

10. *Bottom Line.* Governmental managers rarely have a clear bottom line, while that of a private business manager is profit, market performance, and survival....

. . . Richard E. Neustadt, in a fashion close to Dunlop's, notes six major differences between presidents of the United States and chief executive officers of major corporations.[11]

1. *Time Horizon.* The private chief begins by looking forward a decade, or thereabouts, his likely span barring extraordinary troubles. The first term president looks forward four years at most, with the fourth (and now even the third) year dominated by campaigning for reelection (what second-termers look toward we scarcely know, having seen but one such term completed in the past quarter century).

2. *Authority over the Enterprise.* Subject to concurrence from the Board of Directors which appointed and can fire him, the private executive sets organization goals, shifts structures, procedure, and personnel to suit, monitors results, reviews key operational decisions, deals with key outsiders, and brings along his Board. Save for the deep but narrow sphere of military movements, a president's authority in these respects is shared with well-placed members of Congress (or their staffs): case by case, they may have more explicit authority than he does (contrast authorizations and appropriations with the "take-care" clause). As for "bringing along the Board," neither the congressmen with whom he shares power nor the primary and general electorates which "hired" him have either a Board's duties or a broad view of the enterprise precisely matching his.

3. *Career System.* The model corporation is a true career system, something like the Forest Service after initial entry. In normal times the chief himself is chosen from within, or he is chosen from another firm in the same industry. He draws department heads [and other key employees] from among those with whom he's worked or whom he knows in comparable companies. He and his principal associates will be familiar with each other's roles—indeed, he probably has had a number of them—and also usually with one another's operating styles, personalities, idiosyncrasies. Contrast the president who rarely has had much experience "downtown," probably knows little of most roles there (much of what he knows will turn out wrong), and less of most associates whom he appoints there, willy nilly, to fill places by Inauguration Day. Nor are they likely to know one another well, coming as they do from "everywhere" and headed as most are toward oblivion.

4. *Media Relations.* The private executive represents his firm and speaks for it publicly in exceptional circumstances; he and his associates judge the exceptions. Those aside, he neither sees the press nor gives its members access to internal operations, least of all in his own office, save to make a point deliberately for public-relations purposes. The president, by contrast, is routinely on display, continuously dealing with the White House press and with the wider circle of political reporters, commentators, columnists. He needs them in his [day-to-day] business, . . . and they need him in theirs: the TV network news programs lead off with him some nights each week. They and the president are as mutually dependent as he and congressmen (or more so). Comparatively speaking, these relations overshadow most administrative ones much of the time for him.

5. *Performance Measurement.* The private executive expects to be judged, and in turn to judge subordinates, by profitability, however the firm measures it (a major strategic choice). In practice, his Board may use more subjective measures; so may he, but at risk to morale and good order. The relative virtue of profit, of "the bottom line," is its legitimacy, its general acceptance in the business world by all concerned. Never mind its technical utility in given cases; its apparent "objectivity," hence "fairness," has enormous social usefulness: a myth that all can live by. For a president there is no counterpart (except, *in extremis,* the "smoking gun" to justify

impeachment). The general public seems to judge a president, at least in part, by what its members think is happening to them, in their own lives: congressmen, officials, interest groups appear to judge by what they guess, at given times, he can do for or to their causes. Members of the press interpret both of these and spread a simplified criterion affecting both, the legislative box score, a standard of the press's own devising. The White House denigrates them all except when it does well.

6. *Implementation.* The corporate chief, supposedly, does more than choose a strategy and set a course of policy; he also is supposed to oversee what happens after, how in fact intentions turn into results, or if they don't to take corrective action, monitoring through his information system, and acting, if need be, through his personnel system. A president, by contrast, while himself responsible for budgetary proposals, too, in many spheres of policy appears ill-placed and ill-equipped to monitor what agencies of states, of cities, corporations, unions, foreign governments are up to or to change personnel in charge. Yet these are very often the executants of "his" programs. Apart from defense and diplomacy the federal government does two things in the main: it issues and applies regulations and it awards grants in aid. Where these are discretionary, choice usually is vested by statute in a Senate-confirmed official well outside the White House. Monitoring is his function, not the president's except at second hand. And final action is the function of the subjects of the rules and funds; they mostly are not federal personnel at all. In defense, the arsenals and shipyards are gone; weaponry comes from the private sector. In foreign affairs it is the *other* governments whose actions we would influence. From implementors like these a president is far removed most of the time. He intervenes, if at all, on a crash basis, not through organizational incentives.

Underlying these lists' sharpest distinctions between public and private management is a fundamental *constitutional difference.* In business, the functions of general management are centralized in a single individual: the chief executive officer. The goal is authority commensurate with responsibility. In contrast, in the U.S. government, the functions of general management are constitutionally spread among competing institutions: the executive, two houses of Congress, and the courts. The constitutional goal was "not to promote efficiency but to preclude the exercise of arbitrary power," as Justice Brandeis observed. Indeed, as *The Federalist Papers* makes starkly clear, the aim was to create incentives to compete: "the great security against a gradual concentration of the several powers in the same branch, consists in giving those who administer each branch the constitutional means and personal motives to resist encroachment of the others. Ambition must be made to counteract ambition."[12] Thus, the general management functions concentrated in the CEO of a private business are, by constitutional design, spread in the public sector among a number of competing institutions and thus shared by a number of individuals whose ambitions are set against one another. For most areas of public policy today, these individuals include at the federal level the chief elected official, the chief appointed executive, the chief career official, and several congressional chieftains. Since most public services are actually delivered by state and local governments, with independent sources of authority, this means a further array of individuals at these levels.

AN OPERATIONAL PERSPECTIVE:
HOW ARE THE JOBS AND RESPONSIBILITIES
OF DOUG COSTLE, DIRECTOR OF EPA,
AND ROY CHAPIN, CEO OF AMERICAN MOTORS,
SIMILAR AND DIFFERENT?

If organizations could be separated neatly into two homogeneous piles, one public and one private, the task of identifying similarities and differences between managers of these enterprises would be relatively easy. In fact, as Dunlop has pointed out, "the real world of management is composed of distributions, rather than single undifferentiated forms, and there is an increasing variety of hybrids." Thus for each major attribute of organizations, specific entities can be located on a spectrum. On most dimensions, organizations classified as "predominantly public" and those "predominantly private" overlap.[13] Private business organizations vary enormously among themselves in size, in management structure and philosophy, and in the constraints under which they operate. For example, forms of ownership and types of managerial control may be somewhat unrelated. Compare a family-held enterprise, for instance, with a public utility and a decentralized conglomerate, a Bechtel with ATT and Textron. Similarly, there are vast differences in management of governmental organizations. Compare the Government Printing Office or TVA or the police department of a small town with the Department of Energy or the Department of Health and Human Services. These distributions and varieties should encourage penetrating comparisons within both business and governmental organizations, as well as contrasts and comparisons across these broad categories, a point to which we shall return in considering directions for research.

Absent a major research effort, it may nonetheless be worthwhile to examine the jobs and responsibilities of two specific managers, neither polar extremes, but one clearly public, the other private. For this purpose, and primarily because of the availability of cases that describe the problems and opportunities each confronted, consider Doug Costle, Administrator of EPA, and Roy Chapin, CEO of American Motors.[14]

Doug Costle, Administrator of EPA, January 1977

The mission of EPA is prescribed by laws creating the agency and authorizing its major programs. That mission is "to control and abate pollution in the areas of air, water, solid wastes, noise, radiation, and toxic substances. EPA's mandate is to mount an integrated, coordinated attack on environmental pollution in cooperation with state and local governments."[15]

EPA's organizational structure follows from its legislative mandates to control particular pollutants in specific environments: air and water, solid wastes, noise, radiation, pesticides, and chemicals. As the new administrator, Costle inherited the Ford administration's proposed budget for EPA of $802 million for federal 1978 with a ceiling of 9,698 agency positions.

The setting into which Costle stepped is difficult to summarize briefly. As Costle characterized it:

"Outside there is a confusion on the part of the public in terms of what this agency is all about; what it is doing, where it is going."

"The most serious constraint on EPA is the inherent complexity in the state of our knowledge, which is constantly changing."

"Too often, acting under extreme deadlines mandated by Congress, EPA has announced regulations, only to find out that they knew very little about the problem. The central problem is the inherent complexity of the job that the agency has been asked to do and the fact that what it is asked to do changes from day to day."

"There are very difficult internal management issues not amenable to a quick solution: the skills mix problem within the agency; a research program with laboratory facilities scattered all over the country and cemented in place, largely by political alliances on the Hill that would frustrate efforts to pull together a coherent research program."

"In terms of EPA's original mandate in the bulk pollutants we may be hitting the asymptotic part of the curve in terms of incremental clean-up costs. You have clearly conflicting national goals: energy and environment, for example."

Costle judged his six major tasks at the outset to be:

- Assembling a top management team (six assistant administrators and some 25 office heads).
- Addressing EPA's legislative agenda (EPA's basic legislative charter— the Clean Air Act and the Clean Water Act—was being rewritten as he took office; the pesticides program was up for reauthorization also in 1977).
- Establishing EPA's role in the Carter Administration (aware that the Administration would face hard tradeoffs between the environment and energy, energy regulations and the economy, EPA regulations of toxic substances and the regulations of FDA, CSPS, and OSHA. Costle identified the need to build relations with the other key players and to enhance EPA's standing).
- Building ties to constituent groups (both because of their role in legislating the agency's mandate and in successful implementation of EPA's programs).
- Making specific policy decisions (for example, whether to grant or deny a permit for the Seabrook Nuclear Generating Plant cooling system. Or how the Toxic Substance Control Act, enacted in October 1976, would be implemented; this act gave EPA new responsibilities for regulating the manufacture, distribution, and use of chemical substances so as to prevent unreasonable risks to health and the environment. Whether EPA would require chemical manufacturers to provide some minimum information on various substances, or require much stricter reporting requirements for the 1,000 chemical substances already known to be hazardous, or require companies to report all chemicals, and on what timetable, had to be decided and the regulations issued).
- Rationalizing the internal organization of the agency (EPA's extreme decentralization to the regions and its limited technical expertise).

No easy job.

Roy Chapin and American Motors, January 1967

In January 1967, in an atmosphere of crisis, Roy Chapin was appointed Chairman and Chief Executive Officer of American Motors (and William Luneburg, President and Chief Operating Officer). In the four previous years, AMC unit sales had fallen 37 percent and market share from over 6 percent to under 3 percent. Dollar volume in 1967 was off 42 percent from the all-time high of 1963 and earnings showed a net loss of $76 million on sales of $656 million. Columnists began writing obituaries for AMC. *Newsweek* characterized AMC as "a flabby dispirited company, a product solid enough but styled with about as much flair as corrective shoes, and a public image that melted down to one unshakable label: loser." Said Chapin, "We were driving with one foot on the accelerator and one foot on the brake. We didn't know where the hell we were."

Chapin announced to his stockholders at the outset that "we plan to direct ourselves most specifically to those areas of the market where we can be fully effective. We are not going to attempt to be all things to all people, but to concentrate on those areas of consumer needs we can meet better than anyone else." As he recalled, "There were problems early in 1967 which demanded immediate attention, and which accounted for much of our time for several months. Nevertheless, we began planning beyond them, establishing objectives, programs and timetables through 1972. Whatever happened in the short run, we had to prove ourselves in the marketplace in the long run."

Chapin's immediate problems were five:

- The company was virtually out of cash and an immediate supplemental bank loan of $20 million was essential.
- Car inventories—company owned and dealer owned—had reached unprecedented levels. The solution to this glut took five months and could be accomplished only by a series of plant shutdowns in January 1967.
- Sales of the Rambler American series had stagnated and inventories were accumulating: a dramatic merchandising move was concocted and implemented in February, dropping the price tag on the American to a position midway between the VW and competitive smaller U.S. compacts, by both cutting the price to dealers and trimming dealer discounts from 21 percent to 17 percent.
- Administrative and commercial expenses were judged too high and thus a vigorous cost reduction program was initiated that trimmed $15 million during the first year. Manufacturing and purchasing costs were also trimmed significantly to approach the most effective levels in the industry.
- The company's public image had deteriorated: the press was pessimistic and much of the financial community had written it off. To counteract this, numerous formal and informal meetings were held with bankers, investment firms, government officials, and the press.

As Chapin recalls, "With the immediate fires put out, we could put in place the pieces of a corporate growth plan—a definition of a way of life in the auto industry for American Motors. We felt that our reason for being, which would enable us not just to survive but to grow, lay in bringing a different approach to the auto market—in picking our spots and then being innovative and aggressive." The new corporate growth plan included a dramatic change in the approach to the market to establish a "youthful image" for the company (by bringing out new sporty models like the Javelin and by entering the racing field), "changing the product line from one end to the other" by 1972, [and] acquiring Kaiser Jeep (selling the company's non-transportation assets and concentrating on specialized transportation, including Jeep, a company that had lost money in each of the preceding five years but that Chapin believed could be turned around by substantial cost reductions and economies of scale in manufacturing, purchasing, and administration).

Chapin succeeded for the year ending September 30, 1971. AMC earned $10.2 million on sales of $1.2 billion.

Recalling the list of general management functions in Table 1-2, which similarities and differences appear salient and important?

Strategy

Both Chapin and Costle had to establish objectives and priorities and to devise operational plans. In business, "corporate strategy is the pattern of major objectives, purposes, or goals and essential policies and plans for achieving these goals, stated in such a way as to define what business the company is in or is to be in and the kind of company it is or is to be."[16] In reshaping the strategy of AMC and concentrating on particular segments of the transportation market, Chapin had to consult his board and had to arrange financing. But the control was substantially his.

How much choice did Costle have at EPA as to the "business it is or is to be in" or the kind of agency "it is or is to be"? These major strategic choices emerged from the legislative process which mandated whether he should be in the business of controlling pesticides or toxic substances and if so on what timetable, and occasionally, even what level of particulate per million units he was required to control. The relative role of the president, other members of the administration (including White House staff, congressional relations, and other agency heads), the EPA Administrator, congressional committee chairmen, and external groups in establishing the broad strategy of the agency constitutes an interesting question.

Managing Internal Components

For both Costle and Chapin, staffing was key. As Donald Rumsfeld has observed, "the single most important task of the chief executive is to select the right people. I've seen terrible organization charts in both government and business that were made to work well by good people. I've seen beautifully charted organizations that didn't work very well because they had the wrong people."[17]

The leeway of the two executives in organizing and staffing were considerably different, however. Chapin closed down plants, moved key managers, hired and fired, virtually at will. As Michael Blumenthal has written about Treasury, "If you wish to make substantive changes, policy changes, and the Department's employees don't like what you're doing, they have ways of frustrating you or stopping you that do not exist in private industry. The main method they have is Congress. If I say I want to shut down a particular unit or transfer the function of one area to another, there are ways of going to Congress and in fact using friends in the Congress to block the move. They can also use the press to try to stop you. If I at Bendix wished to transfer a division from Ann Arbor to Detroit because I figured out that we could save money that way, as long as I could do it decently and carefully, it's of no lasting interest to the press. The press can't stop me. They may write about it in the local paper, but that's about it."[18]

For Costle, the basic structure of the agency was set by law. The labs, their location, and most of their personnel were fixed. Though he could recruit his key subordinates, again restrictions like the conflict of interest laws and the prospect of a Senate confirmation fight led him to drop his first choice for the Assistant Administrator for Research and Development, since he had worked for a major chemical company. While Costle could resort to changes in the process for developing policy or regulations in order to circumvent key office directors whose views he did not share, for example, Eric Stork, the Deputy Assistant Administrator in charge of Mobile Source Air Program, such maneuvers took considerable time, provoked extensive infighting, and delayed significantly the development of Costle's program.

In the direction of personnel and management of the personnel system, Chapin exercised considerable authority. While the United Auto Workers limited his authority over workers, at the management level he assigned people and reassigned responsibility consistent with his general plan. While others may have felt that his decisions to close down particular plants or to drop a particular product were mistaken, they complied. As George Shultz has observed: "One of the first lessons I learned in moving from government to business is that in business you must be very careful when you tell someone who is working for you to do something because the probability is high that he or she will do it."[19]

Costle faced a civil service system designed to prevent spoils as much as to promote productivity. The Civil Service Commission exercised much of the responsibility for the personnel function in his agency. Civil service rules severely restricted his discretion, took long periods to exhaust, and often required complex maneuvering in a specific case to achieve any results. Equal opportunity rules and their administration provided yet another network of procedural and substantive inhibitions. In retrospect, Costle found the civil service system a much larger constraint on his actions and demand on his time than he had anticipated.

In controlling performance, Chapin was able to use measures like profit and market share, to decompose those objectives to subobjectives for lower levels of the organization and to measure the performance of managers of particular models, areas, divisions. Cost accounting rules permitted him to compare plants within AMC and to compare AMC's purchases, production, and even administration with the best practice in the industry.

Managing External Constituencies

As chief executive officer, Chapin had to deal only with the Board. For Costle, within the executive branch but beyond his agency lay many actors critical to the achievement of his agency objectives: the president and the White House, Energy, Interior, the Council on Environmental Quality, OMB.

Actions each could take, either independently or after a process of consultation in which they disagreed with him, could frustrate his agency's achievement of its assigned mission. Consequently, he spent considerable time building his agency's reputation and capital for interagency disputes.

Dealing with independent external organizations was a necessary and even larger part of Costle's job. Since his agency, mission, strategy, authorizations, and appropriations emerged from the process of legislation, attention to congressional committees, congressmen, congressmen's staff, and people who affect congressmen and congressional staffers rose to the top of Costle's agenda. In the first year, top-level EPA officials appeared over 140 times before some 60 different committees and subcommittees.

Chapin's ability to achieve AMC's objectives could also be affected by independent external organizations: competitors, government (the Clean Air Act that was passed in 1970), consumer groups (recall Ralph Nader), and even suppliers of oil. More than most private managers, Chapin had to deal with the press in attempting to change the image of AMC. Such occasions were primarily at Chapin's initiative and around events that Chapin's public affairs office orchestrated, for example, the announcement of a new racing car. Chapin also managed a marketing effort to persuade consumers that their tastes could best be satisfied by AMC products.

Costle's work was suffused by the press: in the daily working of the organization, in the perception by key publics of the agency and thus the agency's influence with relevant parties, and even in the setting of the agenda of issues to which the agency had to respond.

For Chapin, the bottom line was profit, market share, and the long-term competitive position of AMC. For Costle, what are the equivalent performance measures? Blumenthal answers by exaggerating the difference between appearance and reality: "At Bendix, it was the reality of the situation that in the end determined whether we succeeded or not. In the crudest sense, this meant the bottom line. You can dress up profits only for so long—if you're not successful, it's going to be clear. In government there is no bottom line, and that is why you can be successful if you appear to be successful—though, of course, appearance is not the only ingredient of success."[20] Rumsfeld says, "In business, you're pretty much judged by results. I don't think the American people judge government officials this way.... In government, too often you're measured by how much you seem to care, how hard you seem to try— things that do not necessarily improve the human condition.... It's a lot easier for a President to get into something and end up with a few days of good public reaction than it is to follow through, to pursue policies to a point where they have a beneficial effect on human lives."[21] As George Shultz says, "In government and politics, recognition and therefore incentives go to those who formulate policy and maneuver legislative compromise. By sharp contrast, the kudos and incentives in business go to the persons who can get something done. It is execution that counts. Who can get the plant built, who can bring home the sales contract, who can carry out the financing, and so on."[22]

This casual comparison of one public and one private manager suggests what could be done if the issue of comparisons were pursued systematically, horizontally across organizations and at various levels within organizations. While much can be learned by examining the chief executive officers of organizations, still more promising should be comparisons among the much larger numbers of middle managers. If one compared, for example, a regional administrator of EPA and an AMC division chief, or two comptrollers, or equivalent plant managers, some functions would appear more similar, and other differences would stand out. The major barrier to such comparisons is the lack of cases describing problems and practices of middle-level managers.[23] This should be a high priority in further research. . . .[24]

Notes

1. To reiterate: this is not a report of a major research project or systematic study. Rather, it is a response to a request for a brief summary of reflections of a dean of a school of government who now spends his time doing a form of public management—managing what Jim March has labeled an "organized anarchy"—rather than thinking, much less writing. Moreover, the speculation here will appear to reflect a characteristic Harvard presumption that Cambridge either is the world or is an adequate sample of the world. I say "appear" since as a North Carolinian, I am self-conscious about this parochialism. Nevertheless, I have concluded that the purposes of this conference may be better served by providing a deliberately parochial perspective on these issues—and thereby presenting a clear target for others to shoot at. Finally, I must acknowledge that this article plagiarizes freely from a continuing discussion among my colleagues at Harvard about the development of the field of public management, especially from Joe Bower, Hale Champion, Gordon Chase, Charles Christenson, Richard Darman, John Dunlop, Phil Heymann, Larry Lynn, Mark Moore, Dick Neustadt, Roger Porter, and Don Price. Since my colleagues have not had the benefit of commenting on this presentation, I suspect I have some points wrong, or out of context, or without appropriate subtlety or amendment. Thus I assume full liability for the words that follow.

2. Selma J. Mushkin, Frank H. Sandifer, and Sally Familton, *Current Status of Public Management Research Conducted by or Supported by Federal Agencies* (Washington, D.C.: Public Services Laboratory, Georgetown University, 1978), p. 10.

3. Ibid., p. 11.

4. Though frequently identified as the author who established the complete separation between "policy" and "administration," Woodrow Wilson has in fact been unjustly accused. "It is the object of administrative study to discover, first, what government can properly and successfully do, and, secondly, how it can do these proper things with the utmost possible efficiency. . ." (Wilson, "The Study of Public Administration," published as an essay in 1888 and reprinted in *Political Science Quarterly,* December 1941, p. 481). For another statement of the same point, see Brooks Adams, *The Theory of Social Revolutions* (Macmillan, 1913), pp. 207–208.

5. See Dwight Waldo, "Organization Theory: Revisiting the Elephant," *PAR* (November-December 1978). Reviewing the growing volume of books and articles on organization theory, Waldo notes that "growth in the volume of the literature is not to be equated with growth in knowledge."

6 See *Cases in Public Policy and Management,* Spring 1979, of the Intercollegiate Case Clearing House for a bibliography containing descriptions of 577 cases by 366 individuals from 79 institutions. Current casework builds on and expands earlier efforts on the Inter-University Case Program. See, for example, Harold Stein, ed., *Public Administration and Policy Development: A Case Book* (Orlando, Fla.: Harcourt Brace Jovanovich, 1952), and Edwin A. Bock and Alan K. Campbell, eds., *Case Studies in American Government* (Englewood Cliffs, N.J.: Prentice-Hall, 1962).

7. Luther Gulick and Al Urwick, eds., *Papers in the Science of Public Administration* (Washington, D.C.: Institute of Public Administration, 1937).

8. See, for example, Chester I. Barnard, *The Functions of the Executive* (Cambridge, Mass.: Harvard University Press, 1938), and Peter F. Drucker, *Management*

Tasks, Responsibilities, Practices (New York: Harper & Row, 1974). Barnard's recognition of human relations added an important dimension neglected in earlier lists.

9. See, for example, "A Businessman in a Political Jungle," *Fortune* (April 1964); "Candid Reflections of a Businessman in Washington," *Fortune* (January 29, 1979); "A Politician Turned Executive," *Fortune* (September 10, 1979); and "The Abrasive Interface," *Harvard Business Review* (November-December 1979) for the views of Romney, Blumenthal, Rumsfeld, and Shultz, respectively.

10. John T. Dunlop, "Public Management," draft of an unpublished paper and proposal, Summer 1979.

11. Richard E. Neustadt, "American Presidents and Corporate Executives," paper prepared for a meeting of the National Academy of Public Administration's Panel on Presidential Management, October 7–8, 1979.

12. Clinton Rossiter, ed., *The Federalist Papers* (New York: New American Library, 1961), No. 51. The word *department* has been replaced by *branch*, which was its meaning in the original papers.

13. Failure to recognize the fact of distributions has led some observers to leap from one instance of similarity between public and private to general propositions about similarities between public and private institutions or management. See, for example, Michael Murray, "Comparing Public and Private Management: An Exploratory Essay," *Public Administration Review* (July-August, 1975).

14. These examples are taken from Bruce Scott, "American Motors Corporation" (Intercollegiate Case Clearing House #9-364–001); Charles B. Weigle with the collaboration of C. Roland Christensen, "American Motors Corporation II" (Intercollegiate Case Clearing House #6-372–359); Thomas R. Hitchner and Jacob Lew under the supervision of Philip B. Heymann and Stephen B. Hitchner, "Douglas Costle and the EPA (A)" (Kennedy School of Government Case #C94-78–216), and Jacob Lew and Stephen B. Hitchner, "Douglas Costle and the EPA (B)" (Kennedy School of Government Case #C96-78–217). For an earlier exploration of a similar comparison, see Joseph Bower, "Effective Public Management," *Harvard Business Review* (March-April, 1977).

15. U.S. Government Manual, 1978/1979, p. 507.

16. Kenneth R. Andrews, *The Concept of Corporate Strategy* (New York: Dow-Jones-Irwin, 1971), p. 28.

17. "A Politician-Turned-Executive," *Fortune* (September 10, 1979), p. 92.

18. "Candid Reflections of a Businessman in Washington," *Fortune* (January 29, 1979), p. 39.

19. "The Abrasive Interface," *Harvard Business Review* (November-December 1979), p. 95.

20. *Fortune* (January 29, 1979), p. 36.

21. *Fortune* (September 10, 1979), p. 90.

22. *Harvard Business Review* (November-December 1979), p. 95.

23. The cases developed by Boston University's Public Management Program offer a promising start in this direction.

24. The differences noted in this comparison, for example, in the personnel area, have already changed with the Civil Service Reform Act of 1978 and the creation of the Senior Executive Service. Significant changes have also occurred in the automobile industry: Under current circumstances, the CEO of Chrysler may seem much more like the Administrator of EPA. More precise comparison of different levels of management in both organizations, for example, accounting procedures used by Chapin to cut costs significantly as compared to equivalent procedures for judging the costs of EPA-mandated pollution control devices, would be instructive.

Working for the Government Is Cool

GARTH COOK

One week, Dana Scully and Fox Mulder are rescuing New Hampshire school children from a ring of Satanic parents. The next they are exploring a series of unexplained murders near a traveling circus. Scully is a trained physician and Mulder has an advanced degree in psychology, but neither chose to set up a private practice. Instead, they opted for jobs that take them to the distant corners of the country—from the Arctic Circle to the Arizona desert. They are FBI agents on "The X-Files," one of television's hottest shows.[1]

An advertisement for the show features a shot of Scully and Mulder with a striking headline: "Working for the government is cool." It's a clever attention getter, an ironic message not to be taken seriously. Indeed, when you set aside the glamorous gun-toters (who themselves risk the "jackbooted fascist" label), the image of the government worker is decidedly *uncool*.

It's amazing what a bad rap government workers get. People who work in all levels of government—federal, state, and local—are written off with a label that has a powerful hold over the country's imagination: bureaucrat. The word evokes images of monotonous and pointless office jobs, reams of unneeded paperwork, lazy and dimwitted workers. A *Wall Street Journal* editorial writer, for example, recently wrote without a hint of shame that the typical bureaucrat is "a pudgy, middle-aged woman slowly applying polish to her fingernails. Every few minutes, she picks up the phone to conduct a conversation with one of her cronies in an adjoining office." A newspaper ad by R.J. Reynolds features a middle-aged man, triple jowled and smiling creepily, underneath the headline "Who Should Be Responsible For Your Children, a Bureaucrat or You?"

It has not always been this way. "In the nineteenth century," says Scott Fossler, president of the National Association of Public Administrators, "'Good enough for government work meant high quality." Even in this century, great presidents inspired Americans to join the government and honor its work. FDR called on the nation to conquer the Depression, largely through government projects, and to win World War II. President Kennedy was able to generate a real excitement for the work of government—you could go to Ethiopia with the Peace Corps or to the moon with NASA. "With FDR and Kennedy, the government had a noble, respected mission," says Fossler. "People had a sense that the government was doing important things." "Ask not what your country can do for you," Kennedy famously declared. Now, egged on by politicians who've made careers of bashing government, many Americans publicly ask whether anyone can do much of anything.

Certainly, the American public sector has plenty of maddening bureaucrats. Rooting out bad government is one of the *Washington Monthly*'s founding causes.[2] Because of overly zealous civil service protections, it can be almost impossible to fire mediocre, or even incompetent, employees. This is a problem not only for those who want service—I doubt I am the only one who has left the local Department of Motor Vehicles feeling angry and exhausted—but it can also be bad for morale. The public employee unions need to see that nobody's interest is served in keeping a lug on the job.

But the perception that all government employees are indolent, ineffective bureaucrats cloistered inside the Beltway is simply wrong. First, most government employees do not work for the federal government. The federal government employs 3 million people, while state and local governments employ 15 million. Second, most federal employees don't even work in Washington: Some 85 percent of them are out in the field.

More to the point, there are many good people in government, and many have interesting jobs. Consider a few pop-culture heroes: Clint Eastwood, the Secret Service agent protecting the president in *In the Line of Fire;* the engineers of *Apollo 13;* the doctors and nurses of "ER"; or "Quincy," the medical examiner who always gets his man. All of these are government jobs.

Plenty of other jobs haven't been the topic of a movie or TV show, but easily could be. You could be one of the National Transportation Safety Board investigators who pores through the twisted metal and plastic of a plane wreck, in search of the clue that will explain the cause of the accident—and, hopefully, prevent it from happening again. Or you could work for the Securities and Exchange Commission, trying to figure out the cons of some of the nation's most devious criminal minds. Or maybe a park ranger job—a historian and preservationist, who has plenty of contact with people, and does most of the day's work in nature's glory—is more your style. "Our big secret" says Greg Carlisle, a game warden with Washington state who, among other things, catches salmon poachers, "is that we're getting paid to do work that we love."

Yet I can't count the number of times that I've heard the familiar refrain from my twentysomething friends: "I'm not sure what I want to do; I guess I'll go to law school." "I don't really want to be a lawyer," they usually protest, as if the almost inevitable path to a fairly tedious legal job will not be followed. . . . Why is law school their fall-back position, when they could go into work that is both interesting and satisfying?

THE NAME GAME

One answer has to be the perverse pride that government at all levels seems to take in devising dreary job titles. How boring does a job as an "Animal Health Technician" sound? That's actually the title for what would better be described as the government's cowboys. Their job is to track down and lasso wild livestock that has wandered over the Mexican border carrying diseases. They spend the work week far from civilization, on horseback in the vast spaces between Brownsville and Del Rio, camping under the stars at night. Who would have guessed?

Or consider the dreary-sounding Texas Office of the State Comptroller. The words evoke rich images—flickering fluorescent lights, tortuous standard forms, bleary-eyed lifers counting the days to retirement. So why does Alan Pollock, a 40-year old father of two and the director of the office's "performance review" division, love his job? And why is the Austin-based comptroller's office described in heroic terms by the citizens of Texas?

The answer is that Pollock and his colleagues are a far cry from the unimaginative pencil-pushers you might have envisioned and much closer to being the shock troops of good government—part journalists, part detectives, part problem-solvers, part enforcers. Their small office, with a creative, can-do attitude reminiscent of a start-up software company, is charged with examining the way the state government does just about everything—from welfare to the work of state troopers—in search of ways to do it better.

One of their most public successes was also one of Pollock's most personally satisfying: a plan for sweeping changes at the Texas Department of Criminal Justice (TDCJ) that was adopted with praise. For years, there had been talk of waste and mismanagement in the prison system, so Pollock and his colleagues were called in.

They found plenty to fix. Pollock tells of his amazement at seeing the 3x5 cards—with tiny writing scrawled over front and back and stored in what looked like shoe boxes—which were being used to keep track of the prisoners. Meanwhile, the computer terminals scattered all over the complex went unused. When Pollock's team noticed guards standing around with little to do, they did a little digging and discovered that the Texas prisons had about 1.5 times as many guards as comparable systems in other states. TDCJ officials tried to say that none of the changes needed to be made. "But we knew their operations backwards and forwards," says Pollock, "so we were calling their bullshit 'bullshit.'"

Today the prisons are doing away with the old card system, guards are being used more intelligently, and the comptroller's work has already saved grateful Texans hundreds of millions of dollars. Now Pollock is gearing up for a major investigation of the state mental health system. "It's great," says Pollock. "Every project is different, and you can see that you're actually changing things." Publicity about their success has brought another change: The office is flooded with résumés from people who want a job at a place called the "Texas Office of the State Comptroller." And there are many other fascinating jobs like Pollock's in the government, at places with unlikely sounding names like the "Government Accounting Office" and the "Office of Management and Budget."

The fun jobs don't always get a lot of publicity, though. A friend of mine went to her college career office to look at job descriptions for federal positions she had heard were interesting. "They were virtually unreadable," she says. "You could not even tell what the person did." Unfortunately, sometimes, that's the whole idea. Those who are already in the know don't necessarily want a lot of outside competition for great jobs that they'd rather give to their own pals. This, long-time readers of the *Washington Monthly* will recognize, is what's known as the "buddy system": Write job descriptions for the good jobs to match the qualifications of friends, and make the jobs sound uninviting to strangers. The unfortunate side effect, of course, is that it feeds the public's view of drones at work and scares away young talent. The actual process of applying for government jobs can also be off-putting—it can take too long to move through the process.

For those who take the plunge, though, the excitement of some government jobs can be addictive. Try to imagine the rush of knowing that swarms of 400-ton jet aircraft, filled with passengers, are depending on you to help them navigate through crowded skies. You could ask the air traffic controllers who were fired by Reagan: Many simply could not find work that was as satisfying in the private sector. They always dream of coming back.

And very few private sector jobs can compare to being a homicide detective. Consider Jerry Giorgio, a detective with the New York Police Department's 34th precinct, and the subject of a fascinating profile in *The New York Times*. One fall evening in 1981, John Chase Wood, a surgery resident at the Columbia-Presbyterian Medical Center, was shot through the heart during a mugging. He bled to death at the hospital where he worked, leaving behind a young, pregnant wife. Long after most of the city had forgotten the slaying, Det. Giorgio continued to painstakingly track down leads. He finally cracked the case and made an arrest last summer. Earlier this year, he arrested the criminal's partner.

Giorgio prides himself on never forgetting a case. Three years ago, he solved a case from 1974. The family of Guadalupe Diaz, a 56-year-old widow whose killer Giorgio collared, still sends him Christmas cards. "[He] is a legend," Assistant Chief John Hill told the *Times*. "If there were 1,000 Jerry Giorgio's, there would be no need for the city's 29,000 policemen."

A question for the law-school bound: Which sounds more interesting—helping to decipher the latest corporate tax rules or piecing together the clues that point the way to a killer on the loose? One of the central facts that has been lost in the latest paroxysm of government bashing is that government workers are serving the public. In fact, the desire to do something more satisfying than devising a better way to market high-top sneakers is what draws many talented people to these jobs in the first place. Consider the researchers with the Centers for Disease Control who wrestle with the latest viruses to prevent another plague. Or think about the case worker who saves children from truly awful situations—the raging drug-addicted mother, the father who won't stop beating his family. Tough jobs, but, as the workers will tell you, it genuinely feels good to do their part to improve society.

To judge from letters that Joe Hoffman gets, New Yorkers remember the day that he saved the city. Hoffman is the man in charge of keeping the city's subways—750 miles of track and 168 stations—running under sometimes crazy conditions. So he was the one who got the phone call at 5 A.M. on a Sunday morning in July. A 4-foot water pipe, among the city's largest, had burst under Times Square. Whole trains were under water, and the flooding was flowing south down Manhattan, burying the two main north-south lines in water and mud. With morning rush hour only 24 hours away, it looked like the entire city would be filled with snarled traffic and hundreds of thousands of angry commuters. Just about everyone agreed that the next few days would be trying for a city not known for its patience.

Just about everyone, that is, except Hoffman, a tough-talking former Marine who doesn't believe in excuses. "Joe Hoffman said 'I'll have it back up in 24 hours, in time for [morning] rush hour,'" recalls one of his co-workers.

Hoffman organized nearly 1,000 transit workers and put them on the enormous job: Hundreds of electric switch boxes were covered in muck and had to be hand-cleaned, electric relays needed to be replaced, mud needed to be removed from under the third rails by hand. Hoffman even pitched in himself. He was seen mopping the floors and showing new workers how to operate the pumps. By Monday morning, just before rush hour, Hoffman was riding the test train through the flood zone. He had kept his promise. To get the subways running again, he had to stay up for 24 hours straight. "This is my job," he says. "You would do exactly the same thing if it were your job."

Or would you? How many people feel that their work affects so many people's personal lives that they cannot go home until their job has been done right? The popular conception of a government job is that it is removed from people and essentially powerless. But public workers often have much more power than their private counterparts, because their work has a real impact on lives. The reason that Hoffman was willing to forgo sleep—beyond his dogged determination—is that people depend on him. The same could be said of emergency medical technicians, who spend their days saving lives. Or consider Jim Bradford, a rehabilitation therapist with the Veterans Administration in Long Beach, California. Instead of providing the usual physical therapy, with monotonous leg lifts and arm extensions, he redesigned a garden for his patients to work in, complete with wheelchair-accessible sidewalks and planting beds. These disabled veterans of war get their exercise, and a measure of satisfaction, by cutting flowers and planting vegetables for the hospital cafeteria.

You also do not need to be one of the top guys—one of the "political appointees" with a fancy title—to have real influence. In the first issue of the *Washington Monthly*, Bill Moyers told of how two civil servants, Chester Cooper and George Carver, were able to convince President Johnson's highest policy advisors to stop the escalation in Vietnam. And Thomas Joe, a federal welfare official, told *The Washington Post* of how he personally put a 26-word clause into a law, virtually unnoticed, that expanded the Social Security Insurance program and cost the government billions of dollars a year. In the second case, the influence was not as admirable, but the point remains: You do not need a high-profile job to make a huge difference.

The ambitious who see glamour in high-profile private sector jobs should talk to Bill Crowfoot, who was recently profiled in the *Los Angeles Times*. He had hit the big time: a well-paying job as a corporate lawyer for Paul, Hastings, Janofsky & Walker, specializing in Latin American work. But one day this past spring, as he was drafting a particularly dull promissory note, he thought: "I can't go on with this."

So Crowfoot gave up a lucrative future as a corporate lawyer and decided to take a job with the Pasadena public schools. Fluent in Spanish, he was able to receive an emergency certification and land a teaching position.

Like any first-year teacher, Crowfoot finds the work exhausting. His classes include students of all levels—in one of his classes, he is supposed to be teaching 11th graders World History at the same time he is teaching 10th graders American History—and some of them are recent immigrants who don't know the first thing about either topic. The kids aren't allowed to take their textbooks home because, Crowfoot says, "we might never see them again." Many of the kids come from poor backgrounds; some of them are involved with gangs. Some kids fear being seen carrying around books or notepaper because they might be labeled a "school boy" and become a target of harassment.

But even in these circumstances, Crowfoot is able to make a difference in a few lives. He set up a file cabinet in his room with a folder for each student, so they can keep their notes without fearing the "school boy" label. In his 12th grade economics class, where many eyes glaze over almost instinctively, Crowfoot broke through by having them read an article in *Inc.* magazine about entrepreneurs. "The lowest paid one earned $72,000 to distribute VW auto parts," says Crowfoot, "and the kids said, 'I can do that.'" Crowfoot also phoned the parents of one kid who shows real academic promise but had been dressing the part of a gang-banger; "I wanted the parents to know that he could be a star if he doesn't make some bad choices," says Crowfoot. And he's even invited kids to his house on the weekend to catch up on English.

I don't want to overstate the amount of impact that teachers have," insists Crowfoot, and with the moments of job satisfaction comes plenty of frustration. Yet he knows that he now has real power to do something positive in people's lives. So Crawfoot laughs when asked if he misses the old job. "Sure, I make less money now, but even most lawyers are mortgaged to the hilt," he says. "People live to their incomes." And as hard as teaching gets, he says, few things could be worse than "getting up at 4 A.M. to revise and proof legal documents."

Indeed, imagine what a bad rap the *private* sector would have if everyone devoted the same energies to bashing it as they devote to pillorying public employees: Who would want to spend their time, people could say sarcastically, shuffling from sales meeting to sales meeting where nothing ever gets decided? Or would you prefer to find obscure tax loopholes for a faceless corporation? Or do you want to work for the same idiots who managed to spill crude oil across 45 miles of Prince William Sound? It wouldn't be long before just about any job would sound like the seventh circle of Hades.

But it shouldn't be the aim of our political dialogue to demonize work, should it? What we need is for our national leaders—Democrats, Republicans, and Independents—to agree that the work government does, be it federal, state, or local, is important, and that the people who do it deserve respect. Even as they disagree about the scope of government, or whether the federal government should devolve responsibility downward, they should put aside reflexive bureaucrat-bashing and call on the nation's best and brightest to serve.

Some might say that this message doesn't make any sense in a time of government downsizing. But the opposite is much nearer to the truth. When we are asking more and more of fewer people, isn't it all the more important to have the very best? Isn't that something that Democrats and Republicans can agree on?

Imagine if Clinton kept reminding the nation that public service is noble. Think of Newt Gingrich encouraging people to join the revolution by working to transform the public sector. Others could pick up the non-partisan message that we all want a government that works for the people, that we need a constant supply of talent, and that government employees deserve respect.

Perhaps then, more of my friends who feel lost, or who are taking the Law School Admissions Test out of inertia, would hear the call. And, perhaps, it wouldn't be too long before everyone would be saying it: "Working for the government is cool."

Notes

1. Additional research and reporting provided by Renée Swanson.
2. Where this article first appeared. —*Ed.*

PART TWO

Bureaucracy, Politics, and Public Policy

2 The Political Setting of Public Administration

In the Introduction to this collection, we learned that politics is a process and that public policies are the results. We referred to the political system as the policy system in order to make explicit the important stakes in politics. This is not a game without consequences—to all of us, almost every day.

In Chapter 1, Allison stressed how important the political environment was in public administration. In this chapter, we examine carefully the relationship between administrative agencies and politics. Here we have two articles that use both historical and political analysis to illuminate the complexity of this relationship.

In the first article, James Q. Wilson seeks to explain how "Big Government" and especially "Big Bureaucracy" came about. He focuses on the interactions of administrative agencies with their clients, a phenomenon often called *clientelism*. Wilson uses clientelism to explain the growth of governmental activities and especially the increased power of bureaucratic agencies in the policy-making process. Much of his attention is on regulatory agencies.

The federal policy makers we see most often are the president, Congress, the courts (especially the Supreme Court), and administrative agencies. In this sense, administrative agencies are best understood as *the fourth branch of government,* as depicted in Figure 2-1. At least as described here, there is no "executive branch." Rather, there is the presidency—an institution as well as an individual—and many administrative agencies (the bureaucracy).

Figure 2-1. The Four Branches of the Federal Government

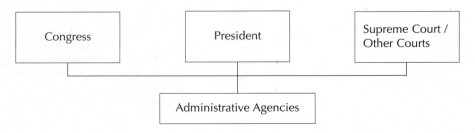

In the second article in this chapter, Francis E. Rourke carefully examines three recent political developments affecting administrative agencies: divided government, where one political party controls the presidency while another political party has a majority in the legislative branch; the rise of political movements and public interest lobbying groups; and increased policy volatility, where public dissatisfaction and changes in public policies can sometimes be very rapid.

These two articles raise many questions:

- How are politics and bureaucracy related?
- What does Wilson mean by "clientelism"? How has it affected administrative agencies?
- How do the three recent trends described by Rourke change the political setting for public administration?

The Rise of the Bureaucratic State

JAMES Q. WILSON

During its first 150 years, the American republic was not thought to have a "bureaucracy," and thus it would have been meaningless to refer to the "problems" of a "bureaucratic state." There were, of course, appointed civilian officials: Though only about 3,000 at the end of the Federalist period, there were about 95,000 by the time Grover Cleveland assumed office in 1881, and nearly half a million by 1925. Some aspects of these numerous officials were regarded as problems—notably, the standards by which they were appointed and the political loyalties to which they were held—but these were thought to be matters of proper character and good management. The great political and constitutional struggles were not over the power of the administrative apparatus, but over the power of the President, of Congress, and of the states.

The Founding Fathers had little to say about the nature or function of the executive branch of the new government. The Constitution is virtually silent on the subject and the debates in the Constitutional Convention are almost devoid of reference to an administrative apparatus. This reflected no lack of concern about the matter, however. Indeed, it was in part because of the Founders' depressing experience with chaotic and inefficient management under the Continental Congress and the Articles of Confederation that they had assembled in Philadelphia. Management by committees composed of part-time amateurs had cost the colonies dearly in the War of Independence and few, if any, of the Founders wished to return to that system. The argument was only over how the heads of the necessary departments of government were to be selected, and whether these heads should be wholly subordinate to the President or whether instead they should form some sort of council that would advise the President and perhaps share in his authority. In the end, the Founders left it up to Congress to decide the matter.

There was no dispute in Congress that there should be executive departments, headed by single appointed officials, and, of course, the Constitution specified that these would be appointed by the President with the advice and consent of the Senate. The only issue was how such officials might be removed. After prolonged debate and by the narrowest of majorities, Congress agreed that the President should have the sole right of removal, thus confirming that the infant administrative system would be wholly subordinate—in law at least—to the President. Had not Vice President John Adams, presiding over a Senate equally divided on the issue, cast the deciding vote in favor of presidential removal, the administrative departments might conceivably have become legal dependencies of the legislature, with incalculable consequences for the development of the embryonic government.

THE "BUREAUCRACY PROBLEM"

The original departments were small and had limited duties. The State Department, the first to be created, had but nine employees in addition to the Secretary. The War Department did not reach 80 civilian employees until 1801; it commanded only a few thousand soldiers. Only the Treasury Department had substantial powers—it collected taxes, managed the public debt, ran the national bank, conducted land surveys, and purchased military supplies. Because of this, Congress gave the closest scrutiny to its structure and its activities.

The number of administrative agencies and employees grew slowly but steadily during the nineteenth and early twentieth centuries and then increased explosively on the occasion of World War I, the Depression, and World War II. It is difficult to say at what point in this process the administrative system became a distinct locus of power or an independent source of political initiatives and problems. What is clear is that the emphasis on the sheer *size* of the administrative establishment—conventional in many treatments of the subject—is misleading.

The government can spend vast sums of money—wisely or unwisely— without creating that set of conditions we ordinarily associate with the bureaucratic state. For example, there could be massive transfer payments made under government auspices from person to person or from state to state, all managed by a comparatively small staff of officials and a few large computers. In 1971, the federal government paid out $54 billion under various social insurance programs, yet the Social Security Administration employs only 73,000 persons, many of whom perform purely routine tasks.

And though it may be harder to believe, the government could in principle employ an army of civilian personnel without giving rise to those organizational patterns that we call bureaucratic. Suppose, for instance, that we as a nation should decide to have in the public schools at least one teacher for every two students. This would require a vast increase in the number of teachers and school rooms, but almost all of the persons added would be performing more or less identical tasks, and they could be organized into very small units (e.g., neighborhood schools). Though there would be significant overhead costs, most citizens would not be aware of any increase in the "bureaucratic" aspects of education—indeed, owing to the much greater time each teacher would have to devote to each pupil and his or her parents, the citizenry might well conclude that there actually had been a substantial reduction in the amount of "bureaucracy."

To the reader predisposed to believe that we have a "bureaucracy problem," these hypothetical cases may seem farfetched. Max Weber, after all, warned us that in capitalist and socialist societies alike, bureaucracy was likely to acquire an "overtowering" power position. Conservatives have always feared bureaucracy, save perhaps the police. Humane socialists have frequently been embarrassed by their inability to reconcile a desire for public control of the economy with the suspicion that a public bureaucracy may be as immune to democratic control as a private one. Liberals have equivocated, either dismissing any concern for bureaucracy as reactionary quibbling about social progress, or embracing that concern when obviously nonreactionary persons (welfare recipients, for example) express a view toward the Department of Health, Education, and Welfare indistinguishable from the view businessmen take of the Internal Revenue Service.

POLITICAL AUTHORITY

There are at least three ways in which political power may be gathered undesirably into bureaucratic hands: by the growth of an administrative apparatus so large as to be immune from popular control, by placing power over a governmental bureaucracy of any size in private rather than public hands, or by vesting discretionary authority in the hands of a public agency so that the exercise of that power is not responsive to the public good. These are not the only problems that arise because of bureaucratic organization. From the point of view of their members, bureaucracies are sometimes uncaring, ponderous, or unfair; from the point of view of their political superiors, they are sometimes unimaginative or inefficient; from the point of view of their clients, they are sometimes slow or unjust. No single account can possibly treat all that is problematic in bureaucracy; even the part I discuss here—the extent to which political authority has been transferred undesirably to an unaccountable administrative realm—is itself too large for a single essay. But it is, if not the most important problem, then surely the one that would most have troubled our Revolutionary leaders, especially those that went on to produce the Constitution. It was, after all, the question of power that chiefly concerned them, both in redefining our relationship with England and in finding a new basis for political authority in the Colonies.

To some, following in the tradition of Weber, bureaucracy is the inevitable consequence and perhaps necessary concomitant of modernity. A money economy, the division of labor, and the evolution of legal-rational norms to justify organizational authority require the efficient adaptation of means to ends and a high degree of predictability in the behavior of rulers. To this, Georg Simmel added the view that organizations tend to acquire the characteristics of those institutions with which they are in conflict, so that as government becomes more bureaucratic, private organizations—political parties, trade unions, voluntary associations—will have an additional reason to become bureaucratic as well.

By viewing bureaucracy as an inevitable (or, as some would put it, "functional") aspect of society, we find ourselves attracted to theories that explain the growth of bureaucracy in terms of some inner dynamic to which all agencies respond and which makes all barely governable and scarcely tolerable. Bureaucracies grow, we are told, because of Parkinson's Law: Work and personnel expand to consume the available resources. Bureaucracies behave, we believe, in accord with various other maxims, such as the Peter Principle: In hierarchical organizations, personnel are promoted up to that point at which their incompetence becomes manifest—hence, all important positions are held by incompetents. More elegant, if not essentially different, theories have been propounded by scholars. The tendency of all bureaus to expand is explained by William A. Niskanen by the assumption, derived from the theory of the firm, that "bureaucrats maximize the total budget of their bureau during their tenure"—hence, "all bureaus are too large." What keeps them from being not merely too large but all-consuming is the fact that a bureau must deliver to some degree on its promised output, and if it consistently underdelivers, its budget will be cut by unhappy legislators. But since measuring the output of a bureau is often difficult—indeed, even *conceptualizing* the output of the State Department is mind-boggling—the bureau has a great deal of freedom within which to seek the largest possible budget.

Such theories, both the popular and the scholarly, assign little importance to the nature of the tasks an agency performs, the constitutional framework in which it is embedded, or the preferences and attitudes of citizens and legislators. Our approach will be quite different: Different agencies will be examined in historical perspective to discover the kinds of problems, if any, to which their operation gave rise, and how those problems were affected—perhaps determined—by the tasks which they were assigned, the political system in which they operated, and the preferences they were required to consult. What follows will be far from a systematic treatment of such matters, and even farther from a rigorous testing of any theory of bureaucratization: Our knowledge of agency history and behavior is too sketchy to permit that.

BUREAUCRACY AND SIZE

During the first half of the nineteenth century, the growth in the size of the federal bureaucracy can be explained, not by the assumption of new tasks by the government or by the imperialistic designs of the managers of existing tasks, but by the addition to existing bureaus of personnel performing essentially routine, repetitive tasks for which the public demand was great and unavoidable. The principal problem facing a bureaucracy thus enlarged was how best to coordinate its activities toward given and noncontroversial ends.

The increase in the size of the executive branch of the federal government at this time was almost entirely the result of the increase in the size of the Post Office. From 1816 to 1861, federal civilian employment in the executive branch increased nearly eightfold (from 4,837 to 36,672), but 86 percent of this growth was the result of additions to the postal service. The Post Office Department was expanding as population and commerce expanded. By 1869 there were 27,000 post offices scattered around the nation; by 1901, nearly 77,000. In New York alone, by 1894 there were nearly 3,000 postal employees, the same number required to run the entire federal government at the beginning of that century.

The organizational shape of the Post Office was more or less fixed in the administration of Andrew Jackson. The Postmaster General, almost always appointed because of his partisan position, was aided by three (later four) assistant postmaster generals dealing with appointments, mail-carrying contracts, operations, and finance. There is no reason in theory why such an organization could not deliver the mails efficiently and honestly: The task is routine, its performance is measurable, and its value is monitored by millions of customers. Yet the Post Office, from the earliest years of the 19th century, was an organization marred by inefficiency and corruption. The reason is often thought to be found in the making of political appointments to the Post Office. "Political hacks," so the theory goes, would inevitably combine dishonesty and incompetence to the disservice of the nation; thus, by cleansing the department of such persons these difficulties could be avoided. Indeed, some have argued that it was the advent of the "spoils system" under Jackson that contributed to the later inefficiencies of the public bureaucracy.

The opposite is more nearly the case. The Jacksonians did not seek to make the administrative apparatus a mere tool of the Democratic party advantage, but to purify that apparatus not only of what they took to be Federalist subversion but also of personal decadence. The government was becoming not just large, but lax. Integrity and diligence were absent, not merely from government, but from social institutions generally. The Jacksonians were in many cases concerned about the decline in what the Founders had called "republican virtue," but what their successors were more likely to call simplicity and decency. As Matthew Crenson has recently observed in his book *The Federal Machine,* Jacksonian administrators wanted to "guarantee the good behavior of civil servants" as well as to cope with bigness, and to do this they sought both to place their own followers in office and—what is more important—to create a system of depersonalized, specialized bureaucratic rule. Far from being the enemies of bureaucracy, the Jacksonians were among its principal architects.

Impersonal administrative systems, like the spoils system, were "devices for strengthening the government's authority over its own civil servants"; these bureaucratic methods were, in turn, intended to "compensate for a decline in the disciplinary power of social institutions" such as the community, the professions, and business. If public servants, like men generally in a rapidly growing and diversifying society, could no longer be relied upon "to have a delicate regard for their reputations," accurate bookkeeping, close inspections, and regularized procedures would accomplish what character could not.

Amos Kendall, Postmaster General under President Jackson, set about to achieve this goal with a remarkable series of administrative innovations. To prevent corruption, Kendall embarked on two contradictory courses of action: He sought to bring every detail of the department's affairs under his personal scrutiny and he began to reduce and divide the authority on which that scrutiny depended. Virtually every important document and many unimportant ones had to be signed by Kendall himself. At the same time, he gave to the Treasury Department the power to audit his accounts and obtained from Congress a law requiring that the revenues of the department be paid into the Treasury rather than retained by the Post Office. The duties of his subordinates were carefully defined and arranged so that the authority of one assistant would tend to check that of another. What was installed was not simply a specialized management system, but a concept of the administrative separation of powers.

Few subsequent postmasters were of Kendall's ability. The result was predictable. Endless details flowed to Washington for decision but no one in Washington other than the Postmaster General had the authority to decide. Meanwhile, the size of the postal establishment grew by leaps and bounds. Quickly the department began to operate on the basis of habit and local custom: Since everybody reported to Washington, in effect no one did. As Leonard D. White was later to remark, "the system could work only because it was a vast, repetitive, fixed, and generally routine operation." John Wanamaker, an able businessman who became Postmaster General under President Cleveland, proposed decentralizing the department under 26 regional supervisors. But Wanamaker's own assistants in Washington were unenthusiastic about such a diminution in their authority and, in any event, Congress steadfastly refused to endorse decentralization.

Civil service reform was not strongly resisted in the Post Office; from 1883 on, the number of its employees covered by the merit system expanded. Big-city postmasters were often delighted to be relieved of the burden of dealing with hundreds of place-seekers. Employees welcomed the job protection that civil service provided. In time, the merit system came to govern Post Office personnel almost completely, yet the problems of the department became, if anything, worse. By the mid-twentieth century, slow and inadequate service, an inability technologically to cope with the mounting flood of mail, and the inequities of its pricing system became all too evident. The problem with the Post Office, however, was not omnipotence but impotence. It was a government monopoly. Being a monopoly, it had little incentive to find the most efficient means to manage its services; being a government monopoly, it was not free to adopt such means even when found—communities, Congressmen, and special-interest groups saw to that.

THE MILITARY ESTABLISHMENT

Not all large bureaucracies grow in response to demands for service. The Department of Defense, since 1941 the largest employer of federal civilian officials, has become, as the governmental keystone of the "military-industrial complex," the very archetype of an administrative entity that is thought to be so vast and so well-entrenched that it can virtually ignore the political branches of government, growing and even acting on the basis of its own inner imperatives. In fact, until recently the military services were a major economic and political force only during wartime. In the late eighteenth and early nineteenth centuries, America was a neutral nation with only a tiny standing army. During the Civil War, over two million men served on the Union side alone and the War Department expanded enormously, but demobilization after the war was virtually complete, except for a small Indian-fighting force. Its peacetime authorized strength was only 25,000 enlisted men and 2,161 officers, and its actual strength for the rest of the century was often less. Congress authorized the purchase and installation of over 2,000 coastal defense guns, but barely six percent of these were put in place.

When war with Spain broke out, the army was almost totally unprepared. Over 300,000 men eventually served in that brief conflict, and though almost all were again demobilized, the War Department under Elihu Root was reorganized and put on a more professionalized basis with a greater capacity for unified central control. Since the United States had become an imperial power with important possessions in the Caribbean and the Far East, the need for a larger military establishment was clear; even so, the average size of the army until World War I was only about 250,000.

The First World War again witnessed a vast mobilization—nearly five million men in all—and again an almost complete demobilization after the war. The Second World War involved over 16 million military personnel. The demobilization that followed was less complete than after previous engagements, owing to the development of the Cold War, but it was substantial nonetheless—the Army fell in size from over eight million men to only half a million. Military spending declined from $91 billion in the first quarter of 1945 to only slightly more than $10 billion in the second quarter of 1947. For the next three years it remained relatively flat. It began to rise rapidly in 1950, partly to finance our involvement in the Korean conflict and partly to begin the construction of a military force that could counterbalance the Soviet Union, especially in Europe.

In sum, from the Revolutionary War to 1950, a period of over 170 years, the size and deployment of the military establishment in this country was governed entirely by decisions made by political leaders on political grounds. The military did not expand autonomously, a large standing army did not find wars to fight, and its officers did not play a significant potential role except in wartime and occasionally as presidential candidates. No bureaucracy proved easier to control, at least insofar as its size and purposes were concerned.

A "MILITARY-INDUSTRIAL COMPLEX"?

The argument for the existence of an autonomous, bureaucratically led military-industrial complex is supported primarily by events since 1950. Not only has the United States assumed during this period worldwide commitments that necessitate a larger military establishment, but the advent of new, high-technology weapons has created a vast industrial machine with an interest in sustaining a high level of military expenditures, especially on weapons research, development, and acquisition. This machine, so the argument goes, is allied with the Pentagon in ways that dominate the political officials nominally in charge of the armed forces. There is some truth in all this. We have become a world military force, though that decision was made by elected officials in 1949-1950 and not dictated by a (then nonexistent) military-industrial complex. High cost, high-technology weapons have become important and a number of industrial concerns will prosper or perish depending on how contracts for those weapons are let. The development and purchase of weapons is sometimes made in a wasteful, even irrational, manner. And the allocation of funds among the several armed services is often dictated as much by interservice rivalry as by strategic or political decisions.

But despite all this, the military has not been able to sustain itself at its preferred size, to keep its strength constant or growing, or to retain for its use a fixed or growing portion of the Gross National Product. Even during the last two decades, the period of greatest military prominence, the size of the Army has varied enormously—from over 200 maneuver battalions in 1955, to 174 in 1965, rising to 217 at the peak of the Vietnam action in 1969, and then declining rapidly to 138 in 1972. Even military hardware, presumably of greater interest to the industrial side of the military-industrial complex, has often declined in quantity, even though per unit price has risen. The Navy had over 1,000 ships in 1955; it has only 700 today. The Air Force had nearly 24,000 aircraft in 1955; it has fewer than 14,000 today. This is not to say the combat strength of the military is substantially less than it once was, and there is greater firepower now at the disposal of each military unit, and there are various missile systems now in place, for which no earlier counterparts existed. But the total budget, and thus the total force level, of the military has been decided primarily by the President and not in any serious sense forced upon him by subordinates. (For example, President Truman decided to allocate one third of the federal budget to defense, President Eisenhower chose to spend no more than 10 percent of the Gross National Product on it, and President Kennedy strongly supported Robert McNamara's radical and controversial budget revisions.) Even a matter of as great significance as the size of the total military budget for research and development has proved remarkably resistant to inflationary trends: In constant dollars, since 1964 that appropriation has been relatively steady (in 1972 dollars, about $30 billion a year).

The principal source of growth in the military budget in recent years has arisen from congressionally determined pay provisions. The legislature has voted for more or less automatic pay increases for military personnel with the result that the military budget has gone up even when the number of personnel in the military establishment has gone down.

The bureaucratic problems associated with the military establishment arise mostly from its internal management and are functions of its complexity, the uncertainty surrounding its future deployment, conflicts among its constituent services over mission and role, and the need to purchase expensive equipment without the benefit of a market economy that can control costs. Complexity, uncertainty, rivalry, and monopsony are inherent (and frustrating) aspects of the military as a bureaucracy, but they are very different problems from those typically associated with the phrase "the military-industrial complex." The size and budget of the military are matters wholly within the power of civilian authorities to decide—indeed, the military budget contains the largest discretionary items in the entire federal budget.

If the Founding Fathers were to return to review their handiwork, they would no doubt be staggered by the size of both the Post Office and the Defense Department, and in the case of the latter, be worried about the implications of our commitments to various foreign powers. They surely would be amazed at the technological accomplishments but depressed by the cost and inefficiency of both departments; but they would not, I suspect, think that our Constitutional arrangements for managing these enterprises have proved defective or that there had occurred, as a result of the creation of these vast bureaus, an important shift in the locus of political authority.

They would observe that there have continued to operate strong localistic pressures in both systems—offices are operated, often uneconomically, in some small communities because small communities have influential congressmen; military bases are maintained in many states because states have powerful senators. But a national government with localistic biases is precisely the system they believed they had designed in 1787, and though they surely could not have then imagined the costs of it, they just as surely would have said (Hamilton possibly excepted) that these costs were the defects of the system's virtues.

BUREAUCRACY AND CLIENTELISM

After 1861, the growth in the federal administrative system could no longer be explained primarily by an expansion of the postal service and other traditional bureaus. Though these continued to expand, new departments were added that reflected a new (or at least greater) emphasis on the enlargement of the scope of government. Between 1861 and 1901, over 200,000 civilian employees were added to the federal service, only 52 percent of whom were postal workers. Some of these, of course, staffed a larger military and naval establishment stimulated by the Civil War and the Spanish-American War. By 1901 there were over 44,000 civilian defense employees, mostly workers in government-owned arsenals and shipyards. But even these could account for less than one fourth of the increase in employment during the preceding 40 years.

What was striking about the period after 1861 was that the government began to give formal, bureaucratic recognition to the emergence of distinctive interests in a diversifying economy. As Richard L. Schott has written, "whereas earlier federal departments had been formed around specialized governmental functions (foreign affairs, war, finance, and the like), the new departments of this period—Agriculture, Labor, and Commerce—were devoted to the interests and aspirations of particular economic groups."

The original purpose behind these clientele-oriented departments was neither to subsidize nor to regulate, but to promote, chiefly by gathering and publishing statistics and (especially in the case of agriculture) by research. The formation of the Department of Agriculture in 1862 was to become a model, for better or worse, for later political campaigns for government recognition. A private association representing an interest—in this case the United States Agricultural Society—was formed. It made every President from Fillmore to Lincoln an honorary member, it enrolled key congressmen, and it began to lobby for a new department. The precedent was followed by labor groups, especially the Knights of Labor, to secure creation in 1888 of a Department of Labor. It was broadened in 1903 to be a Department of Commerce and Labor, but 10 years later, at the insistence of the American Federation of Labor, the parts were separated and the two departments we now know were formed.

There was an early nineteenth-century precedent for the creation of these client-serving departments: the Pension Office, then in the Department of the Interior. Begun in 1833 and regularized in 1849, the Office became one of the largest bureaus of the government in the aftermath of the Civil War, as hundreds of thousands of Union Army veterans were made eligible for pensions if they had incurred a permanent disability or injury while on military duty; dependent widows were also eligible if their husbands had died in service or of service-connected injuries. The Grand Army of the Republic (GAR), the leading veterans' organization, was quick to exert pressure for more generous pension laws and for more liberal administration of such laws as already existed. In 1879 congressmen, noting the number of ex-servicemen living (and voting) in their states, made veterans eligible for pensions retroactively to the date of their discharge from the service, thus enabling thousands who had been late in filing applications to be rewarded for their dilatoriness. In 1890 the law was changed again to make it unnecessary to have been injured in the service—all that was necessary was to have served and then to have acquired a permanent disability by any means other than through "their own vicious habits." And whenever cases not qualifying under existing law came to the attention of Congress, it promptly passed a special act making those persons eligible by name.

So far as is known, the Pension Office was remarkably free of corruption in the administration of this windfall—and why not, since anything an administrator might deny, a legislator was only too pleased to grant. By 1891 the Commissioner of Pensions observed that his was "the largest executive bureau in the world." There were over 6,000 officials supplemented by thousands of local physicians paid on a fee basis. In 1900 alone, the Office had to process 477,000 cases. Fraud was rampant as thousands of persons brought false or exaggerated claims; as Leonard D. White was later to write, "pensioners and their attorneys seemed to have been engaged in a gigantic conspiracy to defraud their own government." Though the Office struggled to be honest, Congress was indifferent—or more accurately, complaisant: The GAR was a powerful electoral force and it was ably and lucratively assisted by thousands of private pension attorneys. The pattern of bureaucratic clientelism was set in a way later to become a familiar feature of the governmental landscape—a subsidy was initially provided, because it was either popular or unnoticed, to a group that was powerfully benefited and had few or disorganized opponents; the beneficiaries were organized to supervise the administration and ensure the funding of the program; the law authorizing the program, first passed because it seemed the right thing to do, was left intact or even expanded because politically it became the only thing to do. A benefit once bestowed cannot easily be withdrawn.

PUBLIC POWER AND PRIVATE INTERESTS

It was at the state level, however, that client-oriented bureaucracies proliferated in the nineteenth century. Chief among these were the occupational licensing agencies. At the time of Independence, professions and occupations either could be freely entered (in which case the consumer had to judge the quality of service for himself) or entry was informally controlled by the existing members of the profession or occupation by personal tutelage and the management of reputations. The latter part of the nineteenth century, however, witnessed the increased use of law and bureaucracy to control entry into a line of work. The state courts generally allowed this on the grounds that it was a proper exercise of the "police power" of the state, but as Morton Keller has observed, "when state courts approved the licensing of barbers and blacksmiths, but not of horseshoers, it was evident that the principles governing certification were—to put it charitably—elusive ones." By 1952, there were more than 75 different occupations in the United States for which one needed a license to practice, and the awarding of these licenses was typically in the hands of persons already in the occupation, who could act under color of law. These licensing boards—for plumbers, dry cleaners, beauticians, attorneys, undertakers, and the like—frequently have been criticized as particularly flagrant examples of the excesses of a bureaucratic state. But the problems they create—of restricted entry, higher prices, and lengthy and complex initiation procedures—are not primarily the result of some bureaucratic pathology but of the possession of public power by persons who use it for private purposes. Or more accurately, they are the result of using public power in ways that benefited those in the profession in the sincere but unsubstantiated conviction that doing so would benefit the public generally.

The New Deal was perhaps the high water mark of at least the theory of bureaucratic clientelism. Not only did various sectors of society, notably agriculture, begin receiving massive subsidies, but the government proposed, through the National Industrial Recovery Act (NRA), to cloak with public power a vast number of industrial groupings and trade associations so that they might control production and prices in ways that would end the depression. The NRA's Blue Eagle fell before the Supreme Court—the wholesale delegation of public power to private interests was declared unconstitutional. But the piecemeal delegation was not, as the continued growth of specialized promotional agencies attests. The Civil Aeronautics Board, for example, erroneously thought to be exclusively a regulatory agency, was formed in 1938 "to promote" as well as to regulate civil aviation and it has done so by restricting entry and maintaining above-market-rate fares.

Agriculture, of course, provides the leading case of clientelism. Theodore J. Lowi finds "at least 10 separate, autonomous, local self-governing systems" located in or closely associated with the Department of Agriculture that control to some significant degree the flow of billions of dollars in expenditures and loans. Local committees of farmers, private farm organizations, agency heads, and committee chairmen in Congress dominate policy-making in this area—not, perhaps, to the exclusion of the concerns of other publics, but certainly in ways not powerfully constrained by them.

"COOPERATIVE FEDERALISM"

The growing edge of client-oriented bureaucracy can be found, however, not in governmental relations with private groups, but in the relations among governmental units. In dollar volume, the chief clients of federal domestic expenditures are state and local government agencies. To some degree, federal involvement in local affairs by the cooperative funding or management of local enterprises has always existed. The Northwest Ordinance of 1784 made public land available to finance local schools and the Morrill Act of 1862 gave land to support state colleges, but what Morton Grodzins and Daniel Elazar have called "cooperative federalism," though it always existed, did not begin in earnest until the passage in 1913 of the Sixteenth Amendment to the Constitution allowed the federal government to levy an income tax on citizens and thereby to acquire access to vast sources of revenue. Between 1914 and 1917, federal aid to states and localities increased a thousandfold. By 1948 it amounted to over one tenth of all state and local spending; by 1970, to over one sixth.

The degree to which such grants, and the federal agencies that administer them, constrain or even direct state and local bureaucracies is a matter of dispute. No general answer can be given—federal support of welfare programs has left considerable discretion in the hands of the states over the size of benefits and some discretion over eligibility rules, whereas federal support of highway construction carries with it specific requirements as to design, safety, and (since 1968) environmental and social impact.

A few generalizations are possible, however. The first is that the states and not the cities have been from the first, and remain today, the principal client group for grants-in-aid. It was not until the Housing Act of 1937 that money was given in any substantial amount directly to local governments, and though many additional programs of this kind were later added, as late as 1970 less than 12 percent of all federal aid went directly to cities and towns. The second general observation is that the 1960s mark a major watershed in the way in which the purposes of federal aid are determined. Before that time, most grants were for purposes initially defined by the states—to build highways and airports, to fund unemployment insurance programs, and the like. Beginning in the 1960s, the federal government, at the initiative of the President and his advisors, increasingly came to define the purposes of these grants—not necessarily over the objection of the states, but often without any initiative from them. Federal money was to be spent on poverty, ecology, planning, and other "national" goals for which, until the laws were passed, there were few, if any, well-organized and influential constituencies. Whereas federal money was once spent in response to the claims of distinct and organized clients, public or private, in the contemporary period federal money has increasingly been spent in ways that have *created* such clients.

And once rewarded or created, they are rarely penalized or abolished. What David Stockman has called the "social pork barrel" grows more or less steadily. Between 1950 and 1970, the number of farms declined from about 5.6 million to fewer than three million, but government payments to farmers rose from $283 million to $3.2 billion. In the public sector, even controversial programs have grown. Urban renewal programs have been sharply criticized, but federal support for the program rose from $281 million in 1965 to about $1 billion in 1972. Public housing has been enmeshed in controversy, but federal support for it rose from $206 million in 1965 to $845 million in 1972. Federal financial support for local poverty programs under the Office of Economic Opportunity has actually declined in recent years, but this cut is almost unique and it required the steadfast and deliberate attention of a determined President who was bitterly assailed both in the Congress and in the courts.

SELF-PERPETUATING AGENCIES

If the Founding Fathers were to return to examine bureaucratic clientelism, they would, I suspect, be deeply discouraged. James Madison clearly foresaw that American society would be "broken into many parts, interests and classes of citizens" and that this "multiplicity of interests" would help ensure against "the tyranny of the majority," especially in a federal regime with separate branches of government. Positive action would require a "coalition of a majority"; in the process of forming this coalition, the rights of all would be protected, not merely by self-interested bargains, but because in a free society such a coalition "could seldom take place on any other principles than those of justice and the general good." To those who wrongly believed that Madison thought of men as acting only out of base motives, the phrase is instructive: Persuading men who disagree to compromise their differences can rarely be achieved solely by the parceling out of relative advantage; the belief is also required that what is being agreed to is right, proper, and defensible before public opinion.

Most of the major new social programs of the United States, whether for the good of the few or the many, were initially adopted by broad coalitions appealing to general standards of justice or to conceptions of the public weal. This is certainly the case with most of the New Deal legislation—notably such programs as Social Security—and with most Great Society legislation—notably Medicare and aid to education; it was also conspicuously the case with respect to post–Great Society legislation pertaining to consumer and environmental concerns. State occupational licensing laws were supported by majorities interested in, among other things, the contribution of these statutes to public safety and health.

But when a program supplies particular benefits to an existing or newly created interest, public or private, it creates a set of political relationships that make exceptionally difficult further alteration of that program by coalitions of the majority. What was created in the name of the common good is sustained in the name of the particular interest. Bureaucratic clientelism becomes self-perpetuating, in the absence of some crisis or scandal, because a single interest group to which the program matters greatly is highly motivated and well-situated to ward off the criticisms of other groups that have a broad but weak interest in the policy.

In short, a regime of separated powers makes it difficult to overcome objections and contrary interests efficiently to permit the enactment of a new program or the creation of a new agency. Unless the legislation can be made to pass either with little notice or at a time of crisis or extraordinary majorities—and sometimes even then—the initiation of new programs requires public interest arguments. But the same regime works to protect agencies, once created, from unwelcome change because a major change is, in effect, new legislation that must overcome the same hurdles as the original law, but this time with one of the hurdles—the wishes of the agency and its client—raised much higher. As a result, the Madisonian system makes it relatively easy for the delegation of public power to private groups to go unchallenged and, therefore, for factional interests that have acquired a supportive public bureaucracy to rule without submitting their interests to the effective scrutiny and modification of other interests.

BUREAUCRACY AND DISCRETION

For many decades, the Supreme Court denied to the federal government any general "police power" over occupations and businesses, and thus most such regulation occurred at the state level and even there under the constraint that it must not violate the notion of "substantive due process"—that is, the view that there were sharp limits to the power of any government to take (and therefore to regulate) property. What clearly was within the regulatory province of the federal government was interstate commerce, and thus it is not surprising that the first major federal regulatory body should be the Interstate Commerce Commission (ICC), created in 1887.

What does cause, if not surprise, then at least dispute, is the view that the Commerce Act actually was intended to regulate railroads in the public interest. It has become fashionable of late to see this law as a device sought by the railroads to protect themselves from competition. The argument has been given its best-known formulation by Gabriel Kolko. Long-haul railroads, facing ruinous price wars and powerless to resist the demands of big shippers for rebates, tried to create voluntary cartels or "pools" that would keep rates high. These pools always collapsed, however, when one railroad or another would cut rates in order to get more business. To prevent this, the railroads turned to the federal government seeking a law to compel what persuasion could not induce. But the genesis of the act was in fact more complex: Shippers wanted protection from high prices charged by railroads that operated monopolistic services in certain communities; many other shippers served by competing lines wanted no legal barriers to prevent competition from driving prices down as far as possible; some railroads wanted regulation to ease competition, while others feared regulation. And the law as finally passed in fact made "pooling" (or cartels to keep prices up) illegal.

The true significance of the Commerce Act is not that it allowed public power to be used to make secure private wealth but that it created a federal commission with broadly delegated powers that would have to reconcile conflicting goals (the desire for higher or lower prices) in a political environment characterized by a struggle among organized interests and rapidly changing technology. In short, the Commerce Act brought forth a new dimension to the problem of bureaucracy: not those problems, as with the Post Office, that resulted from size and political constraints, but those that were caused by the need to make binding choices without any clear standards for choice.

The ICC was not, of course, the first federal agency with substantial discretionary powers over important matters. The Office of Indian Affairs, for a while in the War Department but after 1849 in the Interior Department, coped for the better part of a century with the Indian problem equipped with no clear policy, beset on all sides by passionate and opposing arguments, and infected with a level of fraud and corruption that seemed impossible to eliminate. There were many causes of the problem, but at root was the fact that the government was determined to control the Indians but could not decide toward what end that control should be exercised (extermination, relocation, and assimilation all had their advocates) and, to the extent the goal was assimilation, could find no method by which to achieve it. By the end of the century, a policy of relocation had been adopted *de facto* and the worst abuses of the Indian service had been eliminated—if not by administrative skill, then by the exhaustion of things in Indian possession worth stealing. By the turn of the century, the management of the Indian question had become the more or less routine administration of Indian schools and the allocation of reservation land among Indian claimants.

REGULATION VERSUS PROMOTION

It was the ICC and agencies and commissions for which it was the precedent that became the principal example of federal discretionary authority. It is important, however, to be clear about just what this precedent was. Not everything we now call a regulatory agency was in fact intended to be one. The ICC, the Antitrust Division of the Justice Department, the Federal Trade Commission (FTC), the Food and Drug Administration (FDA), the National Labor Relations Board (NLRB)—all these *were* intended to be genuinely regulatory bodies created to handle under public auspices matters once left to private arrangements. The techniques they were to employ varied: approving rates (ICC), issuing cease-and-desist orders (FTC), bringing civil or criminal actions in the courts (the Antitrust Division), defining after a hearing an appropriate standard of conduct (NLRB), or testing a product for safety (FDA). In each case, however, Congress clearly intended that the agency either define its own standards (a safe drug, a conspiracy in restraint of trade, a fair labor practice) or choose among competing claims (a higher or lower rate for shipping grain).

Other agencies often grouped with these regulatory bodies—the Civil Aeronautics Board, the Federal Communications Commission, the Maritime Commission—were designed, however, not primarily to regulate, but to *promote* the development of various infant or threatened industries. However, unlike fostering agriculture or commerce, fostering civil aviation or radio broadcasting was thought to require limiting entry (to prevent "unsafe" aviation or broadcast interference); but at the time these laws were passed few believed that the restrictions on entry would be many, or that the choices would be made on any but technical or otherwise noncontroversial criteria. We smile now at their naïveté, but we continue to share it—today we sometimes suppose that choosing an approved exhaust emission control system or a water pollution control system can be done on the basis of technical criteria and without affecting production and employment.

MAJORITARIAN POLITICS

The creation of regulatory bureaucracies has occurred, as is often remarked, in waves. The first was the period between 1887 and 1890 (the Commerce Act and the Antitrust Act), the second between 1906 and 1915 (the Pure Food and Drug Act, the Meat Inspection Act, the Federal Trade Commission Act, the Clayton Act), the third during the 1930s (the Food, Drug, and Cosmetic Act, the Public Utility Holding Company Act, the Securities Exchange Act, the Natural Gas Act, the National Labor Relations Act), and the fourth during the latter part of the 1960s (the Water Quality Act, the Truth in Lending Act, the National Traffic and Motor Vehicle Safety Act, various amendments to the drug laws, the Motor Vehicle Pollution Control Act, and many others).

Each of these periods was characterized by progressive or liberal Presidents in office (Cleveland, T. R. Roosevelt, Wilson, F. D. Roosevelt, Johnson); one was a period of national crisis (the 1930s); three were periods when the President enjoyed extraordinary majorities of his own party in both houses of Congress (1914–1916, 1932–1940, and 1964–1968); and only the first period preceded the emergence of the national mass media of communication. These facts are important because of the special difficulty of passing any genuinely regulatory legislation: A single interest, the regulated party, sees itself seriously threatened by a law proposed by a policy entrepreneur who must appeal to an unorganized majority, the members of which may not expect to be substantially or directly benefited by the law. Without special political circumstances—a crisis, a scandal, extraordinary majorities, an especially vigorous President, the support of media—the normal barriers to legislative innovation (i.e., to the formation of a "coalition of the majority") may prove insuperable.

Stated another way, the initiation of regulatory programs tends to take the form of majoritarian rather than coalitional politics. The Madisonian system is placed in temporary suspense: Exceptional majorities propelled by a public mood and led by a skillful policy entrepreneur take action that might not be possible under ordinary circumstances (closely divided parties, legislative-executive checks and balances, popular indifference). The consequence of majoritarian politics for the administration of regulatory bureaucracies is great. To initiate and sustain the necessary legislative mood, strong, moralistic, and sometimes ideological appeals are necessary—leading, in turn, to the granting of broad mandates of power to the new agency (a modest delegation of authority would obviously be inadequate if the problem to be resolved is of crisis proportions), or to the specifying of exacting standards to be enforced (e.g., *no* carcinogenic products may be sold, 95 percent of the pollutants must be eliminated), or to both.

Either in applying a vague but broad rule ("the public interest, convenience, and necessity") or in enforcing a clear and strict standard, the regulatory agency will tend to broaden the range and domain of its authority, to lag behind technological and economic change, to resist deregulation, to stimulate corruption, and to contribute to the bureaucratization of private institutions.

It will broaden its regulatory reach out of a variety of motives: to satisfy the demand of the regulated enterprise that it be protected from competition, to make effective the initial regulatory action by attending to the unanticipated side effects of that action, to discover or stretch the meaning of vague statutory language, or to respond to new constituencies induced by the existence of the agency to convert what were once private demands into public pressures. For example, the Civil Aeronautics Board, out of a desire both to promote aviation and to protect the regulated price structure of the industry, will resist the entry into the industry of new carriers. If a Public Utilities Commission sets rates too low for a certain class of customers, the utility will allow service to those customers to decline in quality, leading in turn to a demand that the Commission also regulate the quality of service. If the Federal Communications Commission cannot decide who should receive a broadcast license by applying the "public interest" standard, it will be powerfully tempted to invest that phrase with whatever preferences the majority of the Commission then entertains, leading in turn to the exercise of control over many more aspects of broadcasting than merely signal interference—all in the name of deciding what the standard for entry shall be. If the Antitrust Division can prosecute conspiracies in restraint of trade, it will attract to itself the complaints of various firms about business practices that are neither conspiratorial nor restraining but merely competitive, and a "vigorous" antitrust lawyer may conclude that these practices warrant prosecution.

BUREAUCRATIC INERTIA

Regulatory agencies are slow to respond to change for the same reason all organizations with an assured existence are slow: There is no incentive to respond. Furthermore, the requirements of due process and of political conciliation will make any response time-consuming. For example, owing to the complexity of the matter and the money at stake, any comprehensive review of the long-distance rates of the telephone company will take years, and possibly may take decades.

Deregulation, when warranted by changed economic circumstances or undesired regulatory results, will be resisted. Any organization, and *a fortiori* any public organization, develops a genuine belief in the rightness of its mission that is expressed as a commitment to regulation as a process. This happened to the ICC in the early decades of this century as it steadily sought both enlarged powers (setting minimum as well as maximum rates) and a broader jurisdiction (over trucks, barges, and pipelines as well as railroads). It even urged incorporation into the Transportion Act of 1920 language directing it to prepare a comprehensive transportation plan for the nation. Furthermore, any regulatory agency will confer benefits on some group or interest, whether intended or not; those beneficiaries will stoutly resist deregulation. (But in happy proof of the fact that there are no iron laws, even about bureaucracies, we note the recent proposals emanating from the Federal Power Commission that the price of natural gas be substantially deregulated.)

The operation of regulatory bureaus may tend to bureaucratize the private sector. The costs of conforming to many regulations can be met most easily—often, *only*—by large firms and institutions with specialized bureaucracies of their own. Smaller firms and groups often must choose between unacceptably high overhead costs, violating the law, or going out of business. A small bakery producing limited runs of a high-quality product literally may not be able to meet the safety and health standards for equipment, or to keep track of and administer fairly its obligations to its two employees; but unless the bakery is willing to break the law, it must sell out to a big bakery that can afford to do these things, but may not be inclined to make and sell good bread. I am not aware of any data that measure private bureaucratization or industrial concentration as a function of the economies of scale produced by the need to cope with the regulatory environment, but I see no reason why such data could not be found.

Finally, regulatory agencies that control entry, fix prices, or substantially affect the profitability of an industry create a powerful stimulus for direct or indirect forms of corruption. The revelations about campaign finance in the 1972 presidential election show dramatically that there will be a response to that stimulus. Many corporations, disproportionately those in regulated industries (airlines, milk producers, oil companies), made illegal or hard-to-justify campaign contributions involving very large sums.

THE ERA OF CONTRACT

It is far from clear what the Founding Fathers would have thought of all this. They were not doctrinaire exponents of laissez-faire, nor were eighteenth-century governments timid about asserting their powers over the economy. Every imaginable device of fiscal policy was employed by the states after the Revolutionary War. Mother England had, during the mercantilist era, fixed prices and wages, licensed merchants, and granted monopolies and subsidies. (What were the royal grants of American land to immigrant settlers but the greatest of subsidies, sometimes—as in Pennsylvania—almost monopolistically given?) European nations regularly operated state enterprises, controlled trade, and protected industry. But as William D. Grampp has noted, at the Constitutional Convention the Founders considered authorizing only four kinds of economic controls, and they rejected two of them. They agreed to allow the Congress to regulate international and interstate commerce and to give monopoly protection in the form of copyrights and patents. Even Madison's proposal to allow the federal government to charter corporations was rejected. Not one of the 85 *Federalist* papers dealt with economic regulation; indeed, the only reference to commerce was the value to it of a unified nation and a strong navy.

G. Warren Nutter has speculated as to why our Founders were so restrained in equipping the new government with explicit regulatory powers. One reason may have been the impact of Adam Smith's *Wealth of Nations*, published the same year as the Declaration of Independence, and certainly soon familiar to many rebel leaders, notably Hamilton. Smith himself sought to explain the American prosperity before the Revolution by the fact that Britain, through "salutary neglect," had not imposed mercantilist rules on the colonial economy. "Plenty of good land, and liberty to manage their own affairs in their own way" were the "two great causes" of colonial prosperity. As Nutter observes, there was a spirit of individualistic venture among the colonies that found economic expression in the belief that voluntary contracts were the proper organization principle of enterprise.

One consequence of this view was that the courts in many states were heavily burdened with cases testing the provisions of contracts and settling debts under them. In one rural county in Massachusetts the judges heard over 800 civil cases during 1785. As James Willard Hurst has written, the years before 1875 were "above all else, the years of contract in our law."

The era of contract came to an end with the rise of economic organizations so large or with consequences so great that contracts were no longer adequate, in the public's view, to adjust corporate behavior to the legitimate expectations of other parties. The courts were slower to accede to this change than were many legislatures, but in time they acceded completely, and the era of administrative regulation was upon us. The Founders, were they to return, would understand the change in the scale and social significance of enterprise, would approve of many of the purposes of regulation, perhaps would approve of the behavior of some of the regulatory bureaus seeking to realize those purposes, but surely would be dismayed at the political cost resulting from having vested vast discretionary authority in the hands of officials whose very existence—to say nothing of whose function—was not anticipated by the Constitutional Convention, and whose effective control is beyond the capacity of the governing institutions which that Convention had designed.

THE BUREAUCRATIC STATE AND THE REVOLUTION

The American Revolution was not only a struggle for independence but a fundamental rethinking of the nature of political authority. Indeed, until that reformulation was completed the Revolution was not finished. What made political authority problematic for the colonists was the extent to which they believed Mother England had subverted their liberties despite the protection of the British constitution, until then widely regarded in America as the most perfect set of governing arrangements yet devised. The evidence of usurpation is now familiar: unjust taxation, the weakening of the independence of the judiciary, the stationing of standing armies, and the extensive use of royal patronage to reward office-seekers at colonial expense. Except for the issue of taxation, which raised for the colonists major questions of representation, almost all of their complaints involved the abuse of *administrative* powers.

The first solution proposed by Americans to remedy this abuse was the vesting of most (or, in the case of Pennsylvania and a few other states, virtually all) powers in the legislature. But the events after 1776 in many colonies, notably Pennsylvania, convinced the most thoughtful citizens that legislative abuses were as likely as administrative ones: In the extreme case, citizens would suffer from the "tyranny of the majority." Their solution to this problem was, of course, the theory of the separation of powers by which, as brilliantly argued in *The Federalist* papers, each branch of government would check the likely usurpations of the other.

This formulation went essentially unchallenged in theory and unmodified by practice for over a century. Though a sizeable administrative apparatus had come into being by the end of the nineteenth century, it constituted no serious threat to the existing distribution of political power because it either performed routine tasks (the Post Office) or dealt with temporary crises (the military). Some agencies wielding discretionary authority existed, but they either dealt with groups whose liberties were not of much concern (the Indian Office) or their exercise of discretion was minutely scrutinized by Congress (the Land Office, the Pension Office, the Customs Office). The major discretionary agencies of the nineteenth century flourished at the very period of greatest congressional domination of the political process—the decades after the Civil War—and thus, though their supervision was typically inefficient and sometimes corrupt, these agencies were for most practical purposes direct dependencies of Congress. In short, their existence did not call into question the theory of the separation of powers.

But with the growth of client-serving and regulatory agencies, grave questions began to be raised—usually implicitly—about that theory. A client-serving bureau, because of its relations with some source of private power, could become partially independent of both the executive and legislative branches—or in the case of the latter, dependent upon certain committees and independent of others and of the views of the Congress as a whole. A regulatory agency (that is to say, a truly regulatory one and not a clientelist or promotional agency hiding behind a regulatory fig leaf) was, in the typical case, placed formally outside the existing branches of government. Indeed, they were called "independent" or "quasi-judicial" agencies (they might as well have been called "quasi-executive" or "quasi-legislative") and thus the special status that clientelist bureaus achieved *de facto,* the regulatory ones achieved *de jure.*

It is, of course, inadequate and misleading to criticize these agencies, as has often been done, merely because they raise questions about the problem of sovereignty. The crucial test of their value is their behavior, and that can be judged only by applying economic and welfare criteria to the policies they produce. But if such judgments should prove damning, as increasingly has been the case, then the problem of finding the authority with which to alter or abolish such organizations becomes acute. In this regard the theory of the separation of powers has proved unhelpful.

The separation of powers makes difficult, in ordinary times, the extension of public power over private conduct—as a nation, we came more slowly to the welfare state than almost any European nation, and we still engage in less central planning and operate fewer nationalized industries than other democratic regimes. But we have extended the regulatory sway of our national government as far or farther than that of most other liberal regimes (our environmental and safety codes are now models for much of Europe), and the bureaus wielding these discretionary powers are, once created, harder to change or redirect than would be the case if authority were more centralized.

The shift of power toward the bureaucracy was not inevitable. It did not result simply from increased specialization, the growth of industry, or the imperialistic designs of the bureaus themselves. Before the second decade of this century, there was no federal bureaucracy wielding substantial discretionary powers. That we have one now is the result of political decisions made by elected representatives. Fifty years ago, the people often wanted more of government than it was willing to provide—it was, in that sense, a republican government in which representatives moderated popular demands. Today, not only does political action follow quickly upon the stimulus of public interest, but government itself creates that stimulus and sometimes acts in advance of it.

All democratic regimes tend to shift resources from the private to the public sector and to enlarge the size of the administrative component of government. The particularistic and localistic nature of American democracy has created a particularistic and client-serving administration. If our bureaucracy often serves special interests and is subject to no central direction, it is because our legislature often serves special interests and is subject to no central leadership. For Congress to complain of what it has created and it maintains is, to be charitable, misleading. Congress could change what it has devised, but there is little reason to suppose it will.

American Bureaucracy in a Changing Political Setting

FRANCIS E. ROURKE

Marked changes in the American political culture in recent years have made life considerably more difficult for national administrative agencies and greatly complicated the task of executive officials charged with managing their affairs. These governmental agencies have had to respond to a continuing public demand both for government services and for a wide range of controls over social and economic activities in American society. This two-fold public demand has persisted even in the face of the deeply antigovernment politics of recent decades.

The fact that government agencies are having trouble doing their work has never been of serious concern in American democracy. After all, constitutional arrangements in the United States were not designed to smooth the way for the exercise of power by the instrumentalities of the state. No amount of anti-bureaucratic rhetoric, however, can obscure the fact that effective national policymaking in the United States, as in other democracies, requires that the elected officials responsible for making policy decisions receive as much help as possible from the permanent organizations of government. The principal question examined here is how changes in American political culture have affected the ability of career civil servants to provide such assistance.

This discussion focuses on three of the changes in modern American politics that have had the most significant effect on the bureaucratic role in the policy process in the United States. The first change is the system of "divided government" that now prevails at the national level—the habit Americans have lately fallen into of putting one political party, the Republicans, in charge of the presidency, while electing a majority of Democrats to a dominant position in either or both houses of the Congress. This unusual form of coalition government has often operated in a surprisingly harmonious way, as each party has gladly seized the opportunity both to have power and to avoid responsibility for its exercise. (A persuasive argument to this effect can be found in Mayhew 1989.) It is, however, an arrangement that has greatly affected the part that career civil servants can play in the development of national policy.

The second important change is the ascent of political movements and public-interest lobbies in American politics. These groups now provide the chief impetus behind policy development in a great variety of government programs in the United States, especially in areas of social policy such as civil rights, environmental protection, and consumer health and safety. The emergence of these new forces on the political scene has disrupted traditional relationships between administrative agencies and the groups they serve, presenting these agencies with the difficult task of defining and carrying out policies that will satisfy conflicting demands from an increasingly variegated political support system. Many of the clientele groups within this system are both less supportive and considerably less deferential toward their administrative patrons than was once the case.

The third change is that, along with much of the world, the United States has moved into an era of policy volatility. Dramatic shifts in the direction of government programs have become so commonplace that the old models predicting that public policy would change only at an incremental or gradualist pace look increasingly obsolete.[1] This decline in the incremental style of policy change has had a very visible impact on the role of administrators in the evolution of national policy. Policy volatility is a world that bureaucrats never made, and it is one in which their influence has steadily diminished. The bureaucrats' forte has always been the gradual alteration of existing policy to cope with emerging demands or sudden disturbances in their agencies' environments. They cope with change by adhering to routines that are carefully scripted to deal with similar situations encountered in the past. These routines are often poorly suited to a political culture in which the present radically and frequently departs from the past.

Given these three changes, the question to be confronted here is how they have affected the ability of administrative agencies to contribute to the discourse through which free societies decide on the policies that their governments should follow. Have these changes led to a significant erosion in the opportunities open to career officials to make their voice heard in shaping national policy in the United States? If so, does this erosion of bureaucratic participation in policymaking have a negative impact on the achievement of policy goals? Modern presidents have certainly seemed to believe that it does not. The White House has often operated in recent years on the alternative assumption that national policymaking will most prosper if it is entirely dominated by presidential appointees.

DIVIDED GOVERNMENT

Reformers tend to look at the separation of powers as a source of policy stalemate in American political life. For much of this century, they proposed the development of cohesive political parties that—in the pursuit of common policy goals—would bind the president and the Congress together after an election.[2] In the past three decades, this long-standing aspiration of reformers has finally been realized, and American political parties have indeed achieved such ideological cohesion: Democrats have now become more reliably liberal and Republicans are certainly more consistently conservative.

Irony of ironies, however: this development has served not to bring the two branches of government together but to drive them even further apart. The voters confounded the calculations of reformers by putting a more unified Democratic party in charge of one or both branches of the Congress, even as they were electing Republicans to the presidency.

Observers disagree as to why this odd political coupling has come about.[3] Some suggest the unlikely possibility that it reflects a devious Machiavellian design on the part of the American electorate. In this view, voters—in conformity with the American political tradition—are fearful of putting too much power in the hands of elected officials. They have thus been unwilling to trust either political party with full control over the reins of government. So they have added a political dimension to the institutional separation between the president and the Congress that the Constitution initially prescribed as the most reliable check on the abuse of power by public officials.

Others argue that the emergence of divided government reflects a natural inclination on the part of voters to have their cake and eat it too. The customarily generous Democrats in the Congress give citizens the services and subsidies that they want from government, while a more frugal Republican president provides assurance that the financial burdens necessary to sustain such programs are kept as light (or at least as invisible) as possible for the taxpaying public.

Whatever the validity of these and other explanations for its advent, divided government has had a significant effect on the operation of American political institutions. Not least in importance is the way in which divided government has diminished the ability of civil servants to influence the character of national policy in the United States. It has done so by restricting the discretion allowed to administrative agencies in making day-to-day decisions as they pursue the policy goals entrusted to their care.

Two political developments generated by divided government have played a major role in this respect. The first is the rise of an administrative presidency through which the White House has sought in a variety of ways to centralize executive power in the hands of presidents and their political appointees. The second is the growing tendency of the Congress and congressional committees to subject the decisions of administrative agencies to much closer outside scrutiny, or what its critics describe as legislative "micromanagement."

The Administrative Presidency

When presidents have found themselves confronted with a Congress under the control of the opposition party, as has been the situation normally facing Republican presidents since the 1960s, they have inevitably been tempted to go it alone. They have tried to bring about major policy changes through unilateral executive action rather than by drafting legislation and submitting it to the Congress, where it might easily be derailed. During the Nixon administration, the White House very often saw its strategic alternatives in just such stark terms: the prospect of failure if it sought approval from a Democratic Congress for its policy initiatives; the prospect of success if it was somehow able to finesse the legislative role in policy development altogether.[4]

What the administrative presidency requires more than anything else is the advantageous use of the discretion ordinarily vested in the hands of executive officials. This discretion may come either from the president's constitutional authority, as the White House staff is wont to claim, or from statutes enacted by the Congress that allow executive organizations to enjoy wide latitude in their pursuit of national policy objectives. President Nixon made extensive use of such executive discretion in his efforts to achieve his administration's policy goals. This was particularly visible in his handling of congressional appropriations, where he undertook to impound funds that the Congress had appropriated for programs to which he was opposed. While the courts eventually disallowed this presidential strategy, Nixon's impoundment decisions did impede the implementation of social and economic programs that would have been high on the president's "enemies" list, if the Nixon White House had kept such a list for policies as well as for persons.

The appointment process also presents abundant opportunities to a president determined to follow an administrative strategy of "going it alone"—a strategy under which not only the Congress but much of the executive branch outside the White House is viewed as hostile territory. Both Nixon and subsequently President Reagan appointed executives to run administrative agencies who were openly opposed to many of the goals these agencies were legally mandated to attain. Reagan used this technique in the case of the agency set up to provide legal services for the poor. Alternatively, the White House may deliberately delay appointing an executive to run an agency whose programs it dislikes, so as to weaken the agency's ability to speak with a strong voice in behalf of its programmatic goals or fiscal needs.

While the administrative presidency is mainly designed to increase presidential power at the expense of the Congress, it also serves to reduce the influence of senior career officials in policy discussions within the executive branch. As the system has recently operated, political appointees and sometimes military officers (as in the case of Colonel Oliver North and Admiral John Poindexter in the Iran-Contra affair during the Reagan administration) are the only executive officials whom the White House wants to use their discretion to advance its policy objectives: political appointees because they are expected to share the president's policy outlook, and military officers because they are thought to be more inclined to defer to their commander-in-chief.

During recent administrations, the number of presidential appointees within the executive branch has multiplied in all directions, and the role of career officials in policy development has correspondingly diminished. This is, as one executive official described it, the equivalent of giving "the federal bureaucracy a lobotomy" (quoted in Heclo 1987, 209). The result is that fewer and fewer career officials are called upon to play important roles in shaping major policy decisions, a development that threatens to make the public service less and less attractive to talented young persons looking for meaningful and challenging job opportunities in government.

Growing Congressional Oversight

In part at least because of its conviction that presidents were ignoring or usurping legislative authority by governing in a unilateral way through the administrative presidency, the Congress has reacted against this presidential strategy. In recent years, the Congress has both strengthened its own surveillance of the executive branch and sought to subject the decisions and actions of executive officials to closer scrutiny by outside forces. Ironically for career officials, this congressional backlash has reinforced the effect of the administrative presidency on the bureaucracy by placing new curbs on the ability of administrators to use their own judgment in exercising their discretionary authority. Under the administrative presidency, both the president and the Congress tend to see bureaucracy as being in the camp of the enemy. Therefore, each institution has a powerful incentive to limit the influence of bureaucrats in the policy process.

The congressional reaction against the administrative presidency has both partisan and ideological roots. The liberal Democrats in the Congress commonly face a Republican regime in the White House that controls and, in their view, often puts a conservative "spin" on the discretion that the Democratic majority in the Congress has intended administrators to use for the pursuit of liberal policy objectives. Congressional Democrats have responded to this threat by strengthening their own ability to oversee and, if necessary, reverse administrative rulings that tilt in a conservative direction. The Congress has also created opportunities for other instruments of oversight—such as public-interest groups and the courts—to challenge or, in the case of the judiciary, to overrule such decisions.

In its various efforts to improve its own oversight capabilities, the Congress has gone a long way toward closing the "expertise gap" that once prevailed in the relationship between the legislature and the executive in this country. In the process of doing so, it has become, as Lawrence Dodd (1989) describes it, almost as "technocratic" as the bureaucracy itself. The Congress has hired an increasingly professionalized staff, created or strengthened its expert advisory institutions (CBO, OTA, CRS, and GAO), and through the proliferation and specialization of its own subcommittees, is now able to conduct a much more sophisticated review of administrative activities. According to Dodd, the principal effect of recent reforms in congressional organization and procedure has been to "put in place a new technocratic government in the Congress, with power passing increasingly to technical experts, including both elected members and nonelected staffers" (pp. 106–7).

Equally important, however, are the efforts that the Congress has made to enhance the ability of groups and organizations outside of government to challenge the way in which administrative agencies use their discretionary authority. The growing influence of public-interest groups in American society is due in no small measure to the fact that liberal Democrats in the Congress have recognized these groups as useful allies in preventing a Republican White House from exploiting administrative discretion to achieve its own conservative policy goals. As one observer notes:

> Republican control of the presidency made liberal Democrats even more wary of placing discretion in the hands of administrators. Encouraging greater participation by "public interest" groups and by "average citizens" was an inviting solution to the problem of administrative discretion. (Melaick 1989, 197)

Environmental statutes, for example, were written by the Congress so as to facilitate challenges in court by public-interest groups opposed to decisions made by the Environmental Protection Agency or other agencies whose decisions had an important environmental impact. They were also designed to strengthen the ability of these groups to prod government agencies to take action to protect the environment whenever the latter seemed reluctant to do so.

The same statutes that eased the ability of private groups to challenge agency action or inaction by taking the executive organization to court also provided an avenue through which the judiciary could become more deeply involved in the task of administrative oversight. This congressional effort to encourage outside challenges to agency decisions can be seen as another example of the risk avoidance at which the national legislature has long been so skilled. Better that tenured judges should make tough policy calls than that members of the Congress who have to run for reelection should do so.

Whatever its motives, the invitation that the legislature handed to the courts to review, and where necessary to reverse, the decisions of administrators was quickly accepted. Even more striking, perhaps, is that the courts began to enjoin administrative agencies to be more energetic in the exercise of their power. The deference to administrative expertise that judges had been practicing since the latter days of the New Deal is now, so to speak, history.

As noted earlier, a strong case can be made that divided government has had much less impact on relations between the president and the Congress than might be expected. There is evidence aplenty that the White House can be just as frustrated by a national legislature dominated by its own party as it is when the Congress is controlled by the political opposition.[5] Moreover, Timothy Conlan (1990) presents convincing evidence that there are situations, like the conflict surrounding enactment of the Tax Reform Act in 1986, where "party competition under divided government can actually propel the enactment of legislation rather than hinder it."[6]

But while its impact on relations between the president and the Congress may have been minimal, the political divergence between the two major governmental institutions in the United States has clearly had pronounced effects on the role of bureaucracy in the American political system. By bringing about the rise of the administrative presidency, divided government has disrupted the alliance that used to exist between presidents and the bureaucracy. Another of its effects, the emergence of a high-powered congressional staff, has eroded the advantage in expertise that executive bureaucrats once enjoyed in dealing with the legislature. Last but not least, divided government has opened a door through which the courts, an old adversary of bureaucracy, have been able to renew and strengthen their influence over agency decisionmaking.

THE TRANSFORMATION IN AGENCY CONSTITUENCIES

In the past, administrative agencies were able to maintain a highly stable relationship with the outside groups that benefited from their activities, and these groups could usually be counted on to be highly supportive of the work that an agency did. The durability of the relationship in these earlier days is underlined by the fact that it was conventional to describe it as being one leg in an "iron triangle" system, in which executive agencies drew enduring support not only from their outside clientele but also from the congressional committees that had immediate jurisdiction over their programs.

As it was used in the past, the metaphor of the iron triangle always suggested two of the most salient characteristics of an administrative agency's traditional relationship with its political support system—the strong bonds that held the separate participants together and the power of these participants to prevent outsiders from influencing policy decisions made within the triangular system, or "triocracy," as Louis Galambos has aptly described it (1982, esp. 51–68). Thus, the iron triangle was a highly exclusionary if not actually a closed policymaking system. It maintained the agency's programs as a privileged policy enclave, where an agency might confine itself for many years to cohabiting with groups that had been "present at the creation"— involved, that is, with the organization's birth and early development.

For most administrative agencies today, this closed system is long gone, a casualty of the "glasnost" that swept over American government beginning in the 1960s—long before Soviet President Mikhail S. Gorbachev introduced the Russian term for "openness" into the American vocabulary. In the American case, glasnost was chiefly driven by two developments. The first was the opening up of the internal affairs of public bureaucracies to much greater outside scrutiny—a process that began with the congressional investigations of government secrecy by the so-called "Moss subcommittee" in the late 1950s and that led inexorably to the enactment of freedom of information or "sunshine" legislation in the decades that followed.[7]

Secondly, the American glasnost drew a great deal of impetus from the extraordinary increase in grassroots political activism that began in the 1960s with the civil-rights movement and then spread in a variety of other directions in support of varied causes, such as consumer protection, environmentalism, and worker health and safety. Iron triangles, or "subgovernments" as they were often called, suddenly found themselves beset on all sides by new groups clamoring for a piece of the policy action, or by congressional investigations sparked by charges from such groups that the agency was lax in administering the protective statutes it had been created to enforce.[8]

The enhanced openness of administrative agencies and the ever-increasing intrusion of outside groups into their internal affairs both reflected and have since fostered the growing power of the media in national policymaking. It was pressure from the news organizations that led to the Moss subcommittee investigations into government secrecy in the 1950s and to the eventual triumph of the freedom of information movement. Since that time the media have provided public-interest groups with a platform from which they can draw the country's attention to issues like toxic waste that have now become priority items on the national policy agenda. Moreover, through their own investigative reporting, news organizations have sometimes blazed trails for such public-interest groups to follow.[9]

In the wake of these developments, the political environment in which the average administrative agency now operates has become considerably less supportive and increasingly more adversarial. The number of groups interested in what an agency does has multiplied, and their attitudes toward it, even when the agency is pursuing objectives to which the groups are deeply attached, are often quite hostile. No one has been more critical of the efforts of the National Highway Traffic Safety Administration to promote safety in automobile travel than Ralph Nader, the consumer advocate who has long crusaded in behalf of this cause. As Jeffrey Berry notes, "For many administrators . . . the quiet bargaining of the subgovernment has been replaced by a much more complex and conflictual environment" (1989, 251).

In this new political context, the task of maintaining a favorable balance in their political accounts becomes considerably more difficult for agency executives, who are already operating in a political culture that is highly suspicious of government and all its works. The difficulties that agency officials confront in this new setting are compounded by the fact that many groups within their organization's increasingly diverse constituency are not only inclined to take a more negative view of the agency's performance than was true in the past but also tend to be much better informed than was once the case. Where such constituents relied in the past on agency personnel as their chief source of expertise on the problems with which they were concerned, they are now able to look elsewhere for such professional advice, or even to bring in-house expertise of their own to bear on policy issues in dispute.

The proliferation of expertise on subjects that bureaucrats may once have monopolized is thus a fact of life for every agency today. As noted earlier in the discussion of increased congressional oversight, expertise has begun to multiply within governmental institutions, as the legislature has begun to catch up with the executive in the quality of its professional staff. Even more important, perhaps, the private sector now abounds with think tanks, consulting firms, and watchdog groups that are widely regarded as more reliable sources of information and advice than the government itself. The specialized knowledge that Max Weber once saw as the comparative advantage that bureaucrats would always enjoy in debates on national policy is now much more widely distributed throughout American society.

In a very influential article, Hugh Heclo (1978) has argued that many agency constituencies today can be more appropriately described as "issue networks" than as "iron triangles." As Heclo describes these networks, they differ from traditional triangles in that their qualification for membership is based not on having some economic or other tangible stake in the decisions that an agency makes, but on being highly knowledgeable about the policy issues that the organization confronts. Hedo's paradigm seems to fit very well for areas of policymaking that are quite technical in character—monetary policy in the economic arena, for example, or the evaluation and application of strategic doctrines in the area of national defense. Whether there is an equally suitable fit in other areas of policy is still being argued.[10]

In any case, if it is true that issue networks are beginning to replace iron triangles as the prime movers in many policy arenas, then further weight is added to the argument that administrative constituencies are increasingly becoming better informed as well as more diversified. It should be noted, however, that this development does not automatically open up the policy dialogue to broader public participation. The issue network's requirement of expertise as a prerequisite for legitimate participation in the policy debate is no less exclusionary than the iron triangle's old precondition that a participant have an economic or other tangible stake in the issues being contested.

But, of course, debates among experts do attract an audience, and as Schattschneider (1960) once noted, this is one of the principal avenues through which a conflict among "insiders" is transformed into a struggle in which outsiders can also participate and make their weight felt in decisions on national policy. Expertise regarding the dangers posed by the depletion of the "ozone layer" or the impact of the "greenhouse effect" on the environment is not widely shared in American society, but the disagreements and debates among scientists who are knowledgeable about such atmospheric phenomena may allow the views of the audience to play a pivotal role in determining which side of the argument carries the day, or as Schattschneider writes, "the audience determines the outcome of the fight" (p. 22).

These twin developments—the increased diversity of constituency groups and the diffusion of expertise on policy issues—have conspired to make the policy views of government organizations less authoritative and consequently more vulnerable to outside criticism in modern American politics. The issue networks on the contemporary scene are much less consensual than were the old-fashioned iron triangles; as Heclo puts it, issue networks provide "a way of processing dissension" (1978, 120). Public administration is thus carried on today in a highly unstable political setting where major segments of its constituency are frequently dissatisfied with an agency's efforts on their behalf and where outside experts constantly question whether the agency is doing the right thing.

For an example of the highly complicated kind of political setting in which an agency might find itself today, witness the case of wetlands management, where the Congress placed policy development under the dual control of the Corps of Engineers and Environmental Protection Agency (EPA). This dual jurisdiction brought environmental policymaking under simultaneous pressure from (a) the economic-development interests traditionally prominent in the Corps' iron-triangle system and (b) the cluster of ecological experts who have always played a leading role in the EPA issue network. Rather than being alternative policymaking systems to which individual agencies may be linked, iron triangles and issue networks may sometimes reinforce one another as sources of potential opposition to agency decisions.[11]

POLICYMAKING VOLATILITY

No area of public policy better exemplifies the changing pattern of policy-making, the shifting role of bureaucracy in the policy process, and especially the volatility of policymaking than does the Social Security system. Originally designed in the 1930s as a retirement program for American wage earners, this system was for decades a model of incremental change, a model in which career officials exercised substantial influence over the direction and pace at which the program developed. A leading student of the program, Carolyn Weaver, goes so far as to claim that the Social Security bureaucracy was the principal force in charting the agency's policies throughout much of its early history. As she writes:

> My reexamination of the history of social security suggests that the bureaucracy, working with and fueling the demands of politicians, played a decisive role in the evolution of the program in the postwar years. The interests of the citizenry, or even the long-term interest of the elderly, cannot be said to have been governing. . . . A complex program, the details of which could be mastered only by experts, removed social security from direct voter as well as legislator control. (Weaver 1987, 54-55)

Weaver's view of the role of bureaucracy in the growth of the Social Security system rests not only on her reading of its history, but also on a theoretical framework she devised for explaining the development of its policies. This model centers attention on the role played by supply-side forces, especially the bureaucracy, in shaping the course of policy change in the United States. Her perspective differs markedly from the conventional view that the evolution of public policy in a democratic society is primarily driven by the shifting demands of citizen groups for public goods. She argues instead that this "demand side" view of the policy process ignores the extent to which self-interested parties supplying government services, such as executive agency officials, are active participants in the process through which policy decisions are made.

But, as Weaver herself concedes, her supply-side model is no longer as handy as it once was in explaining Social Security policymaking. During the 1980s, the landmark reforms in this retirement program were initiated by outside groups like the Greenspan Commission, whose report in 1983 led to broad changes in the Social Security financing system,[12] or by policy entrepreneurs in the executive and legislative branches of government, such as Dr. Otis Bowen, Secretary of Health and Human Services during the Reagan administration, who was the driving force behind the Medicare Catastrophic Care Act of 1988.[13]

In this new setting in the 1980s, there have been abrupt and stunning reversals of Social Security policy. Witness Bowen's Catastrophic Care Act itself, which was both enacted and repealed within the short space of twelve months. The same pattern of policy volatility characterized the agency's administration of its disability program during the 1980s, when, under conflicting pressures from the Reagan White House and the courts, the agency went back and forth on the standards it sought to apply in approving or rejecting disability claims. In the end, the Congress had to step in to untie the policy knots into which the agency had tied itself; see Mezey (1988).

The recent history of the Social Security system has thus been dominated by two interacting changes: the increasing volatility of policymaking in the field and the diminishing ability of the agency's administrative apparatus to shape the course of its own development. In the early days of the program, when the bureaucracy controlled the evolution of policy, innovations were gradual, centering on an incremental expansion in the number of wage earners included within the system.[14] As outsiders have begun to play a more decisive role in policymaking, the pattern has greatly changed. Shifts in policy have more often been a "great leap forward," or in some cases a sharp break with past practice.

The volatility characteristic of these changes in the Social Security system has been visible in other areas of national policymaking as well. Since the 1960s, for example, there has been an explosive growth in political activism coming from both the left and the right in American politics in support of radical shifts in regulatory policy. Liberals and conservatives have joined in support of far-reaching measures aimed at deregulating key sectors of the economy. Traditional conservative opponents of economic regulation pushed for this deregulation as a means of freeing business organizations from restraints damaging to their effectiveness, while liberals supported it in the belief that it would provide consumers with easier access to goods and services such as airline travel.[15]

But even as the American economy was being deregulated, intense pressure mounted for highly innovative forms of government control in such areas as women's rights, cleaning up the environment, and consumer protection. Regulatory policymaking has thus come under pressure for radical change from opposite directions. One set of reformers has assiduously sought to deregulate the economy, while another has been attempting with equal fervor to break new ground in what is loosely called "social regulation," where noneconomic objectives are of paramount concern.

Even more volatility looms on the horizon in the regulatory field today, in the wake of recent experience in sectors of the economy, such as the financial and telecommunications fields, where deregulation has had some disappointing results, and where pressure is building for some measure of reregulation.

Whatever its other implications, the volatility that has been so common in the recent history of American policymaking both reflects and contributes to a diminishing role for career civil servants in the policy process. The growing use of presidential task forces, commissions, and other kinds of "adhocracies" in major sectors of policymaking in recent years has commonly been interpreted as a no-confidence vote in the ability of the career bureaucracy to generate the policy initiatives required to deal with major problems confronting the country.[16] The working habits of bureaucratic organizations are better adapted to handling the continuing and inescapable tasks of government than they are to implementing the "brave new worlds" in both foreign and domestic policy that liberal and conservative activists have been zealously trying to fashion in recent American politics. As postmortems on Lyndon Johnson's pathbreaking Great Society programs and the counterrevolution led by Ronald Reagan both testify: innovations in policy are much easier for political activists to design than they are for government officials to carry out.

In their pioneering study of how the policy agenda emerges in the United States, Cobb and Elder make the point that policy changes can be driven by both institutional and systemic forces. The primary role in identifying the problems that public officials need to confront may be played by either governmental institutions or by political forces outside of government (1983, 1416, 85-87). One way of describing what has happened to the role of bureaucracy in this new era of American policymaking is to suggest that administrative institutions have become much less influential in defining the issues with which elected officials should deal, and that systemic forces within the outside political community have become much more important in shaping the policy agenda in the United States, especially in the domestic arena.

BUREAUCRACY AND THE POLICY DISCOURSE

The general tendency of the political changes examined here has been toward diminishing the influence that career civil servants exert over the design and execution of national policy. As this analysis has tried to show, both the president and the Congress have looked elsewhere for advice on policy issues and restricted the discretion allowed to bureaucrats in making the everyday decisions necessary to put policies into effect. In each of these ways the influence of bureaucrats in the policymaking process has been scaled back.

Moreover, the outside groups on which executive agencies could once rely for support are much less likely today to endorse agencies' policy positions. And the movement from incremental to nonincremental styles of decisionmaking in American politics has given other organizational forms, such as the adhocracies represented by either the commission or the task force, an increasingly prominent role at the cutting edge of policy development.

How, if at all, can these changes be said to have affected the success of national policymaking? What, if anything, does the policy process lose when bureaucrats play a less-important role in policy development than they once did? In the literature on policymaking the contribution that career civil servants can make to the national policy discourse is generally downgraded. Bureaucrats are alleged to be excessively cautious in the advice they give on major policy issues—a timidity rooted in their fear of being held responsible for mistakes.

Their critics also contend that when immediate action is called for, career administrators tend to counsel delay. Or that they shun the possibility of taking bold or unconventional steps—preferring instead the safer path of traditional procedures. In the dramaturgy of American politics, bureaucrats are generally seen as obstructing the pursuit of innovative and imaginative policy options—much to the detriment of the public they serve.[17]

As always, there is an element of truth in such a caricature. In a variety of policy domains, large public organizations and the people who work in them are the chief custodians of whatever wisdom experience has generated in those domains. What these people do best is to apply the knowledge gained from the past to resolve the issues currently facing them. The problems that give them the greatest difficulty are those for which there is no precedent in their organization's previous history. This is why American presidents have so often sought to create new organizations to deal with novel issues confronting the White House. And this is not the least of the reasons for the bureaucratic proliferation in the rapidly changing environment of twentieth-century American politics.

But if there is something in the culture of executive organizations that the standard caricature of bureaucracy captures, there is also much that it misses. In the development of national policy, there are always strong and conflicting pressures between doing something quickly and doing it right. The political sphere commonly generates highly intense pressures for the "quick fix." By way of contrast, bureaucracies are typically focused on the necessity of "getting it right," since these organizations usually have painful memories of mistakes that were made in the past in launching or carrying out policy initiatives that departed widely from past practice.[18]

To be sure, no policymaking system can be effective if it is paralyzed by memories of past mistakes or chooses to focus primarily on the avoidance of error rather than the achievement of results; yet, an abundance of forces in the American political system today are pushing toward radical changes in the direction of national policy. In this volatile political context, there is surely an important role in the policy process for a set of institutions that is primarily committed to the avoidance of error in a political setting otherwise tilted in the direction of achieving short-term results.

Bureaucracies also play an important if not indispensable role in American politics by serving as the chief habitat of professional norms within the policymaking culture. The negative stereotype of bureaucracy commonly emphasizes the close identification of bureaucrats with their own organization and their penchant for promoting its status and power, even when the merits of continued public support for some of its activities may seem highly questionable. What this portrait of administrative behavior chiefly emphasizes is the strong interest that bureaucrats sometimes take in feathering their own nests. What this perspective fails to recognize, however, is that bureaucracies also serve today as the natural habitat of highly trained and very skilled professionals who bring to policy deliberations a critical capacity for both defining the sources of the problem that policymakers confront and identifying the weaknesses of remedies that may be proposed. Moreover, it is common for these experts in scientific and other fields to put adherence to the norms of their craft well ahead of any loyalty they may feel for the government organization by which they happen to be employed.

So if bureaucracies tend to stifle dissent, as is often alleged, it is also true that they provide a haven for very independent or even maverick professionals who are always ready to go public with their disagreement on policy issues more often than not by "leaking" their critical views to a friendly outside audience.

The promotion of widespread discussion and debate preceding the execution of national policy decisions has always been looked upon as a major practical advantage as well as a moral virtue of policymaking in a democratic society. Bureaucrats, like the other interested parties normally involved in the policy process, have a contribution to make to such a free-wheeling discourse on national policy, even when this contribution is no more than a cautionary tale about the possibility of failure.

Consider, for example, the lesson taught by a recent examination of American involvement in the Vietnam war. The authors point out that a wargame simulation was conducted in 1965 by "a cross section of the best informed and most expert middle-level officials of government" on the eve of a massive expansion in this country's military commitment to the war. The study was "eerily prophetic" of the stalemate to which American intervention eventually led—but its findings never made their way "through the Johnson policy process to the Oval Office."[19]

To be sure this lesson would not find ready acceptance in the arena of American politics. In this political setting it is always easy to find an audience for the unassailable proposition that a policy debate completely dominated by bureaucrats is a violation of the public's right to rule. It is a much greater challenge to elicit support for the alternative possibility that major public policies may sometimes suffer because there has been too little bureaucratic involvement in their design, even though the evidence suggests that administrative agencies can provide the president and the Congress with a very valuable early warning system against costly mistakes in launching new policy ventures.

Notes

1. The classic study of incrementalism is, of course, Braybrooke and Lindblom (1963). For an interesting analysis of incrementalism in recent American policymaking, see Jones (1984, 238–46).
2. James L. Sundquist (1988-89) provides an excellent critique of this reformist orientation.
3. James P. Pfiffner (1989) reviews the varied efforts that have been made to explain the advent of divided government.
4. For a recent discussion of the concept of the administrative presidency by its inventor, see Richard P. Nathan (1986); however, Richard W. Waterman (1989) presents a less sanguine view of the way in which this White House strategy has operated.
5. See Mayhew (1989). Note, however, that Mayhew's argument is not that divided government makes "no difference," but rather that it makes "very little difference" (p. 87).
6. Conlan cites the Clean Air Act of 1970 as another example of legislation that drew much of its force and inspiration from rivalry for political credit between the White House and Congress.
7. For a discussion of the pioneering efforts of the Moss subcommittee to promote openness in government, see Rourke (1961), esp. pp. 107–10, 218–20.
8. "Creedal passion" is the phrase Samuel P. Huntington (1981) uses to describe the primal force that lies behind much of the political action by reform movements today. See especially pp. 85–166.
9. There is a very revealing analysis of the alliance between the media and public interest groups in contemporary American politics by Benjamin Ginsberg and Martin Shefter (1985, esp. pp. 7–8).
10. For a review of some of these arguments, see Berry (1989).
11. I am indebted here to a study of wetlands management policy prepared by Andrew Pavord, a graduate student at Johns Hopkins University.
12. For an analysis of the Greenspan Commission's work, see Light (1985).
13. Bowen's success in overcoming opposition within the Reagan administration to this catastrophic insurance plan is described in Thompson (1990).
14. The classic study of the way in which policy changes in the Social Security program evolved over the years is by Martha Derthick (1979).
15. Compare the discussion of the crosspressures to which regulatory agencies are now subject in Harris and Milkis (1989).
16. The role of these temporary organizations in the policymaking process is examined in Rourke and Schulman (1989).
17. For a spirited challenge to these stereotyped images of bureaucracy see Charles T. Goodsell (1983).

18. Two recent studies of policymaking in domestic and foreign affairs provide inter-esting illustrations of conflicts between the rival imperatives of "getting it right" and "getting it done." David J. Kling (1990) examines this problem in a study of an asbestos cleanup operation managed by EPA. William Bacchus (1990) looks at it from the perspective of the State Department's efforts to develop a better method of handling the flow of refugees from the Soviet Union.

19. See Fred I. Greenstein and John P. Burke (1989-90, 576). Garry Wills (1982) suggests that there was a similar failure to consult knowledgeable bureaucrats before the Kennedy White House launched its ill-fated Bay of Pigs invasion of Cuba in 1961. What the policy process needed in this case, Wills argues, was "more procedure and bureaucratic checking" (p. 230).

Bibliography

Bacchus, William (1990). "U.S. Refugee and Diplomatic Programs in a Rapidly Evolving Foreign Policy Climate: Measuring Program Success." Paper presented at the annual meeting of the American Political Science Association, San Francisco.

Berry, Jeffrey M. (1989). "Subgovernments, Issue Networks, and Political Conflict." In Richard A. Harris and Sidney M. Milkis, eds. *Remaking American Politics*. Boulder, Col.: Westview Press, pp. 239–60.

Braybrooke, David L., and Lindblom, Charles E. (1963). *A Strategy of Decision*. New York: The Free Press.

Cobb, Roger W., and Elder, Charles D. (1983). *Participation in American Politics: The Dynamics of Agenda-Building*, 2nd ed. Baltimore: Johns Hopkins University Press.

Conlan, Timothy J. (1990). "Competitive Government: Policy Escalation and Divided Party Control." Paper presented at the annual meeting of the American Political Science Association, San Francisco.

Derthick, Martha (1979). *Policymaking for Social Security*. Washington, D.C.: Brookings Institution.

Dodd, Lawrence C. (1989). "The Rise of the Technocratic Congress: Congressional Reform in the 1970s." In Richard A. Harris and Sidney M. Milkis, eds. *Remaking American Politics*. Boulder, Col.: Westview Press, pp. 89–111.

Galambos, Louis (1982). *America at Middle Age: A New History of the United States in the Twentieth Century*. New York: McGraw-Hill.

Ginsberg, Benjamin, and Shefter, Martin (1985). "A Critical Realignment? The New Politics, the Reconstituted Right, and the Election of 1984." In Michael Nelson, ed. *The Elections of 1984*. Washington, D.C.: The Congressional Quarterly.

Goodsell, Charles T. (1983). *The Case for Bureaucracy: A Public Administration Polemic*. Chatham, N.J.: Chatham House.

Greenstein, Fred I., and Burke, John P. (1989-90). "The Dynamics of Presidential Reality Testing: Evidence from Two Vietnam Decisions." *Political Science Quarterly* 104 (Winter):557–81.

Harris, Richard A., and Milkis, Sidney M. (1989). *The Politics of Regulatory Change: A Tale of Two Agencies*. New York: Oxford University Press.

Heclo, Hugh (1978). "Issue Networks and the Executive Establishment." In Anthony King, ed. *The New American Political System*. Washington, D.C.; American Enterprise Institute, pp. 87–124.

——— (1987). "The In-and-Outer System: A Critical Assessment." In G. Calvin Mackenzie, ed. *The In-and-Outers: Presidential Appointees and Transient Government in Washington*. Baltimore: Johns Hopkins University Press.

Huntington, Samuel P. (1981). *American Politics: The Promise of Disharmony*. Cambridge, Mass.: Harvard University Press.

Jones, Charles O. (1984). *An Introduction to the Study of Public Policy*. Monterey, Calif.: Brooks/Cole Publishing.

Kling, David J. (1990). "Federal Asbestos Funding for Schools: Public Administration in a Pinch." Paper presented at the annual meeting of the American Political Science Association, San Francisco.

Light, Paul (1985). *Artful Work: The Politics of Social Security Reform.* New York: Random House.

Maybew, David R. (1989). "Does It Make a Difference Whether Party Control of the American National Government Is Unified or Divided?" Paper presented at the annual meeting of the American Political Science Association, Atlanta.

Melnick, R. Shep (1989). "The Courts, Congress, and Programmatic Rights." In Richard A. Harris and Sidney M. Milkis, eds. *Remaking American Politics.* Boulder, Col.: Westview Press, pp. 188–212.

Mezey, Susan Gluck (1988). *No Longer Disabled: The Federal Courts and the Politics of Social Security Disability.* New York: Greenwood Press.

Nathan, Richard P. (1986). "Institutional Change under Reagan." In John L. Palmer, ed. *Perspectives on the Reagan Years.* Washington, D.C.: Urban Institute Press, pp. 121–45.

Pfiffner, James P. (1989). "Divided Government and the Problem of Governance." Working Paper of the Center for Congressional and Presidential Studies (89–4). Washington, D.C.: The American University, November 8.

Rourke, Francis E. (1961). *Secrecy and Publicity: Dilemmas of Democracy.* Baltimore: Johns Hopkins University Press.

Rourke, Francis E., and Schulman, Paul R. (1989). "Adhocracy in Policy Development." *The Social Science Journal* 26:131–42.

Schattschneider, E. E. (1960). *The Semi-Sovereign People.* Holt, Rinehart and Winston.

Sundquist, James L. (1988-89). "The New Era of Coalition Government in the United States." *Political Science Quarterly* 103 (Winter):613–35.

Thompson, Carolyn R. (1990). "The Political Evolution of the Medicare Catastrophic Health Care Act of 1988." Ph.D. diss. Johns Hopkins University.

Waterman, Richard W. (1989). *Presidential Influence and the Administrative State.* Knoxville, Tenn.: University of Tennessee Press.

Weaver, Carolyn L. (1987). "The Social Security Bureaucracy in Triumph and in Crisis." In Louis Gallambos, ed. *The New American State: Bureaucracies and Policies since World War II.* Baltimore: Johns Hopkins University Press, pp. 54–84.

Wills, Garry. (1982). *The Kennedy Imprisonment: A Meditation on Power.* Boston: Little, Brown.

3   Public Policy and Administration in a Federal System

Policy making in America does not occur only at the national level. We are in a federal system, which consists of national, state, and local levels. Interactions among these levels of policy making are critical in understanding the process and the results; in our federal system, policy-making roles are shared, and the relationships among the levels are constantly changing. In the end, federalism is a contradiction: it tries to marry diversity and central direction.

A number of trends in intergovernmental relations (IGR) should be recognized:

- The emergence of local government, especially cities, as a full partner in the federal system
- The demand for a national urban policy since the late 1960s, but the failure of several administrations to come to grips with these issues
- The historic default of the states in policy leadership, although this is changing
- Increased competition for federal funding among the regions of the country, especially the "Frost Belt" and the "Sun Belt"
- Attempts at simplification to make federal grant programs work better because of fewer restrictions and regulations
- Calls for a "new federalism" by President Reagan to shift greater governmental responsibility to states and localities), which again appear in the 1990s.

Federalism has three principal dimensions: political, economic (or fiscal), and administrative. The political aspect is the most visible, as when President Clinton meets with a group of mayors about the nation's drug problem. Administrative federalism often seems nearly invisible, as when specialists in criminal justice discuss state and local implementation of a federal program.

Economist and public executive Alice Rivlin has suggested that the federal government has taken on too much responsibility and should return some of its functions to the states. She also seeks a clearer division of responsibilities between the states and the federal government so, she says, both levels could operate more effectively. Yet her own historical analysis of federalism and intergovernmental relations indicates that this has not been the case. In the first article here, Rivlin provides a short, analytical history of the way federalism has worked in this century.

In the second article in this chapter, two well-known experts in public administration examine the administrative dimension of federalism with greater attention than is typically found. The starting point for John DiIulio and Don Kettl is the Contract with America associated with Republicans in the 1994 congressional elections in the middle of President Clinton's first term. Drawn from a much longer report, their discussion of possible devolution of authority in our federal system reaches well beyond the "contract."

Some discussion questions for Chapter 3 are:

- What are the principal patterns of federalism—political, fiscal, and administrative—that have developed in the United States?
- Could the public policy roles between the states and the federal government be rearranged in a more rational way? What are the obstacles?
- What are the administrative realities of American intergovernmental relations as discussed by DiIulio and Kettl? How much does the average citizen know about them? How might management issues affect any attempt to alter our federal system?

The Evolution of American Federalism

ALICE M. RIVLIN

. . . For much of the twentieth century, power has flowed toward Washington and the functions of federal and state government have become increasingly intertwined. Why did this happen? Are the reasons for the blurring of distinctions between federal and state government still valid today?

CHANGING VIEWS OF FEDERALISM

To the Founding Fathers, the division of responsibility between the states and the federal government was a crucial issue with high emotional and intellectual content. Most of them believed that the states should retain a large measure of autonomy. Their experience with the English crown made them nervous about lodging too much power in any central government. Life under the Articles of Confederation, however, demonstrated that the national government could not function effectively if its powers were too narrow or if it depended on state contributions for revenue. Hence the drafters of the Constitution gave the federal government limited but quite specific powers, including the power to levy and collect taxes. To reduce misunderstanding, they later added a Tenth Amendment stating explicitly that "the powers not delegated to the United States by the Constitution, nor prohibited by it to the States, are reserved to the States respectively, or to the people."

The Tenth Amendment seems clear enough, but the Constitution itself was a document drafted by a committee. It contained some language suggesting more comprehensive powers for the national government, such as the statement that Congress should provide for "the general welfare." Hence the Constitution did not permanently settle the controversies about which level of government should have which functions. It did, however, create a framework for debating and resolving conflicts between the federal government and the states that has stood the test of more than two centuries.

From 1789 to about 1933, all levels of government were small by modern standards, but the states were clearly more important than the federal government, except possibly in time of war. Moreover, the two levels of government usually ran on separate tracks, each in control of its own set of activities. Scholars called the arrangement "dual federalism."

From the Great Depression through the 1970s, all levels of government expanded their activities, but power shifted to Washington. The federal government took on new responsibilities, and the distinction between federal and state roles faded. Scholars talked about "cooperative federalism."

By the beginning of the 1980s, the drive for centralization had peaked, and power began shifting back to state capitals. No new concept emerged, however, of how responsibilities should be divided. The current era has been called a period of "competitive federalism," meaning the federal government and the states are competing with each other for leadership in domestic policy.[1]

SMALL GOVERNMENT AND DUAL FEDERALISM

The national government created by the Constitution was charged with defending the new country and dealing with the rest of the world. It sent diplomats to foreign capitals, dealt with the Tripoli pirates, fought the invading British, invaded Mexico, and warred with Spain. Above all, it kept the nation together despite the disaster of the Civil War and the tensions of reuniting North and South.

In the nineteenth century, much of the national government's attention was devoted to acquiring territory and encouraging its settlement and development. Washington granted land to settlers and developers and encouraged the entry of new states. It fostered trade and interstate commerce and subsidized canals and railroads. It arranged the delivery of mail, managed the national currency—often with conspicuous lack of success—and encouraged the growth of banks.

Sometimes economic development shaded into what is now called "social policy." For example, new states were given land grants for public schools. In 1862 the national government endowed land grant colleges to teach agriculture and the "mechanical arts" and later (in 1890) granted these institutions a modest annual subsidy. The federal government also engaged in a few public health activities early in its history, such as maintaining hospitals for merchant seamen. In general, however, social policy matters such as education, health, and aid to the poor were the concern of state and local governments or private charity.

By the end of the nineteenth century, the excesses of big business and the human cost of unfettered profit seeking were arousing public anger and creating pressure for federal intervention. Antitrust laws reined in monopolies. In the early years of the twentieth century, the "muckrakers" pointed to scandalous health, safety, and labor practices, and the Progressive movement fought for corrective action. The federal government moved to regulate food adulteration, child labor, and other abuses. Progressives had more success in some states, however, than they did in Washington, in part because the courts took a narrow view of the role of the federal government.

Dual federalism was never absolute. Even in the nineteenth century, there were instances of federal-state cooperation on law enforcement or public works and modest overlaps of functions.[2] Scope for intertwining of functions was minimal, however. The national government was remote from most citizens and its activities were few.

Until the early years of the twentieth century, the modest scope of the federal government did not require a broad-based tax system. Revenues from customs duties and the sale of public lands amply covered peacetime spending. Indeed, there was often a surplus of funds. A federal income tax, although used briefly to help finance the Civil War, was thought to be unconstitutional.

In 1913 the Constitution was amended to permit the federal government to levy an income tax, and the Federal Reserve System was created to put banking and credit on a more solid basis. The Federal Reserve was eventually to give Washington a powerful set of tools for influencing the economy by controlling money, credit, and interest rates. The federal income tax was ultimately to finance a huge expansion in federal activities. Both developments, however, lay in the future. In the 1920s, conservatives dominated Washington and the federal role remained limited. In 1929 total federal spending was under 3 percent of GNP. States and localities spent almost three times as much as the federal government.[3]

TWO REASONS FOR FEDERAL GROWTH

In the great Depression of the 1930s, the federal government took on new responsibilities, and its budget grew rapidly. Federal domestic functions continued to expand after World War II, even as America's worldwide responsibilities were growing (Figure 3-1). By the late 1950s federal domestic outlays exceeded amounts spent by state and local governments from their own sources.

This escalation of Washington's role is often seen as a single juggernaut of centralization, sweeping power toward Washington. Two sources of growth, however, should be distinguished. One was the evolving conviction, dramatically reinforced by the Great Depression, that new national institutions were needed to strengthen the economy and perform functions that states could not be expected to perform on their own. This conviction prompted a wave of institution building that included both purely federal activities and joint federal-state efforts.

A second source was the escalating perception, reinforced by the civil rights movement, that states were performing badly even in areas that almost everyone regarded as properly assigned to them. Frustrated with the states, reformers urged the federal government to augment state spending and redirect state and local priorities. The result was a rapid proliferation of grants to states—and directly to their localities—designed to strengthen their capacities and influence their decisions.

Figure 3-1. Domestic Government Expenditures, Selected Periods, 1947-90

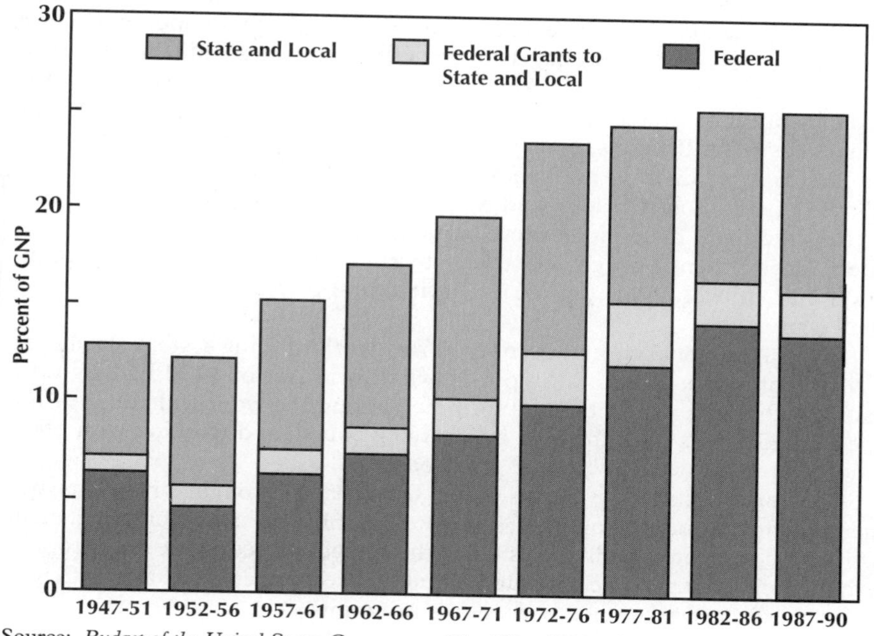

Source: *Budget of the United States Government, Fiscal Year 1992*, tables 1.2, 3.1, 15.2.

BUILDING NATIONAL INSTITUTIONS

The Great Depression brought the economy close to collapse and radically altered the role of the federal government. The stock market crash of October 1929 presaged an economic freefall. Factories and businesses closed, millions of workers lost their jobs, the banking system tottered, and citizens were frightened and insecure. President Herbert Hoover, unable to stem the tide of economic disintegration, lost the 1932 election in a landslide to Franklin D. Roosevelt, who proclaimed a "New Deal."

The Roosevelt government took over in mid-crisis. Its first task was to get the economy functioning again. To stop a disastrous run on the banks, the new administration briefly closed all banks and then reopened them under new rules. Over a quarter of the labor force was unemployed. The federal government handed out emergency relief. It put people to work on a vast array of projects from building dams and schools to painting murals and recording folk music. The federal government created institutions to buy home and farm mortgages from hard-pressed banks and reschedule them so families could retain their homes and farms. It lent money to businesses on favorable terms and prodded industry to produce and hire. These efforts helped to revive the economy, but unemployment was still high at the end of the 1930s. Only World War II got the economy booming again.

The Great Depression revealed weaknesses of a highly unregulated and decentralized economic system. It changed the public's view of the desirable role of the federal government and impelled the president and the Congress, despite initial resistance from the Supreme Court, to create federal institutions and programs to reduce the chances of economic disaster striking again.

Since the weakness of the banks had nearly brought the economy to a halt, the architects of reform were eager to strengthen banking, credit, and financial systems. Deposit insurance, bank and thrift regulation, and housing and farm credit institutions greatly increased the stability of the banking system and made it easier for business, homeowners, and farmers to obtain credit.

Agricultural distress and rural poverty, aggravated by the worldwide collapse of commodity prices, bad weather, and poor farming practices, dramatized the need for regional development and agricultural assistance. The federal government brought electricity to rural areas, built dams to supply power and control floods, supported agricultural prices, and aided large and small farmers.

A strong national commitment to a freer world trading system also began in the Depression. The U.S. Smoot-Hawley Tariff Act of 1930 had set off a tariff war that was widely blamed for precipitating the worldwide depression. The United States took the lead in reversing course and working with other nations for reciprocal lowering of trade barriers.

The human suffering of the Great Depression, brought on by massive unemployment and falling wages, created public pressure for permanent institutions to protect individuals from the impact of economic catastrophes beyond their control. The institution builders responded with two different approaches: social insurance and welfare programs.

Social Insurance

Social insurance enables the population to pool certain risks, such as losing income because of unemployment, disability, retirement, or death of the family breadwinner. Workers pay a portion of their wages (usually matched by their employer) into a government fund while they are working and are entitled to benefits when they retire or when specified disasters strike. Social insurance taxes are analogous to insurance premiums or private pension contributions. Those who have contributed long enough do not have to prove that they are destitute to get benefits—just that they are disabled or unemployed or retired. Unlike welfare, there is no means test and no shame in accepting benefit checks.

The Social Security System   The biggest social insurance program, social security, evolved from small beginnings in 1935 into a strong and extremely popular national institution. Workers covered by social security pay a tax on their earnings, matched by their employer. In return, when they retire they receive a pension whose level is related to their past earnings. Benefits are paid to disabled workers and to survivors if the worker dies. The social security system gradually expanded to include virtually all workers; benefits increased over several decades. In 1965 medical benefits for the elderly (the medicare program) were added to the social security system.

Unemployment Insurance   Unlike social security, the unemployment insurance system, set up in response to the massive unemployment of the Great Depression, was a joint state and federal effort. The federal government assisted the states in setting up unemployment insurance funds and established many of the rules, but left the level of contributions and benefits up to the states themselves.

Social insurance proved a popular, successful, and enduring concept. Part of its popularity relates to the contributory feature and the specificity of the benefits. People feel they are paying for identifiable benefits that will be there if they need them. They object less to social insurance taxes than to the general taxes that support government services whose benefits are widely dispersed and hard to identify.

Welfare Programs

Social insurance was a response to the economic hardships of the 1930s, but could not be an immediate solution. Workers had to build up eligibility for future benefits. Meanwhile, people were destitute. State welfare programs were totally swamped. To meet part of the need, the federal government put in place a set of means-tested welfare programs to provide income to some poor families and individuals. The elderly, blind, and disabled and women supporting children were entitled to payments if they could prove that they had inadequate means. Like the social insurance programs, these welfare programs were "entitlements": people who met the requirements specified in the law were entitled to benefits. However, the benefits were paid out of general government revenues, not out of a fund to which beneficiaries contributed.

The welfare programs were expected to become less necessary as social insurance coverage widened and gave people who were unemployed, retired, or disabled a means of support. The hope was that widows with children would increasingly be covered by survivors' benefits under social security; the subsequent growth of the number of divorced and single women with children was not anticipated.

Social insurance did reduce poverty, but the means-tested programs did not disappear. Indeed, rising concern about low-income families (especially women with children) prompted not only the expansion of aid to families with dependent children (AFDC), but the addition of other federal means-tested programs in the 1960s and 1970s, including food stamps, expanded housing assistance, and medicaid (the joint federal-state program that finances medical care for low-income people).

Funding and responsibility for welfare programs were shared by federal and state governments (and in some states, by local governments as well) in complex and interlocking ways. In general, the federal government made the rules about who would be eligible for benefits on what conditions, but states set the actual benefit levels and administered the funds. The federal government matched the money paid out by the state according to a formula that gave more federal money (per dollar of state money) to poorer states. Benefit levels varied substantially, with poor states generally providing low benefits despite proportionately higher assistance from the federal government.[4]

Stabilizers for the Economy

Social insurance and welfare programs not only provided income to individuals and families facing economic disaster, they also made economic disaster less likely. If economic activity dropped off sharply, the downward spiral would be cushioned, since individuals drawing social insurance benefits and welfare would be able to buy necessities and pay their rent or mortgages. This increased purchasing power would bolster the income of producers and prevent layoffs of workers and forced sales of homes. Thus both welfare programs and social insurance would act as automatic stabilizers for the economy.

Other National Initiatives

Growing federal activities cost money, but Washington was not short of funds. Federal income tax rates were raised to high levels to finance World War II, and withholding was introduced in 1943. Both personal and corporate taxpayers got used to paying a significant portion of their income to the federal government. Moreover, in the good news period . . . , personal incomes and business profits rose rapidly. Even after taxes, almost everyone was doing well. The federal tax system was generating so much revenue that new programs could be funded while tax rates were reduced. Moreover, the share of GNP devoted to defense declined gradually after the Korean War buildup in the early 1950s. Domestic spending growth could be accomplished without commensurate increases in the overall federal share of GNP.

By 1960 the federal government's budget for domestic programs alone had grown to 8.1 percent of GNP.[5] Between 1933 and 1960, the role of the federal government had changed from that of a minor player on the domestic government scene to a major one.

INFLUENCING AND REFORMING THE STATES

Despite the growth in some types of federal programs, many types of public services were still considered very much the business of the states until the early 1960s. Elementary and secondary education, health services, police and fire protection, sanitation, social services, and most other direct services to citizens were still viewed as overwhelmingly state and local matters.

Only occasionally did Washington intervene in these areas to further an objective deemed worthy of national attention. For example, the federal government began giving the states grants for vocational education programs in high schools as early as 1917. In the late 1950s, when the Soviet Union's Sputnik launch focused attention on technical education, Washington set up grant programs designed to improve science, mathematics, and language teaching in the schools (the National Defense Education Act). These "categorical" grant programs accumulated slowly over the years and then exploded in the 1960s and 1970s.

In the 1960s, President Lyndon B. Johnson's Great Society programs reflected mounting dismay that the states were not performing effectively and were shortchanging the poor, urban dwellers, and minorities. States and their local governments were seen as lacking the means and the capability to provide services in a modern society. Federal programs were designed explicitly to change the way states performed their own functions.

The Sad State of the States

Dissatisfaction with the states had been building for several decades, starting with the Great Depression. State governments were unable to cope with the nation's economic crisis. Reformers turned to the federal government, which responded with a blizzard of new activity. Some began to regard the states as anachronisms that might eventually fade from the American governmental scene. Political scientist Luther Gulick declared in the depths of the Great Depression, "It is a matter of brutal record. The American State is finished. I do not predict that the states will go, but affirm that they have gone."[6]

The challenges of World War II further augmented the powers of the federal government, and activists continued to turn to Washington to deal with perceived needs of the postwar economy for housing, hospitals, and an interstate highway system. Bashing the states was a popular sport. Writing in 1949, Robert S. Allen characterized state government as "the tawdriest, most incompetent and most stultifying unit of the nation's political structure."[7]

By the early 1960s, when national concern about minorities and the poor was rising, states were seen as perpetrators of discrimination. The southern states were overtly racist, defiant of federal efforts to desegregate schools and other public facilities and to ensure the participation of all races in the political process. Moreover, the indictment of states went far beyond the South and beyond issues of race and poverty. As Frank Trippett put it: "One glaring truth of the times is that most of the perplexing domestic problems confronting the country today would not exist if the states had acted."[8] Terry Sanford, a former governor of North Carolina, concurred: "Because many groups and people have encountered evasion of duty by the state, they have felt that they had no choice but to try the road to Washington. The trek to Washington could have been expected, for government is not static." Sanford, a strong believer in the necessity and feasibility of state reform, conceded, "If nothing much can be done, then indeed the states will soon be finished."[9]

The weakness of state government involved both the executive and legislative branches. In many states, governors had relatively few powers and short terms of office. They had small staffs composed of political appointees with limited professional qualifications. They presided over executive branch departments that were often fragmented, poorly organized, and staffed with bureaucrats who had limited training and education and few of the tools and skills of modern government. The office of governor itself often attracted "good-time Charlies" at the end of careers in the private sector. Abler politicians gravitated toward the federal government, where there was more scope for their talents.

State legislatures, before the reforms that began in the 1960s, were far from models of strong democratic institutions. Legislatures often met for only a few weeks every other year. Members served part time, were paid little, and were dependent on their primary jobs. They had hardly any staff, usually not even clerical support.

Rural areas typically dominated the legislature. Cities and their growing suburbs were underrepresented, as were minorities and lower-income people. Rural overrepresentation was often built into state constitutions that required equal representation of sparsely populated rural counties and densely populated urban ones. In many states, entrenched rural interests had simply prevented reapportionment of the legislature for years or even decades. In 1962 Tennessee had not reapportioned its legislature since 1901. Eight states had not redistricted in more than fifty years, and twenty-seven states had not redistricted in more than twenty-five years.[10] "Some of the resulting inequalities were spectacular. In 1960 the five largest counties in Florida had half the population and 5 of 38 Senate seats; the Senate districts ranged in population from 10,000 to 935,000. Los Angeles County had 40 percent of California's population and only 1 of 40 seats."[11]

Although larger, richer states, such as New York and California, tended to have more capable governments, states in general did not inspire confidence. They were seen as "errand boys" of the federal government, helping to carry out policy formulated at the national level. Even this role diminished as the federal government increasingly bypassed states and dealt directly with local governments.

The Civil Rights Revolution

The civil rights movement, which gathered steam in the 1950s and reached a climax in the 1960s, profoundly altered the relationship of the federal government to states and localities. The Civil War, nearly a century earlier, had freed the slaves and amended the Constitution in an attempt to guarantee equal rights for all races. In fact, however, blacks, especially but not exclusively in the South, were denied basic political rights (including the right to vote), excluded from public facilities and services, discriminated against in employment, educated in separate and inferior schools, denied access to higher education, and otherwise relegated to second-class citizenship and economic deprivation.

After World War II, growing outrage on the part of blacks and a rising proportion of the whole population swelled into a national movement. State segregation laws were challenged in the federal courts under the U.S. Constitution, and the federal government passed legislation spelling out equal rights in greater detail. In 1954, in *Brown* v. *Board of Education,* the Supreme Court rejected the idea that separate schools could be regarded as equal. Gradually, schools, universities, and other public facilities were desegregated, but not without dramatic confrontations between state and federal officials.

Enforcing civil rights laws involved the assertion of federal authority in schools, parks, hospitals, restaurants, hotels, and other facilities that had not heretofore been seen as areas of federal concern. Efforts to right past wrongs involved increasingly complex intrusion on state and local autonomy. Even after legal segregation of school systems was abrogated, for example, de facto racial segregation remained because blacks and whites lived in different neighborhoods. As a result, the courts searched for ways of achieving racial desegregation of the schools by redrawing school boundaries and busing children out of their neighborhoods.

The War on Poverty

The civil rights movement, by focusing attention on economic as well as political deprivation of minorities, aroused concern about the general prevalence of poverty. Americans rediscovered that even in their prosperous country a large population, in both rural and urban areas, lived at the margin of subsistence. The poor included low-wage workers in agriculture, manufacturing, and service industries, dwellers in depressed areas such as Appalachia and the Mississippi Delta, native Americans, and Hispanics. Blacks were only about a quarter of the poor.

In 1964 President Johnson called for a war on poverty. He sent an avalanche of proposals to Congress designed to change the lives of the poor in a variety of ways. Most were enacted in a frenzy of legislative activity that rivaled the early days of the New Deal.

The Investment Strategy   The strategists in the war on poverty saw the poor as mired in a cycle of poverty from which they were ill equipped to escape because of bad health, lack of skills, and lack of experience, both in the workplace and in the political process. They emphasized an investment strategy of providing the poor not with money, but with services that would help adults and children break out of the poverty cycle. Providing these services to the poor involved federal intervention in a whole range of government functions previously regarded as state and local prerogatives.

A prime example of the investment strategy was the Head Start program, whose premise was that because poor children came to school less ready to learn than middle-class children, they fell behind and were never able to catch up. Head Start provided intensive preschool education to improve the skills, health, and nutrition of low-income children and enhance their chances of succeeding in school. Other federal programs provided special services for low-income youngsters to help them progress through school, get jobs, or go to college. (Principal programs included follow through, teacher corps, title I of the Elementary and Secondary Education Act, job corps, neighborhood youth corps, and upward bound.) In addition, neighborhood health centers offered health resources in areas with few doctors and medical facilities. Legal services helped poor people obtain redress of grievances and claim benefits to which they were entitled under the law. Community action programs, perhaps the most controversial of all, tried to mobilize the poor to be more effective politically in their own behalf.

Some programs were intended to demonstrate that a broad range of coordinated services could turn a deteriorating area into an improving one. Riots in Los Angeles, Detroit, Washington, and other big cities in the late 1960s directed attention to blighted urban areas. Urban renewal, model cities, and other programs channeled federal funds directly to city governments.

The investment strategy of the war on poverty involved a great many programs and projects. Most were relatively small, however. They reached only a minority of the population in poverty and did so in ways that were usually too fleeting to make a life-changing difference.

Income Strategy Proposals   Many people concerned about the poor thought the investment strategy was too slow and indirect. Better education, beginning in preschool, might eventually enable poor children to earn more, but four-year-olds would not be in the labor force for about fourteen years. Meanwhile, they were growing up amid deprivation and blight. What the poor needed most urgently was money—a means of paying for necessities such as food, housing, and medical care.

Some scholars and politicians were attracted to the idea of a guaranteed income, sometimes known as a negative income tax (NIT). They believed that existing welfare programs were demeaning and undermined incentives to work because family earnings were deducted from the welfare grant. A poor family was effectively subject to a 100 percent tax on earnings. Under an NIT, a family with no income would be guaranteed a minimum income and would be encouraged to work because the grant would be reduced (or "taxed") by less than their earnings.[12] Thus an NIT would both provide income for families who could not work and encourage those who could work to do so. Some thought that such a system could be administered by the Internal Revenue Service (IRS). Families with adequate incomes would pay positive taxes, those with low incomes would get checks (or negative taxes), and only the IRS would know the difference.

The NIT was an intriguing idea, although it would have been more expensive and difficult to administer than its initial proponents imagined. Efforts to convert President Johnson to the idea failed. He was committed to the investment strategy, especially to opening educational opportunities for poor children, and had little interest in reforming welfare. In any case, by the end of Johnson's presidency in 1968, escalating defense spending was squeezing domestic programs. The NIT was ruled out by cost as well as philosophy.

To the surprise of most liberals, President Richard M. Nixon endorsed a welfare reform proposal in 1969 that bore striking resemblance to an NIT. Nixon proposed guaranteeing a minimum income to all families and encouraging work by reducing the guarantee less than the amount of earnings. The proposed guarantee level was below the welfare benefits paid to AFDC families in urban states, but above the benefits in the South. The proposal would have put a national floor under income for the first time and substantially benefited low-wage workers.

President Nixon's family assistance plan, as it was called, passed the House of Representatives twice, but was defeated in the Senate by a coalition of conservatives, who thought it too generous to the poor, and liberals, who thought it not generous enough. The idea survived in the supplementary security income program, which was essentially an NIT for people who were elderly, blind, or disabled.

Despite the absence of an income strategy in the war on poverty and the failure of Nixon's reform, welfare programs grew rapidly in the 1960s and even faster in the 1970s. Collectively, these programs had a much bigger impact on federal budgets than the investment strategy programs. AFDC increased as larger proportions of the poor applied for aid and benefit levels rose. Medicaid, passed at the same time as medicare, provided health benefits for many low-income families, especially those eligible for AFDC. The food stamp program, which went to a broader group of low-income people than AFDC, grew rapidly. Public housing and other housing subsidies for low-income families increased.

The Proliferation of Grants

Federal activism in the 1960s and 1970s spread from poverty and civil rights into many other areas. Turning to Washington for help became routine. Pollution, transportation, recreation, economic development, law enforcement, even rat control, evoked the same response from politicians: create a federal grant. National concern shifted from one problem to another, but existing grants were never terminated. The result was an accumulation of more than 500 categorical programs, each with detailed rules, formulas for matching and distributing the money, bureaucracies charged with carrying out and overseeing the program, and beneficiaries and professional groups with an interest in perpetuating and enlarging the grant.

Some critics worried that the pervasiveness of federal grants reduced state and local autonomy. Others were more concerned that the proliferation of grants allowed state and local authorities to do whatever they wanted and send the bill to the federal government.

States and cities learned to tailor their budgets to maximize federal funding. Unfortunately, they sometimes neglected more routine activities. According to New York City Mayor Edward I. Koch:

> Left unnoticed in the cities' rush to reallocate their budgets so as to draw down maximum categorical aid were the basic service-delivery programs. . . . New roads, bridges, and subway routes were an exciting commitment to the future, but they were launched at the expense of routine maintenance to the unglamorous, but essential, infrastructure of the existing systems.[13]

Another problem was that less affluent jurisdictions often lacked the savvy or the staff to take full advantage of the federal largesse, especially when it took the form of project grants for which they had to compete. Wealthier states and cities were able to put together more sophisticated or better-documented project proposals.

Revenue Sharing

In 1964, Walter Heller, chairman of the Council of Economic Advisers in the Johnson administration, proposed "revenue sharing" to channel federal money to the states without the detailed specifications of categorical grants. Revenue sharing responded to several problems besides the growing concern about categorical grants. Needs for public services at the state and local level were rising more rapidly than revenues; state and local revenues grew more slowly and fell more heavily on low-income people than the federal income tax; federal income tax revenues tended to rise faster than the need for federal spending; and poor states could not be expected to bring services up to acceptable national levels without help. Revenue sharing would address all these concerns by channeling a portion of federal income tax receipts to the states—no strings attached—with low-income states receiving disproportionate shares.[14]

President Johnson rejected the revenue sharing proposal. He favored social programs managed directly by Washington or categorical grants with tight federal controls. During his administration, the number of categorical grants exploded, and the revenue sharing idea remained buried deep in the White House files.

President Nixon, however, was attracted to revenue sharing, which fit well with his "New Federalism" philosophy of increasing state autonomy.... His proposal, known as general revenue sharing, was enacted in 1972 with the enthusiastic support of state and local politicians.

General revenue sharing funds were specified in the law, not tied to the federal income tax. The money was disbursed under a formula that benefited poor states disproportionately. The money was divided into two parts, one to be spent at the state level and one to be "passed through" to local governments. The earmarking of a local share reflected the fears of mayors that they would not get enough money if they had to lobby for it in their state capitals.

Rules were also introduced to try to prevent the recipients from substituting federal money for existing funding.

That revenue sharing was popular with state and local officials is hardly surprising. It provided financial support and made no onerous demands. It was not, however, equally popular with members of Congress, who preferred more control over how federal funds were used. Hence categorical grant programs continued to grow in the 1970s, while revenue sharing did not.

The Reagan Revolution

President Ronald Reagan was a conservative former governor of California with strong views about the role of government, at both the federal and state levels. He won a landslide victory over President Jimmy Carter in 1980 after vociferously attacking federal domestic spending in his campaign and advocating deep cuts in federal income taxes, more defense spending, and a balanced budget. Within weeks of taking office, Reagan confronted Congress with a drastic budget proposal involving major increases in defense spending, deep cuts in domestic programs, and reductions in federal income taxes over a three-year period. Congress, awed by the electorate's evident desire for change and skillfully manipulated by Reagan's energetic director of the Office of Management and Budget, David Stockman, passed both the tax and budget proposals with astonishing rapidity.

Reagan administration budget policy profoundly influenced the future of relations among federal, state, and local governments. As Richard Nathan and Fred Doolittle put it:

> The cuts made in grants-in-aid in Reagan's first year in office were historic. This was the first time in over thirty years that there had been an actual-dollar decline in federal aid to state and local governments. The cuts produced a 7 percent reduction for fiscal year 1982 in overall federal grants-in-aid to state and local governments.... This amounted to a 12 percent decline in real terms.[15]

Federal grants were both reduced and restructured. Categorical programs were grouped into block grants that gave state and local governments more latitude in spending the funds. The Reagan cuts fell heavily on the poor, especially the working poor, and hit cities more dramatically than states.

Most of the reductions in domestic spending came during Reagan's first year in office. Subsequent requests for additional cutbacks met increasing opposition from Congress and the public. Some of the funds cut in the initial reductions were later restored, and modest increases in grants occurred late in the 1980s. Huge federal deficits, however, kept downward pressure on federal spending, especially discretionary spending, which is easier to control than entitlements. Very few new federal grant programs were created in the 1980s. Federal aid to state and local governments (as a percentage of GNP, the federal budget, or state and local spending) stayed well below the level of the late 1970s. The pattern of increasing state and local dependence on federal grants had been broken.

One of the casualties of the Reagan revolution was general revenue sharing. Opponents pointed out that huge deficits left no federal revenue to share. Congressional support for revenue sharing was weaker than support for the categorical programs that affected identifiable clients and professional groups.

First the state and then the local components of revenue sharing were eliminated.

Unexpectedly, the Reagan cuts energized state and local governments. The cuts created what Richard Nathan has called "the paradox of devolution." With less federal help, states, and to some extent localities, were forced to strengthen their own capacities and resources to meet the rising social problems of the 1980s. The federal pullback came at a fortunate moment—after two decades that had greatly enhanced states' ability to move into the breach.

THE STATES RISE TO THE CHALLENGE

The dissatisfaction with state government that reached a crescendo in the 1960s not only prompted an explosion of federal activity, it also brought a wave of reform in the states themselves. Goaded partly by the federal government and partly by pressure from their own citizens, states took steps to turn themselves into more modern, responsive, competent governments. By the time the Reagan revolution of the 1980s thrust new responsibilities on them, state governments were far more ready to rise to the challenge than they would have been two decades earlier.

Executive Branch Reforms

One theme of the state reform movement was strengthening the capacity of governors to provide state leadership. Colonial antagonism toward a strong executive had left a legacy of state constitutions with strict separation of powers between the executive and legislative branches and carefully circumscribed gubernatorial powers. As a result, governors frequently lacked the tools and resources needed to lead a modern state.

Presidents, of course, faced the same problem for the same reason, but in the first half of the twentieth century there were major improvements in the organization and staffing of the White House. For example, the Bureau of the Budget (later called the Office of Management and Budget) was created in 1921 and the Council of Economic Advisers was established in 1946.

Efforts to improve the capacity of governors came later. In the early 1960s, many governors served only two years, not long enough to articulate and carry out a strategy for state action. Many were lame ducks, prohibited from succeeding themselves. Many governors had limited powers of appointment; other state officials were directly elected and had their own power bases. Many appointments were made by boards or commissions whose members were elected, controlled by the legislature, or served fixed terms from which they could not be removed. Governors often had neither the authority nor the staff to prepare an executive budget for the legislature. Indeed, states' chief executive officers frequently lacked powers that CEOs of corporations would regard as absolutely essential to leadership and effectiveness.

A common reform was shifting to longer terms, as well as lifting restrictions on succession. In 1955 governors had four-year terms in only twenty-nine states. By 1988 the number had risen to forty-seven. In the same period, the number of states in which governors were barred from a second successive term dropped from seventeen to three.[16]

Other reforms shortened the ballot and reduced the number of independently elected state officials. A widely quoted report by the Committee for Economic Development in 1967 urged that only two state executives, the governor and the lieutenant governor, be elected and that they run as a team from the same party, like the president and vice president. More states now elect the governor and lieutenant governor as a team, but the effort to reduce the number of elected officials has met with only modest success. Over the period 1960-80, the number of states electing four or fewer executives rose only from three to nine.[17] Between 1956 and 1988, the number of separately elected officials besides the governor dropped from 709 to 514, still an astonishingly high average of more than 10 per state.[18] Some governors obtained more formal powers of appointment and removal. Longer terms also tended to increase the governors' control of boards and commissions whose members are appointed for fixed terms.

During this era there were also substantial increases in the size and professional qualification of staffs, with the average size of the staff rising from eleven in 1956 to forty-eight in 1988.[19] Governors also created budget and planning offices charged with developing an executive budget reflecting the governor's priorities, formulating longer-term plans for the state and its government, and monitoring the effectiveness of state programs. Almost all governors now prepare an executive budget and submit it to the legislature with extensive back-up analysis.[20]

In this period, state agency officials, like the staffs they supervised, became visibly more professional. They had more degrees and were more likely to be career civil servants. State officials became more diverse, although women and minorities are still underrepresented at the top of state governments.

Governors themselves have been described as a "new breed"—younger, better educated, less likely to be lawyers, more likely to seek careers in public service. Many of them have been state legislators or agency executives. Many go on to the U.S. Senate or to other federal positions.[21]

None of these changes, of course, guarantees that governors will be successful or effective. Leadership qualities are in short supply at the state, as at the federal, level. Judgment and luck, as well as formal qualification and power of office, play an enormous role in determining a governor's effectiveness. Nevertheless, an able governor now has far more opportunity in most states to formulate and carry out policy than he (and now occasionally, she) would have had in the early 1960s.

Reforming the Legislative Branch

Reform of state legislatures in the 1960s came partly in reaction to stronger governorships. The American system of separation of powers invites such swings of reformist zeal from one branch to the other. The creation of the Congressional Budget Office in 1974 was in part the result of the strengthening of the presidential budget-making capacity in the 1960s and creation of policy analysis staffs in cabinet agencies. Congress needed professional help in responding to the increasingly sophisticated budget presentations of the president's staff. State legislatures, after the strengthening of governors' offices, found themselves in a similar position.

A more urgent impetus, however, came from the Supreme Court. In *Baker v. Carr* (1962), the Court indicated its willingness to hear cases in which voters in a state claimed that malapportionment of their legislature denied them equal protection of the laws under the Fourteenth Amendment to the U.S. Constitution. Then in *Reynolds* v. *Sims* (1964) the Court took the startling position that equal protection required *both* houses of the state legislature to be apportioned on a population basis, despite the fact that the U.S. Constitution specifies equal representation for all states in the U.S. Senate regardless of population. States rapidly reapportioned their legislatures to conform to the court's principle of "one person, one vote." This redrawing of the lines, now repeated after every census, brought a new and far more diverse group of legislators to state capitols and added pressure for other kinds of reform.[22]

In general, reapportionment favored metropolitan areas, especially growing suburban communities. It put urban problems on state agendas and eventually led to increased state aid to cities. Political fallout varied. Democrats gained more seats in the Northeast and Midwest, but Republicans benefited in the South.[23]

At the same time, the work load of legislatures was increasing. Short sessions every other year were no longer adequate. More and more states found that part-time citizen-legislators were unable to cope with the demands of modern state activity. Legislative sessions were lengthening, and pay had to be raised to compensate legislators who were now spending a substantial part of their working hours on state business. Legislatures also began to demand better working conditions and more professional and clerical assistance. Members needed staff both to service constituent requests and to work on increasingly technical legislative matters. Committees became more active and utilized more professional staff.

Strengthening State Revenue Systems

In recent years, states have strengthened and diversified their revenue systems. States and localities generally have become much less dependent on property taxes, which used to be almost the sole source of local revenue and an important one for states as well. Sales taxes, whose bases have been significantly broadened, now bring in more total revenue than property taxes. More important, many states and some cities have begun to rely more heavily on income taxes. States and localities have also turned for revenue to a broad range of fees and charges designed to make the actual users of state and local services pay a larger share of the costs. Between 1960 and 1990, property taxes dropped from 37.7 percent to 21.8 percent of the revenue state and local governments raised from their own sources, while individual income taxes grew from 5.7 to 14.8 percent and fees and charges grew from 16.8 to 28.9 percent.[24]

The trend to broader-based state and local revenue systems in this period has been called "one of the most dramatic turnarounds in the annals of American public finance."[25] Although states and localities are still hard-pressed to raise enough revenue to pay for the services demanded by their citizens, their revenue systems are stronger, more responsive to economic growth, and less regressive than they were a few decades ago.

Moreover, states and localities have raised more revenue, despite frequent protests from taxpayers. State and local revenue, exclusive of federal grants, has gone up from 7.6 percent of GNP in 1960 to 10.3 percent in 1990.[26]

Meanwhile, the federal government's fiscal strength has declined. There was a time when revenues from the highly progressive federal income tax tended to grow faster than the economy as a whole. Rising incomes moved taxpayers into higher brackets, where they paid a higher proportion of their income in tax. Even if people's real income had not increased, inflation tended to increase the government's revenue by pushing taxpayers into higher brackets. This phenomenon was known as "bracket creep."

In 1981, however, the federal income tax was made less progressive by reducing rates on high incomes. Moreover, beginning in 1985 the tax brackets were adjusted for inflation to remove bracket creep. Hence federal revenues no longer grow faster than the economy. Moreover, except for social security payroll taxes, federal revenues as a share of GNP have been declining. Federal revenues (excluding social security taxes) fell from 15.4 percent of GNP in 1960 to 12.0 percent in 1990....

MANDATES

The federal government's own fiscal weakness has not made it any less eager to tell states and localities what to do. Indeed, when its ability to make grants declined, the federal government turned increasingly to mandates as a means of controlling state and local activity without having to pay the bill.

Mandates take several forms. Some are direct orders to states and localities to comply with certain rules (such as waste-water treatment standards) or face civil or criminal penalties. Some of them are cross-cutting requirements routinely attached to federal programs (compliance with anti-discrimination rules or minimum wages). Others impose conditions on a whole system (access for disabled people to mass transit or schools) as a condition of receipt of federal grants for any part of the system.

In the 1960s and early 1970s, when federal money was flowing to states and localities in increasing amounts, the recipients expressed little concern about the conditions attached to grants. As money tightened, however, and mandates became more pervasive and expensive, state and local officials became increasingly strident in criticizing federal mandates. David R. Beam noted that the character of the dialogue went from "cooperative" to "other 'c' words—like compulsory, coercive, and conflictual."[27] Complaints from the state and local level were hardly ever about the purposes of federal mandates, which were acknowledged to be laudable. Rather, they were about the federal government's asserting the authority to write complex and costly regulations that then had to be implemented by states and localities. "Cities and states feared that they were becoming the 'field hands of federalism'—simply, tools for implementing national policy directives in environmental protection, race, sex and age nondiscrimination, handicapped access and education, bilingual education, health planning, and other areas."[28]

Mayor Koch expressed the views of many state and local officials on the receiving end of multiple federal mandates in a satirical list of rules that appeared to be followed by the "mandate mandarins" in Washington: (1) "Mandates solve problems, particularly those in which you are not involved"; (2) "Mandates need not be tempered by the lessons of local experience"; (3) "Mandates will spontaneously generate the technology required to achieve them"; (4) "The price tag of the lofty aspiration to be served by a mandate should never deter its imposition on others."[29]

Although state and local governments have challenged federal mandates in the courts in recent years, they have generally lost. New mandates continue to be added. Among the most costly, although the cost has been shared by the federal government, are mandates for additional services to low-income families under medicaid.

Mandates add to citizen confusion about who is in charge. When the federal government makes rules for state and local officials to carry out, it is not clear to voters who should be blamed, either when the regulations are laxly enforced or when the cost of compliance is high.

WHITHER FEDERALISM?

In the last decade, the tide of centralization has turned and the balance of power has generally shifted from the federal government toward the states. The states have strengthened their capacity for governance and their revenue systems, while the federal government has found itself overstretched and short of funds. The intertwining of roles, however, has not diminished. Federal grant programs have received less funding, but their number remains huge—a recent publication lists more than 600 federal grant programs for state and local government.[30] Mandates have been used to enforce federal policy when funds were limited. No new concept of federal and state roles has yet emerged....

Notes

1. John Shannon and James Edwin Kee, "The Rise of Competitive Federalism," *Public Budgeting and Finance,* vol. 9 (Winter 1989), pp. 5-20.
2. Daniel J. Elazar, *The American Partnership: Intergovernmental Cooperation in the Nineteenth-Century United States* (University of Chicago Press, 1962).
3. *Economic Report of the President, February 1991,* pp. 310, 379.
4. The food stamp program is an exception. The funds are federal and the benefit formula is the same in all states.
5. *Budget of the United States Government, Fiscal Year 1992,* p. 182.
6. Quoted in Ann O'M. Bowman and Richard C. Kearney, *The Resurgence of the States* (Prentice-Hall, 1986), p. 4.
7. Quoted in Morton Keller, "State Government Needn't Be Resurrected Because It Never Died," in Thad L. Beyle, ed., *State Government: CQ's Guide to Current Issues and Activities, 1989-90* (Washington: Congressional Quarterly, 1989), p. 174.
8. Frank Trippett, *The States: United They Fell* (New York: World Publishing, 1967), p. 2.
9. Terry Sanford, *Storm over the States* (McGraw-Hill, 1967), pp. 36, 1.
10. Sanford, *Storm over the States,* p. 35.
11. Malcolm E. Jewell, "What Hath *Baker v. Carr* Wrought?" in Beyle, ed., *State Government,* pp. 85–95, quotation on p. 86.
12. Suppose the guarantee were $8,000 a year for a family of four. If the tax rate were 50 percent and the family earned $4,000, the grant would be reduced by $2,000 and the family would end up with a total income of $10,000.

13. Edward I. Koch, "The Mandate Millstone," *The Public Interest,* no. 61 (Fall 1980), p. 43.
14. Specifically, the federal government would annually deposit funds equal to 2 percent of the federal income tax base in a trust fund for the states. The money would be divided among the states on the basis of population and could be used for any purpose except highways (a trust fund for highways already existed). Each state would work out its own way of sharing the money with its local governments. Task Force on Intergovernmental Fiscal Cooperation, "Strengthening State and Local Government: A Report to the President of the United States," November 11, 1964 (unpublished). The task force was chaired by Joseph A. Pechman. President Johnson, allegedly angry because Heller had leaked the proposal to the *New York Times,* refused to release the report.
15. Richard P. Nathan, Fred C. Doolittle, and Associates, *Reagan and the States* (Princeton University Press, 1987), p. 4.
16. Thad L. Beyle, "From Governor to Governors," in Carl E. Van Horn, ed., *The State of the States* (Washington: Congressional Quarterly, 1989), pp. 35–36. The holdouts for two-year terms are all small New England states: Rhode Island, New Hampshire, and Vermont. Kentucky, Virginia, and New Mexico still bar succession.
17. Bowman and Kearney, *Resurgence of the States,* chap. 2.
18. Beyle, "From Governor to Governors," p. 36.
19. Beyle, "From Governor to Governors," p. 36.
20. By 1983, the governor shared the power to put together an initial budget with the legislature in only three states (South Carolina, Texas, and Mississippi). Bowman and Kearney, *Resurgence of the States,* p. 61.
21. Larry Sabato, *Goodbye to Good-Time Charlie: The American Governorship Transformed,* 2d ed. (Washington: Congressional Quarterly Press, 1983).
22. Alan Rosenthal, "The Legislative Institution: Transformed and at Risk," in Van Horn, ed., *State of the States,* pp. 69–102.
23. Jewell, "What Hath *Baker v. Carr* Wrought?"
24. Advisory Commission on Intergovernmental Relations, *Significant Features of Fiscal Federalism,* vol. 2: *Revenues and Expenditures* (Washington, 1991), p. 132.
25. Shannon and Kee, "Rise of Competitive Federalism," p. 14.
26. *Budget of the United States Government, Fiscal Year 1992,* table 15.1.
27. David R. Beam, "On the Origins of the Mandate Issue," in Michael Fix and Daphne A. Kenyon, eds., *Coping with Mandates: What Are the Alternatives?* (Washington: Urban Institute Press, 1990), p. 23.
28. Beam, "Origins of the Mandate Issue," p. 23.
29. Koch, "The Mandate Millstone," pp. 43–44.
30. U.S. General Accounting Office, *Federal Aid: Programs Available to State and Local Governments,* HRD-91-93FS (May 1991).

Fine Print: The Contract with America, Devolution, and the Administrative Realities of American Federalism

JOHN J. DIIULIO JR.
DONALD F. KETTL

This report of the Brookings Institution's Center for Public Management (CPM) is intended to help inform the contemporary debate about federalism, most specifically as it relates to the Contract with America. One of the animating ideas of the Contract is the belief that the absolute size and scope of the national government can and should be greatly reduced, while responsibility for many remaining non-defense federal responsibilities can and should either be devolved to state and local governments, or, where possible and appropriate, removed altogether from governmental hands and made the responsibility of private citizens, families, churches, or other civic institutions....[1]

At the outset, let it be clear that this Brookings-CPM report is *not* about the desirability of the Contract with America, or of any particular provisions or sub-sections thereof, or of any given substantive policy goals of the Republican-led 104th Congress. Rather, our principal concern here is to measure as dispassionately as possible the distance between the Contract and its language of devolution, on the one side, and the administrative realities of contemporary American federalism, on the other.

We find that this distance must now be measured in-miles, not inches. *The Contract with America contains virtually no administrative fine print. The language of devolution does more to hide than to highlight the administrative realities of federal-state relations, more to distort than to delineate the facts about how existing intergovernmental policies are implemented, and more to delay nitty-gritty implementation decisions than to define precisely how "devolved" domestic policies can be administered so that they might succeed where existing federal policies have ostensibly failed.*

As Herbert Kaufman stated neatly, policy is enunciated in rhetoric; it is realized (or not) in action.[2] Since the 1960s, policymakers at all levels, but especially at the federal level, have enacted new policies or recast old ones without thinking through how best the policies can be administered, or whether, in fact, they can be implemented at all. Successive Democratic-controlled Congresses established broad (and not infrequently unreachable) goals and delegated to others (either federal bureaucracies, state and local governments, or vast networks of private contractors) the task of administration.

One obvious way to avoid the administrative complexities of American federalism is simply to have less government, especially less government from Washington. Rhetorically, that is what the Contract with America and the language of devolution are all about. And relative to the ambitious national policy plans that Democrats have favored since the days of the New Deal and the Great Society, the Contract does represent "less government."

But make no mistake: *the Contract with America is a big government—and a big government from Washington—document, fly paper for virtually all the same intergovernmental administrative problems that have bedeviled successive generations of national policymakers since the end of the Second World War....*

Conceptually, one way to approach questions about sorting federal responsibilities is to recognize that there are at least three activities of every governmental function: *setting* policy, *financing* policy, and *administering* policy. In any given area of domestic policy, Washington can be involved in one, two, three, or none of these activities. The content and character of federal-state relations thus depends not only on whether the national government is expanding or contracting its activities in given areas, but on which mix of responsibilities Washington is assuming or shedding, centralizing or devolving. . . .

. . . Americans now have about $3 trillion worth of government, about half of it national, the other half of it state and local. Some want to shrink both halves of this pie. Others want to shrink only the federal half. And still others prefer to reslice it in ways that improve government performance. In recent years many policy intellectuals and political leaders of both parties have used the term devolution to describe their ideas about how to reorder and sort federal responsibilities. But do Republicans and Democrats mean even roughly the same thing by "devolution"?

To be sure, the administrative politics of devolving given federal responsibilities after as much as a half-century of nationalizing them are bound to be controversial and complicated. But this is only the beginning of what dedicated devolutionists must face.

The problems with devolution go much deeper, right down to the core belief that the growth of the national government has been fueled mainly by an expansion of the Washington-based federal bureaucracy. The Reagan administration railed against "waste, fraud, and abuse" by federal bureaucrats. The Clinton administration has made cutting the size of the federal civilian work force the popular political centerpiece of its campaign to "reinvent government."[3] With few exceptions, national politicians of both parties, the public, and the press are highly and uniformly receptive to this blame-the-federal-bureaucracy article of devolutionist faith. There is just one problem: it is totally and demonstrably false.

Since 1960 the only persistent personnel growth in federal agencies has occurred among senior executives and presidential political appointees (from 451 in 1960 to 2,393 in 1992).[4] The rest of the federal work force has thinned, not thickened. As Figure 3-2 shows, between 1965 and 1994 the volume of federal regulations issued and the amount of federal money spent rose much faster than did the number of federal civilian employees who wrote the regulations and disbursed the funds. Between 1960 and 1990 the number of federal civilian workers fluctuated between 2.2 million and 3.2 million. In recent years the number of federal civilian employees has been dropping and is now at 2.08 million. Over the last several decades, the fraction of federal civil servants who work in the Washington area has held steady at around 11 percent. Most federal bureaucrats do not work "inside the beltway"—or anywhere near it.

The real "Washington bureaucracy" is composed mainly of the large number of people who work *indirectly* for the national government as employees of private firms and state and local agencies that are largely, if not entirely, funded by federal dollars. Outside the defense area, the federal government revolves around three basic functions: (1) paying subsidies to particular individuals, groups and organizations in society (farmers, veterans, schools,

Figure 3-2. Federal Government Growth

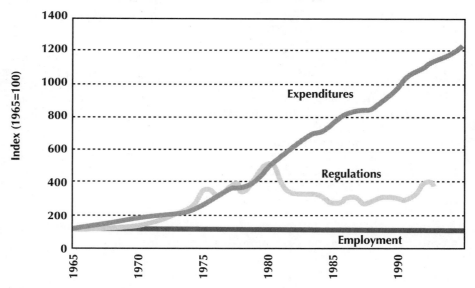

Source: *Budget of the U.S. Government, Fiscal Year 1996.*

hospitals); (2) transferring money from the federal government to state and local governments; and (3) enforcing congressionally mandated regulations for various sectors of society and the economy.

For several decades now, in accordance with increasingly detailed acts of Congress, federal civilian employees, state and local government employees, and vast networks of private contractors and non-profit organizations have performed these and related functions *together.* Contrary to the devolutionist creed, federal bureaucrats are neither always the dominant partners in inter-governmental administration nor the chief culprits in clear-cut cases of "waste, fraud, abuse," or outright policy or program failure.

Since the end of World War II, virtually every major domestic policy initiative in the United States has involved state and local governments: medicare, medicaid, antipoverty, interstate highways, environmental cleanup, and much, much more. This pattern is illustrated in the shared Social Security financing and payment arrangements under the Social Security Act (administered by the states subject to federal review for compliance with min-imum standards set by the Secretary of Health and Human Services), the management for active state and local participation in land use under the Federal Land Policy and Management Act (regionally administered subject to federal review for compliance with planning criteria set by the Secretary of the Interior), and the state implementation of the Clean Air Act, under which state officials develop specific plans for environmental cleanup (subject to standards set by the Environmental Protection Agency). . . . [5]

In addition to the huge role that state and local governments play in the "Washington bureaucracy," almost every major federal domestic policy directly involves either private contractors, or non-profit organizations, or both. In many federal programs these private agents make important decisions as well as implement them. To cite just a few examples, Environmental Protection Agency (EPA) contractors have answered the agency's Superfund hotline and advised callers about which projects might be eligible for funding. Other contractors have helped develop the Department of Transportation's safety policy. Each involvement meant using the discretion granted federal bureaus by Congress and shaping fundamental policy decisions. At EPA, in fact, contractors developed criteria for how the agency ought to define inherently governmental functions that should not be contracted out.

Relying on contractors to deliver services is one thing; relying on them to make government policy is another. Many federal agencies lack the staff, in numbers or training, to conduct such work. Sometimes, as with the Superfund program, these shortages flow directly from congressional restrictions on agency hiring. Drawing the line between policy execution and policymaking, moreover, is difficult. Public administration has been struggling for a century, with increasing frustration, to solve this problem....

WHICH WAY TO DEVOLUTION?

Zeroing in on the federal bureaucracy, cutting the federal payroll, and consolidating federal programs are ways of avoiding, not confronting, the hard work of sorting federal responsibilities and mastering the administrative realities of the "Washington bureaucracy" and American federalism itself. There are at least three additional ways that devolutionists could proceed.

First, devolution could mean the *total or near-total national withdrawal* of federal responsibilities. Devolution could be wielded as an axe in many areas where the federal government now plays a big role in making, administering, or financing domestic policy. There are, for example, many conservatives who believe that Washington should simply stop all involvement in most areas of social policy.

But the Contract with America does not trumpet any such retreat. Rather, the Contract is practically a catalogue of all the areas in which the federal government has become deeply involved since the end of the Second World War. No more than the Eisenhower administration rolled back the New Deal does the Contract even contemplate rolling back major elements of both the New Deal and the Great Society.

A second possibility is devolution as the *radical privatization* of federal responsibilities. In this scenario, Washington would play paymaster to private firms which assumed a greater and greater share of existing federal responsibilities. The Contract would encourage a resumption of Reagan-era efforts to privatize more federal functions than ever before.

A third potential path of devolution is the *new "new federalism."* This road would need to be paved brick-by-brick with block grants and the repeal of so-called unfunded mandates. Steps on this road have already been taken by the Republican-led, Contract-bound 104th Congress.

At present, the first path remains politically irrelevant, while the latter two are littered with major administrative obstacles, not to mention barriers imposed by contemporary judicial doctrines about federalism....

REINVENTING BLOCK GRANTS?

Whatever the fate of devolution efforts that center on the further privatization of federal responsibilities, there can be no doubt that the Contract with America is a midwife at the birth of the third "new federalism" of the last quarter-century.

In the 1970s, President Nixon pushed for block grants as part of his "New Federalism" initiatives. In the 1980s, President Reagan waved the same banner, but with a crucial difference: Reagan tried to block welfare-type grants, whereas Nixon's block grants were for services that states and localities themselves perform.[6]

Let us begin, however, with a more detailed overview of the twentieth-century history of block grants—a guided preview to a history that may be about to repeat itself once again.[7]

In 1915 the federal government gave less than $6 million in grants-in-aid to the states. By 1925, over $114 million was spent; by 1937 nearly $300 million. The great growth began in the 1960s: between 1960 and 1966 federal grants to the states doubled; from 1966 to 1970 they doubled again; between 1970 and 1975 they doubled yet again. By 1985 they amounted to over $100 billion a year and were spent through more than four hundred separate programs. The five largest programs accounted for over half the money spent and reflected the new priorities that federal policy had come to serve: housing assistance for low-income families, medicaid, highway construction, services to the unemployed, and welfare programs for mothers with dependent children and the disabled.

Until the 1960s most federal grants-in-aid were conceived by or in cooperation with the states and were designed to serve essentially state purposes. Large blocs of voters and a variety of organized interests would press for grants to help farmers, build highways, or support vocational education. During the 1960s, however, an important change occurred: the federal government began devising grant programs based less on what states were demanding and more on what federal officials perceived to be important *national needs* (See Table 3-1). Federal officials, not state and local ones, were the principal proponents of grant programs to aid the urban poor, combat crime, reduce pollution, and deal with drug abuse.

The rise in federal activism in setting goals and the efforts, on occasion, to bypass state officials occurred at a time when the total amount of federal aid to states and localities had become so vast that many jurisdictions were completely dependent on it for the support of vital services. Whereas federal aid amounted to less than 2 percent of state and local spending in 1927, by 1970 it amounted to 19 percent and by 1980 to 26 percent (see Table 3-2 and Figure 3-3).

LESS GOVERNMENT?

Americans say they want less government, especially less government from Washington. The Contract with America and the drive for devolution are responses to this popular outcry. Today only 22 percent of Americans (versus 73 percent in 1958) "trust the government in Washington to do what is right most of the time/always." About 67 percent of Americans (versus 35 percent in 1965) think "big government" poses "the biggest threat" to the country's

Table 3-1
The Changing Purposes of Federal Grants
to State and Local Governments
1960-1992 [percent]

	1960	1992
Transportation and highways	43	12
Income security	38	24
Health	3	40
Education and training	7	16
Miscellaneous	9	8

Source: *Budget of the U.S. Government, Fiscal Year 1994,* pp. 51-58.

future. Some 80 percent feel that the value they get from federal taxes is "only fair/poor," and 60 percent favor "a smaller government with fewer services" to a "larger government with many services." Finally, 73 percent are convinced that the federal government "is much too large and has too much power."[8]

It is perfectly clear how negatively Americans now feel toward government in general and the federal government in particular. What remains entirely unclear, however, is whether the mass public, national lawmakers, and state

Table 3-2
Federal Aid to State and Local Governments
1955-1995

		Federal Aid as a Percentage of:	
Year	Total Federal Aid (in billions)[a]	Federal Outlays	State and Local Outlays
1955	$15.1	4.7	10.1
1960	29.1	7.6	14.7
1965	41.8	9.2	15.3
1970	73.6	12.3	19.2
1975	105.4	15.0	23.0
1980	127.6	15.5	26.3
1985	113.0	11.2	21.0
1990	119.7	10.8	20.0
1995	175.3(est)	15.3(est)	NA

[a]In constant 1987 dollars.

Source: Total aid figures, percentages of federal outlays, and 1995 estimates from *Budget of the U.S. Government, Fiscal Year 1993,* Table 12.1, part 5, pp. 164-165. Percentages of state and local outlays 1955-1985 from *Budget of the U.S. Government, Fiscal Year 1991,* Table 12.1, pp. A321. Percentage of state and local outlays in 1990 from *Budget of the U.S. Government, Fiscal Year 1994,* p. 79.

and local government leaders are prepared to do what would be necessary to shrink substantially the size and scope of the national government, devolve major chunks of federal responsibilities, and live with the huge changes in American life that must result from any serious and sustained effort to reverse a half-century of "big government." Some evidence suggests that the anti-government, anti-Washington consensus is 3,000 miles wide but only a few miles deep. . . .

And just how much "less government" do Americans really want and what, if anything, can be done from Washington to deliver it? After one subtracts the military and defense spending, the fact remains that most government spending in America has been, and continues to be, state and local. No other modern democratic nation in the world has the vibrant and politically consequential subnational governance that America does. . . .

The balance of federal-state powers is today, as it has always been, a bone of political and jurisprudential contention. But even those who insist on "less government" must agree that federalism lives and that America, even on its worst day, remains one of the most well-governed, well-ordered free societies that the world has ever known. In the language of the very first paragraph of the first number of *The Federalist,* is there anyone who truly believes that the American political experience has been a failure, or that, in the absence of the rapid-fire adoption of the Contract with America and full-speed efforts at devolution, America will soon enter the ranks of societies governed not by "reflection and choice" but by "accident and force"? Somehow, we doubt it.

In a monumental empirical study of post-1970 efforts in Italy to devolve certain central government responsibilities to regional governments, Robert D. Putnam summons the intellectual spirit of Alexis de Tocqueville to reveal the civic traditions (associationism, trust, and cooperation) that make democracy work. Like other modern democratic peoples, today's Americans have civic traditions that can hardly be described simply as anti-government. As Putnam keenly observes,

> We want government to *do* things, not just *decide* things—to educate children, pay pensioners, stop crime, create jobs, hold down prices, encourage family values, and so on. We do not agree on which of these things is most urgent, nor how they should be accomplished, nor even whether they are all worthwhile. All but the anarchists among us, however, agree that at least some of the time on some issues, *action* is required of government institutions. This fact must inform the way we think about institutional success and failure.[9]

When cut-government push comes to address-problems shove, how many contemporary Americans really do not want government in general, or the national government in particular, to act on reducing crime, encouraging family values, and all the rest? Unless we have misplaced or completely misread the last half-century's worth of public opinion data, and unless the $3 trillion worth of government Americans have voted for themselves is a mirage, the only reasonable answer is "a minority."

CIVIC EDUCATION ABOUT PUBLIC MANAGEMENT

Whether one agrees fully or disagrees entirely with the Contract with America, the country will fare better in the future if national lawmakers, state and local government officials, the press, and the public come to grips with the administrative realities of American federalism. . . .

Figure 3-3. Federal Aid to State and Local Governments, 1980-1995

Total federal aid to state and local governments, in billions of 1987 constant dollars, and the aid as a percentage of total federal spending, for each fiscal year.

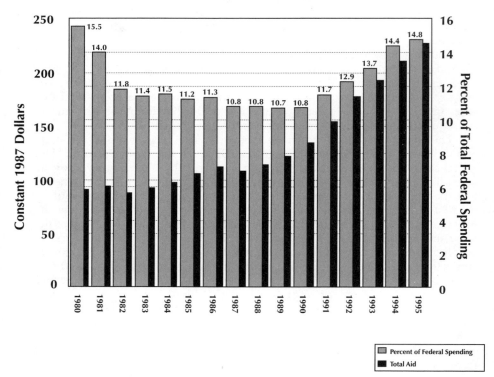

Source: *Budget of the United States Government, Fiscal Year 1996, Historical Tables,* Table 12-1, pp. 175-76.

Note: Data for 1995 [are] estimated.

Not without justification, the case has often been made that civic education about public management—practical knowledge of how government does what it does and how, if at all, it could do things better—promotes a sort of prudential conservative bias. For when public management noses sniff government policies, they almost always smell something burning—or something likely to burn before too long. No one who understands what it actually takes to translate complicated public policy mandates into administrative action; alter out-moded government personnel or procurement practices; foster and maintain cooperation among disparate public and private bureaucracies; promote effective leadership and build productive organizational cultures within the public sector; coordinate a network of federal, state, and local agencies, private contractors, and non-profit organizations; institutionalize meaningful ways of measuring and evaluating government performance; or devise ways of cutting "red tape" without destroying democratically enacted procedural safeguards, knows that none of these things can be done without lots of political foresight and forbearance, plenty of hard work by public administrators, and no shortage of sheer good luck. Many government policy or program failures are in fact administrative failures in disguise. Likewise, the perverse and unintended consequences of any given government policy often owe much to the ways in which that policy was (or was not) implemented.

Yet after a half-century of big-government policy initiatives were put into law by national political leaders who hardly ever gave federalism, implementation, or management issues a thought, we are now witnessing efforts to change the course of American governance by leaders who seem no less blissfully ignorant of these issues.

Whatever one's particular policy preferences or ideological outlook on what government ought to be doing (or to refrain from doing), it should be possible to concede the need for civic education about public management. It is revealing, for example, that the 1994 *National Standards for Civics and Government,* a fine guide to much that children K-4 through high school should know about the theory and practice of American government, conveys almost nothing about what most government agencies actually do; how given types of bureaucracies at given levels of government are monitored, organized, and evaluated; the administrative realities of intergovernmental relations; and other facts, figures, and first-order ideas about how a federal, state, or local bill which has become law gets implemented (or not). . . . [10]

REDISCOVER GOVERNMENT

Whether American government needs to be razed or reinvented, devolved or downsized, we cannot say. But we are certain that American government needs to be rediscovered by policy elites and average citizens alike. By "rediscovering government" we mean:

1. Empirically documenting what government does and the actual range of administrative successes and failures in government bureaucracies;

2. Analyzing carefully the reasons for the interagency, intraagency, and historical variance in the performance of government policies and programs;

3. Figure out how, if at all, well-substantiated instances of managerial excellence in government bureaucracies can be replicated widely; and

4. Producing and disseminating widely a body of reliable applied administrative knowledge about what public leadership and management strategies work best, under what conditions, and at what human and financial costs.[11]

Unless we are totally mistaken, a generation from now America is still going to have lots and lots of government, much of it from Washington. Whatever else happens, therefore, we hope that the debate over the Contract with America, devolution, and the administrative realities of American federalism causes many Americans, and not just public management specialists, to begin to rediscover government.

Notes

1. Ed Gillespie and Bob Schellhas, eds., *Contract with America: The Bold Plan by Rep. Newt Gingrich. Rep. Dick Armey and the House Republicans to Change the Nation* (New York: Times Books, 1994), esp. pp. 125–141.
2. Herbert Kaufman, *The Forest Ranger* (Baltimore: Johns Hopkins Press, 1960), p. 3.
3. Donald F. Kettl and John J. DiIulio, Jr., eds., *Inside the Reinvention Machine: Assessing Governmental Reform* (Washington, D.C.: Brookings Institution, forthcoming March 1995).
4. Paul C. Light, *Thickening Government* (Brookings Institution and the Governance Institute, 1995), p. 7.
5. John J. DiIulio, Jr., Donald F. Kettl, and Gerald J. Garvey, *Improving Government Performance: An Owner's Manual* (Brookings, 1993), p. 39. Also see Kettl, *Sharing Power: Public Governance and Private Markets* (Brookings, 1993).
6. Richard P. Nathan and Fred Doolittle, *Reagan and the States* (Princeton, NJ: Princeton University Press, 1987), Chapter 2.
7. Portions of this account are based directly on or adapted from James Q. Wilson and John J. DiIulio, Jr., *American Government: Institutions and Policies,* Sixth Edition (Lexington, MA: D.C. Heath and Company, 1995), Chapter 3.
8. Data from the Roper Center for Public Opinion Research, as reported in Karlyn Bowman and Everett Carll Ladd, "Opinion Pulse: Disillusionment with Washington," *The American Enterprise,* March/April 1995, p. 101.
9. Putnam, *Making Democracy Work,* pp. 8–9. Emphasis in original.
10. Center for Civic Education, *National Standards for Civics and Government* (Calabasas, CA: Center for Civic Education, 1994).
11. John J. DiIulio, Jr., *Rediscovering Government: Leadership, Administration, and Culture in the Federal Bureaucracy,* a Twentieth-Century Fund Book, forthcoming.

4

Public Administration in a Democratic Society

Hostility toward administrative authority is nothing new in this country. It started with colonists revolting against a distant king and his local administrators and continued through the Articles of Confederation and the Constitutional Convention right into the twentieth century. However, the fear that government bureaucracy is too powerful, almost out of control, has probably never been as strong as it is today. This chapter treats the place of bureaucracy in modern society, especially the clash between bureaucracy and democracy.

There are inherent contradictions between the concepts of bureaucracy and democracy. One question is whether public bureaucracies can be controlled at all.

Students of public administration have long realized that a *system* of restraints in effect controls the power of public bureaucracies. Always undergoing change, these restraints may be divided into two basic types: intragovernmental and extragovernmental.

Regarding *intragovernmental vehicles* for control, most notable in the American context is the separation of powers. Through hearings and investigations, review of the budget, audits, confirmation of appointments, staff assistance, and individual monitoring of constituency complaints, legislative control of bureaucratic power has been especially important. The courts are increasingly active, and judicial review is also significant.

Hierarchical administration, sometimes referred to as "overhead democracy," is also an important vehicle. Chief political executives are usually elected in our republican form of government, and citizens expect them to hold the bureaucracy accountable.

Chief executives at all levels of American government have increased the size of their staffs to assist them in this function. Consolidation and centralization of agency structures is one common device. Increasingly, chief executives also use modern management techniques and information systems to supervise public agencies under their control.

The final intragovernmental factor that merits attention, but is often neglected in the literature, is internal control within the bureaucracy. Included here is administrative self-restraint, because—as many believe—total outside control is probably impossible. Increasing the sense of personal responsibility among public employees at all levels of government is one of the critical issues of our time.

Extragovernmental forces are represented primarily by a variety of competing interest groups, political parties, public opinion, and direct citizen participation. Scholarly research can also be included here.

Some observers place particular emphasis on the role of the press with its First Amendment privileges. They want to help the media and citizens obtain better access to government: through "sunshine" laws that require governmental meetings to be open, and through freedom of information (FOI) legislation facilitating access to government records. They feel that less secrecy in government means greater control over the power of officeholders.

Trends in the political control of bureaucratic power and the effectiveness of this system are the principal topics of discussion in this chapter. With revelations about the activities of the CIA, FBI, and IRS—not to mention Abscam and President Nixon's "enemies list"—controlling the bureaucracy is a topic of permanent importance as well as contemporary controversy.

There are other related issues. Many Americans believe that government does too much, whereas others contend that government does too little. Business people complain about too much regulation, and citizens of all kinds complain about the red tape and paperwork they encounter in dealing with government.

American society appears to be in the midst of a fundamental rethinking about the scope of government activity. Much of this discussion centers on the role and functions of large public bureaucracies. We will give additional attention to this in Chapters 9 and 10.

The 1980s were a decade of decentralization and deregulation. Previous to President Clinton, the last five presidents—Nixon, Ford, Carter, Reagan, and Bush; four Republicans and a Democrat—were all against Big Government and especially Big Bureaucracy. Public opinion seems to be moving toward a reconsideration of the government's ability to solve societal problems, which has not been seriously challenged since the presidency of Franklin D. Roosevelt.

In the first article in Chapter 4, Theodore Lowi, one of America's most prominent political scientists, first raises the issue of political ideology. But, as it turns out, he is more interested in the discretion exercised by administrative agencies.

In the second article here, William Gormley attempts to assess the current condition of administrative accountability, focusing on the states. Gormley reminds us of the variety of devices available to constrain administrative agencies as well as covering relevant current developments.

In the final selection in this chapter, the nation's leading theorist in public administration, Dwight Waldo, turns his attention to ethics in the public service. First Waldo attempts to sort out to whom or to what public employees are obligated. Then he speculates about putting ethics into practice.

This chapter raises some of the most important issues surrounding the practice of public administration today. Just a few of the questions to contemplate in connection with this chapter are:

- What perspectives do liberals and conservatives bring to the question of administrative power?
- How would Lowi deal with the administrative discretion typically found in government agencies?
- What is new in administrative accountability, at least as affects state-level agencies?
- Are administrative ethics possible? Why or why not?
- Looking back at the articles in the first four chapters of this anthology, do you think that administrative agencies at all levels of government are too powerful today? Are they sufficiently controlled and, if so, by whom and how?

Two Roads to Serfdom: Liberalism, Conservatism, and Administrative Power

THEODORE J. LOWI

*You must first enable the government to control
the governed; and in the next place oblige
it to control itself.* — JAMES MADISON

This is a revisit to the well of delegated, discretionary power and the politics of administrative agencies. It is the same as it was twenty years ago, the same well in the same place with pretty much the same contents, only deeper and more polluted. As in the past, my concern is for the political consequences of delegated power (see Lowi 1969, 1979).

Delegation of power is an inevitable and necessary practice in any government. No theory of representative government is complete without it. An absolutist position against delegation would be utter foolishness. However, there are relatively uncontrollable spillover effects from delegated power. Delegation of power does something to the giver and to the receiver. From the very first to the very last act delegation is a calculated risk. If it is to be done rightly, its consequences must be understood.

The consequences in question are of constitutional importance. As far as I am concerned, they embody the key constitutional issue of our time—precisely in the spirit of Madison's epigraph. The intent of the framers is not what is at issue; the *concern* of the framers is. The purpose of the Constitution is the regulation or regularization of power in at least three ways. First, and foremost, the Constitution regulates through limitations on power. This is the essence of "the social contract" as understood by Americans. Second, substantive calculability is used to regulate power. This translates into "rule of law" as understood by Americans, and is embraced as the main antidote to tyranny, that being defined as arbitrariness. Third, power is regularized by procedural calculability. This means relatively rigid formalism defined as due process. This is captured very well in Richard Stewart's notion of constitutive law, which "consists of rules that make legally recognized practices possible" (Stewart 1987).

It is my contention that the delegation of broad and undefined discretionary power from the legislature to the executive branch deranges virtually all constitutional relationships and prevents attainment of the constitutional goals of limitation on power, substantive calculability, and procedural calculability. My argument, although a hypothesis about tendencies, has appeared to be absolutist to my critics (see, e.g., Gellhorn 1987; Sargentich 1987; Stewart 1987, 328). But fortunately, that is a consequence of my style rather than inherent in the proposition itself. Let me meet my critics and contribute to constructive exchange by putting forth one important point of clarification, which is that, because the delegation of power is a matter of degree, the change of relationship between giver and receiver is also a matter of degree; this holds true until some indeterminate point when the relationship can be said to be deranged. I like the way Ernest Gellhorn (1987, 352) puts it, with some slight translation to meet my needs. He states that delegations become excessive when they are "used to create private goods." My version would be that *all* discretion delegated to administrative agencies, by degree, provides the conditions for the creation of private goods. This is the very essence of patronage, in the feudal sense of the term, and therefore of serfdom—the capacity to distribute material resources or privileges on a personalized, individualized basis. This incorporates Gellhorn's theory as a clarification of my own criterion: At what point can duly constituted authority be turned into patronage? Although it would be improbable that the precise point would be the same for each agency, it may be possible to agree that the question of the relationship between authority and patronage is the right question.

This returns us to the direct connection between delegated discretion and constitutional derangement. Because I am not an absolutist, I have no rigid commitment to a particular set of constitutional forms, ours or anyone else's. But forms do exist for a purpose, and if broad delegation changes the form and interferes with the attainment of the purpose, then we can begin to speak of derangement and its attendant consequences, and we can do so not in absolute terms but empirically and as a matter of degree.

As I began arguing nearly twenty-five years ago (Lowi 1969), liberalism was undoing itself not because its policy goals would alienate the American people but because of its failure to appreciate the constitutional and political limitations inherent in broad delegation that would interfere with attainment of liberal policy goals by contributing to the impression and the reality of patronage, with privilege and private goods going not to the deserving but to the best organized. The reasoning was as follows: every delegation of discretion away from electorally responsible levels of government to professional career administrative agencies is a calculated risk because politics will always flow to the point of discretion, the demand for representation would take place at the point of discretion, and the constitutional forms designed to balance one set of interests against another would not be present at the point of discretion.

Such arguments in the 1960s were largely disregarded or ridiculed as unrealistic. The biggest horse laugh was given to the idea of considering the revival of the *Schechter* rule.[1] Consequently, government by broad and undefined delegated discretionary power was given a forty-year test. As liberal programs advanced toward completion of the New Deal agenda, so did the breadth of delegated discretion. My 1969 critique (Lowi 1969, 101-24) coincided with the first year of a five-year binge in the enactment of important regulatory policies. Depending on who is doing the counting, an argument can be made that Congress enacted more regulatory programs in the five years between 1969 and 1974 than during any other comparable period in our history, including the first five years of the New Deal. It is possible to identify 130 major regulatory laws enacted during the decade (see Lowi 1979, 115). Moreover, an even stronger argument can be made that the regulatory policies adopted during that period were broader in scope and more unconditional in delegated discretion than any other programs in American history.

What makes this epoch of policy creativity all the more significant is that the national government during that decade was headed by two right-of-center Republican administrations (Nixon, Ford) and one Democratic administration elected on an explicit anti-Washington campaign (Carter). Yet, most of the votes for these programs in the House and the Senate were overwhelmingly favorable, with dissents coming from both parties. Although there was occasional grumbling heard from the White House, no important bills passed by Congress were vetoed by these three presidents.

In other words, the goals and methods, and the broad, virtually unconditional delegations of power were supported by strong, bipartisan consensus. Moreover, no evidence can be found that opposition to any of these programs included arguments about unduly or dangerously broad delegations of power. Thus, those who rose then, and those who rise now to defend delegated legislative power, have had their way. Also, oblivious to the consequences that might flow from broad delegation, the lawyers and the policymakers would naturally search for other explanations when the collapse of regulatory government came. And it did come, at the very time of the regulation binge itself. I recognize that many factors may have contributed to the constitutional derangements observed here, but this in no way reduces the possibility of the causal linkage between these derangements and the rise of delegated power.

CONSTITUTIONAL DERANGEMENTS
AND THE DELEGATION OF POWER

From Congressional to Presidential Government

In the 1880s, political science professor Woodrow Wilson characterized American national government as "congressional government," and he published an important book under that title (see Wilson 1908). At some point toward the end of the 1930s, a book characterizing American national government as "presidential government" would have been equally appropriate. Recognized by virtually all, and embraced by most, the rise of presidential government has been explained by any number of factors, ranging from the growth of the large economy to the expansion of mass communication. But the factor most immediately and obviously involved in the change from congressional to presidential government was the voluntary, self-conscious rendering of legislative power to the president, thence to the agencies in the executive branch. I call the process "legiscide" (see Lowi 1985, 28-30).

The conversion to presidential government directly contributed to the transformation of national politics, broadly defined. The most noticeable aspect of that was the decline of national political parties and their loss of control of the presidency. The transition can be understood as one from party democracy to mass democracy, where consent is conveyed not merely by election but by regular plebiscite, expressed in weekly and monthly public opinion polls. The center of initiative has become the presidency, the center of gravity has become the executive branch, and the focus of expectations on the part of the American people follows accordingly (Lowi 1985, 67–92).

Undermining the Welfare State Consensus

The last of the great expansions of the welfare state, Supplemental Security Income and the indexing of social security benefits on top of a 20 percent boost in those benefits, occurred in 1972. These were followed within a year by official recognition of a fiscal crisis in the welfare state. The problem was less one of financing, however, than of political support. There had been considerable political support for Medicare and Medicaid, adopted in 1965.[2] There had been initial support for the boost in social security benefits and for indexing pegged to the cost of living. But over the years after 1965, many corporate and middle-class supporters of welfare were one-by-one jumping ship, despite the fact that many of the expansions of the welfare state had been aimed at benefiting the middle classes themselves. They were jumping ship largely because of the welfare programs of Aid to Families with Dependent Children, public assistance, welfare in kind, and other "means tested" programs associated with the War on Poverty. Why? Because these were discretionary welfare programs, in contrast to the first several social security titles adopted after 1935, which were relatively nondiscretionary (see Lowi 1979, 232-35).

The abandonment of the relatively clear categoric criteria of the original social security titles in favor of the highly discretionary, open-ended approach of the newer programs contributed to grievous insecurity among the very persons that welfare sought to assist, cut a deep wedge between the minority poor and city hall, and alienated large segments of formerly middle-class supporters (Lowi 1979, 207–17, 226). During the 1970s, it became de rigueur to attack the welfare state. Ironically, efforts to establish welfare as a right were coming just in the wake of the successful efforts to render the very concept of welfare increasingly vague.

Undermining Regulation

To a great extent, the undermining of the welfare categories contributed to the undermining of regulation because the problems with welfare were the most important reasons for the binge of regulatory programs and the vast expansion of the scope of each (see Lowi 1979, 220-36). Regulatory programs adopted in this period have been referred to as "social regulation," for the very good reason that they had to be society-wide in order to control the costs of the welfare state. Cost containment in welfare can only go so far through such practices as controlling rate charges and cleansing the welfare roles of chiselers. If the welfare state assumes responsibility for indemnifying all injuries and the dependencies attributable to them, then a maximum effort had to be made to reduce cost by reducing the number of injuries themselves. This meant more regulation. In each instance, the purpose was good; an ounce of prevention may be worth a pound of cure. But legislation merely ordaining a desired goal was bound to undermine the process itself. Demands for remedies escalated from demands for relief against specific conduct to demands for the general outcome itself as a collective right—not a right asserted by an individual to a specific remedy for a specified act of damage,[3] but a generalized "class action" right to the safe water, the safe machine.[4]

Interest-Group Liberalism, Continued

The long-established pattern of officially sponsored interest group access and representation in agency decision-making processes continued, but there were some new twists in the 1970s. New groups, emerging in what is now called "the new politics" or "public interest politics," achieved close coalitional relationships with some agencies, especially the new regulatory agencies with the broadest discretion. Many of the new groups adopted a "politics of rights," attempting to put their own interests in a safe position beyond the access of majoritarian politics (see Schoenbrod 1987). This was not an illogical development; it was in fact a predictable one, considering that all legislation tends to convey some rights to some and the new, broad "goals statutes" convey some rights absolutely (Schoenbrod 1987, 1983). Although this gave some agencies an adversarial environment that they had not before had, the general pattern of privileged relations between groups and agencies continued, and so did the declining consensus for regulation itself. There were no regular political forces or processes in the national government that had the capacity of regularly pushing interest groups back toward the more public and generalized legislative process, where confrontations and competition among groups might tend to contribute to the self-regulation of which Madison spoke so longingly in *The Federalist* no. 10.

Derangements in the Judiciary

Widespread and generally critical references to activist courts and the imperial judiciary are entirely misleading (see Pierce and Shapiro 1981). The federal courts have been activist, perhaps imperial, but only in regard to state actions. At the national government level, virtually the reverse is true. As national executive power has grown and federal agencies have grown larger as well as more numerous, the federal courts have acted as though they are seeking to maintain their power as a coordinate branch of government by joining, supplementing, and generally embracing agency powers—often by pushing agencies beyond where agency chiefs want to go and by pushing agencies to act more vigorously than agency chiefs wish to act. Relaxation of the rules of standing to sue (Friedenthal, Kane, and Miller) and the filing of class action suits seem to me to be as often as not motivated by a willingness to accommodate new politics groups who are seeking to push agencies more vigorously in a direction of statutory obligations.[5] There may be a few instances in which federal courts resist federal agencies, but the fact remains that this resistance has rarely been articulated at the level of constitutional discourse. The federal courts follow the rule of statutory construction that will render the statute constitutional, and then they proceed to interpret the statute in order to help dispose of the issues brought forth in the case being litigated. The logic of this situation is generally to expand agency powers because, in most instances, especially those involving social regulation, the terms of the delegation from Congress to the agency are so broad, and contain such high-flown rhetoric about the goals, that any but an expansive interpretation would be contrary to the spirit of the statute.[6] Among other things, this leads me to ask a very important question of experts such as Richard Stewart: Why is a court that is competent to interpret existing statutes and to develop rules from its decisions within the context of this broad and ill-defined statute institutionally incompetent to judge the absence of enforceable rules in the statute? And why is it politically more acceptable and less hazardous for judges to create an operational statute out of an empty legislative enactment than it is for judges to state honestly and forthrightly that the original statute is too empty to permit judges to enforce it? (See Stewart 1987, 325–28.)

Derangement of Agency Professionalism

The derangement of agency professionalism takes two paradoxical forms. First, a substantive specialization and the reputation for professional judgment are displaced by formula decision making, formalistic analysis, and the appearance of theoretical science. Second, law of power from the legislature is not merely a straightforward grant of authority to an agency. It is that and more. The language of these broad statutes is a systems language, a language that attempts to incorporate all of the variables that might tend to explain the existence of the problem and might provide a lead toward a solution of the problem. We talk about a systems analysis today as though that were an established fact and a phenomenon capable of being analyzed. In fact, a system is a figment of imagination, an artifact of someone's theory. This has become so much a part of our thinking that it takes on the appearance of reality when, in reality, a system is at best hypothetical. Embracing the system as the universe of analysis led policy-makers to think of regulation as embracing that entire system. This imposed upon the perspective of the lawmaker and the administrator a complexity beyond human capacity—to incorporate for the purpose of empirical causal analysis, and then for the purpose of control, the totality of interdependent causes and effects (see Lowi 1991, 1992). Note the language of the Occupational Safety and Health Act (OSHA): "To assure so far as possible every working man and woman in the Nation safe and healthful working conditions and to preserve our human resources."[7] Or, take the language of President Nixon's message to the Congress as they were setting up the Environmental Protection Agency, in which he said that the purpose of his reorganization plan was to respond to "environmentally related activities" and organize them "rationally and systematically." He went on to argue that "we need to know more about the *total environment*" [emphasis added] if we are effectively to "ensure the protection, development . . . and enhancement of the total environment."[8]

In order to reach the entire system, a systems analysis is obviously called for, and that comes not from the substantive expertise of the professions around which the agency is organized, but from a more general, theoretical science or a language indicative of such a science. It seems fairly clear that the significantly expanded use of science and technology in decision making is, as a consequence, compromising or otherwise weakening substantive specialization and the reputation of agencies for substantive judgment. At the same time, and in response to the same set of forces, economics has been replacing law as the language of the state. Formula decision making and formalistic analysis are governed more by budgetary data, aggregate data drawn from a whole variety of extra-agency sources, and systems analytic cookbooks than from solid knowledge of the sector and the problem at hand that is built up over a lifetime of direct, sensory experience. In other words, the new requirements of system analysis tend to violate the long-established theory of administrative expertise on which our whole system is built. That is not necessarily a bad thing, but it deserves some examination.

Although some skeptical scholars such as Richard Nelson have tried to demonstrate the limits of formal reasoning in policy-making, the science/ technology methodologies, ranging from aggregate quantitative indices and benefit-cost analysis to zero-based budgeting, are replacing the very professional judgments for which Congress claims to have so much respect when it leaves its statutes so inadequately constructed (Nelson 1977). The involvement of science/technology as a decision-making methodology can be explained in part by America's faith in science and technology. However, another important part of the explanation is that the provision for science/technology methodology *tends to compensate for the absence of legal integrity.* Once a systems concept is combined with general, aggregate, theoretical science and generalized cookbook decision-making formulas, the boundaries of agencies are surpassed or eradicated, as the case may be. At this point, who needs the agency at all? To whom is the legislative authority being delegated? Or, I should ask, to *what* is agency authority being delegated?

Derangement of Procedure

There has been an important transition from procedure to proceduralism. We have had quite a fill already of what Stewart (1987) calls "constitutive law." Just as Congress has relied upon science and technology, so Congress also has used procedure as an effort to compensate for the absence of legal integrity in its legislative draftsmanship. On the eve of the 1970s regulatory policy binge, the leading student of administrative law, Kenneth Culp Davis, observed that broad administrative discretion is unavoidable, but that safeguards are available, thereby making administrative discretion desirable, as long as discretion is "guided by administrative rules adopted through procedure like that prescribed by the federal Administrative Procedure Act" (Davis 1969).[9] That is the classic rationalization for broad delegations and poor legislative drafting.

It is certainly better to have procedure than to have nothing. But a closer look at the politics of Congress's adoption of regulatory policies will reveal that there are at least four other reasons why procedures are provided and why, in the period of the regulation binge, procedures went *well beyond* the requirements of the APA. First, as already suggested, the procedural provisions that go well beyond the APA are adopted to compensate for unconstitutionally vague and unguided delegations of power. Second, certain kinds of procedures are adopted to open access to agency decision making in order to co-opt citizens and to add legitimacy to their processes. Although some observers are dubious that broad delegations of legislative power to administrative agencies endanger legitimacy, Congress and the agencies themselves operate as though that is a real problem, and both go out of their way to use procedure to shore up legitimacy with the various organized constituencies (see Mashaw 1985). Third, and this point is closely related to the second, procedures that provide for easy access and participation by citizens and groups to the rule-making process enable officials to encourage or channel citizens and groups into the administrative process rather than to pursue the same issues prematurely in a court. This procedure-laden rule-making process has had a significant impact on interest group politics, shifting more and more of it from the lobbies of Congress to the corridors of agencies. We need a new word for the administrative equivalent to lobbying. I propose "corridoring." Fourth, and finally, many of the procedural provisions that go beyond the APA are proposed by *opponents* of the legislation in order to reduce the effectiveness of the programs themselves.

For all of these reasons, the time span of agency decision making, from the moment a rule is proposed to the point at which it is adopted and published in the *Federal Register,* is now exceeding an average of thirty-five months. This is used in the arguments against the legitimacy and efficiency of administrative agencies when in fact a good part of that decision-making span is attributable to the deliberate, strategic, antagonistic, or dilatory imposition of procedures.

Derangement of Presidential Power

Presidential government was a direct and immediate product of the 1930s delegations of power from Congress (see Lowi 1979; 1985). The development of the office in practice and in theory took longer, although it began in 1937 with the appeal of the President's Committee on Administrative Management, whose second sentence was, "The President needs help." Help was forthcoming, to such an extent that observers were very soon referring to the "institutional presidency" and to management as an essential feature of the presidency (Neustadt 1954, 1955). It did not stop there, and it has not stopped since that time. Every president has said, or has appointed a commission to say for him, that the president continues to need help; and every president has gotten virtually all the help he has asked for, without eliminating any of the innovations and additions inherited from his predecessors.

Presidential power has been given the stamp of approval by scholarly and journalistic experts and also by the Supreme Court. One of the greatest sources of derangement has been from the scholars, many of whom stepped forward in the 1940s, 1950s and 1960s to proclaim that the presidency was not only part of democratic theory, but was a superior form of democracy to democracy based upon the legislature. In effect, the presidency represents the "real majority." This view was reflected in decisions of the Supreme Court. Even in the historic steel seizure case, although the Supreme Court denied President Truman's claim that the president had inherent powers to seize the steel mills, the justices otherwise actually strengthened presidential power by the dictum that the president could very probably have succeeded in the seizure if he had claimed the authority to do so under an existing statute.[10]

Another important case, *United States v. Nixon,*[11] also advanced presidential power while appearing to delimit it. The court rejected President Nixon's claim to executive privilege as a constitutional protection against delivery of the Watergate tapes, but at the same time, the court stated only that the claim to executive privilege did not protect documents from a subpoena in a criminal prosecution. In all other instances, such as when there is a specific need to protect military, diplomatic, or sensitive national security secrets, executive privilege for the presidency is a privilege—qualified, but nonetheless a privilege.

The constitutional basis of presidential power was advanced again in 1983 when the Supreme Court declared the legislative veto unconstitutional.[12] The purpose of this device, which Congress had applied to 295 provisions in 196 laws, was to take back in bits and pieces what Congress had given away since the 1930s in increasingly large chunks of delegated legislative power (Abourezk 1977). Although not of fundamental importance, the decision tipped the balance between the two branches still further toward the presidency. The only other case of any importance in advancing presidential power was, in 1986, *Bowsher v. Synar*,[13] which involved the constitutionality of parts of the Gramm-Rudman-Hollings law. Here again, the Court appeared at first blush to be cutting down on presidential as well as congressional power by its ruling that Congress was relying on nonexecutive offices to make executive decisions. This threw back on Congress the burden of deficit containment and left open for the future a crisis in all independent regulatory commissions. Although the Supreme Court did not adopt the circuit court's explicit argument on this point, they have left the door open to a future attack that will require Congress to put all the independent regulatory commissions directly within presidential authority.[14]

This suggests that both Congress and the Court, having granted and approved, respectively, the enormous delegations of discretion in a long series of enactments and decisions, have locked themselves into a kind of imperative to grant additional powers, constitutional validation, and ideological embrace to the presidency in order to accomplish the impossible task of meeting the obligations that the statutes impose. If lawyers would spend half as much time expressing concern over the impossibility of presidential control of administrative agencies as they do on the impossibility of Congress's formulating decent rules of law, both presidential control and congressional lawmaking would improve immeasurably.

THE CONSERVATIVE REACTION

As I predicted earlier (Lowi 1969), liberalism was eventually its own undoing. Liberalism's electoral collapse was due to the structure of its laws, the increasingly discretionary character of its administrative agencies, and the disappointment and indignation that arose out of frustrated expectations built on high-flown rhetoric about collective rights to statutory goals. There were actually two reactions to liberal excesses. One was libertarianism and the other conservatism (see, generally, Newman 1984; Lowi, forthcoming). Libertarians and conservatives made common cause against big national government. Both sought to make the domestic part of the government smaller, especially in the area of the regulatory agencies. The two reactions, however, are far from identical.

The libertarian reaction was a genuine demand for deregulation. Libertarians are the descendants of the nineteenth-century, free-market liberals and had been screaming, pretty much in the wilderness, against all forms of government intervention since the 1930s. The size and strength of the libertarian critique did not really begin to revive until the liberalism of the New Deal was already in a virtual shambles in the 1970s. The growth of the popularity of the libertarian position must be attributed more to the failure of New Deal liberalism than to the strength of the libertarian position itself.

Because it was suspected all along of being a front for and a sycophant to important economic interests, libertarians attempted to show in the 1970s that the costs of these regulatory programs clearly outweighed any benefits they produced. The data base for this argument, however, was extremely questionable.

Much of the data came from research done in the 1970s by Murray Weidenbaum (1978), who went on to serve as President Reagan's first Chairman of the Council of Economic Advisers. Because compliance costs are so varied across the different businesses and industries, and because firm data are hard to obtain and are usually mixed with highly subjective experiences, Weidenbaum and his team took a single year, 1976, and assimilated various studies of their own and those of a variety of other scholars to arrive at a rough estimate of $62 billion for the compliance costs to businesses (Weidenbaum 1978, 4).[15] Wiedenbaum then estimated the bureaucratic costs of regulation, deriving these from the budgets of the various regulatory agencies, and came up with a figure of $3.1 billion. This gave him a total cost of regulation for 1976 as $65 billion. But more important, Weidenbaum noted the twenty-to-one ratio between compliance costs and administrative costs and used this as the multiplier for all other years. Thus, in 1979, the estimated administrative costs came to $4.8 billion and, with the application of the multiplier of twenty, resulted in an easy estimate of $97.9 billion. Adding the $97.9 billion to the $4.8 billion, he calculated an overall cost of $102.7 billion.[16] This produced an impressive absolute figure for each year and a spectacular impression of growth—55 percent in a mere three-year period. A later reevaluation (Schwarz 1988, 90–106) of Weidenbaum's figures revealed that actual regulatory costs stayed at exactly the same percentage of GNP in 1979 as they had been in 1976.[17] In other words, modern liberalism was its own worst enemy; its failings produced such a large target that it was almost impossible for libertarianism to miss.

The genuine conservatives make a much more important and interesting case because they are no more against government regulation than are the New Deal liberals. Contrary to the expectations of most people, there was more real deregulation in the four years of the Carter administration than during all the years of the Reagan administration. President Reagan only once confronted Congress with a request for legislation actually terminating any regulatory authority, that of the Interstate Commerce Commission (ICC). Instead, the Reagan administration sought and took on significant increases in managerial power to reduce the regulatory burden, not by terminating or shrinking any of the authority now held in the executive branch, but by retaining the power and using it to control the agencies so as to reduce or delay the output of rules. The difference here is quite significant and is consonant with the history of the growth of executive power. President Reagan could reduce significantly the level and intensity of government intervention while leaving the *capacity for intervention* intact for himself and his successors. The following are examples of the conservative approach to *regulation management* as distinct from deregulation.

Impoverishing the Agencies

Budget cuts such as 15 percent of the Federal Trade Commission budget and 30 percent of the Consumer Product Safety Commission budget suggest a strategy of weakening agencies into submission. But note well that there was no equivalent shrinkage of their statutory authority.

Appointing Commissioners Hostile to Their Programs

Appointing hostile commissioners to preside over agencies while leaving statutory authority intact maximizes the president's opportunity to engage in discretionary deregulation as an aspect of regulation management. And note from the scandals in agencies such as the Environmental Protection Agency that discretionary deregulation has not been an across-the-board, evenhanded, downward pressure on regulation.

Strengthening Presidential Oversight

With the demise of the legislative veto, the regulatory review power lodged in the Office of Management and Budget (OMB) gives the president substantive item veto through the back door even as he fails to get constitutional item veto through the front door. The route to substantive item veto in the regulatory field is largely through the cost-benefit review process. It extends as a mandatory process to all departmental regulatory agencies and, as a matter of strong obligation, even to the independent regulatory commissions.

This amounts to a significant increase in the centralization of the executive branch. It has actually come at the expense of the budget process, a price, however, that a conservative president is obviously willing to pay. Increased centralization has meant the reversal of traditional budgeting from "bottom-up" budgeting, in which OMB assembles all the agency requests and constructs a budget from them, to a "top-down" approach, in which the White House sets the budgetary ceilings on goals and these are reconciled by the agencies before they go to Congress for the prescribed congressional reconciliation. This puts OMB in the position to set the terms of regulatory discourse. OMB officials are quick to protest that no more than 10 percent of the proposed rules submitted to OMB are actually turned down. But there seems to be a general consensus that this review process affects a far larger number of rules by influencing the form of their drafting prior to the review process, and far more than 10 percent are probably sent back to agencies for revision prior to ultimate approval. Thus, although it is true that the Reagan administration reduced the total amount of regulation, as measured by the number and cost of rules emanating from regulatory agencies, it achieved this result through executive centralization rather than through the actual shrinkage of executive authority (Seidman and Gilmore 1986).

Regulating the Poor

The Reagan administration significantly expanded regulatory authority over welfare cases and welfare clients. Cleansing the eligibility lists, stigmatizing welfare to reduce demands, and using the conditions of welfare to teach moral lessons in work and prudence are good examples of conservative approaches to regulation. This is not small government or decentralized government, but *different* government.

Using the Deficit as Regulation Management

There are at least two different theories of deficits. One is the Keynesian theory, which treats the deficit as a fiscal instrument. The other is the supply-side theory in which the deficit is, among other things, a regulatory instrument;

it works as an automatic control over domestic commitments. Never mind that the immense and growing deficits of the 1980s contributed significantly to the revival of the economy after the fairly deep recession of 1981-82. The fact is that these tremendous deficits will put very severe ceilings on what Congress can do in the domestic field long after conservatives are out of office.

Restoring Regulatory Power to the States

Although neither President Reagan nor President Bush tried as hard as their far right wing demanded, it is nevertheless an indication of the attitude of contemporary conservatism toward government power that the two administrations unqualifiedly endorsed the restoration of the many powers taken from the states by the Supreme Court since the 1950s. These include the drastic reduction of the power of the states over persons accused of crimes; the virtual elimination of the power of the states over religious observances in the public schools; the virtual elimination of the power of the states over pregnant women and their fetuses; the restriction of the authority of local and county welfare administrators over welfare clients in the determination of eligibility without entitlement; and restoration of the power of states, counties, and cities to apply their own interpretation of national voting rights laws. These demonstrate that there is almost nothing about conservative administrations at the national, state, or local levels that indicates any inclination to reverse the fifty-year tendency toward discretionary agencies and centralized executive power. On the contrary, the purpose of decentralizing powers is to restore moral hegemony to state and local governments.

THE TWO ROADS TO SERFDOM

The governmental and political institutions shaped during the fifty-plus years since 1933 have not been put under siege by the first serious alternative to liberalism this century. Whatever the "Reagan revolution" may amount to in terms of a change of policy direction, it does not amount to a revolution against liberal institutions because nothing about the Reagan revolution was aimed at the overly powerful presidency, the mass base of the presidency, the peripheral (albeit occasionally pesky) Congress, the discretionary agencies, or the cooperative courts. Here are two reasons why.

First, liberal national institutions suit conservatives. Conservatism should have tried to tone down the vulgar, mass democracy of the plebiscitary presidency and the immense size and power of the executive branch. But conservatives also need a bully pulpit; if it happens to have been built by liberalism, so be it.

This points to the second reason why conservative administrations have embraced liberal institutions: conservatives are *not* libertarians. Conservatives need a solid structure, just as modern liberals do, but a structure with a different orientation. George F. Will, one of the few writers who grasps the difference between conservatism and libertarianism, made the point best. Conservatives have no interest, Will points out, in dismantling the strong national government. Rather, according to Will (1983, 23), they believe in strong government, "including the essentials of the welfare state."[18] Conservatives, however, in Will's view, reject liberal "uncertainty about . . .

human nature" (Will 1983, 56-57).[19] In other words, Will argues, "state-craft" must attempt "soulcraft." Let there be regulatory policy—but for the purpose of restoring moral hegemony to traditional elites. Let there be welfare policy—but for the primary purpose of teaching the moral lessons required to bring the poor and self-indulgent classes into the realm of proper comportment within proper authority. Justice William Rehnquist, not William Simon or David Stockman, is the correct personification of the conservative era; the free market comes second to a strong state capable of exercising moral leadership, moral education, moral mobilization, and moral authority.

Because conservatives need a large discretionary state as much as the liberals, there is at present no constituency for the rule of law. Interest group liberals have been impatient to get on with goals defined by sentiment and by the claims of the best-organized groups. New politics groups are even more concerned with getting a favorable administrative environment. Conservative groups seek their own economic goals for the national government and moral hegemony for their new federalism. But why should that be otherwise? The surprising thing is that the legal experts offer no counterpoise. In their struggle for the power they have enjoyed as a profession throughout most of their history, lawyers have joined the flow rather than fight or shape it. Defense of the rule of law by old-fashioned lawyers and older liberals was wiped away as a mask for the status quo (see Ackerman 1984). Legal realists debunked the rule of law as a mere rationalization for private values. Later, legal realists proposed essentially to exchange the rule of law for the artificial science of economics and economic reasoning. Worst of all, the largest number of mainstream legal scholars hammer more nails in the coffin of the rule of law by providing reasoned arguments for why the effort to establish the rule of law, especially in legislative drafting, is unrealistic, unnecessary, counterproductive, and, in some instances, downright undesirable.

Let us take Stewart's position as an illustrative (and illustrious) case in point. First, to make his case for broad delegation, Stewart posits a false dichotomy: Congress cannot "write detailed commands" (1987, 324) or "precise rules of conduct" (328), *therefore,* broad and undefined delegation is the only alternative. Stewart then adds to this a second false dichotomy: federal courts are not "institutionally competent" to "invalidate wholesale" congressional statutes (326), *therefore,* broad delegation to administrative agencies is not only desirable but unreviewable (327-28). That is, the judiciary, for reasons not given, would have to condemn entire statutes on the grounds that the policies are too important to be left to administrators or that such delegations are not necessary and proper, and because this would "usurp judgments which we as a nation have concluded ever since 1937 ought to be resolved through political mechanisms," *therefore,* courts must not review the propriety of a delegation at all (326).

It is inexplicably ideological not to examine any middle points or other alternatives. Stewart leaves no room whatsoever for a bad first effort to be improved by successive efforts, unless he believes that Congress cannot learn from the experience of the administrative agencies in trying to implement the vague first effort at lawmaking (Stewart 1987, 324). Good legislation ought to be a matter of successive approximations—through later amendments, and, best of all, through codification.[20] Stewart, like so many others, apologizes for congressional incompetence by telling us how busy Congress is already (doing what?), and by telling us how much more complex our society is today (Stewart 1987, 329-30). Because no data or arguments are given to support such an apology, it remains in the realm of pure ideology. In fact, to the state legislators of the 1840s, society must have seemed immeasurably more complex than ours seems to us today. They were, after all, living in the midst of the Industrial Revolution; there was not yet any established economic theory of capitalism, no clear grasp of fractional reserve banking or insurance; and, according to the legal historians I read, even the tort law was only barely emerging (Horowitz 1977). Meanwhile, there was less continuity among legislators and less education. They had fewer staff members and a smaller budget with which to buy expertise and research. There were also problems such as greater party domination and more corruption. Yet, there was much more legal integrity in the average statute produced by the state legislatures of the 1840s than in the average statute coming out of Congress today.

Turn now to that part of the apology where Stewart (1987, 328) and others argue that it is next to impossible to formulate good rules of law for such a "vast and varied nation." The fact is that *proposals* for legislation are usually very clear and provide a very sound basis for articulating a general rule. When organized interest groups come before Congress, they tend to know exactly what they want and can generalize their wants into a rule that would be clearly understood and applicable to a known category of people or conduct. It is true that the rules they would have Congress adopt tend to be much too self-serving and often patently contrary to the public interest. It is the job of Congress to take these proposals and to work out compromises with the various contrary and conflicting proposals until a majority is ready to vote final passage. Thus, the burning question here is not why Congress is unable to formulate legislation with clear rules, but why Congress, in the process of compromise, takes proposals that embody clear rules and turns them into the vague and meaningless delegations of power that apologists call inevitable. All of this gives the ring of eternal verity to the observation (attributed to Bismarck) that "those who love laws and sausages would do well not to watch either one being made." Granted compromise is required in a system of majority rule and, granted also, compromise is not very pretty; but there is more than one kind of compromise. In fact, there are at least two kinds of compromise: compromise through weakness and compromise through vagueness.

The classic illustration of compromise through weakness is the compromise typical of business transactions in which the seller is asking far too much and the purchaser is willing to pay far too little. Each side weakens its initial position until the point where a transaction can be made, ordinarily to their mutual satisfaction. Bear in mind, however, that the item being exchanged (or, more generally, the point at issue) remains pretty much the same.

The second type of compromise, compromise through vagueness, is one in which two parties may start out with a clear understanding of the item to be exchanged or the point at issue between them, but they reach the compromise by altering the definition of the item or the point at issue, rendering the definition sufficiently vague so that each side can leave with its own kind of definition of what was at issue, what was exchanged, and how much was actually paid for it. In any of the numerous instances when original proposals are clear regarding the point at issue, there is absolutely no compelling reason why Congress chooses compromise through vagueness over compromise through weakness. But with apologists like law professors, why not?[21]

Then there is the famous court defense. For years, the federal courts have been regularly displacing the judgment of administrators—and that is not seen as an interference into the political functions. This underscores once again how curiously ideological it is for the apologists merely to assert that for courts to engage in constitutional review of delegation would mean a leap into invalidating most of the regulatory statutes on the books and that this would reverse court positions over the past two centuries (see Stewart 1987, 325–27). In the first place, even if courts courted the apocalypse by making constitutional issues out of delegation, this would not immediately and patently mean that all regulatory statutes would be invalidated wholesale, nor would it mean that the courts would be forced to wipe out entire statutes. It should not be necessary to remind lawyers that cases come up one by one and that most important statutes embodying broad delegations are composed of sections and titles, with each subject to separate legal attack. Second, the courts would not have to invalidate a provision of the statute in so many words, such as "this provision is unconstitutional because it violates the separation of powers." Although not a lawyer, I do not believe my picture of the process is all that inaccurate. First, as already proposed, the court would not have to pass on the entire statute, but only on a particular section or title that is at issue. Second, the court would not have to invalidate, in the positive sense implied by that term, but could actually take a *Shelley v. Kraemer* approach—in effect, "Congress can pass an empty section 1066 or a totally opaque title V, but the courts cannot enforce them."[22] Third, courts, in the words of President Andrew Jackson, are not the only interpreters of the Constitution. If the court finds itself without efficient guidelines to enforce a particular provision, Congress could respond by revising that section of the law, or administrators could find some means of enforcement other than court orders.

Finally, although I have utmost respect for Stewart's (1987, 335–41) proposal for resort to "constitutive law," I am unable to see this as any kind of a solution to the problem of excessive delegation or excessive centralization. First, as Stewart himself confesses, "constitutive rules necessarily have prescriptive elements . . . [and] prescriptive rules are created by constitutive processes" (336). Second, although it is true that constitutive rules "allow subsystem actors a measure of discretion that permits incorporation of subsystem interests and values in decisions about conduct" (336–37), it is very unfair to suggest that a clear rule of law cannot permit interaction with subsystem values. If a clear rule of law required absolute, lockstep obedience through which everyone "must act as federal officials direct," (Stewart 1983, 336–37) then no one in his right mind would be in favor of clear rules of law under any conditions. To be equal and opposite in my argument, I would be forced to say that we must oppose constitutive rules because we would be absolutely obliged to accept the decisions made by the constitutive process, even if those go contrary to basic values or national goals (whatever those might be). I see no need to take that position, however, because common sense tells me that for every constitutive law there is very likely to be a prescriptive rule or a set of rules, or some well-understood limit as to the permissible range of outcomes.

CONCLUSION

Prospect of rule of law has too often been cast as a debate between formalist and antiformalist models. As a formalist, I will close with some comments about the consequences of antiformalism. My problem with antiformalism, or informalism, is that it amounts to a rationalization for government grounded in nothing. Liberal antiformalists rationalize their position with the authority of process allegedly grounded in science—which means methodology, a process. That is a bed of sand. Conservative antiformalists rationalize their position with the authority of morality arising out of virtuous character, or "soulcraft." That is a swamp. In both cases, antiformalism is a rationalization for government by authority rather than government by rule.

For most of the twentieth century, the national government was dominated by a liberal consensus, and the antiformalist rationalization was a defense of liberal authority. With the rise of conservatism on a national scale during the past decade, we acquired a second system of authority, for which antiformalism is equally rationalization. Government being what it is, these opposite approaches come to the same end as serfdom or the moral equivalent thereof.

Serfdom is a condition of dependency on patronage. Patronage in the medieval sense, as in "to patronize," is a relationship between holders of resources (patrons) and seekers to resources (clients), where the holders have the discretion or power to share their resources—material goods or privileges—on a personal basis. This can be in response to meritorious personal claims, or on a personal basis in which the patron seeks to recruit the client's loyalty or a general reputation for virtue or goodwill. In our modern context, patronage remains the same: *The greater the discretion that accompanies the delegation of power, the greater the capacity of agencies to become patrons because discretion enables them to convert regulatory or welfare policies into resources for group or individual patronage.*

The antidote to government by patronage is not termination of the policies or the agencies, but *reduction of their discretion.* Otherwise, conservatism and liberalism speak to each other with nothing better than alternative roads to serfdom. I have said this a dozen different ways over the past years, but Charles Hamilton (1979) of Columbia University may have said it best when he expressed his concern that American blacks may have moved from the status of slavery to the status of subject to the status of recipient, without ever having enjoyed the status of citizenship.[23] It would be a great pity if that became the new equality for everybody.

Notes

1. *A.L.A. Schechter Poultry Corp. v. United States,* 295 U.S. 495, 529–50 (1935).
2. Health Insurance for the Aged Act, Pub. L. No. 89-97, 79 Stat. 290 (codified as amended in scattered sections of 26 U.S.C.). Democrats in the House voted 237 for and 48 against, with Republicans voting 70 for and 68 against (H.R. 6675, 89th Cong.,1st Sess., 111 Cong. Rec. 18,393 [1965]. In the Senate, Democrats voted 57 for and 7 against, while Republicans voted 13 for and 17 against (H.R. 6675, 89th Cong., 1st Sess., 111 Cong. Rec. 18,514 [1965].
3. In "Returning to First Principles," Ernest Gellhorn (1987, 349) suggested that I have taken the extreme position of limiting all executive discretion "to a specific remedy for a specified act of damage." That was an incorrect interpretation of the

passage. I use the passage here to indicate a change in what individuals are demanding. If I were to use this passage for anything more than that, I would take it as virtually the limiting extreme of what an ideal piece of legislation would contain. But I would certainly not be so extreme or unrealistic as to reject all legislation that went beyond a specific remedy for a specified act of damage. Stewart (1987, 331) attempts to discredit the nondelegation doctrine by characterizing it as "requiring that all regulatory statutes contain detailed rules of conduct." They do not have to be all that detailed to be good rules of conduct. Detailed rules also would be a limiting case.

4. An example from the Occupational Safety and Health Act of 1970 (OSHA) will suffice: "The Secretary . . . shall set the standard which most adequately ensures, to the extent feasible, on the basis of the best available evidence, that no employee wilt suffer material impairment of health or financial capacity even if such employee has regular exposure to the hazard dealt with by such standard for the period of his working life." Occupational Safety and Health Act of 1970, 29 U.S.C. 655(b)(5) (1982).

5. On filing class action suits", see Fed. R. Civ. P. 23.

6. Consider, e.g., the Clean Air Act Amendments of 1970 (Publ. L. No. 91-604, 84 Stat. 1676, codified at 42 U.S.C. 7401-7626 (1982) to effectuate the far-reaching goal of improving the quality of the nation's air "so as to promote the public health and welfare and the productive capacity of its population."

7. Occupational Safety and Health Act of 1970, Pub. L. No. 91-596, 84 Stat. 1590 (codified at 29 U.S.C. 651-678 [1982]).

8. *President's Message to Congress Transmitting Reorganization Plans to Establish Two Agencies,* 6 Weekly Comp. Pres. Doc. 908 (9 July 1970).

9. 5 U.S.C. 551-59 (1982). The federal Administrative Procedure Act (APA) was intended to set forth requirements for three types of procedures available to agencies: formal adjudication, formal rule making, and informal rule making.

10. *Youngstown Sheet & Tube Co. v. Sawyer,* 343 U.S. 579 (1952) esp. 585-86, which notes that the Selective Service Act and the Defense Production Act authorized the president to take both personal and real property under certain circumstances.

11. 418 U.S. 683 (1984).

12. *INS v. Chadha,* 462 U.S. 919 (1983).

13. 106 S. Ct. 3183 (1986).

14. The probability of this increased significantly with the presence of Antonin Scalia and Clarence Thomas on the Supreme Court.

15. The study found the aggregate cost of complying with federal regulation came to $62.6 billion in 1976 or over $300 for each man, woman, and child in the United States.

16. This consists of $4.8 billion of direct expenses by federal regulatory agencies and $97.9 billion of cost of private sector compliance.

17. Schwarz's recalculation of Weidenbaum's own figures produces a total cost of federal regulation for 1979 at $27 billion *less* than Weidenbaum's public figures claim.

18. In this same discussion (Will 1985, 126-32), he states that if conservatism is to engage itself with present ways of living, it must address government's graver purposes with an affirmative doctrine of the welfare state.

19. In the nineteenth century, a growing uncertainty about the very idea of a known or even knowable human nature was the reason for people to desire a statecraft that made an attempt at soulcraft. Recently, however, the reason for rejecting the state's engagement in soulcraft is nervousness about the very idea of human nature.

20. In the first edition of *The End of Liberalism,* I left myself open to criticism that I was relying on the judiciary to solve all the problems of democracy by proposing that we revive the *Schechter* rule in order to force Congress to do its job by making decent rules of law. "Juridical democracy" was interpreted to mean "judicial

democracy," despite my insistence that the two were far from identical (Lowi 1969, chap. 10). Efforts to correct that impression in the second edition and in other writings did not fully succeed. The purpose of the later efforts was to move the issue to a middle ground, recognizing the inevitability of broad "policy-with-out-law" in the first instance, followed by "successive approximations" of decent rules of law (Lowi 1979, 307). But there will be no such middle ground as long as legal experts tell legislators that their accomplishments are historically inevitable and the best possible under the circumstances.

21. Because there are so few good examples of compromise through weakness (which is the same as saying there are so few good examples of law with legal integrity), I will offer the very imperfect example of the Civil Rights Act of 1964, Pub. L. No. 88-352, 78 Stat. 241 (codified as amended at 28 U.S.C. 1447; 42 U.S.C. 1971, 1975a-1975d, 2000a-2000h-6, [1982]). Because the major provisions were (1) fairly clear about the rule of law embodied therein; and (2) very controversial, compromises of a most delicate sort were called for. Proponents of the legislation enlisted the efforts of the "Great Compromiser," Hubert Humphrey. For most of the provisions, the Humphrey forces did not seek majority support by redefining the point at issue into a vague goal statute such as, "let there be fair treatment by 1974." Instead, they usually kept the point at issue close to the original proposals that the civil rights forces devised and sought compromise by weakening the sanctions or lengthening the time span for implementation. For example, they even agreed to provide jury trials for contempt of court in some of the enforcement procedures See 42 U.S.C. 2000h (1982), which allows for jury trial in criminal contempt proceedings.

22. 334 U.S. 1 (1948), esp. 13–21.

23. This is a slight variation on a theme set forth in Hamilton (1979).

References

Abourezk, James. 1977. "The Congressional Veto: A Contemporary Response to Executive Encroachment on Legislative Prerogative." *Indiana Law Journal* 52(2):323–95.

Ackerman, Bruce. 1984. *Reconstructing American Law.* Cambridge, Mass.: Harvard University Press.

Davis, Kenneth C. 1969. *Discretionary Justice: A Preliminary Inquiry.* Baton Rouge: Louisiana State University Press.

Friedenthal, Jack H., Mary Kay Kane, and Arthur R. Miller. 1985. *Civil Procedure.* St. Paul, Minn.: West Publishers.

Gellhorn, Ernest. 1987. "Returning to First Principles." *American University Law Review.* 36(2):345–54.

Hamilton, Charles V. 1979. "The Patron-Recipient Relationship and Minority Politics in New York City." *Political Science Quarterly* 94(2):211–28.

Horowitz, Morton. 1977. *The Transformation of American Law.* Cambridge, Mass.: Harvard University Press.

Lowi, Theodore J. 1969. *The End of Liberalism: Ideology, Policy and the Crisis of Public Authority.* New York: W. W. Norton.

———. 1979. *The End of Liberalism: The Second Republic of the United States.* 2d ed. New York: W. W. Norton.

———. 1985. *The Personal President; Power Invested, Promise Unfulfilled.* Ithaca, N.Y.: Cornell University Press.

———. 1991. "Toward a Legislature of the First Kind." In *Knowledge, Power and the Congress.* Edited by W. H. Robinson and C. H. Wellhorn. Washington, D.C.: Congressional Quarterly.

———. 1992. "The State in Political Science: How We Become What We Study." *American Political Sciences Review* 86(1):1–7.

————. 1993. "Before Conservatism and Beyond: American Ideology and Politics in the 1990s." Norman, Okla.: University of Oklahoma Press (forthcoming).

Mashaw, Jerry L. 1985. "Prodelegation: Why Administrators Should Make Political Decisions." *Journal of Law, Economics and Organization* 1(1):81-100.

Nelson, Richard R. 1977. *The Moon and the Ghetto.* New York: W. W. Norton.

Neustadt, Richard E. 1954. "Presidency and Legislation: The Growth of Central Clearance." *American Political Science Review* 48(3):641–71.

————. 1955. "Presidency and Legislation: Planning the President's Program." *American Political Science Review* 29(4):980–1021.

Newman, Stephen L. 1984. *Liberalism at Wit's End: The Libertarian Revolt against the Modern State.* Ithaca, N.Y.: Cornell University Press.

Pierce, Richard J., and Sidney A. Shapiro. 1981. "Political and Judicial Review of Agency Action." *Texas Law Review* 59(7): 1175–1222.

Sargentich, Thomas O. 1987. "The Delegation Debate and Competing Ideals of the Administrative Process." *American University Law Review* 36(2): 419–42.

Schoenbrod, David. 1983. "Goals, Statutes or Rules Statutes: The Case of the Clean Air Act." *University of California Los Angeles Law Review* 30(4):740–828.

————. 1987. "Separation of Powers and the Powers That Be: The Constitutional Purposes of the Delegation Doctrine." *American University Law Review* 36(2):355–90.

Schwarz, John E. 1988. *America's Hidden Success.* Rev. ed. New York: W. W. Norton.

Seidman, Harold, and Robert Gilmour. 1986. *Politics, Position, and Power.* 4th ed. New York: Oxford University Press.

Stewart, Richard. 1987. "Beyond the Delegation Doctrine." *American University Law Review* 36(2):323–44.

Weidenbaum, Murray. 1978. "The Costs of Government Regulation of Business." Study prepared for the use of the Subcommittee on Economic Growth and Stabilization of Joint Economic Congressional Commission of the United States. Washington, D.C.: Government Printing Office.

Will, George F. 1983. *Statecraft as Soulcraft.* New York: Simon & Schuster.

Wilson, Woodrow. 1908. *Constitutional Government in the United States.* New York: Columbia University Press.

Accountability Battles in State Administration

WILLIAM T. GORMLEY JR.

State bureaucracies have paid a price for their growing importance, and that price is a loss of discretion. In recent years, state bureaucracies have become more permeable, more vulnerable, and more manipulable. They are subject to a growing number of controls, as governors, state legislators, state judges, presidents, members of Congress, federal bureaucrats, interest groups, and citizens all attempt to shape administrative rule making, rate making and adjudication at the state level. Of equal significance, they are subject to tougher, more restrictive, and more coercive controls.

In other words, state bureaucracies have become more accountable for their actions. In a sense, this is both understandable and desirable. Even state bureaucrats concede the virtues of accountability, at least in theory. Yet accountability is a multidimensional concept. Increasingly, the question is not whether state bureaucracies shall be accountable but to whom. A related question is how accountability can best be structured to avoid damage to other important values, such as creativity and flexibility.

A variety of controls that limit the discretion of state bureaucracies recently has proliferated, primarily in the areas of legislative oversight, executive management, due process, and regulatory federalism. For example, "coercive controls" rely on coercion for bureaucratic performance, while "catalytic controls" may yield comparable progress with fewer adverse side-effects. The emergence of accountability battles pit competing claimants against one another, in bitter struggles over authority, with state bureaucracies as the ultimate prize. Courts increasingly are being asked to resolve these disputes, but the courts are not disinterested claimants. Often they wish to shape the behavior of state bureaucracies. Thus, judges have emerged as key arbiters and managers, deciding accountability battles in some instance, triggering them in others.

THE PROLIFERATION OF CONTROLS

During the 1970s and the 1980s, as state bureaucracies grew larger and more important, politicians, judges, and citizens strengthened their leverage over state bureaucracies by institutionalizing a wide variety of control techniques. Some of these techniques, such as sunset laws and ombudsmen, were new. Others, such as executive orders and conditions of aid, were old but not much utilized. Control techniques also differed in their directness, formality, durability, and coerciveness. However, they all shared a common purpose—to make state bureaucracies more accountable to other public officials or to the people.

Legislative Oversight

During the 1970s, state legislatures discovered oversight as a form of bureaucratic control. Legislative committees took an active interest in bureaucratic implementation or nonimplementation of state statutes and conducted hearings aimed at identifying and resolving problems. This became easier as the legislator's job became a full-time profession in most states and as legislative staffs became larger and more professional. More than their congressional counterparts, state legislators decided not to leave oversight to chance. Perhaps oversight needed an extra push at the state level. In any event, state legislatures established regular mechanisms for legislative review.

Following the lead of Colorado, approximately two-thirds of the state legislatures adopted sunset laws, which provide for the automatic expiration of agencies unless the state legislature acts affirmatively to renew them. Although the threat of extinction is far-fetched in the case of large agencies, the threat of review must be taken seriously by all agencies. The sunset review process is especially important for obscure agencies that might otherwise escape scrutiny by legislative committees.

In addition to sunset laws, many state legislatures substantially upgraded the quality of their legislative audit bureaus. Gradually, these organizations came to place greater emphasis on program evaluation and policy analysis, less emphasis on auditing and accounting. To ensure careful, well-crafted evaluations, state legislatures augmented the staffs assigned to these organizations.

Finally, the overwhelming majority of state legislatures provided for legislative review of administrative rules and regulations. In sixteen states, legislative vetoes enable the legislature to invalidate an administrative rule or regulation. Through the legislative veto process, state legislatures have exercised closer scrutiny of administrative rule making. The U.S. Supreme Court declared the legislative veto unconstitutional at the federal level,[1] and state courts have invalidated legislative vetoes in eight states.[2] Nevertheless, the legislative veto continues to be an important mechanism for legislative control in one-third of the states.

In thinking about legislative controls, a useful distinction can be made between inward-looking and outward-looking legislative changes. As political scientist Alan Rosenthal has observed, state legislatures have become more fragmented, more decentralized, and less cohesive in recent years. In some sense, this might be characterized as legislative decline. However, a fragmented legislature is not necessarily weaker in its dealings with other units of government, such as state bureaucracies. A highly fragmented legislature may provide more occasions for legislative oversight and more incentives for individual legislators to engage in oversight. Thus, as legislatures become weaker internally, they may become stronger externally. This is especially true of those forms of legislative control that do not require a legislative majority.

Executive Management

For years, governors have complained about the fragmented character of the executive branch. Many executive branch officials are elected or appointed to office for fixed terms that do not coincide with the governor's term. The number of state agencies, boards, and commissions can be overwhelming and disconcerting. Also, agencies have their own traditions and habits and may be reluctant to follow the priorities of a new governor. All of these factors have inhibited executive integration, coordination, and leadership.

During the 1970s and the 1980s, many governors took steps to deal with these problems. Most governors spearheaded major reorganizations of the executive branch, striving for greater rationality and for a reduction in the number of boards and commissions. Minor reorganizations also were commonplace. In Minnesota, for example, five governors issued a total of 155 reorganization orders between 1970 and 1988.[3]

Governors also institutionalized cabinet meetings, subcabinet meetings, or both to secure greater coordination and integration. During the 1970s, approximately fourteen governors established a cabinet for the first time and approximately twenty-five governors established subcabinets to advise and coordinate in broad policy domains.[4] The hope was that these meetings would ensure that key executive branch officials marched to the same drumbeat.

In addition, governors relied on new budget techniques, such as zero-based budgeting, to increase their control over agency budget submissions and, ultimately, agency budgets themselves. Under zero-based budgeting, the previous year's budget base is not taken for granted, although it may be incorporated into alternative budget submissions. During the 1970s, approximately twenty-five states adopted a modified form of zero-based budgeting.[5]

At the same time, governors fought successfully for shorter ballots to bring more top state officials under gubernatorial control. Between 1962 and 1978, the number of elected state executives declined by 10 percent.[6] As a result of these reforms, governors today are more likely to deal with state agencies headed more often by gubernatorial appointees in whom they can have confidence.

Finally, executive orders have become more popular in recent years. In Wisconsin, Gov. Lee Sherman Dreyfus issued more executive orders in 1979 than his predecessors had issued during the 1960s and 1970s.[7] Dreyfus's successor, Anthony S. Earl, issued even more executive orders than Dreyfus.[8] Similarly, in Massachusetts, the number of executive orders issued between 1965 and 1980 rose 206 percent over the preceding fifteen years.[9] Many of these executive orders were aimed at controlling state bureaucracies.

Interest Representation

Unable or unwilling to control state agencies directly in every instance, politicians relied on surrogates to ensure better representation for favored points of view, such as consumers, environmentalists, and the elderly. Political scientists Matthew McCubbins and Thomas Schwartz referred to this phenomenon as "fire-alarm oversight" because politicians in effect depend on citizen or other public officials to spot fires in the bureaucracy and help stamp them out.[10] During the 1970s and the 1980s, states took a number of steps to improve representation for broad, diffuse interests or other underrepresented interests, especially before state regulatory agencies—a "representation revolution" occurred.[11]

For example, many established "proxy advocacy" offices to represent consumer interests in state public utility commission proceedings, such as rate cases. In some instances, attorneys general served this function; in other instances, separate consumer advocacy offices were established. Wisconsin, meanwhile, established a Citizens Utilities Board, funded by citizens through voluntary contributions but authorized by the state legislature to include membership solicitations in utility bills.[12] State legislatures in Illinois, Oregon, and New York subsequently established similar organizations, though without provisions for inserts.[13]

Disappointed in the performance of occupational licensing boards, state legislatures mandated lay representation on the boards in the hope that fewer anti-competitive practices would result. Wisconsin law specifies that at least one public member shall serve on each of the state's occupational licensing boards. California goes even further. Since 1976, California has required that all occupational licensing boards have a majority of public members, except for ten "healing arts" boards and the Board of Accountancy.[14]

Many state legislatures require public hearings in various environmental policy decisions. Pursuant to the California Coastal Act of 1972, a coastal zoning commission must call for a public hearing whenever a developer submits a construction permit request for a project that might have an "adverse environmental impact" on coastal resources.

Some interest representation reforms that occurred on the state level were mandated by or encouraged by the federal government. For example, Congress required states to cooperate with the Environmental Protection Agency (EPA) in providing for public participation under the Federal Water Pollution Control Act; the Resource Conservation and Recovery Act; the Comprehensive Environmental Response, Compensation, and Liability Act; and other statutes. Through the Older Americans Act, Congress required states to establish long-term care ombudsman programs to investigate complaints by nursing home residents and to monitor the development and implementation of pertinent laws and regulations.

Regulatory Federalism

The dynamics of regulatory federalism differ significantly from those of interest representation reforms. In both cases, politicians exercise indirect control over state bureaucracies, relying on surrogates to articulate their concerns. However, regulatory federalism is much more intrusive. If a consumer advocacy group recommends a new rule or regulation, a state agency may consider and reject it. If a federal agency instructs a state agency to adopt a rule or face a sharp cutback in federal funds, the state agency does not have much of a choice.

Regulatory federalism is a process whereby the federal government imposes conditions on state governments that accept federal funding.[15] Regulatory federalism arose as an adjunct to the new social regulations of the 1970s and as an antidote to the laissez faire of general revenue sharing. Regulatory federalism includes a variety of techniques, such as direct orders (unequivocal mandates), crossover sanctions (threats in one program area if actions are not taken in another program), crosscutting requirements (obligations applicable to a wide range of programs), and partial preemptions (the establishment of minimal federal standards if states wish to run their own programs).[16] Some of these techniques apply to state legislatures; some apply to state agencies; many apply to both.

The number of federal statutes imposing significant new regulatory requirements increased dramatically during the 1970s. Given the Reagan administration's public support for federalism and deregulation, many observers expected regulatory federalism to decline during the 1980s. However, as political scientist Timothy Conlan has shown, the number of federal statutes with significant intergovernmental controls directed at the states increased even further.[17] Moreover, a disproportionate increase came about in the most coercive regulatory control techniques—namely, direct orders and crossover sanctions. In Conlan's words, "the 1980s rivaled the previous decade as a period of unparalleled intergovernmental regulatory activity."[18]

In some cases, Congress imposed new regulatory requirements on the states despite Reagan's philosophical reservations. This was especially true in environmental policy. In other cases, however, the Reagan administration fully supported tougher controls on the states. For example, in transportation policy, it endorsed a variety of crossover sanctions,[19] and in welfare policy, it advocated limits on eligibility to receive public subsidies.[20]

Several regulatory federalism initiatives of recent years have been challenged in court. However, the courts have routinely upheld the federal government's right to impose constraints on state governments accepting federal funds.[21] The courts also have upheld partial preemptions,[22] crossover sanctions,[23] and direct orders.[24]

Due Process

In addition to serving as arbiters in intergovernmental disputes, federal judges have been active participants in efforts to control state bureaucracies. They have intervened vigorously in pursuit of such constitutional rights as "due process of law" and freedom from "cruel and unusual punishment." Dissatisfied with progress at the state level, they have gone so far as to seize, for example, state prisons and homes for the mentally ill or the mentally retarded, substituting their managerial judgment for that of state public administrators.

Wyatt v. Stickney[25] was the first in a long line of institutional reform cases in which federal judges decided to play a strong managerial role. Alabama's homes for the mentally ill and the mentally retarded were overcrowded, understaffed, dangerous, and unsanitary. In response to a class action suit, Judge Frank Johnson held that mental patients have a right to adequate and effective treatment in the least restrictive environment practicable. To secure that right, he issued extremely specific treatment standards and ordered rapid deinstitutionalization.

Shortly after the *Wyatt* decision, Judge Johnson found himself embroiled in an equally bitter controversy over Alabama's prisons. By most accounts, conditions in the state's prisons were deplorable. Rapes and stabbings were widespread; food was unwholesome; and physical facilities were dilapidated. In response to inmate complaints, Judge Johnson issued a decree calling for adequate medical care, regular fire inspections, and regular physical examinations.[26] When conditions barely improved, he issued detailed standards, including cell-space requirements, hiring requirements, and a mandatory classification system.[27]

The Alabama cases set the stage for a large number of similar cases throughout the country. In state after state, federal judges mandated massive changes in physical facilities, staffing ratios, health services, and amenities. They specified the size of prison cells, the credentials of new employees, and plumbing and hygiene standards. They shut down facilities and prohibited new admissions, even where alternative facilities were not available.

The U.S. Supreme Court finally applied the brakes on mental health orders in *Youngberg v. Romeo.*[28] In that decision, the Court ruled that mentally retarded clients are constitutionally entitled to minimally adequate treatment and habilitation but that professionals, including state administrators, should be free to decide what constitutes minimally adequate training for staff. Thus, the decision was viewed as a partial victory for state administrators.

The Supreme Court has yet to focus on prison reform cases, which continue to drag on in many states. In Texas, for example, Judge William Justice has been locked in a bitter battle with the Texas Department of Corrections since he called for sweeping reforms in *Ruiz v. Estelle.*[29] By 1992, thirty-seven states were under some kind of court order for their prisons. In nine states, the entire state prison system was under court order.[30]

As Republican presidents have appointed more conservative judges to the federal bench, court takeovers of prisons and other public institutions would be expected to decrease. However, as political scientist Robert Bradley has noted, judges appointed by Republican presidents are no more likely than judges appointed by Democratic presidents to issue structural reform decrees in state prison cases.[31] Additional reasons exist to doubt that this phenomenon will diminish. As John DiIulio, Jr., has observed, "Demographic and sentencing trends make it likely that institutional overcrowding will worsen over the next decade. If that happens, and if prison and jail officials prove unable to maintain any semblance of safe and humane conditions behind bars, then sweeping judicial intervention into prisons and jails may be more of a growing prospect than a fading memory."[32]

TYPES OF CONTROLS

Useful in thinking about recent efforts to control state bureaucracies is to imagine a spectrum ranging from catalytic controls, at one end, to coercive controls, at the other end, with hortatory controls falling in between. Catalytic controls stimulate change but preserve a great deal of bureaucratic discretion. Coercive controls require change and severely limit bureaucratic discretion. Hortatory controls involve more pressure than catalytic controls but more restraint than coercive controls.[33]

Moreover, different types of controls have different types of effects. In their public policy implications, catalytic controls have been surprisingly effective and coercive controls have been notably counterproductive.

Catalytic Controls

Catalytic controls require state bureaucracies to respond to a petition or plea but do not predetermine the nature of their response. As a result, such controls are action-forcing but not solution-forcing. They alter bureaucratic behavior, but they permit the bureaucracy a good deal of discretion and flexibility. Examples of catalytic controls include public hearings, ombudsmen, proxy advocacy, and lay representation.

Public hearings have enabled environmentalists to win important victories in their dealings with state bureaucracies. For example, citizens have used public hearings on state water quality planning in North Carolina to secure important modifications of state plans concerning waste water disposal, construction, and mining.[34] Similarly, citizens used public hearings before the California Coastal Commission to block permits for development projects that would have an "adverse environmental impact" on coastal resources.[35]

Ombudsmen have been active in several areas but especially on nursing home issues. According to one report,[36] nursing home ombudsmen have been effective in resolving complaints on a wide variety of subjects, including Medicaid problems, guardianship, the power of attorney, inadequate hygiene, family problems, and the theft of personal possessions. Another study[37] found that nursing home ombudsmen provide useful information to legislators and planners.

Proxy advocates have effectively represented consumers in rate cases and other proceedings held by state public utility commissions. As a result of the interventions, utility companies have received rate hikes substantially lower than those originally requested. Proxy advocates also have been instrumental in securing policies on utility disconnections and payment penalties that help consumers who are struggling to pay their bills.[38] Even in complex telecommunications cases, proxy advocates have successfully promoted competition on behalf of consumers.[39]

Catalytic controls may be too weak in some instances. In several Southern states, for example, public hearing requirements in utility regulatory proceedings have been pointless because consumer groups and environmental groups have not materialized to take advantage of such hearings.[40] Lay representation on occupational licensing boards also has been a disappointment. Lacking expertise, lay representatives typically have deferred to professionals on these boards.[41]

Overall, though, catalytic controls have been remarkably successful in making state bureaucracies more responsive to a vast array of formerly underrepresented interests. In effect, they have institutionalized what political scientist James Q. Wilson refers to as "entrepreneurial politics"[42] or the pursuit of policies that offer widely distributed benefits through widely distributed costs. Moreover, catalytic controls have achieved results without engendering bureaucratic hostility and resentment. Studies show that state administrators welcome citizen participation[43] and interest group interventions.[44] At their best, catalytic controls provide state bureaucrats with ammunition to justify policies that promote the public interest.

Hortatory Controls

Hortatory controls involve political pressure or "jawboning," usually by someone in a position of authority. They strike a balance between bureaucratic discretion and bureaucratic accountability. Some, such as sunset laws and administrative reorganizations, are relatively mild; others, such as partial preemptions and crossover sanctions, are relatively strong.

The strength of hortatory controls depends primarily on two factors: their specificity (are the goals of the controllers clear?) and the credibility of the threat (how likely is it that penalties will be invoked?). Thus, sunset laws are relatively weak because the threat of termination is remote, except in the case of extremely small agencies.

To argue that some hortatory controls are mild is not to say that they are ineffective. A study of legislative audit bureau reports reveals that they do lead to changes in legislation, administrative practice, or both. Research by legislative audit bureaus is more likely to be utilized by state legislators than other types of research.[45] The literature on administrative reorganizations reveals that they do not reduce government spending but that they can promote coordination and integration if they are well-crafted and well-executed.[46] The key seems to be to put agencies with interrelated missions under the same roof.

Research on sunset laws roughly parallels the findings on administrative reorganizations. As a cost-containment device, sunset legislation has been a failure. However, as a mechanism for focusing legislative attention on agencies and issues low in visibility, sunset legislation has been a success. In a number of states, such as Connecticut and Florida, sunset laws have resulted in significant changes in statutes and agency rules.[47]

Stronger hortatory controls have been even more effective, though they also have been dysfunctional in some respects. In response to quality control systems in welfare, "errors of liberality" have declined, but "errors of stringency" have increased.[48] In effect, states have sacrificed accuracy for cost-containment. States also have enforced federal regulations that they know to be unreasonable, in response to partial preemptions in environmental policy. For example, the Minnesota Pollution Control Agency enforced a rigid EPA definition of hazardous waste, even though it meant that a lime sludge pile could not be removed from a highway site, could not be used for waste-water treatment, and could not be used to clean an electric utility company's smoke-stack emission.[49]

Strong hortatory controls place a premium on uniform standards and universal compliance with such standards. In some instances, such as civil rights, no practical alternative exists to strong controls, because local prejudices are too deeply ingrained to permit cooperation. In others, however, strong hortatory controls may impose premature closure, discouraging innovation and experimentation and proving difficult for the states to serve as "laboratories" for the nation and for other states.

Despite the new federalism, strong hortatory controls have been particularly prominent in intergovernmental relations. Although federal aid to state and local governments has declined, no commensurate decrease has taken place in federal regulations. Political scientist Richard P. Nathan cites state reforms in health, education, and welfare as evidence of a growing state role in a conservative era.[50] Yet state administrators cite precisely these issue areas, along with environmental policy, as ones where federal influence is relatively strong.[51] States can be both innovating and responding. Or perhaps the state legislatures are innovating, while the state agencies are responding. In any event, regulatory federalism has not abated in recent years, even if the goals and purposes of federal overseers have changed during the Reagan and Bush administrations.

Coercive Controls

Coercive controls rob state bureaucracies of their discretion. They compel a specific response, often within a specific time frame. Neither the solution nor the deadline may be reasonable, but the state bureaucracy does not have the luxury of responding reasonably. Immediate compliance becomes more important than rationality, and short-term "outputs" become more important than long-term "outcomes."

Coercive controls often trigger bureaucratic circumvention or resistance. In the former case, bureaucrats comply with the letter, but not the spirit, of a tough requirement. In the latter case, the bureaucracy goes to court. In both cases, an adversarial relationship develops that precludes cooperation, bargaining, and persuasion.

As a response to legislative vetoes, some state agencies have issued emergency rules, which are not subject to the usual legislative review process. In Wisconsin, for example, state agencies issued a total of fifty-four emergency rules during the 1985-1986 legislative session—a sharp increase over earlier years.[52] Reliance on emergency rules is especially unfortunate, because they do not involve public hearings. Thus, to escape highly threatening legislative vetoes, agencies have escaped less-threatening public hearings as well.

Court orders have triggered some of the more dysfunctional bureaucratic responses. When Judge Frank Johnson required state prisons to reduce their overcrowding, Alabama prison officials simply released large numbers of prisoners, forcing county jails to take up the slack. Unfortunately, county jails were poorly equipped for the task; they lacked adequate space and personnel. Consequently, many prisoners, shipped to county jails, were forced to endure conditions even worse than those they experienced in the state prisons.[53] Yet the state agency was technically in compliance with the court decree.

A key problem with coercive controls is that they place far too much emphasis on formal authority. Many state agencies depend considerably on a series of informal understandings. This is especially true of prisons, where quick-thinking guards and cooperative inmates help to maintain a delicate balance between order and chaos. When that balance is disrupted, tragedy may result. This is precisely what happened in Texas, where Judge Justice's court orders dissolved the informal networks that enabled the prisons to function on a daily basis. As guards became more timid, direct challenges to authority rose sharply. Disciplinary reports reveal abrupt and dramatic increases in incidents where a guard was threatened or assaulted.[54] Inmates also turned on themselves, with their fists or with makeshift weapons. By generating rising expectations and undermining bureaucratic morale, Judge Justice created a temporary power vacuum that prison gangs quickly filled. The tragic result was a series of riots and violent episodes that left fifty-two inmates dead within two years.[55]

ACCOUNTABILITY BATTLES

Accountability battles have become more prominent in state politics for three principal reasons: (1) the proliferation of controls; (2) the intensification of controls; and (3) the judicialization of controls. As controls multiply, some are likely to be contradictory. Competing claimants emerge. As controls intensify, contradictory controls generate more friction. Competing claimants press their claims. As controls spill over into the courts, disputes are resolved according to legal criteria. Moreover, the courts themselves become active participants in these battles. Frustrated with both state politicians and state bureaucrats, judges have decided that they can do a better job and that they are entitled to do so under the U.S. Constitution, the state constitution, or both.

State Legislatures versus Governors

Accountability battles between state legislatures and governors have erupted in recent years. Although such disputes are not new, they seem to focus increasingly on directives to administrative agencies and on questions of legal authority instead of political preference. As a result, state judges have found themselves playing a key role in arbitrating disputes between governors and state legislatures.

Legislative vetoes have aroused considerable conflict between state legislatures and governors, even when the same party controls both branches of government. In New Jersey, for example, the Democratic state legislature and

Democratic governor Brendan T. Byrne clashed in court over a generic legislative veto and a more specific veto, whereby certain building authority proposals must be approved by both houses or the presiding offices of the legislature, depending on the nature of the proposal.[56] The New Jersey state supreme court upheld the specific legislative veto[57] but ruled the generic veto unconstitutional, citing violations of separation of powers and the presentment clauses of the state constitution.[58]

Executive orders also have triggered conflict between state legislatures and governors. In Pennsylvania, for example, Republican governor Dick Thornburgh issued an executive order "privatizing" the state's liquor control store system. The Democratic state legislature, which had just rejected such a plan, promptly took the governor to court. A Commonwealth Court judge ruled in favor of the legislature, noting that the governor's privatization plan was "without authority and contravenes the Sunset Act." He also accused both sides of playing an unseemly game of political football at the public's expense.[59]

Money, the "mother's milk of politics," has fueled many disputes between state legislatures and governors. In Wisconsin, Republican governor Tommy Thompson refused to accept a decision by the Democratic state legislature to maintain welfare benefits at existing levels. Stretching the outer limits of his line-item veto authority, Thompson vetoed two digits and a decimal point from the state legislature's benefit formula, thereby effecting a 6 percent reduction in welfare benefits. The legislature promptly took the governor to court, but the Wisconsin supreme court upheld a generous interpretation of the governor's line-item power.[60]

The most striking aspect of accountability battles between state legislatures and governors is that they often have a partisan edge, pitting a Republican governor against a Democratic state legislature or vice versa. As divided government has become more common at the state level, state agencies find determining whether they are in Democratic or Republican hands increasingly difficult. Thus, the voters' ambivalence has triggered important legal battles with high stakes.

Federal Politicians versus State Politicians

State bureaucracies increasingly are being asked to implement federal statutes, such as environmental protection statutes. Often these federal statutes contradict state statutes or the policy preferences of the state's governor. Under such circumstances, a showdown is likely, with the federal government citing the "commerce clause" or the "take care clause" of the U.S. Constitution, while the state government cites the Tenth Amendment.

The U.S. Supreme Court and other federal courts have routinely sided with the federal government in accountability battles where the allocation of federal funds is at issue. If states accept federal funding, they also must accept the conditions the federal government attaches to those funds. However, many intergovernmental disputes do not involve federal funding but a federal effort to preempt state activity in a particular policy domain. Here, also, the U.S. Supreme Court has sided with the federal government, though with occasional exceptions.

In *National League of Cities v. Usery,*[61] the Supreme Court surprised many observers by rejecting the federal government's attempt to extend minimum wage and maximum hour provisions to municipal employees. In doing so, the Court said that the Tenth Amendment prohibited any federal action that impaired "the State's freedom to structure integral operations in areas of traditional governmental functions." Thus a key provision of the 1974 Fair Labor Standards Act Amendments was ruled unconstitutional. The decision was an important victory for both state and local governments.

In subsequent cases, the Supreme Court wrestled gamely with the "traditional governmental functions" criterion and offered further clarification. For example, in *Hodel v. Virginia Surface Mining and Reclamation Association,*[62] the Court articulated a three-fold test for determining when Tenth Amendment claims shall prevail. Specifically, the Court extended protection to the states if federal regulations: (1) regulate the states as states; (2) address matters that are indisputable attributes of state sovereignty; and (3) impair the states' ability to structure integral operations in areas of traditional function. In Hodel—a strip mining case involving a partial preemption statute—the Court concluded that Congress had acted properly and with restraint. Similarly, in *FERC v. Mississippi,*[63] the Court applauded Congress for imposing modest constraints on state public utility commissions, when it could have preempted the field entirely.

Finally, after years of painful efforts to distinguish between "traditional government functions" and other functions, the Supreme Court abandoned that doctrine outright in *Garcia v. San Antonio Metropolitan Transit Authority.*[64] Writing for the majority, Justice Harry A. Blackmun concluded that "State sovereign interests . . . are more properly protected by procedural safeguards inherent in the structure of the federal system than by judicially created limitations of federal power."[65] In effect, the states would have to protect themselves through vigorous lobbying on Capitol Hill. The Supreme Court no longer would invoke a rule that was "unsound in principle and unworkable in practice."[66]

Although most accountability battles between federal and state politicians have focused on the commerce clause, one celebrated dispute involved the constitutional provision (in Article I) that the states shall have the authority to train state militia. A number of governors, opposed to the Reagan administration's Central America policies, objected to White House orders, backed by Congress, to use the National Guard for training exercises in Honduras. The governors feared that their troops would directly or indirectly support the contras' efforts to overthrow the Sandinista government in Nicaragua. Gov. Rudy Perpich of Minnesota and ten other governors sued the federal government to protest the deployment of National Guard troops without gubernatorial consent. The governors did not dispute the president's authority to federalize the Guard to deal with a national emergency, but they noted pointedly that no state of emergency existed.

On August 5, 1987, a federal district court upheld the federal government's right to deploy National Guard units while the Guard is on active duty. In the words of Judge Donald Alsop, "All authority to provide for the national defense resides in the Congress, and state governors have never had, and never could have, jurisdiction in this area."[67] That decision was subsequently affirmed by the U.S. Court of Appeals and by the U.S. Supreme

Court.[68] Here, as in other disputes between federal and state politicians, the federal government has been successful in establishing its preeminence.

Federal Judges versus State Politicians

In accountability battles between federal politicians and state politicians, federal judges have served as arbiters. In other disputes, however, federal judges have served as both arbiters and combatants. In numerous institutional reform cases, federal district court judges have ordered sweeping changes that are attainable only if state legislatures allocate more money than they wish to spend in a particular policy domain. These decisions have had tangible effects on state budgets.[69] The decisions also have raised important questions concerning both federalism and the power of the purse.

Confronted by shocking conditions in Alabama's prisons, Judge Frank Johnson ordered the entire prison system overhauled. He required immediate action to provide adequate food, clothing, shelter, sanitation, medical attention, and personal safety for inmates. He ordered individual cells, with each cell being at least 60 square feet. He required educational and rehabilitative services. And to ensure swift implementation, he established human rights committees.

Other federal judges have acted with equal vigor. Judge William Justice, appalled by conditions in Texas prisons, ordered an end to quadruple cells, triple cells, and double cells. He restricted the use of force by prison guards and ordered an end to the state's "building tender" system, in which inmates in effect guarded other inmates. In addition, he ordered sharp improvements in health care, fire and safety standards. He also insisted on prompt punishments for violations of constitutional rights.

In other institutional reform cases, federal judges have ordered sweeping changes in state treatment of the mentally ill and the mentally retarded. In New York, Judges Orrin Judd and John Bartels demanded more ward attendants, eighty-five more nurses, thirty physical therapists, and fifteen more physicians at the Willowbrook Developmental Center on Staten Island. They prohibited seclusion of patients and called for the immediate repair of broken toilets. They also ordered a sharp decrease in the Willowbrook population, stressing the advantages of deinstitutionalization. To implement these reforms, they appointed and preserved a Willowbrook Review Panel, which developed into a powerful agent of change.

In Pennsylvania, Judge Raymond Broderick went ever further, after learning of unsanitary, inhumane, and dangerous conditions at the Pennhurst State School and Hospital for the mentally retarded. In a strongly worded opinion, Broderick ordered the eventual closing down of the Pennhurst facilities, with residents being relocated in community facilities. In the meantime, he insisted on clean, odorless, and insect-free buildings, no new admissions, and less reliance on forcible restraint and unnecessary medication. To achieve these results, he appointed a special master and set deadlines for compliance.

More often than not, accountability battles between federal judges and state politicians have been won by federal judges. In reviewing lower court decisions, appeals court judges and the U.S. Supreme Court have agreed that "cruel and unusual punishment" is intolerable in state prisons and that the mentally ill have a constitutional right to "treatment" if admitted to a state facility. However, appeals courts also have raised questions about the extraordinarily detailed and specific remedies mandated by federal district court judges.

In *Newman v. Alabama*,[70] the U.S. Court of Appeals for the Fifth Circuit ruled that Judge Johnson went too far in specifying the size of new prison cells, in appointing human rights committees, and in insisting on rehabilitation opportunities for all prisoners. In the words of the court: "The Constitution does not require that prisoners, as individuals or as a group, be provided with any and every amenity which some person may think is needed to avoid mental, physical and emotional deterioration." In *Ruiz v. Estelle*,[71] the U.S. Court of Appeals for the Fifth Circuit ruled that Judge Justice went too far in outlawing double cells in Texas prisons (but supported his ban on triple and quadruple cells). In *New York State Association for Retarded Children v. Carey*,[72] the U.S. Court of Appeals for the Second Circuit concluded that Gov. Hugh Carey could not be held in contempt of court for failing to provide funding for the Willowbrook Review Panel. In *Pennhurst State School and Hospital v. Halderman*,[73] the U.S. Supreme Court ruled that a right to treatment exists only if a state accepts federal funds and if federal conditions of aid are clearly and unambiguously stated. In *Youngberg v. Romeo*,[74] the U.S. Supreme Court ruled that even when a right to treatment exists, it should be operationalized by qualified professionals, not judges.

Thus, accountability battles between federal district court judges and state politicians have given way to battles between federal district court judges and federal appeals court judges. On questions of constitutional rights, the appeals court judges generally have deferred to federal district courts, to the chagrin of the states. On questions of remedies, however, the appeals courts have cautioned lower courts against excessive specificity that stretches the limits of judicial expertise.

CONCLUSION

State administrative agencies once enjoyed considerable autonomy. Ignored by virtually everyone but clientele groups, they were "semisovereign" entities. In the early 1970s, that began to change. As state budgets grew and state bureaucracies increased in importance, this era came to a close. To make state agencies more accountable, politicians and judges institutionalized a wide variety of reforms. Through direct and indirect means, they attempted to bring state bureaucracies under control.

Ironically, this occurred at precisely the same time as the growing professionalization of state agencies. Thanks to civil service reforms, budget increases, rising education levels, and growing pressure for specialization, state bureaucracies acquired greater experience and expertise. They now are more adept at problem solving than ever before and arguably more deserving of discretion Thus, they chafe at external pressure, particularly when it is highly coercive.

General agreement exists that state agencies ought to be accountable. Even state bureaucrats cheerfully concede that point. However, consensus on the need for bureaucratic accountability has given way to "dissensus" on lines of authority. If governors and state legislators both claim an electoral mandate, who is right? If presidents and governors both cite constitutional prerogatives, who is correct? If federal judges and state politicians disagree on spending priorities, who deserves the power of the purse?

In the 1990s, state agencies are living in a different world—one character-ized by growing emphasis on hierarchy, oversight, and judicial review. State agencies are more accountable to their sovereigns than they used to be. Yet accountability has become a murky concept. Principal-agent theories of politics[75] work only when the principal's identity is clear to the agent. In numerous policy areas, state bureaucratic agents face dual principals or even multiple principals.

Thus, accountability battles rage, as competing sovereigns press their claims. As one might expect in a federal system, different actors have won accountability battles in different settings and at different times. Increasingly, however, federal judges are settling the most difficult of these battles. In the process of resolving disputes, federal judges have themselves become inter-ested parties. Ultimately, federal judges decide how accountability shall be defined, how authority shall be structured, and how power shall be wielded in a federal system. If accountability battles persist, the judicialization of state administration is the most probable result.

Notes

1. *Immigration and Naturalization Service v. Chadha,* 462 U.S. 919 (1983).
2. L. Harold Levinson, "The Decline of the Legislative Veto: Federal/State Comparisons and Interactions," *Publius* 17:1 (Winter 1987): 115–132.
3. Thad L. Beyle, "The Executive Branch: Organization and Issues, 1988-1989," in Council of State Governments, *The Book of the States, 1990-1991* (Lexington, Ky.: Council of State Governments, 1990), 76.
4. Lydia Bodman and Daniel Garry, "Innovations in State Cabinet Systems," *State Government* 55:3 (Summer 1982): 93–97.
5. Thomas Lauth, "Zero-Base Budgeting in Georgia State Government: Myth and Reality," in *Perspectives on Budgeting,* ed. Allen Schick (Washington, D.C.: American Society for Public Administration, 1980), 114–132.
6. Larry J. Sabato, *Goodby to Good-time Charlie: The American Governorship Transformed* (Washington, D.C.: CQ Press, 1983).
7. Susan King, "Executive Orders of the Wisconsin Governor," *Wisconsin Law Review* 2 (1980): 333–369.
8. Justin Kopca, "Executive Orders in State Government;" unpublished manu-script, Madison, Wis., May 1987.
9. E. Lee Bernick, "Discovering a Governor's Power: The Executive Order," *State Government* 57:3 (1984): 97–101.
10. Matthew McCubbins and Thomas Schwartz, "Congressional Oversight Overlooked: Police Patrols versus Fire Alarms," *American Journal of Political Science* 28:1 (February 1984): 180–202.
11. William Gormley, Jr., "The Representation Revolution: Reforming State Regulation through Public Representation," *Administration and Society* 18:2 (August 1986): 179–196.
12. Involuntary bill inserts later were ruled unconstitutional in a California case that effectively invalidated a key provision of the Wisconsin law. See *Pacific Gas and Electric v. Public Utilities Commission of California,* 106 S. Ct. 903 (1986).
13. Beth Givens, *Citizens' Utility Boards: Because Utilities Bear Watching* (San Diego, Calif.: Center for Public Interest Law, University of San Diego Law School, 1991).

14. Howard Schutz, "Effects of Increased Citizen Membership on Occupational Licensing Boards in California," *Policy Studies Journal* 2 (March 1983): 504–516.

15. Regulatory federalism also may be used to describe the relationship between state and local governments. For more on the growing burdens placed by state governments on local governments, see Catherine Lovell and Charles Tobin. "The Mandate Issue," *Public Administration Review* 41:3 (May/June 1981): 318–331. See also Joseph Zimmerman, "Developing State-Local Relations: 1987-1989," in Council of State Governments, *The Book of the States, 1990-1991,* 533–548.

16. Advisory Commission on Intergovernmental Relations, *Regulatory Federalism: Policy, Process, Impact and Reform* (Washington, D.C.: Advisory Commission on Intergovernmental Relations, 1983).

17. Timothy Conlan, "And the Beat Goes On: Intergovernmental Mandates and Preemption in an Era of Deregulation," *Publius* 21:3 (Summer 1991): 43–57.

18. Ibid., 50.

19. James Gosling, "Transportation Policy and the Ironies of Intergovernmental Relations," in *The Midwest Response to the New Federalism,* ed. Peter Eisinger and William Gormley (Madison: University of Wisconsin Press, 1988), 237–263.

20. Sanford Schram, "The New Federalism and Social Welfare: AFDC in the Midwest," in *The Midwest Response to the New Federalism,* 264-292.

21. *Massachusetts v. U.S.,* 435 U.S. 444 (1978); and *Connecticut Department of Income Maintenance v. Heckler,* 105 S. Ct. 2210 (1985).

22. *Hodel v. Virginia Surface Mining and Reclamation Association,* 452 U.S. 264 (1981); and *FERC v. Mississippi,* 456 U.S. 742 (1982).

23. *South Dakota v. Dole,* Slip Opinion No. 86-260, U.S. Supreme Court, June 23, 1987.

24. *EEOC v. Wyoming,* 460 U.S. 226 (1983); *Garcia v. San Antonio Metropolitan Transit Authority,* 105 S. Ct. 1005 (1985); *City of New York v. FCC,* 108 S. Ct. 1637 (1988); and *Mississippi Power and Light v. Mississippi,* 108 S. Ct. 2428 (1988).

25. *Wyatt v. Stickney,* 324 F. Supp. 781 (M.D. Ala., 1971).

26. *Newman v. Alabama,* 349 F. Supp. 278 (M.D. Ala., 1972).

27. *James v. Wallace,* 406 F. Supp. 318 (M.D. Ala., 1976); and *Pugh v. Locke,* 406 F. Supp. 318 (M.D. Ala., 1976).

28. *Youngberg v. Romeo,* 102 S. Ct. 2452 (1982).

29. *Ruiz v. Estelle,* 503 F. Supp. 1265 (S.D. Tex. 1980).

30. Joel Rosch, "Will the Federal Courts Run the States' Prison Systems?" in *State Government: CQ's Guide to Current Issues and Activities 1987-1988,* ed. Thad L. Beyle (Washington, D.C.: Congressional Quarterly Inc., 1987), 165–168.

31. Robert Bradley, "Judicial Appointment and Judicial Intervention: The Issuance of Structural Reform Decrees in Corrections Litigation," in *Courts, Corrections, and the Constitution,* ed. John DiIulio, Jr. (New York: Oxford University Press, 1990), 249-267.

32. John DiIulio, Jr., "Conclusion: What Judges Can Do to Improve Prisons and Jails," in *Courts, Corrections, and the Constitution,* 288–289.

33. William Gormley, Jr., *Taming the Bureaucracy: Muscles, Prayers, and Other Strategies* (Princeton, N.J.: Princeton University Press, 1989).

34. David Godschalk and Bruce Stiftel, "Making Waves: Public Participation in State Water Planning," *Journal of Applied Behavioral Science* 17:4 (October-December 1981): 597–614.

35. Judy Rosener, "Making Bureaucrats Responsive: A Study of the Impact of Citizen Participation and Staff Recommendations on Regulatory Decision Making," *Public Administration Review* 42:4 (July/August 1982): 339–345.

36. Administration on Aging, U.S. Department of Health and Human Services, *National Summary of State Ombudsman Reports for U.S. Fiscal Year 1982* (Washington, D.C.: U.S. Government Printing Office, 1983).

37. Abraham Monk et al., *National Comparative Analysis of Long Term Care Programs for the Aged* (New York: Brookdale Institute on Aging and Adult Human Development and the Columbia University School of Social Work, 1982).
38. William Gormley, Jr., *The Politics of Public Utility Regulation* (Pittsburgh, Pa.: University of Pittsburgh Press, 1983).
39. Paul Teske, *After Divestiture: The Political Economy of State Telecommunications Regulation* (Albany: SUNY Press, 1990), 63–85.
40. Ibid.
41. Gerald Thain and Kenneth Haydock, *A Working Paper: How Public and Other Members of Regulation and Licensing Boards Differ: The Results of a Wisconsin Survey* (Madison, Wis.: Center for Public Representation, 1983).
42. James Q. Wilson, ed., *The Politics of Regulation* (New York: Basic Books, 1980).
43. Cheryl Miller, "State Administrator Perceptions of the Policy Influence of Other Actors: Is Less Better?" *Public Administration Review* 47:3 (May/June 1987):239–245.
44. Glenn Abney and Thomas Lauth, *The Politics of State and City Administration* (Albany: SUNY Press, 1986).
45. David Rafter, "Policy-Focused Evaluation: A Study of the Utilization of Evaluation Research by the Wisconsin Legislature," Ph.D. dissertation, University of Wisconsin, Madison, Wis., 1982.
46. Kenneth Meier, "Executive Reorganization of Government: Impact on Employment and Expenditures," *American Journal of Political Science* 24:3 (August 1980): 396–412; and Karen Hult, *Agency Merger and Bureaucratic Redesign* (Pittsburgh, Pa.: University of Pittsburgh Press, 1987).
47. Doug Roederer and Patsy Palmer, *Sunset: Expectation and Experience* (Lexington, Ky.: Council of State Governments, June 1981).
48. Evelyn Brodkin and Michael Lipsky, "Quality Control in AFDC as an Administrative Strategy," *Social Service Review* 57:1 (March 1983): 1–34.
49. Eric Black, "Why Regulators Need a Don't-Do-It-If-It's-Stupid Clause," *Washington Monthly* 16:12 (January 1985): 23–26.
50. Richard P. Nathan, "The Role of the States in American Federalism" (Paper delivered at the annual meeting of the American Political Science Association, Chicago, September 3-6, 1987).
51. Richard Elling, "Federal Dollars and Federal Clout in State Administration: A Test of 'Regulatory' and 'Picket Fence' Models of Intergovernmental Relations" (Paper delivered at the annual meeting of the Midwest Political Science Association, Chicago, April 17-20, 1985).
52. Douglas Stencel, "Analysis of Joint Committee for Review of Administrative Rules Caseload 1985-1986," unpublished manuscript, Madison, Wis., April 1987.
53. Tinsley Yarbrough, *Judge Frank Johnson and Human Rights in Alabama* (University: University of Alabama Press, 1981).
54. James Marquart and Ben Crouch, "Judicial Reform and Prisoner Control: The Impact of *Ruiz v. Estelle* on a Texas Penitentiary," *Law and Society Review* 19:4 (1985): 557–586.
55. Aric Press, "Inside America's Toughest Prison," *Newsweek*, October 6, 1986, 46–61.
56. Levinson, "The Decline of the Legislative Veto," 121.
57. *Enourato v. New Jersey Building Authority*, 448 A. 2d 449 (N.J. 1982).
58. *General Assembly v. Byrne*, 448 A. 2d 438 (N.J. 1982).
59. Gary Warner, "Despite Ruling, Future of Liquor Stores Up in Air," *Pittsburgh Press*, December 30, 1986, 1.
60. Charles Friederich, "Lawmakers to Sue Thompson over Budget Vetoes," *Milwaukee Journal*. September 2, 1987, B3; and Doug Mell, "Thompson Vetoes Win in Court," *Wisconsin State Journal*, June 15, 1988, 1.
61. *National League of Cities v. Usery*, 426 U.S. 833 (1976).

62. *Hodel v. Virginia Surface Mining and Reclamation Association,* 452 U.S. 264 (1981).
63. *FERC v. Mississippi,* 456 U.S. 742 (1982).
64. *Garcia v. San Antonio Metropolitan Transit Authority,* 105 S. Ct. 1005 (1985).
65. 105 S. Ct. 1018 (1985).
66. 105 S. Ct. 1016 (1985).
67. Robert Whereatt, "State Loses Guard Suit," *Minneapolis Star and Tribune,* August 5, 1987, 1.
68. *Perpich et al. v. Department of Defense,* Slip Opinion NO. 89-542, U.S. Supreme Court, June 11, 1990.
69. Linda Harriman and Jeffrey Straussman, "Do Judges Determine Budget Decisions?" *Public Administration Review* 43:4 (July/August 1983): 343–351.
70. *Newman v. Alabama,* 559 F. 2d 283 (5th Cir., 1977).
71. *Ruiz v. Estelle,* 679 F. 2d 1115 (1982).
72. *New York State Association for Retarded Children v. Carey,* 631 F. 2d 162 (1980).
73. *Pennhurst State School and Hospital v. Halderman,* 101 S. Ct., 1531 (1981).
74. *Youngberg v. Romeo,* 102 S. Ct. 2452 (1982).
75. Jonathan Bendor and Terry Moe, "An Adaptive Model of Bureaucratic Politics," *American Political Science Review* 79:3 (September 1985): 755–774.

Public Administration and Ethics

DWIGHT WALDO

"No process has been discovered by which promotion to a position of public responsibility will do away with a man's interest in his own welfare, his partialities, race, and prejudices."—JAMES HARVEY ROBINSON

"You are welcome to my house; you are welcome to my heart ... my personal feelings have nothing to do with the present case.... As George Washington, I would do anything in my power for you. As President, I can do nothing."
—GEORGE WASHINGTON, to a friend seeking an appointment

"There is not a moral vice which cannot be made into relative good by context. There is not a moral virtue which cannot in peculiar circumstances have patently evil results." —STEPHEN BAILEY

"The big organization dehumanizes the individual by turning him into a functionary. In doing so it makes everything possible by creating a new kind of man, one who is morally unbounded in his role as functionary.... His ethic is the ethic of the good soldier: take the order, do the job, do it the best way you know how, because that is your honor, your virtue, your pride-in-work."
—F. WILLIAM HOWTON

"It seems to be inevitable that the struggle to maintain cooperation among men should destroy some men morally as battle destroys some physically."
—CHESTER BARNARD

"The raising of moral considerations in any discussion on organizations usually causes discomfort. . . . Nonetheless, if morality is about what is right and wrong, then behavior in organizations is largely determined by such considerations."—
DAVID BRADLEY AND ROY WILKIE

"The first duty of a civil servant is to give his undivided allegiance to the State at all times and on all occasions when the State has a claim on his service."
—BOARD OF INQUIRY, UNITED KINGDOM, 1928

. . . The several heterogeneous epigraphs are directed toward emphasizing the central theme of this presentation, namely, that moral or ethical[1] behavior in public administration is a complicated matter, indeed, *chaotic*. While some facets of the matter have been treated with insight and clarity, nothing in the way of a comprehensive and systematic treatise exists—or if so I am unaware of it.[2] This situation may not reflect just accident or lack of interest. What may be reflected is the fact that a systematic treatise is impossible, given the scope, complexity, and intractability of the material from which it would have to be constructed and given an inability to find acceptable or defensible foundations of ideas and beliefs on which it could be grounded.

In this discussion I hope to indicate some of the subjects that might be given attention in a systematic treatise. I appreciate that even this hope may represent pretentiousness.

PUBLIC MORALITY AND PRIVATE MORALITY

An appropriate beginning is to note a distinction between public and private morality and the possibility of a conflict between them.[3] This is a very elementary distinction, but much evidence indicates that it is little understood. As presented in the media, including the columns of the pundits, morality in public office is a simple matter of obeying the law, being honest, and telling the truth. *Not so.*

Public morality concerns decisions made and action taken directed toward the good of a collectivity which is seen or conceptualized as "the public," that is, as an entity or group larger than immediate social groups such as family and clan. Conventionally, "the public" in the modern West is equated with "the nation," or "the country." Thus when decisions are made and actions taken vis-à-vis other nations or countries a public interest is presumed to be in view. Similarly, when the decision or action is directed inward toward the affairs of the nation-state, a public or general interest is presumed to come before private or group interests.

In either case a decision or action justified as moral because it is judged to be in the interest of the public may be immoral from the standpoint of all, or nearly all, interpretations of moral behavior for individuals. The most common example is killing. When done by an individual it is, commonly, the crime of homicide. When done in warfare or law enforcement on behalf of the public it is an act of duty and honor, perhaps of heroism—presuming the "correct" circumstances. All important governments have committed what would be "sins" if done by individuals, what would be "crimes" if done under their own laws by individuals acting privately.

Those in government who decide and act on behalf of the public will from time to time, of *necessity* as I see it, be lying, stealing, cheating, killing.

What must be faced is that all decision and action in the public interest is inevitably morally complex, and that the price of any good characteristically entails some bad. Usually the bad is not as simple and stark as the terms just listed signify; but sometimes it *is*, and honesty and insight on our part can begin with so acknowledging.

Ironically, the concept of "the public" is regarded, and I believe properly, as a good and even precious thing. It is a heritage from Greek and Roman antiquity. Its projection, elaboration, nurture, and defense are generally represented as the work of inspired thinkers, virtuous statesmen, and brave warriors. How can this be, when sins and crimes are committed in the name of the public? The answer is twofold. First, my favorite question: Compared to what? Assuming government is desirable, or at least inevitable, what legitimating concept is better? At least the idea of government in the name of a public advances that enterprise beyond purely personal and often tyrannical rule. Second, once in motion, so to speak, the concept of the public becomes invested with, a shelter for, and even a source of, goods that we identify with words such as citizenship, security, justice, and liberty.

THE STATE AND HIGHER LAW

To see the matter of public and private morality in perspective it is necessary to understand the complicated relationship of both moralities to the concept of *higher law*. The concept of higher law, simply put for our purposes, holds that there is a source and measure of rightness that is above and beyond both individual and government. In our own history it is represented prominently in the justification of the Revolution against the government of George III, and it inspired the Declaration of Independence.

The classical Greek philosophers, from whom much of our tradition of political thought derives, sought a moral unity. Are the good man and the good citizen the same? Both Plato and Aristotle answered the question affirmatively, though Plato more certainly than Aristotle. In the comparatively simple world of the city-state this answer could be made plausible, given the Greek conviction of superiority and the elitist nature of citizenship: the polity creates citizens in its admirable image and is thus the source of man's morality; there can be no legitimate appeal from what it holds to be right.

But as Sophocles' *Antigone* signifies, the idea of a higher law—in this case the laws of Zeus as against those of the king, Creon—existed even in Athens. During the Hellenistic period, after the decline of the city-state, the idea of a natural law above and beyond the mundane world was elaborated, especially by the Stoics. A sense of personhood apart from the polity, and of the essential equality of humans *as* humans was developing, and this was accompanied by a growing belief that right and wrong rested on foundations beyond the polity. As Sabine put it in his history of political theory: "Men were slowly making souls for themselves." With Christianity these ideas were of course broadened and deepened. The idea of God's law, or natural law—and characteristically the two became conflated—was to become a powerful force in relation to both private and public morality.

For more than a millennium after the fall of Rome, during a period in which government all but disappeared in the West, the relationship of the two powers, the sacred and the secular—for most purposes to be equated with

Church and secular authority—was at the center of political philosophy and political controversy; but the theoretical and logical supremacy of the higher law was seldom questioned. With the emergence of the modern state a new era opened. The authority of a state, even a secular state, to determine right and wrong for its citizens was powerfully asserted by political theorists, notably Machiavelli and Hobbes. On the other hand, the long era of higher-law thinking had left an indelible imprint on thought and attitude. That there is something to which one's conscience gives access and which provides guidance on right and wrong remains a strong feeling even among those who regard themselves as completely secular.

The discussion of higher law has indicated that the initial duality of public morality and private morality was simplistic. There is an important, and insufficiently appreciated, distinction between the two, as I hope was demonstrated. But two important matters are now apparent. One is that higher law does not equate with or relate only to private morality as against public. Its sanction can be claimed by the polity if the polity represents the sacred as well as the secular, that is, if there is no separation of church and state—or perhaps even if there is.

The other matter is that the public-private distinction is but one example, albeit a crucial one for our purposes, of a class of relationships that can be designated *collectivity-person*. The biological person is of course distinguishable from any collectivity: nation, party, union, family, whatever. But whether the person can have or should have moral standing apart from the collectivities that have created him and given him meaning is a large part of what ethics is about; for all collectivities of any durability and significance will claim, explicitly or implicitly, to be the source of moral authority. While the state may well, and in some cases inevitably will, claim moral supremacy, the individual will have to weigh its claims against his or her interpretations of competing claims of other collectivities *and* the claims of higher law and "conscience."

Plainly, the ethical landscape is becoming very cluttered and complex. More to this shortly. But first a few words on *reason of state*. Reason of state is public morality at its extreme reach. Plainly put, it is conduct that violates all or nearly all standards of right conduct for individuals; this in the interests of the creating, preserving, or enhancing state power, and rationalized by "the ends justify the means" logic. A few years ago I had occasion to review the literature on this subject in Political Science in the United States. Significantly, what I found was very little, and this mostly by émigré scholars. Unbelievably, there is no entry for this important subject in the seventeen-volume *International Encyclopedia of the Social Sciences,* even though it was planned and executed during the moral-ethical hurricane of the Vietnam War. A number of historical factors, beyond exploring here, have led us to gloss over and even deny the complexities and contradictions that exist when public and private morality conflict, as inevitably they sometimes will.

A MAP—OF SORTS

A few years ago, attempting to address the subject "Ethical Obligations and the Public Service," I made a rough sketch of the ethical obligations of the public administrator as seen from one point of view. Later, this sketch was somewhat elaborated and refined in collaboration with Patrick Hennigan in a yet unpublished essay. It will serve present purposes to indicate the nature of this endeavor.

The sketch, or "map," as we called it, is of ethical obligations of the public administrator with special reference to the United States. The perspective taken is that of the *sources* and *types* of ethical obligations to which the public administrator is expected to respond. We identify a dozen, but as we indicate, the list is capable of indefinite expansion and does not lend itself to logical ordering.

First. Obligation to the Constitution

This is a legal obligation of course, but it is also a source of ethical obligations, which may be symbolized and solemnized by an oath to uphold and defend the Constitution. The upholding of regime and of regime values is a normal source of public-service obligation, and the Constitution is the foundation of regime and of regime values for the United States. But note: not an unambiguous foundation. A great deal of our history, including a civil war, can be written in terms of different interpretations of the Constitution.

Second. Obligation to Law

Laws made under the Constitution are a source not just of legal obligation but also of ethical obligations, as public-service codes of ethics normally underscore. Note again the ambiguities and puzzles. What if the law is unclear? What if laws conflict? What if a law seems unconstitutional, or violates a tenet of higher law? What is the ethical status of regulations made under the law?

Third. Obligation to Nation or Country

By most interpretations, a nation or country or people is separable from regime, and plainly this sense of identity with a nation, country, or people creates ethical obligations. Indeed, in many situations the obligation to country—Fatherland, Motherland, Homeland, however it may be put—overrides the obligation to regime. Lincoln, justifying his actions in 1864: "Was it possible to lose the nation, and yet preserve the constitution?"

Fourth. Obligation to Democracy

As indicated in previous discussions, this is separable from obligation to Constitution, granted that the relationship is complicated and arguable. Whatever the intent of the Framers—and I do not expect agreement on that, ever—democracy happened: it came to be accepted as an ideology or ethic and as a set of practices that somewhat overlie and somewhat intertwine with the Constitution. The emotional and intellectual acceptance of democracy creates obligations that are acknowledged and usually felt by the public administrator. But again, note the ambiguities: Is the will of the people *always* and *only* expressed in law? If in other ways, how? And how legitimated? Is the *will* of the people, however expressed, to be put ahead of the *welfare* of the people as seen by a public official with information not available to the people?

Fifth. Obligation to Organizational-Bureaucratic Norms

These may be logically divided between those that are *generic* and those that are *specific*. The generic obligations are deeply rooted, perhaps in human nature, certainly in history and culture. They are associated with such terms as loyalty, duty, and order, as well as, perhaps, productivity, economy, efficiency. Specific obligations will depend upon circumstance: the function, the clientele, the technology.

Sixth. Obligation to Profession and Professionalism

The disagreements among sociologists as to what precisely *profession* entails may be disregarded here. All would agree that a profession, indeed a well-developed occupation, has an ethos that acts to shape the values and behavior of members. This ethos concerns actions pertaining to fellow professionals, clients, patients, employers, and perhaps humanity in general. We have become much more aware of the strength and effects of professional values and behavior in public administration since the publication of Frederick Mosher's *Democracy and the Public Service*.

Seventh. Obligation to Family and Friends

Obligation to family is bedrock in most if not all morality. But in countries shaped by the Western political tradition it is formally accepted that *in principle* obligation to country and/or regime as well as to the public is higher than that to family. While the newspaper on almost any day will indicate that the principle is often breached, we are very clear and insistent on the *principle,* and on the whole we believe that the principle prevails. But in countries in which the concept of public is recent and inchoate and in which family or other social group remains the center of loyalty and values, the principle is breached massively, so much so that the creation of an effective government may be impossible.

Friendship is less than family, but shares with it the immediate, personal bond; and friendship as well as family is honored in moral tradition. To indicate the ethical problems that may arise from this source one has only to set forth a name: Bert Lance.

Eighth. Obligation to Self

Yes, to self: this is a respectable part of our moral tradition, best epitomized in the Shakespearean "This above all, to Thine own self be true." Selfishness and egocentrism are by general agreement bad. The argument for *self* is that self-regard is the basis for other-regard, that proper conduct toward others, doing one's duty, must be based on personal strength and integrity. But, granting the principle, how does one draw the line in practice between proper self-regard and a public interest?

Ninth. Obligation to Middle-Range Collectivities

In view here is a large and heterogeneous lot: party, class, race, union, church, interest group, and others. That these are capable of creating obligations felt as moral is quite clear, and that these obligations are carried into public administration is also quite clear. When, and how, is it proper for such obligations to affect administrative behavior, to influence public decisions?

Tenth. Obligation to the Public Interest or General Welfare

This obligation is related to Constitution, to nation, to democracy. But it is analytically distinct. It is often explicitly embodied in law, but also has something of a separate existence. The concept is notoriously difficult to operationalize, and has been repeatedly subject to critical demolition. But presumably anyone in public administration must take it seriously, if only as a myth that must be honored in certain procedural and symbolic ways.

Eleventh. Obligation to Humanity or the World

It is an old idea, and perhaps despite all a growing idea, that an obligation is owed to humanity in general, to the world as a total entity, to the future as the symbol and summation of all that can be hoped. All "higher" religions trend in this direction, however vaguely and imperfectly. It is certainly an ingredient in various forms of one-world consciousness, and it figures prominently in the environmental ethic and in ecological politics.

Twelfth. Obligation to Religion, or to God

Immediately one must ask, are these two things or the same thing? The answer is not simple. But that obligations are seen as imposed by religion or God is not doubted even by atheists. One could quickly point to areas of public administration in which these felt obligations are at the center of "what's happening"—or possibly not happening.

A NEED FOR MAPS

Obviously, this listing of sources and types of ethical obligations involved in public administration is rough. The number, twelve, is plainly arbitrary. Perhaps some of the items were wrongly included, or should be combined. Perhaps some should be further divided and refined. Certainly other items might be included: *science,* for example, since science is interpreted not just to require a set of proper procedures but to be an ethos with accompanying ethical imperatives. As we know, *face-to-face groups* develop their own norms and powerfully influence behavior, but were not even mentioned. And what of *conscience?* Is it to be regarded as only a passive transmitter of signals or as in part at least an autonomous source of moral conduct?

You will have noticed that I did not attempt to order the twelve types of obligations, that is, list them in order of importance or ethical imperative. This was neither an oversight nor—I believe—a lack of intelligence on my part, but rather reflected the untidiness of the ethical universe. Perhaps the list included incommensurables. In any event, we lack the agreed beliefs which would enable us to construct an order of priority, one to twelve, with the higher obligation always superior to the lower.

How are we to proceed? How can we achieve enough clarity so that we can at least discuss our differences with minimum confusion, the least heat and the most light? My own view is that a desirable, perhaps necessary, preliminary activity is to construct more and better maps of the realm we propose to understand. Granted that this expectation may reflect only the habits of academia; professors are prone to extensive preparation for intellectual journeys never undertaken. But I do not see how we can move beyond a confused disagreement until there is more agreement on what we are talking about.

If I am essentially correct, then what would be useful would be a serious and sizable mapmaking program. We need various types of maps, analogous to maps that show physical features, climatic factors, demographic data, economic activity, and so forth. We need maps of differing scale, some indicating the main features of a large part of the organizational world, some detailing particular levels, functions, and activities. Despite common elements, presumably—no, certainly—the ethical problems of a legislator are significantly different from those of a military officer, those of a regulatory commissioner different from those of a police chief, those of a first-line supervisor from those of a department head.

Simply put: If we are going to talk about ethics in public life it would be useful to know what we are talking about.

A NEED FOR NAVIGATION INSTRUMENTS

The metaphor of maps may not have been the most apt, but I now use one that may be less felicitous, that of navigation instruments. But at least the second metaphor is complementary: given maps, how do we navigate? How do we find our way through what the maps show us? Let me indicate the nature of some navigation equipment that would be of use.

First, it would be useful to have an instrument to guide us through the historical dimensions of our ethical problems in public administration. Above all, it would be useful to have an explication of the implications and consequences of the disjunction, noted in earlier discussions, between the rise of political self-awareness and the rise of administrative self-awareness. Both as a part of that inquiry and independently, what do we know about the rise and growth of administrative morality, of notions of stewardship, duty and obligations, reciprocal or unilateral? With respect to estate management, which has been so large a part of administrative history, have rules of proper conduct been widely divergent, or has the nature of the function disposed toward uniformity? Since estate management has been centrally involved in royal governance, from Sumer to the Sun King—and beyond—what effect has this had on bureaucratic morality? Perhaps it is worth more than mere mention that *estate* and *state* are cognates, both derived from the Latin *stare:* "to be *or* stand"; the essential notion in both cases is of substance, firmness, an organizing center.

Second, it would be useful to have instruments provided by the social sciences or derived from a survey of them. Immediately, we face the fact indicated in the epigraph from Bradley and Wilkie at the head of this chapter: "The raising of moral considerations in any discussion on organizations usually causes discomfort." In addressing organizational behavior as in contemporary social science generally, ethics is not just a neglected interest, it is a rejected interest. I shall return to this point; but what I have in mind presently need not cause serious discomfort, though it no doubt would strike many as a peculiar interest and a waste of energy. What I have in view is not an addressing of ethical issues as such, but rather a survey to determine what the several social sciences have to say about ethical matters, either directly or indirectly. For example, are ethical issues present in disguise—morality pretending to be science? We can see that the *yes* answer has often been true in the past, and not a few claim it is true now. What would the most honest, nonideological view reveal? Aside from this question, do the paradigms and tools of the several social sciences offer any handles for ethical inquiry?

Political Science, presumably, would be most centrally involved. And that brings me, inevitably, back to the theme of disjunction: what are the consequences for both Political Science and Public Administration, more broadly, *politics* and *administration,* of the fact that politics reached self-awareness in classical Greece and administration not until the late nineteenth century—this despite the fact that, even (especially?) in small and simple polities, politics and administration were inevitably intermingled.

The other social sciences, even Anthropology, need also to be surveyed. "Even Anthropology?"—an argument could be made that its determined lack of normativeness plus its comparativeness make it particularly germane. Sociology—beginning with its ancestry in Montesquieu and others, and certainly decisively in Comte, Spencer, Durkheim, Weber, Parsons, and other major figures—is rich with relevant material; whether in spite of or because of its scientific stance is hard to say. And Economics? One should not, of course, be put off with its scientific aura and impressive technical apparatus. Adam Smith, in his own view and that of his contemporaries, was a moral philosopher; and Irving Kristol has recently reminded us that Smith's *An Inquiry into the Nature and Causes of the Wealth of Nations* was not intended as a defense of the *morality* of free enterprise. Economics, both in what it attends to and in what it refuses to attend to, in the behavior it licenses and in the behavior it forbids, is very central to any inquiry into ethical conduct in administration: As a random illustration, the recent realization that noxious waste chemicals simply have been dumped in tens of thousands of locations. What sins are committed in the name of externalities and exogenous variables?

Third, ethics as a self-aware enterprise, together with the philosophic matrices from which differing ethical theories are derived, needs to be searched and ordered for the purposes of ethical analysis and judgment in public administration. It may be thought peculiar, to say the least of it, that only well into this discussion ethical theory as such is brought to the fore. But as I view the matter it deserves no high priority. For ethics has little attended to proper behavior in large-scale organization. Its central interests have been elsewhere, tending to oscillate between the probing of traditional relationships such as those of family and friendships and rather abstract and bloodless general principles of conduct. While there is to be sure a great deal in the literature that is relevant, its relevance becomes clear only by extrapolation and application.

Fourth, religion also needs to be surveyed with the object of determining what instruments of navigation it can provide. For our purposes attention should be centered on the Judeo-Christian stream of religious thought and practice, but all major religions should be included. Among the many subjects on which I am not expert are theology and religious history. However, it takes only a little knowledge and understanding to appreciate three things. The first is that theology as such, like ethics to which it is linked in many ways, has attended very little to proper conduct in formal organizations, at least those not religious. Second, as with ethics, there is in theology a great deal that can be made relevant by extrapolation and application. In fact, the writings of Reinhold Niebuhr moved vigorously in this direction; and perhaps I do less than justice to others of whose work I may be unaware. Third, the history and effect of religious institutions and the second, third and X-order effects of religious thought and practice are of so great import for organizational life that one could devote a career to the matter without doing more than explore a few areas. The point is made simply by referring to the work under the heading of Protestant Ethic.

THE PYRAMID PUZZLE

Not surprisingly, many of the most interesting and significant questions concerning administration and ethics concern the theory and practice of hierarchy. Some of these questions are generic, in the sense that they apply to business and nonprofit private organizations as well as to public administration. But some have a special relevance to public administration, as they concern governmental institutions and political ideology. It will be instructive to focus briefly on this pyramid puzzle in the public context.

Central, at least to my own interest, is the fact that hierarchy is represented both as a force for morality and a source of immorality. Both cases are familiar to us, though perhaps not in the context of ethics.

The affirmative case has it that hierarchy is a force that works both for the soft values of democracy and the hard values of effectiveness, efficiency, and economy; indeed, that the achievement of the soft and hard values is complementary, not two things but a single thing. This is a central theme of old-line Public Administration, and the reasoning and conclusions are familiar: Democracy is, realistically, achievable only if power is concentrated so that it can be held accountable, and this is possible only through hierarchy. Otherwise, responsibility bleeds into the social surround. The devices for focusing citizen attention so that it could be made effective—devices such as the short ballot and party reform—were part of the old-line package. Responsibility was viewed as owed upward, subordinate to superordinate, to the top of the pyramid, then bridged over by the electoral principle to the people. Authority was viewed as moving the other direction, upward from the people through their elected representative, then bridged over to the top of the pyramid and descending, echelon by echelon, to every officer and employee.

That this way of viewing things has considerable logic and force strikes me as self-evident. It is plausibly, though hardly unarguably, based on Constitution and history, and can be bolstered with much evidence. It can be, and has been, buttressed by arguments from foreign experience and from business practice.

Able and honorable persons have supported the main tenets of the argument. Thus Paul Appleby in his *Morality and Administration in Democratic Government:*[4] The hierarchical principle forwards effective government, but above all it is necessary to democratic government, insuring through its operation the triumph of the general interest over special interests. Thus Marver Bernstein in "Ethics in Government: The Problems in Perspective,"[5] arguing that serious ethical irregularities as well as inefficiencies are all but assured through the absence of hierarchical control in the arrangements for some regulatory agencies, which create conflicts of interest or in effect make the regulatory agencies captives of the interests to be regulated. Thus Victor Thompson in his *Without Sympathy or Enthusiasm: The Problem of Administrative Compassion,*[6] where he argues that the prescriptions for participation equal an invitation for the unauthorized to steal the "tool" of administration from its "owners," the public.

The case against hierarchy in turn has considerable logic and force. It also has roots in Constitution and history, and can be bolstered with much evidence. In this case persons who are able and honorable have stressed the contradictions involved in using hierarchy as a means of promoting democracy, the limitations of hierarchy as a means of achieving effectiveness and efficiency, and its complicity in forwarding immorality. Thus Vincent Ostrom in his *The Intellectual Crisis in American Public Administration,*[7] arguing the spuriousness of the case for centralization, and the greater democracy achievable by organizing public administration into smaller units more in accord with "consumer" will and control. Thus the advocates of a New Public Administration,[8] who take social equity as guiding principle and seek to achieve it "proactively," through client-oriented and client- involving devices. Thus F. William Howton—quoted in one of the epigraphs[9]—who speaks for many who believe that hierarchy with its accustomed corollaries creates deformed humans with deadened consciences. Thus Frederick Thayer in his *An End to Hierarchy! An End to Competition!*[10] who finds hierarchy implicated in immorality as well as promoting inefficiency, and necessarily to be abolished if there is to be a tolerable future—indeed, perhaps, a *future.*

My aim is not to weigh the arguments, much less render a verdict, but rather to emphasize the tangle of ethical problems in and related to the principle and practice of hierarchy; this by way of illustrating the central position of ethical concerns in our professional business—whether or not we care to attend to them *as* ethical questions. But before passing on, let me pose one question that many would regard as the paramount one: What difference does democracy make with respect to the morality of actions taken by government? Rousseau, if I understand him correctly, argued that while the people can be *mistaken,* they cannot be *wrong.* Two examples to ponder, the first from history, the second hypothetical. (1) If the bombing of Haiphong was "immoral," was the firebombing of Hamburg and Dresden—which was massively greater—also immoral? If not, why not? (2) If the Holocaust had been carried out under a democratic government rather than a dictatorship, would an Eichmann have been any more or less immoral? In reflecting on this, bear in mind Herman Finer's notable essay on "Administrative Responsibility in Government,"[11] in which he holds with regard to the public servant: "The first commandment is subservience."

OBSERVATIONS AND REFLECTIONS

. . . At most I can hope to point to some of the matters that would be worthy of attention in a more serious and systematic inquiry. In conclusion, the following further observations and reflections. I shall proceed discontinuously, serially.

First

The twentieth century has hardly been distinguished either by its observance of agreed moral codes or by its concentration on ethical inquiry. On the contrary, it has been distinguished by a "decay" of traditional moral codes, a widespread feeling that morality is "relative" if not utterly meaningless, and a disposition to regard ethical inquiry as frivolous, irrelevant. These currents of thought and feeling have been associated with a "falling away" from religious belief and a concomitant rise of "belief" in science and its philosophical—or antiphilosophical—aura.

These developments have coincided with the Organizational Revolution: an unprecedented increase in the variety, number, size, and power of organizations, at the center of which is government, public administration. It has coincided also, and relatedly, with the arrival of administrative self-awareness, with a new type of "scientific" interest in administrative study and a resulting increase in administrative technology.

So we confront this historical situation: Just at the time the organizational world is thickening and thus the need for ethical guidance increasing, not only does old morality erode but no serious effort is made to create new codes of conduct appropriate to the new situation; and the scientific mentality that is largely responsible for the Organizational Revolution simultaneously makes it difficult to take ethical matters seriously.

Second

In no country does the level of conscious ethical conduct in government reach the level of complex reality, but the United States may have one problem to an unusual degree. It has often been observed that Americans tend to view morality very heavily if not exclusively in sexual and pecuniary terms: in the public area, Elizabeth Rays on payrolls and Tongsun Parks passing envelopes of currency behind closed doors.

As I see it, a concern for *public* morality must indeed include a concern with the ordinary garden varieties of sexual and pecuniary misconduct within or affecting public life; we would have to be ignorant of history and oblivious to contemporary political life to think otherwise. However, as even my few shallow probes indicate, the matter of ethically proper conduct reaches far, far beyond the popular images of sex and money. It presents problems of conduct for which traditional morality, growing in and shaped to simpler times, provides little guidance. Or worse, it provides *mis*guidance.

Third

Some of the better writings bearing on our subject emphasize the prevalence, perhaps even the necessity, of "moral ambiguity" in organizational life. Thus Stephen Bailey in his "Ethics and the Public Service";[12] I refer back to the epigraph from this essay emphasizing the "contextuality" of good and evil. Thus Melville Dalton in his *Men Who Manage*,[13] who concluded that persons from a middle-class background are more likely to become successful managers than persons from a working-class background, not because of superior ability or technical skill but because of a socialization that better prepares them to cope with moral ambiguity.

If we cannot *clarify* the ethics of the organizational world, perhaps it will help if we can advance *understanding* of the complexity and confusion. If ambiguity cannot be eliminated, then a "tolerance for ambiguity" becomes an essential operating skill. A *moral* quality as well as an operating skill? I shall not try to answer that.

Fourth

The following seems to be true, almost axiomatically: Moral complexity increases as memberships in organizations increase; persons in formal organizations in addition to traditional/nonformal organizations face greater moral complexity than those only in the latter; those in formal *public* organizations face more moral complexity than those in nonpublic organizations; and moral complexity increases as responsibilities in an administrative hierarchy increase.

If this is a correct view, then high-placed administrators (managers, executives) in public organizations are at the very center of ethical complexity. In this connection I refer you to the probing of morality in relation to administration in Chester Barnard's *The Functions of the Executive*[14]—from which comes the epigraph at the head of this chapter. *The Functions* is of course widely and correctly viewed as a seminal work. But it is a commentary on the interests of the past generation that this discussion of morality has been generally ignored.

Barnard believed that "moral creativeness" was an essential executive function. As the quoted sentence indicates, he believed also that the burden assumed could lead to moral breakdown. In a similar vein Stephen Bailey, in the essay cited in observation Third above, uses the metaphor "above the timber line" to signify the severe moral climate in which the high executive must operate and the dangers to which he is exposed.

Fifth

We have recently seen, and we presently see, the growth of a gray area, an area in which any clear distinction between the categories of *public* and *private* disappears, disappears in a complex and subtle blending of new organizational modes and legal arrangements. In this gray area, hierarchy is diminished, but does not disappear; new lateral and diagonal relationships grow up and operate along with it, making it formally and operationally difficult to answer the question: Who's in charge here?

As I view it, our ethical problems are compounded in this growing gray world. Who will be responsible for what to whom? In what will duty consist and by what can honesty be judged? One view is that, with hierarchy relaxed and freedom increased, the way is open for the development of authentic *personal* morality. Harlan Cleveland seeks a solution in the hope and prescription that managers in the "horizontal"[15] world that is emerging will regard themselves as "public managers"—because in fact they will be. I confess that on most days I find it hard to share either of these two varieties of optimism.

Sixth

As the epigraph from David Bradley and Roy Wilkie indicates, "the raising of moral considerations" in the study of organizations has not been popular. Indeed, the chapter on Morality and Organizations in their *The Concept of Organization*[16] is, to my knowledge, without a parallel in the scores of general treatments of organizational behavior or theory.

A number of factors, some pertaining to American public affairs and without need of mention, and some pertaining to the general climate of our intellectual life that are beyond explicating here, suggest that there may be a change in the situation, that we will begin to address seriously the ethical dimensions of our organizational world—here I allow myself a bit of optimism. This may be best done—perhaps it can be done only—by working from the empirical base legitimated in recent social science. It might begin, for example, with mapmaking, along the lines suggested earlier. Later, just possibly, we may be able to address the ethical as such.

One point of view has it that ethical inquiry is dangerous. Samuel Butler put it this way: "The foundations of morality are like all other foundations: if you dig too much about them, the superstructure will come tumbling down." But in our case, the digging has been done; the superstructure is already down. But then, the old superstructure was not to our purpose anyway. Perhaps on a new foundation we can use some of the fallen materials to build a superstructure that *is* to our purpose?

Notes

1. Strictly speaking, *moral* signifies right behavior in an immediate and customary sense; *ethical* signifies right behavior as examined and reflected upon. But no warranty is given that this distinction is always made in what follows.
2. Certainly Robert T. Golembiewski's *Men, Management, and Morality: Towards a New Organizational Ethic* (New York: 1965) is an able and useful work, and I do not wish to demean it. But the picture in my mind is of a work even broader in scope, one taking into account developments of the past decade. Neither do I mean to slight the useful work of Wayne A. R. Leys, done when ethics was *really* unfashionable: *Ethics and Social Policy* (New York: 1946), and *Ethics for Policy Decisions: The Art of Asking Deliberative Questions* (New York: 1952).
3. The analysis set forth in this section is a brief version of that in my "Reflections on Public Morality" (6 *Administration and Society* [November 1974], pp. 267–282).
4. Paul Appleby, *Morality and Administration in Democratic Government* (Baton Rouge, La.: 1952).
5. Marver Bernstein, "Ethics in Government: The Problems in Perspective" (*61 National Civic Review* [July 1972], pp. 341–347).

6. Victor Thompson, *Without Sympathy or Enthusiasm: The Problem of Administrative Compassion* (University, Ala.: 1975).

7. Vincent Ostrom, *The Intellectual Crisis in American Public Administration* (University, Ala.: 1973).

8. See the symposium, H. George Frederickson, ed., "Social Equity and Public Administration" (*34 Public Administration Review* [January/February 1974], pp. 1–51).

9. F. William Howton, *Functionaries* (Chicago: 1969).

10. Frederick C. Thayer, *An End to Hierarchy! An End to Competition! Organizing the Politics and Economics of Survival* (New York: 1973).

11. Herman Finer, "Administrative Responsibility in Democratic Government" (*1 Public Administration Review* [Summer 1941], pp. 335–350).

12. Stephen Bailey, "Ethics and the Public Service" (*23 Public Administration Review* [December 1964], pp. 234–243).

13. Melville Dalton, *Men Who Manage* (New York: 1959).

14. Chester Barnard, *The Functions of the Executive* (Cambridge, Mass.: 1947). See especially Chapter 17, The Nature of Executive Responsibility.

15. Harlan Cleveland, *The Future Executive: A Guide for Tomorrow's Managers* (New York: 1972).

16. David Bradley and Roy Wilkie, *The Concept of Organization: An Introduction to Organizations* (Glasgow: 1974).

PART THREE

The Management of Government Agencies

5 Understanding Public Organizations

In this part of *Current Issues in Public Administration,* attention shifts from external relations to the internal dynamics of public agencies. Chapter 5 introduces organization theory, the many different approaches and theories to help explain behavior in organizations.

This chapter begins with Russ Linden's interpretation of the evolution of work in both business and public bureaucracies. While public administration is as old as Imperial China, Ancient Egypt, and the Roman Empire, Linden begins with the rise of the railroads, which he considers the first modern business in America. Linden traces work from craft to mass production, and then he focuses on the post office, schools, hospitals, and police departments. Linden tries to explain why public agencies so often have been fragmented and bureaucratic.

In the second article in this chapter, Bolman and Deal bring four perspectives to understanding organizations and especially to understanding organizational leadership. These four perspectives are:

- the structural frame,
- the human resource (or human relations) frame,
- the political frame, and
- the symbolic (or cultural) frame.

They are largely derived from sociology, psychology, political science, and anthropology, respectively.

Bolman and Deal take on one of the most slippery but most important of all organizational topics—leadership. They seek to clarify the definition of leadership and effective leadership behavior.

Most of their examples come from public schools, a context about which most of us know something. Few public organizations touch citizens—young people, their parents, and their communities—the way schools do. And the contemporary critique of schools, especially big city school systems, in many ways mirrors a larger concern about all public organizations. Education is an important segment of public administration—over half of all state and local employees work in education.

Computers, the Internet, the World Wide Web, software, artificial intelligence, telecommunications—all these terms are increasingly familiar to anyone in modern society and certainly to those who work in governmental administration. In the third article, James Perry and Kenneth Kraemer attempt to sort out the implications of rapidly changing information technology on public administration and public administrators. Perry and Kraemer examine the impact of technology on the nature of work and challenges presented. They stress state and local governments, where the vast majority—over fifteen million—of public employees in the United States work.

Chapter 5 looks at behavior inside public organizations. The key questions for students are:

- How did the evolution of work foster the bureaucratization of public agencies? How does this fit with Weber's theory of bureaucracy, which was covered by Blau and Meyer in the first article in Chapter 1?

- Which one of Bolman and Deal's four frames explains the most to you about how government bureaus actually work? Or does it take more than one frame?

- Why is administrative leadership so difficult, and how could it be improved in public agencies?

- In the terms suggested by Bolman and Deal, how would you describe the leadership of your high school principal (or some other top level public executive)?

- What are the main challenges to public agencies and public employees presented by the current trends in technology, and, as a result, what changes are necessary in public administration?

The Evolution of Work in Public and Private Bureaucracies

Russell M. Linden

The effort to provide a seamless experience for consumers may evoke a pleasant sense of déjà vu for many. Organizations that move quickly, that provide variety, customization, and personal service are actually relearning something that once came naturally. Indeed, the seamless organization is a kind of reincarnation of the individualized craft approach to producing goods and services, an approach that dominated the U.S. economy prior to the mid nineteenth century. It's not the same today, of course, because of vast changes in the scale of operations and the speed of communications and transportation. But the emerging seamless organization shares highly significant features with the general merchants, craftspeople, artisans, and farmers who were the backbone of the country's commerce two hundred years ago; it is reintroducing a holistic approach to work and direct, personal relationships with the consumers of its work.

PREVIEW

This [article's] purpose is to show how, and why, our public and private organizations have become fragmented and bureaucratic. I believe it is essential to understand this history so that we can avoid making the mistakes that led to the fragmentation of government in the first place.

While government and business differ in fundamental ways, they have many things in common. One commonality is a history of bureaucratic growth. As we will see, U.S. business and government organizations went through the same developmental stages, as industrial models provided the major influence on development of our governmental structures. Both industry and government began with small craftlike units led by a few generalists; they grew into large, segmented, fragmented bureaucracies characterized by division: of labor, of specialists, of management levels, of producers from consumers. For most of the past two centuries these divisions seemed to produce far more benefits than costs. Today, the costs have become unbearable, compelling us to learn how to replace division with a seamless focus on outcomes.

SEAMLESSNESS IN CRAFT PRODUCTION

As Alfred D. Chandler (1977) tells us, until the 1840s, the U.S. economy was dominated by generalists. Most people, of course, still worked on farms, and farmers understood all aspects of farming because they performed all, or almost all, of its tasks. In commerce, the general merchant dominated the scene. He performed all of the trading functions, from purchasing goods to financing and insuring the transactions. These generalists typically had a direct and personal relationship with the users of their products. Since most working Americans knew that they would see their customers over and over, they felt a sense of accountability. Trust developed, not trust born of some romantic ideal, but the kind of trust that comes from mutual interdependence and long-term relationships. Perhaps most important to us today, the gener-- alist was highly responsive to the customer's needs and could customize goods or services to the customer's taste.

As the nineteenth century progressed, the nature of work changed radically. Personal relationships yielded to impersonal ones, a holistic understanding and performance of work evolved into the division of labor and the fragmentation of work into its smallest elements, and work became a job for many Americans. No middle managers supervised the work of other managers prior to the 1840s. No staff specialists told line managers what to do: they didn't appear until the late 1850s. Then the industrial revolution separated the roles of producer and consumer, of owner and manager, and the modern organizational hierarchy segregated people into departments and divisions, managers and workers. Americans who once identified themselves by their craft or trade increasingly described themselves by which company they worked for.

FROM CRAFT TO MASS PRODUCTION: EFFICIENCY AND FRAGMENTATION IN WORK

In *The Wealth of Nations,* published in 1776, Adam Smith expressed his enthusiasm for a new idea, the principle of division of labor. He had observed two types of production in a pin factory: craft production and a group that divided their work into small, narrow tasks. The group that divided its labor showed vastly higher productivity.

Seventeen years later, in 1793, Eli Whitney invented the cotton gin, which quickly transformed the production of cotton in the United States. Again according to Chandler's (1977) account, cotton exports more than quintupled in the next eight years. Such quantities required financing, management, and distribution systems. A sequence of specialists—from jobber, importer, and cotton factor (who marketed the crop and financed the farmer) to broker and commission agent—participated in an efficient and impersonal chain that brought cotton to market. These changes brought to an end the personal and direct relations of the farmer and general merchant. As Chandler notes, "Rarely did a merchant know both the producer and consumer at either end of the long chain of middlemen, transporters, and financiers who moved the goods through the economy" (p. 48). Specialization had arrived on at least one major front in our economy.

Railroads as Our First Modern Hierarchies

Technology also gave rise to the railroads, which led to development of the first modern business enterprises in the United States. The railroads faced an unprecedented task: management of a large, dispersed organization spreading rapidly across an entire continent with thousands of workers and thousands of cars. The task was as daunting as it was risky. In an age of crude information management tools, it was very difficult to know the exact location of rolling stock. Many roads ran multiple trains on the same tracks; a mistake in scheduling could prove fatal. After one such disaster occurred in 1841 in Massachusetts, the resulting outcry moved the state legislature to investigate. An early version of a blue ribbon commission looked into the matter and issued a report that would bring a knowing smile to any government employee. The commission's recommendations produced our first developed bureaucratic hierarchy.

The hierarchy included several levels of supervisors and managers. It established clear responsibility and authority for each of three railroad divisions and created functional managers to run them. It included a headquarters in which senior managers were to oversee the divisional managers. Other managerial positions were added (master of transportation, assistant masters of transportation, master mechanics, superintendent), and each level was given a set of reports to complete and pass up the chain. Precise timetables were established, and detailed instructions on how to handle breakdowns were given to conductors. In the interest of safety and efficiency, an elaborate and highly rational organization was designed. It soon became the blueprint for other railroads and for large organizations in other industries.

By the 1880s, railroad leaders completed the modern business hierarchy, developing the line-staff-concept and modern accounting procedures, as well as information systems to control and evaluate the work of the many managers running the system. The organization chart of a typical railroad in the 1870s could be the chart of most large scale bureaucracies, then or now.

The impact of the railroads was widespread, both industrially and organizationally. Their growth required new financial arrangements. The new telegraph technology spread along the railroads' rights of way, providing a communications system that complemented the railroads. The railroads' speed of delivery led to a huge increase in the volume of mail. That new volume, in turn, required the U.S. postal system to develop a hierarchical system very closely resembling that of the railroads.

The Beginning of Scientific Management

The specialization and fragmentation of work advanced by several more steps toward the turn of the twentieth century, as a group of engineers began employing scientific methods to root out inefficiencies and waste in factories and organizational systems and to increase productivity through improved accounting, cost control, and gain-sharing plans to motivate workers.

The most famous of this group was Frederick W. Taylor. Obsessed with the rationalization of work, Taylor did scientific time and motion studies of the most productive workers in various plants to identify specific work methods that all should follow, as well as to document the amount to be paid in gain-sharing plans. The goal was to break a job down into the simplest tasks that could be done quickly and learned by someone with little education: "In his [Taylor's] system the judgment of the individual workman was replaced by the laws, rules, principles, etc., of the science of the job which was developed by management. . . . The whole attitude of Taylor in this respect was described by a mechanic who worked with him. . . . Taylor would tell him that he was 'not supposed to think, there are other people paid for thinking around here'" (Marshall and Tucker, 1992, p. 5).

In order to rationalize factory work processes, Taylor proposed development of a planning department made up of highly specialized "functional foremen" who divided up the activities of the general foremen they were to replace (Chandler, 1977). This new department would oversee operations of the entire plant, scheduling daily work plans for each unit and each worker. It would recruit, hire and fire, monitor workers' output, and analyze costs. Another generalist, the plant foreman, was about to be replaced by specialists.

Although there is little evidence of factory owners adopting Taylor's system just as he proposed it, he had a tremendous impact on the nature of management and the organization of work. His ideas influenced managers in both private and public sectors, and many factories incorporated the responsibilities of Taylor's functional foreman into an expanded group of staff specialists reporting to the plant manager. His work furthered the movement toward division of labor, specialization, rigid controls, and the separation of line and staff.

Ford and Sloan: System and Structure

The development of auto manufacturing is a microcosm of the country's movement from craft to mass production. Prior to Henry Ford's innovations, most auto manufacturers used a system of craftspeople to make and assemble the car. Highly skilled workers used flexible tools to make custom ordered cars, one at a time. Customers didn't shop at car dealerships—there were none to visit. Rather, they would visit a machine tool company and order a car to their specifications. The car was made by small groups of craftspeople, who thoroughly understood its engineering and design principles.

This craft system was decentralized. A small number of machine shops made the various parts, coordinated by an owner entrepreneur who had a direct relationship with everyone involved. No two cars were exactly alike, because they were made to order and because machine tools could not yet cut hardened metal to precise dimensions and mass produce a design. Such tools became available in 1906, and with them automakers were able to produce interchangeable parts. This technological advance meant that auto production would soon soar and the craftspeople would lose their place in the infant industry (Womack, Jones, and Roos, 1990).

Henry Ford followed in the spirit of Frederick Taylor, continually studying the production process and looking for ways to standardize it, rationalize it, root out waste, and improve productivity. By using the new precision machine tools, reducing the number of parts needed to build the car, and making them easy to attach, Ford made revolutionary gains in productivity—and brought the final demise of the craftsperson's usefulness in auto production.

Ford had a genius for organization and a profound distrust of anyone but himself. This combination led him to divide up everything that mattered about mass production.

> Ford took it as a given that his workers wouldn't volunteer any information on operating conditions—for example, that a tool was malfunctioning—much less suggest ways to improve the process. These functions fell respectively to the foreman and the industrial engineer, who reported their findings and suggestions to

higher levels of management for action. So were born the battalions of narrowly skilled indirect workers—the repairman, the quality inspector, the housekeeper, and the rework specialists, in addition to the foreman and the industrial engineer.... Ford was dividing labor not only in the factory, but also in the engineering shop. Industrial engineers took their places next to the manufacturing engineers who designed the critical production machinery. They were joined by product engineers, who designed and engineered the car itself [Womack, Jones, and Roos, 1990, p. 32].

In addition, Womack and coauthors show how the original "knowledge workers"—staffers who managed information but didn't understand how a car was built or even what the inside of a factory looked like—took the place of skilled craftsmen who in the past had handled all facets of production.

Ford's innovations didn't end there. He also invented the interchangeable worker. Ford was dealing with workers so diverse it makes our current work force look homogeneous. His employees spoke over fifty languages, and many spoke no English at all. To meet these challenges, he took division of labor to the extreme. He gave assemblers just one task. A worker would perform the same repetitive movement (such as put two nuts on two bolts) thousands of times a day. Ford also built on Taylor's concept of the staff specialist, creating quality inspectors, rework specialists, repairmen, and other workers never needed when craftsmen built the entire car and inspected their own work (Womack, Jones, and Roos, 1990).

Ford provided steady employment to thousands of workers at the then unheard-of industrial wage of $5 a day, and his productivity improvements and high sales volumes brought the Model T's cost within reach of working people. At the same time, he contributed mightily to the "de-skilling" of the U.S. worker, a problem we are only now beginning to confront.

Alfred Sloan completed the modern mass production system with his creation of the divisional structure at General Motors. Sloan took specialization another step when he established separate divisions for each car model (Oldsmobile, Buick, Pontiac, Chevrolet, and Cadillac), plus additional units for separate components (generators by Delco, steering gears by Saginaw, and so on). Divisions were organized by function (such as accounting, manufacturing, engineering), and each function was run by specialists. Sloan also created new staff specialists of financial management and marketing, giving each division its own dedicated experts. The division of labor had become complete.

The automakers' relations with labor unions only added to the system's fragmentation. Eventually, unions accepted the basic tenets of the mass production model and fought for job seniority and job rights. They wanted more—more security, more rights based on seniority, more job rules, and, of course, more money and benefits within the system. One could hardly blame them for such demands. Unfortunately, union priorities and management's treatment of unions only led to a more rigid work force that focused on equity, not organizational success and improvement.

In the mass production model, few people understood what it took to build a car from start to finish, but everyone knew what his or her individual job and unit did. The divisional structure, using the principles of mass production, became the model for virtually all manufacturing industries and most services. Work, and the workplace, had been rationalized and fragmented in ways that lowered prices, increased volume, and provided work for millions. Few Americans in the 1920s would have believed that organizational systems producing such manifest benefits would be overcome by their own built-in limitations.

FROM CRAFT TO MASS PRODUCTION IN GOVERNMENT: POST OFFICE, EDUCATION, HEALTH CARE, POLICE WORK

Our government agencies and their structures mirrored the movement from craft to mass production in U.S. business. Just as commerce two hundred years ago was dominated by generalist merchants, farmers, and craftspeople, the government was also run by a small number of generalists. A typical federal department in 1800 was administered by the secretary, aided by clerks and a small field establishment (White, 1963). There were no bureaus, no middle managers, few specialists. This simplicity was primarily a function of size; the county's population simply didn't require a large, central governmental bureaucracy. It was also due to ideology. As Matthew Crenson (1975) notes in his study of early U.S. bureaucracy, "Hostility toward 'bureaucracy' has been a durable feature of American political life for generations" (p. ix).

But as the country and its government grew, our government agencies were influenced by new management thinking. They developed a specialized, hierarchical form that reflected the bureaucracies emerging in the private sector. Growth and new technologies were partly responsible. In addition, fraud and corruption created demands for improved controls, and those demands led to checks and balances, more hierarchy, more layers of management. The organizational forms that emerged resembled those of the railroads and, later, the automakers. The move to rationalize and the need to control wrongdoing spawned bureaucracies heavy with senior administrators and staff specialists, bureaucracies that fragmented the work once done holistically by professionals. And in each case, the professional was further separated from the end user of services.

The country didn't want a large, controlling federal government; it distrusted the notion of career civil servants, yet it needed certain business done. Our first presidents found an answer to this dilemma by placing government departments in the hands of people chosen on the basis of character. There is a certain irony here, given that our Constitution had established a government of laws, not of people. But it was not until Andrew Jackson became president in 1829 that the notion of formal rules and regulations, impersonal standards, and performance measures was established. For an entire generation prior to Jackson, public officials were selected for their personal virtue and reputation for honesty.

The government that Jackson inherited was a highly personal, informal one: "Command ... was personal. Authority and responsibility for the affairs of an agency were concentrated in a single human being. The functioning of a department depended less upon its formal organizational apparatus than upon the personality and preferences of its chief. Indeed, formal organizational apparatus hardly existed. To a considerable extent, the agency was the creature of its chief—his character, his commands, and his personal taste" (Crenson, 1975, p. 51).

But Jackson didn't leave government as he found it. In spite of his own preferences, he began the growth of bureaucracy and specialization in U.S.

government. His change of heart was caused by abuses of public office. Just as hierarchical, bureaucratic systems were begun by the railroads in response to a problem (safety), the federal government created administrative layers to deal with a different problem: the use of public office for private gain. Since Jackson had been roundly criticized for expanding the spoils system in government, he had to be especially sensitive to allegations that his appointees were guilty of corruption. The abuses were first discovered in the Post Office Department, and it was there that our first nonmilitary government hierarchies grew.

Postal Service

Until the 1850s, the entire postal system was administered by three assistant postmaster generals and a few clerks: no middle managers, staff specialists, or transportation hubs. Each of the almost seventeen thousand local post offices in 1849 was run locally (Chandler, 1977). In essence, the system had been run during its first three decades by one man. Abraham Bradley, one of the first public officials to come to Washington when the government was established there in 1800, was the department's real power. The department became a "thing of his own making," as he supervised the letting and performance of contracts, all financial matters, and the behavior of local postmasters (Crenson, 1975, p.112). When he was forced out during Jackson's first term, his successors confronted a major dilemma. It seems that old Bradley had written very little down! There were a few official records, but most important information was noted on old scraps of paper or remained in his head. He must have been one of the first U.S. bureaucrats to use the strategy of building a power base by making himself indispensable.

Abraham Bradley's personal approach to administration didn't outlast him in the post office, because of the problems discovered there during Jackson's presidency. The major problems concerned the letting and oversight of contracts to deliver the mail. Since the Post Office Department had no transportation capability, it paid contractors to get the mail through. When a House committee investigated these contracts, it found plenty to report. A mail delivery route awarded to one contractor for $4,500 a year increased to $38,500 just twenty-four months later. Contractors provided unnecessary services to jack up prices; some charged for services that they never delivered (Crenson, 1975).

Congress's investigation of postal abuses led to a thorough housecleaning and a new postmaster general, Amos Kendall. Taking charge in 1835, Kendall brought in a trusted colleague to control finances. He then did what many bureaucrats do today when they want to make a splash and get people's attention: he reorganized. He split the country into two regions and assigned an assistant postmaster to each. More significantly, he separated the supervision of financial accounts from all other management responsibilities and took responsibility for overseeing the accounts himself. He thus established the principle of separation of powers in the federal administration. Checks and balances were being extended from the Constitutional framework to departments and agencies within the executive branch.

Congress furthered the trend a year later when it added a treasury department auditor to the post office staff. This auditor (and forty staff) oversaw department accounts, keeping a special eye out for abuses of contracts. Then, it created an additional system to control expenditures and abuse, which added to governmental fragmentation. It directed that all postal revenues be sent to the U.S. treasury, only to be returned later in the form of annual appropriations. Congress was far more concerned about curbing misconduct than about administrative productivity. As has often been noted, the framers of the Constitution worried about abuse of power, not about efficiency, and Congress followed in the same path. Finally, Kendall compounded the fragmentation when he replaced his two-region organization with a tripartite model: offices for appointments, contracts, and inspections, each run by an assistant postmaster. In a very short time, Amos Kendall and the Congress brought division of labor, specialization, and a degree of hierarchical bureaucracy to one of the country's largest government agencies.

In the ensuing decades, the Post Office Department developed an organizational structure very similar to that of the railroads. In 1855, to meet the increasing pace and volume of mail, Congress funded fifty distribution centers staffed by middle managers. They were given detailed position descriptions on how to coordinate the flow of mail. Specialized mail cars came into use. Difficult as it may be to imagine today, the newly organized postal system was considered highly efficient. By this time it was the government's largest operating agency, and as such it had no lack of political patronage. Still, it developed a highly professional cadre of managers who oversaw its growth (which continued until, in 1992, Postmaster General Marvin T. Runyon responded to a $2 billion deficit with the largest government reorganization in several decades, eliminating thirty thousand management and support positions and prompting the early retirement of forty-seven thousand workers). Hierarchy and bureaucracy were spreading in the federal government.

Education

Through the first half of the nineteenth century, those Americans who went to public schools were taught all their subjects by the same teacher. This individual passed on both the knowledge and the morals of the community and was expected to model the high standards taught in the classroom. Usually single, often male (females came to dominate later in the century), the generalist teacher had the important responsibility of helping to pass on the community's culture and beliefs.

As Marshall and Tucker (1992) have shown, a new model began to spread by the early 1850s. The one-room schoolhouse gave way to buildings in which students were divided by age. Some classes were led by teachers who specialized in different subjects. And students began to be separated into different ability groups.

By the turn of the twentieth century, the nature and purposes of public schools changed. The numbers of children going to school mushroomed, and for the first time many children went on to high school. Compulsory education meant mass education, and mass education required a new organizational approach. Reformers of the nineteenth and early twentieth century, indignant over the corruption and abuse of public office by politicians and their cronies, had been remaking local governments through the introduction of council-manager plans, giving the policy-making function to the elected officials while maintaining the ongoing administrative functions for a professional manager. The reformers were enthusiastic about the promise of scientific management and sought to apply its principles to education.

They began by replacing the ward system of school board appointments with a corporate style, giving a smaller number of (business)people a policy-making role. The boards would then select the superintendent, a professional to run the schools. The superintendents selected were attracted to the new scientific management methods and apparently borrowed from Taylor's concept of the large planning department in building their own central administrative staffs. Result: an explosion of administrators. According to the U.S. Office of Education, in 1899 there was an average of four central staffers in the 484 cities surveyed. Between 1890 and 1920, staff numbers grew exponentially: from 9 to 144 in Baltimore, 7 to 159 in Boston, 10 to 159 in Cleveland, and 235 to 1,310 in New York (Marshall and Tucker, 1992). The trend has continued to this day, unfortunately. In the New York public schools, the ratio of administrators to students is sixty times higher than in the New York City parochial school system (Peters, 1992).

More significant than the change in school governance was the application of scientific management methods to the schools' curricula and staff management. In order to fill the needs of the country's booming industries and to meet the perceived needs of the influx of immigrant children for whom English was a second language, schools were transformed into deliverers of an educational "product," one that fit the requirements of Henry Ford's mass production plants. Thus, conformity, precision, and regularity, the skills and attitudes needed in industrial employees, were emphasized. Factory labor required workers who showed up every day on time, took orders willingly, and did their repetitive tasks without complaint, and schools learned how to turn out such a product. Franklin Bobbitt, professor of educational administration at the University of Chicago and an influential proponent of Taylorism for the schools, said that efficiency depended on "centralization of authority and definite direction by the supervisors of all processes performed.... The worker [that is, the teacher] must be kept supplied with the detailed instructions as to the work to be done, the standards to be reached, the methods to be employed, and the appliances to be used.... [T]here can never be any misunderstanding as to what is expected of a teacher in the way of results or in the matter of method" (Marshall and Tucker, 1992, p. 17).

Schools divided knowledge into "subjects"—science, social science, math, reading—and each of those subdivided again and again. Following in the spirit of Adam Smith, many school leaders concluded that the nation's schools would be most efficient by dividing up the curriculum and giving teachers specialized roles. Just as there was "one best way" to organize work in the factory, there must be one best way to teach and to learn.

The schools, operating with scientific management efficiency, performed a wondrous achievement. They turned out millions of children, including many immigrants, who were literate in English, knew basic math, were punctual, understood the rules of work, and were willing to do the jobs required in the factories. That is no small accomplishment. The price we paid wouldn't show up until the second half of the century, when our economic competitors' productivity and quality started to exceed our own, in part because of the advanced skills of their workers. While other countries were investing in the education and development of their youth, we were mass producing an obedient but largely de-skilled work force. The "scientific" approach that reduced learning to its smallest, most fragmented elements and micromanaged teachers by dictating their every move, would prove disastrous for the country.

Health Care

Most Americans born before 1950 can remember being treated by a family doctor. Memories of the good old general practitioner are not a nostalgic fiction: for much of this century doctors had a generalist role, providing most, if not all, of the outpatient's medical care. And hospital staffs were far less specialized than they are now. The catalyst, again, was technology. Prior to the development of penicillin and other miracle drugs, most doctors were generalists because little specialization was possible.

The family doctor of the 1940s and 1950s would scarcely recognize the medical field today, as physicians increasingly engage in specialties and subspecialties. Prior to World War II, 77 percent of physicians were general practitioners. That number declined to 56 percent in 1955 and 31 percent in 1966 (Starr, 1982). According to an Associated Press article published in the *Daily Progress* of Charlottesville, Virginia (June 6, 1993), by 1992, the percentage of graduating medical students opting for generalist roles dropped to 15 percent. Today's hospitals are bastions of segmentation, for the patient (who encounters forty-eight different personnel during an average hospital visit) and for the professional. The 629-bed St. Vincent Hospital in Indianapolis, for instance, had 598 separate job classifications before it was reorganized, and over half of those slots had but a single occupant (Lathrop, 1991).

And the problem involves more than specialization. The entire field of health care providers is caught up in a range of activities that add little to the patient's health. A three-year study by Booz Allen & Hamilton described the situation in hospitals in stark terms: record keeping, scheduling, transporting, supervising, meetings, cleaning up, meal service, and idle time consume 84 percent of hospital personnel activity. "Put another way, for every dollar spent on direct care, we spend $3 to $4 waiting for it to happen, arranging to do it, and writing it down," noted J. Philip Lathrop, Booz Allen's vice president of health care practice (Weber, 1991, p. 24).

The Booz Allen study looked at one 650-bed acute care facility that provides a full range of health care services. It has a favorable financial position relative to comparable facilities in its state. The study found that, of each dollar this facility spends on employee wages,

- fourteen cents goes to scheduling and coordinating care,
- twenty-nine cents goes to documenting what is going on,
- twenty cents pays for idle time,
- eight cents goes to the hotel services hospitals provide,
- six cents pays for transportation services, and
- seven cents goes for management and supervision.

That leaves a paltry sixteen cents for actual health care. Lathrop (1991) places most of the blame on the health care industry itself: "No one told us to fragment our large hospitals into 150 responsibility centers or to manage our business—patient care—in a way that requires seven to nine layers of management between the CEO and the bedside caregiver.... No one dictated to us that to provide a chest film for an inpatient we should perform forty discrete tasks, involve fifteen different employees, or take three hours to do it all" (p. 18).

It hasn't always been this way, of course. Our health care system has evolved through many of the same stages that characterize private industry's development. In the first half of the nineteenth century, most Americans dealt with illness themselves. It was a personal and family problem, and they went to doctors rarely. As urbanization became a fact of life and more Americans separated work from home life, it became more difficult to care for the ill at home, and specialization crept into health care. Physicians became an accepted part of daily life. Two hundred hospitals existed by the 1870s, but they were dedicated more to charity and mental health problems than to the general public's health.

Spurred by the growing American love affair with science and technology, the number of hospitals exploded to over six thousand by 1920. Technological advances as well as financial incentives led more and more doctors into specialized practices. Hospitals could afford the newly developed equipment needed for many of the tests and procedures becoming popular. In addition, doctors (never a well-paid profession during the nineteenth century) found that they could treat more patients in their offices than at home; those too sick to go to the office were hospitalized. The result: home visits became obsolete as hospitals were transformed from communal, informal places to highly bureaucratic organizations. An orientation to wellness changed into treatment for disease. And hospitals went from the "periphery to the center of medical education and medical practice." What once were "refuges mainly for the homeless poor and insane" had become "doctors' workshops for all types and classes of patients" (Starr, 1982, p. 146).

Fragmentation, compartmentalization, and specialization characterize the organization of health care today. In health care, as in education and private industry, we have fragmented the work such that the once proud craftsperson/professional no longer performs the full scope of work and is increasingly separated from the patient.

Police Work

Those who can remember being cared for by the family doctor may also recall knowing the cop on the neighborhood beat. It wasn't long ago that most police departments in the United States were organized to support the patrolman or woman who walked the streets of a neighborhood, knew many of the residents, and often got their cooperation in preventing crime and apprehending suspects. Technology and applications of "modern" management systems have changed that, generally for the worse. But now many departments are becoming aware of this problem and returning to a holistic role for the police officer.

The evolution from the all-purpose cop on the beat to the highly trained, technology-driven police officer of the 1990s paralleled the development of our health care system, with one major difference. Like physicians, police officers played a generalist role through the nineteenth and early twentieth centuries. They knew the residents; they knew the community; they understood community issues and concerns. Specialization came with increasing professionalization of police work beginning in the 1930s and with the advent of sophisticated technology and exploding urban problems of the 1960s. The one major difference between the bureaucratization of police work and that of health care lies in the element of corruption.

Police were victims of the political spoils system that did so much damage to U.S. government through the mid to late nineteenth century. Municipal police departments began to form as early as the 1830s, often as a response to urban unrest and riots. Police chiefs were usually appointed by elected officials, who used their appointment power to reward political supporters. Many departments became corrupt tools of politicians, going after their political enemies and turning their heads when politicians' friends broke the law. Late nineteenth-century reforms helped reduce some of the corruption, especially that associated with hiring, but abuses continued, largely because corrupt elected officials continued appointing the department leaders. Major reforms followed in the 1930s, when a commission established by President Hoover made recommendations leading to the professionalization of the police. Higher education requirements, systematic training, professional standards for hiring and promotion, establishment of crime prevention units, and professionally appointed leadership turned politicized departments into professional ones (Trojanowicz and Bucqueroux, 1990).

Ironically, the very professionalization that led to major police improvements during the 1930s, 1940s, and 1950s led to serious problems in the 1960s and 1970s. For as departments became more professional, they began using scientific management tools that separated the patrolman from the community. Police division of labor, overreliance on technology, and specialization created a feeling of isolation in many communities, and that isolation was magnified by the urban explosions of the 1960s.

By the 1960s, the police were under siege. Excesses of radical protest movements spilled into the streets, and cops were often on the receiving end of the violence. The protest movements died down, but urban violence continued and escalated. Most departments pulled patrol officers off their walking beats and went to a random patrol/rapid response method. They put the cops into cars, equipped them with the latest technology, took them out of the neighborhoods they once patrolled, and instead gave them large areas to cruise. It seemed to make sense. As crime spread, as criminals became more sophisticated and their use of guns increased, police roles became narrower and more specialized. Investigations, narcotics, and youth divisions developed subspecializations to cope with escalating gang problems, drugs, and violence. Further, the spread of 911 emergency systems rapidly increased the numbers of calls going to the departments.

The situation was complicated by the courts. A tide of decisions protecting the rights of the accused forced police to spend huge amounts of time documenting what they were doing. Like the hospital personnel who devote far more time to paperwork, management, and reporting than to actual health care, police across the country faced a rising tide of paper in the 1970s and 1980s. It's doubtful that the social problems plaguing us would be any better if police had less paper to handle. However, like their colleagues in the schools and hospitals, police officers have found themselves separated from the work they signed on to perform and increasingly distanced from their chiefs by the ranks of middle managers who push paper and manage information. They work in highly specialized roles, they feel extremely limited in their range of options, and they have lost contact with people in the neighborhoods who once were their potential partners.

THE END, AND COST, OF MASS PRODUCTION

Thus, in several important parts of the private and public sectors we see the same patterns repeated. Individual generalists who work in personal relationships with their consumers are replaced by large, impersonal hierarchies in which work is reduced to its smallest elements and workers are separated from the consumers and from each other. Given the technologies developed during the nineteenth and early twentieth centuries and the country's need to feed and manage its growing numbers, it's doubtful that any other pattern could have developed. A producer-oriented era called for centralized, segmented organizations.

Separation in business (division of labor, specialized positions, separate "line" and "staff," and so on) was mirrored in government. Public agencies adopted similar management models. Moreover, many governmental reforms used the principle of separation to meet public demands for accountability and honesty. For instance, the Pendleton Act of 1883 tried to separate politics from administration in federal hiring; the council manager form of local government that emerged in the early twentieth century separated policy making from policy administration; and the rise of oversight boards and commissions created an additional layer of review, which separated management functions among two or more bodies.

The costs of separation have been enormous. While division of labor and specialization have allowed government agencies to manage complex problems, they also led to enormous fragmentation, overlap, and duplication. Worse, these relics of the mass production era have tied the hands of bright and committed civil servants and reduced the quality and effectiveness of government programs.

The costs show up in the proliferation of programs: the federal government has over 150 employment and training programs, administered by fourteen different departments (Gore, 1993). It shows up in the numbers of people whose job it's to check on, audit, or control others—700,000 employees, fully one-third of the federal nonpostal work force, according to one U.S. Office of Management and Budget estimate. And it shows up throughout state and local government as well. A study by the National Commission on the State and Local Public Service describes state and local government as "fragmented and balkanized." The budgetary process in many states is a nightmare, splitting one budget into several hundred bills. Authority at the local government level is fragmented among dozens of commissions and boards, which divides executive and legislative authority and makes it difficult to form coalitions around common interests. The legislative process sifts bills through endless committees, which break what should be broad comprehensive bills into hundreds of pieces. Personnel systems become absurd, which results in narrow job classification systems containing anywhere from 551 job titles (South Dakota) to as many as 7,300 (New York). As the commission concludes, the fifteen million state and local employees need to be turned loose from "command and control" and rule-bound systems that tie their hands and be given clear missions with authority and responsibility to achieve them (Ehrenhalt, 1993).

The costs show up in the turf wars that managers fight, encouraged by personnel systems that reward people by the size of their staffs and budgets. The costs show up in poor service to customers who have to put up with delays, shoddy quality, runarounds, and lack of accountability. And perhaps most insidiously, the costs are reflected in unspoken *assumptions*—that government *has* to be slow, will *always* buy from the lowest bidder, can *only* be organized in a fragmented manner. It's such assumptions, as well as outmoded structures and systems, that force otherwise smart and conscientious civil servants to do stupid things.

The rise of the consumer society, along with the development of review technologies, has transformed some organizations, giving them the capability to provide seamless service to their customers.

References

Chandler, A. D., Jr. *The Visible Hand: The Managerial Revolution in American Business.* Cambridge, Mass.: Harvard University Press, 1977.

Crenson, M. A. *The Federal Machine: Beginnings of Bureaucracy in Jacksonsian America.* Baltimore: Johns Hopkins University Press, 1975.

Ehrenhalt, A. "Hard Truths, Tough Choices: Excerpts from the First Report of the National Commission on the State and Local Public Service." *Governing,* August, 1993, pp. 47–56.

Gore, A. *Creating a Government That Works Better and Costs Less.* Washington: U.S. Government Printing Office, 1993.

Lathrop, J. P. "The Patient-Focused Hospital." *Healthcare Forum Journal.* July/August, 1991, pp. 16–20.

Marshall, R., and Tucker, M. *Thinking for a Living: Education and the Wealth of Nations.* New York: Basic Books, 1992.

Peters, T. J. *Liberation Management.* New York: Knopf, 1992.

Starr, P. *The Social Transformation of American Medicine.* New York: Basic Books, 1982.

Trojanowicz, R., and Bucqueroux, B. *Community Policing: A Contemporary Perspective.* Cincinnati: Anderson, 1990.

Weber, D. O. "Six Models of Patient-Focused Care." *Healthcare Forum Journal,* July/August, 1991, pp. 23–31.

White, L. D. *The Jacksonians: A Study in Administrative History. 1829-1861.* New York: Macmillan, 1963.

Womack, J. P., Jones, D. T., and Roos, D. *The Machine That Changed the World: The Story of Lean Production.* New York: HarperCollins, 1990.

Reframing
Organizational Leadership

LEE G. BOLMAN
TERRENCE E. DEAL

America's quest for better public organizations is also a plea for better leadership. Whenever an organization is not working, people look for leadership to make it better. Leadership is a hardy perennial that returns season after season to offer hope of reliable and effective ways to improve organizations. Yet the hopes have been repeatedly dashed. Is the promise of leadership illusory? Or have we not yet understood it well enough to bring it to fruition? Despite countless books and studies, no one has developed a widely accepted definition of what leadership is, nor what makes some leaders effective and others ineffectual. Yet Americans remain optimistic:

> For many—perhaps for most—Americans, leadership is a word that has risen above normal workaday usage as a conveyer of meaning and has become a kind of incantation. We feel that if we repeat it often enough with sufficient ardor, we shall ease our sense of having lost our way, our sense of things unaccomplished, of duties unfulfilled. (Gardner, 1985, p. 1)

COMMON-SENSE IDEAS OF LEADERSHIP

In the absence of any consensual view of leadership, a series of common-sense views of leadership have arisen. Debates about which is better confuse leaders and followers alike. The problem is that each view captures only part of what leadership is about.

The most prevalent common-sense conception equates leadership with power: "Leadership is the ability to get others to do what you want." This definition is too broad because it includes coercion and the naked exercise of force, very different from leadership. It is too limited because it omits the art and poetry of leadership: such things as values, vision, and passion.

A second lay definition suggests that leaders "motivate people to get things done." This idea emphasizes persuasion and example rather than force or seduction, and implies that leadership is to be judged by its product. But how do we assess leadership outcomes? Still missing from the definition is the question of purpose and values.

A third definition sees leadership as a participative, democratic process that helps followers to find their own way. Leaders help followers do what *they* want, rather than what the leader wants. This view rejects images of powerful leaders who manipulate sheep-like followers, but it risks turning leaders into weathervanes who simply turn in the direction of the prevailing winds.

A fourth common-sense definition is that "leaders provide a vision." This adds needed elements of meaning, purpose and mission, but it implies that vision is the solitary creation of a brilliant, forward-looking prophet. It also neglects to ask what happens if no one else shares or supports the leader's vision. This definition can be intimidating to potential organizational leaders who wait expectantly for the brilliant flash of insight that will finally free them to lead.

These views are only a sample of existing images of leadership. If this array is not confusing enough, consider the definitions offered by experts, scholars, and famous leaders in Table 5-1. The idea of leadership has survived for centuries, and almost everyone believes that it is important. The public keeps searching for more of it to solve the great social problems, including those in education. Yet the concept remains shrouded in controversy and confusion. School leaders, like leaders in other sectors, are often bewildered and puzzled. When they look to academics and consultants for help, they encounter a cacophonous chorus that adds to the confusion. In this article, we attempt to decompose the concept of leadership, and to distinguish it from related ideas. Our purpose is to provide a way out of the continuing conceptual confusion and give organizational leaders at least a rough map of the territory. We present several propositions that outline our view of what leadership is, what it is not, and what it might become. Our examples are primarily from education, our principal area of research, but the concepts here are applicable to a wide variety of other public and nonprofit organizations.

Table 5-1
Conceptions of Leadership

"Leadership is any attempt to influence the behavior of another individual or group." (Paul Hersey in *The Situational Leader*)

"Managers do things right. Leaders do the right thing." (Warren Bennis and Burt Nanus in *Leaders: Strategies for Taking Charge*)

"Leadership is the ability to decide what is to be done and then get others to want to do it." (Dwight D. Eisenhower)

"Leadership is the process of moving a group in some direction through mostly noncoercive means. Effective leadership is leadership that produces movement in the long-term best interests of the group." (John Kotter in *The Leadership Factor*)

"Leadership is the process of persuasion or example by which an individual (or leadership team) induces a group to pursue objectives held by the leader or shared by the leader and his or her followers." (John Gardner in *On Leadership*)

"Leadership over human beings is exercised when persons with certain motives and purposes mobilize, in competition or conflict with others, institutional, political, psychological, and other resources so as to arouse, engage and satisfy the motives of followers." (James MacGregor Burns in *Leadership*)

"Leadership is a particular kind of ethical, social practice that emerges when persons in communities, grounded in hope, are grasped by inauthentic situations and courageously act in concert with followers to make those situations authentic." (Robert Terry in "Leadership—A Preview of a Seventh View")

1. Leadership and Power Are Not the Same.

Most images of leadership suggest that leaders get things done by getting people to do something. Yet powerful people are not always leaders. Armed robbers, extortionists, bullies, traffic cops, prison guards, and used-car dealers all get people to do things, but few would see them as "leaders." We expect leaders to influence noncoercively and to generate cooperative effort toward goals that transcend the leader's narrow self-interest.

2. Leadership Is Different from Authority.

Leadership is also distinct from authority, even though leaders may have authority and authorities may be leaders. In many ways, the concept of authority is as controversial as leadership. Max Weber (1947) linked it to legitimacy. People voluntarily obey authorities when they believe their requests are legitimate and cease to obey if legitimacy is lost. Legitimate authority comes from three sources (Weber, 1947):

a. Traditional—we obey a particular custom or official because our ancestors did   .
b. Legal-rational—we obey people who hold certain offices, such as school principals, because we believe that they have the right to make decisions, a right based on the premise that the system will work better if we follow their directives
c. Charismatic—we obey a particular person because of an "uncommon and extraordinary devotion of a group of followers to the sacredness or the heroic force or the exemplariness of an individual and the order revealed or created by him" (Weber, 1947, pp. 358–359)

A leader cannot lead without legitimacy. The cooperation that leaders get must be primarily voluntary rather than coerced. But authority refers broadly to the phenomenon of voluntary obedience, including many examples (such as obedience to law) that fall outside the domain of leadership. As Gardner (1985, p. 7) put it, "The meter maid has authority, but not necessarily leadership."

3. Leadership and Management Are Not the Same.

One can be a leader without being a manager, and many managers could not "lead a squad of seven-year-olds to the ice cream counter" (Gardner, 1989, p. 2). The fact that managers are *expected* to lead can make it more likely that they will. But many teachers will attest vehemently that, if anyone in their school is providing leadership, "it sure isn't the principal."

Gardner argues against contrasting leadership and management too sharply because of the risk that leaders "end up looking like a cross between Napoleon and the Pied Piper, and managers like unimaginative clods" (Gardner, 1989, p. 3). He suggests several dimensions for distinguishing leadership from management. Leaders think longer-term and look beyond their unit to the larger world. They reach and influence constituents beyond their immediate jurisdictions. They emphasize vision and renewal. They have the political skills to cope with the challenging requirements of multiple constituencies (Gardner, 1989, p. 4).

4. Leadership Is Not Always Heroic.

Popular images of John Wayne, Bruce Lee, and Sylvester Stallone provide a distorted, romanticized, male-dominated view of how leaders function. Murphy (1988) wisely calls for recognition of the unheroic side of leadership. We need to recognize that leadership is always situational and relational, and that leaders are often not the most potent or visible force for change or improvement. Leaders may exemplify and represent important values without being flamboyant. Often, their most important and heroic achievement is to recognize and anoint unsung heroes and heroines whose day-to-day actions are the real basis for an organization's success.

5. The Demands for Leadership Vary by Context.

Images of the solitary, heroic leader focus too much on the actors and too little on the stage. We often overemphasize the influence of stars and underemphasize the significance of the supporting cast or the people backstage. Against the assumption that "leaders make things happen," it is important to consider the alternative proposition that "happenings make leaders." That proposition is reflected in Figure 5-1.

Requirements for effective leadership differ greatly in different situations. The Chancellor of the New York City Public Schools and the Superintendent of Schools in Cosmos, Minnesota (who is also principal of the district's elementary school) face very different challenges. Brookline High School (in a wealthy suburb of Boston) and Jamaica Plain High School (in inner-city Boston) are about two miles apart geographically, but light years apart in the problems facing their respective principals. No single formula for leadership is possible or advisable for the great range of situations that school leaders encounter.

6. Leadership Is Relational.

Leadership is often seen as a one-way process: leaders lead and followers follow. In reality, leadership is fundamentally a complex relationship between leaders and their constituents. Despite its many contributions, the "effective schools" tradition has sometimes added to the confusion by emphasizing "strong leadership" from principals, while deemphasizing collegiality and collaboration (Barth, 1990). Even the most sophisticated current models of school leadership typically accept the "one-way" assumption. Ames and Maehr (1989) and Bossert, Dwyer, Rowan, and Lee (1982) present

Figure 5-1

one-way causal models. They depict principals' instructional leadership as a consequence of factors *external* to the school, but solely as an independent variable with respect to *internal* school variables. Such an assumption misleads both research and practice. Cronin (1984) captures this issue well:

> The study of leadership needs inevitably to be linked or merged with the study of followership. We cannot really study leaders in isolation from followers, constituents or group members. The leader is very much a product of the group, and very much shaped by its aspirations, values and human resources. The more we learn about leadership, the more the leader-follower linkage is understood and reaffirmed. A two-way engagement or two-way interaction is constantly going on. When it ceases, leaders become lost, out of touch, imperial, or worse (Cronin, 1984, pp. 24-25).

Experienced public administrators feel and know all too well that leaders are not independent actors, and that their relationship with those they lead is not static. It is a two-way street: leaders both shape and are shaped by their constituents. Leaders often promote a new idea or initiative only *after* large numbers of their constituents already favored it (Cleveland, 1985). Leaders respond to what is going on around them. Their actions generate responses from others that, in turn, affect the leaders' capacity for further influence (Murphy, 1985). Leadership never occurs in a vacuum. It requires an organic relationship between leaders and followers.

7. Leadership Is Different from Position.

It is common to regard "school leadership" and "school administration" as synonymous. Although we look to administrators for leadership, it is both elitist and unrealistic to look *only* to them (Barth, 1988). Assuming that leadership is solely the job of administrators relegates everyone else to the pale and passive role of "follower." It also encourages managers to try to do everything, taking on more responsibility than they can adequately discharge.

Administrators are leaders only to the extent that others grant them cooperation and see them as leaders. Conversely, one can be a leader without holding an administrative position. There are opportunities for leadership from a variety of roles or groups. Good schools are likely to be those that encourage leadership from many quarters (Kanter, 1983; Bolman, Johnson, Murphy, and Weiss, 1990; Murphy, 1990):

> The relationship between teacher and principal is currently under sharp scrutiny. The top-down model is too unwieldy, is subject to too much distortion, and is too unprofessional. Problems are frequently too big and too numerous for any one person to address alone. Schools need to recognize and develop many different kinds of leadership among many different kinds of people to replace the venerable, patriarchal model. While much of the current literature suggests that effective principals are the heroes of the organization, I suspect that more often effective principals enable others to provide strong leadership. The best principals are not heroes; they are hero makers (Barth, 1990, pp. 145-146).

8. Good Leaders Need the "Right Stuff."

The last decade has spawned a series of studies of "good leadership," both in education (Brookover and others, 1987; Lezotte and others, 1980) and in the private sector (Bennis and Nanus, 1985; Clifford and Cavanagh,

1985; Conger, 1989; Kotter, 1982, 1988; Konzes and Posner, 1987; Levinson and Rosenthal, 1984; Maccoby, 1981; Peters and Austin, 1985; Vaill, 1982). The literatures in the two sectors have followed divergent methodological paths, and each has reached somewhat different conclusions.

Research on school leadership has been mostly correlational and based primarily on survey data. Test scores in reading and mathematics have served almost exclusively as the dependent variable (Bossert, 1988; Chubb, 1988; Murnane, 1981; Persell, Cookson, and Lyons, 1982; Rowan, Bossert, and Dwyer, 1983). By comparing schools with similar demographics but dissimilar test scores, researchers have concluded that effective schools are likely to have a principal "who is a strong programmatic leader and who sets high standards, observes classrooms frequently, maintains student discipline, and creates incentives for learning" (Bossert, 1988, p. 346).

The flurry of recent leadership in the private sector consists almost entirely of qualitative studies of organizational leaders, mostly corporate executives. Methodology has varied from casual impressions to systematic interviews and observation. Vision is the one characteristic of effective leadership that is universal across the private-sector reports. Effective leaders help to establish a vision, to set standards for performance, and to create a focus and direction for organizational efforts. While no other characteristic is universal, several appear repeatedly. One that is explicit in some studies (Clifford and Cavanagh, 1985; Konzes and Posner, 1987; Peters and Austin, 1985) and implicit in most of the others is the ability to communicate a vision effectively to others, often through the use of symbols. Another frequently mentioned characteristic is commitment or passion (Clifford and Cavanagh, 1985; Vaill, 1982; Peters and Austin, 1985). Good leaders care deeply about whatever their organization or group does. They believe that nothing in life is more important than doing something well, and they communicate that belief to others. A third frequently mentioned characteristic is the ability to inspire trust and build relationships (Kotter, 1988; Maccoby, 1981; Bennis and Nanus, 1985). Kouzes and Posner (1987) found that "honesty" came first on a list of traits that managers said they most admired in a leader.

Beyond vision, the ability to communicate the vision, and the capacity to inspire trust, consensus breaks down. The studies cited above, along with extensive reviews of the leadership literature (Bass, 1981; Hollander, 1978; Gardner, 1989), provide a long list of attributes associated with effective leadership: risk-taking, flexibility, self-confidence, interpersonal skills, "managing by walking around," task competence, intelligence, decisiveness, understanding of followers, and courage, to name a few. The problem is that nearly everyone has a different list.

9. School Leadership Takes Place in Organizations.

Research on school leadership is often disconnected from research on school organization. Bossert (1988) correctly notes that "a classical model of bureaucratic organization underlies much of the thinking about school effectiveness." Bossert argues for a "multi-level" view of the principal's leadership that emphasizes the leader's role in shaping instructional organization and school climate. Yet, even this view takes only partial account of the significant organizational features affecting school leadership.

Bolman and Deal (1984; 1991) argue that organizational research and administrative practice are seriously impaired because scholars and practitioners focus on only one or two of four critical aspects of multidimensional organizations. They propose that organizations need to be understood through four perspectives: structural, human resource, political, and symbolic. The *Structural Frame* emphasizes the importance of formal roles and relationships. Structures—commonly depicted in the form of organization charts—are created to fit an organization's environment and technology. Organizations allocate responsibilities to participants and create rules, policies, and management hierarchies to coordinate diverse activities.

The *Human Resource Frame* starts with the premise that organizations are inhabited by people who have needs, feelings, prejudices, skills, and limitations. They have great capacity to learn, and an even greater capacity to defend old attitudes and beliefs. From a human resource perspective, the key to effectiveness is to tailor organizations to people—finding an organizational form that enables people to get the job done while still feeling good about what they are doing.

The *Political Frame* views organizations as arenas where different interest groups compete for power and scarce resources. Conflict arises because of differences in needs, perspectives, and lifestyles among different individuals and groups. Bargaining, negotiation, coercion, and compromise are all part of everyday life in organizations. Every practitioner knows that politics are a major part of the school leader's job, yet much of the literature on the principalship says little about these issues. Even the intensely political features of the superintendency have been largely ignored by educational researchers (with a few significant exceptions, such as Cuban, 1988). A recent wave of "critical," "postmodern," and "deconstructionist" theory is explicitly political, but primarily offers a critique of existing institutions rather than offering guidance to practitioners wondering how to get on with the job in an imperfect world.

The *Symbolic Frame* abandons the assumptions of rationality that appear in the other frames. It treats organizations as tribes, theaters, cathedrals, or carnivals. In this view, organizations are cultures, propelled more by rituals, ceremonies, stories, heroes, and myths than by rules, policies, and managerial authority. Organization is theater: the drama engages actors inside, and outside audiences form impressions based on what they see occurring onstage. Myer and Rowan's (1977, 1978) work on formal structure as myth and ceremony, and Cohen and March's (1974) model of garbage-can decision-making are among the clearest applications of the symbolic frame to educational organizations, but such concepts have only partially been integrated into research and theory on school leadership.

10. Effective Leaders Are Flexible Thinkers.

Each of the four organizational frames offers a different view of leadership (summarized in Table 5-2). Structural leadership is reflected in the calls for more attention to instruction (Bossert, 1988). Structural leaders lead through analysis and design rather than charisma and inspiration. Their success depends on developing the right blueprint for the relationship between their school's goals and structure, and on their ability to get that blueprint

Table 5-2
Reframing Leadership

Frame	Effective Leadership		Ineffective Leadership	
	Leader Is:	Leadership Process	Leader Is:	Leadership Process
Structural	Social architect	Analysis, design	Petty tyrant	Management by detail and fiat
Human resource	Catalyst, servant	Support, empowerment	Weakling, pushover	Abdication
Political	Advocate	Advocacy, coalition-building	Con artist, hustler	Manipulation, fraud
Symbolic	Prophet, poet	Inspiration, framing experience	Fanatic, fool	Mirage, smoke and mirrors

Source: Adapted from Bolman and Deal, 1991.

widely accepted. Successful structural leaders create schools with high expectations and a clear sense of direction. Structural leaders who pay too little attention to other dimensions of organizational life are likely to be dismissed as shortsighted tyrants or insensitive bureaucrats.

Human resource leadership focuses on school climate, interpersonal relationships, and the values of shared governance, participation, and openness. Successful human resource leaders are catalysts and servant leaders. They build organizations whose success derives from highly committed and productive employees. Calls for the principal to build a positive school climate (Bossert, Dwyer, Rowan and Lee, 1982), to create a community of learners (Barth, 1990), and to empower teachers (Johnson, 1989) reflect the human resource view. But it is abundantly clear that many school administrators fear the negative side of this perspective: being labeled as wimp and weakling.

Most practicing school administrators recognize the political nature of the job. A group of big-city superintendents, gathered at a conference at the Harvard Graduate School of Education in early 1989, were asked, "What is the most vexing challenge that you currently face in your job?" Consider some of their responses:

> Getting a board of seven diverse people to become visionaries for the school district, while addressing their own personal and political needs—getting them to recognize that they are leaders for the entire district.

> I thought first of the vexing problem of giving a school board vision, but it's like teaching a pig to sing: the results are poor and it annoys the pig. I think the biggest challenge is the issue of minority achievement. Urban schools catch the dark and the different. I often talk about the relentless intractability of the job. Most of the problems don't seem to have solutions. You're choosing between the lesser of two evils, and that has personal costs.

One of my critical problems is getting people to love and care for these young people—having high expectations and being committed—and getting various publics to care about these young people, when 70 percent of our population does not have children in the schools.

My most critical problem is developing a comprehensive vision of what needs to be done to improve schooling in America, and getting stakeholders to buy into it. Having a vision does not help unless stakeholders buy it, add to it, make it their own.

All of those descriptions reflect central dimensions of political leadership: the need to deal with multiple publics with diverse interests and agendas, the ubiquity of conflict, and the problematic nature of the superintendent's capacity to influence. Only a few studies of school leadership have begun to deal with this reality (examples include Blumberg and Greenfield, 1988; Cuban, 1988; Murphy, 1990). Effective political leaders, like many of the superintendents quoted above, know how to develop agendas, build coalitions, and move their organizations forward. But political dynamics play themselves out on an elusive and slippery slope. Less effective or principled political leaders are likely to be seen as manipulators and con artists.

In the private sector, visionary leadership became the great fad of the late 1980s. Like many corporate fads, it seeped rapidly into discussions of school leadership but produced almost no careful discussion of what symbolic leadership is really all about. Several accounts of visionary and charismatic leaders in the private sector have appeared (for example, Carlzon, 1987; Conger, 1989; Konzes and Posner, 1988), but comparable studies of school leaders are scarce. A few case studies of charismatic school leaders (examples include Lightfoot, 1983; Stahl and Johnson, no date; Kauler and Leader, 1987a, 1987b) demonstrate that such leaders exist. Much more research is needed on the process by which vision emerges, and on the relationship of symbolic to other elements in leadership. Faith and meaning are central problems in education. The key dilemma for symbolic leaders is how to bring vision and inspiration without being seen as fools or shamans who use smoke and mirrors to create empty hope.

Each of the frames has its own vision or image of reality. Each is incomplete, but each captures a significant and powerful slice of organizational reality. Only when both scholars and practitioners can use all four are they likely to appreciate the depth and complexity of organizational life.

NEW POSSIBILITIES

Leadership is indispensable to significant improvement and reform in America's public schools and many other public agencies. It plays a central role in shaping missions, articulating values, setting directions, and building motivation. Leadership helps people move forward in the face of uncertainty about what to do, disagreement about how to do it, and doubts that it can be done. But leadership is a very challenging and arduous enterprise. When leaders in the public sector look for help on how to lead, they encounter a jangled, cacophonous chorus of ideas. Both academic literature and common-sense ideas about leadership confuse and frustrate highly motivated, well-intentioned administrators who want to do whatever they can to help their organizations succeed.

This article tries to sketch a better map of the terrain of organizational leadership. The map is incomplete, because the territory is only partly charted. We hope that readers can take the map, study it, revise it, fill in some of the gaps, and make it their own. In the process, they will experience both the joy of discovery and the satisfaction of knowing more clearly where they have been and where they might go next. *Far Side* creator Gary Larson once drew a cartoon showing dozens of heavily armed sheriff's deputies and police officers on a manhunt. They enthusiastically follow a single bloodhound who charges forward, nose to the ground, with only one unspoken thought: "I can't smell a damn thing!" School and governmental leaders need better maps. Otherwise, like the bloodhound, they may take a lot of people with them even when they have no idea where they are going. With the help of their colleagues and constituents, leaders will need to find or blaze new paths. Better maps make it easier to know which paths are likely to be roads to hell, and which might lead to the promised land of real and lasting improvement in educational and other public organizations.[1]

Note

1. This article is based in part on the research of the National Center for Educational Leadership, funded under a grant from the Office of Educational Research and Improvement of the U. S. Department of Education. Some ideas in this paper originally appeared in *Reframing Organizations: Artistry, Choice and Leadership* (Bolman and Deal, 1991). We are grateful to our colleagues in NCEL, whose insights and counsel have enriched and expanded the ideas in this paper.

Bibliography

Ames, R. and Maehr, M. A research agenda for the Center for Research and Development on School Leadership. Paper presented at AERA, San Francisco, March, 1989.

Barth, R. "Principals, Teachers, and School Leadership." *Phi Delta Kappan,* **69** (9), May 1988, 639–642.

Barth, R. *Improving Schools from Within.* San Francisco: Jossey-Bass, 1990.

Bass, B. M. *Stogdill's Handbook of Leadership: A Survey of Theory and Research.* New York: Free Press, 1981.

Bennis, W., and Nanus, B. *Leaders: Strategies for Taking Charge.* New York: Harper, 1985.

Blumberg, A., and Greenfield, W. *The Effective Principal: Perspectives on School Leadership.* Boston, MA: Allyn and Bacon, 1988.

Bolman, L. G., and Deal, T. E. *Modern Approaches to Understanding and Managing Organizations.* San Francisco: Jossey-Bass, 1984.

Bolman, L. G. and Deal, T. E. *Reframing Organizations: Artistry, Choice and Leadership.* San Francisco: Jossey-Bass, 1991.

Bolman, L. G., Johnson, S. M., Murphy, J. T., and Weiss, C. H. Re-Thinking School Leadership. Cambridge, Massachusetts: National Center for Educational Leadership, Harvard University, Occasional Paper No. 1, 1990.

Bossert, S. T., Dwyer, D. C., Rowan B., and Lee, G. "The Instructional Management Role of the Principal." *Educational Administration Quarterly,* 18, 1982, 34–64.

Bossert, S. T. "School Effects." In Boyan, N. J. (Ed.) *Handbook of Research on Educational Administration.* New York: Longman, 1988.

Brookover, W., Bready, C., Flood, P., Schweitzer, J., & Wisenbaker, J. *School Social Systems and Student Achievement: Schools Can Make a Difference.* New York: Praeger, 1987.

Burns, J. M. *Leadership.* New York: Harper, 1978.

Carlzon, J. *Moments of Truth.* Cambridge, MA: Ballinger, 1987.

Chubb, J. E. "Why the Current Wave of School Reform Will Fail." *Public Interest,* 90, Winter 1988, 28–49.

Cleveland, H. *The Knowledge Executive: Leadership in an Information Society.* New York: Dutton, 1985.

Clifford, D. K., and Cavanagh, R. E. *The Winning Performance.* New York: Bantam Books, 1985.

Cohen, M., and March, J. G. *Leadership and Ambiguity.* New York: McGraw-Hill, 1974.

Conger, J. A. *The Charismatic Leader.* San Francisco: Jossey-Bass, 1989.

Cronin, T. E. "Thinking and Learning about Leadership." *Presidential Studies Quarterly,* 1984, 22–34.

Cuban, L. *The Managerial Imperative and the Practice of Leadership in Schools.* Albany, NY: State University of New York Press, 1988.

Gardner, J. *The Nature of Leadership.* Washington, DC: The Independent Sector, 1985.

Gardner, J. *On Leadership.* New York: Free Press, 1989.

Hersey, P. *The Situational Leader.* New York: Warner, 1984.

Hollander, E. P. *Leadership Dynamics.* New York: Free Press, 1978.

Johnson, S. M. Teachers, power, and school change. Paper presented at Conference on Choice and Control in American Education, University of Wisconsin-Madison, May, 1989.

Kanter, R. M. *The Change Masters.* New York: Simon and Schuster, 1983.

Kaufer, N., and Leader, G. C. "Diana Lam (A)." Boston: Boston University, 1987a.

Kaufer, N., and Leader, G. C. "Diana Lam (B)." Boston: Boston University, 1987b.

Kotter, J. P. *The General Managers.* New York: Free Press, 1982.

Kotter, J. P. *The Leadership Factor.* New York: Free Press, 1988.

Kouzes, J. M., and Posner, B. Z. *The Leadership Challenge: How to Get Extraordinary Things Done in Organizations.* San Francisco: Jossey-Bass, 1987.

Levinson, H., and Rosenthal, S. *CEO: Corporate Leadership in Action.* New York: Basic Books, 1984.

Lezotte, L., Hathaway, D. V., Miller, S. K., Passalacqua, J., & Brookover, W. B. School Learning Climate and Student Achievement: A Social Systems Approach to Increased Student Learning. Tallahassee: The Site Specific Technical Assistance Center, Florida State University Foundation, 1980.

Lightfoot, S. L. *The Good High School.* New York: Basic, 1983.

Maccoby, M. *The Leader.* New York: Ballantine, 1981.

Meyer, J., and Rowan, B. "Institutionalized Organizations: Formal Structure as Myth and Ceremony." *American Journal of Sociology,* 30, 1977, 431–450.

Meyer, J., and Rowan, B. "The Structure of Educational Organizations." In M. W. Meyer and Associates, *Environments and Organizations: Theoretical and Empirical Perspectives.* San Francisco: Jossey-Bass, 1978.

Murname, R. J. "Interpreting the Evidence on School Effectiveness." Teachers College Record, 83(1), Fall 1981, 19–35.

Murphy, J., "Preparing School Administrators for the Twenty-First Century: The Reform Agenda." In B. Mitchell & L. L. Cunningham (Eds.), *Educational Leadership and Changing Contexts of Families, Communities, and Schools* (the 1990 NSSE yearbook). Chicago: University of Chicago Press, 1990.

Murphy, J. T. *Managing Matters: Reflections from Practice.* Monograph, Harvard Graduate School of Education, Cambridge, Massachusetts, 1985.

Murphy, J. T. "The Unheroic Side of Leadership: Notes from the Swamp." *Phi Delta Kappan,* 69(9), May 1988, 654–659.

Murphy, J. T. "Searching for Leadership: From Hacksaw to Pogo." *Phi Delta Kappan,* in press.

Persell, C. H., Cookson, P. W., & Lyons, H. "Effective Principals: What Do We Know from Various Educational Literatures?" Paper prepared for the National Conference on the Principalship, convened by the National Institute of Education, October 1982.

Peters, T. J., and Austin, N. *A Passion for Excellence.* New York: Random House, 1985.

Rowan, B., Bossert, S. T., and Dwyer, D. C. "Research on Effective Schools: A Cautionary Note." *Educational Researcher,* April 1983, 24–31.

Stahl, E., and Johnson, S. M. "The Josiah Quincy School." Cambridge, MA: Harvard Graduate School of Education, no date.

Terry, R. "Leadership: A Preview of a Seventh View." Minneapolis: Humphrey Institute of Public Affairs, University of Minnesota, 1986.

Vaill, P. B. "The Purposing of High-Performance Systems." *Organizational Dynamics,* Autumn 1982, 23–29.

Weber, M. *The Theory of Social and Economic Organization.* Translated by T. Parsons. New York: Free Press, 1947.

The Implications of Changing Technology

James L. Perry
Kenneth L. Kraemer

New technologies are frequently described as "transforming," or "having the potential to transform," state and local governments and society more generally. In fact, however, technology has rarely been shown to have such effects. Rather than transforming state and local governments, technology has been adapted by government leaders to fit their perceptions of the opportunities and threats of its application. For the most part, such adaptive application of technology has been incremental and evolutionary rather than dramatic and revolutionary. Taken together, however, incremental, evolutionary change can, and often does, affect the way in which state and local governments operate. And these effects have implications for the public service.

We examine three broad questions with respect to changing technology:

1. What will be the effects of technological developments on the state and local public service during the 1990s?
2. What are the implications of these technological effects for the recruitment, development, and retention of government personnel?
3. What are ways of dealing with these implications?

This chapter seeks to address these questions with respect to technology generally, and with respect to information technology in particular. We focus on information technology because it is pervasive in governments and will become more so during the next decade and beyond. Ninety percent or more of all state and local governments have adopted computing, and computing accounts for about 3 percent of state and local government operating budgets

(Kraemer, King, Dunkle, and Lane, 1989; Caudle and Marchand, 1989). The ratio of computing devices to state and local government employees currently is about 1:200 and is expected to reach 1:1 by early in the twenty-first century. Most applications of computing in government currently are conventional and oriented toward business functions rather than service delivery. The productivity improvements from these applications are marginal for the most part, or confounded with other improvements and difficult to identify and measure. However, productivity gains are expected to be greater in the future as more emphasis is placed on applications that radically restructure service delivery. These developments will only increase the pervasiveness of information technology.

THE EFFECTS OF TECHNOLOGICAL CHANGE

Our review of research and practice indicates that the effects of information technology can be broadly classified into two general areas: (1) the activities performed by government and (2) the nature of work. These effects are generally well documented by individual studies, empirical surveys (both cross-sectional and longitudinal), and/or literature reviews. However, not all effects are equally well understood, as will become apparent below.

Activities Performed by the Government

Over the last twenty years or more, it has become apparent that information technology is altering the activities performed by state and local governments. It has resulted in the creation of new government functions and institutions—the information systems function and the management information specialist (MIS) department, the telecommunications function and the Office of Telecommunications, the information resources management (IRM) function and the IRM Office (Andersen and Dawes, 1991). Information technology also is altering the social organization and distribution of activities in government and is changing the broad processes by which work is carried out within and between government institutions.

Social Organization and Distribution. Information technology facilitates more diverse forms of social organization and distribution of governmental activities. For example, it permits either centralized or decentralized organization and central or local distribution of the activities of government while also permitting greater central monitoring and control. Historically, mainframe computers have been viewed as facilitating greater centralization. The advent of microcomputers is viewed as facilitating greater decentralization. In fact, computing has always facilitated either approach, or a mix thereof, and still does today (Attewell and Rule, 1984; Robey, 1981).

It is also the case that particular advances in the technology seem to coincide with administrative reforms or trends and reinforce one another. This was true in the 1950s with the introduction of the computer and centralized accounting and budgeting, in the 1960s with time sharing and intergovernmental systems such as the National Crime Information Center/Computerized Criminal History (NCIC/CCH), and in the 1970s with large-scale computer networks and service integration. Throughout the eighties, there has been a trend toward decentralization of federal government activities to the states and, in turn, from the states to local governments. This decentralization trend will continue and perhaps even accelerate during the nineties. It will be facilitated by the increasing availability of computer networks, databases, electronic mail systems, and microcomputers at each level of government and throughout the federal system.

It is important to recognize that information technology has not brought about the trend toward decentralization, just as it did not bring about the earlier centralizing trends. Rather, it has been brought about by changes in perceptions of what governments can and should do, and by political or managerial ideologies (King, 1984; Kraemer, Dickhoven, Tierney, and King, 1987). However, information technology does facilitate the trend toward decentralization and will do so even more in the future because of decreases in cost combined with increases in the processing power and storage capacity of newer computer systems.

Information technology also changes the terms on which small-scale information processing competes with mass processing. It permits rapid and frequent changes of products and services, and it permits frequent changes in processes themselves. A possible effect therefore is that government workplaces will be smaller and more distributed, more flexible and changeable, and closer to the clients they serve. This can be seen in various efforts over the years to create "little city halls" and distributed service centers with the aid of computerized information systems that allow central records to be directly accessed and changed locally (Kling, 1978; Kraemer and King, 1988).

A related change is the distribution of workers themselves. The bulk of government workers will continue to be located in central places like the statehouse, the county hall of administration, and city hall. Some will be decentralized to distributed workplaces such as regional offices, metropolitan subcenters, and little city halls. Still others will work at home with a link to the office via the computer and telecommunications; that is, they will "telecommute." The proportion of such workers is estimated to be around 10 million nationally by the year 2000. Whether it reaches such numbers or not, government workers are likely to be among such telecommuters because of the "services" nature of their jobs. The type of workers who will telecommute first and foremost are those who already work at home, such as computer professionals, writers and editors, handicapped workers, and "piece workers." For the most part, work at home will not replace work at the office but will supplement it. That is, workers will work certain days (or parts of days) at the office and the remainder at home (Vitalari and Venkatesh, forthcoming).

Changes in Work Processes. The foregoing changes in social organization and distribution of activities will be reflected in changes in the processes by which work is carried out within and between institutions. Although the possible changes are many, four are especially important: co-production, sophisticated coordination and optimization, automation of direct services to citizens, and electronic communication with citizens.

Co-production refers to the increasing mix of public, private, and voluntary institutions in the provision of services to citizens. Although there are more sophisticated examples of co-production, the simplest is found in the volunteer fire and emergency services found in many small communities. The municipal governments provide and maintain the equipment and train and insure the volunteers, but the actual services are carried out by citizens who are notified of emergencies by beepers and other special signaling devices and who can call a special number where a recording tells them the nature of the emergency and the response that is to be mounted. Information technology will enable such innovation in other services as well.

Coordination and optimization refers to the ability of government agencies in far-flung locations to coordinate their activities and to optimize them in terms of some overall interest. Although such systems seldom currently exist in state and local governments, the prototypes exist in the federal government and can be extended to state and local governments for purposes such as job matching and eligibility determination.

A modest example at the state level is Colorado's job bank, a system that exists in other states as well. Most of Colorado's major cities and counties are linked through a central computer to a system that keeps track of participants in job training programs and job openings and allows social service personnel to match job openings to clients' backgrounds and qualifications. A logical extension of this system is to provide terminals for both employers and employees so that they can enter job openings and resumes and do searches for a match on their own (Gurwitt, 1988).

Automation of service delivery refers to the completely computerized handling of requests for information or service. Many examples are already in operation around the country. Several cities have automated citizen access to public services such as building inspections and bibliographic retrieval (from public libraries) and to public records such as land records, tax records, vital records, business licenses, and other "public" information.

For example, Dallas, Texas, has a system for the scheduling of building permit inspections. Instead of calling a city office that is only open from eight to five to schedule an inspection, builders can now call the building inspection office at any time of the day or night. The phone is answered by a microcomputer with a voice response system, which asks them to key in information about the building on a push-button phone. It then gives them a time for an inspection. At the inspection office, that information is then fed automatically to a mainframe computer, which goes on to arrange inspectors' daily schedules and routes (Gurwitt, 1988).

Another example is provided by experiments in Ramsey County (St. Paul), Minnesota, the state of Washington, and Berks County, Pennsylvania, that involve rethinking the way in which public assistance payments are made to individuals. Instead of issuing checks, which the welfare recipients then have to take to the bank to get cashed, the county is issuing bank cards for welfare recipients who can then use them at ATMs around the county to draw out cash against their public assistance accounts. Like any other bank cards, these cards have an expiration date and so the individual's eligibility and assistance is reexamined before a new card is issued. In addition, the cards and/or the ATMs can be programmed with information that limit the amount of any one cash withdrawal, the number of cash withdrawals within any time period, or other user options to encourage cash management (Gurwitt, 1988).

Electronic communication with citizens can occur in a variety of ways, but most frequently it is occurring through the automated handling of citizen requests for information and complaints and through two-way, interactive electronic mail and dialogues. An example is provided by Santa Monica. California's Public Electronic Network (PEN). Anyone with access to a personal computer, once registered with the city, can use PEN to obtain information about city council hearings or city commission activities; to communicate with city staff, city council members, and other city officials; or to engage in a "public dialogue" on community issues such as rent control, the environment, the economy, women's issues, or senior citizens' issues. Computer terminals are located in city hall, public libraries, senior citizen centers, other public buildings, and shopping malls to facilitate access by people without computers (Richter, 1991).

The Nature of Work

As might be expected from the foregoing changes, the new information technologies are changing the nature of work in state and local governments. Empirical research conducted over the last twenty years shows that the increasing automation of work processes is producing several changes, including (1) a speed-up of work, (2) a tighter coupling of work, (3) greater independence for professional and staff workers and greater interdependence for operations workers, (4) greater control over people for managers and professionals and greater control over jobs for clerical and administrative workers, and (5) greater flexibility in work organization.

Speed-up. Computerization has produced a speed-up of work at all levels within government, ranging from street-level workers to office workers to professional workers to policy makers and managers. The speed-up has occurred because the technology allows individuals to work faster, shortens the cycles for processes such as billing, paying and collecting, and records information in real time, as events and actions occur, and thereby creates an expectation for fast response. An important effect of this speed-up is a general increase in time pressures felt by all types and levels of workers (Danziger and Kraemer, 1986).

Tighter Coupling. Information technology is also creating a tighter coupling of work, especially where individuals from several different governmental departments and functions are tied together in a single system such as a financial system, personnel system, geographic information system, or emergency dispatch system. A tighter coupling of work means that what a person does in one part of the organization triggers decisions or action by others, or that what people do in their own parts of the organization creates a picture of something happening that all must respond to in a coordinated fashion. The former is illustrated by the case of a building inspection that discovers serious health, safety, and environmental hazards and triggers the need for response by the fire department (hazardous materials), health department, and police department. The latter is illustrated when the independent actions of these departments result in determinations that taken together suggest that a building must be vacated, sealed off, and torn down because of the total set of hazards present and the improbability of their amelioration.

Greater Independence and Interdependence. There is growing interdependence among some work groups as a result of automation, but there is also a growing independence for others. Information technology appears to increase the independence of highly professional and specialized work groups such as engineers, planners, economists, statisticians, management analysts, and staff analysts. These groups have always been able to function relatively independently, and computing has only increased their independence at the margins. It has done so by providing them with direct hands-on access to the technology, to data, and to the power to manipulate data in order to produce information relevant to their jobs. This increased capability has tended to heighten their stature and their independence of action (Danziger and Kraemer, 1986).

In contrast, the extension of computing into government has increased the interdependence of office work groups at the operational level, especially when they rely upon one another for input of data (and its accuracy, timeliness, format), for processing cases and clients in a sequence of steps, or for manipulations of data that form the basis for action by others (for example, forecasts or work schedules). The groups most often affected are the clerical, administrative, and managerial in both operational and staff functions such as finance and personnel, planning and building, fire and police, and across these functions (for example, geographic information systems, financial systems, and personnel systems).

Control over People and Jobs. Information technology (IT) has been shown to increase potential for control of individuals and jobs while actually increasing the autonomy of particular roles. First, IT provides a higher level of organizational control and greater capacity for judging performance via computerized monitoring systems built into the operating systems of government. This capacity for work monitoring via the computer is now a reality for professionals as it has been for clerical and administrative workers (Bjorn-Anderson, Eason, and Robey, 1986).

Second, managers and professionals generally enjoy greater increases in control attributed to computing than do clerical and administrative workers (Danziger and Kraemer, 1986). However, computerized systems also can make the task of control more difficult, especially for those in superordinate roles who themselves become dependent on the technology. For example, a study of supervisors and customer service representatives in a large public utility (Kraut, Dumais, and Koch, 1989) found that as a result of installing a new customer inquiry system, the supervisors' work was made both more difficult and more technology-dependent. In the past, supervisors had known the jobs of their subordinates because they themselves had previously been customer service representatives. However, with the introduction of the new computerized system, supervisors' knowledge was suddenly obsolete, and, they did not possess nor were they provided with training to develop the skills they needed to operate in the new computerized environment.

Third, computerization has increased workers' sense of control over certain aspects of the job, including mastery over relevant information and improved communications. This has especially been the case for clerical and administrative jobs, and it has been accompanied by an increase in time pressures (Kraemer and Danziger, 1990).

Greater Reliability. The most significant impact of IT on work organization is that the technology enables managers and policy makers to choose whatever structural arrangements they desire, including combinations of structural arrangements. IT does not determine work organization; it facilitates it. Although information technology may enhance employee skill and autonomy, thereby facilitating decentralization and distribution of work, it also facilitates hierarchical control and task fragmentation (Bjorn-Anderson, Eason, and Robey, 1986). For example, hierarchical control and task fragmentation are facilitated by information technology when efficiency is the primary goal, the organizational scope is limited, capital cost is low, equipment reliability is high, workforce interest is low, and computerized monitoring is effective (for example, in the mail room or central records department of a state or local government organization). This fact highlights the importance of recognizing that the organization of work is at least as much a matter of political/managerial choice as it is of function/task necessity. It is a matter of choice about the structure of governance in organizations (Kraemer, 1991).

Summary

As the foregoing suggests, the effects of information technology are being felt at all levels of state and local government. There are many areas where we do not yet know or have a completely clear idea of the effects, but we have been able to draw some conclusions. IT has generated opportunities to reconfigure relationships, including those between levels of government, among subunits of the same jurisdiction, and between levels within state and local governments. The effects of IT on the activities of state and local governments and the organization of work have had ramifications for the nature of work itself. State and local government employees are experiencing greater time pressures, tighter coupling of their work activities, and changes in dependence and autonomy. In toto, the effects of technological change on state and local governments require the greatest adjustments for public service since the reform movement of the early twentieth century.

TECHNOLOGY'S CHALLENGE FOR THE STATE AND LOCAL PUBLIC SERVICE

The processes of technological change will have substantial implications for the composition, skills, organization, and psychological disposition of the state and local public service. They pose substantial challenges for public service in five respects: (1) worker displacement; (2) the creation of new jobs; (3) skill transformation; (4) redefinition of the temporal, physical, and social meaning of public service; and (5) technology-induced stress. These challenges and their linkages to effects of technological change are discussed next.

Worker Displacement

The restructuring of work will displace large numbers of employees. For example, information technology has reduced, and will continue to reduce, the demand for middle managers through the creation of organizationwide information networks (Millman and Hartwick, 1987). These networks through the capabilities they provide for messaging, broadcasting, scheduling, and so forth, eliminate or at least reduce the need for some middle manager functions related to the collection, reduction, transmission, and distribution of information. At the same time, middle managers will have increased requirements to help define and manage automation projects both within their own area and with others (Osterman, 1986).

Information technology will continue the long-standing automation of the less skilled workforce and the impact will be greater in the office than at the street level. IT will also result in greater automation of physical processes such as waste water treatment, flood control, and traffic signal control, and consequently it will reduce the number of blue-collar workers in state and local governments. For example, in waste water treatment the opening and closing of valves, the monitoring of flows, and the testing for water quality, which were previously done by people, are now done automatically by IT applications. Moreover, the use of IT in the planning and design of these facilities and processes has increased the ability of engineers and designers to simulate the systems in advance of their construction and to make changes that further reduce the need for people to operate them.

The shifts in the occupational structure of the state and local public service, however, are not likely to mirror those of the American economy as a whole. Worker displacement in the state and local government sector due to technological change is likely to differ radically from most other sectors of the American economy because of a variety of institutional factors. One of these is the nonmarket character of most state and local government activities, which is likely to affect displacement in several ways. First, relatively few workers will be displaced through ordinary processes of displacement—plant shutdowns, business failures, or relocations—because of the essential character of most public services and their restriction to a specific geographic area. Displacement in a traditional sense will be limited to workers whose jobs (in contrast to organizations) are eliminated or who may be placed on long-term or permanent layoff, although decisions to privatize certain public services could have more far-reaching consequences.

Another reason that the role of technological innovation in state and local government, particularly information technologies, is likely to differ from the economy as a whole is that the role of technological innovation is more ambiguous. Technological changes may be adopted as a means for enhancing efficiency, but other non-efficiency-inducing motivations might also influence their adoption. State and local officials may pursue an innovation as a means of enhancing the quality of services or their own professional or political standing and visibility. To the extent that technologies are adopted for nonefficiency reasons, worker displacement is less likely to be one of the human resource consequences of the decision.

Traditional sources of displacement are also likely to be attenuated by job security practices in state and local governments, which will direct policy makers toward other strategies, such as attrition, as adjustment mechanisms. Thus, to the extent that certain occupational groups suffer from technological change, the manifestations of the displacement are likely to be managed either through changes in in-flows (for example, recruitment) and out-flows (for example, attrition) or hidden within the internal labor markets of state and local government organizations. Given the probable processes of worker displacement in the state and local government sector, compositional shifts in skill levels (Spenner, 1988), that is, occupational changes, occurring as a result of worker displacement are likely to be dramatic only when viewed in the long term.

Creation of New Jobs

Another long-term consequence of technological change will be the creation of entirely new functions and jobs in government. Completely new categories of organizational activity, such as technology policy, technology development, information resources management, and telecommunications management, have already been recognized in many large state and local governments (Caudle and Marchand, 1989). New job titles and classifications, both in particular technologies such as information technology and in technology generally, also have been recognized. Positions such as network specialist, information analyst, information resources manager, technology policy analyst, technology transfer agent, and technology adviser will become more commonplace with regard to technology development in state and local governments (U.S. Advisory Commission on Intergovernmental Relations, 1990).

The growing use of information technology requires not only the introduction of more technical personnel into government but also new kinds of personnel, both in the functional areas of government and in the IT function itself. In the functional areas, IT is creating the need for new specialists who are knowledgeable and skilled in both their functional specialty and in IT, for example, police systems analysts.

In the IT function, several new developments are bringing about the need for new kinds of people. First, the introduction of telecommunications, computing, and office automation is creating the need for people who can work at the interface of these three technologies to bring about their integration. Second, the diffusion of personal computers (whether stand-alone, networked, handheld, or portable) is creating the need for end-user specialists who can act as trainers, consultants, troubleshooters, and planners. Third, the increasing accumulation of data is requiring computer specialists in data management. Finally, and most important, IT demands the creation of information analysts—people who know how to work with the technology in order to produce useful information for decision making.

Skill Transformation

The skill implications of new technologies, particularly information technologies, are likely to be highly variable, depending on the technology itself and arrangements of organizational and environmental variables (Spenner, 1988). At the risk of overgeneralizing, however, the long-run implications of the types of technological changes state and local governments are presently experiencing or are likely to experience will require enlargement and upgrading of employee skills. There already is and will continue to be an upgrading of skills as a result of computerization, and of automation more broadly (Attewell, 1987, Danziger and Kraemer, 1986).

The basis for arguing that skills will generally need to be upgraded is that the automation that underlies many information technologies tends to broaden responsibilities, increase the abstractness of tasks and goals, and increase and broaden forms of task interdependence (Adler, 1984; Zuboff, 1988). The skill requirements can be described broadly as falling into four categories. The first is user literacy, which refers to the ability to understand and to use the technology in one's work regardless of the type of work or the level in the organization. The second is information literacy, which refers to the ability to recognize, locate, evaluate, and use meaningful information (American Library Association, 1989). The third is technical literacy, which refers to the ability to create with the technology. And the fourth is managerial literacy, which refers to the ability to make intelligent and wise choices about the application of the technology to government.

Although state and local government organizations could choose to fractionate work to overcome changing skill requirements associated with automation, several factors are likely to militate against job simplification as a means for coping with the skill transformations inherent in many new technologies. Given the decline in the growth rate of the labor pool, narrow definition of the skill requirements of new jobs is not likely to be an optimal strategy. The need for state and local governments to maintain their attractiveness to job seekers in the face of increasingly tight labor markets (Johnston and Packer, 1987; Johnston, 1988) is likely to stimulate the enrichment of jobs rather than their simplification. Reported trends that employee preferences for satisfying work are increasing also diminish the viability of simplification as a strategy for adjustment. Thus, the dominant pressure on state and local governments will be to respond to needs for a workforce with enlarged and enhanced skills.

The implication of these developments for the public service is that electronic communication will increasingly be a complement to face-to-face communication with other officials, other governments, and the public. For the most part, it will not substitute for existing communication, but will reinforce and enhance such communication.

Temporal, Physical, and Social Meaning of Public Service

The transformation of the social organization of work accompanying the evolution of information technologies in state and local governments also will have far-reaching implications for public service. For example, office automation technologies have tended to redefine the social space in which work is conducted. Telecommunications and networking technologies widen the prospects for personal isolation by increasing the feasibility of work-at-home or remote-site activity. These technologies potentially expand opportunities for novel scheduling arrangements such as flextime and compressed work weeks.

The redefinition of physical, temporal, and social space will not be received in the same way by all employees, and its effects are likely to be both positive and negative. For example, Bair (1987), extrapolating from interviews with office workers that these employees experience strong needs for connectedness with each other as well as with organizational levels above and below, identified personal isolation as a secondary consequence of office automation. On the other hand, voluntary work-at-home arrangements have been reported to increase employee satisfaction. In addition to altering employee perceptions about the physical and social space in which they work, managers will be challenged to motivate employees they cannot physically supervise and to respond rapidly to changing demands for service. These by-products of changing information technologies must be monitored, diagnosed, and managed.

Technology-Induced Stress

Another threat to achieving the potential of new technologies is the failure of state and local governments to assist employees to adapt physically and emotionally to the demands of new technology. Only recently have some of the forms of physical and emotional stress associated with the revolution in information technologies become widely known. These adaptive problems have taken a variety of forms, creating an entirely new vocabulary in occupational medicine. Among the physical manifestations of technology-induced stress are repetitive-motion syndrome and VDT-related eye, back, and neck strains. Emotional manifestations of technology-induced stress are equally common. Some employees experience *technostress,* which results from an inability to adapt to the introduction and operation of new technology (Nykodym, Miners, Simonetti, and Christen, (1989). Others may experience even more intense phobias, called cyberphobia or computerphobia, which produce physical symptoms such as dizziness, shortness of breath, and sweating palms.

The consequence of these pathologies is reduced performance effectiveness. Furthermore, there is some evidence to indicate that technology-induced stress is not distributed randomly but is more prevalent among female and older workers (Elder, Gardner, and Ruth, 1987), demographic groups who will be even more vital components in the future workforce of state and local governments (Johnston and Packer, 1987; Johnston, 1988).

RESPONDING TO THE CHALLENGES POSED BY CHANGING TECHNOLOGY

What types of responses have state and local governments made to the human resource consequences of changing technology? For the most part, few governments have responded explicitly. What responses would be necessary if state and local governments pursue the types and rate of technological changes that permit them to improve efficiency and effectiveness? What types of responses to technological change would give state and local governments an advantage in competing for employees in the environment predicted by *Workforce 2000* and *Civil Service 2000*? These questions are addressed in this concluding section.

Worker Adjustment Policies

The concept of worker adjustment is typically used to refer to labor market policies that assist displaced workers to find new jobs with reasonable earnings prospects (Cyert and Mowery, 1987). We believe the meaning of worker adjustment should be broadened to encompass not only public policies but also organizational policies that represent the social contract between employers and employees who may be affected by technological change. In order to expeditiously and effectively integrate new technologies into the workplace, state and local governments must be prepared to deal comprehensively with some of the negative side effects of technological change. Among the side effects most likely to be viewed negatively by employees are displacement and technology-induced stress. A comprehensive policy to deal with these problems is likely to have several components: a formal statement of policy, training, advance notice, job security, and career counseling and outplacement opportunities.

An Explicit Statement of Policy. This is one way of allaying employee fears about how new technology will affect them and building trust within the workforce. The policy statement should articulate the state or local government's vision about a range of human resource issues arising from the introduction of new technology, including the role of employee involvement, opportunities for advance notice, training commitments, and job security. The impetus for such policy statements may come from employee interests rather than management. For example, the International Association of Machinists and Aerospace Workers has developed a "Worker's Technology Bill of Rights," which articulates its approach to dealing with job security, retraining, and job protection (Deutsch, 1987). The bill of rights has been the basis for negotiated agreements in both the public and private sectors.

Training. Long-term ability to maximize the benefits of technological change and to minimize adverse consequences is crucially dependent on the provision of appropriate education and training. In a recent survey, local government officials identified computer literacy as the greatest training and education need confronting local governments (Slack, 1990). That local officials would identify computer literacy, an early stage in training for new information technologies, as the greatest need reflects both the breadth of impact of information technologies and the long road most state and local governments still have to travel to meet their needs.

An example of the magnitude of the commitment that state and local organizations must devote to training is provided by Long Beach, California's approach to implementing office automation, beginning in 1984 (McMillen, 1984). Several extraordinary steps were taken by the Information Services Department in fulfilling the city manager's directive to install office automation throughout the city. One was the creation of a training center that was used for group training sessions and hardware and software demonstrations. Another step was to assign full-time personnel to support tasks such as ordering supplies, ongoing training, and problem resolution. Training was provided at both the training center and the worksite. Backup personnel were provided to replace staff who were trained off site.

The Long Beach example illustrates some generalizable requirements for workforce training. For all but small cities, state and local governments will need to prepare in-house training programs to augment vendor or contractor training. They will also have to devise ways to train workers for new technology without interfering with current operations.

Formal training and education programs will probably not suffice to ensure adequate support for adoption and utilization of new technologies. State and local government organizations must recognize that user-to-user interaction may be important for overcoming employee fears about new technology and enhancing the utility of formal training. For example, based on his study of information technology in cities ranging in size from 5,000 to

55,000, Rocheleau (1988) recommended that cities should use the informal system to train personnel and should seek to encourage the informal sharing of information. Among the examples he provides is the location of a microcomputer in the police department lunch room to encourage sharing about the new technology. Support services provided by an information center are another means of informally training personnel.

The training needed simply to keep pace with the operation of new information technologies per se is vast, but secondary training needs associated with changing technological/organizational interrelationships are likely to be even more substantial and far reaching (Helfgott, 1988). For example, managers and supervisors will require training in job design to improve their ability to structure jobs mediated by technology.

Advance Notice. Although the concept of advance notice is controversial, it may become an essential component of human resource practices in future labor markets. We noted earlier that certain features of the state and local government sector make outright displacement of employees less likely, but state and local governments may reap substantial benefits from full and early disclosure of their plans for technological changes regardless of the disemployment effects associated with a particular change. One example of a broad disclosure policy is that of Boeing Aircraft, which annually briefs members of the International Association of Machinists about company plans for the introduction of new technology that may affect employees (Deutsch, 1987). The adoption of similar policies by state and local governments would help to alleviate anxieties associated with the introduction of new technologies, build employee commitment, and speed workforce adaptations. Research indicates that advance notice policies have widely favorable effects, with few adverse effects either to organizations or to employees (Addison and Portugal, 1987; Ehrenberg and Jakubson, 1989).

Job Security. In an earlier time, guarantees of job security would have been viewed with alarm, but in the future, assurances of continued employment may pay big dividends (O'Brien and Kroggel, 1989). Job security can be an effective device to convince employees that technological progress is not threatening to their well-being. It is one way of diminishing resistance to technological change in state and local workforces. Given the shrinking rate of growth in the size of the labor pool, job security is also a means for ensuring that an organization retains potentially scarce employees. An organization's promise of job security may be made contingent on an employee's willingness to retrain for a new job at comparable pay.

Career Counseling and Outplacement Assistance. As jobs in state and local organizations increase in complexity and historical patterns of job ladders and job families change, state and local governments will have to become more proactive in career counseling for their employees. This will probably require a series of changes in the ways that state and local governments presently manage employee careers. One of the changes will be essentially managerial—to vest line managers with more responsibility to counsel their subordinates about career opportunities and to prepare them to undertake new jobs.

Not all employees will be ready or able to adjust to newly defined jobs and therefore will need job search assistance. For employees who prefer to leave the organization rather than adapt, some form of outplacement assistance policies for displaced employees would be appropriate. AC Transit (Oakland, California) used outplacement as part of a seven-point downsizing plan to humanize the layoff for fourteen nonunionized and management employees for whom there was no other alternative (Settles, 1988). Similarly, Anaheim Memorial Hospital used an outplacement service together with workshops on resume preparation, interviewing skills, action planning, and emotional adjustment to soften the hardships for employees when it closed Fullerton Community Hospital (Newman, 1987). In situations where relatively large numbers of employees face loss of their jobs, state and local government organizations may choose to provide job search workshops either directly or in conjunction with employee representatives.

Restructuring Human Resource Management Systems

The sweeping changes attendant to information technology not only require adjustments in work itself but also in the management and control systems that support state and local government activities. Most of the changes will occur in personnel systems, but other management and control systems will also need to be modified; among them the governmental unit's planning, procurement, and budgeting systems. Planning systems will have to be modified so that they take better account of potential strategic constraints imposed by human resource flows. Similar advances are needed in the procurement of information technologies and in managing the complex, long-term, large-scale, and inherently risky projects these systems entail. Capital and operating budgets will need to more completely reflect training and other human-resource-related costs.

It is difficult to predict precisely how state and local government recruitment practices will be altered by technological change. To the extent that government becomes a player in high-technology labor markets, it will probably have to recruit more from regional and national markets. Although this may require few adjustments for state governments, local governments will have to reassess traditional residency requirements that may limit their attractiveness. High demand in many technology specialties will necessitate rapid assessment and hiring of applicants. This is likely to require streamlining government hiring practices and shifting merit system controls from input practices (for example, testing) to post audit.

Career ladders will need to be altered to fit new distributions in occupations and transitions between occupations and to facilitate movement between jobs (Debons, King, Mansfield, and Shirey, 1981). Narrowly defined job categories will have to be replaced by broader job classifications to provide incentives to workers in the form of on-the-job learning opportunities.

State and local government organizations will have to reassess their relationships with organized labor. Adjusting successfully to technological change will demand large doses of cooperation between labor and management. Management and labor will increasingly need to approach negotiations as a problem-solving rather than adversarial process. Issues such as advance notice and job security will be of central importance to labor organizations, but labor can also help to forge innovative solutions for training and career development.

Incentives

State and local government organizations can encourage employees to voluntarily respond to technological change and future workforce needs by providing appropriate incentives. Previous experience indicates, however, that such incentives will not occur without explicit attention from state and local government managers and policy makers. For example, Iacono and Kling (1987, p. 75) note that the introduction of new technologies has not altered organizational incentive systems for clerical workers: "A new generation of integrated computer-based office systems will not automatically alter the pay, status, and careers of clerks without explicit special attention."

A starting point for restructuring incentives must be organizational pay systems. The shifting occupational and skill requirements associated with changing technology will require state and local governments to adopt pay systems that are congruent with the new technologies and consistent with a government's goals. Pay systems will increasingly need to be structured to reward the acquisition, modification, and development of individual competencies. Such a pay system will encourage workers to acquire new skills and thus facilitate redeployment and job redesign. One pay philosophy that seeks to increase organizational flexibility in these ways is pay for knowledge or skills-based pay. Pay for knowledge developed as a support system for team development in quality of working life programs. It typically includes three design features: (1) an employee's rate of pay is adjusted as new skills are mastered and demonstrated in performing job duties; (2) an employee will perform several assignments requiring different kinds and levels of knowledge and skills; and (3) employees will be involved in planning, setting standards, and measuring results from their work (Henderson, 1989).

A reassessment of existing educational incentives would also be a move in the right direction. Many governments presently provide for some type of tuition reimbursement, but such reimbursements are often restricted to job-related or job-specific courses. These programs will have to be liberalized to accommodate the need for retraining.

To the extent that employees affected by technology resist its adoption or implementation, state and local government organizations will be unable to realize technology's promise. The likelihood of resistance increases the importance of the process governments use to introduce new technologies. State and local government managers must seek out a variety of means to reduce resistance to appropriate technological changes. One means is to involve employees in the design and implementation of new technologies (O'Brien and Kroggel, 1989). User involvement in information systems development and implementation increases both systems usage and user satisfaction. Another step is to build employee trust and to avoid threats by adopting the type of worker protection policies discussed at the beginning of this section. These steps could be augmented by programs designed to reduce stress associated with a technology's use. For example, New York City has passed an ordinance that provides employees with extra breaks to diminish possible effects of prolonged exposure to VDTs (Halachmi, 1991).

Executive Leadership

As information technology becomes an integral part of service delivery, the education and training of public servants in the future must convey this state of the practice and instill habits of thinking about the role of technology in services innovation. The need for such thinking is important for all managers and professionals in the public service, but it is particularly critical for senior executives where the authority and resources exist to make bold decisions about services innovation. The need is not for senior executives to generate the innovations. Rather, it is for them to evaluate innovations presented to them by subordinates and staff professionals and to sift the effective from the ineffective and the marginal. The need is also for senior executives to take the lead in developing relationships with the private sector as well as with other public agencies to mobilize the technical and social support required for these innovations and to create the conditions for successful implementation and use.

Perhaps the single factor that most limits the executive's ability to exercise leadership in the application of technology will be the continuing serious fiscal shortfalls of state and local governments. This suggests that government might be encouraged to use information technology to help reduce costs, but that executives will have much less money to do so effectively, and it will cost more to innovate in the 1990s than in the 1980s. For example, while the costs of hardware of given capability are declining, modern systems require wider distribution of hardware than their predecessors, and the costs of skilled computer staff and user training are increasing. As a result, executives will have to make much more careful decisions about the innovations in which to invest. Moreover, they will have to focus attention on getting the most from the information systems in which they do invest, as well as those in which they have already invested. Careful investment analysis and continuous user training will be critical tools for senior executives to ensure payoffs from information systems investments.

CONCLUSION

Technological change is transforming public service in state and local governments. The transformation is an evolutionary process, still probably in its early to middle stages, judging by its effects across all state and local governments. Despite the early stage, many of the implications of technological change for the state and local public service have become apparent, such as worker displacement; creation of entirely new job classifications; skill transformation; redefinition of the temporal, physical, and social meaning of public service; and technology-induced stress.

These consequences of technological change will require vigorous and thoughtful responses from state and local governments if they hope to achieve their productivity and service improvement objectives. The cornerstone of a vigorous response is a comprehensive worker adjustment policy that represents a state or local government's commitment to its employees as reflected in a vision statement, training programs, guarantees of advance notice and job security, and other provisions designed to diminish anxiety and displacement.

State and local government organizations will also have to reassess their management and control systems to ensure that they are aligned with the new organizational realities. Appropriate incentives will be needed to reinforce organizational objectives.

Finally, it is important to consider a comment by Erich Bloch (1986), former director of the National Science Foundation, in the *Journal of State Government*. He pointed out that "technological strength results from a chain of events that *ends* with new products competing successfully on international markets" (p. 144). The key to technological strength is skilled people and knowledge, both of which are created and fostered in universities. What public servants need more than anything is the transfer of knowledge and skill to understand and deal with technology. That knowledge and skill exists in universities, and the universities should be challenged to provide them through degree programs, executive education, and continuing education aimed at ensuring that there is a competent public service for today's technological society.

The authors gratefully acknowledge the helpful comments of Enid Beaumont, Walter Broadnax, Thomas Galvin, Thomas Kinney, Rob Kling, Eugene McGregor, Sally Marshall, Richard Nathan, John Ottensman, and Frank Thompson.

References

Addison, J. I., and Portugal, P. "The Effect of Advance Notification of Plant Closings on Unemployment." *Industrial and Labor Relations Review,* Oct. 1987, *41,* 3–16.

Adler, P. *Rethinking the Skill Requirements of New Technologies.* Cambridge, Mass.: Harvard Business School, 1984.

American Library Association, Presidential Committee on Information Literacy. *Report of the American Library Association Presidential Committee on Information Literacy.* Chicago: American Library Association, 1989.

Andersen, D. F., and Dawes, S. S. *Government Information Management.* Englewood Cliffs, NJ.: Prentice-Hall, 1991.

Attewell, P. "The Deskilling Controversy." *Work and Occupations,* 1987, *14*(3), 323–346.

Attewell, P., and Rule, J. "Computing and Organizations: What We Know and What We Don't Know." *Communications of the ACM,* Dec. 1984, *27,* 1184–1192.

Bair, J. H. "User Needs for Office Systems Solutions." In R. E. Kraut (ed.), *Technology and the Transformation of White-Collar World.* Hilledale, NJ.: Erlbaum, 1987.

Bjorn-Anderson, N., Eason, K., and Robey, D. *Managing Computer Impact: An International Study of Management and Organization.* Norwood, NJ.: Ablex, 1986.

Bloch, E. "The Challenge of Science and Technology in the States." *Journal of State Government,* 1986, *59*(4), 144–145.

Caudle, S. L., and Marchand, D. *Managing Information Resources: New Directions in State Government.* Syracuse, N.Y.: Syracuse University, School of Information Studies, Center for Science and Technology, 1989.

Cyert, R. M., and Mowery, D. C. (eds.). *Technology and Employment: Innovation and Growth in the U. S. Economy.* Washington, D.C.: National Academy Press, 1987.

Danziger, J. N., and Kraemer, K. L. *People and Computers.* New York: Columbia University Press, 1986.

Debons, A., King, D., Mansfield, U., and Shirey, D. *The Information Professional: Survey of an Emerging Field.* New York: Marcel Dekker, 1981.

Deutsch, S. "Successful Worker Training Programs Help Ease Impact of Technology." *Monthly Labor Review,* Nov. 1987, *110,* 14–20.

Ehrenberg, R. G., and Jakubson, G. H. "Advance Notification of Plant Closings: Does It Matter?" *Industrial Relations,* Winter 1989, *28,* 60–71.

Elder, V. B., Gardner, E. P., and Ruth, S. R. "Gender and Age in Technostress: Effects on White Collar Productivity." *Government Finance Review,* Dec. 1987, *17,* 17–21.

Gurwitt, R. "The Computer Revolution: Microchipping Away at the Limits of Government." *Governing,* 1988, *l*(8), 35–42.

Halachmi, A. "Productivity and Information Technology: Emerging Issues and Considerations." *Public Productivity and Management Review,* Summer 1991, *14,* 327–350.

Helfgott, R. B. "Can Training Catch Up with Technology?" *Personnel Journal,* Feb. 1988, *67,* 67–72.

Henderson, R. *Compensation Management.* (5th Ed.) Englewood Cliffs, NJ.: Prentice-Hall, 1989.

Iacono, S., and Kling, R. "Changing Office Technologies and Transformation of Clerical Jobs: A Historical Perspective." In R. E. Kraut (ed.), *Technology and the Transformation of White-Collar Work.* Hillsdale, NJ.: Erlbaum, 1987.

Johnston, W. B., and Packer, A. H. *Workforce 2000: Work and Workers for the 21st Century.* Indianapolis, Ind.: Hudson Institute, 1987.

Johnston, W., and others. *Civil Service 2000.* Indianapolis, Ind.: Hudson Institute, 1988.

King, J. L. "Ideology and Use of Large-Scale Decision Support Systems in U.S. Economic Policy Making." *Systems, Objectives, Solutions,* Apr. 1984, 81–104.

Kling, R. "Automated Welfare Client Tracking and Service Integration." *Communications of the ACM,* June 1978, *21,* 484–493.

Kraemer, K. L. "Strategic Computing and Administrative Reform." In C. Dunlop and R. Kling (eds.), *Computerization and Controversy: Value Conflicts and Social Choices.* Orlando, Fla.: Academic Press, 1991.

Kraemer, K. L., and Danziger, J. "The Impacts of Computer Technology on the Worklife of Information Workers." *Social Science Computer Review,* 1990, *8*(4), 592–613.

Kraemer, K. L., Dickhoven, S., Tierney, S. F., and King, J. L. *Datawars: The Politics of Modeling in Federal Policymaking.* New York: Columbia University Press, 1987.

Kraemer, K. L., and King, J. L. "Computing and Public Organizations." *Public Administration Review,* Nov. 1986, *46,* 488–496.

Kraemer, K. L., and King, J. L. "Centralization, Decentralization and the Role of Information Technology in Managing the Metropolis." *Local Government Studies,* 1988, *14*(2), 23–47.

Kraemer, K. L., King, J. L., Dunkle, D. E., and Lane, J. P. *Managing Information Systems: Change and Control in Organizational Computing.* San Francisco: Jossey-Bass, 1989.

Kraut, R., Dumais, S., and Koch, S. "Computerization, Productivity, and Quality of Work-Life." *Communications of the ACM,* 1989, *32*(2), 220–238.

McMillen, S. "Office Automation: A Local Government Perspective." *Public Administration Review,* Jan.-Feb. 1984, *44,* 64–67.

Millman, Z., and Hartwick, J. "The Impact of Automated Office Systems on Middle Managers and Their Work." *MIS Quarterly,* 1987, *11*(4), 479–491.

Newman, L. "Hospital Closure: Managing the Pain of Going Out of Business." *Healthcare Forum,* July-Aug. 1987, *30,* 35–37.

Nykodym, N., Miners, I., Simonetti, J. L., and Christen, J. C. "Computer Phobia." *Personnel Journal,* Aug. 1989, *68,* 54–56.

O'Brien, J. P., and Kroggel, L. P., Jr. "Technology: Training, Not Trauma." *Personnel Journal,* Aug. 1989, *68,* 32–41.

Osterman, P. "The Impact of Computers on the Employment of Clerks and Managers." *Industrial and Labor Relations Review,* 1986, *39,* 175–186.

Richter, M. L. "The Real Advantages of Putting Government on Line." *Governing,* 1991, *4*(8), 60.

Robey, D. "Computer Information Systems and Organization Structure." *Communications of the ACM,* Oct. 1981, *24,* 679–686.

Rocheleau, B. "New Information Technology and Organizational Context: Nine Lessons." *Public Productivity Review,* Winter 1988, *12,* 165–177.

Settles, M. F. "Humane Downsizing: Can It Be Done?" *Journal of Business Ethics,* 1988, *7,* 961–963.

Slack, J. D. "Local Government Training and Education Needs for the Twenty-First Century." *Public Productivity and Management Review,* Summer 1990, *13,* 397–404.

Spenner, R. In R. M. Cyert and D. C. Mowery (eds.), *The Impact of Technological Change on Employment and Economic Growth.* Cambridge, Mass.: Ballinger, 1988.

U.S. Advisory Commission on Intergovernmental Relations. *State and Local Initiatives on Productivity, Technology, and Innovation: Enhancing a National Resource for International Competitiveness.* Washington, D.C.: U.S. Advisory Commission on Intergovernmental Relations, 1990.

Vitalari, N., and Venkatesh, A., "An Emerging Distributed Work Arrangement: An Investigation of Computer-Based Supplemental Work at Home." *Management Science,* 1992, *38*(12), 1687–1706.

Zuboff, S. *In the Age of the Smart Machine: The Future of Work and Power.* New York: Basic Books, 1988.

6 Human Resources Management

In government, we really have *three* public personnel systems: the patronage system, based on political appointments to positions; the merit or civil service system, designed to employ the ablest in public jobs; and the labor relations or collective bargaining system, the most recent.

Most public employees in America are employed under a merit system. The concept of a merit system is really quite elitist, suggesting that citizens prefer "the best and the brightest" individuals to be employed in government.

The determination "where to draw the line" between patronage and merit systems is always difficult, and there is almost always conflict between the staffing purposes of political groups and civil service systems. Official contempt for the civil service and federal civil servants probably reached its height under President Nixon, when there was a conscious effort to subvert the federal civil service system.

What constitutes a modern merit personnel system? The U.S. Office of Personnel Management suggests two dozen elements for any governmental jurisdiction of about five hundred employees or more. These are:

Provision for *equal employment opportunity applicable to all personnel actions* without regard to political affiliation, race, color, national origin, sex, age, religious creed, marital status, or physical handicap.

A plan for systematic *job analysis* involving collecting data and making certain judgments about the nature of individual jobs to provide a basis for such things as classifying positions, developing minimum qualification requirements, constructing job-related tests, identifying training needs, and reviewing individual performance. Job analysis is a major component of affirmative action for equal employment opportunity. The courts have specifically cited job analysis as a required basis for qualification standards and written tests.

Grouping or classification of positions by occupation according to similarities or differences in duties, responsibilities, and qualification requirements.

A realistic *pay system* tied to sound job analysis and position classification, which assures equity within the system and comparability with pay offered by other employers in the same labor market area for similar work.

Job-related *minimum qualification requirements* which describe the nature and amount of experience, training, knowledge, and skills needed for successful performance as well as a means for determining that applicants possess such requirements.

Recruiting, examining, rating certification, and selection procedures which reach all parts of the labor market; which apply the established qualification requirements in a fair, job-related fashion in testing and selecting the best-qualified persons from among all eligible candidates; and which make special affirmative action provisions for assuring equal opportunity to members of minority groups, women, and those disadvantaged by educational, economic, physical, or social handicaps.

A *placement* system which not only assures the sound initial placement of new employees but also provides for follow-up and for remedial placements.

An adequate *probationary period* which must be satisfactorily completed before permanent tenure or status is conferred.

A continuing *performance evaluation* system providing employees and managers feedback aimed at strengthening employee and organizational performance.

An *incentive awards* program which provides recognition for exceptional performance and successful ideas for improving operations.

A *training and career development program* which, among other things, fills the gaps between the qualifications required for the positions in question and the qualifications possessed either by employees already in or on the career ladder for such positions or by outside candidates for such positions; which prepares employees to meet the future needs of the public service; and which keeps the public service up-to-date in its use of modern techniques, technology, and equipment.

A *promotion* system which provides for fair and objective consideration of eligible employees for the promotion opportunities which arise; and which assures that selection for promotion is job-related and based on merit, not political or personal patronage or racial or other favoritism.

Provision for *lateral transfers and reassignments* of employees among different agencies or parts of agencies, and for details and temporary duty assignments to meet short-term needs.

Provision for *reprimands, suspensions, demotions, and removals* of employees for disciplinary reasons or unsatisfactory performance.

Objective and effective *appeals and grievance* systems for employees.

A *labor-management relations* provision which enables employees to be involved in personnel policies and practices affecting their employment consistent with merit principles, the preservation of management rights, and the protection of the public interest.

An orderly and fair method of making necessary *cutbacks in the work force* due to budget reductions, decrease in workload, reorganizations, or other reasons.

Fringe benefits, such as *age and disability retirement, group life and health insurance, vacation and sick leave, paid holidays, and employees' compensation for job-connected injuries and sickness.*

An *occupational safety and health program* and provision for employee counseling and guidance services.

A statutory or executive code of *ethical conduct* for all public service personnel which includes prohibitions against conflict of interest, nepotism, and political coercion.

A system of *policy, regulatory, and operational issuances* published by the central personnel agency for the direction and guidance of employing agencies of the government.

A system of *personnel records, reports, and statistics* as needed for legal or personnel management purposes.

Provision for *personnel planning, overall program planning, and continuing program evaluation* which recognizes the critical role of effective personnel management in the delivery of government services to the public.

A sound basic *public personnel law, positive support from top management, adequate financial resources for essential operations, and competent professional personnel staffs* both in the central personnel agency and in the line departments.

However, merit goals have not always brought meritorious results. There are many critics of contemporary civil service procedures—federal, state, and local. They claim that there is little scientifically supportable evidence that many civil service examinations are directly related to later on-the-job performance, that too much job security for public employees limits managerial effectiveness, that past performance receives too little credit for promotions as opposed to the reliance on written examinations, and that salary increases are virtually automatic, thereby eliminating an important possible incentive for improved performance. To this some critics would add that collective bargaining systems in state and local government have the tendency to reinforce some of the worst aspects of civil service systems.

In this chapter's first article, Patricia Ingraham and David Rosenbloom look at the condition of the federal government's merit personnel system. They provide a short history of the civil service and then examine hiring, classification and pay, and training. They also examine relevant court rulings and the meaning of "merit" in the federal government.

In the second article, Sonia Ospina looks at the topic of workforce diversity. She makes explicit the benefits of diversity and the concrete steps required to achieve those benefits. In her essay, Ospina provides a perspective with which to better understand some of the issues of the day in an increasingly diverse nation.

Chapter 6 has dealt with people as personnel and with the management of human resources. Here are some questions in connection with Chapter 6:

- What are some of the current issues and problems confronting personnel management in the federal government?
- Ingraham and Rosenbloom conclude that "neither the essential definition of merit nor fundamental merit principles is clear" today. If the Pendleton Act was passed in 1883 and the Civil Service Reform Act was approved in 1978, how can that be?
- Many Americans celebrate both their common heritage and their differences. Why has diversity—gender, race, ethnicity—become such a controversial issue today?
- Is affirmative action a useful tool to promote diversity?
- Do you agree with Ospina about the benefits of diversity? Do you agree with her plan to promote diversity in the workforce? Why or why not?
- What other personnel issues seem important in public administration today? Political patronage? Collective bargaining and public employee unionism? Sexual harassment? Civil service procedures? Workers with disabilities? Downsizing? Personnel management is a large area, with important implications for all of government operations.

The State of Merit in the Federal Government

Patricia W. Ingraham
David H. Rosenbloom
(With the research assistance of John P. Knight)

The merit system, by raising the character and capacity of the subordinate service, and by accustoming the people to consider personal worth and sound principles, rather than selfish interest and adroit management as the controlling elements of success in politics, has also invigorated national patriotism, raised the standard of statesmanship, and caused political leaders to look more to the better sentiments and the higher intelligence for support.

The Eaton Report to President Rutherford B. Hayes, 1879

THE PROBLEM

For over one hundred years, the American civil service has been guided by merit principles. Those principles, underpinning a system intended to protect federal employment and employees from partisan politics, were simple and direct: fair and open competition for federal jobs, admission to the competitive service only on the basis of neutral examinations, and protection of those in the service from political influence and coercion. The system that has grown from these principles, however, is not simple and direct. Today, rules and regulations related to federal personnel administration fill thousands of pages. Today, the federal government's merit system *does not work*. These procedures have created a system in which the recruitment, testing, and hiring of employees is often conducted independently of those who will manage and be responsible for the employees' performance. The personnel function is often viewed independently—indeed, often in isolation—from management concerns and priorities. Many continue to define merit only in terms of entrance to the federal service through centralized neutral and objective examinations, but in a diverse and complex society, tests alone are not an accurate measure of merit. It is abundantly clear that the construction and administration of such examinations create as many problems as they solve. Many federal managers argue that the time spent trying to understand the system overshadows whatever benefits the merit system provides.

In 1978, President Jimmy Carter declared that there was "no merit in the merit system." Others have argued that there is no system in the merit system. Incremental laws and procedures, accumulating over a one-hundred-year period, have created a jerrybuilt set of rules and regulations whose primary emphasis is on negative control of federal personnel, rather than on a positive affirmation of merit and quality in the federal service. The design of a system intended to screen large numbers of applicants for a limited number of positions is outdated and inappropriate for contemporary technology and the changing demographics of the twenty-first century. The elimination of the discriminatory Professional and Administrative Career Examination (PACE) in 1982 demonstrated how entrance procedures should not look, but failed to specify how they should. The gradual accretion of often conflicting objectives, rules, and regulations has created, not a coherent national system of merit, but a confusing maze of procedure. At the same time, the long-term effectiveness of the federal government rests on the ability to recruit and retain a quality workforce. The many restrictive components of the contemporary merit system severely inhibit that ability. Merit has come to signify a narrow and negative focus on positions and jobs, rather than competence, accountability, and effective public service.

It is not the intent of this article to propose or endorse specific reforms, although there are many. Instead, the purpose is to describe the disjointed evolution and current state of the federal merit system—the status quo from which future reforms must proceed. Very clearly, those reforms cannot build on a clear and coherent foundation, for no such foundation exists. Future reforms, therefore, must address fundamental questions: What does "merit" mean for contemporary federal personnel administration?[1] What are the critical components of a merit system for the future? Is it possible to replace rules and regulations with flexibility and discretion for federal personnel, but still to ensure accountability and responsiveness to the public and to elected officials? Without this fundamental analysis, current proposals for reform may only contribute to the system's baggage; the ability of the federal government to be an effective and competitive employer will not be addressed.

THE ORIGINS

The passage of the Pendleton Act in 1883 began the process of creating a civil service based on merit for the American national government. Strongly anchored in the experience of the British civil service, the American system nonetheless reflected uniquely American politics and government. The public excesses of the patronage system were viewed as a national disgrace and as a serious burden on the presidency. The assassination of President James Garfield by a demented office seeker dramatically demonstrated the problem. The glut of office seekers in Washington and their constant demands on the president and his staff created other problems; they reportedly led President Abraham Lincoln to request, when he contracted smallpox, that all the office seekers be sent to him, for "now I have something I can give to each of them."[2]

The passage of the legislation reflected political realities as well. There were strong civil service leagues in many states. They had successfully placed personnel reform on the agenda for the 1882 congressional elections. The support expressed for reform in those midterm elections ensured that it would become a national issue. Political demands, however, were tempered by a serious constitutional question: Did the creation of a centralized personnel system and Civil Service Commission violate the powers of both the president and Congress over personnel matters?[3]

The dilemma posed by the political need to act and questions of constitutional legitimacy produced a classically political solution: The initial legislation covered only 10 percent of the federal workforce. But Congress granted the president power to include additional federal employees in the classified civil service by Executive Order. Patronage would be controlled, but slowly. Van Riper notes, "If the act permitted an orderly retreat of parties from their prerogatives of plunder, it made possible as well the gradual administrative development of the merit system."[4]

At the heart of the new merit system was one fundamental principle: Admission to the classified civil service would be *only* through open competitive examinations. Unlike the British system, which relied on formal academic training, the American system hailed the practical American spirit; the examinations would focus on common sense, practical information, and skills. The examination system would be designed to provide all who desired federal employment a fair, equal, and objective opportunity to enter the civil service. The act created decentralized Boards of Examiners to administer the tests and specified that they "be so located as to make it reasonably convenient and inexpensive for applicants to attend before them."[5]

The American system also differed from its British heritage in its definition and treatment of neutrality. Very clearly, political neutrality was to be a hallmark of the new classified civil service. The need for a competent civil service that would serve either political party well was widely accepted. At the same time, neither members of Congress, the president, nor the reformers were willing to commit to the British tradition of an elite higher civil service whose members were active participants in policy debates. Policy participation was not viewed as a legitimate administrative function. For the American civil service, neutrality was a protection against politics, but also an exclusion from policy. Herbert Kaufman offered the following assessment: "the civil service was like a hammer or a saw; it would do nothing at all by itself, but it would serve any purpose, wise or unwise, good or bad, to which any user put it."[6]

THE GROWTH OF THE CLASSIFIED SERVICE

The origins of the merit system in the federal government are important for a number of reasons. First, because the system had a purposefully limited beginning, growth could, and did, occur in an unplanned and unpredictable way. Second, the system was formed in a way designed to gather the largest possible number of applicants for a limited number of government jobs. The "fair and open competition" principle was interpreted from the outset to be national competition for what were then largely Washington-based jobs (postmasters were not included in the original legislation). The system was, in short, designed to be a screening system and was based on the fundamental assumption that there would be many more job seekers than jobs. Further, since most positions would be in Washington, centralizing the personnel function within the Civil Service Commission made good sense. Third, despite the emphases on objective merit and free and open competition, the Pendleton Act included provisions whose intent and impact was to attenuate those emphases. The act specifically noted, for example, that veterans were to continue to be given preference in federal hiring, a practice that had been formally established in 1865. In addition, the Pendleton Act reaffirmed the nation's commitment to a geographically "representative" federal workforce, an emphasis first articulated during George Washington's presidency. Merit, veterans' preference, and geographic representativeness did not necessarily coincide, even in 1883. In the ensuing years, veterans' groups, in particular, have often pursued objectives clearly at odds with those of federal personnel experts and managers.

Finally, the provision for presidential determination of increased coverage did not remove politics from the development of the civil service system; instead, it ensured that the growth of "merit" would be dependent on political cycles. Presidents who chose to extend the merit system often came under attack from their own parties for doing so; each extension of civil service coverage meant fewer patronage appointments and fewer payoffs for party loyalty. As a result, commitment by presidents to merit and the classified civil service fluctuated dramatically in the early years. Generally, presidents such as Theodore Roosevelt (also a former civil service commissioner) who succeeded a president of their own party found advancing merit to be somewhat easier than those who did not. President William McKinley, for example, included 1700 additional employees in the classified service by Executive Order, but also exempted about 9,000 employees through rollback and new exemption procedures.[7] Woodrow Wilson took the reins of a federal government that had been controlled for sixteen years by Republicans. Despite his association with the National Civil Service Reform Association, the Wilson administration was under intense pressure for patronage. President Wilson said of this pressure, "The matter of patronage is a thorny path that daily makes me wish I had never been born."[8]

Congress, too, retained a keen interest in patronage. As new governmental tasks and functions were approved, Congress could choose to place the jobs created outside the classified service. From the time of the first Wilson term to the New Deal, that option was often pursued. It was pushed to new heights—this time at presidential initiative—in Franklin Roosevelt's New Deal. The experience of the civil service in the New Deal years is treated differently by different analysts; Van Riper, for example, offers an exceedingly harsh assessment. More pragmatically, Kaufman notes that Franklin Roosevelt managed to "kill two birds with one stone," when he "put into effect all of the programs and projects he considered vital for the welfare of the country. And he excepted the positions in these agencies from the classified service, thus enabling him to fill many of the patronage demands threatening the merit system."[9] In any case, prior to Roosevelt's election in 1932, approximately 80 percent of federal employees were in the competitive civil service. By 1936, that proportion had declined to about 60 percent.[10]

The percentage of the federal workforce under merit protection gradually increased during and after World War II. That time period also saw notable efforts to bring cohesion to the previously haphazard development of the civil service system. The Ramspeck Act in 1940, for example, gave the president the authority to eliminate existing exemptions, including those created by the Pendleton Act. By 1951, about 87 percent of total federal employment was in the classified service.[11] The percentage expanded still further throughout the 1960s and 1970s, so that, by 1980, well over 90 percent of the federal workforce was covered by civil service laws and regulations.

THE GROWTH IN COMPLEXITY

The Pendleton Act itself contained the seeds for the disjointed growth, internal contradictions, and enormous complexity of the American merit system. The very limited initial coverage and the presidential power to extend merit created "blanketing in" procedures. As each new group of employees was thus included in the system, employees who had been appointed by patronage became members of the merit system. As the Civil Service Commission noted, "Although the practice represents a deviation from the merit principle, it makes future appointments to the 'blanketed in' positions subject to merit rules."[12] In addition, the provisions for veterans' preference flatly repudiated the merit principles that applied to everyone else in the competitive system. It was not until 1953, for example, that veterans were required to achieve a passing score on the competitive examinations before having their five- or ten-point veterans' preference added.[13] All other applicants, of course, were not considered for federal employment if they failed the examination.

HIRING

There were other deviations from merit principles. Almost from the beginning, the Civil Service Commission divided the classified civil service into "competitive" (competitive exam required), "noncompetitive" (noncompetitive exam required) and "excepted" (no exam required). Schedule A authority, which exempted from examination some positions that were technically within the classified service, formalized these distinctions. Until 1910, all noncompetitive and excepted categories were lumped under Schedule A authority. In 1910, Schedule B was created to include all noncompetitive positions. In 1953, an Executive Order from President Dwight Eisenhower removed confidential and other policy-sensitive positions from Schedule A and placed them in the newly created Schedule C, whose intent was to permit the president greater numbers of political appointees in policy-sensitive posts (as well as in other lower-level positions, such as chauffeurs and receptionists).[14] Although Schedule A authority is now used primarily for appointing in specialized professions such as law and accounting, Schedule B authority became the primary vehicle for federal hiring in the period immediately following the abolition of PACE. Because federal hiring during this period was limited to a few major agencies with the greatest employment needs, most federal agencies had no systematic hiring authority available to them and little, if any, experience with Schedule B. In 1985, one of the last years of heavy reliance on Schedule B, 98 percent of all appointments under the authority were made by nine of the twenty-one largest departments and agencies.[15] The use of Schedule C, although fairly limited initially, has also expanded in the past twenty years, primarily at upper grade levels.[16]

It is also important to consider the large number of special authorities under which federal agencies now hire. Reliance on such authorities (as well as on Schedule B) was necessitated by the abolition of the Professional and Administrative Career Examination (PACE) in 1982. PACE, which replaced the earlier Federal Service Entrance Examination (FSEE), had provided a single centralized means of recruitment and entry for many federal jobs. When PACE was abolished with no replacement, it became necessary for the Office of Personnel Management (OPM) and the many federal agencies to fall back on existing limited authorities and to use them for purposes for which most had never been intended.

Temporary appointment authority, intended to simplify hiring and separation, as well as to limit the expansion of government, is one such special authority. Temporary appointments have increased substantially in both numbers and duration in recent years, particularly since 1984, when the OPM permitted expansion of their use. Of equal significance, methods of appointing to temporary positions have increased dramatically. At the present time in the federal government, there are *thirty-five* ways to appoint to temporary positions alone.[17] Part-time appointments are an additional option; they, too, are not consistently made through competitive examination procedures.

Direct-hire authority was created for hard-to-hire occupations such as engineers, nurses, and scientists. Direct-hire appointments are made on the basis of unassembled examinations. In 1989, a new direct-hire authority was created for Vietnam veterans. The Outstanding Scholar authority permits on-the-spot hiring of college graduates who have completed four-year degrees with a GPA of 3.5 or better. Simplified hiring procedures also exist for affirmative-action hires, for returned Peace Corps volunteers, and for students enrolled in the Cooperative Education Program, among others. A precise and current list of the many authorities available to federal employers is difficult because the OPM has not updated and distributed such a list since 1980. It is important to note, however, that in 1989, 45 percent of federal career appointments were made under provisions that delegated either examining or hiring authority (or, in some cases, both) to the individual agencies. Another 25 percent were direct-hire appointments in hard-to-hire occupations, while about 15 percent were specialized mid- to senior-level appointments for which there was no register. Only about 15 percent of the appointments were made through "traditional" civil service procedures; that is, through centralized examination or from central registers administered by OPM.[18]

Finally, the federal merit hiring "system" is made more complex by the inclusion of entire agencies (FBI, CIA, Postal Service) in excepted authorities and by the creation of separate but parallel merit systems in others (TVA, for example). The Foreign Service operates with a separate system; so too does the Public Health Service. In some organizations, such as the Department of Health and Human Services and the State Department, more than one system is in place.

In 1978, major civil service reform legislation was passed. A centerpiece of Carter administration domestic policy, the Civil Service Reform Act of 1978 (CSRA) was intended to simplify federal personnel policy through decentralization and delegation, as well as to increase the accountability and responsiveness of federal employees through performance appraisal and evaluation. CSRA created financial incentives linked to performance for top career executives and mid-level managers. The act created the Senior Executive Service (SES) in an effort to make the senior management cadre of the federal career service more flexible and more responsive. It codified federal labor-management practices for the first time, reaffirmed the federal government's commitment to representativeness and affirmative action, and provided new protection for whistleblowers. The act abolished the Civil Service Commission and replaced it with the Office of Personnel Management, the Merit Systems Protection Board, and the Federal Labor Relations Authority. These new institutions were to be leaders in shaping a new and more coherent federal personnel and human resource management strategy.

Because CSRA was the first comprehensive reform of the civil service in nearly a hundred years, expectations for improvements were high. In fact, however, many of those expectations have not been met.[19] This is due to a modest understanding and shallow level of support for many of the reforms; the new political environment of the Reagan administration also had a profound impact on many of the primary implementation activities. The budgetary cutbacks in the early years of the Reagan administration accompanied implementation of critical components of the reform. Much of the political rhetoric accompanying proposed policy changes was directed at the career bureaucracy: the "permanent government." Morale was very low. Delegation, decentralization, and simplification proceeded in fits and starts; attention was again paid to this issue only because the abolition of PACE removed the major central means of recruiting and testing for the federal service.

Most significantly, however, for all its emphasis on greater clarity and simplicity in the federal merit systems, the Civil Service Reform Act did not replace the tangle of procedures related to federal personnel practices. In many respects, it merely added another layer of complexity and confusion to an already complex system. Decentralization and delegation of recruiting and hiring, for example, is not simplification if 6,000 pages of rules, regulations, and guidelines remain in effect. The ability to understand and monitor such a system is extremely difficult, and probably impossible in the absence of any central guiding principles and objectives. The ability to understand and manage effectively in such a system is made even more difficult when other characteristics of the federal personnel system are considered.

CLASSIFICATION AND COMPENSATION

Classification of federal employees was formally authorized in 1923 with the passage of the Classification Act. This legislation not only classified positions according to duties and responsibilities but also assigned salary levels to those positions. It therefore established in law the principle of nationally uniform compensation levels. The act was passed shortly after the Budget and Accounting Act of 1921, and clearly fell under the umbrella of the economy and efficiency movement so prevalent in government at that time. Van Riper notes that "the Bureau of the Budget [created by the 1921 act] tended to emphasize economy at the expense of almost everything else. But the pressing need for careful estimates of personnel and personnel costs, if any budget was to really mean anything, stimulated further concern with the standardization ... of federal wages and functions."[20]

The administration of the new act was supervised by a newly created Personnel Classification Board.

In addition, the act established in law the American principle of "rank in job," rather than the European practice of "rank in person." This meant that the salary or wages for each job was determined solely by the position and by the necessary qualifications for that position, not by the personal qualifications of the person filling the position (although presumably they matched fairly closely). Finally, the act institutionalized the very specialized nature of the American civil service. The jobs to be classified were narrow and specific; again, in keeping with the economy and efficiency movement, flexibility and discretion were limited whenever possible.

Although an analysis of the Classification Act's effectiveness in 1929 indicated that it had not created a "consistent and equitable system of ... pay for positions involving the same work,"[21] there was no additional reform in this area until 1949. There were, however, fairly consistent calls for change during that twenty-year period. The Commission of Inquiry on Public Service Personnel noted in 1935, for example, that "the most obvious fault to be found with all classifications made on the American plan is their complexity—the great number of classes and occupational hierarchies that are set up. What seem to be the most trifling differences in function or difficulty are formally recognized and duly defined...." The commission noted further that "classifications of such complexity are to be condemned because of the fetters that they place upon department heads in the management of their business."[22]

The Ramspeck Act extended the Civil Service Commission's authority for classification to the entire field service in 1940; in 1945 a presidential order directed the commission to begin that task. By that time, the commission was responsible for about half of the total federal civil service positions.[23] The complexity of the federal personnel system was now much in evidence. The absence of a comprehensive wage-and-salary policy had become a notable problem. The final report of the first Hoover Commission detailed the issues related to pay and personnel and concluded: "Probably no problem in the management of the Government is more important than that of obtaining a capable and conscientious body of public servants. Unfortunately, personnel practices in the federal government give little room for optimism that these needs are being met."[24]

In 1949, at least partially in response to Hoover Commission recommendations, the Classification Act of 1949 was passed. The act created the "supergrade" system, which preceded the Senior Executive Service, and simplified the occupational series by merging the previous five into two. The Classification Act of 1949 is important for another reason: It marked an early point on what has now come to be considered the "cycle" of centralization and decentralization in federal personnel policy. Excessive centralization of classification activities was perceived to be a major cause of an overly rigid and slow system. As a result, the 1949 act delegated classification authority for positions below the supergrades back to the agencies. It gave the Civil Service Commission postaudit review authority for those delegations. With other authority such as examining still residing with the Civil Service Commission, with very limited experience in classification activity at the agency level, and with extensive central regulations and procedures still governing the activity, however, this delegation set the precedent for others to follow. Authority was gradually pulled back into the commission until, when the Civil Service Reform Act of 1978 was written, excessive centralization was again perceived to be the problem.

Despite the centrality of classification activities to federal personnel policy and pay, classification has not been thoroughly analyzed since before the passage of the 1949 act. In the intervening forty years, the procedures and regulations associated with classification—most notably the classification and qualification standards[25]—have become seriously outdated and burdensome. The Merit Systems Protection Board recently found, for example, that *63 percent* of the white-collar classification standards currently in use were issued before 1973.[26] In addition, for the 1982-84 period, OPM declared a moratorium on writing new classification standards and the problem was exacerbated. Because grade levels flow directly from classification and qualification standards (or they *should*), the link between these standards and pay is immutable. Obsolescent standards inevitably influence the ability to determine fair pay for an occupation or grade. There are more than 900 occupations in the federal classified service and over 30 different pay systems. The links between the two cannot be ignored in reform, and simplification or total redesign of federal classification schemes is also necessary.

The Civil Service Reform Act of 1978, which did not address the issue of pay, did give the Office of Personnel Management authority to delegate classification activities to the agencies. It did so, however, without addressing or eliminating the plethora of rules and regulations that had accumulated over the years and without directly reforming the Classification Act of 1949. As noted earlier, this failure to address the procedural "baggage" added yet another layer of complexity to a very murky system. To date, OPM has limited such delegation to a very small number of demonstration projects. "Reform" of classification and qualification standards has occurred primarily through efforts to write "generic" standards, which provide greater flexibility. Without a fundamental reexamination of classification procedures, however, other efforts at personnel and pay reform necessarily remain somewhat tangential to change.

TRAINING AND DEVELOPMENT

Training and development of the federal workforce has had a somewhat checkered history. Although a limited number of agencies created education and training programs for their employees, general direction and support was clearly lacking until the passage of the Government Employees Training Act of 1958. Indeed, Van Riper notes that, before 1940, "the excess of applicants compared to available jobs had suggested to both Congress and many administrators that extensive in-service training programs were essentially wasteful."[27] The very limited supply of labor during World War II mandated that federal personnel policy include provisions for training and retraining of federal personnel. At the end of the war, however, many of these activities were cut back or eliminated. The training void was duly noted by the first Hoover Commission and, partly in response to the Hoover Report, President Truman directed the Civil Service Commission to attack what the commission itself called the "curse of excessive specialization."[28] By most accounts, this attack garnered only modest results.

During the presidency of Dwight Eisenhower, whose military training convinced him of the benefits of the enterprise, training began to achieve more credibility. In Eisenhower's first term, the Federal Training Policy Statement was issued. This directive advocated formulation of training plans and emphasis on employee development opportunities. The Civil Service Commission was given lead responsibility for these training efforts. In 1958, during the second Eisenhower term, his administration followed up with the Government Employees Training Act of 1958. Although passage of the act involved intense political negotiation, this act legitimized the training function and provided funds for training and centralized training programs. In its 1974 report, *Biography of an Ideal*, the Civil Service Commission argued that the provisions of the 1958 act "make the training function in the United States Government the envy of even the most advanced of nations."[29] That statement was undoubtedly an exaggeration in 1974; it is clearly not accurate today.

Like much else in the federal personnel system, training and development have not grown in a systematic and coherent way. Despite the provisions of the 1958 act (which has never been revisited), training has remained a fairly low priority. In times of budget cuts and constraints, training costs are often the first to be eliminated from the budget. In its report to the National Commission on the Public Service, the Task Force on Education and Training said, "There are significant shortcomings in federal government human resource policies. Government agencies spend far too little on training of all kinds and concentrate their efforts on meeting narrow, short-term needs. The area of greatest concern is the plainly inadequate attention paid to the development of management and executive leadership in the civil service."[30]

The Civil Service Commission and, later, the Office of Personnel Management, did not develop a government-wide training strategy until Constance Newman assumed the directorship of OPM in the Bush administration. Financial support for training at both central and agency levels remains very limited. At the same time, the need for training and retraining has never been more clear. The demographics of the twenty-first century, changing skill demands, and dramatic technological progress all point to new development needs. Merit and competence are inextricably intertwined.

THE COURTS AND THE MERIT SYSTEM

In the 1970s and 1980s, the federal judiciary played a substantial role in defining and redefining the merit system. The Supreme Court, in particular, has been an ardent supporter of two historical tenets of merit: (1) depoliticization of the public service, and (2) assuring that operational definitions and applications of merit in public personnel administration are strongly job related.

Depoliticization

A major goal of the merit system has been to remove partisan politics from public personnel management. George William Curtis, a leading nineteenth-century civil service reformer, noted that the merit system made it possible to take "the whole non-political public service out of politics."[31] The effort had two prongs: to prohibit public employees from taking an active part in partisan political management and campaigning, and to eliminate patronage hiring and dismissal from the public service. The Supreme Court has embraced both elements of depoliticization.

The effort to remove public employees from partisan politics has been most generally embodied in the first and second Hatch Acts (1939 and 1940) and in various state and local equivalents. The first Hatch Act applies only to federal employees; it prohibits them from using their "official authority or influence for the purpose of interfering with or affecting the result of an election," or from taking an "active part in political management or political campaigns." The second Hatch Act applies similar restrictions to state and local government employees whose positions are at least partially funded by the federal government. These measures carve out a legal and political status for public employees that is remarkably different from that of ordinary citizens. While partisan political participation is considered virtuous for citizens generally, it is simply illegal for public employees. Not surprisingly, both acts have been subject to challenge in the courts on the grounds that they violate the First and Fourteenth Amendment rights of public employees. They have also been attacked for vagueness because both acts lack a comprehensive definition of the activities they proscribe.

The constitutional arguments against the Hatch Acts and similar political neutrality statutes have filled volumes of law reviews and many court briefs. In 1973, however, the Supreme Court seemed to put the constitutional issues to rest in an opinion that strongly supported depoliticization of the public service and afforded Congress great latitude in seeking to achieve that end. In *U.S. Civil Service Commission* v. *National Association of Letter Carriers* (NALC),[32] the Court held:

> We unhesitatingly reaffirm ... that Congress ... has the power to prevent [federal employees covered by the first Hatch Act] from holding a party office, working at the polls and acting as party paymaster for other party workers.... Our judgment is that neither the First Amendment nor any other provision of the Constitution invalidates a law barring this kind of partisan political conduct by federal employees.

> Such a decision on our part would no more than confirm the judgment of history, a judgment made by this country over the last century that it is in the best interests of the country, indeed essential, that federal service should depend upon meritorious performance rather than political service.

The *NALC* decision effectively allows Congress to take virtually any reasonable steps to remove the federal service from partisan political activity. The Court went even further in supporting depoliticization when, in *Elrod* v. *Burns* (1976),[33] it ruled patronage dismissals from ordinary public-service positions *unconstitutional*.

Elrod concerned the constitutionality of patronage dismissals from the Cook County, Illinois, Sheriff's Office. The discharged employees claimed that their First and Fourteenth Amendment rights to freedom of belief and association had been violated. A majority of the Supreme Court's justices agreed that the dismissals were unconstitutional, but the Court was unable to reach a majority opinion as to precisely why.

The issue was more fully clarified in *Branti* v. *Finkel* (1980),[34] in which the Court came close to "constitutionalizing" merit. In assessing the patronage dismissal of two public defenders in Rockland County, New York, Justice John Paul Stevens, speaking for the Court's majority, reasoned that patronage dismissals are unconstitutional unless "the hiring authority can demonstrate that that party affiliation is an appropriate requirement for the effective performance of the public office involved." As Justice Lewis Powell argued in dissent, however, the only logical alternative to a patronage system is one that is merit oriented: "Many public positions previously filled on the basis of membership in national political parties now must be staffed in accordance with a constitutionalized civil service standard that will affect the employment practices of federal, state and local governments."

An important aspect of the *Branti* ruling is that the Court reasoned that merely labeling positions "policy making" or "confidential" is not enough to justify patronage dismissals from them. In practice, this means that some traditional public personnel classifications, such as "excepted" and "exempt," will no longer be synonymous with "at the pleasure" of the political official at the head of an agency or government.

In sum, the Supreme Court has been very sympathetic to the nineteenth-century civil service reformers' ideal of taking politics out of the public service and the public service out of politics. It has declared that patronage dismissals will generally be unconstitutional and has held that the Constitution can easily accommodate restrictions on public employees' partisan political activities. At the same time, it must be noted that Congress has recently raised questions about the overall utility of the Hatch Act and about its infringement on the rights of public employees. Each of the last several sessions has seen the introduction of legislation intended to roll back Hatch provisions. Those in favor of reform argue that federal employees are severely disadvantaged by the inability to participate in politics on their own behalf. Those opposing reform argue that continued political restrictions on federal employees are essential to maintaining any semblance of a merit system. It is important to note that the strength of the proreform group has increased recently; in fact, some observers predicted reform of the Hatch Acts before the end of 1990.[35] The Supreme Court's view of such legislation, should it pass, could be an important redefinition of merit.

Making Sure That the Merit System Assures Merit

A second aspect of the judiciary's involvement in public personnel administration has concerned the very meaning of *merit*. Here, too, the thrust of judicial activity has been two pronged.

All merit systems afford covered employees protection against arbitrary, capricious, illegal, or unconstitutional dismissals. These same systems provide for dismissals in the interests of the efficiency of the public service. During the aftermath of the loyalty-security programs of the late 1940s and early 1950s, the federal judiciary began to look more closely at the government's claims that particular dismissals promoted efficiency. In *Board of Regents* v. *Roth* (1972),[36] the Supreme Court held that public employees are constitutionally entitled to procedural due process protection when dismissals abridged their constitutional rights or liberties, damaged their reputations, seriously impaired their future employability, or infringed upon a property interest, such as tenure, in their jobs. By 1985, the Court had expanded the application of due process considerably. In *Cleveland Board of Education* v. *Loudermill*,[37] it found that a public employee had a "property right" in a job because the Ohio civil service statute made him a "classified civil service" employee, who was entitled to retain his position "during good behavior and efficient service."

Constitutional due process in dismissals from the civil service does not necessarily require elaborate procedures. It does require that the government, as employer, state its reasons for the dismissal and allow the public employee to try to rebut its claims. Once the record contains each side's perspective, review by an administrative official or a court is generally possible. Unsubstantiated claims that dismissals will promote efficiency have been vulnerable to successful challenge. Thus, where there is a merit system, the government cannot simply purport that dismissals serve efficiency objectives; it must demonstrate conclusively that they do so.

The federal judiciary has also sought to assure that merit systems yield merit by requiring, under some circumstances, that standard civil service examinations be strongly job related. In a series of cases beginning in the early 1970s, the courts have held that employment practices having a negative impact on the employment interests of members of minority groups and women are illegal unless they are valid in the sense of being job related.[38] These rulings have been under the Civil Rights Act of 1964, as amended, and the Constitution's equal protection clause (limited to the public sector). There have been numerous instances in which public agencies have been unable to demonstrate efficient job relatedness to make the practices at issue legally or constitutionally acceptable. One remedy that the judiciary may impose in such cases is quota hiring from among qualified minority-group members for a limited period of time, as in *United States* v. *Paradise* (1987).[39]

These cases have forced public-sector jurisdictions to rethink their definitions and applications of merit principles and to attempt to eliminate cultural bias in their hiring and promotional procedures. In *Johnson* v. *Santa Clara County* (1987),[40] the Supreme Court accepted a broad definition of merit that included an effort to establish a socially representative workforce. It specifically embraced the principle that exam scores do not have to be the sole determinant in promotions. Instead, jurisdictions are free to consider a range of factors, including sex and minority-group status. In *Johnson,* the Court noted that merit systems can be flexible because "there is rarely a single, 'best qualified' person for a job. An effective personnel system will bring before the selecting official several fully-qualified candidates who each may possess different attributes that recommend them for selection."[41]

Thus the federal judiciary and the Supreme Court have strengthened two aspects of the merit system. They have protected depoliticization by upholding regulations prohibiting federal employees from engaging in partisan political activity. They have required depoliticization by finding that patronage dismissals from the public service will generally be unconstitutional. The courts have also strengthened the merit system by requiring that dismissals, selections, and promotions done in the name of merit actually embody merit.

THE MERIT SYSTEM AND MERIT PRINCIPLES

This, then, is the procedural and legal environment of the contemporary federal "merit system." The remarkable growth of complexity in both the environment and the system has been reflected in restatements of the underlying principles: Not surprisingly, there are more merit principles today than there were in 1883. After a long period of formal silence about what the merit principles actually ensured, they have been enunciated in legislation twice in the past twenty years. In 1970, the Intergovernmental Personnel Act formally listed the merit principles for the first time:

1. Hiring and promoting employees on the basis of relative ability, with open consideration for initial appointment.
2. Providing fair compensation.
3. Retaining employees on the basis of performance, correcting inadequate performance and separating those whose inadequate performance cannot be corrected.
4. Training employees as needed for high quality performance.
5. Assuring fair treatment of applicants and employees in all aspects of personnel administration without regard to political affiliation, race, color, national origin, sex, or religious creed, and with proper regard for their privacy and constitutional rights as citizens.
6. Protecting employees against partisan political coercion; and prohibiting use of official position to affect an election or nomination for office.[42]

It is worth noting that the Intergovernmental Personnel Act, by using the lever of federal funding, applied these merit principles to state and local governments, just as the second Hatch Act had earlier prohibited state and local employees from partisan political activity.

In 1978, the principles were restated and somewhat redefined again in the Civil Service Reform Act. Now there were nine, much more complex, principles:

1. Recruitment should be from qualified individuals from appropriate sources in an endeavor to achieve a workforce from all segments of society, and selection and advancement should be determined solely on the basis of relative ability, knowledge and skills, after fair and open competition that assures that all receive equal opportunity.
2. All employees and applicants for employment should receive fair and equitable treatment in all aspects of personnel management without regard to political affiliation, race, color, religion, national origin, sex, marital status, age, or handicapping condition, and with proper regard for their privacy and constitutional rights.
3. Equal pay should be provided for work of equal value, with appropriate consideration of both national and local rates paid by employers in the private sector, and appropriate incentives and recognition should be provided for excellence in performance.
4. All employees should maintain high standards of integrity, conduct, and concern for the public interest.
5. The federal workforce should be used efficiently and effectively.
6. Employees should be retained on the adequacy of their performance, inadequate performance should be corrected, and employees should be separated who cannot or will not improve their performance to meet required standards.
7. Employees should be provided effective education and training in cases in which such education and training would result in better organizational and individual performance.
8. Employees should be (a.) protected against arbitrary action, personal favoritism, or coercion for partisan political purposes, and (b.) prohibited from using their official authority or influence for the purpose of interfering with or affecting the result of an election or a nomination for election.

9. Employees should be protected against reprisal for the lawful disclosure of information that the employee reasonably believes evidences (*a.*) a violation of any law, rule, or regulation, or (*b.*) mismanagement, a gross waste of funds, an abuse of authority, or a substantial and specific danger to public health and safety.[43]

Whatever else might be said about the merit principles as we near the year 2000, they are no longer simple and straightforward. Even the principles without their baggage do not provide clear guidance to the federal manager or personnel director who seeks to ensure merit within the overarching objective of effective service delivery. Further, the principles themselves now contain conflicting purposes and objectives. They are more comprehensive, but they are much, much more confusing.

COPING WITH THE MERIT SYSTEM

How do federal managers deal with the constraint, confusion, and complexity of merit as it exists today? In an effort to examine this question, staff members of the National Commission conducted a series of interviews with personnel directors and others in agencies that have made extensive and recent use of existing hiring procedures. Representatives from different agencies, different regions of the country, and central and field offices were interviewed to determine whether and where differences in attitudes toward merit existed. Many persons interviewed requested confidentiality. To honor those requests, no persons or agencies are identified [here]. In the interviews, commission staff focused on entrance to the federal service, rather than on promotion once inside.

Two findings from our interviews are paramount: first, there continues to be remarkable support for the merit *principles*. Second, there is almost unanimous dissatisfaction with the merit *system*. Furthermore, although there is strong support for reforming and removing what many refer to as the "procedural baggage" of the merit system, there is a continuing awareness of the potential for political and other abuse of the merit system and for the need for some protection of career employees and positions. There was, nonetheless, a very strong conviction that federal personnel directors and other federal managers, left on their own, would actively pursue merit. One group of managers said, "If the slate were clean, most of the agencies, most of the time, would create procedures that make good sense. Those procedures that they would re-create would look like the merit principles."[44]

Other managers affirmed this commitment, but emphasized that both the definition of merit and the means of pursuing it need to be examined. Arguing that managers must focus on purpose, not problems, one personnel director said, "The merit system has come to be a way of life, but we must remember that the principles are the basis."[45] Another noted that merit "is confused and it is struggling, but it is there. The system, however, is beyond repair; it needs to be totally rethought. Delegating bad procedures to us does not solve problems; we need to go back to the fundamental principles and guidelines."[46]

The central agency personnel directors interviewed were unanimous in their assessment that the basic design of the current merit system is not appropriate for either current or future recruiting and hiring needs. One director said, "The days of national recruiting are over; the reality is that if you waste the time advertising nationwide, you lose the opportunity to hire the people you really need."[47] Representatives of an agency noted for its innovation and foresight in relation to personnel summarized the situation in these terms: "the goal is to find the best person for the job. The principles are fundamental and they shape the process, but you cannot control merit in a centralized way.... The system is arcane and archaic and we have not done a good job of articulating the new realities."[48]

The interviews uncovered strong differences between central agency staff and field staff in relation to the status of merit. The view of the merit system as archaic and procedure bound was echoed in the field office interviews, but those interviews reflected serious concerns about protecting merit as well. One manager put it in the following terms, "The merit system has little credibility . . . only a few remaining bureaucrats and a few conscientious managers are keeping it from being totally disregarded."[49] Another manager said, "Until merit is defined as something other than test scores, we will continue to reach merit goals, but the quality of the workforce and the quality of the work, will go steadily down."[50]

Underlying many of these concerns is the conviction that while the merit system does not work well or consistently anymore, no coherent replacement or direction has been advanced. Without that replacement and additional guidance, field managers fear replacing even an unworkable system. Indeed, a recent report of the General Accounting Office found that in the face of extensive decentralization and inadequate central-to-field communication, many field managers simply did not know how they were supposed to operate in relation to merit. There has been virtually no systematic monitoring of field experience and precedent; GAO found that even keeping adequate records was problematic.[51]

Overall, then, while there continues to be strong support for the fundamental principles of merit, dissatisfaction with and confusion about the current system is high. Further, the split between central agency personnel and field personnel in terms of how well agencies are coping in the current environment is cause for concern. The inability, or unwillingness, of central personnel to trust and train other personnel in their own agencies is damning evidence of the problems with merit today. The problem highlighted by National Commission interviews has been noted elsewhere. A recent MSPB survey reported that "personnel specialists view delegation of authority from agency personnel offices to line managers somewhat less favorably than they view delegation from OPM to agencies. Whereas 83 percent of respondents believe that delegation of authorities from OPM to agency personnel offices can lead to improved personnel management, only 60 percent believe the same is true of delegation from personnel offices to line management."[52]

It may be that, lacking confidence in field managers, central agency personnel have failed to take the responsibility of decentralization and delegation seriously. The same may be said of the Office of Personnel Management. The ensuing lack of reporting and monitoring is a serious deficiency that needs to be corrected. A more accurate record of experience with decentralized merit is necessary for effective reform. In addition, the need for training and education—about the new environment, the new accountability, and the new responsibility—is very clear. It must be given high priority.

CONCLUSIONS AND RECOMMENDATIONS

Today, neither the essential definition of merit nor fundamental merit principles is clear. Merit cannot mean, as one would assume from examining the system, excessive constraint and blind obedience to a nearly unintelligible maze of procedure. No manager or personnel director can work consistently or effectively in a system defined by over 6,000 pages of rules and regulations. One hundred years of accumulated rules and regulations are the baggage of merit. They do not clarify and define; they obscure. The current system essentially assumes that public managers must be coerced into meritorious behavior; there is no presumption that, left to their own skills and conscience, members of the federal service will nonetheless pursue quality and effective service.

The basic components of the system continue to reflect demographic realities of the late nineteenth century. For many federal agencies, many occupations, and many regions of the country, the contemporary reality is that personnel systems cannot screen out potential employees, but must gather them in. Demographic projections for the next twenty years demonstrate very clearly that to be competitive in these activities, the federal government must be flexible, aggressive, and innovative. The current system is set up precisely to discourage such qualities.

Key components of the current system have not been reexamined for many years. Classification and training are leading examples. A crazy quilt of rules and regulations, patched together as new needs and demands appeared over the past hundred years, provides false assurance that important protections are in place. Rhetoric creates both complacency about the status quo and an unnecessarily negative view of the career civil servants the system is intended to protect.

Today, it is inconceivable that a major nation could govern well, resolve social and economic problems, or play an effective global role in the absence of a strong civil service that is well integrated into its political institutions and culture. Throughout the world, national civil services are being reformed and restructured. Virtually everywhere, government is considered a tool for formulating and implementing public policies. But as Alexander Hamilton noted two centuries ago in *The Federalist Papers,* "the true test of a good government is its aptitude and tendency to produce a good administration."

Good government in the United States requires much better public administration. There is no doubt that public personnel administration, always the cornerstone of public administration, must be redesigned—or perhaps designed for the first time—if the United States is to meet the challenges of the present and the future. There is no "quick fix" for the civil service and public administration. There is a dramatic need to decide, for the first time in over a hundred years, what kind of public service the American national government needs and deserves. Proceeding from that base, future reforms must provide the map and the tools for a new system.

Notes

1. Throughout this [article], "merit" is defined primarily in terms of entrance to the federal service. Very clearly, promotion and protection of employees' rights are also part of the merit mosaic. Both, however, are worthy of separate treatment.

2. Civil Service Commission, *Biography of an Ideal* (Washington, D.C.: CSC, 1974), 28.
3. Paul P. Van Riper, *History of the United States Civil Service* (Evanston, Ill.: Row, Peterson, 1958), 106.
4. Ibid., 105.
5. The Civil Service Act of 1883 (Pendleton Act), *Statutes at Large of the United States of America,* vol. 20, p. 403, sec. 3.
6. Herbert Kaufman, "The Growth of the Federal Personnel System," in The American Assembly, *The Federal Government Service* (New York: Columbia University Press, 1954), 36.
7. Stephen Skrowronek, *Building a New American State: The Expansion of National Administrative Capacities, 1877-1920* (New York: Cambridge University Press, 1982), 70–71.
8. Woodrow Wilson, quoted in Van Riper, *History of Civil Service,* 234.
9. Herbert Kaufman, "Growth of Federal Personnel System," 39. For Van Riper's dissenting view, see Van Riper, *History of Civil Service,* chap. 13.
10. See the Civil Service Commission, *Biography of an Ideal,* 66.
11. See the discussion of the Ramspeck Act and its implementation in Van Riper, *History of Civil Service,* 344–46.
12. Civil Service Commission, *Biography of an Ideal,* 49.
13. Ibid., 89.
14. Van Riper, *History of Civil Service,* 207.
15. Merit Systems Protection Board, *In Search of Merit: Hiring Entry Level Federal Employees* (Washington, D.C.: MSPB, September 1987), i.
16. The greatest increase occurred in the Carter presidency; the elevated levels from that administration were increased still further under President Reagan. See Patricia W. Ingraham, "Building Bridges or Burning Them? The President, the Appointees and the Bureaucracy," *Public Administration Review,* September/ October 1987, 425–35.
17. This number is based on research conducted by the U.S. Navy, Office of Civilian Personnel.
18. Data from the U.S. Office of Personnel Management, Office of Career Entry.
19. For extensive discussion of CSRA, see Patricia W. Ingraham and David Rosenbloom, Co-Editors, "Symposium on Ten Years of Civil Service Reform," *Policy Studies Journal,* Winter 1989.
20. Van Riper, *History of Civil Service,* 298.
21. Ibid., 304.
22. Lucius Wilmerding Jr., *Government by Merit* (New York: McGraw-Hill, 1935), 57.
23. See Van Riper, *History of Civil Service,* 426–27.
24. *Final Report of the First Hoover Commission,* in *Basic Documents of American Public Administration, 1776-1950,* ed. Frederick C. Mosher (New York: Holmes and Meier, 1976), 210.
25. Standards are the tools actually used to describe a job and the necessary qualifications for it. The Merit Systems Protection Board notes that "typically, each occupation is covered by a standard that describes the work of the occupation at various grade levels ... to function, the classification process must bring together three elements—position descriptions, classification standards, and human judgment—to arrive at appropriate conclusions.... OPM's qualification standards determine what skills are needed and evaluate whether candidates who apply are basically qualified to perform the work." Merit Systems Protection Board, *OPM's Classification and Qualification Systems: A Renewed Emphasis, A Changing Perspective* (Washington, D.C.: MSPB, November 1989), 6–7.
26. Ibid., 12.
27. Van Riper, *History of Civil Service,* 380.
28. Ibid., 432.
29. Civil Service Commission, *Biography of an Ideal,* 97.
30. Task Force on Education and Training, National Commission on the Public Service, *Investment for Leadership: Education and Training for the Public Service* (Washington, D.C., 1989), 120.

31. George William Curtis, *The Situation* (New York: National Civil Service Reform League, 1886), 17.
32. 413 U.S. 548 (1973).
33. 427 U.S. 347 (1976).
34. 445 U.S. 507 (1980).
35. For a full discussion of the issues surrounding Hatch reform, see chap. 2 of [*Agenda for Excellence: Public Service in America,* ed. Patricia Ingraham and Donald F. Kettl (Chatham, N.J.: Chatham House Publ., 1992)].
36. 408 U.S. 564 (1972).
37. 470 U.S. 532 (1985).
38. See David H. Rosenbloom, "What Every Public Personnel Manager Should Know about the Constitution," in *Public Personnel Administration,* ed. Steven Hays and Richard Kearney (Englewood Cliffs, N.J.: Prentice-Hall, 1990), 49–52, for a brief recent analysis.
39. 94 L. Ed.2d 203 (1987).
40. 94 L. Ed.2d 615 (1987).
41. 413 U.S. 548 (1973).
42. This summary of the principles contained in the Intergovernmental Personnel Act is taken from Civil Service Commission, *Biography of an Ideal,* 99–100.
43. P.L. 95-454, 13 October 1978, Civil Service Reform Act of 1978, Title I.
44. Personal interview, National Commission on the Public Service staff, February 1990.
45. Ibid.
46. Personal interview, National Commission on the Public Service staff, March 1990.
47. Ibid.
48. Personal interview, National Commission on the Public Service staff, February 1990.
49. Telephone interview, National Commission on the Public Service staff, December 1989.
50. Ibid.
51. General Accounting Office, *Federal Recruiting and Hiring* (Washington, D.C.: GAO, May 1990).
52. Merit Systems Protection Board, *Federal Personnel Management Since Civil Service Reform* (Washington, D.C.: MSPB, November 1989), 10.

Realizing the Promise of Diversity

Sonia M. Ospina

This [article] discusses the benefits of work force diversity for public sector organizations. It proposes an approach to diversity that takes into account the difficulties managers may face as organizations develop their work force. It also discusses some practical strategies for achieving diversity, dilemmas related to meeting the diversity challenge, and lessons drawn from previous experiences in public sector organizations.

The promise of diversity in the workplace is to create an environment in which employees' different identities and abilities are not only respected but also appreciated. Such an environment is conducive to motivating and rewarding high performance in all employees, regardless of social background. The approach proposed in this chapter invites managers to engage in four developmental tasks—considering, pursuing, managing, and maximizing diversity—to promote a shift from homogeneous to diverse organizations. This approach resembles an engineering project, where activities at each stage are meant to establish the foundation upon which future building blocks will rest. The particular conditions that exist in each organization define the types of strategies that will best fit each developmental task.

The [article] has four main sections. The first one defines work force diversity and discusses the mixed results of previous diversity efforts in the public sector (which point to the need to work harder on achieving this goal). The second section introduces and explains a proposed framework for moving toward diversity. The third section suggests strategies for developing each of the tasks in the framework, drawing illustrations from public sector experiences. The fourth section provides practical suggestions for change efforts centered on achieving diversity.

WORK FORCE DIVERSITY: THE REALITY

The work force of any organization can be characterized by the degree of its individual, professional, and social diversity (Jackson and Hardiman, 1990). Individual diversity refers to variations in the internal predispositions of an organization's employees. Professional diversity concerns various work-related attributes within an organization, such as occupations, organizational rank, and job functions. Both influence work relationships.

Nevertheless, work force diversity efforts in organizations focus primarily on social diversity. This refers to variations in the characteristics that identify a person with a given "cultural" community. Such a social identity typically stems from attributes such as age, race, ethnicity, gender, physical ability, sexual orientation, nationality, and class. Secondary attributes that may also affect this identity include income, education, religious beliefs, lifestyle, marital status, military experience, geographical location, functional background, union status, and others (Loden and Rosener, 1991). Social identity involves both self-definition and attributes perceived by others (Cox, 1993).

The infinite combinations of these primary and secondary social attributes produce the particular "social types" that make up a given work force. In theory, each employee is a unique individual worker that managers must attempt to optimize. In practice, however, some categories have become more relevant than others in defining who gets hired and who gets ahead. For historical reasons beyond the scope of this discussion, attributes like ethnicity, race, and gender, among others, have become social "marks" that play a critical role in determining the workplace experience of entire groups in our society (Williams, 1990). For example, in many organizations entire job clusters are occupied by individuals with similar social traits that are unrelated to the job. This is what experts call occupational and job segregation. Job segregation often results in the assignment of positive or negative social value to particular jobs, which in turn affects their associated rewards and working conditions (Tomaskovic-Devey, 1993; Ospina, forthcoming). For example, jobs occupied by a large proportion of white males tend to have better salaries and promotion prospects than jobs occupied by women of color. The resulting inequality creates obstacles to realizing the promise of diversity.

These practices are not the result of conspiracies against certain groups; they are the product of the fact that American workplaces were constructed around traditional values and the expectations of a homogeneous work force. Attitudinal, organizational, and institutional changes are thus required to incorporate the needs and values of the wide variety of types of employees that makes up the contemporary work force (Gottfredson, 1992). This may also require developing strategies to eliminate situations that contribute to maintaining formal or informal conditions of exclusion in identifiable organizational areas.

The most common social groups discussed in the diversity literature include women, people of color, individuals from ethnic or national groups (Gotteredson, 1992), gay men and lesbians (Gentile, 1994), older workers (Mayrand, 1992), physically challenged individuals (Equal Employment Opportunity Commission, 1992), employees with HIV or AIDS (Stone, 1994), and individuals with particular needs in areas as varied as family obligations (Merit Systems Protection Board, 1991) and religious mandates that affect their appearance or require dietary restrictions. (Schachter, 1993).

The barriers encountered by these groups can be illustrated with metaphors that have become part of the everyday vocabulary of the workplace in both the public and private sectors: women may encounter the "glass ceiling" and people of color may face "career plateauing" as they approach the upper echelons of an organizational hierarchy; employees may experience "sticky floors" as they try to leave entry-level jobs. "Glass walls" may impede their movement between functional areas. Other images convey practices that affect individuals who face particular demands outside the workplace. An example is the so-called maternal wall and the much debated "mommy track," which may also affect "modern" fathers who want to share family responsibilities at home. Individuals with disabilities and older workers may be confronted with "lazy physical environments" and "anti-gray" practices that reduce their chances for effective performance. For immigrant employees, there may very well be "accent ceilings," and for gays and lesbians, implicit and explicit "homophobic climates." These examples may not represent the only dimensions to consider in formulating a diversity agenda, but they do highlight groups who have traditionally experienced the effect of direct and indirect patterns of exclusion in the workplace and who presently question the traditional values embedded in organizational practices.

Managerial commitment to diversity is, however, less rooted in a desire to redress previous and present injustices than in a pragmatic acknowledgment that diversity makes good business sense—in both the private and public sectors (Coleman, 1994; Morrison and Herlihy, 1992). Managerial concerns for attracting and retaining a diverse work force stem from the confluence of three systemwide factors: the dramatic change in the demographic composition of the American work force; the societal trend to preserve and celebrate cultural differences and the value of multiculturalism; and changes in the nature of work (Johnson and Packer, 1987; Thomas, 1993). Indeed, the globalization of the economy, the shift from an industrial to an information-based society, and the shift from a manufacturing to a service economy have produced profound changes in today's workplace (Jackson and Alvarez, 1992). These circumstances highlight the relevance of the diversity challenge in the 1990s. The following list (drawn from Jackson and Holvino, 1988; Saltzstein, 1989; Jackson, 1992; Cox, 1993; Thomas, 1993; Merit Systems Protection Board, 1993a, 1993b; Ferran, 1994; Gentile, 1994; and Gowing and Payne, 1992) provides an inventory of the benefits of diversity applied to public organizations. I have classified the benefits according to the nature of the gain. The list includes ethical benefits, legal and public policy benefits, human resource (HR) management benefits, and organizational benefits, supporting the assertion that work force diversity makes good management sense all around.

Ethical Benefits

- Promotes fairness and justice in the workplace
- Creates economic opportunity and reduces social inequality

Legal and Public Policy Benefits

- Ensures compliance with personnel-related legal requirements
- Balances the government's need for productive employees against the rights of employees as free citizens of a constitutional democracy
- Increases representation and responsiveness in the bureaucracy
- Increases the potential for grassroots support for agency programs and policies

Human Resource Management Benefits

- Increases competitiveness in HR acquisition: enhances organizations' reputation and ability to attract and keep the best employees
- Reduces labor costs: reduces absenteeism, turnover, and employee dissatisfaction, resulting in improved delivery of services
- Increases productivity and innovation: reduces "group think"; minimizes reliance on traditional problem-solving strategies; promotes creative and innovative approaches

Organizational Benefits

- Increases internal capabilities: enhances organizations' flexibility and ability to address change; promotes fluidity in organizational design, as broader pools of candidates are available to take varied assignments
- Increases "marketing" advantages and responsiveness, as work force mirrors client population: extends organizational reach into more market niches (that is, new clients and services); enhances organizational insight and cultural sensitivity in addressing client needs and values
- Decreases discrimination litigation
- Increases organizational legitimacy due to enhanced reputation and higher effectiveness

Public sector organizations have fared better than private sector ones in their efforts to include diverse groups in their ranks. Studies indicate, for example, that proportional representation of particular groups has been achieved in many government bureaucracies. However, there is still a long way to go, as attention moves from mere representation to inclusion. Efforts to increase representation have occurred via formal Equal Employment Opportunity (EEO) and Affirmative Action (AA) policies. These have been helpful in opening the door, but they have not produced equality at all levels of the bureaucracy (Newman, 1994). For example, African Americans and women working in government are still overrepresented in clerical and menial jobs and underrepresented in supervisory, managerial, and executive positions. They also tend to be clustered in certain occupations and agencies while being virtually excluded from others (Page, 1994; Lewis, 1994; Kim and Lewis, 1994). Moreover, fiscal difficulties in federal, state, and local governments have threatened AA gains in government employment because layoffs hit those with the least seniority hardest (Mathews, 1994).

Even the most aggressively enforced EEO and AA policies cannot affect institutionalized practices nor change organizational cultures that perpetuate traditional assumptions bred in the workplace of the past. Hence, these efforts alone will not produce work environments that welcome, appreciate, and support employees from diverse backgrounds (Merit Systems Protection Board, 1993a). In addition to EEO and AA policies, public sector managers need other strategies to realize the benefits of work force diversity.

A FRAMEWORK FOR PROMOTING DIVERSITY

Work force diversity varies considerably from one organization to the next. Hence, a specific organizational diversity profile becomes the logical point of reference to decide the characteristics and priorities of a diversity agenda. Cox (1993) has developed a classification of organizational "types" that can be very helpful in achieving this diagnosis.

Three Organizational Types

Organizations can be placed on a continuum ranging from totally homogeneous (monolithic) to mixed (plural) to diverse (multicultural). These points represent stages of development in the diversity agenda, according to an organization's demographic composition and the consequent cultural dynamics. In organizations that are in the first, most primitive stage of development, employees who do not fit a dominant social type are totally excluded or relegated to marginal or subordinate roles. Jackson and Hardiman (1990) further distinguish two additional phases within this first stage of development: in the "exclusionary" phase, differences are openly viewed as defects; in the "club" phase, by contrast, organization members reject open discrimination (although the formal and informal organizational structures are still dominated by a majority culture, and minorities are accepted only if they conform).

Plural organizations exhibit proportional representation of minority groups, but their culture and systems remain typified by the dominant group's values. Jackson and Hardiman (1990) further distinguish "compliance" and "affirmative action" phases in this stage. In the first, decision makers take formal steps to reduce discrimination, usually through enforcement of AA and EEO regulations. While this allows individuals to enter the organization, inequality at each level of the hierarchy, as well as the culture that sustains it, remains untouched. In the latter phase, managers take a more active role in affirming a commitment to valuing and supporting minority members. These employees, however, continue to be evaluated according to the standards of the majority group.

In a multicultural organization, people of diverse backgrounds share privileges and responsibilities equally at every organizational level and in every type of job. In this (ideal) stage, the culture fosters and values differences; the process by which employees learn about organizational values and preferences espouses pluralism; organizational structures and systems facilitate integration, even at the level of informal networks; HR managers actively target biases embedded in the HR system; and management makes a proactive effort to effectively address intergroup conflict (Cox, 1993). Jackson and Hardiman (1990) also break this organizational stage down further, into "redefining" and "multicultural" phases. In the former, the dominant cultural perspective gradually incorporates new values and practices. The latter phase represents the fully developed promise of diversity (still to be achieved). In the view of Jackson and Hardiman, a truly multicultural organization

- Reflects the contributions and interests of diverse cultural and social groups in its mission, operations, and products or services

- Creates mechanisms for inclusion of diverse groups as full participants at all levels, especially in decisions that shape the organization

Moving toward the last stage requires managerial commitment and an understanding of multiculturalism. In this type of organization, managers view the mix of employees as a mosaic, in contrast to the image of a melting pot or a salad bowl (Pomerleau, 1994). The shift toward a multicultural organization requires, in Pomerleau's view, an organizational worldview that produces an increased degree of trust, mutually agreed upon processes for win-win conflict resolution, honest modes of communication, and the opening up of structures to facilitate responsiveness.

Four Managerial Tasks

Many diversity strategies fail because they are not integrated into a broader managerial approach that considers where the organization is and where it will be in the future. Such a diagnosis is required in order to design appropriate diversity strategies for each stage of organizational development. Indeed, moving from one stage to another requires at least four critical tasks. First, organizational stakeholders must become aware of the benefits of increased work force diversity. Only then can they engage in the second task, a serious pursuit of diversification in the workplace. Third, once a critical mass is available, the manager must find strategies to appropriately motivate, develop, and reward individual members of the diversified work force. The fourth task consists of ensuring the added value gained by having a diverse workplace is maximized in relation to the organization's strategic goals. Figure 6-1 presents an overview of these managerial tasks.

Managers may be tempted to work on the four tasks simultaneously. It is, however, important to recognize that the first two tasks (considering and pursuing diversity) contribute to generating the right mix of employees required for the success of the next two tasks. In fact, the task of maximizing the value of a diverse workplace applies only in organizations where the cultural shift to embrace multicultural values has taken place.

Each of the managerial tasks involved in promoting diversity—considering, pursuing, managing, and maximizing diversity—requires a creative com-

Figure 6-1. The Developmental Stages of Diversity

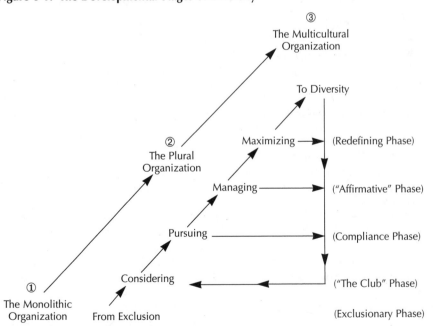

Source: Adapted from Cox, 1993, and Jackson and Hardiman, 1990.

bination of strategies and tools. Defining tasks, developing strategies, and fashioning tools are, in turn, part of a continuous process. As an organization changes its profile, new strategies are added, and earlier ones are changed. For example, managers of an already diverse work force must still monitor demographic changes in the labor market and reevaluate their strategies so as to pursue further diversity.

A truly multicultural organization may never be fully accomplished. Feedback loops at every stage suggest that managers' diversity tasks may be as permanent as those proposed by the POSDCORB acronym from classic administration theory (referring to an administrator's seven basic tasks: planning, organizing, staffing, directing, coordinating, reporting, and budgeting) or those suggested by more modern managerial frameworks such as strategic planning and the management of innovation.

REALIZING THE PROMISE

To be effective, a diversity agenda must follow a systemic logic linked to an organization's bottom line. Every diversity tool and activity must be chosen and implemented not only in reference to multiculturalism but also with the goal of enhancing organizational performance. The following sections illustrate this concept for each of the four managerial tasks described above. Each section begins with an example of a diversity issue encountered in an actual workplace.[1]

Considering Diversity: Strategies to Increase Awareness

In a large municipal agency whose female population represents only 14 percent of its work force of over fifty thousand, about a half dozen informal women's groups have emerged.[2] These groups address the frustrations of working in a historically male-dominated service delivery area where women face an unfriendly work environment. Recently the agency launched a formal initiative to create a women's advisory council. While welcoming the idea, members of the grassroots women's groups expressed general discomfort: they felt they had been excluded from the decision-making process used to create and design the new body. The agency's executive director then charged the EEO officer with addressing this concern. The EEO officer first performed a count of the informal women's groups in the agency. He then convened a meeting where representatives from each group discussed their needs and ideas.

Work force homogeneity is a potential source of morale problems. In the situation described above, the conflict was generated by the fact that the women's council was not created within a context of addressing the broad concerns of female employees (namely, the unequal distribution of organizational resources such as status, rewards, jobs, and authority in this male-dominated agency).

The example illustrates the problem of introducing the concept of diversity in an "exclusionary" or "club" organization. Managers in such organization focus on strategies such as the following:

- Performing a diversity audit to assess the type and amount of existing diversity, the agency's developmental stage, and areas requiring urgent, intermediate, and long-term attention. Informal techniques may include taking the organization's "pulse" by checking the number of EEO complaints, looking at retention figures, conducting exit interviews, and even visually checking the tables in the employee lounge to see the level of informal segregation. Formal techniques include conducting regular attitudinal surveys, forming focus groups to study the problem, and implementing the traditional EEO diagnostic practices discussed in the next section.

- Explicitly including diversity goals in mission statements and in recruitment policies and practices.
- Looking for mechanisms to increase awareness of the benefits of diversity among all organizational members.

Organizations at higher levels along the diversity continuum also need to use strategies to increase awareness of the need for diversity. Such strategies include the following:

- Instituting formal sensitivity training and "understanding differences" programs or workshops tailored to the agency's diversity profile
- Supporting informal grassroots (identity-based) groups
- Promoting "core groups" of managers who meet regularly to have frank talks on diversity
- Including diversity topics in orientation programs
- Organizing agency-sponsored social events and cultural celebrations with a diversity component

Pursuing Diversity: Strategies to Create a Diverse Work Force

Changes in the external environment (coupled with significant litigation) have motivated the U.S. Forest Service to become more professionally and demographically representative. Professional diversification has changed the dominance of the forester's role as other natural resource professionals have joined the agency. Demographic diversification has targeted the most valued career ladder in the agency to ensure wider social representation among rangers. After the agency modified its traditional career paths and system for promotion, a larger number of women and minorities were actively recruited and supported in their upward movement. This effort has been accompanied by new policy initiatives that stress the principles of participation, sustainability, collaboration, and integration. The overall effect has been stormy and imperfect, but it has introduced profound organizational change into the service (see Tipple and Wellman, 1991).

Pursuing diversity involves using strategies to ensure representation of members from different social categories at all levels of an organization. The example illustrates how the task directly overlaps with formal EEO policies and AA programs. But as a managerial task, this effort must frame such specialized policies within a broader agenda. The goal is to influence all areas where exclusion has occurred, promoting representation as well as equality in treatment within units, functional specialties, career paths, jobs, and ranks. Hence this change effort should simultaneously affect the organization's demographics, structure, and culture. Strategies to support this agenda include the following:

- Conducting periodic voluntary surveys to poll employees on management practices, barriers to contribution, and information deficits and feeding the results back to managers, thus making them accountable for the presence or absence of progress in identified weak areas
- Focusing diversity audits on two areas: EEO techniques (such as ranking, clustering, and pay equity analyses) and cultural assessments (to identify shared assumptions and values that represent barriers to diversity)
- Offering EEO training to managers and supervisors and requesting their input into the AA goal-setting process
- Articulating a strategy to communicate diversity goals and explain the components of the diversity policy throughout the organization
- Setting up a record-keeping process to keep track of staffing practices that reproduce exclusionary patterns
- Creating orientation programs for new employees at entry, intermediate, and management levels to continue the aggressive diversity strategy initiated with the active recruitment and hiring of underrepresented groups
- Offering staff training in team development, conflict resolution, and multiculturalism
- Ensuring diversity in key committees
- Creating task forces to propose innovative plans (detailing objectives, phases, schedules, and accountability) for pursuing diversity

Managing Diversity: Supporting an Effective Work Force

The Great Lakes regional office of the Federal Aviation Administration (FAA) developed a comprehensive effort to manage diversity after women and employees of color described many instances of discrimination in hearings to the House Subcommittee on Government Operations. The FAA identified and strengthened areas of its personnel system that were critical to the initiative, adding benefits such as flextime and child care. It developed a comprehensive training program, covering employees from orientation to retirement. For example, a three-day experiential cultural diversity workshop dealt with feelings, attitudes, and perceptions and issues such as sexual harassment, discrimination, and racism. Trained employees were later used as resources to conduct one-day workshops and to address diversity issues in the workplace. As employees became more sensitized to diversity, they were offered skills training in a follow-through support program. This program included team-building workshops for supervisors, diversity skill training for managers, leadership training to help employees create support groups and establish networking groups, a mentoring program available to all new hires, and a marketing effort to disseminate information about the initiative and clarify misconceptions about it. Assessment of the process included surveys of employees' feelings about the training and about their work environment, exit interviews, and listening sessions (see Merit Systems Protection Board, 1993b).

Managing diversity means actively searching for ways to eliminate any subtle or blatant barriers that keep employees from reaching their full potential. The goal is to create a work environment where employees feel welcome, appreciated, and supported. Since barriers to such an environment may crop up at any stage in an employee's career, managers must consider various human resource management (HRM) functions simultaneously. For example, the described initiative encompassed training, career development, recruitment, and compensation components of the HR system.

Managers must constantly search for ways to break down identified obstacles. On an organizational level, this means searching for permanent mechanisms that will minimize the need for case-by-case responses to solve diversity problems. The result is a workplace where employees feel they are treated with fairness and consistency while experiencing a response to their specific needs (Geber, 1990). Examples of successful strategies to achieve this goal include the following:

- Including diversity goals as an item in managers' and supervisors' performance appraisals
- Designing appraisal systems that use behavioral and performance-based evaluation criteria, thus minimizing the potential for individual biases to affect HR decisions
- Offering conflict-management training to managers and supervisors
- Targeting training programs to support identified developmental needs of specific employee populations (needs such as English as a second language and pronunciation or phonics classes)
- Creating mentoring and sponsorship programs and career development programs with counseling, diagnosing, and planning services available (including early-, mid-, and late-life career planning), as well as offering paid and unpaid sabbaticals
- Designing job rotation programs to facilitate employee exposure, visibility, and workplace learning
- Redesigning career paths to create bridges that open new opportunities and correct inequities in earlier designs (for example, career ladders with low ceilings or few steps)
- Offering alternative work arrangements (part-time employment, flextime, compressed work weeks, job sharing and flexible placement, telecommuting, term positions, and phased retirements) and life cycle benefit packages (child care, elder care, alternative work schedules, and leave-sharing programs)
- Correcting pay inequities throughout the system

Maximizing Diversity: Using the Work Force Strategically

The Albuquerque, New Mexico, School District was having difficulty in hiring enough minority teachers. The district employed 1,200 educational assistants most of them minority women. The job was characterized by low salaries and a high turnover rate. Viewing the support staff as a natural pool from which to recruit new minority and bilingual teachers, a labor-management committee designed a developmental program to achieve this goal. It had three components: an internship in which experienced assistants coached newly hired paraprofessionals, a new career ladder that would lead the educational assistants into other positions in the school system, and a tuition-subsidized training program developed with a local community college that would lead to an advanced degree in child development and eventually to teacher certification. In this way, the school district and the educational assistants association created a joint program that combined staff members' career aspirations with the school's human resource needs (see American Federation of Labor and Congress of Industrial Organizations, 1992).

The school district maximized its diversity by searching for ways to fully utilize its existing mix of employees, taking advantage of environmental opportunities in the process of accomplishing organizational objectives. This example highlights the difference between achieving some diversity and utilizing a diverse work force (Thomas, 1993). A strategic approach to diversity focuses on the latter, not the former.

In this managerial task, the same strategies described for managing diversity are used to convert components of the strategic plan into human resource programs that support it. For example, the recruitment, staffing, training, promotion, and separation functions of the school district's HR system were used to tap a natural labor pool whose underutilization had led to a high turnover rate and low motivation. The diversity edge of this HR planning exercise consisted of customizing the program's services to the expressed needs of specific employees. Offering a broad range of choices ensures that an organization has the right people in the right place at the right time—managed, supported, and rewarded in the right way—to achieve its goals.

Other strategies worth mentioning because of their specific focus on population segments include the following:

- Adding new benefits and new choices and making them available to more employees. Cafeteria benefits and benefits for nontraditional groups such as same-sex partners are two examples of new benefits. Broadened choices include (in child care, for example) providing informational and financial assistance, offering direct day care, and providing time-off policies (Merit Systems Protection Board, 1991).

- Introducing new policies as new issues are identified. For example, an agency might create a policy defining its position and procedures in relation to sensitive issues such as sexual harassment, physical accommodations for the disabled, and HIV and AIDS, or it might reassess existing rules in areas like dress code and physical appearance (Schachter, 1993).

- Finding and using external resources to support new efforts. For example, Business Responds to AIDS is a cooperative effort between the U.S. Centers for Disease Control and the business sector to provide technical assistance to meet the workplace challenges this disease creates (Stone, 1994).

- Starting a managerial succession plan that identifies openings and diverse internal candidates to fill them. This requires strengthening HR practices with innovations such as job and talent banks, improved career-planning services, and the use of forecasting and other human power modeling techniques to assess labor supply and demand.

EMBARKING ON A DIVERSITY CHANGE EFFORT

The managerial tasks described in the previous section follow a developmental more than a chronological order. They are part of a systematic process of change designed to move an organization from monolithic to multicultural. For example, although a monolithic organization cannot, by definition, successfully manage diversity, managers in a plural organization must develop activities associated with the less complex tasks of considering and pursuing diversity.

Developing a diversity agenda is not easy. Studies of diversity efforts have identified, among others, the following potential pitfalls:

- Difficulty convincing relevant stakeholders that multiculturalism is needed

- Difficulty marketing the diversity plan, as the costs associated with it are easier to quantify than its benefits

- Potential employee resentment or disillusionment stemming from, among other things, disappointed hopes for rapid improvement, fear of exclusion or of a loss of benefits, and general uncertainty

- The fact that a decision to change standards may be perceived by some as a decision to "reduce" standards, with a consequent loss of program credibility

- Increased danger of group polarization resulting from changing the existing distributive order

These and other risks can be minimized by clearly stating the rationale behind the change process and designing a solid strategy to communicate it. In addition, according to Cox (1993), a successful effort must include the following:

Leadership: top management commitment and support, steering and advisory groups, communications strategy

Research measurement: comprehensive organizational assessments, baseline data, benchmarking

Education: awareness and advanced training, development of in-house expertise, orientation programs

Changes in culture and management systems: using HRM strategies

Follow-up: evaluation processes, accountability, ensuring continuous improvement

Managers may feel paralyzed by the complexity of the process. They may be reluctant to take the time and dedicate the resources required to follow it through. Public sector managers may be particularly vulnerable in this area, given that agency cultures and the political environment do not lend themselves to long-range planning. Diversity scholars are adamant, however, that diversity considerably increases an organization's chances for success. Research in organizational change supports this assertion. The key is to remember that the process of creating a comprehensive diversity plan is part of the change effort itself, not just its precondition.

It is true that managers may find it difficult to influence the personnel systems of public sector organizations. Yet it is important to emphasize that most of the strategies reviewed in this chapter, as well as some of the advice that follows, were drawn from experiences in public agencies (for additional illustrations of public sector diversity efforts see Merit Systems Protection Board, 1993a, 1993b; Mathews, 1994).

The following guidelines summarize lessons drawn from specific diversity efforts surveyed in the literature. They can help the public sector manager anticipate hurdles and capitalize on what others have learned in the past.

Begin with yourself:

- Understand diversity. Recognize types of diversity and clarify their strategic nature. Clarify your motivation and your vision.
- Assess your readiness to accept the roles of advocate (to gain the buy-in of important stakeholders) and change agent (to lead the pioneering implementation process).
- Adopt a long-term view. Avoid quick fixes, but do celebrate small wins.

At the program level:

- Anticipate possible problems and be prepared to address them. Be prepared to change the direction of the program, and remind team members of this possibility.
- Combine cultural and structural strategies. Organize programs that develop individuals, not groups; stress variance, not just average differences; treat group differences as important but not special; and seek out and strengthen common bonds.
- Reexamine assumptions, but maintain high standards. Set high but realistic goals. Test assumptions and support claims with evidence.
- Do not underestimate the power of communicating directly with program participants about the importance of the program and the requirements involved, independently of top management support. Solicit negative as well as positive feedback from your "customers" (that is, your employees).

At the organizational level:

- Foster mind-set shifts (for example, foster the idea that diversity includes everyone and that it is of strategic managerial benefit).
- Audit and modify organizational culture and systems as necessary.
- Gain the support of top management and first-level supervisors in your organization. Enlist the support of other relevant organizations (such as regulatory agencies) affected by the program.
- Stay close to the customer throughout the design, marketing, and evaluation phases of the change effort. In particular, involve stakeholders in problem definition, program implementation, and evaluation by using mechanisms such as advisory committees, surveys, and focus groups.

SUMMARY

Employee diversity is only one of several critical diversity trends affecting the workplace. Administrators also face diversity in markets, products and services, professional specialties, workplace structures, management processes, and organizational cultures (DeLuca and McDowell, 1992). The interdependencies among these trends are clear. After all, the reconsideration of assumptions, styles, and practices traditionally used to manage people in the workplace is taking place at the same time that external social forces are pressuring decision makers to question present work arrangements.

Public administrators have not been exempt from these pressures. Today they are required to deliver better services with fewer financial and human resources. In this competitive environment, promoting work force diversity enhances managers' ability to attract and retain the right type of employees and motivate them to perform at their best. Yet the challenges of diversity are not the same for all managers in all organizations. Diversity strategies must respond to the specific requirements of an organization's work force profile and the demands posed by its environment.

Notes

1. The strategies described in the following sections are from an inventory collected over the years from innumerable sources, including but not limited to those presented in the references. For a self-contained discussion of these strategies, see Cox, 1993.
2. This example reports an actual situation described to the author in a confidential interview. The name of the agency has been withheld and its characteristics concealed due to the confidential nature of the information.

References

Note: The author thanks Peter Del Toro for his help in preparing this [article].

American Federation of Labor and Congress of Industrial Organizations. *Reinvigorating the Public Service: Union Innovations to Improve Government.* Washington, D.C.: American Federation of Labor and Congress of Industrial Organizations, 1992.

Coleman, T. "Managing Diversity: Keeping It in Focus." *Public Management,* 1994, 76(10), 10–16.

Cox, T., Jr. *Cultural Diversity in Organizations: Theory, Research and Practice.* San Francisco: Berrett-Koehler, 1993.

DeLuca, J., and McDowell, R. "Managing Diversity: A Strategic 'Grass Roots' Approach." In S. E. Jackson and others (eds.), *Diversity in the Workplace: Human Resources Initiatives.* Vol. 1. New York: Guilford Press, 1992.

Equal Employment Opportunity Commission. U.S. Department of Justice. *The Americans with Disabilities Act: Questions and Answers.* Washington, D.C.: Government Printing Office, 1992.

Ferran, E. "Workplace Cultural Diversity: A Manager's Journal." *Journal of Child and Family Studies,* 1994, 3(1), 1–5.

Geber, B. "Managing Diversify." *Training,* 1990, 27(7), 23–32.

Gentile, M. (ed). *Differences That Work: Organizational Excellence through Diversity.* Boston: Harvard Business School Press, 1994.

Gottfredson, L. "Dilemmas in Developing Diversity Programs." In S. E. Jackson and others (eds.), *Diversity in the Workplace: Human Resources Initiatives.* Vol. 1. New York: Guilford Press, 1992.

Gowing, M., and Payne, S. "Assessing the Quality of the Federal Workforce: A Program to Meet Diverse Needs." In S. E. Jackson and others (eds.), *Diversity in the Workplace: Human Resources Initiatives.* New York: Guilford Press, 1992.

Jackson, B., and Hardiman, R. "Assessing Organizational Diversity." Document from the Multicultural Organization Development Training Seminar offered by New Perspectives, Inc., 1990 (Mimeographed).

Jackson, B., and Holvino, E. "Developing Multicultural Organizations." *Creative Change*, Fall 1988, pp. 14–19.

Jackson, S. E. "Stepping into the Future: Guidelines for Action." In S. E. Jackson and others (eds.), *Diversity in the Workplace: Human Resources Initiatives*. Vol. 1. New York: Guilford Press, 1992.

Jackson, S. E., and Alvarez, E. "Working through Diversity as a Strategic Imperative." In S. E. Jackson and others (eds.), *Diversity in the Workplace: Human Resources Initiatives*. Vol. 1. New York: Guilford Press, 1992.

Johnson, W., and Packer, A. *Workforce 2000: Work and Workers for the Twenty-First Century.* Indianapolis, Ind.: Hudson Institute, 1987.

Kim, P., and Lewis, G. "Asian Americans in the Public Service: Success, Diversity and Discrimination." *Public Administration Review,* 1994, *54*(3), 285–290.

Lewis, G. B. "Women, Occupations, and Federal Agencies: Occupational Mix and Interagency Difference in Sexual Inequality in Federal White-Collar Employment." *Public Administration Review,* 1994, *54*(3), 271–275.

Loden, M., and Rosener, J. *Workforce America: Managing Employee Diversity as a Vital Resource.* Homewood, Ill.: Business One Irwin, 1991.

Mathews, A. (ed.). The Public Manager Forum—Diversity: Fact Not Fashion. *The Public Manager (The New Bureaucrat),* 1994, *23*(3), 15–42.

Mayrand, P. "Older Workers: A Problem or the Solution?" In American Association of Retired Persons, *Fifth Textbook Authors' Conference Proceedings.* Washington, D.C.: American Association of Retired Persons, 1992.

Merit Systems Protection Board. *Balancing Work Responsibilities and Family Needs: The Federal Civil Service Response.* Washington, D.C.: Government Printing Office, 1991.

Merit Systems Protection Board. *Evolving Workforce Demographics: Federal Agency Action and Reaction.* Washington, D.C.: Government Printing Office, 1993a.

Merit Systems Protection Board. *A Report on the Proceedings of "The Changing Face of the Federal Workforce: A Symposium on Diversity."* Washington, D.C.: Government Printing Office, 1993b.

Morrison, E., and Herlihy, J. M. "Becoming the Best Place to Work: Managing Diversity at American Express Travel-Related Services." In S. E. Jackson and others (eds.), *Diversity in the Workplace: Human Resources Initiatives.* New York: Guilford Press, 1992.

Newman, M. "Gender and Lowi's Thesis: Implications for Career Advancement." *Public Administration Review,* 1994, *54*(3), 277–284.

Ospina, S. *Illusions of Opportunity: Employee Expectations and Workplace Inequality.* Ithaca, N.Y.: Cornell University Press/Industrial Labor Relations Press, forthcoming

Page, P. "African-Americans in Executive Branch Agencies." *Review of Public Personnel Administration,* Winter 1994, *15*, 24–47.

Pomerleau, R. "A Desideratum for Managing the Diverse Workplace." *Review of Public Personnel Administration,* 1994, *14*(1), 85-100.

Saltzstein, G. "Enhancing Equal Employment Opportunity" In J. L. Perry (ed.), *Handbook of Public Administration.* (1st ed.) San Francisco: Jossey-Bass, 1989.

Schachter, H. L. "A Case for Moving from Tolerance to Valuing Diversity: The Issue of Religiously Distinctive Dress and Appearance." *Review of Public Personnel Administration,* 1993, *13*(2), 29–46.

Stone, R. "AIDS in the Workplace: An Executive Update." *The Academy of Management Executives,* 1994, *8*(3), 52–64.

Thomas, R. R. "Managing Diversity: An Evolving Managerial Concept." In A. R. Cohen (ed.), *The Portable MBA in Management.* New York: Wiley, 1993.

Tipple, T., and Wellman, D. "Herbert Kaufman's Forest Ranger Thirty Years Later: From Simplicity and Homogeneity to Complexity and Diversity." *Public Administration Review,* 1991, *51*(5), 421–428.

Tomaskovic-Devey, D. *Gender and Racial Inequality at Work: The Sources and Consequences of Job Segregation.* Ithaca, N.Y.: Industrial Labor Relations Press, 1993.

Williams, R. *Hierarchical Structures and Social Value.* New York: Cambridge University Press, 1990.

7 Public Budgeting and Financial Management

Budgeting is one of the most important games in government, complete with players, roles, strategies, and prizes. And how the game is played determines what government does (or does not do). The budget may be the most important document in public administration. It is a statement, more or less, of what government is going to do for the next year—with price tags attached.

In the first article in this chapter, one of the nation's most respected budget experts, Allen Schick, examines the federal budgetary process. He provides both some historical perspective and a glimpse at the steps followed in developing the annual federal budget. Schick also provides a sense of some of the complexity that goes with governmental budgeting. While Schick's focus is the federal government, many of these same basic steps exist in state and local budgeting as well.

No topic about budgeting in our time has caused as much political controversy as the federal budget deficit. In the second article in this chapter, economist Robert Eisner feels that the public may be confused about deficits. Eisner takes a contrarian view of budget deficits, even going so far as to suggest that budget deficits might be increased.

With the help of a healthy economy, the federal budget deficit declined dramatically during the Clinton years. A political budget deal was crafted between the Democratic President and a Republican Congress in 1997. Although budget surpluses have been projected by the year 2002, many deficit related issues still remain to be addressed in the period after that year.

In fiscal year 1995, the federal government spent over $200 billion for more than 600 grant programs to state and local governments. This is about 15 percent of all federal expenditures. One federal budget trend has been to devolve authority for public programs to the states, but federal dollars have not always followed.

Budgeting not only includes annual operating revenues and expenditures, but it also includes paying for large capital projects, like bridges and airports. This is America's nagging *infrastructure* problem.

Budgeting is inseparable from other aspects of governmental financial management. Financial management is concerned with a wide variety of other issues:

- Accounting, auditing, and financial reporting
- Budget execution and control
- Cash management, involving the handling of cash receipts, investment of idle funds, relations with financial institutions like banks, cash flow, and general treasury management
- Risk management and insurance, preventing and reducing a governmental unit's exposure to the accidental loss of its assets

- Revenue and expenditure forecasting
- Capital improvement planning and debt management, particularly long-term indebtedness and bonds
- Appraising the financial condition of a governmental jurisdiction
- Determining the actuarial soundness of financial schemes, like pension systems
- Purchasing and procurement

Some questions to discuss about public budgeting are:

- Who are the participants in the budgetary process—federal or local— and what roles do they play?
- Although both Senator Dole and President Clinton talked about it during the last presidential election, are budget deficits all that bad? And exactly why is it so difficult to reduce the annual federal deficit? How successful has the federal government been in doing this in the 1990s, and why?

Mapping the Federal Budget Process

ALLEN SCHICK

Budgeting differs from many other government responsibilities in that its tasks must be completed each year. No matter how difficult the choices or uncertain the outlook, the president must submit a budget each year and Congress must make appropriations. If the president and Congress decide that the time is not ripe to act on a particular legislative proposal, they can lay it aside until more information is available or an agreement has been hammered out. But they cannot default on their responsibility to deal with the budget each year. If they did, federal programs and agencies would shut down for lack of money and the work of government would come to a halt.

Budgetary procedures regulate conflict by parceling out tasks and roles, establishing expectations and deadlines for action, and limiting the scope of issues that are considered. Conflict is dampened by the routines of budgeting, the repetitive tasks that are completed with little change year after year, and the behavior of participants. Budget makers generally display a willingness to compromise that is often lacking when other kinds of matters are in dispute.

The rules of budgeting affect the outcomes. How much is taxed and spent, who pays and who benefits, which programs grow and which shrink— these and other matters are influenced by formal procedures and informal behavior. Throughout this book, therefore, the discussion shifts back and forth between the process and the politics of budgeting. No explanation of budgeting is complete unless it takes both into account.

The process and the politics revolve around two main institutions of government power: the presidency and Congress. The evolution of federal budgeting has been a long contest for political power; the weapons used by the combatants have been the rules and procedures of budgeting. For two hundred years these institutions have vied for power of the purse, with the advantage sometimes held by one and sometimes by the other. The struggle over the past two centuries has resulted in parallel budget processes in the executive and legislative branches.

The evolution not only bequeathed budgetary roles to the president and Congress, it also left the federal government with two budget processes, one centered on annual appropriations, the other dispersed among many entitlement programs. The two are sometimes merged to compile a budget for the entire federal government. But on key matters, such as the route taken by legislation in Congress and the rules of deficit control, the processes go their separate ways.

The final section of this chapter introduces the annual budget process and the roles of the many participants in federal budgeting.

THE EVOLUTION OF FEDERAL BUDGETING

The history of federal budgeting is intertwined with the growth of the nation's revenues, expenditures, and deficits. Large federal budgets and huge deficits are a recent development (table 7-1). The first Congress in 1789 appropriated only $639,000 to cover the expenses of the new government. This amount is now spent by the federal government every ten or fifteen seconds. The growth of government transformed budgeting from a Congress-centered activity to one in which both it and the president have prominent roles, and from a process that (except for wartime) usually produced balanced budgets into one in which deficits are common. These transformations are associated with three periods of federal budgeting. The first, stretching from 1789 to 1921, began with small government and rare deficits and ended with a much enlarged government and financial difficulties. The second began with the Budget and Accounting Act of 1921, which gave the president a central role in managing the nation's finances, and ended with a vastly larger government and efforts to make Congress more responsible for budget policy. The third period began with the Congressional Budget Act of 1974 and includes the Gramm-Rudman-Hollings legislation in 1985 and 1987 and the Budget Enforcement Act of 1990.

Legislative Dominance, 1789-1921

The Constitution gives Congress the power to levy taxes and provides that funds may be drawn from the treasury only pursuant to appropriations made by law. The Constitution does not specify how these legislative powers of the purse are to be exercised, nor does it expressly provide any role for the president in financial matters or for a federal budget process. In fact, the concept of budgeting was imported from Europe more than a century after the Constitution was adopted.

Table 7-1
Federal Receipts, Outlays, Deficit, and Public Debt,
Selected Fiscal Years and Periods, 1789-1995[a]

Billions of dollars

Fiscal years	Revenues	Outlays	Surplus or Deficit	Public Debt[b]
1789-1900	16	17	-1	1
1910	1	1	★	1
1920	7	6	★	24
1930	4	3	1	16
1940	7	9	-3	43
1950	39	43	-3	219
1960	92	92	★	237
1970	193	196	-3	283
1980	517	591	-74	709
1990	1,031	1,253	-221	2,410
1993	1,154	1,408	-265	3,247
1995[c]	1,354	1,519	-165	3,646

Sources: *Historical Statistics of the United States: From Colonial Times to 1970*, series Y 335-338; and *Budget of the United States Government, Fiscal Year 1995, Historical Tables*, tables 1.1, 7.1.
★Less than $0.5 billion.
a. Amounts shown are on a unified or consolidated budget basis. They include social security, other trust funds, and other off-budget transactions. The amounts for 1789-1900 are the total receipts, outlays, deficit, and public debt accumulated during this period. The amounts shown for other years are the receipts, outlays, surplus or deficit, or public debt recorded for the relevant year.
b. The public debt is the portion of the gross federal debt held by the public. It does not include the portion of the federal debt held by government accounts, such as the social security trust funds. At present, the gross federal debt is about $1.3 trillion higher than the public debt.
c. Estimated.

In the early years of American government, revenue and spending legislation, as well as other financial matters, were concentrated in the House Ways and Means and the Senate Finance Committees. Federal revenues and spending grew sporadically during the nineteenth century. Growth spurts, usually occasioned by war (table 7-2) were followed by periods of stability. Federal spending tripled during the War of 1812, doubled during the Mexican-American War, and increased twenty-fold during the Civil War. Spending receded after each war, but still remained well above prewar levels. Total spending usually was stable between wars. For example, the government spent $358 million in 1867 (the first full fiscal year after the Civil War) and $366 million in 1897 (the last year before the Spanish-American War). The government typically accumulated debt during wartime, was burdened by high interest payments after a war, and gradually undertook new expenditures as debt was retired and interest charges decreased. The paydown of the public debt was made possible by revenues (mostly from tariffs) that were ample to cover expenditures during peacetime. With budgets consistently at or near balance, the public debt dropped from $2.8 billion in 1866 to $1.3 billion in 1900.

Table 7-2
Impact of War on Federal Spending,
Selected Fiscal Years, 1811-1975

Millions of current dollars

War	Prewar Level[a]		Wartime Peak[a]		Percentage Change	Postwar Low[a]		Percentage Change
War of 1812	8	(1811)	35	(1814)	331	22	(1817)	-37
Mexican-American War	28	(1846)	57	(1847)	106	45	(1849)	-21
Civil War	67	(1861)	1,298	(1865)	1,850	358	(1867)	-72
Spanish-American War	366	(1897)	605	(1899)	65	521	(1900)	-14
World War I	713	(1916)	18,493	(1919)	1,678	6,358	(1920)	-50
World War II	9,468	(1941)	92,712	(1945)	879	59,232	(1946)	-36
Korean War	42,562	(1950)	76,101	(1953)	79	68,444	(1955)	-10
Vietnam War	118,528	(1964)	183,640	(1969)	55	332,332	(1975)	81

Sources: *Historical Statistics of the United States: Colonial Times to 1970,* series Y 335-338, Y 457-465; and *Budget of the United States Government, Fiscal Year 1993, Historical Tables,* tables 1.1, 3.1.

a. Fiscal year in parentheses.

Remarkably, financial balance was achieved despite the lack of a budget system that coordinated all legislative or executive revenue and expenditure action. As long as the federal government was small and its financial operations stable, a budget was not considered necessary. Two related developments, however, brought this comfortable situation, in which the government achieved satisfactory outcomes without a coordinated process, to a close. One was the fragmentation of congressional action, the other the growth of federal spending and peacetime deficits.

The first step in fragmenting legislative action occurred as a by-product of the Civil War, which greatly added to the financial burdens of government. Both the House (1865) and the Senate (1867) separated spending and revenue jurisdiction and assigned spending to newly established appropriations committees. The second step, which occurred late in the nineteenth century, was the assignment of half the appropriations bills to various legislative committees, with the result that the appropriations committees no longer had jurisdiction over all federal spending. The dispersion of appropriations control led to higher spending, especially in those bills in the jurisdiction of legislative committees.

Legislative fragmentation was mirrored by decentralization in the executive branch. The president had a limited role in overseeing financial operations. Most agencies submitted their spending estimates directly to the relevant congressional committees without having their requests reviewed by him. Agency requests were compiled in an annual Book of Estimates, but little policy control was exercised over the amounts requested. Fragmentation and the progressive increase in federal spending (which doubled between 1894 and 1914) as the United States expanded social and regulatory programs and became more active in international matters led to persistent deficits. Spending exceeded revenues in eleven of the seventeen years between 1894 and 1910. Then came World War I. Federal spending soared from $700 million in 1914 to more than $18 billion five years later, and the public debt exploded from $1 billion to $25 billion. Shortly after the war, Congress turned to the president to coordinate financial decisions. The key legislation was the Budget and Accounting Act of 1921, which established the executive budget system that is still in operation. This and other landmarks in federal budgeting are listed in table 7-3.

Presidential Budgeting, 1921-74

The 1921 act did not directly alter the procedures by which Congress made revenue and spending decisions (although it did spur the House and Senate to return jurisdiction over all spending bills to the appropriations committees). The main impact was in the executive branch. The president was required to submit a budget to Congress each year, and the Bureau of the Budget, renamed the Office of Management and Budget (OMB) in 1970, was established to assist him in carrying out his budget responsibilities. These responsibilities were organized around an elaborate executive budget process in which agency requests were reviewed by the president's budget staff. Agencies were barred from submitting their budgets directly to Congress, as they had in the past. Under the new procedures the president and his budget aides decided how much would be requested.

In effect, the 1921 act made the president an agent of congressional budget control. Congress, it was expected, would coordinate its revenue and spending decisions, and thereby eliminate deficits, by acting on comprehensive recommendations from the president. Although the 1921 act does not bar Congress from appropriating more than the president requests, the expectation was that it would weigh his recommendations in making its own budget decisions.

The Budget and Accounting Act had immediate success in controlling federal finance. Taxes were reduced, and both spending and the public debt declined during the 1920s (table 7-1). These accomplishments may have been partly due to the conservative temperament of postwar America, but they also were the result of the fiscal discipline imposed by the new budget system. Throughout the 1920s the president's budget office maintained a tight grip on agency spending.

Then came the Great Depression, and with it the New Deal and a vast expansion in the scale of government. On the eve of the depression in 1929, federal spending was only 3 percent of GDP; a decade later it was 10 percent. Although expenditures tripled, revenues failed to keep pace, and the government incurred substantial deficits. World War II, however, brought a massive inflow of revenue as Congress enacted a broad-based income tax with high rates. As a result, federal revenues were seven times higher in 1945 than they had been five years earlier. Following the pattern set after previous wars, Congress lowered taxes but retained sufficient additional revenue to enlarge government programs. Although outlays averaged 18 percent of GDP during the 1950s, the surge in revenues enabled the president to produce budgets that were at or near balance.

Table 7-3
Milestones in Federal Budgeting,
1789-1990

Year	Event	Significance
1789	Constitution	Gives Congress the power to levy taxes and requires appropriations by Congress before funds are disbursed
1802-67	Committee structure	House Ways and Means Committee established as standing committee in 1802; House Appropriations Committee established in 1865. Senate Finance Committee established in 1816; Senate Appropriations Committee in 1867
1837, 1850	House and Senate rules	House and Senate bar unauthorized appropriations
1870, 1905-1906	Antideficiency Act	Requires apportionment of funds to prevent overexpenditure
1921	Budget and Accounting Act	Provides for an executive budget; establishes the Bureau of the Budget and the General Accounting Office
1939	Reorganization Plan No. 1	Transfers Bureau of the Budget to the new Executive Office of the President and expands the bureau's role
1967	President's Commission on Budget Concepts	Adoption of the unified budget, including trust funds
1974	Congressional Budget and Impoundment Control Act	Establishes the congressional budget process, House and Senate budget committees, and the Congressional Budget Office. Also establishes procedures for legislative review of impoundments
1980	Reconciliation process	Reconciliation used for the first time at start of congressional budget process
1985, 1987	Gramm-Rudman-Hollings Acts	Set deficit reduction targets and sequestration procedures
1990	Budget Enforcement Act	Shifts from fixed to adjustable deficit targets, caps discretionary spending, establishes pay-as-you-go rules for revenues and direct spending, and establishes new budgeting rules for direct and guaranteed loans
1990	Chief Financial Officers Act	Provides for a chief financial officer in all major agencies to oversee financial management and integrate accounting and budgeting

The additional revenues and expanded government enabled the president to use the budget to develop an annual legislative program and to manage federal agencies. It became customary in the 1950s for the president to compile a set of legislative proposals each year in tandem with the formulation of the annual budget. The president's budget staff actively used the budget process to improve the management of federal programs and agencies. With the budget's increased share in GDP, the president became increasingly active in steering the economy and keeping it on a high-growth, low-inflation course. Despite the steady rise in federal spending—real outlays doubled between 1949 and 1966—the booming economy enabled the government to balance its books or hold deficits sufficiently low that they did not give rise to budget difficulties.

The Vietnam War and the growth of mandatory expenditures brought this idyllic period in federal budgeting to an end. Because the war was unpopular, Congress was reluctant to pay for it with tax increases. It did enact a small surtax, and the additional revenue produced a small surplus in fiscal year 1969, but the tax expired and deficit spending resumed before the war ended. Attitudes toward the deficit were conditioned by distaste for the war. Rather than considering the deficit an appropriate means of financing military operations, as it had been thought of in previous wars, many Americans regarded it as evidence of an abandonment of fiscal responsibility. To make matters worse, when the war ended, federal spending did not recede and the budget did not return to balance. In fact, there was no postwar year in which federal spending did not surpass the wartime peak. There was a small drop in the ratio of expenditures to GDP, but not enough to balance the budget.

The post-Vietnam pattern differed from the budgetary patterns after previous wars because the composition of federal spending had changed. Past spending had been determined by annual presidential and congressional actions. In the past, when war ended, Congress appropriated less for military purposes, cut some or all of the taxes levied to finance the war, and applied surplus funds to domestic programs. After the Vietnam War, however, an expanding share of the budget went for mandatory payments—social security, medicare and medicaid, food stamps, and other entitlements—that had to be made regardless of the government's financial condition. Less than one-quarter of total spending a generation ago, entitlement payments are now more than one-half (table 7-4). After Vietnam the increase in these payments exceeded the decrease in defense expenditures. Between 1969 and 1973, defense spending declined by $6 billion, but payments to individuals soared by $50 billion. Instead of a post-Vietnam peace dividend, the budget was hobbled by large and persistent deficits.

With an increasing share of the budget driven by eligibility rules and payment formulas, the president's budget became more a means of estimating the future cost of existing obligations than of deciding the program and financial policies of the government. The president's budget capacity was also weakened by the Vietnam War, which undermined confidence in his leadership and soured his relationship with Congress. President Nixon warred with Congress over budget priorities and the impoundment of funds. Spurred by belief that the budget was out of control and that the president could not lead, Congress sought to bolster its own role in budgeting.

Table 7-4 Federal Payments to Individuals, Selected Programs, Fiscal Years 1970, 1980, 1990, and Estimated, 1994, 1997					
Program	*1970*	*1980*	*1990*	*1994*	*1997*
Outlays (billions of dollars)					
Social security (OASDI)	30	117	246	317	336
Federal retirement	3	15	31	36	38
Supplemental security income	0	6	11	24	28
Medicare (HI)	5	24	66	102	183
Medicaid	3	14	41	87	106
Food stamps	1	9	15	26	27
Family support (AFDC)	4	7	12	16	17
Veterans' assistance	5	11	14	19	19
Total payments for individuals	65	279	584	830	994
Percent of total federal outlays	33	47	47	56	59
Recipients (millions)					
Social security	26	35	39	42	45
Medicare (HI)	n.a.	28	33	36	38
Medicaid	15	22	25	36	39
Food stamps	9	19	19	27	27
Family support (AFDC)	7	11	11	14	17

Sources: *Budget of the United States Government, Fiscal Year 1995, Analytical Perspectives,* p. 204; and *Budget of the United States Government, Fiscal Year 1995, Historical Tables,* tables 11.3, 6.1.

n.a. Not available.

Grappling with the Deficit, 1974-94

Congress's quest for its own budget process culminated in the Congressional Budget Act of 1974, which President Nixon signed into law less than a month before he was driven from office by the Watergate scandal. This measure provided for Congress to adopt a budget resolution that sets forth budget totals and functional allocations. The budget resolution is the only occasion for Congress to vote on the size of the deficit, total spending, and budget priorities.

In bolstering Congress's budget capacity, the legislation did not alter the formal role of the president. As before, the president submits a budget each year, and Congress can defer to his recommendations if it wishes to do so. Now, however, Congress has the option of relying on its own budget resolution rather than on the president's budget for guidance on revenue and expenditure decisions. The budget resolution retains the congressional processes for enacting revenue and spending legislation, but it provides a framework within which the many separate measures affecting federal finances can be considered. Congress can assess the financial implications of revenue appropriations and other spending measures in the light of the policies adopted in its budget resolution.

The Congressional Budget Act did not ordain that the budget be balanced, nor did it bar Congress from adopting resolutions that have big deficits. Nevertheless, the act was spurred by the expectation that deficits would be smaller if Congress expressly had to vote for them. This expectation has not been fulfilled. The economy went into a tailspin just about the time that Congress began implementing the new process, so that the deficit was much higher than had been incurred before 1974. During the first decade (fiscal years 1976-85) of the new process, the budget deficit averaged more than $110 billion a year. It had been $15 billion a year during the previous decade. The deficit averaged 3.8 percent GDP during the decade; in the previous decade it averaged 1.4 percent.

The soaring deficit had various causes: economic stagflation during the 1970s, the built-in escalation in entitlement expenditures, and President Reagan's success in prodding Congress to cut taxes at the same time it was boosting defense expenditures. Whatever the cause, no one could claim that having Congress vote on a budget resolution generated lower deficits.

As the budget crisis deepened in the 1980s—the deficit averaged more than $200 billion a year during fiscal years 1983-86—Congress established annual targets to reduce the deficit. The Balanced Budget and Emergency Deficit Control Act of 1985, commonly referred to as the Gramm-Rudman-Hollings (GRH) Act, called for the progressive reduction in the deficit in each fiscal year from 1986 through 1990 and for a balanced budget in 1991. It also provided for the cancellation of budget resources if the projected deficit exceeded the target by more than an allowed amount. Congress amended the law in 1987 and postponed the target year for a balanced budget to 1993.

Despite the threat of sequestration—the withholding of funds when deficit targets have been exceeded—the deficit exceeded the GRH target in each fiscal year from 1986 through 1990. The law was defective in a number of ways. It did not require that the actual deficit be within the target, only that the deficit projected at the start of the fiscal year be within that year's allowed level. An increase in the deficit during the fiscal year, whether because of estimation errors, changes in economic conditions, or new policies, did not require compensatory action to offset the increase, even if the actual deficit exceeded the target. Reliance on projected rather than actual deficits led to manipulation of budget estimates, bookkeeping tricks in lieu of genuine savings, and deficits much higher than had been budgeted.

BUDGET ENFORCEMENT RULES

One of the lessons Congress derived from the failure of GRH is that it is futile to set fixed dollar limits on annual deficits. Fixed limits can be overtaken by unforeseen developments such as the recession that began in the summer of 1990. To contain the deficit, Congress concluded, it is necessary to control the amount of revenue raised and money spent. In line with this reasoning, the Budget Enforcement Act of 1990 established a new deficit control process that distinguishes between discretionary spending, controlled by annual appropriations decisions, and direct spending, controlled by substantive legislation outside the jurisdiction of the appropriations committees. The BEA rules were to be effective only for fiscal years 1991-95, but they were subsequently extended through fiscal year 1998, and there is a strong probability that they will be extended for additional years.

BEA has three sets of rules: adjustable deficit targets, caps on discretionary spending, and pay-as-you-go (PAYGO) rules for revenues and direct spending.

The Gramm-Rudman-Hollings law set targets that were not adjusted for changes in economic conditions or for reestimates of program expenditures. BEA, however, gives the president the option of adjusting the maximum deficit amount when he submits his budget to Congress. President Clinton exercised this option for both the 1994 and the 1995 fiscal years, thereby eliminating the possibility that funds would be sequestered because the maximum deficit amount had been exceeded. In effect, under the rules now in place, whatever the deficit is is what it is permitted to be. Removal of direct control of the deficit has not, however, ushered in an anything goes era in federal budgeting: strong controls are imposed on the revenue and spending decisions that affect the size of the deficit.

One of these controls pertains to the one-third of federal spending that is controlled by annual appropriations. This discretionary spending includes virtually all defense expenditures, the operating costs of most federal agencies, and many of the grants made each year to state and local governments. Discretionary spending does not include the many billions of dollars appropriated each year for entitlement programs. These *appropriated entitlements* are classified as direct rather than discretionary spending because they are controlled by the legislation that establishes eligibility criteria and payment formulas. Appropriations for entitlements must be sufficient to finance the payments the government is obligated to make. The appropriations committees do not have discretion to fund these entitlements at levels that differ from those mandated by law.

For each year through fiscal year 1998 BEA sets a dollar limit on total discretionary budget authority and outlays (table 7-5). The limits may be adjusted for emergency spending and certain other factors; if they are not adjusted, total discretionary spending will be frozen at approximately fiscal year 1993 levels for each of the next five years. If appropriations cause the limits on either budget authority or outlays to be breached, the president must sequester sufficient budget resources to compensate for the excess spending. Under BEA rules, a uniform percentage would be taken from all discretionary programs, projects, and activities. If the excess spending were to occur during the last quarter of the fiscal year (between July 1 and September 30), the next year's discretionary spending limits would be reduced by the amount of the excess.

Only two tiny sequesters have been applied to discretionary spending during the first four fiscal years (1991-94) that the caps have been in place. Congress has been determined to stay within the caps, even to the extent of turning down some of President Clinton's spending proposals. Doing so was not difficult during the early years of BEA because the caps were set at a sufficiently high level to accommodate expected spending. But now that the caps have been frozen at 1993 levels through 1998, they are likely to be increasingly onerous.

The final set of BEA rules pertains to the PAYGO (pay-as-you-go) parts of the budget, revenues and direct spending. The basic rule is that legislation increasing direct spending or decreasing revenues must be fully offset so that the deficit is not increased. Direct spending consists mostly of entitlement programs that have either annual or permanent appropriations, but it also includes other budgetary resources (such as control authority for the highway trust fund) provided outside the appropriations process.

Table 7-5
Discretionary Spending Limits, Fiscal Years 1994-98[a]

Billions of dollars

Limits	Baseline Projection and Outlays	1994	1995	1996	1997	1998
Original statutory	Ba	510.8	517.7	519.1	528.1	530.6
caps	OL	534.8	540.8	547.3	547.3	547.9
Adjustments,	Ba	2.9	2.9	0	0	0
special allowances	OL	3.4	2.7	1.2	0.5	0.1
IRS, IMF, debt	Ba	0.2	0.2	0	0	0
forgiveness	OL	0.4	0.4	0	0	0
Changes in inflation	Ba	-9.5	-11.8	n.a.	n.a.	n.a.
	OL	-5.8	-8.8	n.a.	n.a.	n.a.
Credit reform and	Ba	8.6	9.8	0	-0.1	-0.1
other changes	OL	2.8	3.9	-0.2	-0.2	-0.3
Emergency	Ba	2.3	0	0	0	0
appropriations	OL	8.2	3.2	0.4	0	0
Discretionary limits,	Ba	515.3	518.7	519.1	528.0	530.0
February 1994	OL	543.8	542.4	548.6	547.8	547.7
President's fiscal year	Ba	n.a.	515.3	517.7	520.3	526.0
1995 budget	OL	n.a.	542.4	546.1	547.8	544.4

Source: *Budget of the United States Government, Fiscal Year 1995, Analytical Perspectives, Preview Report*, tables 14.1, 14.2, 14.3.

n.a. Not available

a. Early in each session, OMB and CBO issue sequestration preview reports estimating discretionary spending limits with the adjustments prescribed by law. In August the two agencies issue update reports to reflect the impact of legislation enacted up to that point in the session. They issue final sequestration reports after the session has concluded.

   This table sets forth the original spending limits enacted in 1990 for fiscal years 1994 and 1995 and in 1993 for fiscal years 1996-98. It also shows the adjustments made as of February 1994 in the limits for each of these years. Additional adjustments will be made for the later years in subsequent sequestration reports. By the time Congress makes appropriations for fiscal 1996 and beyond, the spending limits will differ from those displayed here.

PAYGO does not require any offsetting action when the change in revenue or spending occurs pursuant to existing law, such as a drop in revenue caused by a weakening economy or an increase in medicare payments caused by inflation in health costs. Nor does PAYGO bar Congress from passing revenue or spending legislation that would add to the deficit. Rather, it requires that the deficit increase caused by such legislation be fully offset by legislation raising revenues or cutting direct spending, or by the sequestration of funds from certain direct spending programs. In practice, however, Congress has been unwilling to approve direct spending legislation unless it has already decided how the deficit increase would be offset. In 1994, for example, action on the GATT (General Agreement on Tariffs and Trade) Treaty was delayed because the measure would have reduced tariff revenue.

A determination of whether a PAYGO sequestration is required is made after each session of Congress. At that time OMB, which makes the official estimates of the impact on the budget of enacted legislation, calculates the net impact on the deficit of revenue and direct spending legislation enacted during

Table 7-6
Deficit Impact of Pay-as-You-Go (PAYGO) Legislation,
Fiscal Years 1993-98[a]

Millions of dollars

Legislation	1993[b]	1994	1995	1996	1997	1998	1993-98
			Impact on Baseline Deficit				
Legislation enacted in 1991 and 1992							
OMB estimate	-2,676	-910	-803	—	—	—	-4,389
CBO estimate	-2,676	-910	-803	—	—	—	-4,389
Legislation enacted in 1993							
Phaseout of programs for wool and mohair							
OMB estimate	0	0	-47	-103	-183	-181	-514
CBO estimate	0	0	-57	-103	-176	-169	-505
Unemployment Compensation (P.L. 103-152)							
OMB estimate	0	853	-164	-429	-286	-383	-409
CBO estimate	0	1,070	-137	-285	-270	-372	6
National Defense Authorization (P.L. 103-163)							
OMB estimate	0	52	47	43	41	45	228
CBO estimate	0	13	3	5	6	8	35
Naval Vessels Transfer Act (P.L. 103-174)							
OMB estimate	0	-27	-17	-15	-11	-6	-75
CBO estimate	0	-27	-17	-15	-11	-6	-75
All other 1993 legislation							
OMB estimate	-20	6	13	31	29	4	63
CBO estimate	-20	16	8	28	28	3	63
Subtotal: bills enacted in 1993							
OMB estimate	-20	884	-168	-473	-410	-521	-707
CBO estimate	-20	1072	-198	-370	-423	-536	-475
Total: all bills enacted as of December 3, 1993							
OMB estimate	-2,696	-26	-971	-473	-410	-521	-5,097
CBO estimate	-2,696	162	-1001	-370	-423	-536	-4,864

Source: *Office of Management and Budget, Final Sequestration Report to the President and Congress for Fiscal Year 1994* (December 1993), table 7.

a. Effects on the deficit of all revenue and direct spending legislation enacted since the 1991 session.

   In addition to periodic sequestration reports, OMB must report to Congress within five days after the enactment of direct spending or revenue legislation on the budgetary impact of that measure.

   An OMB estimate that an increase in the deficit due to revenue or direct spending legislation has not been fully offset would trigger a sequestration. The report excerpted here estimates that PAYGO legislation enacted in 1993 decreased the deficit for 1993-98 by $700 million.

b. The Omnibus Reconciliation Act of 1993 reduced the deficit for fiscal years 1993-98 (according to OMB) by almost $500 billion. However, that act provided that these savings were to be excluded from the PAYGO computations.

the session. PAYGO scorecards show the effects for a multiyear period going back to legislation enacted in 1991 and projecting the impact on each year's budget through 1998 (table 7-6). Social security legislation and other direct spending or revenue legislation designated by the president and Congress as emergency measures are excluded from estimates of the deficit impact. If OMB were to find a net increase in the deficit, nonexempt direct spending programs would be sequestered by a uniform percentage. Because most direct spending is exempted from sequestration, the brunt of any mandated cutback would fall on a few programs.

Although PAYGO has not curtailed deficits resulting from existing revenue or spending laws, it has had a marked effect on new legislation. Since it went into effect in the 1991 session, Congress and the president have applied the emergency designation only sparingly. In fact, Congress blocked the use of PAYGO to expand direct spending by decreeing that the savings achieved in the 1993 deficit reduction legislation should not be included in PAYGO computations. A complete reckoning of what has happened since the rules were devised in 1990 would show that Congress has achieved substantial deficit reduction by increasing revenue and cutting direct spending under existing law while also offsetting any deficit increases resulting from new legislation.

The deficit control rules established by the Budget Enforcement Act are the most recent step in the evolution of federal budgeting. They will not be the last. Other proposals to revise federal budget practices are discussed in chapter 10.

THE ANNUAL BUDGET PROCESS

Each reform has layered federal budgeting with distinctive roles, rules, and procedures. The various processes added over the years revolve around an annual budget cycle that begins with the formulation of the president's budget in the executive branch, then moves to Congress, which has four separate processes for making budget decisions, and then on to agencies as they implement their approved budgets. The cycle concludes with the review and audit of expenditures. Table 7-7 provides a timetable of the major steps in the process. It represents an ideal; it assumes that each stage is completed on schedule, something that has rarely happened in the past fifteen years. But the basic steps are repeated from year to year with little change, even though particular procedures may vary in accord with the style of the president and his relations with Congress or in response to changes in political or economic conditions....

The President's Budget

Preparation of the executive budget involves the three sets of participants whose principal functions are listed in table 7-8. These are federal agencies, which request funds; the Office of Management and Budget, which reviews the requests and compiles the budget; and the president, who is responsible for submitting a budget to Congress in early February each year. Budget preparation generally begins in a decentralized manner, with each agency using its own procedures and guidelines for assembling its request. Some presidents such as Bill Clinton issue policy directives through OMB to guide agencies in compiling their budgets; others such as George Bush do not become engaged in the process until agencies have made their submissions.

The process takes eight to ten months in most agencies, longer in some of the largest. At the time they are preparing the new budget, agencies also are implementing the budget for the year in progress and seeking funds from Congress for the fiscal year immediately ahead. Because of the long lead times, agencies assemble their budgets with great uncertainty about the conditions that will prevail when the funds actually become available.

Agency work on the budget is concentrated during the spring and summer of the year preceding its submission to Congress. OMB examines agency requests in the fall, after which it notifies them (via a passback) of its recommended spending levels for their programs. Agencies have a brief period during which they may appeal to the president for more than was recommended by OMB. Once the appeals have been decided, the budget is printed and submitted to Congress.

The Congressional Budget Resolution

Congressional action on the budget involves the four sets of committees whose functions are listed in table 7-9. Each set of House and Senate

Period	Activities
Table 7-7	
Timetable of the Fiscal Year 1995 Budget	
Period	*Activities*
1993	
March-June	Development of budget guidelines and preliminary policies; call for estimates issued by agency budget office to operating units
July-September	Agencies formulate detailed requests, which are submitted to OMB
October-December	OMB reviews agency requests and issues passbacks; agency appeals to OMB and/or president. Final decisions
1994	
January	Compilation and printing of executive budget.
February	President submits budget to Congress no later than first Monday in February
March 15	Congressional committees submit views and estimates on the budget to budget committees
April 15	Deadline for adopting the fiscal year 1995 budget resolution
May 15-July	House action on regular appropriations bills for 1995
July-September	Senate action and conference on regular appropriations; enactment of appropriations
October 1	Fiscal year 1995 starts. Continuing resolutions enacted if all appropriations have not been enacted
October-November	CBO and OMB issue final sequestration reports for the past session of Congress. Reports are due ten and fifteen days respectively after end of session
October 1994- September 1995	Agencies spend resources and carry out activities as authorized by Congress
1995	
January-September	Congress may make supplemental appropriations for fiscal year 1995 in progress
September 30	Fiscal year ends
October 1	Fiscal year 1996 begins
October-December	Agencies, Treasury, and OMB close the books on fiscal year 1995
1996	
February	Actual revenue and expenditure data included in fiscal year 1997 budget
January-December and beyond	Agencies prepare financial statements; postaudits and evalutions are conducted

committees has custody over one of the four types of congressional budget actions: the annual budget resolution, revenue measures, authorizing, legislation, and appropriations bills. In performing these tasks, Congress is aided by several legislative staff agencies (table 7-10).

The budget committees produce a resolution that is an internal framework for Congress; it has no legal effect. Its principal purpose is to guide Congress in its consideration of revenue and spending measures. The budget resolution which covers a five-year period, sets forth budget totals and functional allocations. In addition, the resolution often contains reconciliation instructions directing certain House and Senate committees to report legislation that conforms existing revenue or spending laws to the policies adopted in the budget resolution. Legislation developed by committees pursuant to these instructions is packaged in an omnibus reconciliation bill (commonly labeled the deficit reduction bill), which is considered by the House and Senate under special procedures that expedite its passage.

Table 7-8
Budget Functions of Executive Institutions

President	Office of Management and Budget (OMB)	Federal Agencies
Establishes executive budget policy and submits annual budget to Congress	Operates executive budget system and advises president on financial and other issues	Submit budget requests to OMB; appeal to president for more funds
Submits supplemental requests, budget amendments, and updates to Congress	Issues procedural and policy guidelines to agencies	Justify president's budget recommendations before congressional committees
Signs (or vetoes) revenue, appropriations, and other budget-related measures passed by Congress	Issues passbacks to agencies and recommends budget levels to the president	Allot funds among subunits
	Compiles annual budget submitted to Congress	Maintain accounting systems and systems of internal control
Notifies Congress of proposed rescissions and deferrals	Reviews proposed legislation and testimony and monitors congressional action on appropriations and other measures	Obligate funds and preaudit expenditures
Issues sequestration orders to cancel budget resources		Carry out activities for which funds were provided
Appoints the director of OMB and other executive officials	Apportions funds and oversees implementation of the budget	Prepare annual financial statements in accord with accounting standards
	Scores revenue and spending legislation, as provided by BEA	Measure performance and develop performance-based budgets
	Conducts management activities to improve efficiency of federal operations	

Revenue Measures

The budget resolution is Congress's only means of considering the whole budget, albeit in highly aggregated terms. All other budget-related actions deal with particular revenue or spending matters. Although Congress takes some action affecting revenues just about every year, it has no regular schedule for taking up major tax legislation. In some years it hardly does anything; in a few it makes truly significant changes in the tax laws.

Revenue legislation is in the jurisdiction of the House Ways and Means and the Senate Finance Committees, two of the oldest and most powerful committees in Congress. The Ways and Means Committee usually acts first because the Constitution stipulates that revenue measures shall originate in the House. Although the Senate takes up the measure after the House, it often makes major changes, setting the stage for the conference at which much of Congress's tax legislation is written.

Authorizing Legislation

Under the rules, before the House or Senate can appropriate funds, the program or agency to receive the money must be authorized in law. This requirement contemplates a sequence in which Congress authorizes a program,

Table 7-9 **Budget Functions of Congressional Committees**			
Authorizing Committees	*Appropriations Committees*	*Revenue Committees*	*Budget Committees*
Report authorizing and direct spending legislation	Report regular and supplemental appropriations	Report revenue legislation	Report budget resolution
Oversee executive agencies	Review proposed rescissions and defer-rals	Report legislation, social security, and certain other entitlements	Draft reconciliation instructions and compile reconcilia-tion bill
Recommend changes in laws pursuant to reconciliation instructions	Submit views and estimates to budget committees	Submit views and estimates to budget committees	Allocate new budget authority, outlays, and other aggregates to committees
Submit views and estimates to budget committees on matters in their jurisdiction	Subdivide budget authority and outlays among their subcommittees	Recommend changes in laws pursuant to reconciliation instructions	Monitor budget and advise Congress on budget impact of leg-islation
Include CBO cost estimates in reports on their legislation	Establish account structure for federal agencies		
	Establish rules for reprogramming		
	Provide guidance to agencies on expendi-ture of funds		

then appropriates money to it. There are many variations to this sequence. . . . Sometimes the authorization is permanent and Congress need only act on appropriations for the particular program or agency to continue in operation; other times the authorization is annual and Congress must pass both it and the appropriations bill. Most authorizations are discretionary: the amount available is determined by annual appropriations. But for some the authorizing legislation provides direct spending.

Most congressional committees are involved in formulating authorizing measures. Each committee goes about the task in its own way. There is no standard structure or style to authorizations and no prescribed volume of this type of legislation. In some sessions the authorizing committees are active and produce much new legislation; in others, they are relatively dormant and authorizing activity is depressed.

Appropriations Bills

Annual appropriations are provided in thirteen regular appropriations bills, each of which is in the jurisdiction of parallel House and Senate subcommittees. Shortly after the president submits his budget to Congress, the various appropriations subcommittees hold hearings at which agency officials justify the amounts requested. Although the thirteen sets of subcommittees

---

Table 7-10
Budget Functions of Congressional Support Agencies

Congressional Budget Office (CBO)	General Accounting Office (GAO)	Congressional Research Service (CRS)
Issues reports with five-year projections on the budget and the economy	Issues accounting guidelines and reviews agency accounting systems	Analyzes legislative issues and proposals affecting agencies and programs
Estimates five-year cost of reported bills; prepares baseline budget projections and maintains database for scorekeeping	Audits operations of certain federal agencies; evaluates programs and recommends improvements	Assists committees and members by providing data and analyses relevant to their legislative responsibilities
Assists the budget, tax, appropriations, and other committees	Issues legal opinions concerning the use of funds	Compiles legislative histories of particular legislation and programs
Issues reports on options for deficit reduction	Reviews deferrals and rescissions to determine whether they have been properly reported and funds released as required	Issues report on the status of legislation
Reviews the president's budget and other proposals	Investigates expenditures and agency operations as requested by congressional committees	Analyzes proposals to change federal budget practices
	Settles certain claims and debt collection issues or disputes	

act independently, each is limited by the amount of appropriations allowed by the discretionary spending caps. Before any of the subcommittees marks up its bill, the House Appropriations Committee divides the total discretionary funds among them. (A parallel procedure is used by the Senate Appropriations Committee.) When an appropriations bill is considered by the House or Senate, the spending provided in it is compared to the amount allocated to the relevant subcommittee. In some circumstances floor consideration of an appropriations bill may be barred if the subcommittee allocation has been exceeded. This rarely occurs, however, because appropriations subcommittees take care to stay within their allocations.

The House takes up the appropriations bills one at a time, usually beginning in June and continuing through July. The Senate also acts on appropriations one by one, after which a conference committee irons out differences between the House and Senate versions. If the process operates on schedule, the thirteen regular appropriations bills should be enacted by October 1, the start of the new fiscal year. When Congress fails to enact all of these bills on time, it provides interim funding in a *continuing resolution.* Congress also enacts supplemental appropriations measures to provide additional funds during the fiscal year.

Budget Implementation

Agencies cannot spend appropriations until the funds have been apportioned by OMB among the time periods (usually quarters) or projects. Most federal agencies have an allotment process that distributes their apportioned funds among administrative units. Agencies generally are not permitted to spend in excess of their apportionments or allotments.

Although agencies must spend funds according to the terms and conditions set by Congress, they sometimes reprogram funds (shift them from one use to another in the same account) to meet unanticipated needs or changing conditions. Deviation from spending plans also occurs when funds are impounded— withheld from obligation of expenditure. Special procedures, described in chapter 9, are brought into play when this happens.

Review and audit constitute the final phase of the budget cycle. Agencies have the primary responsibility for ensuring the propriety and efficiency of their expenditures, and most audits are conducted by them or under their auspices. A number of changes have been made recently in the financial management practices of federal agencies. These have been spurred by legislative developments, in particular the Chief Financial Officers Act of 1990 and the Government Performance and Results Act of 1993. These and other developments have impelled agencies to give increased attention to the manner in which they implement the budget

CONCLUSION

One of the frequent complaints about federal budgeting is that the process has grown too complicated and labyrinthine. There are so many rules and requirements, so many opportunities for obstruction and delay, so many deals that have to be made and interests that have to be harmonized, so much confusion and frustration. Just about every committee and member of Congress has a piece of the budgetary action, but nobody has all of it. The same issues come up again and again; they never are finally resolved, nor is there any sure means of bringing them to closure. Fragmentation of responsibility is pervasive, as is duplication of effort. In federal budgeting, it seems, timetables and deadlines are established to be ignored and violated.

The developments described in this [article] have encrusted budgeting with many procedures. Each can be justified on its own, but the cumulative effect is to overload the process with more than it can handle in the time that is available. Clearly, budgeting is far more complex than it was before there were congressional budget resolutions, reconciliation bills, PAYGO rules, discretionary spending caps, impoundment procedures, and so on. Isn't it time, the complainers ask, to divest the process of much of the baggage accumulated over the years? . . . For the present, it should be noted that the complexities and conflicts of budgeting have more to do with the size and sprawl of the budget and the difficulties of grappling with the deficit than with the multiplicity of processes that have to be completed each year. The only way to simplify budgeting and get it to operate as clockwork would be to cut back the size of the budget and eliminate or significantly reduce the deficit. Since neither action is likely to occur soon, the many processes and rules introduced in this [article] will continue to vex federal budgeting.

Sense and Nonsense about Budget Deficits

ROBERT EISNER

Almost everybody talks about federal budget deficits. Almost everybody is against them in principle. And almost no one knows what he or she is talking about.

Maybe it goes back to something deep in our Calvinist heritage, that we must suffer rather than borrow. "No gain without pain," goes the modern version. We must raise taxes or cut useful government spending now to pay for a better future.

Or perhaps it has more recent political roots. Franklin D. Roosevelt pledged but never managed to "balance the budget," and Republicans attacked Democrats over budget deficits for the next 50 years. Then, with the huge Reagan-era deficits, Democrats thought they had their chance and turned the tables on the issue. In charting his independent course, Ross Perot has made the deficit his principal issue and has advanced a number of extreme "solutions" to the problem, including a balanced-budget amendment to the Constitution. President Clinton, in his initial State of the Union address on the economy, was constrained to present a comprehensive deficit reduction package.

The public has always agreed in wide proportions that the deficit should be eliminated. But it is far from clear that any candidate—Republican, Democrat, or Independent—has ever won an election with this position. In fact, many have lost by opposing popular deficit-increasing measures or by supporting tax increases to reduce it. With all the hoopla about deficit reduction, a Gallup poll reported at the time of Clinton's first State of the Union address is significant. Asked, "Which is more important, creating jobs or reducing the deficit?" 65 percent of respondents chose "creating jobs" and only 28 percent "reducing the deficit."

The public may well not understand the choice, but, as we shall confirm, deficits can indeed create jobs. Deficits can be good for us, as well as bad. And deficits can be too small as well as too large. To know which, you at least have to measure them right.

WHAT IS THE DEFICIT AND HOW IS IT MEASURED?

Few people have any notion how the federal budget deficit is measured. Many, including the major TV news anchors, editorialists in leading newspapers such as *The New York Times,* and countless politicians, do not even seem to know the difference between deficit and debt. The deficit is the amount by which expenditures exceed tax revenues in a given period or, in the more comprehensive official jargon, "outlays" exceed "receipts," and hence the amount that must be borrowed or added to the debt over that period. The debt is the amount owed at any point in time—what has been borrowed and not paid back.

President Clinton himself, in his Inaugural Address, succumbed to the public looseness of phrase, if not general confusion, in saying that we must "cut our massive debt." If he meant the federal debt, that in fact is quite beyond reasonable possibility in the foreseeable future. Clinton has more realistically talked of cutting the *deficit* by $140 billion as against forecasts of what it will be in 1997. But that would still leave a deficit of some $206 billion and the debt hence *growing* by that amount annually. Only a budget *surplus* would reduce the debt.

Yet we still hear the President and others talking about reducing the debt. Witness the pious Mobil advertisement that argues, "Clearly, one of President Clinton's and the 103rd Congress's primary tasks must be to reduce the federal debt to the extent practical as soon as possible," adding inexplicably the internally redundant clause, "and to balance the budget to prevent further deficits."

Many do not understand the measures of the debt about which they speak so much. The most frequently cited figure, something over $4 trillion now, is a gross "total," which includes over $1 trillion of "debt" held within the government, largely by trust funds such as those for Social Security for old age and retirement. But a more meaningful figure, relevant to household spending financial markets, and business decisions, and excluding accounting transactions between one arm of government and another, is for what is called the "gross federal debt held by the public." This came, at the end of the 1992 fiscal year, to almost exactly $3 trillion.

We have a vast number of measures of the federal deficit, most of which would horrify any private or public accountants worth their salt. Aside from differences between the Bureau of Economic Analysis national income accounts and the Office of Management and Budget and Congressional budgets, budgets with and without "deposit insurance" outlays (chiefly for the Savings and Loan bailout), our federal accounting violates a basic principle of accounting for private business, most state and local governments in the United States, and national governments across the globe: it does not distinguish between current or operating outlays and capital expenditures.

If there were no separate capital accounts, almost every large corporation in the United States would be reporting "deficits" or losses. Of course, this is not so. Private businesses exclude capital outlays from their current accounts and charge only depreciation when presenting their income (or profit) and loss statements. In a growing company, current investment is virtually always greater than depreciation, which is an average of past investment. Including depreciation rather than current investment thus permits profitable companies to keep their bottom line in the black. And many state and local governments in the United States, required by their constitutions to balance their current or operating budgets, finance capital outlays (like roads and bridges and new water systems or school buildings] separately, by borrowing.

Even this, however, would not now do much for the federal government deficit. Assume, counterfactually, that federal accounting conformed to private business practice and included in the budget only the depreciation on past tangible investment, not current tangible capital investment. The resulting U.S. federal budget deficit would be virtually the same as the overall deficits generally reported. This is a manifestation of something of which we should be much more aware—virtually zero net public investment in physical infrastructure. Our public physical plant is wearing out at least as fast as it is being replaced. A more comprehensive measure of investment, though, would include the OMB's estimates of "Major Federal Capital Outlays" for research and development and education and training as well as physical capital. If we used this measure, net investment, reflecting (however inadequately) the needs of our growing population, would be positive. Its exclusion would reduce the measure of the deficit by perhaps $80 billion of the $290 billion reported for our last fiscal year.

Given some $175 billion per year of federal grants to state and local governments, it might make some sense to present a consolidated account for all of government, as the U.S. Bureau of Economic Analysis does in its national income and product accounts. If we do that and then separate out all capital expenditures, for both tangible and intangible investment, we find that while the total consolidated 1991 budget retains a deficit of $193 billion, the current account portion of that deficit is only $24 billion.

A large part of the deficit is accountable directly to our slow economy and high unemployment. The U.S. Congressional Budget Office indeed estimates that each percentage point of unemployment adds, in the short term, $50 billion to the deficit, with the amount growing over time as additional deficit adds more to debt and subsequent interest payments.

If national unemployment in 1993 were merely back at its 5.3 percent average of the years 1988 to 1990—instead of hovering at nearly 7 percent—the deficit would be $100 billion less; by 1996, as a consequence of interest payment savings on a lesser accumulated debt, it would be some $130 billion less. Virtually all of the Clinton-Gore Administration's commitment to deficit reduction could be realized by that minimal reduction in unemployment.

Achieving a 4 percent unemployment rate, which has long been a target, or a 3 percent rate such as during the Vietnam War, could bring about an even greater reduction in the deficit.

The Office of Management and Budget, in its final document released by President Bush, offered "baseline" deficit estimates grounded on the relatively pessimistic economic outlook of 51 private "blue chip" forecasters. They foresaw real GDP growth of only 3 percent in 1993, 2.9 percent in 1994, and then down to 2.5 percent from 1995 to 1998; unemployment was still projected at 5.7 percent for 1998.

The OMB also presented deficit estimates on the basis of "high-growth" projections, which had the GDP increasing in successive years at 3.5 percent, 4.0 percent, 3.7 percent, 3.4 percent, 3.2 percent, and 3.0 percent, with unemployment down to 5.0 percent in 1998, its level in March, 1989 at the beginning of the Bush Administration. I have added estimates of what the deficit would have been in any year over which unemployment had averaged 5 percent. These were calculated on the assumption, consistent with Congressional Budget Office calculations, that each percentage point reduction in unemployment is associated in the short run, without including eventual interest savings, with a reduction in the deficit equal to 0.8 percent of the GDP.

I have compared deficit projections under the different assumptions as to growth and employment, and the results are striking. With no additional spending cuts or tax increases, the deficit would have fallen, in the high-growth scenario, from 4.9 percent of the GDP in 1992 to 2.1 percent in 1998, more than meeting the Clinton Administration's goals. If unemployment had been down to 5 percent throughout the period, instead of just in any given year, there would have been growing interest savings on a lower debt, and the deficit would have shrunk even more than shown in my short-run 5 percent unemployment curves.

THE DEFICIT IN A GROWING ECONOMY

In an expanding economy with an increasing population, almost everything grows: births and deaths, marriages and divorces, borrowing and repayment, income and wealth, and assets and debt. The criterion for increasing debt—how much borrowing there should be—is directly related to income. This is true for the government as well as for prudent private borrowers, banks, and businesses. Governments, as well as people, should not indefinitely allow their debt to grow faster than their income.

One may well argue that a responsible deficit target, similar to responsible targets for private business and households, is that debt over the long run grow no faster than income or, for the nation, gross domestic product (GDP). At the end of the 1939 fiscal year, as the New Deal was giving way to World War II, the gross federal debt held by the public came to $41 billion, 47 percent of GDP. In 1946, after World War II, it reached $242 billion, or 114 percent of GDP. By 1980, with federal budget deficits in all of the years from 1961 on, the debt had grown to $709 billion, but had fallen, relatively, to 27 percent of GDP. At the end of the 1992 fiscal year, the debt held by the public was $2,999 billion, up to 51 percent of GDP, but still only a little more than it was in 1939 and less than half of its proportion just after World War II. We may note both the short-period changes and the secular swings of the debt-GDP ratio in the graph "Some Say to Watch the Debt-GDP Ratio." [See Figure 7-1.]

There is nothing sacrosanct about any particular debt-GDP ratio. In periods of recession we may expect deficits to rise and the debt to grow more rapidly than GDP, which will itself be growing much less rapidly, if at all. If there is need for major investment, debt may again grow faster than GDP.

But suppose we were to keep the debt-GDP ratio constant. It is instructive to note what this "equilibrium" target would imply for our current situation. If we maintained the approximate 1992 debt-GDP ratio of 0.5 and assumed an estimated 7 percent growth, then the projected 1993 deficit would be $210 billion. Compare this with the final Bush OMB projected 1993 deficit of $327 billion as well as with the $227 billion that deficit would be if unemployment were two percentage points less.

The Bush OMB's final deficit projections are based on the "blue chip" private forecasters' anticipation of an unemployment rate averaging 7.2 percent for all of calendar 1993! Greeted with much expression of concern, the OMB had its mismeasured deficit declining from $327 billion in 1993 to $270 billion in 1994 and $230 billion in 1995 before beginning to rise again to $266 billion in 1996, $305 billion in 1997, and $320 billion in 1998. They assumed unemployment above 6 percent through 1995 and at 5.7 percent in 1998. The OMB also assumed interest rates on 91-day Treasury bills would rise, unaccountably, from their current rate of less than 3 percent to over 5 percent, thus adding perhaps another $50 billion to the annual deficit.

Those projections, though, even if correct, would still have the deficit-to-GDP ratio below 3.9 percent, with the debt-GDP ratio virtually stable, at 57 percent, by 1998. The debt would then be growing at a 6.67 percent per annum rate with a projected nominal GDP growth of 5.93 percent. If the rate

Figure 7-1. Some Say to Watch the Debt-GDP Ratio

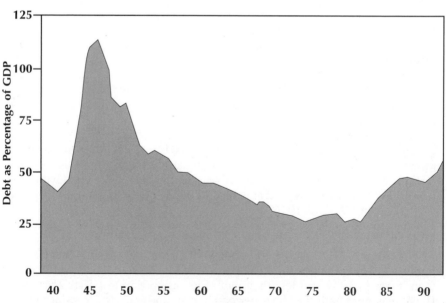

of growth of GDP were over 6.67 percent, the debt-GDP ratio would be declining. If unemployment were down only to its 5.2 percent rate of 1989 and Treasury bill rates were still around 3 percent, the resulting 1997 deficit would be not $305 billion but on the order of $200 billion, or 2.5 percent of GDP. With a slightly more ambitious 7 percent rate of growth of GDP, the debt-GDP ratio would then be headed for an equilibrium ratio of 36 percent, well below its current figure of about 51 percent. In a meaningful, relative sense, President Clinton would have reduced "our massive debt."

HOW DO DEFICITS HURT? OR DO THEY?

Much of what is written and said about the damage done by federal budget deficits is sheer nonsense, no matter how often repeated. First, of course, the notion that the federal government will go bankrupt because it is unable to pay off or service its debt is absurd. A sovereign government need never overtly repudiate a debt in its own currency. It can always tax those subject to its laws, including bondholders, to get the necessary proceeds. Or it can simply print the money needed—in the case of the United States, have the Federal Reserve buy Treasury securities. That may have other consequences, which we will consider. But in any event, there is no issue of bankruptcy for debt in dollars. (Debt denominated in a foreign currency, which is not the case for the United States, is quite another matter.) The debt may be repaid in cheaper dollars, but there is no reason why it cannot be repaid.

Ross Perot warned repeatedly that we are "spending our children's money." But our children's money has not yet been printed and will of course be printed or supplied when our children need it, in whatever quantities the interaction of the monetary authorities and our banking and financial system then determine. Alan Greenspan's successors in the Federal Reserve will always be able to supply money for our children. What they cannot supply and, we shall see, what may be lacking are the real resources of capital—public and private, tangible and intangible, human and nonhuman—with which we are failing now to endow our children.

We are also told that our continuing deficits mean we are passing ever greater debt on to our children. This is literally true. Our children will be the *owners* of all those Treasury bills, notes and bonds that constitute the debt. That will give them a nice cushion of accumulated savings. Is that necessarily so bad?

We are further told that the interest burden of the debt, currently about $185 billion per year, is a heavy drag on the economy. In fact it comes to only about 3 percent of GDP. But, more fundamentally, the interest payments of the Treasury are, after all, income to their recipients. Any taxes that may be levied to finance the payments are then matched by added income.

There are those who call this a regressive redistribution of income, on the assumption that the rich receive interest income financed by taxes paid by the poor. A moment's reflection casts major doubt on that assumption. The ultimate beneficiaries of the interest receipts—via pension funds, insurance, and banking services, as well as savings bonds—must for the most part be in the large middle class. And relatively little is paid in taxes by the very poor. The social cost of debt and deficits will have to be found elsewhere.

On a more sophisticated level, some might argue that if marginal tax rates are three percentage points higher to finance interest payments, work-effort may be discouraged. People receiving large proportions of their income in the form of interest would not wish to work to earn more with Uncle Sam taking still another three cents out of every additional dollar. But with interest income only 3 percent of GDP (a bit higher as a percentage of national income), we are a long way from having to worry about that.

It is also said that large deficits will cause inflation. The first answer to this is that we have had some large deficits in the last decade, and inflation has declined sharply. It is running currently at no more than 3 percent by official measure and is probably less, perhaps zero with full adjustment for product improvement. Indeed, the times series relation between deficits and inflation in the United States has generally been negative; bigger deficits have come with less inflation and smaller deficits with more inflation. To be fair, however, this reflects primarily the effect of the economy on the deficit, rather than the deficit on the economy. In recessions, inflation tends to be less, and, with lesser tax revenues and greater outlays for unemployment benefits, deficits are larger. In booms, inflation may be more while tax revenues are greater and unemployment benefits less, so that deficits are less.

An appropriate test of the effect of deficits on inflation, or on any other economic variables, would have then to abstract from the reverse effect of those variables on the deficit. One way to get at this is to work with a measure of the deficit that is not affected by the fluctuations of the economy. For this purpose we may use what has variously been called the structural, the cyclically-adjusted, or the "high-employment" budget. This indicates what tax revenues, outlays, and the deficit *would* be if the economy were on some fixed path as, say, a 6 percent unemployment path for a measure that has been published periodically by the Bureau of Economic Analysis. The size of the high-employment deficit may then be a measure of fiscal stimulus. But larger high-employment deficits have also not been associated with more inflation.

The reason for this negative finding brings us closer to the fundamental relation of government deficits and government debt to the economy. That depends very considerably on the state of the economy, whether it is zooming along at top speed or is in a sluggish, slack-resources, unemployment mode. Recognizing this will lead us to the conclusion, however shocking to some, that *deficits can be good for us*. This is not to say that they are always beneficial, but they will be good if they generate otherwise lacking purchasing power for the products of American business. In general, deficits can be too small as well as too large. And for most of the past half-century, including right now, contrary to the conventional wisdom, we will find that deficits have been too small. Far from struggling to reduce the deficit, as President Clinton has constrained himself, or offering demagogic appeals for zero deficits (or even surpluses to "pay off" the debt), as has Mr. Perot, we should be looking for the most productive ways to increase it.

ARE DEFICITS IRRELEVANT?

There is a school of thought, led by Harvard's Robert Barro, which argues that deficits essentially do not matter. This is not my argument. What Barro and his many followers (still a minority among economists) claim is that financing government expenditures by borrowing and by taxes at least nondistortionary "lump-sum" ones) are equivalent in their effects on the economy. This proposition is called "Ricardian equivalence," after the great classical economist, David Ricardo, who first suggested the possibility before later rejecting it. It reasons that if taxpayers have greater after-tax incomes because government expenditures are financed by borrowing instead of by taxes, they will not spend their extra income. Instead, they will save it to pay the future taxes necessary to service the resulting debt, or else leave the money to their children, who will pay those taxes.

The arguments against Ricardian equivalence are myriad: the difference between borrowing and lending costs of government and private agents who frequently have liquidity constraints; the lack of certainty or even knowledge by any of us that taxes will in fact be higher in the foreseeable future or that others, including the parents of our children's spouses or the other grandparents of our grandchildren, will not pay those taxes; and finally the case where we have no children or else consider them worthless and not worth providing for. But I leave that debate to the economics journals, which have filled many pages with it.

HOW DEFICITS DO MATTER

We return then to the mainstream argument that deficits do matter; the question is how. Simply enough, deficits, as opposed to government outlays financed by taxes, matter because they add to the purchasing power and aggregate demand of the private sector. A person or business is likely to spend more when holding a government security than a receipt for payment of taxes. The former, after all, is part of the person's or business's wealth. All of our economic theory and empirical evidence indicate that people with more wealth, other things being equal, will spend more.

That increases in the real value of the government debt to the private sector increase consumption and aggregate demand is old neoclassical economics, a line of reasoning to be found in the works of Gottfried Haberler and A.C. Pigou. The Keynesian argument is parallel, that real deficits increase consumption by adding to current real disposable income. Keynes also included changes in the value of wealth as an argument of his consumption function, warning that ignoring them would be perilous in times in which they changed.

Failure to take into account the huge increase in debt held by the public during World War II—the debt-GDP ratio was well over 100 percent in 1946—was a major factor in the alarmist, erroneous predictions that the end of the war would bring on a major recession. And that failure was part of the background and motivation for the path-breaking work of Nobel Laureates Milton Friedman and Franco Modigliani in developing our modern theory of the consumption function. Wealth, or the permanent income to be expected from the wealth, are critical determinants of consumption expenditures.

If we doubt that theory, we can try a quick mental experiment. Suppose I could arrange with Lloyd Bentsen, our new Secretary of the Treasury, for each reader of this article to be given $100,00 in new Treasury bills. How many would feel poorer? How many would spend none of their new holdings? And how many might just buy a new car or take a more expensive vacation trip? If even some fall into that last category, the result is higher consumption expenditures and more business to those producing the additional goods or services purchased. But this additional holding of Treasury bills—or other Treasury securities, or cash to the extent that the Federal Reserve buys some of the additional debt—is exactly what happens when the government runs a deficit.

There is one important qualification, however, too often overlooked: inflation. If prices today are 3 percent higher than a year ago, then today's $100,000 are the equivalent, roughly, of $97,000 in last year's purchasing power. We may be expected to feel richer and spend more only to the extent that the deficit raised our wealth in government securities by more than enough to keep up with inflation. A deficit is a *real* deficit only to the extent that it adds to the real value, that is the value in constant dollars, of our holdings of government debt. We may view the loss in real value of outstanding debt due to inflation as an "inflation tax" levied by the government on debt holders, thus reducing that real deficit. Another way of looking at this is to see that of the $185 billion of interest payments swelling the nominal deficit, some $90 billion represents the amount the government finds it necessary to pay, because of higher nominal interest rates, to compensate bondholders for their inflation losses.

THE SHORT RUN: CONSUMPTION, OUTPUT, AND EMPLOYMENT

While the greater wealth the public holds in government debt as a result of deficits will induce more consumption, greater deficits are actually often accompanied by less consumption. This is because recessions and associated unemployment reduce consumption and also, as we have noted, increase deficits. As warned before, we have to avoid confusing cause and effect, the effect of deficits on the economy and the effect of the economy on deficits.

To ascertain the effect of an independent increase in the deficit, one not brought on by the decline of the economy, we need again to consider the high-employment budget, which indicates what the deficit *would be,* aside from fluctuations of the economy, if unemployment were fixed. And further, since we can expect that it is only real increases in the wealth in the form of government debt held by the public that can be expected to affect consumption, we should also adjust the deficit for the loss in the real value of the debt due to changes in the price level.

The impact of deficits on the economy should then be found in the relation between an inflation-adjusted and cyclically adjusted deficit and the economic variables with which we are concerned. I have accordingly constructed [along with Paul J. Pieper of the University of Illinois at Chicago, my collaborator in many of these investigations) time series of what I call the price-adjusted, high-employment deficit. And I have worked these into simple charts and tables and more rigorous least-squares regressions as well as, more recently, VARs (vector autoregressions). These latter put together past and current values of the presumably underlying variables and try to estimate their relations and interrelations without preconditions or confining specifications as to lags or what determines what. The results have confirmed, over and over as I have tested the relations for robustness over time as well as for variations in formulations, that deficits, over the past three decades at least, have been good for us.

Specifically, we have found that higher values of the price-adjusted, high-employment deficit, taken as a percent of GNP or GDP, have been associated with more rapid subsequent growth in real product, as may be seen in [Figure 7-2], "As Goes Deficit, So Goes Product," sparing readers of this article more sophisticated statistical presentation. (This may be found in my 1986 book, *How Real is the Federal Deficit?*, and in numerous periodical articles.) And since more rapid growth in real product is associated with alleviated unemployment, it comes as no surprise that we have also found that larger deficits have been associated with less subsequent unemployment.

There is one condition that must have been necessary for this result. There must have been slack resources for most of the last 30 years over which I have estimated these relations. Unemployment could not have been reduced by bigger deficits if it were already at its rock-bottom, full-employment level. And output could not have increased faster if there were no additional workers and no additional capacity for increased production. Sadly, this slack-resource condition was met.

It must be recognized that, except for wartime—unemployment reached the 3 percent level during the Vietnam War—we have rarely if ever had truly full employment. Herein is a vital caution to President Clinton and the Congress as they put into place a program for economic recovery and sustained, high-investment growth. We entered 1993 with unemployment still over 7 percent and most forecasts, including those used by the OMB, the Congressional Budget Office, and the Clinton Administration itself, indicating that this unemployment rate would subside only very slowly.

Figure 7-2. As Goes Deficit, So Goes Product

Changes in Price-Adjusted High-Employment Deficit and
Real Gross Domestic Product as Percentages of GDP, 1961-91

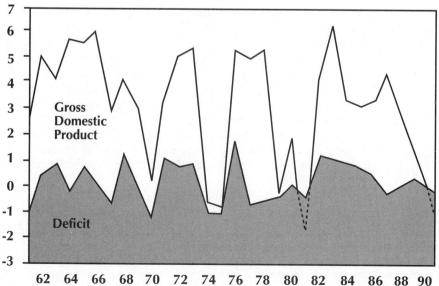

Yet the economic program the President presented in his February 17 address to Congress included a reduction of the structural deficit by $55 billion from 1993 to 1994. Is this a time for the restraint of deficit reduction or for the stimulus of *more* government spending—preferably for public investment—and *lower* taxes?

This fundamental fact of excess unemployment may be challenged by devotees of the pernicious "natural rate" of unemployment or "non-accelerating-inflation-rate of unemployment (NAIRU]." They may find 6 percent or $6^1/_2$ percent or even the 7+ percent of the past year to be natural. They may think that in our perfect market economy whatever *is* must be optimal and natural. I recall the joke about the graduate student who in January, 1983 wrote on the board the flash, depth-of-recession news from the Bureau of Labor Statistics: "The natural rate of unemployment has just reached 10.7 percent."

But I will maintain that involuntary unemployment due to a lack of aggregate demand or purchasing power is a fundamental fact of our economy, as confirmed by these effects of deficits. And this fundamental fact makes all the difference, making a mockery of most arguments for reducing the deficit at this time, and exposes the error of the conventional wisdom of too many, although not all, macroeconomic theorists.

THE LONG RUN: NATIONAL SAVING

The fact that increases in the real, structural deficit have usually ushered in growth or greater growth in output and reductions in unemployment becomes central to the one legitimate possible argument that deficits may be too large. It relates to the future, not to their current effect. As long as there is some slack in the economy, fiscal stimulus in the form of bigger deficits will in the short-term raise output and employment. But, some insist, these deficits reduce "national saving." In so doing they reduce the capital we will have in the future and hence reduce future product. That is—or would be, if it were true—the real burden that deficits place on our children and grandchildren and indeed, except for those near the end of their lives, on all of us.

Is it true, though? Do our deficits reduce national saving and investment or capital accumulation? There is one argument that gives the false impression that this is inevitable. Conventional gross national saving, GS, is defined as the sum of private saving—personal saving, PS, and business saving, BS—and public saving, or the consolidated federal, state, and local budget surpluses, FS plus SLS. And the total of gross national saving (except for a statistical discrepancy) is identically equal to the total of gross investment, GI:
$$GS = PS + BS + FS + SLS = GI$$

Deficits are then seen as negative surpluses, or negative public saving that offsets positive private saving. Bigger federal deficits constitute a still greater negative value to PS and hence mean less total or national saving, GS, and less gross investment, GI, or less accumulation of capital for the future. Reducing the deficit would raise national saving and investment. All this may seem apparent from the identity above.

This argument is alas just too simplistic. It entails the elementary fallacy of assuming *ceteris paribus*: other things being the same. But imagine more realistically, for example, that the federal deficit is reduced—FS is made less negative—by cutting grants to state and local governments, which have been running about $175 billion per year. Would this not immediately reduce state and local government surpluses, SLS, and thus offset the reduction in the federal deficit or algebraically higher value of FS?

Or suppose the federal deficit is reduced by raising income taxes. This would reduce disposable personal income and surely reduce personal saving, PS, the difference between disposable personal income and consumption, even if, as is likely, consumption were also reduced. So here we would have another offset to the increase in public saving or reduction in public spending. Similarly, an increase in corporate profits taxes would reduce undistributed corporate profits ant thus reduce business saving, BS. And a like consequence, it should be noted, would flow from a reduction in government expenditures, either in transfer payments like Social Security benefits or in government outlays for goods and services. In both events, disposable income and private saving would be reduced. A decline in business saving and private saving would at least partly offset the algebraic increase in the negative federal surplus.

LOOKING AT INVESTMENT

A nation invests either by accumulating real assets on its own soil or by acquiring claims to assets in the rest of the world. Gross investment is the sum of gross private domestic investment and net foreign investment: $GI = GPDI + NFI$. And gross national saving, GS, we have noted, is identically equal to gross investment. We can thus better consider how reduced federal deficits would affect national saving by finding its effects on the components of gross investment.

By far the larger element here is gross private domestic investment, the sum of business and nonprofit institution expenditures on new equipment and structures, construction of new housing, and increases in business inventories. Would the cuts in consumption and government expenditures for goods and services result in more or less private domestic investment? If we cut our purchases of new cars, is that going to lead the automobile industry to spend more or less on new facilities? If our disposable income is cut, will we buy more or fewer new houses?

I may seem to be loading the questions, but the answer is not that obvious. Classical economists and the conventional wisdom would argue that if the government is borrowing less, interest rates will be lower, and this will stimulate more business investment and purchases of new houses. But will this positive effect outweigh the negative effect of lower sales to ultimate consumers and of lower incomes?

A half-century ago Oscar Lange examined this issue in a seminal review of Keynes's *General Theory*. He pointed out that there was an "optimal propensity to consume" that would maximize investment. This would be reached when the stimulative effect on investment of more consumption was eventually just balanced by the increasing negative effects of higher interest rates.

What happens is that as consumption increases from low levels the developing pressure on capacity stimulates investment, and there is little rise in recession interest rates and little negative effect on investment. As full employment is approached, more consumption begins to crowd out investment simply because there is no more capacity to increase both consumption and investment. In a free market, interest rates rise as business struggles to get the funds to finance additional capital to increase capacity. But these higher interest rates increasingly choke off investment. Thus, whether more consumption or more government expenditures crowd out domestic private investment may again depend on how close the economy is to full employment. If we are at full employment—or some people's "natural rate"—so that output cannot be increased, then it is clear that, aside from getting goods from the rest of the world, more output going to consumption or government must mean less output to private investment. If we are not at full employment, then the outcome of changes in budget deficits and changing consumption and/or government spending is not clear. We can get a pretty good idea, however, by looking at the historical facts.

Here again, my charts, tables, and regressions provide clear results. As shown in [Figure 7-3] "Deficits May Spur Investment . . . ," larger inflation-adjusted, structural deficits have been associated with *more* subsequent gross private domestic investment, and smaller deficits have been associated with less investment. My multiple regression results add the information that easier money, as measured by increases in the real monetary base, has also been associated with increases in real output *and* domestic investment. The remedy to any increases in interest rates would thus appear to be supportive, stimulatory monetary policy by the Federal Reserve.

Figure 7-3. Deficits May Spur Investment . . .

Price-Adjusted High-Employment Deficit and Gross Private
Domestic Investment as Percentages of GDP, 1959-91

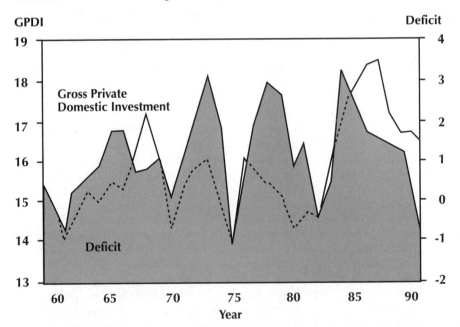

This, however, still does not tell the whole story. Gross investment, which is equal to gross saving, is the sum of gross private domestic investment and net foreign investment. And net foreign investment is largely net exports or, a bit more generally, the current account surplus in our balance of international payments. If we export more than we import, to the extent that we do not give foreigners' payments back to them, we acquire foreign assets. We thus have net foreign investment. But if we import more than we export, we pay for this excess by giving foreigners net additional claims, in debt or equity, on us. We have negative net foreign investment, reducing total gross investment.

Will not increased deficits stimulate the demand for all goods, foreign as well as domestic, and thus increase imports and reduce net foreign investment? Indeed they will. And reductions in the deficit would reduce imports—perhaps by causing a recession—and raise net foreign investment! Whether the cutting of deficits raises or reduces national saving then depends on the balance of the two effects, the increase in net foreign investment and the reduction in gross private domestic investment.

Once more, we can turn to the data. The results of statistical analysis, while not as sharp as in the case of domestic investment alone, take the ground out from the argument that reducing deficits is likely to raise national saving. The historical record has shown the opposite. Larger, real structural deficits have been associated with more saving and smaller deficits with less saving.

DEFICITS AND TOTAL NATIONAL SAVING

The statistical relation involving the conventional, narrow measure of national saving, it must be acknowledged, is not that strong. It is strengthened in a major way, however, when we recognize that what is relevant for our future, and that of our children and grandchildren, is not merely the accumulation of capital in the form of gross private domestic investment and net investment in the rest of the world. Of vital significance is public investment in all of the tangible infrastructure on which private industry depends, as well as all investment, public and private, in education and training and research and the basic services of public security on which social living depends.

Increased federal deficits may well go toward financing increased public investment. They have apparently done so already, if insufficiently. Inflation-adjusted, strategic deficits have been positively related to total government *tangible* investment. As shown in [Figure 7-4] "Encourage Education Spending. . . ," they have also been positively related to total government expenditures on education.

As a start to measuring this broader effect of deficits, I have related our real, structural deficits to expanded measures of national saving, and once again I find a sharp positive relation, as seen in [Figure 7-5] ". . . and Increase National Saving." Larger price-adjusted, high-employment deficits have historically been associated with more, not less, national saving.

Figure 7-4. Encourage Education Spending...

Changes in Price-Adjusted High-Employment Deficit and Real Total
Government Expenditures on Education as Percentages of GDP, 1960-91

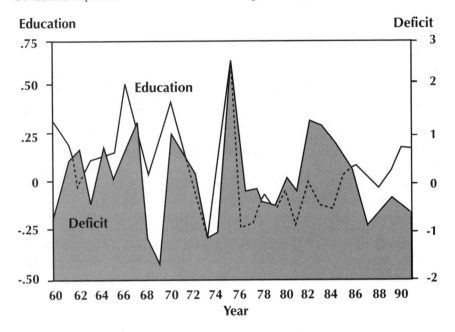

Figure 7-5. ... and Increase National Saving

Changes in Price-Adjusted High-Employment Deficit and Real Total
Tangible National Savings as Percentages of GDP, 1961-91

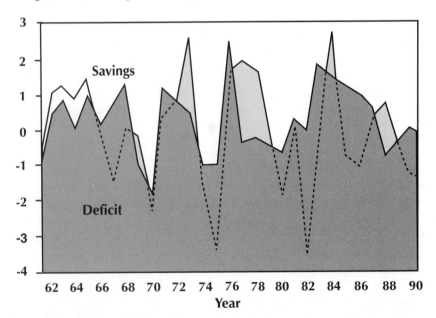

PROVIDING FOR THE FUTURE

Given the state of our economy, present deficits are not too large. They will naturally come down as we reduce unemployment, speed economic growth, and achieve a prosperous economy.

Real, structural deficits have helped and not hurt current output, employment, consumption, and well-being. They also encourage more, not less, investment in our future.

President Clinton, in advancing a broad-based program for investment and economic growth, has stated explicitly, "Deficit reduction is not an end in itself." The purpose of deficit reduction is rather to help provide for our future and our children's future by increasing national saving and investment. But we must then be clearly aware of the danger that deficit-cutting measures will curtail or reduce conventionally measured gross private domestic or business investment, household investment, and the public investment in physical capital and in people that he sees, correctly I believe, as vital to that future.

8   Policy Analysis, Implementation, and Evaluation

A public policy approach to public administration offers considerable insight into the importance of administrative agencies and approaches to improving public administration. The Introduction to this anthology sketched the public policy approach to understanding public administration.

Basically, public policy is what government says or does. In tracing the steps of the policy cycle, three points studied by scholars in this area seem to have great potential for improving public administration:

- policy and program analysis,
- policy implementation,
- policy, program, and organizational evaluation.

In the first article in this chapter, an analyst-turned-professor, Laurence Lynn, explains policy analysis and discusses the need for careful, systematic analysis as a way to improve governmental decision making. Lynn also observes that there are different kinds of policy analysts with different combinations of analytical and political skills. Many policy and program analysts are located within administrative agencies, and analytical techniques are often applied to policies as well as program activities.

In the second article, Paul Sabatier examines what we know about the process of implementing public policies. While policies sometimes originate in administrative agencies and while agencies regularly influence and sometimes set public policies, government agencies spend most of their time and resources on implementation. The implementation of intergovernmental programs is especially difficult.

The policy perspective reminds us of the inseparability of politics and public administration. The same interest groups, coalitions, and other political participants who seek to influence the legislative process also monitor and attempt to influence administrative rules and procedures, program design and organizational allocation of resources as policy is implemented.

In the third article, David Ammons overviews the need for performance measurement in government. Measurement includes a range of approaches, including the evaluation of public programs for efficiency and effectiveness as well as using benchmark data to compare your agency's performance with the leading organizations in a particular area of governmental activity. Underlying the concept of performance measurement is the idea that administrators should explain to the public the degree of their success. This leads to programmatic and organizational improvement as well as greater public accountability.

While Ammons focuses on local government, performance management has received a major push from the federal Government Performance and Results Act (GPRA). GPRA requires federal government agencies to set goals, measure performance, and report of their accomplishments.

Chapter 8 has taken a policy perspective on key aspects of public administration. Here are a few questions for students to consider:

- What is policy analysis? Assess its potential to improve the quality of decisions in government.
- What have we learned about implementation from two decades of research? How might this influence public agencies?
- Can we actually measure the performance of governmental programs and agencies? Exactly what should be measured?
- What does Ammons mean by "benchmarking?" How is this technique used? Is it helpful to public managers?
- If you knew a new city manager in a nearby city, would you recommend anything you learned in this chapter to improve the management of that city? What would you recommend? Why?

Policy Analysis

LAURENCE E. LYNN JR.

Because policy analysis is both a specialized and a controversial activity, it is useful to introduce the basic ideas and approaches that distinguish its practitioners. The evolution of policy analysis as both an intellectual discipline and an institutional process has been shaped by the tension between two conflicting points of view, one supportive and one critical.[1]

THE IDEA

Advocates of the analytic perspective argue that the typical public policy issue is so complex, value-laden, and unstructured that policy analysis is essential if policymakers are to sort through the issues, the alternatives, and the costs and consequences of those alternatives to reach a thoughtful position. As Charles Schultze, former director of the Bureau of the Budget and chairman of the Council of Economic Advisers, puts it: "The most frustrating aspect of public life is ... the endless hours spent on policy discussions in which the irrelevant issues have not been separated from the relevant, in which ascertainable facts and relationships have not been investigated but are the subject of heated debate, in which consideration of alternatives is impossible because only one proposal has been developed, and, above all, discussions in which nobility of aim is presumed to determine the effectiveness of the program."[2]

A meaningful resolution of policy disagreements, in this view, can be achieved only if the relationships between inputs (or means) and outputs can be established. Schultze argues that a primary function of policy planning is identifying "social production functions," that is, the ways in which inputs, such as teachers, school facilities, and curriculum materials, are transformed into outputs, such as specific educational attainments.[3] He goes on to say that policy analysis is necessary to translate values, such as an educated citizenry, into specific objectives, such as eliminating financial barriers to attending college. The policy planner supports the formulation of strategy by saying to the public executive, "If these are your values (say, ensuring equality of opportunity), here are policy objectives consistent with those values (say, improved access to public education by handicapped children), and here are alternative programs together with the costs necessary to achieve these objectives. Now you can make an informed choice."

In this supportive view, [political] conflict ... cannot be intelligently resolved without systematic analysis of the net effects and costs.... Politics inescapably reflects a balancing of economic interests; to remain oblivious to whose wants are satisfied and at whose expense makes no sense.

Criticism of the analytic perspective takes two contrasting forms. According to the first type of criticism, public policymaking is too political to benefit from the formal techniques of policy analysis.[4] Ours is a society of divergent and often conflicting values. The reconciliation of these conflicts often depends on suppressing discussion either of underlying values and goals or of the overall consequences of governmental actions. Focus is concentrated instead on budgets, programs, or "inputs," about which differences of opinion can be adjusted and agreement can be reached. A good decision is one to which every participant can attach satisfactory meanings and thus accept as consistent with particular goals and values. A process that forces debate on the goals, outputs, costs, and priorities of alternatives may be disruptive to the orderly adjustment of conflicting interests. Policy analysis is incompatible with, or irrelevant to, the give-and-take of partisan mutual adjustment.

In this critical view, the impasse over the Simpson-Mazzoli bill should have been resolved not by analysis but by the striking of a bargain between supporters and opponents in which both get something of value.

An alternative criticism of policy analysis takes the opposite tack: public policymaking should be more rather than less principled. Policy analysis takes the process in the wrong direction, making it too narrowly political. In the view of Laurence H. Tribe, policy analysis, with its methodological bias in favor of economic models and concepts, reflects a "wants orientation to public choices and a value system built on ever changing perceptions of immediate self-interest, of benefits and costs expressed in monetary terms."[5] Tribe believes that public policy should instead be founded on bodies of principle to which we are committed or obligated rather than on calculations of who gains and who loses by specific government actions. The discovery and integration of our values rather than repeated reference to analytic frameworks built on self- interest should lie at the heart of policymaking.

In this view, the debate between Reagan and Mondale was as it should have been. Are we to be a nation in which citizens must be issued identity cards by the government? Are we to be a nation in which rapacious employers exploit powerless workers? It is those principles, rather than the matter of net benefits or costs, that are rightly at stake.

Who is right, advocates or critics? In general, the value of substantive policy planning and analysis depends on one's answers to the kinds of questions raised in the first half of this book: How are public policies actually determined? (Do ideas, evidence, and argument make a difference?) Do public executives have a significant role in policy formation? (Do we care about their intellectual competence in policy debate?) What kinds of factors influence the behavior of government organizations? (Do research and analysis help shape the premises for organizational action?) How do personality and cognitive styles influence the performance of executive roles in government? (Is competence in complex substantive matters associated with managerial competence?) How do individuals make choices? (Do they ever refer to analysis of alternatives?)

Since the answer to most of the parenthetical questions is "yes," the question of whether systematic policy analysis should be part of the policymaking process is really not an issue. Charles Lindblom observes that "in all governments all over the world, a standard routine for reaching a policy decision is to gather and analyze facts, doing so with at least implicit theory. If analysis is often hurried and sometimes superficial, it is never wholly absent."[6] Successful public executives no more question the value of analytic support than they question the contributions of other specialists—lawyers, auditors, comptrollers, political tacticians—in their organizations.

THE DISCIPLINE

What is policy analysis?

The short answer is that policy analysis is conducted in whatever way is appropriate to the problem and the circumstances.[7] Policy analysis is often relatively simple, done, as practicing policy analysts like to say, on the backs of envelopes and using "naive" methods. It may be no more extensive, for example, than a list of effects and costs accompanied by rough and partial orders of magnitude. Occasionally—the analysis of national energy policy alternatives is an example—more elaborate approaches are called for in which large-scale policy models are constructed and used to evaluate a sophisticated range of policy choices. The spirit motivating all such work is the same, however: to clarify issues and alternatives for the benefit of policymakers.

Whether simple or elaborate, policy analysis proceeds in a disciplined, logical way. It is worth laying out the general structure of policy analysis to serve as a model by which to determine what might be done in any given circumstance. This structure has four elements: identifying the purposes of government actions; identifying and evaluating alternative ways of achieving given purposes; choosing specific designs for governmental actions; and evaluating the capacity of the government to execute particular actions.

Identifying Purposes

A comprehensive policy analysis begins with a clear formulation of possible justifications for government action. A problem exists—social or economic conditions are not what they should be—and government action of some kind may be justified to correct or ameliorate the situation. Justifying government action (or inaction) is, of course, a fundamentally philosophical and political matter—a high game. It is not self-evident that policy analysts have any special competence in addressing it. Indeed, many experienced political executives forbid their policy planners to take up such large questions, especially if they believe the answers ought to be determined by a consensual process among high-game participants. For several reasons, however, that is a shortsighted view.

First, because controversy is usually associated with justifying public policy, effective public executives devote considerable thought to the rationale for particular proposals. Such preparation enables them to be more persuasive and, by revealing logical or philosophical problems, makes them less vulnerable to unanticipated partisan criticism.

Second, even at a philosophical level, there are many ways of articulating the purposes of governmental activity and many different principles justifying government action. Those principles may have widely different, even conflicting, implications for what kind of action ought to be undertaken. Systematic analysis, as Schultze pointed out, can reveal the principles at stake and the costs and consequences of embracing them or of choosing one principle over another.

Finally, officials are often judged on the consistency of their views and actions. By insisting that policy analyses begin with principles, officials gain some measure of protection against inconsistent, uncoordinated, thoughtlessly expedient actions. They can better communicate the sense of having a bigger picture within which specific issues should be understood. This sense may be an advantage in partisan policy debate.

Evaluating Alternatives

How should government go about achieving its purposes? What means should it employ to achieve desired ends or specific effects? More than any other, those questions challenge the intellectual creativity and the political and bureaucratic sophistication and communications skills of policy analysts. The most important contribution of a policy analysis is often the extent to which it broadens the range of realistic alternatives from among which policymakers can choose a course of action.

The key concept here is "alternatives." To an analytical mind, the idea that one should evaluate alternative ways of achieving a given objective comes naturally; it is the "right" way to approach the making of a choice. Many, perhaps most, policymakers, however, do not think this way. They may view policymaking as reacting to particular proposals for action that "experts" have created rather than solving problems or pursuing substantive goals. Moreover, they are apt to approach policy issues with definite predispositions about how government ought to act. These predispositions may spring from intellectual conviction, but more often they reflect the policymakers' intuitive judgments about what is politically feasible, what is ideologically acceptable, or what "works" in practice.

Nonetheless, in principle and usually in fact, there are alternatives or options for achieving policy goals and for dealing with a pressing problem. Analysis of the alternatives may reveal opportunities for creative contributions to public policy that would otherwise go unrecognized. Actively calling for and paying attention to this kind of analysis can be an important factor in public executive effectiveness.

Designing Specific Actions

When the means have been chosen, the design of public policies is far from complete. This is nowhere more clearly indicated than in legislation that authorizes the performance of a service, actions to control a private activity, or the awarding of grants in accordance with regulations or guidelines established by the relevant public official. It is evident in countless instances of executive decision making during which, in the quest for agreement or under the pressure of deadlines, detailed questions as to how the action is to be designed are postponed until "later." Nothing can happen, however, and no results can be produced until those details have been worked out.

It can be sensed from the foregoing that the bureaucratic problems of resolving these questions confront public executives with difficult issues. For one thing, because of their specialized or technical nature, such matters are of necessity delegated to specialized agencies or staffs or contracted to consultants. For another, the choices to be made may be especially difficult or controversial; had they been easy to resolve, they would have been resolved. Thus, the public executive must be able to supervise the design process without becoming consumed or coopted by it.

An experience in Joan Claybrook's administration of the National Highway Traffic and Safety Administration illustrates the complications associated with designing specific government actions and the problems these pose for public executives.

> There was continuing battle going on between me and many of my assistant administrators over the level of detail that it was necessary for me to know. I felt they didn't have the same kind of judgment as I did about what was and was not important.
>
> For example, when I read the department regulation on odometers, it stated that if an odometer could be turned backwards it would have to have an indication on it that would register the action. . . . Well, I thought, why have the indicator option—why not just say you couldn't turn it backwards? So I wrote a note saying the regulation was not properly written and somebody dutifully knocked out the indicator option and reissued the regulations.
>
> A month later a spinner—a guy who spins odometers backwards—went to see Wendell Ford, the senator who chairs one of the Senate commerce subcommittees that authorizes NHTSA's programs. The spinner showed the senator how our regulation was deficient, since the clip that manufacturers would put in to prevent turning the odometer backwards would stop a normal person but not a spinner. Well, that's a very deficient regulation so I hurried over to the rulemaking engineer who had handled it and asked him, "Why didn't you write the regulation so that it wouldn't be easy for a spinner to avoid?" He said, "Well, it would cost more money." I told him, "Who's the decision maker in the agency? You should tell me you have several different ways to accomplish a goal." We might have, for example, written the regulation so that the whole odometer would be destroyed if you turned it backwards. . . .
>
> As a result of all this, . . . Senator Ford held a public hearing at which I had to testify about why we did this dumb thing. I had to spend five times as much time studying the details of the odometer regulations because this guy made a prejudgment. . . . [8]

The fact that there were alternative ways to write an odometer regulation and that each had different costs and consequences was not evident to Claybrook until she was confronted by time-consuming political controversy over her regulation. While it is impossible to consider every alternative for every detail of policy design, the discipline of asking, "Are there significant alternatives that should be considered?" will improve executive performance.

Assessing Government Capacity

Based on his experience as a public official in New York City, the late Gordon Chase asserted that "an agency head is well advised to consider . . . whether a proposed new or expanded program will be relatively difficult to implement—and therefore eat up a lot of his best staff—or whether it will be relatively inexpensive in drawing down scarce managerial resources."[9] Before deciding on a particular policy design, a good public executive will ask, "How hard will it be to implement?"

Following experiences in the 1960s and 1970s when the expectations of many social policy advocates as to what government could do were disappointed, students of public policy increasingly turned their attention to problems of implementation. The emphasis on implementation is intended to highlight the value to sound decision making of being able to consider governmental capacity when choosing a policy design. Chase, for example, identified three sources of difficulties in implementing public programs:

- operational demands on program agencies and field workers implied by a particular program concept;
- the nature and availability of resources necessary to run the program;
- the extent to which authority over the program would be shared with other political and bureaucratic actors, that is, the extent to which the program administrator would have control over program implementation.

Richard F. Elmore has christened the class of approaches that includes Chase's "backward mapping."[10] "The logic of backward mapping," says Elmore, "begins with a statement of specific behavior at the lowest level of the implementation process that generates the need for a policy." The analysis then states "an objective . . . as a set of effects, or outcomes." Next, "the analysis backs up through the structure of implementing agencies, asking at each level two questions: What is the ability of this unit to affect the behavior that is the target of the policy? And what resources does this unit require in order to have that effect?" Finally, the analyst describes the policy that will produce the necessary resources.[11]

The importance of this kind of thinking is that it brings to the foreground issues of organizational capacity to produce concrete results, issues of critical importance to public executives whose goal is to contribute to public policy. It will not always be possible to complete a comprehensive backward map. It is expensive in terms of staff resources, and the kinds of questions that arise cannot always be answered with available information in a reasonable time. Nonetheless, the discipline of visualizing desired outcomes and anticipating obstacles to achieving them is an effective preventer of policy failure.

THE ANALYSTS

Public executives are often uncomfortable around the policy analysts who do the kind of work just described. Part of that discomfort stems from ignorance or misconceptions concerning policy analysts' professional motivations and methods of work.

The key characteristic of good policy analysts is their intellectual versatility. Policy analysts employ whatever intellectual and computational approaches will clarify issues and alternatives, thereby sharpening and focusing policy debate and choice. In choosing an approach to analyzing a policy issue, policy analysts will, of course, consider the nature of the problem, the public executive's interest, the amount of time available, the availability of data and other information, and their own skills and abilities as well as those of coworkers whose cooperation will be needed. Even though they may be trained in an academic discipline or technical field, good policy analysts are not first and foremost economists, engineers, statisticians, or sociologists who happen to be interested in policy. Rather, they are technically versatile, inquisitive, naturally interdisciplinary individuals whose first loyalty is to clarifying policy issues and alternates for public executives.

In the flesh, policy analysts, like public executives, display wide variations in talents, interests, and styles, which reflect differences in training, experience, and competence. Arnold Meltsner, who has studied policy analysts at work, observes that "they come to their jobs with different incentives. They have different internalized standards of accomplishment and success, and even those with a common education rely on different skills or strengths in the performance of their tasks."[12] As with public executives, it is the peculiar characteristics of their operating style that are often most consequential to their effectiveness in particular roles.

Meltsner has devised a revealing scheme for classifying policy analysts. He ranks them as high or low in two separate dimensions: analytical skill, the ability to do technically competent work, and political skill, the ability to function effectively in a government organization and to communicate with public officials. The classification scheme that results is shown in Figure 8-1.[13]

At first glance, it might be thought that a public executive would want to assemble a policy analysis staff that contains no pretenders and as many entrepreneurs as possible, with politicians and technicians (the one-dimensional analysts) included only out of necessity. In fact, as noted previously, many public executives distrust policy analysts with high political skill, whether technically capable or not. Technicians, who can produce the numbers on demand and who are apt to be comfortable in a role that requires no political acumen, fill the bill nicely for these public executives.

Many policy analysts are unquestionably entrepreneurial, seeing the social function of policy analysis as broadly educational and prescriptive. Beyond improving the basis for specific decisions by specific officials, policy analysis would help a wide audience think about and make judgments concerning what government should do. Many policy analysts believe they should produce ideal policies that can serve as standards by which to judge the performance of policymakers. The social value of policy analysis can, in this view, be unacceptably compromised if analysts lose their independence of view. In other words, if public executives reject sound advice, they, not the policy analysts, are in error.

Many analysts who work in or consult for government have been trained to adopt a vision that transcends the responsibilities of political superiors.

Figure 8-1. Classification of Policy Analysts

		Political Skill	
		High	Low
Analytical Skill	High	Entrepreneur	Technician
	Low	Politician	Pretender

Source: From Arnold S. Meltsner, *Policy Analysts in the Bureaucracy* (Berkeley: University of California Press, 1976). Reprinted by permission.

Some go so far as to view policy analysis as a substitute for partisan political processes rather than as an adjunct to them. Many policy analysis shops maintain staff morale through changing political seasons by adopting the role of a counterculture, advocating "the public interest" rather than a narrow or parochial organizational or political interest. They would prefer a definition of policy analysis framed in terms of the nature of the intellectual tasks to be performed: identifying objectives; developing distinctive ways of accomplishing the objectives; evaluating alternatives in terms of benefits, losses, and risks; and determining the sensitivity of results to key assumptions. Good policy analysis, in this view, is necessarily produced by experts possessing neutral and professional competence.

Public executives are right to be skeptical of such claims and distrustful of the analysis that often accompanies them. Policy analysts may profess to be politically neutral, but the implications of their work are hardly ever neutral. Effective policy analysts are craftsmen, working with the materials of particular policy problems, rather than social scientists seeking universal truth. Public executives are nonetheless well advised to harness the idealism and enthusiasm for ideas and evidence that are characteristic of policy analysts. Breaking away from the status quo, even if only incrementally, often depends on identifying an alternative course of action or a new premise for action that originates in analytic insight stimulated by devotion to the public interest. Original minds may be hard to manage, but the effort is often worth it....

Notes

1. Giandomenico Majone, "Applied Systems Analysis: A Genetic Approach," in *Handbook of Systems Analysis,* edited by Edward S. Quade and Hugh J. Miser, vol. I overview (Laxenburg, Austria: International Institute for Applied Systems Analysis, 1981, processed).
2. Charles L. Schultze, *The Politics and Economics of Public Spending* (Washington, DC: The Brookings Institution, 1968), p. 75.
3. Ibid., pp. 57ff
4. See, for example, Aaron Wildavsky, *The Politics of the Budgetary Process,* 3rd ed. (Boston: Little, Brown, 1979), chapter 6; Charles E. Lindblom, "The Science of 'Muddling Through,'" *Public Administration Review,* XIX (Spring, 1959), pp. 79–88, and Lindblom's subsequent works.
5. Laurence H. Tribe, "Policy Science: Analysis or Ideology?" *Philosophy and Public Affairs* 2:1 (Fall, 1972), pp. 66–110, and "Ways Not to Think about Plastic Trees," in Laurence H. Tribe, Corinne H. Schelling, and John Voss, *When Values Conflict: Essays on Environmental Analysis, Discourse, and Decision,* edited by Laurence H. Tribe, Corinne H. Schelling, and John Voss (Cambridge, Mass.: Ballinger, 1976), pp. 61–91.
6. Charles E. Lindblom, *The Policy-Making Process* (Englewood Cliffs, NJ: Prentice-Hall, 1968), p. 6.
7. The best explication of the spirit of policy analysis is in Giandomenico Majone, "An Anatomy of Pitfalls," in *Pitfalls of Analysis,* edited by Giandomenico Majone and Edward S. Quade (Chichester, England: Wiley, 1980), pp. 7–22.
8. Joan Claybrook and NHTSA, (C), a teaching case prepared by David Whitman, Kennedy School of Government Case Program, C95-81-385, copyright 1981 by the President and Fellows of Harvard College, pp. 14–15.
9. Gordon Chase, "Implementing a Human Services Program: How Hard Will It Be?" *Public Policy,* 27:4 (Fall, 1979), pp. 385–435.
10. Richard F. Elmore, "Backward Mapping: Implementation Research and Policy Decisions," in Walter B. Williams, et al., *Studying Implementation: Methodological and Administrative Issues* (Chatham, NJ: Chatham House, 1982), pp. 18–35.
11. Ibid., p. 21.
12. Arnold Meltsner, *Policy Analysts in the Bureaucracy* (Berkeley: University of California Press, 1976), p. 14.
13. Ibid., p. 16.

Two Decades of Implementation Research: From Control to Guidance and Learning

PAUL A. SABATIER

The 1960s and early 1970s represented a rather remarkable era of policy innovation in Western Europe and North America. Virtually every country instituted one or more reforms to expand educational opportunity, to reduce interregional economic disparities, to expand health and social security programs, to reduce air and water pollution, to improve consumer protection, to protect the rights of minority groups, etc. A decade of relative prosperity made these reforms possible. Activist governments provided the political will. And social scientists and other professionals provided many of the ideas.

It soon became clear, however, that many of the programs were not working as intended. Implementation research arose largely as an effort to explain these apparent failures.

One of the early studies—Pressman and Wildavsky's (1973) analysis of the abortive effort by the Federal Government to create 3,000 jobs in Oakland— was to have an enormous impact on the first generation of implementation research, particularly in the United States. First, starting from the dictionary definition of "implementation" as the "carrying out of a decision," it focused inquiry on the extent to which, and the reasons for which, the formal objectives of a policy decision were (or were not) attained. It thus focused attention squarely on one of the principal topics of this volume, namely, the extent to which official policymakers can use a variety of control mechanisms and institutional arrangements to guide social change (Kaufmann: chapter 11).

Moreover, Pressman and Wildavsky went beyond the bounds of traditional public administration in several critical ways. In so doing, they provided the new field with a separate identity. First, they focused attention on "the complexity of joint action," i.e. the enormous number of clearance points in various bureaucracies and target groups at various levels of government whose assent, if not active cooperation, are usually required for a program to achieve its objectives. They thus pointed to the importance of interorganizational relations and policy networks, a distinguishing feature of implementation research (in contrast to the single-organization focus of traditional administrative studies).

Second, Pressman and Wildavsky chose as their dependent variable not the behavior or decisions of implementing agencies but rather policy *outcomes*, e. g. the number of jobs created or improvements in air quality. In so doing, they identified a program's *causal theory* as a critical explanatory variable. For example, the Oakland program was based on the premise that trickle-down effects from public works projects are an efficient strategy for creating jobs. While this may be true for underdeveloped regions like Appalachia, it is hardly appropriate for the highly developed San Francisco Bay Area — where a much more precise targeting is required. Thus, even if the implementing agencies had behaved in a manner completely consistent with legislative intent, the program would not have achieved its objectives— or would have done so only very inefficiently—because it was based on an inadequate model of the critical factors affecting the problem. As we shall see, this focus on a program's underlying causal assumptions was to become one of the major contributions of implementation research.

In the years following publication of their classic, several distinct approaches to implementation analysis have emerged. Suffice it to say that the "top-down" approach of Pressman and Wildavsky—which starts from a policy decision and then explores the extent to which, and the reasons for which, its objectives are attained—has been refined and tested by a number of scholars (Cerych and Sabatier 1986; Lester and Bowman 1989; Mayntz 1978; Mazmanian and Sabatier 1981, 1989; McFarlane 1989; Rodgers and Bullock 1976; Van Horn 1979). It has also been subjected to considerable criticism. Bowen (1982) has questioned the emphasis on "veto points," while Wildavsky and others have expressed reservations about the frequency with which one can usefully make a clear conceptual distinction between formulation/adoption, on the one hand, and implementation, on the other (Barrett and Fudge 1981; Majone and Wildavsky 1978; Nakamura 1987).

But by far the most fundamental critique has come from a group of largely European scholars who have labeled themselves "bottom uppers" (Hanf 1982). They got their start from a number of studies showing very substantial limits on the ability of central governments to guide the behavior of local implementors and target groups (Barrett and Fudge 1981; Berman and McLaughlin 1976; Derthick 1972; Hanf and Scharpf 1978; Weatherly and Lipsky 1977). When combined with doubts about the utility of separating formulation from implementation, what emerged was a perspective which argued that the appropriate starting point should not be a policy decision but rather the actors involved in addressing a *policy problem*. From this arguably emerges a more accurate portrait of the role of various governmental programs—vis-á-vis other factors—in guiding behavior "on the ground." While the "bottom uppers" have developed some rather imaginative descriptive tools (see Elmore 1979; Hjern and Porter 1981; Hull and Hjern 1987), thus far they have largely been unable to transform their network analyses into a viable causal model which incorporates the often indirect effects which legal and socio-economic factors can have on individual behavior.[1]

It is not the purpose of this chapter to review the voluminous literature on implementation. That has been done elsewhere (Barrett and Fudge 1981; Sabatier 1986). Instead, it attempts to draw a number of conclusions from this literature which are particularly relevant to an understanding of the problems of guidance, control, and performance evaluation in the public sector. In addition, the concluding section suggests a promising strategy for combining the best features of the "top-down" and "bottom-up" approaches in order to understand the factors affecting the ability of governments to guide/change target group behavior over time.

IMPLICATIONS OF THE IMPLEMENTATION LITERATURE
FOR GUIDANCE AND CONTROL IN THE PUBLIC SECTOR

The Importance of Street-Level Bureaucrats in Program Delivery

Implementation studies frequently have found that the most important actors are not the official policymakers in the capital but rather the street-level bureaucrats—classroom teachers, social workers, pollution control inspectors—who interact directly with target groups (e.g. secondary school students, polluting industries). Legislative intent is usually sufficiently vague and the amount of hierarchical control within organizations sufficiently weak that street-level implementing officials have very substantial discretion (Barrett and Fudge 1981; Berman and McLaughlin 1976; Hanf and Scharpf 1978; Weatherly and Lipsky 1977). This is even more so in programs which require a high degree of commitment and skill from on-the-ground professionals: Such commitment normally is contingent upon a rather large domain in which they can exercise their professional judgment. Finally, many implementation efforts involve not simply a single organization but rather a loosely coupled network of organizations from different levels of government, none of which is preeminent (Hjern and Porter 1981). In such a situation a policy program may actually consist of the sum of negotiated settlements among street-level bureaucrats and target groups, drawing upon a variety of laws for its legal justification.

While implementation scholars agree about the substantial discretion usually exercised by street-level bureaucrats, they disagree concerning the ability of elected officials to guide the behavior of implementors and target groups so as to bring their actions within the limits defined as legally acceptable over time.

On the one hand are scholars like Hanf and Scharpf (1978: chapter 1), Elmore (1979), Barrett and Fudge (1981), and probably Bennan (1980) who suggest that control by formal policymakers is virtually impossible and/or undesirable. Thus one should give street-level professionals the resources they need and trust them to do a good job. The evidence suggests that this strategy is used with some frequency in certain countries—most notably, Britain (Hill 1982)—and in policy areas such as mental health with strong professional associations and few clear standards. It is also a preferred strategy in cases—e. g. sulfur oxide emissions in Europe—in which policymakers are preoccupied with not putting "their" target groups at a competitive disadvantage vis-á-vis those in other regions or countries (Knoepfel and Wiedner 1982b).

Nevertheless, there are a number of reasons for believing that formal policymakers are not nearly so impotent as Hanf et al. might suggest.

First, while it would seem obvious that any implementation study should contain a careful content analysis of the formal policy decision being implemented, skeptics of formal guidance mechanisms have not always done so. For example, Berman and McLaughlin's (1976) multi-volume analysis of the implementation of federally sponsored educational innovations by local school districts during the early 1970s contained only the most cursory discussion of the formal decisions of federal authorities: Were these statutorily mandated programs or the result of purely administrative rule making? Were the programs in any sense mandatory, or were they merely innovations offered to local districts for their consideration? Careful analysis of such questions would seem critical to any judgments concerning the relative influence of federal vs. local officials, yet the studies were largely silent on these topics. Similarly, decent scholarship requires that clear distinctions be made between campaign manifestos and the speeches of public officials, on the one hand, and official governmental policy decisions, on the other. The former often contain promises which are not reflected in the negotiated settlements characteristic of most legislative and cabinet decisions. Only the latter, of course, are officially binding on street-level implementors and target groups. To use the former as the benchmark for measuring the shortfall between "policy" and outcome—and thus as an indicator of the power of street-level implementors—is really quite misleading.[2] In sum, any assessment of the (in)capacity of official policymakers to guide local implementors would seem to require a more careful analysis of their stated intent—as contained in the official policy decisions—than has often been the case.

Second, it should be obvious that the ability of central authorities to alter the behavior of local officials varies with a number of factors. Sharpe (1985, 1986) argues that these include the number of formal levels in a political system, the representation of local officials at the center via one of the legislative houses or the *cumul de mandats*, the presence of vertically integrating professional communities or political parties, and the financial autonomy of localities. These factors operate primarily at the systemic (nation-state) level, although a few also vary by policy area within countries. In addition, Mazmanian and Sabatier (1981; 1989) have suggested a number of specific mechanisms available to official policymakers which can improve their ability to guide the behavior of street-level implementors: These include the clarity of the policy directives; the number of veto/clearance points involved; the financial resources available; the formal access of various interests to the implementation process; and, to some extent, the policy preferences of implementing officials. In short, the degree of autonomy of street-level bureaucrats *varies* from country to country, policy area to policy area, program to program. It is virtually never either trivial or total.

Third, the initial preoccupation of implementation scholars with explaining program failures led to an unrepresentative set of policy cases, and almost certainly exaggerated the autonomy of street-level implementors vis-á-vis formal policymakers. The vast majority of early studies dealt with social programs initiated by federal authorities in the U. S. and the Federal Republic of Germany (Berman and McLaughlin 1976; Derthick 1972; Hanf and Scharpf 1978; Pressman and Wildavsky 1973). A moment's application of the Sharpe and Maxmanian/Sabatier variable lists suggests that these should be among the weakest cases of guidance by formal policymakers: Not only did they involve the entire panoply of veto points inherent in federal systems, but they generally also involved programs in which federal officials had only modest ideas of where they wanted to go or how to get there, as well as very little local political support. Small wonder that one found substantial local discretion and variation in program performance. Subsequent research has revealed a number of cases of basically successful program implementation—the 1965 Voting Rights Acts (Rodgers and Bullock 1976), the British Open University (Cerych and Sabatier 1986), the California coastal commissions (Sabatier and Mazmanian 1983)—due in no small part to the ability of official policymakers to enunciate reasonably clear objectives, to affect the preferences of key implementing officials, to reduce the number of negotiators to a manageable level, and to assure that many of them would be supportive of the program.

In sum, while street-level implementators are always important, official policymakers are not always as impotent to affect the outcome of local negotiations as Hanf et al. seem to suggest.

The Need to Take into Account a Fairly Long Time-Span

Most of the early implementation studies attempted to reach judgments concerning a program's outcomes, and the factors affecting them, within 2-4 years of the basic policy decision (usually in the form of a new law). Examples include Derthick's (1972) analysis of new towns within U.S. cities, the Pressman and Wildavsky (1973) classic, and the initial studies of the federal compensatory education legislation (Murphy 1971).

This time-span was explicable given the felt need to explain the apparent inability of programs to meet their mandated objectives. Both policymakers and academics wanted to know why. In some cases, e. g. the Oakland study, the time-frame was perfectly appropriate because it coincided roughly with the program's demise.

But in many other cases this limited time-span proved to be quite misleading. First, it led to premature assessments of a program's effects. In the case of ambitious efforts to significantly change the behavior of large numbers of people, it is clear in retrospect that a 2-4 year time-frame is completely inappropriate. It takes a year or two to get a program to hire personnel, draft the basic implementing regulations, and otherwise get off the ground. To expect major changes after only a few years is quite unrealistic—and perhaps a peculiarly American failing. When it doesn't happen, we are quick to judge a program to have failed. In several cases, such judgments have turned out to be premature and unfair. Second, and directly related, a short time-frame neglects the possibility that program proponents will identify and overcome a series of impediments over a period of years. In such cases, the result can be *cumulative incremental change:* After a decade or so, the program proves to be much closer to achieving its mandated objectives than it was after 2-4 years (Sabatier 1986).

An excellent example is Title I of ESEA, the U. S.'s compensatory education program. It was supposed to funnel federal funds to school districts with large numbers of disadvantaged children in order to improve their educational performance. Studies conducted a few years after passage of the 1965 legislation revealed a dismal failure, with widespread evidence that schools were not targeting the funds on disadvantaged students and, not surprisingly that such students were showing no improvement in basic learning skills (Murphy 1971). Yet studies conducted 6-8 years later—i. e. after a decade or so of implementation—revealed substantial improvements in targeting funds and a number of instances of significant improvements in educational performances (Kirst and Jung 1982).

While a complex story, the improvements can basically be attributed, first, to continued Congressional commitment to compensatory education throughout the 1965-78 period and, second, to a gradual learning process by program proponents (Mazmanian and Sabatier 1989: Ch. 6). For example, early audits—leaked to the press in 1968 by dissatisfied implementing officials—revealed widespread misuse of funds by local school districts. These were attributed to ambiguities in the legislation, to a general unwillingness by federal officials to monitor and improve local compliance, and to the political weakness of program beneficiaries (e.g. the poor) in most local school districts. The resulting scandal led to Congressional clarification of intent, to a strengthening of the authority of program proponents within the federal education ministry, to a variety of efforts to develop supportive constituencies in state and local school agencies (e.g. via the hiring of parents as teachers' aides), and to a tightening of federal regulations concerning targeting of funds. It also became increasingly obvious that educators really had very little idea about *how* to teach children from disadvantaged backgrounds. This led to a rather substantial federal research program designed to identify successful techniques and to promote their adoption by local school districts. That turned out to be a slow and difficult process, in part because of the gradual realization that one could not force innovation upon teachers—an example of the need for professional discretion mentioned earlier.

Of course, there are also cases of initially effective programs whose performance declines over time. For example, there is a substantial American literature indicating that attempts to regulate business in order to benefit consumers are subject to a "cycle of decay" over time (Bernstein 1955; McConnell 1966; Quirk 1981; Sabatier 1975).

In sum, the direction of program change is subject to changes in socioeconomic conditions, interest group support, elections, and learning by both proponents and opponents. But there is a rather remarkable consensus among implementation scholars concerning the desirability of taking a fairly long-term perspective, e. g. 10-15 years, in order to understand the ability of the public sector to guide target group behavior (Barrett and Fudge 1981; Majone and Wildavsky 1978; Sabatier 1986). Shorter time intervals are likely to produce erroneous conclusions about program effects and to mask the critical process of policy evolution and learning.

The Importance of Basing a Program on Sound Causal Assumptions

As previously indicated, one of Pressman and Wildavsky's major contributions to the implementation literature—and to our understanding of the factors affecting governmental efforts to guide behavior in order to obtain desired outcomes—was their focus on the causal assumptions behind a program.

There are several different ways of conceptualizing the notion of a program's (often implicit) causal model. Some authors, including Pressman and Wildavsky (1973) and Bardach (1977), are concerned with understanding the factors contributing to efficiency at least as much as with those affecting efficacy. Others, such as Berman (1978), and Mazmanian and Sabatier (1981, 1989), focus purely on those contributing to effectiveness. For example, the latter authors have developed a concept of a program's (implicit) causal model which includes two aspects:

(1) The cognitive component: To what extent did the policy formulators understand the principal problem-related factors and institutional linkages affecting goal attainment?

(2) The jurisdictional component: To what extent did they give implementing agencies jurisdiction over sufficient linkages to have at least the potential of attaining legal goals?

Their emphasis, then, is on the theory actually *incorporated* into the legislation or other authoritative policy decision rather than merely on the one that some policy formulators may have had in mind (which comprises the cognitive component).

Whatever the precise nature of the concept of causal model (assumptions) underlying a program used by various authors, study after study has shown this to be a critical variable explaining program outcomes. Several examples come from Cerych and Sabatier's (1986) analysis of the implementation of European higher education reforms. In 1968 the planners of the British Open University (OU) predicted an enrollment of approximately 25,000 students in the 1970 entering class. Actual enrollment turned out to be 24,000. Two years before, planners of the French university institutes of technology (IUTs) predicted enrollments in 1972— the fifth year of the program—would attain 160,000 students. The actual figure turned out to be 34,000.

The principal reason for this enormous variation in ability to attain projected enrollments was simply that the British planners were using more accurate causal assumptions and better data than their French colleagues. The French based their projections on an extremely general model indicating the types of manpower training needed for targeted levels of economic development. It implicitly assumed, among other things, that students would radically alter their historic preference for 4-year university (as opposed to short-cycle, technical) education and that the competing short-cycle institutions would simply disappear. Not surprisingly, this turned out to be quite erroneous. In contrast, British planners of the OU calculated the pool of potential applicants from specific subgroups of the population (e.g. teachers without a university degree), made a conservative estimate (e.g. 10 percent) of the percentage likely to enroll, and then supplemented this analysis with a survey of the British population soliciting their degree of interest in attending the OU in the near future. They then interpreted these results in a likewise conservative fashion and, not surprisingly, came up with quite accurate projections.

Again, however, an adequate time horizon is critical for understanding guidance mechanisms. One of the things which happened in many of these cases is that program proponents gradually improved their causal assumptions over time. French educational planners began exploring the reasons behind their grossly inadequate IUT projections. This led to the development of much more differentiated (by region and by market sector) manpower training models; to several unsuccessful attempts to eliminate the competing short-cycle institutions; and finally to what Wildavsky (1979) has termed "a strategic retreat on objectives." Projected IUT enrollments were gradually revised downwards until by 1979 they finally matched the actual enrollment of 52,000 students.

Do Not Assume That Governmental Action Is a Critical Factor

As will be recalled, "top-down" implementation approaches start with a policy decision and then examine the extent to which, and the reasons for which, legal and other objectives are attained over time. One of the principal shortcomings of this approach is a danger of overemphasizing the importance of the program under study in affecting target group behavior and ultimate outcomes. This can be dealt with through careful research design—ideally, an interrupted time series with a pretest-posttest control group. But such quasi-experimental designs frequently present all sorts of practical problems given the time and resource constraints of real-world research.

In this respect, the bottom-up approach presents some methodological advantages (Hull and Hjern 1987). By starting with the actors involved in a policy problem and investigating their perceptions of the range of factors affecting their activities, the researcher is less likely to underestimate the importance of market forces or the unanticipated consequences of programs in other policy areas. For example, the comparative study of sulfur oxide emissions in several European countries directed by Knoepfel and Wiedner (1982b) frequently found that purely market forces (e.g. the efficiency of different production processes) and governmental programs in other policy areas (particularly energy) had at least as much effect on firms' pollution emissions as did pollution control policy.

Of course, pure bottom-up approaches have their own methodological shortcomings, e. g. a tendency to ignore why potentially important actors are *not* in a given implementation network. In addition, their reliance on actors' perceptions produces a tendency to neglect how a variety of legal and socio-economic factors may structure actors' participation, resources, and preferences without their explicit knowledge (Sabatier 1986). But these deficiencies can largely be corrected once more explicit and elaborate causal models get added to the networking technique.

WHERE DO WE GO FROM HERE?

Two decades of implementation research in the U. S. and Europe have produced at least four implications for our understanding of guidance and control in the public sector:

(1) Street-level bureaucrats—classroom teachers, social workers, pollution control inspectors—play a critical role in the provision of governmental services and in attempts to regulate private behavior. Particularly in the case of professionals, it is probably illusory for official policymakers to think they can tightly control the behavior of their supposed subordinates. On the other hand, policymakers can affect what happens on the ground by structuring the implementation process through relatively clear directives and through affecting the number, the resources, and, to some extent, the preferences of street-level bureaucrats and target groups. But the efficacy of such mechanisms will vary by country, policy area, and program.

(2) In assessing the effectiveness of various attempts at guidance and control, one needs to take into account a reasonably long time-period, at

least 10 years. Shorter periods may produce quite erroneous conclusions concerning a program's effects. More importantly, they neglect the importance of learning, as various actors respond to perceptions of performance gaps and to changing conditions by devising a series of strategies to address them.

(3)   The causal assumptions behind a program are a critical factor affecting performance. They are also one of the factors most susceptible to policy learning.

(4)   Rather than start with a *policy decision* and then examine its implementation, it is probably preferable to begin with a *policy problem* and then examine the variety of actors actually and potentially involved in addressing it. But such an approach must be built upon an explicit causal theory of the factors affecting the participation rates, resources, and preferences of various actors if it is to rise beyond purely descriptive network analysis. All of these conclusions derive from research prior to the mid-1980s.

In the latter 1980s, at least two promising advances—one methodological, the other theoretical—have emerged from the implementation literature.

Almost all implementation research has consisted of rather detailed studies of a single case, with the best empirical work consisting of attempts to use quasi-experimental designs involving a few locales (Hull and Hjern 1987; Sabatier and Mazmanian 1983). Given the number of variables affecting any implementation effort, however, the number of cases examined in any of these studies has been too small to draw valid conclusions (Goggin 1986). The solution is to use longitudinal, cross-sectional designs in which policy outputs (or impacts) are examined in, for example, 30 locales for each of 10 years (Goggin et al. 1990). While difficult and expensive, such a design has been used in several recent efforts (Browning et al. 1984; Lester and Bowman 1989; Scholz and Wei 1986). The most ambitious of all implementation studies—the Knoepfel and Wiedner analysis of sulfur oxide policy in several European countries—essentially followed such a design.

A second recent innovation is more conceptual and theoretical. Sabatier (1986; 1988) has synthesized the best features of top-down and bottom-up implementation approaches with contributions from a number of other literatures (policy learning, elite belief systems) into an "advocacy coalition" framework of policy change over periods of a decade or more. A general overview is seen in Figure 8-2.

Consistent with the concerns of "bottom-up" scholars, the framework starts with a policy subsystem, i. e. the actors (public and private) interacting in a given policy area such as air pollution or secondary education. It argues that most actors can be grouped into one or more advocacy coalitions, based upon similar beliefs concerning basic policy objectives and instruments. Over time, each advocacy coalition will attempt to use a variety of governmental and other institutions to further its policy goals, with most governmental programs being a compromise between the wishes of different coalitions. Much of the interaction within a subsystem is the result of policy-oriented learning, as coalitions seek to learn more about the seriousness and the causes of the problems of concern to them, as well as the utility of various approaches to solving those problems. The framework also acknowledges the importance of

Figure 8-2. General Model of Policy Change Focusing on Competing Advocacy Coalitions within Policy Subsystems

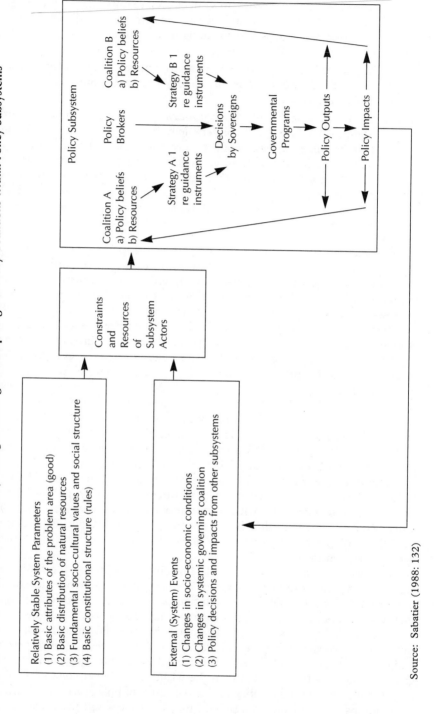

Source: Sabatier (1988: 132)

two sets of factors external to the subsystem—stable system parameters (such as constitutional rules) and external events (such as changes in socio-economic conditions and policy outputs from other subsystems).

The advocacy coalition framework includes a number of specific hypotheses concerning coalition stability, the sources of major policy change, and the conditions conducive to policy-oriented learning. Thus far it has been subjected to a fair amount of empirical testing, largely involving energy and environmental policy in the U.S.[3] In general, coalitions have been found to be quite stable over time, with the other hypotheses drawing more mixed support.

In my opinion, future advances in our understanding of guidance, coordination, and learning in the public sector will depend critically upon scholars' willingness and ability to develop conceptual models which are reasonably comprehensive and empirically falsifiable. The advocacy coalition framework is one such effort. Elinor Ostrom's approach to institutional analysis ... is another, while Andrew Dunsire's cybernetic approach to bureaucracy ... deals with a more limited domain. While we differ on many things, all of us share the conviction that it is better to be clear—and subsequently proven wrong—than to be mushy and think you're always right.

Notes

1. For examples of almost purely descriptive case studies of "implementation networks," see Hanf and Scharpf (1978: Ch. 12), the symposium by Hjern and Hull (1982), and the cases in Barrett and Fudge (1981). Of efforts to develop causal models, that of Scharpf (Hanf and Scharpf 1978: Ch. 13) based on exchange theory is suggestive but rudimentary, while that of Knoepfel and Wiedner (1982a) is comprehensive but completely lacking in parsimony.
2. For example, Burgess has criticized the British Open University for having failed in its (alleged) mission of attracting a significantly greater percentage of working class students than more traditional British universities. While he provides no citations concerning the source of this supposed mission, it was probably Labour's 1966 campaign manifesto. Yet a careful analysis of the *governmental* policy documents—most notably, the 1968 Planning Committee Report—reveal that they were utterly silent on the topic of class representation, while being very explicit that the OU was to be open to anyone on a first-come, first-serve basis (Cerych and Sabatier 1986: Ch.3). In short, not only was Burgess incorrect in contending that the OU was intended to significantly increase working class access to higher education, any attempt to impose quotas for various classes would arguably have been counter to its legal mandate.
3. For several case studies critically exploring various aspects of the framework, see the Fall 1988 issue of *Policy Sciences.* Sabatier and Jenkins-Smith are preparing a book with additional cases by various authors.

References

Bardach, E. (1977): *The Implementation Came.* Cambridge, Mass.: MIT Press.

Barrett, S., and C. Fudge (eds.) (1981): *Policy and Action.* London: Methuen.

Berman, P. (1978): "The Study of Macro- and Micro-Implementation." *Public Policy* 26 (Spring): 157–184.

Berman, P. (1980): "Thinking about Programmed and Adaptive Implementation." In Ingram, H., and D. Mann (eds.), *Why Polities Succeed or Fail,* 205–231. Beverly Hills: Sage.

Berman, R, and M. McLaughlin (1976): "Implementation of ESEA Title 1." *Teacher College Record* 17 (Feb.): 397–415.

Bernstein, M. (1955): *Regulating Business by Independent Commission*. Princeton: Princeton Univ. Press.

Bowen, E. (1982): "The Pressman—Wildavsky Paradox." *Journal of Public Policy* 2 (February): 1–21.

Browning, R., D. R. Marshall, and D. Tabb (1984): *Protest Is Not Enough: The Struggle of Blacks and Hispanics for Equality in Urban Politics*. Berkeley: Univ. of California Press.

Cerych, L., and R Sabatier (1986): *Great Expectations and Mixed Performance: The Implementation of European Higher Education Reforms*. Stoke-on-Trent, U. K.: Trentham Books.

Derthick. M. (1972): *New Towns In-Town*. Washington, D.C.: Urban Institute.

Elmore, R. (1978): "Organizational Models of Social Program Implementation." *Public Policy* 26 (Spring): 185–228.

Elmore, R. (1979): "Backward Mapping." *Political Science Quarterly* 94/4: 601–616.

Goggin, M. (1986): "The Too Few Cases/Too Many Variables Problem in Implementation Research." *Western Political Quarterly* 38 (June): 328–347.

Goggin, M., A. Bowman, J. Lester, and L. O'Toole (1990): *Implementation Theory and Practice: Third-Generation Research*. Glenview, Ill., Scott, Foresman.

Hanf, K. (1982): 'The Implementation of Regulatory Policy: Enforcement as Bargaining." *European Journal of Political Research* 10 (June): 159–172.

Hanf, K., and F. W. Scharpf (eds.) (1978): *Interorganizational Policy Making: Limits to Coordination and Central Control*. London: Sage.

Hill, M. (1982): "The Role of the British Alkali and Clean Air Inspectorate in Air Pollution Control." *Policy Studies Journal* 11 (Sept.): 165–174.

Hjern, B., and C. Hull (1982): "Implementation Research as Empirical Constitutionalism." *European Journal of Political Research* 10 (June): 105–116.

Hjern, B., and D. Porter (1981): "Implementation Structures: A New Unit of Administrative Analysis." *Organization Studies* 2/3: 211–227.

Hull, C., and B. Hjern (1987): *Helping Small Firms Grow*. London: Croom Helm.

Kirst, M., and R. Jung (1982): 'The Utility of a Longitudinal Approach in Assessing Implementation: Title 1, ESEA." In Williams, W. (ed.), *Studying Implementation*, 119-148. Chatham, N.J.: Chatham House.

Knoepfel, P., and H. Wiedner (1982a): "A Conceptual Framework for Studying implementation." In Downing, P., and K. Hanf (eds.), *The Implementation of Pollution Control Programs*, 7–31. Tallahassee: Policy Sciences Program.

Knoepfel, P., and H. Wiedner (1982b): "Implementing Air Quality Control Programs in Europe." *Policy Studies Journal* 11 (Sept.): 103–115.

Lester, J., and A. Bowman (1989): "Implementing Environmental Policy in a Federal System." *Polity* 21: 731–753.

Majone, G., and A. Wildavsky (1978): "Implementation as Evolution." In Freeman, H. (ed.). *Policy Studies Review Annual—1978*, 103-117. Beverly Hills: Sage.

March, J.G., and H. A. Simon (1958): *Organizations*. New York: Wiley.

Mayntz, R. (1978): "Intergovernmental Implementation of Environmental Policy." In Hanf, K., and F. W. Scharpf (eds.), *Interorganizational Policy Making*, 201–214. London: Sage.

Mazmanian, D., and P. Sabatier (eds.) (1981): *Effective Policy Implementation*. Lexington, Mass.: D.C. Heath.

Mazmanian, D., and P. Sabatier (1989): *Implementation and Public Policy*. rev. ed. Lanham: Univ. Press of America.

McConnell, G. (1966): *Private Power and American Democracy*. New York: Alfred Knopf.

McFarlane, D. (1989): "Testing the Statutory Coherence Hypothesis: The Implementation of Federal Family Planning Policy in the States." *Administration and Society* 20 (February): 395–422.

McLaughlin, M. (1975): *Evaluation and Reform: ESEA, Title I*. Cambridge: Ballinger.

Murphy, J. (1971): "Title I of ESEA: The Politics of Implementing Federal Education Reform." *Harvard Educational Review* 41/1: 35–63.

Nakamura, R. (1987): "The Textbook Policy Process and Implementation Research." *Policy Studies Review* 7 (1): 142–154.

O'Toole, L. (1986): "Policy Recommendations for Multi-Actor Implementation: An Assessment of the Field." *Journal of Public Policy* 6 (April): 181–210.

Pressman, J., and A. Wildavsky (1973): *Implementation.* Berkeley: Univ. of California Press.

Quirk, P. (1981): *Industry Influence in Federal Regulatory Agencies.* Princeton: Princeton Univ. Press.

Rodgers, H., and C. Bullock (1976): *Coercion to Compliance.* Lexington, Mass.: D. C. Heath

Sabatier, P. A. (1975): "Social Movements and Regulatory Agencies." *Political Science* 6 (Sept.): 301-342.

Sabatier, P. A. (1986): "Top-Down and Bottom-Up Approaches to Implementation Research." *Journal of Public Policy* 6 (January): 21–48.

Sabatier, P. A. (1988): "An Advocacy Coalition Framework of Policy Change and the Role of Policy-Oriented Learning Therein." *Policy Sciences* 21 (Fall): 129–168.

Sabatier, P. A., and D. Mazmanian (1983): *Can Regulation Work? The Implementation of the 1972 California Coastal Initiative.* New York: Plenum.

Scholz, J., and F. H. Wei (1986): "Regulatory Enforcement in a Federalist System." *American Political Science Review* 80 (December): 1249–1270.

Sharpe, L. J. (1985): "Central Coordination and the Policy Network." *Political Studies* 33 (September): 361–381.

Sharpe, L. J. (1986): "Intergovernmental Policy-Making: The Limits of Subnational Autonomy." In F.-X. Kaufmann, G. Majone, and V. Ostrom (eds.), *Guidance, Control, and Evaluation in The Public Sector,* 159-182. Berlin: de Gruyter.

Van Horn, C. (1979): *Policy Implementation in the Federal System.* Lexington, Mass.: D. C. Heath.

Weatherly, R., and M. Lipsky (1977): "Street Level Bureaucrats and Institutional Innovation: Implementing Special Education Reform." *Harvard Educational Review* 47 (May): 171–197.

Wildavsky, A. (1979): *Speaking Truth to Power.* Boston: Little, Brown.

Williams, W. (1980): *The Implementation Perspective.* Berkeley. Univ. of California Press.

Performance Measurement in Local Government

DAVID N. AMMONS

Aggressive businesses and industries measure performance meticulously. In their popular book on excellence in corporate America, Tom Peters and Bob Waterman characterized top companies as "measurement-happy and performance-oriented."[1] They found that the *very best of the best* complemented their measurement systems with an action orientation that separated them from the pack. Outstanding companies carefully monitor and record the relevant dimensions of performance—they know the important facts and figures—and they act on that knowledge.

Cities, counties, and other public sector agencies confront a far different circumstance. Without the pressure of competition or the unforgiving bottom line of profit or loss, governmental units are apt to neglect performance measurement as they focus on more pressing matters. Carefully conceived systems of performance measurement are more than a little complex; often they are more than a little threatening to the status quo; and they do impose expenses on the organization in terms of development and ongoing administration. Consequently, performance measurement is often allowed to slip in priority, except among local governments that have an extraordinary commitment to management information.

WHY MEASURE PERFORMANCE?

Properly developed and administered, a performance measurement and monitoring system can offer important support to a host of management functions.[2] Each function has important ramifications for local governments that aspire to be excellent.

- *Accountability* Managers in top-performing organizations insist on accountability from their subordinates and, in turn, expect to be held accountable by their organization superiors. Performance measures document what was done by various governmental departments or units, and, ideally, how well it was done and what difference it made. Through such documentation, outstanding departments and entire organizations earn the trust of their clients and citizens as they demonstrate a good return in services provided for tax dollars received.

- *Planning/budgeting* Local governments with an objective inventory of the condition of public services and facilities, a clear sense of service preferences among their citizens, and knowledge of the cost of providing a unit of service at a given level are better equipped to plan their community's future and to budget for that future. Again, performance measurement—incorporating unit costs and indicators of citizen demand or preference—is key.

- *Operational improvement* Local governments that measure performance are more likely to detect operational deficiencies at an early stage. Furthermore, performance records enhance their ability to confirm the effectiveness of corrective actions.

- *Program evaluation/MBO/performance appraisal* Carefully developed performance measures often provide valuable information for the systematic evaluation of program effectiveness. Management-by-objectives (MBO) programs and pay-for-performance systems for managerial employees, where they exist, typically are tied to performance measures. In some cases, employee performance appraisals or other forms of systematic performance feedback have been based, at least in part, on individual performance relative to established measures.

- *Reallocation of resources* A clear indication of program effectiveness and unit costs—in essence, a scorecard on tax dollar investments and returns in various service functions— can aid decision makers in reallocation deliberations, especially in times of financial duress.

- *Directing operations/contract monitoring* Managers equipped with a good set of performance measures are better able to detect operational strengths and weaknesses, to provide feedback to employees and work units, and to deploy close supervision where it is needed most. Performance measures also provide evidence useful in determining whether the service quality specified in contractual arrangements is, in fact, being achieved.

Stated simply, performance measurement provides local governments with a means of keeping score on how their various operations are doing. As noted by Harry Hatry, that scorekeeping function is vital:

> Unless you are keeping score, it is difficult to know whether you are winning or losing. This applies to ball games, card games, and no less to government productivity.... Productivity measurements permit governments to identify problem areas and, as corrective actions are taken, to detect the extent to which improvements have occurred.[3]

TYPES OF PERFORMANCE MEASURES

Efforts to identify different types of performance measures have sometimes yielded lengthy lists.[4] Most measures, however, may be categorized as one of four types: workload measures, efficiency measures, effectiveness measures, or productivity measures.

Workload measures indicate the amount of work performed or the amount of services received. By comparing workload measures reporting, say, the number of applications processed by the personnel department, the number of sets of city council minutes prepared by the city clerk, the number of arrests by the patrol division of the police department, and the number of trees planted by parks crews with the corresponding records from a previous year, a local government official or citizen can see whether workload volume is up or down. Although that information can be of some value, it reveals only how much work was done—not how well it was done or how efficiently.

Efficiency measures reflect the relationship between work performed and the resources required to perform it. Typically, efficiency measures are presented as unit costs, but they can take other forms as well.

Unit costs are calculated by dividing total costs of a service or function by the number of units provided. For example, if 2,000 feet of 8-inch sewer line are installed by municipal crews at a total cost of $80,000, then the unit cost of sewer line installation is $40 per foot. A reversal of the ratio—dividing the number of units by the resources consumed—reveals the number of units produced per dollar and is also an efficiency measure (e.g., three-tenths of an inch of sewer line per dollar.) Other forms of efficiency measures reflect alternative types of resource input (for example, units produced per labor-hour) or production relative to an efficiency standard. If meter readers complete only one-half of their assigned rounds, if repairs by county auto mechanics take twice as long as private garage manuals say they should, or if expensive maintenance equipment is operated only 10 percent of the time it is available, questions of efficiency relative to a prescribed or assumed standard may be raised.

Benchmarking

In order to determine whether a local government's performance is favorable or unfavorable, it is necessary to compare that jurisdiction's performance marks against some relevant peg. Among local governments that monitor their own performance, many compare current performance to figures for the same measures in previous reporting periods. Some compare the performance measures of different units in the same jurisdiction providing similar services or compare performance records with predetermined targets. Until recently, relatively few used national or state standards, private sector performance, or the performance records of other jurisdictions as "benchmarks" for gauging their own jurisdiction's performance.[1]

In the private sector, benchmarking has been widely acclaimed as a technique that contributes to performance improvement. By identifying best-in-class performers and the practices that make them so, industries may refine their own processes in a quest to meet or exceed the benchmarks set by outstanding performers.

Public sector application of the term *benchmarking* has been a bit broader. In some cases, objectives or targets set arbitrarily by a state or local government itself have been labeled benchmarks. In other cases, the term has been used in a manner more consistent with private sector application. Following the corporate pattern the term *benchmark* might be reserved for anticipated or desired performance results anchored either in professional standards or in the experience of respected local governments.

Local governments desiring to identify suitable benchmarks for their operations confront two major issues. One is data availability. Information is needed on standards and on the experience of several other communities for a range of local government functions. In most cases, that information is not easily secured. The second issue is comparability. In assembling suitable benchmarks, each jurisdiction must be vigilant in identifying factors that make some jurisdictions suitable for comparison and others unsuitable. Cost comparisons are especially vulnerable: differences in reporting periods, accounting practices, and cost of living may confound simple comparison. Social and economic factors that may influence the difficulty of a given jurisdiction's incoming workload may similarly set it apart from its counterparts and limit the value of comparisons. Care is therefore in order as communities select their benchmarks.

Cautionary notes are appropriate for jurisdictions embarking on benchmarking, but so are words of encouragement. The principle of accountability demands that department heads and managers be able to tell elected officials how their operations are doing and that elected officials, in turn, be able similarly to inform the public. How a local government is doing in comparison to last year is interesting, but not as interesting as how it is doing in comparison to national standards or to the performance of others in the same line of work. Such comparisons are sometimes difficult and often require explanations. The willingness to grapple with that difficulty and to provide those explanations may well distinguish public officials truly committed to the principle of accountability from those who are not.

1. Harry Hatry, "Performance Measurement Principles and Techniques: An Overview for Local Government," *Public Productivity Review* 4 (December 1980), 312-39.

Source: Adapted from David N. Ammons, "Performance Measurement and Benchmarking," in *Municipal Benchmarks,* 1996. Copyright © 1996 by Sage Publications, Inc. Reprinted by permission of Sage Publications, Inc.

Effectiveness measures depict the degree to which performance objectives are being achieved or otherwise reflect the quality of local government performance. Meter reading error rates of less than 0.5 percent, a consistent record of fire suppression with only minimal spread, and low return rates on auto repairs reflect effective operations. Response times and other measures of service quality are only indirectly related to effectiveness, but are typically included among effectiveness measures for their presumed linkage.

Productivity measures combine the dimensions of efficiency and effectiveness in a single indicator. For example, where "meters repaired per labor hour" would reflect efficiency and percentage of meters repaired properly" (e.g., not returned for further repair within six months) would reflect effectiveness, "unit costs (or labor-hours) per *effective* meter repair" would reflect productivity. The costs (or labor-hours) of faulty meter repairs as well as the costs of effective repairs would be included in the numerator of such a calculation, but only good repairs would be counted in the denominator—thereby encouraging efficiency *and* effectiveness by meter repair personnel.

Examples of each of the four types of performance measures for several common local government functions are provided in Table 8-1. The value of workload measures is limited. Much greater insight into the performance of local government operations may be gained from efficiency, effectiveness, and productivity measures.

CRITERIA FOR A GOOD SET OF PERFORMANCE MEASURES

Properly developed sets of performance measures possess several distinctive characteristics.[5] Good sets include measures that are

- *Valid* They measure what they purport to measure—that is, a high score on a given measure does, in fact, reflect possession of the underlying dimension or quality.

- *Reliable* The measure is accurate and exhibits little variation due to subjectivity or use by different raters (for example, a measuring tape is a reliable instrument in that it is highly objective, and two different persons using the same instrument are likely to get very similar measurements).

- *Understandable* Each measure has an unmistakably clear meaning.

- *Timely* The measures can be compiled and distributed promptly enough to be of value to operating managers or policy makers.

- *Resistant to perverse behavior* The development of a performance measure raises the profile of the performance dimension being examined. That higher profile sometimes brings unintended consequences or even strategies designed to "beat the system"—for instance, if police department performance is measured solely by the number of tickets written, police officers may become overzealous in issuing tickets; if garbage collection workers are rated solely by the number of tons collected, a few enterprising crews may decide to water down the garbage before having it weighed. The best sets of performance measures have little vulnerability to such actions because they have been devised carefully and also because they typically include multiple measures that address

Table 8-1
Examples of the Four Principal Types of Performance Measures

Function	Workload Measure	Efficiency Measure	Effectiveness Measure	Productivity Measure
City clerk	Number of sets of city council meeting minutes prepared	Employee-hours per set of city council meeting minutes prepared	Percentage of city council minutes approved without amendment	Percentage of city council minutes prepared within seven days of the meeting and approved without amendment
Library	Total circulation	Circulation per library employee	Circulation per capita	Ratio of circulation per capita to library costs per capita
Meter repair	Number of meters repaired	Cost per meter repair	Percentage of repaired meters still functioning properly six months later	Cost per properly repaired meter (i.e., total cost of all meter repairs divided by number of meters needing no further repairs within six months)
Personnel	Job applications received	Cost per job application processed; cost per vacancy filled	Percentage of new hires/promotions successfully completing probation and performing satisfactorily six months later	Cost per vacancy filled successfully (i.e., employee performing satisfactorily six months later)

performance from several dimensions and thereby hold potentially perverse behavior in check.

- *Comprehensive* The most important performance dimensions are captured by the set of measures. Some minor facets of performance may be overlooked, but the major elements are addressed.

- *Nonredundant* By favoring unique measures over duplicative measures, the best sets of performance measures limit information overload for managers, other decision makers, and consumers of local government reports. Each measure contributes something distinctive.

- *Sensitive to data collection cost* Most dimensions of local government performance can be measured either directly or through proxies. In some cases, however, measurement costs may exceed their value. Good sets of performance measures include the best choices among *practical* measurement options.

- *Focused on controllable facets of performance* Without necessarily excluding important, overarching, and perhaps relatively uncontrollable characteristics relevant to a particular function, good sets of performance measures emphasize outcomes or facets of performance that are controllable by policy initiatives or management action. For example, while a police department's set of performance measures might include the rate of domestic homicides in the jurisdiction, a good set of measures would also include indicators of public safety more widely considered controllable by police efforts.

SOURCES OF PERFORMANCE DATA

Typically, performance data are secured from various combinations of the following sources: existing records, time logs, citizen/client surveys, trained observer ratings, and specially designed data collection processes.

The simplest and most desirable source of performance measurement data is the set of records already being maintained by a local government. Workload counts, complaint records, and response times for various services are common, even among local governments with modest performance reporting practices. Such information can serve as the foundation of a performance measurement system and sometimes can be converted to higher-level measures. Depending on its level of precision, for example, workload data might be combined with expenditure information to yield efficiency measures.

Time logs completed on either a comprehensive or a random basis provide resource-input information for labor-related efficiency measures (e.g., work units per employee-hour) or for measures comparing actual work completed in a given amount of time to the amount of work expected on the basis of engineered work standards. Apart from vehicle maintenance and perhaps a handful of other services, however, engineered world standards are rarely available for common local government functions.

The surveying of users of particular services or citizens in general is a feedback mechanism used by a number of local governments. That practice may get an additional boost from the customer focus and current popularity of the total quality management (TQM) movement.

Surveys typically tap respondent perceptions regarding the adequacy of selected services, the nature of any perceived deficiencies, and the extent to which respondents avail themselves of various services and facilities. In order for a survey of citizens in general or of users of a particular service to contribute meaningfully to a local government's performance measurement system, the survey must be conducted with sufficient scientific rigor to produce reliable results. Such rigor typically introduces costs that exceed those of tempting, low-cost alternatives, but surveys conducted "on the cheap" are frequently misleading and can be easily discredited. Carefully designed and properly randomized telephone surveys have been found to be a widely accepted, moderately priced alternative to highly desirable but more expensive face-to-face interviews and low-cost, low-response-rate mail surveys.

Trained observer ratings have been used successfully in several cities for evaluating the condition of facilities and infrastructure. Typically, persons employed in clerical or other positions outside the department responsible for facility maintenance are trained to serve on an intermittent basis as raters of street cleanliness or parks maintenance, for example. Instructed on the finer points of distinguishing between various grades of facility condition and customarily armed with photographic depictions of those grades, trained observers can provide a more systematic evaluation of condition than can usually be drawn from records of citizens' compliments or complaints or even from citizen surveys. The effective administration of trained observer programs requires careful attention to training and issues of reliability. Supervisors often spot-check facilities to corroborate ratings and, where two or more raters assess the same facility within a short period of time, supervisors usually re-inspect if the grades of raters are more than one unit apart.

Unfortunately, information already on hand or readily available through customary means does not always meet current performance measurement needs. Analysts may discover, for example, that existing workload counts and random time logs have been based on estimates rather than on precise figures. The citizen survey everyone in town likes to quote may turn out to be suspect because it was conducted using questionable methods—relying on a tear-out questionnaire in the local newspaper. Even federal figures, presumed to be rock solid, may be less comprehensive and conclusive than originally thought; FBI crime statistics, for example, include only *reported* crimes—not all crimes actually committed. Typically, at least a few new data collection procedures must be introduced to support the development of a good set of performance measures.

STATUS OF PERFORMANCE MEASUREMENT IN LOCAL GOVERNMENT

A little more than a half-century ago, a pair of esteemed observers noted the availability of a number of "rough and ready measurement devices," but nevertheless conceded the limited development of performance measurement among city governments.

> It is probably true that in the present state of our knowledge the citizen can often better judge the *efficiency* of his local government by the political odor, be it sweet or foul, which emanates from the city hall than by any attempt at measurement of services.[6]

Over the years, various movements to improve management practices, rationalize decision making, or enhance accountability often have encouraged improved performance measurement. Respected professional associations, including the American Society for Public Administration, the Governmental Accounting Standards Board, the Government Finance Officers Association, and the International City/County Management Association, have promoted the practice. Some local governments have responded to that encouragement. Many of the writings on performance measurement in local government repeat familiar names as exemplars: Sunnyvale, California; Phoenix, Arizona; Charlotte, North Carolina; Dayton, Ohio; Palo Alto, California; Savannah, Georgia; Randolph Township, New Jersey; Dallas, Texas; Aurora, Colorado; New York City; Alexandria, Virginia; Charlottesville, Virginia; and Portland,

Oregon.[7] These communities, however, are far from typical in the advanced status of their performance measurement systems. Despite survey responses suggesting widespread and fairly sophisticated performance measurement in local government, more exacting research involving the examination of actual performance reporting documents reveals far more limited development.[8] Not all cities and counties even engage in performance measurement. Among those that do, most rely heavily on workload measures. Some report a few efficiency or effectiveness measures for various functions. Rarely are productivity measures reported.

Although performance measurement is well developed and still improving in some local governments, most have a long way to go. Speaking of his own city in the not-too-distant past, one Philadelphia official remarked, "If you were to ask how much it cost to pick up a ton of trash, I hope you weren't waiting for an answer the same year."[9] The situation, he noted, had improved greatly in recent years. Perhaps the remarks of an Indianapolis official put the development of performance measurement and program evaluation systems in proper perspective: "We're coming from an era of cleaning our clothes on rocks, and now we have come up with a hand-cranked washing machine. It's a much better life, but of course we'd rather have an automated washing machine, eventually."[10]

OVERCOMING RESISTANCE
TO PERFORMANCE MEASUREMENT

The likelihood is great that some form of resistance will be encountered in efforts to develop or enhance performance measurement systems. Although the precise source often is not predictable, *some* resistance almost inevitably will come from *somewhere*. The proper starting point for developing a coping strategy is to try to understand the reasons for that resistance.

Typically, performance measurement is seen by various groups or individuals in the organization as a threat to their status. Some employees may fear that it is the first step in a process that will lead to tougher work standards and a forced speed-up of work processes, perhaps to be followed by the layoff of workers who are no longer needed or who cannot keep up.

Supervisors and managers may feel threatened by what they perceive to be the insinuations of a performance measurement drive. Believing that executive and legislative satisfaction with their performance would generate no such movement, they may sense an accusation of poor performance. They fear loss of status or even loss of employment if performance measures confirm those accusations, and they feel certain of a loss of discretion as the upper echelons gain yet another means of looking closely over their shoulders.

Even some top local government officials, who would seem to have so much to gain from improved performance measures, may resist their development. Especially prone to do so are those who believe that, by virtue of their own political adeptness or membership in the dominant political coalition, their preferences are more likely to prevail in political negotiations without the influence of performance facts and figures.

Seven Essential Steps in Public Sector Benchmarking

Simply put, benchmarking is a rigorous yet practical process for measuring your organization's performance and processes against those of best-in-class organizations, both public and private, and then using this analysis to improve services, operations, and cost position dramatically. The great news is that the process of benchmarking is neither complex nor scientific. Benchmarking, in fact, consists of seven common-sense steps.

Step 1. Determine which functional areas within your organization will benefit most from benchmarking. Give priority to functions that make up a high percentage of the organization's cost, that are especially influential in shaping customer assessment of services, that appear to show room for improvement, or that are capable of being improved.

Step 2. Identify the key performance variables to measure cost, quality, and efficiency for the functions you have selected.

Step 3. Pick the best-in-class organizations for each benchmark item. Best-in-class organizations are those that perform each function at the *lowest cost* or with the *highest degree of quality or efficiency.* Best-in-class organizations can be comparable directly to yours in size, structure, and organization, but this is not required for every study candidate.

Step 4. Measure the performance of the best-in-class organizations for each benchmarked function.

Step 5. Measure your own performance for each benchmarked item, and identify the gaps between you and the best-in-class.

Step 6. Specify actions and programs to close the gaps in your favor.

Step 7. Implement and monitor your benchmarking results.

Source: Excerpted from Kenneth A. Bruder, Jr., and Edward M. Gray, "Public-Sector Benchmarking: A Practical Approach," *Public Management* 76 (September 1994): S9-S14. *Public Management* is published by ICMA.

Usually, such fears are overblown. Rarely are performance measurement efforts inspired by sinister or mean-spirited motives. Although detractors often fear worker exploitation or loss of supervisory discretion, the most commonly prescribed blueprints for measurement system development call for the involvement of those parties rather than for their exclusion. Measurement initiatives typically are most successful when they secure the input and support of frontline employees and supervisors. When that happens, a new measurement and reporting system—and the clarification of work unit objectives and priorities that accompanies the system's development—is likely to earn accolades from those parties rather than charges of exploitation.

Persons who fear that politics will be displaced in local decision making through the rationalizing influence of objective performance measures need not be overly concerned. Advances in management practices may, at most, supplement political considerations in decision making. In a democratic setting, politics can never be displaced—nor should it be.

Resistance in advances in performance measurement may emanate from a variety of concerns and may be manifested in different forms. A few things in this regard, however, are fairly predictable. Proponents of improved performance measures should expect three common declarations from opponents.

"You can't measure what I do!" If the performance of a department or office has not been measured in the past, it should not be surprising that incumbents might reason that their activities must be unmeasurable. If their performance could have been measured, it already would have been. Offices or departments making this declaration are often characterized by nonroutine work and the absence of an existing data collection system. Both factors can make measurement difficult. Rarely is it impossible.

Sometimes a bit of creativity is necessary to devise either a suitable direct measure or a proxy that measures performance indirectly. Often, interviewing skills are even more important. "If your office closed shop for a few weeks, I know you would be missed," the interviewer might suggest. "But who would suffer the greatest impact, and what aspect of your work would they miss the most?" Gradually, with cooperation from employees and relevant officials, a widely accepted set of performance measures can emerge.

"You're measuring the wrong thing!" Once again, the involvement of service providers is key to resolving their complaints or calming their fears. It could be that relatively insignificant performance dimensions are being measured and that more important dimensions are being ignored. If so, the remedy is to replace the former with the latter. The involvement of service providers can assure corrective action.

On the other hand, it is possible that the debate over appropriate performance measures may have uncovered a fundamental problem. A difference of opinion may exist between upper management and the service delivery unit over desired elements of service, or the unit may simply have labored under a longstanding misconception about what management wants. Such disagreements or misunderstandings should be resolved.

Yet another group of stakeholders in measuring the right thing are citizen-customers. Their involvement, typically through strategic planning processes, focus groups, and citizen commissions, can enhance the likelihood that the right things are being measured.

"It costs too much and we don't have the resources!" Understandably, departmental officials who already feel that their resources are stretched too thin may be reluctant to tackle new, time-consuming measurement and reporting tasks that may syphon program resources. Those officials are a little like the overburdened logger who, facing a stack of uncut logs, felt he could not spare the time to sharpen his dull saw. Well-meaning but reluctant officials must be persuaded of the value of performance measurement as a tool for improving services and making better use of scarce resources.

There is no reason to embark on performance measurement improvements unless better measures are expected to lead to improved services, to make services more efficient, or to make them more equitable. Service providers must be assured of management's commitment to those ends and convinced of management's resolve to use performance measurement to improve, rather than to drain resources from, services to the public. It may be helpful to point out to skeptics that most local government officials in jurisdictions that have performance measurement systems report that their systems have been worth the expense.[11]

DEVELOPING A PERFORMANCE MEASUREMENT AND MONITORING SYSTEM

Performance measures will not lead inevitably to improved performance. Although the act of measuring an operation for its results draws attention to that function and may thereby inspire greater efforts and improved performance, such results cannot be guaranteed. Performance measurement is merely a tool. If wielded properly, it can identify areas of performance adequacy and areas of performance deficiency; however, it can neither explain the former nor prescribe remedies for the latter. Reliable explanations and appropriate prescriptions require subsequent analysis of targeted operations.

Performance measurement and monitoring systems may be developed in a variety of ways. The steps outlined in the accompanying sidebar have been gleaned from the experience of several local governments and distilled from the writings on this topic, but many variations on this pattern are possible and, indeed, perhaps desirable in a given setting.

**Steps in the Development and Administration
of a Performance Measurement and Monitoring System**

1. Secure managerial commitment.
2. Assign responsibility (individual or team) for spearheading/coordinating departmental efforts to develop sets of performance measures.
3. Select departments/activities/functions for the development of performance measures.
4. Identify goals and objectives.
5. Design measures that reflect performance relevant to objectives:
   - Emphasize service quality and outcomes rather than input or workload.
   - Include neither too few nor too many measures.
   - Solicit rank-and-file as well as management input/endorsement.
   - Identify the work unit's customers and emphasize delivery of services to them.
   - Consider periodic surveys of citizens, service recipients, or users of selected facilities.
   - Include effectiveness and efficiency measures.
6. Determine desired frequency of performance reporting.
7. Assign departmental responsibility for data collection and reporting.
8. Assign centralized responsibility for data receipt, monitoring, and feedback.
9. Audit performance data periodically.
10. Ensure that analysis of performance measures incorporates a suitable basis of comparison.
11. Ensure a meaningful connection between the performance measurement system and important decision processes (e.g. goal setting, policy development, resource allocation, employee development and compensation, program evaluation).
12. Continually refine performance measures, balancing the need for refinement with the need for constancy in examining trends.
13. Incorporate selected measures into public information reporting.

Notes

1. Thomas J. Peters and Robert H. Waterman, Jr., *In Search of Excellence: Lessons from America's Best-Run Companies* (New York: Harper & Row, 1982), 240.

2. Mark Glover, "Performance Measurement: Local Government Efforts and Successes," SECOPA 1993 Conference, Cocoa Beach, FL, 7 October 1993; David Osborne and Ted Gaebler, *Reinventing Government: How the Entrepreneurial Spirit Is Transforming the Public Sector* (Reading, MA: Addison-Wesley 1992), 156; Lawrence H. Thompson "Service to the Public: How Effective and Responsive Is the Government?" Statement before the U.S. House of Representatives Committee on Ways and Means, 8 May 1991, U.S. General Accounting Office, GAO/T-HRD-91-26, 14; U.S. General Accounting Office, *Performance Budgeting: State Experiences and Implications for the Federal Government* (Washington, DC: U.S. GAO, February 1993), GAO/AFMD-93-41, 1; Lance L. Decker and Patrick Manion, "Performance Measurement in Phoenix: Trends and a New Direction," *National Civic Review* 76 (March-April 1987), 119–129; Harry P. Hatry, "Local Government Uses for Performance Measurement," *Intergovernmental Personnel Notes* (May-June 1980)

3. Harry P. Hatry, "The Status of Productivity Measurement in the Public Sector," *Public Administration Review* 38 (January/February 1978), 28.

4. Harry P. Hatry, "Performance Measurement Principles and Techniques: An Overview for Local Government," *Public Productivity Review* 4 (December 1980): 312–39.

5. Hatry, "Performance Measurement Principles and Techniques"; Charles K. Bens, "Strategies for Implementing Performance Measurement," *Management Information Services Report* 18 (November 1986); Harry P. Hatry, Louis H. Blair, Donald M. Fisk, John M. Greiner, John R. Hall, Jr., and Philip S. Schaenman, *How Effective Are Your Community Services? Procedures for Measuring Their Quality*, 2d ed (Washington, DC: The Urban Institute and ICMA 1992), 2–3.

6. Clarence E. Ridley and Herbert A. Simon, *Measuring Municipal Activities: A Survey of Suggested Criteria for Appraising Administration* (Chicago: International City Managers' Association, 1943), ix.

7. See, for example, Hatry et al., *How Effective Are Your Community Services?* 1; Bens, "Strategies for Implementing Performance Measurement," 1; Osborne and Gaebler, *Reinventing Government*, 349; and Geoffrey N. Smith, "Mayoral Measures," *Financial World* 161 (18 February 1992): 8.

8. Harry P. Hatry and Donald M. Fisk, *Improving Productivity and Productivity Measurement in Local Governments* (Washington, DC: Urban Institute, 1971); Hatry, "Status of Productivity Measurement"; Charles L. Usher and Gary C. Cornia, "Goal Setting and Performance Assessment in Municipal Budgeting," *Public Administration Review* 41 (March/April 1981), 229–35; Susan A. MacManus, "Coping with Retrenchment: Why Local Governments Need to Restructure Their Budget Document Formats," *Public Budgeting and Finance* 4 (autumn 1984): 568–66; Rosemary B. LeGrotte, "Performance Measurement in Major U.S. Cities" (Ph.D. diss. North Texas State University 1987); Gloria A. Grizzle, "Linking Performance to Funding Decisions: What Is the Budgeter's Role?" *Public Productivity Review* 11 (spring 1987): 33–44, David N. Ammons "Overcoming the Inadequacies of Performance Measurement in Local Government: The Case of Libraries and Leisure Services," *Public Administration Review* 55 (January/ February 1995): 37–47.

9. Katherine Barrett and Richard Greene, "The State of the Cities: Managing for Results," *Financial World* 163 (1 February 1994): 44.

10. Ibid.

11. Robert P. McGowan and Theodore H. Poister, "Impact of Productivity Measurement Systems on Municipal Performance," *Policy Studies Review* 4 (February 1985): 532–40.

PART FOUR

*Public Administration
and Change*

● ●

9 Public Administration in a Three-Sector Society: Relationships among Governmental, Business, and Nonprofit Organizations

Few topics dealing with public administration in the last few years have generated as much controversy and public debate as the relations between business and public administration. The issues are many and varied. They range from the size of government in American society to joint private-public ventures in promoting economic development; from contracting out to private firms for public services to greater governmental scrutiny to protect the environment; from occupational and health safety rules to industry advisory committees for government agencies.

One of the most dramatic examples during the Bush administration was the federal bailout of the savings and loan institutions. Hundreds of financially weak savings and loan associations were closed or taken over. The price tag will be in the hundreds of billions of dollars, primarily to support the government's commitment in guaranteeing the security of depositors' money. The Office of Thrift Supervision in the U.S. Department of the Treasury was created to more closely monitor the S&L industry. Funds are now insured by the Federal Deposit Insurance Corporation, which formerly covered only commercial banks. And a new organization, the Resolution Trust Corporation, was established to liquidate failed savings institutions.

In recent years, we have often heard in the United States that government, or bureaucracy, is too big, is too bloated. One way to measure this is to compare the size of government in this country with the size in other countries. One standard measure of this is governmental expenditures as a percent of gross domestic product (GDP), the total of goods and services produced in a country. For the United States, this involves adding together federal, state, and local expenditures.

The results of comparing the United States with the other industrialized democracies shows that only two countries, Japan and Turkey, are near the United States, and these three are at the bottom of the list. Sweden and Denmark, Belgium and France, Norway and Italy, Germany and Britain and Canada and many others have governments relatively larger than that in the United States. Government expenditures in the United States amount to about one-third of GDP.

Government's role is not fully explained, however, just by its expenditures. In the first selection in this chapter, Richard Lehne provides an overview of government regulation of business. Lehne presents the rationale for regulation, and he also describes the more recent pressures for deregulation. One regulatory agency which was judged to be no longer necessary was the Interstate Commerce Commission, the very first regulatory agency in 1887.

In the second article in this chapter, William Gormley takes a pragmatic look at the trend toward privatization of government services. Gormley finds that privatization has many faces and is more promising under some circumstances than others. Gormley adds that privatization is not just about government and business, but also includes the "third sector," the nonprofit organizations in American society.

The final article attempts to survey the growing trend toward public-private partnerships in solving problems of public importance. Graham Finney and David Grossman provide examples of these partnerships in a wide range of endeavors, and attempt to assess the lessons learned from these experiments to date. They then peek into the next century and speculate about scenarios for the future; they see a partnership scenario as the most likely.

Chapter 9 surveys some of the most important and most controversial questions in public administration today:

- Why does government ever regulate the private sector?
- What are the forms of government regulation of business?
- Is the period of deregulation likely to be followed by a period of re-regulation? Why or why not?
- What does "privatization" mean?
- What explains the trend toward privatization of public services?
- According to Gormley, under what conditions is privatization most likely to work?
- Why have public-private partnerships become so popular? When should they be used to solve public problems?

Understanding
Government Regulation

RICHARD LEHNE

The meltdown of the savings and loan industry has been described as the "greatest regulatory fiasco in American history."[1] Ed Gray, chairman of the Federal Home Loan Bank Board and chief regulator of the industry, remembers being called to a private meeting at a lavishly marbled Senate office building.[2] It was April 1987, and Senator Dennis DeConcini of Arizona took the lead at the meeting. He was joined by senators Alan Cranston of California, John Glenn of Ohio, and John McCain, also of Arizona.

The Senators, DeConcini said, were concerned about Lincoln Savings and Loan, a California S&L, or "thrift" institution, that had been bought by Charles H. Keating. They wanted to know why Gray's examiners were being harsh and unfair in their examination of Lincoln's records. A few weeks earlier the Bank Board had imposed a new regulation limiting investments in speculative ventures by thrifts such as Lincoln. DeConcini asked Gray to withdraw the regulation.[3] The meeting continued for an hour with Gray defending the need for the new rule.

The Senators called a second meeting a week later with the Bank Board officials from San Francisco who were directly responsible for regulating Lincoln. This time, they were also joined by Senator Riegle of Michigan. As the Senators continued to defend Lincoln, the San Francisco officials stressed that procedures at Keating's S&L violated common sense, the Bank Board's regulations, and the law. They compared Lincoln to a ticking time bomb, said it was the worst situation they had ever seen, and promised that a criminal complaint would soon be filed. Shortly after this meeting, the San Francisco regulators recommended to Washington that Lincoln be taken out of Keating's control because it was squandering federally insured funds and violating legal requirements.

Ed Gray soon completed his term at the Bank Board and was succeeded as chair by a former Senate aide. The Lincoln case was then transferred from the San Francisco office to Washington, nothing more was heard about the criminal referral mentioned by the San Francisco regulators, and Lincoln negotiated a favorable new agreement with the Bank Board that allowed Keating to remain in business. Less than a year later, however, in April 1989, Lincoln was finally taken over by the Bank Board, the cost to taxpayers was then estimated to be $2.5 billion, and Charles Keating was subsequently arrested, indicted for fraud, and convicted.

During this period newspapers carried accounts of Charles Keating's extensive political contributions and donations. At a news conference held after Lincoln Savings and Loan was seized by federal regulators, Keating said: "One question, among the many raised in recent weeks, had to do with whether my financial support in any way influenced several political figures to take up my cause. I want to say in the most forceful way I can: I certainly hope so."[4]

One way to interpret the savings and loan industry collapse is to see it as an instance of criminals buying political protection to cover up misconduct and eventually getting caught. Some observers argue, however, that the S&L debacle involved more than crooks and payoffs. They note that financial losses at Lincoln and similar S&Ls "did not account for a significant share of [S&L] association losses."[5] They maintain that the dynamics of the S&L industry need to be understood to explain why the regulatory mess actually occurred.

To open a saving and loan association or a bank, potential owners invest a specific amount of their own funds to serve as the institution's capital and assure it a margin of safety. S&Ls and similar financial institutions then have two operating tasks: first they collect savings, and then they use the savings to earn income.[6] Historically, saving and loan associations undertook these tasks in distinct ways. Originally, deposits made in S&Ls could only be withdrawn after six months, one year, or some specific period of time. In contrast to these "time deposits," accounts in commercial banks were available whenever the depositor wanted funds. These were called "demand deposits." S&Ls originally used the time deposits only to make twenty- or thirty-year mortgage loans to help people purchase homes. Commercial banks earned income by offering a greater variety of loans and services. S&Ls and commercial banks made a profit by earning more from their loans than they had to pay in interest to depositors. To maintain confidence in the banking system, the federal government guaranteed that depositors would not lose their money if individual banks went bankrupt.

During the 1970s, the saving and loan industry faced two major problems. First, interest rates soared. By the end of the 1970s, rates reached 20 percent. Second, advances in communications and data processing made money market funds, a new form of savings account offered by other financial service companies, available throughout the country. Money market funds gathered people's savings and lent those savings to government agencies willing to pay 13 or 14 percent interest. S&Ls were limited by law to paying about 5 percent interest on savings accounts.

As a result of these two developments, S&Ls lost deposits as people shifted their savings from thrifts into money market funds that paid higher interest. Yet the S&Ls were still committed to long-term mortgage loans that yielded only 7 or 8 percent interest per year. As the level of deposits fell, S&Ls lost most of their capital. They turned to Washington for help.

First, Congress ended the rule limiting the rate S&Ls could pay in interest so that they would stop losing deposits to the money market funds. Regulators then reduced the minimum amount of capital required of S&L institutions so that hundreds of S&Ls would not be forced out of business. Third, Congress and the regulators together allowed S&Ls to invest in activities other than home mortgages so they could earn higher returns on their investments. Finally, Congress increased savings insurance to $100,000 per account to make S&Ls more attractive to depositors.

By 1983, Congress and the regulators had responded to four specific S&L problems, but together the four piecemeal changes produced a dangerous regulatory situation. Normally, the managers of banks and S&Ls act responsibly so as not to jeopardize the capital invested by the people who own the bank. By 1983, however, hundreds of S&Ls had lost all their capital. These decapitalized institutions remained in business only because the federal government guaranteed depositors that it would refund their money if the S&L went bankrupt.

The managers of these decapitalized S&Ls had no reason to act prudently. They had nothing to lose. They made risky loans on speculative ventures, often to friends and associates. They recognized that they would reap substantial rewards if the gambles paid off and knew that the federal government would be required to pay off the depositors if the loans went into default.

Furthermore, S&Ls earn immediate profits by processing loans, and they can increase profits by increasing their volume of loans. Decapitalized S&Ls paid abnormally high interest rates to attract deposits from throughout the country so they could sustain a surging tide of loans. During this period the most reckless S&Ls grew to mammoth size. Depositors were unconcerned about the reckless nature of the loans being made by the S&Ls because the federal government had guaranteed them that their deposits would be protected.

In 1985, federal regulators began to recognize the consequences of the regulatory changes that had been made a few years earlier. They asked Congress to grant them authority to halt the developing trends, but they were opposed by S&L managers like Keating and the United States League of Savings Associations, which did not want regulators to take any action against its members. By 1986, regulators could no longer close the worst S&Ls because they lacked funds to pay off the depositors.[7] The issue that brought Ed Gray to the meeting with Senator DeConcini was a Bank Board regulation to limit the riskiest ventures of the decapitalized S&Ls.

While delaying definitive action and hoping the problem would cure itself, legislators like the so-called "Keating Five" Senators diligently solicited political contributions from the S&L industry. Neither the Republican nor the Democratic party wanted to address the S&L fiasco until after the 1988 presidential election season because neither candidate wanted to debate who was most responsible. Regrettably, each day the decapitalized S&Ls remained in operation, the volume of reckless loans increased. Because many of those loans would never be repaid and the federal government had guaranteed the funds of depositors, each day of operations ran up an estimated $30 million in losses that federal taxpayers would eventually be required to pay. This refusal to deal with the regulatory problems of the savings and loan industry in a timely manner turned a $20 billion or $30 billion debacle into a $300 billion disaster. When, in 1990, the federal government faced up to its responsibility to pay off the depositors whose funds it had guaranteed, some observers estimated the total cost to taxpayers would reach $500 billion.

Even the sorriest spectacle can be instructive. This chapter uses the example of the savings and loan industry to consider how best to understand government regulation. The chapter first outlines different perspectives on regulation that emerge from the analyses of scholars and the activities of businesspeople. It then reviews the history of regulation and identifies the features of new and old patterns of regulation. In the last section, the chapter focuses on deregulation and regulatory reform and reviews the stakes that were involved in these movements. The savings and loan saga is certainly not a typical regulatory event, but it can help us decide how to understand best the dynamics of government regulation.

PERSPECTIVES ON REGULATION

Government regulation is "a distinctively American approach to balancing public and private interests."[8] Regulations insist that public purposes must be respected in business operations. While antitrust policies control the competition-related activities of business, regulation restricts business actions involving specific products. (Sometimes the distinctions between antitrust and regulatory policies are blurred.)

Two analytic perspectives have dominated our understanding of the place of regulation in the relationship between government and business: the public interest perspective and the private interest perspective.[9]

Public Interest Perspective

Most analyses present regulation as a response to market failure.[10] Regulation seeks to protect consumers and achieve the benefits of marketplace competition in situations in which competition does not occur.[11] Sometimes the technical factors of an industry's operations prevent competition. Such industries are often called *natural monopolies*. They include local telephone, electric, or water utilities, in which high capital investment makes competing utility systems too costly; and radio and television broadcasting, in which operating rules are needed to prevent broadcasters from disrupting each other's signals.

Regulation may also appear because of a different form of market failure: the failure of the price mechanism. In some industries, prices are not an accurate measure of the true social costs of business activity. Some businesses are regulated because their operations pollute the environment, yet the marketplace prices of the business's product do not include the full social costs of pollution. In other instances, a product is more valuable to the society than to the individual consumer, and it is regulated to assure that enough of that product is provided to meet the society's needs.

Finally, market failure may occur because consumers lack the information needed to make proper judgments about products and producers. S&Ls and other financial institutions are regulated because individual consumers cannot know enough to determine if a firm's lending practices are sound and if the institution itself is safe. Medical products and medical practitioners are required to meet government standards because individual consumers have no basis on which to make medical judgments.

In each of these instances, regulation emerges as a cure for the failures of the marketplace. If regulation fails to achieve its objectives, it is assumed that the regulatory process had been poorly designed or subverted. According to the public interest perspective, the regulation of the saving and loan industry was intended to provide a safe and secure place for citizens to save money, and the collapse of the industry occurred because regulators lacked the intelligence and resources to supervise the industry properly and because unscrupulous managers and politicians exploited the regulatory process for their own selfish goals.

Private Interest Perspective

According to the private interest perspective,[12] it is a pretense to maintain that regulation is a public interest activity.[13] According to this view, people pursue their private interests in the regulatory arena with the same diligence as they pursue their individual interests in the private sector. Regulation should be understood as nothing more than an effort to use governmental authority to redistribute income from one group to another. Since numerous studies show that the actual consequences of many regulatory policies are to enrich specific private groups, students of regulation should acknowledge that the actual effects of regulation are, in fact, the intended effects.

Three groups are in the best position to benefit from regulation. First is business. Business does not act as a class, but as companies or industries. When a company faces a decline in sales, it can cut the price of its product, improve quality, increase its advertising budget, or invest in a lobbying effort to secure beneficial regulatory action.[14] When the S&L industry faced problems in the late 1970s, it launched a campaign to change the governmental rules under which it operated. As a result, it was allowed to pay higher interest rates, reduce its capital, and invest federally guaranteed funds in speculative ventures. Some firms in the industry profited handsomely from these changes until the governmental costs of their actions were publicly recognized.

Members of Congress can also benefit by transforming regulation into porkbarrel politics.[15] Regulatory actions affect specific geographic areas in distinct ways, and members of Congress seek to promote the economic interests of their regions. The corporate headquarters of Charles Keating's firm was in Arizona, and Lincoln Savings and Loan was located in California. The Senators from these states were most active in promoting their cause in the Lincoln S&L case. Members of Congress have influence over regulatory agencies, and the expectation that they will exercise that influence helps legislators raise campaign funds. Keating contributed well over $1 million to the political causes of the five Senators with whom Gray met.

Regulators are in a position to benefit individually and organizationally from regulation.[16] Extensive regulatory authority can lead to bureaucratic aggrandizement with surging budgets and growing personnel rosters. Regulation also benefits individual bureaucrats by giving them an opportunity to advance their careers either by garnering professional esteem or by displaying their qualifications for private sector jobs.

From the private interest perspective, an understanding of regulation is enhanced by acknowledging that regulatory intervention in the marketplace is usually an effort by some group to increase its own wealth and income at the expense of others. Benefits to private groups are neither a subversion nor an aberration but reflect the fundamental nature of regulation.

Empirical Perspective

Regardless of whether regulation is seen as an effort to promote public or private interests, businesspeople recognize that regulations inevitably assist some groups at the expense of others.[17] The old rule that limited S&Ls to paying no more than 5 percent interest on savings accounts helped money market fund managers persuade depositors to withdraw their savings from S&Ls. The federal guarantee of S&L deposits erased for depositors the difference between a prudently managed and a recklessly managed S&L and thus benefited poorly run institutions by making them as attractive as well-managed firms.

Since each company operates in a unique way, the impact of government regulation differs by firm. Nevertheless, there is no escaping the fact that every economic enterprise in the country is affected by the costs and benefits of a myriad of government regulations.

The impact of regulation depends on the details of specific situations, but regulatory disputes follow normal patterns: consumers vs. producers; producers vs. producers; or consumers vs. consumers. Some regulatory issues are disputes between consumers and producers. When a regulated public utility wants to raise the fees it charges for its product, its opponents are those who must pay the higher costs.

Other regulatory disputes are contests between two different groups of producers. In part, the S&L controversy pitted the decapitalized S&Ls against those S&Ls that were well managed. It is common for regulatory issues to be contests between truckers and the railroads, high-cost and low-cost manufacturers, or export-oriented firms and companies serving a domestic market.

Finally, regulatory questions can place the interests of one group of consumers against the interests of others. Automobile insurance rates, for example, can be higher for the residents of crime-ridden urban areas or safer suburban districts, for careful drivers or the accident-prone, for men or women, for experienced drivers or those who have recently learned to drive. Regardless of the original motivation, every governmental regulation has impact on various segments of the economy.

DIMENSIONS OF FEDERAL REGULATION

Government regulation is not a complicated topic. Regulations are policy tools. They are rules that restrict business operations in order to accomplish governmental purposes. Regulation is made to appear more complex than it is when commentators focus on administrative arrangements rather than public purposes. Government regulation is conducted in an infinite variety of ways, but an emphasis on the purposes of regulation rather than the techniques makes regulation easier to comprehend.

There are scores of federal regulatory agencies but only two basic forms of regulation. Governments engage in *economic regulation* when they require firms in a particular industry, such as the savings and loan industry, to behave in specific ways regardless of the forces of the marketplace. Governments' *social regulations* impose rules on how all firms, regardless of industry, conduct specific functional activities, such as labor-management relations or environmental protection. Table 9-1 lists four agencies involved in the economic regulation of specific industries and four other agencies responsible for the social regulation of specific functions. The table also identifies the years in which the agencies were created and their jurisdictions.

Economic Regulation

Federal economic regulation began with the creation of the Interstate Commerce Commission (ICC) in 1887. Article I of the U.S. Constitution gives Congress the power to regulate interstate commerce, but Congress left this authority to the states until 1887.

The emergence of an industrial economy and the growing impact of railroads on society led many states to begin to regulate commerce on their own. In 1877, the U.S. Supreme Court confirmed the authority of government to regulate economic activity in *Munn* v. *Illinois*.[18]

Table 9-1
Selected Federal Regulatory Agencies

Agency	Year Created	Jurisdiction
Economic Regulation		
Interstate Commerce Commission	1887	Railroads, trucking; some water shipping; abolished 12-31-95
Federal Home Loan Bank Board	1932	Savings and loan industry; abolished 1990
Federal Communications Commission	1934	Interstate, foreign telephone; television and radio
Federal Energy Regulatory Commission	1977	Replaced Federal Power Commission (1920); natural gas, electricity
Social Regulation		
Equal Employment Opportunity Commission	1964	Enforces 1964 Civil Rights Act banning discrimination
Environmental Protection Agency	1970	Environmental pollution
Occupational Safety & Health Administration	1970	Health and safety standards in the workplace
Consumer Product Safety Commission	1972	Safety and labeling standards for consumer products

Munn was one of the most unscrupulous grain elevator operators in Illinois. He stored grain for shipment in interstate commerce. Munn was convicted in state court of violating an Illinois law regulating prices that could be charged for storing grain. His attorney argued that the Illinois law was unconstitutional because the state had no power to regulate items in interstate commerce and no power to reduce the value of Munn's property by limiting his prices. The U.S. Supreme Court upheld the Illinois law and defined a doctrine that has sustained government regulation in subsequent decades, "When private property is devoted to a public use, it is subject to public regulation."[19]

Within the next decade, twenty-five states began to regulate rail operations, but the growing volume of state regulation soon impeded interstate commerce. In *Wabash, St. Louis, and Pacific Railway Co.* v. *Illinois,* the Supreme Court severely restricted state regulation of rail operations by expanding congressional power under the commerce clause.[20] This decision led Congress to pass the Act to Regulate Commerce in 1887 that created the ICC and instructed the agency to promote safe, adequate, and economical surface transportation.

The ICC was the federal government's first independent regulatory commission. Independent commissions with five or seven members appointed to lengthy terms developed into a popular administrative device for regulating private economic activity. Commissions were stable agencies that would base their decisions on expert analyses rather than partisan electoral considerations.

Their decisions would reflect the collective judgment of a group rather than idiosyncratic opinions of a single administrator. The popularity of the commission form for regulating economic activity reflects a distrust of government, confidence in expertise, and recognition of the need for a predictable environment in which to make investments and conduct business.

Despite widespread support for the creation of the ICC, the commission was generally ineffective in the first three decades of its history.[21] The ICC's statutory powers were unclear, and most of its actions were challenged in the courts. Congress subsequently passed a series of laws shoring up the commission's authority that culminated in the Transportation Act of 1920. This last law authorized the ICC to establish railroad rates and oversee the development of the industry, and it led to a tremendous expansion of the ICC's role.

During the Great Depression of the 1930s, competition between railroads and lower-cost trucking firms intensified. The ICC consistently took the side of the railroad industry by requiring truckers to match the higher rates charged by the railroads. In the 1960s and 1970s, the Congress and the ICC devised numerous plans to assist the financially troubled railroads, but none of their schemes was able to reverse the industry's decline. In the deregulation era of the late 1970s and early 1980s, Congress said that the industry's problems had been caused by federal regulation and granted railroads more freedom to set prices and govern their own operations.[22]

The Interstate Commerce Commission served as a prototype for other independent regulatory commissions. It focused originally on a single industry, railroads, and later assumed some responsibility for the associated industries of trucking and water shipping. It exercised its authority over the industry by making decisions in three economic areas: *entry,* or what firms are allowed to participate in the industry; the *price* firms may charge for their products; and the *conditions of service,* or the features of the product that is provided consumers. The ICC also regarded itself as the defender of the industry it was to regulate rather than as a watchdog for consumers' interests. Social regulation differs from economic regulation in that it cuts across industry boundaries and seeks to achieve policy goals that extend beyond industry operations.

Social Regulation

Federal social regulation is associated with the expansion of federal regulatory authority that occurred in the 1960s and 1970s. Most of this new regulatory authority involved the areas of equal employment opportunity, environmental protection, occupational safety and health, and consumer protection. Much social regulation, however, comes from an earlier era and concerns such business functions as labor-management relations, corporate finance, and marketing.

Part of the justification for social regulation is the view that imperfections in the market system cause the problems social regulation is intended to correct. A perfectly functioning price system, for example, would somehow account for the social costs of environmental pollution and occupational disease. More importantly, social regulation embodies society's aspirations. It indicates that the society wants to promote certain objectives, such as fair labor-management relations or clean air. Social regulation represents the governmental judgment that these objectives can be achieved by restricting the operations of business and other private institutions.

The Environmental Protection Agency (EPA) was created in December 1970 and embodies the common features of social regulatory agencies. The structure of the newer social regulatory agencies reflects disenchantment with the classic independent regulatory commissions.[23] The older commissions were usually seen to be "captured" by the businesses they were intended to regulate, unconcerned about consumers, and unable to take the actions needed to solve the industry's long-term problems.

The newer social agencies are more likely to be located in the executive branch than be independent and headed by an administrator than a commission. A single administrator is more visible than a commission and held more easily accountable for an agency's actions or inactions. An administrator is also a presidential appointee, and the president will pay the political costs for an administrator's shortcomings. The newer social regulatory agencies administer rules that cut across sectors of the economy, and, thus, these agencies are less likely to be unduly influenced by a single industry or corporation.

The EPA bears symbolic responsibility for the society's anxieties about acid rain, the greenhouse effect, holes in the ozone layer, toxic wastes, and other environmental nightmares, but its actions are based on specific statutes. The agency's authority is derived from single-purpose statutes covering clean air, clean water, solid wastes, toxic wastes, radon, noise, and other pollutants.

Within each of these areas, the EPA first establishes *broad program standards*. In air pollution, for example, the EPA has defined national air-quality standards for common pollutants, factory emission levels for specific substances, emission standards for newly constructed factories, and motor vehicle emission standards. The EPA then defines *narrow performance and design standards* that restrict how companies operate or mandate how products perform so as to achieve the broad program standards. For example, automobile emission standards specify how many grams per mile of hydrocarbons, carbon monoxide, and nitrogen oxides cars are permitted to release. Social regulatory agencies usually enforce compliance with their standards through a system of permits and certifications that firms must obtain to demonstrate that they are abiding by the agencies' rules.

Inherent in the standard-setting and enforcement process are specific problems that social regulatory agencies inevitably face. First, it is often difficult to relate narrow performance and design standards to broad policy objectives.[24] How many grams of nitrogen oxides per mile are permissible? How much health risk is allowable for workers who are employed in factories that use cancer-causing substances like benzene? Second, social regulation invariably involves compliance costs to business, and these costs generate antagonism. Theoretically, although not in every instance, the value of the benefits to the society exceed the costs, but the parts of the society that pay the costs of social regulation are often not those who receive the benefits. Finally, social regulation can be used in a strategic and political way. Eastern coal producers and labor unions, for example, combined to require new power plants to install expensive equipment to remove sulfur emissions regardless of the sulfur content of the coal being burned in the power plant. This regulation used governmental authority to end the cost advantage and reduce sales of western coal, which was naturally low in sulfur content.[25] Table 9-2 summarizes the key differences between economic and social regulation.

Table 9-2
Key Features of Economic and Social Regulation

Regulation Features	Economic Regulation	Social Regulation
Focus of agency	Single industry	Multi-industry activity
Structure	Commission	Executive agency
Focus of rules	Entry, price, service	Standards
Political context	Producers, officials	Diverse interests

Discussions of regulation sometimes emphasize peculiar historic events or administrative structures and lose sight of the general patterns of governmental action.[26] Much of government operates by imposing restrictions on business and other private institutions, even though the term regulation is only applied to specific situations. Criticisms of regulation are motivated by complaints about specific forms of economic and social regulation as well as by unhappiness with government's broader goals and activities.

CONTEST BETWEEN REFORM AND DEREGULATION

Deregulation was a worldwide trend in the 1980s. The movement away from government control of economic decisions took different forms in different countries, but it dominated domestic policy in the United States and the United Kingdom and was quite visible in Germany and Japan. Even though deregulation is associated with the Reagan era, its intellectual origins and some of the key events in the deregulation process occurred in the 1970s. A review of the various criticisms of regulation foreshadows the political conflicts that emerged in the 1980s.

Criticisms of Regulation

The Reagan era's opposition to regulation was based on academic criticisms that had widespread support in the 1970s, but these nonpartisan criticisms were turned to political purposes in the 1980s that were not fully justified.[27] The critiques of economic regulation emphasized different points than the appraisals of social regulation.

The journalistic critics of economic regulation argued that producers had too much influence in the operations of independent regulatory commissions. The Federal Home Loan Bank Board, for example, was more concerned about the problems of S&Ls as institutions than about the overall health of the country's banking system or the welfare of consumers. The ICC sought to protect railroad companies instead of concentrating on the development of a comprehensive surface transportation system.

Economic critics accepted the goals of economic regulation but maintained that the actions of regulatory commissions had blocked rather than facilitate the achievement of statutory goals. Airlines, truckers, railroads, and other regulated industries were incurring unnecessary costs, providing worse service, and sacrificing economic efficiencies because of the regulatory frameworks established by the various commissions. The statutory goals of providing safe and efficient services in these industries could be achieved more effectively if the regulatory commissions abandoned or at least changed their regulatory approach.

The criticisms of social regulation argued with both its goals and its techniques. The critics insisted that the health, safety, environmental, and equity objectives were not worth the costs the society would incur to achieve them. In one observer's words, "... the problem is mainly that there are too many instances of regulations that generate large social costs without commensurate social benefits...."[28]

Furthermore, the statutes creating social regulatory programs frequently contained rigid goals that no political system could realistically achieve.[29] Precise deadlines focused attention on short-term, quick fixes that often stood in the way of long-term solutions to basic problems. The statutes asserted the importance of one policy and were often unwilling to acknowledge alternative approaches to achieving goals in that policy area or the need to balance one social goal with a variety of competing objectives. Analysts recommended that regulatory agencies rely on market incentives rather than command-oriented regulations to achieve their goals.

In the 1970s and early 1980s, there was substantial economic evidence to support the view that some deregulation and some regulatory reform would better achieve the public goals of industry-oriented, economic regulation. There was political disagreement about the goals of social regulation, and some ambiguous evidence that the techniques of the social agencies were costly and ineffective. In the 1980s, various criticisms of economic and social regulation were combined into a general attack on regulation that ignored the merits of individual programs and was offered as evidence of the need for comprehensive deregulation.

Deregulation

Presidential interest in regulation had been infrequent until the 1970s, when Presidents Ford and Carter spotlighted the importance of regulatory issues. The period from 1978 to 1982 witnessed a flurry of legislative activity that deregulated a number of critical industries. (See Table 9-3.)

The statutory initiatives of the years between 1978 and 1982 appeared exclusively in the areas of economic regulation and attracted bipartisan support.[30] During the later years of the Reagan administration, however, regulation became a more partisan issue. The Reagan government regarded both social and economic regulation as unnecessary burdens that had to be relieved if the country's economy was to be revitalized. The statutory framework for social and economic regulation changed little after 1982, but the administration reduced the significance of regulation by reducing the budgets of regulatory agencies and appointing officials to run the agencies who were more sympathetic to the administration's policy goals than to the agencies priorities. Throughout the Reagan years, there was a contest between those who sought to deregulate various areas of social and economic life and others who proposed to reform the regulatory process by making regulation less burdensome but more effective.

Table 9-3 Major Deregulation Statutes, 1978-1982		
Year	*Name of Act*	*Purpose*
1978	Airline Deregulation Act	Ended price, entry, route, regulation by 1985
	Natural Gas Policy Act	Eliminated intra- and interstate price controls by 1989
1980	Motor Carrier Reform Act	Allowed more flexible pricing in trucking industry
	Staggers Rail Act	Allowed railroads flexibility in pricing and in discontinuing uneconomical routes
	Depository Institutions Deregulation Act	Eliminated ceiling on S&L interest rates
1982	Bus Regulatory Reform Act	Allowed price, entry competition in bus industry
	Depository Institutions Act	Expanded range of permissible investments for S&Ls

Regulation, however, remains a policy tool. The standard for evaluating regulatory initiatives is whether they have a positive or negative effect on society. The regulation of the S&L industry offers one example of the significance of regulation. Since the airline industry was the first major industry to be deregulated, it offers another basis for making judgments about deregulation.

Impact of Airline Deregulation

The Airline Deregulation Act of 1978 gave companies greater flexibility to enter the airline industry, determine prices, and decide themselves how they would service different routes.[31] The legislation did not, however, remove all controls. Carriers are still required to demonstrate that they meet financial and technical qualifications before they begin service and to satisfy safety and maintenance standards during operations.

Most analysts agree that airline deregulation has resulted in lower fares. By one study, the cost of flying fell 23 percent between 1977 and 1986; and, by another estimate, airline deregulation is saving passengers approximately $16 billion per year in comparison with prederegulation prices.[32] Fare reductions, of course, have not occurred on every flight. Fares fell most sharply between major airports served by competing airlines, and fares rose between lesser airports that were only served by a single carrier. About one hundred smaller communities have lost jet service, but most are now served by commuter airlines that usually operate more frequently.

The long-term downward trend of airline accident rates continued during the deregulation period.[33] Between 1979 and 1987, accidents on large jet carriers fell 36 percent in comparison with the 1970 to 1978 years, and fatalities declined 32 percent. Concerns about airline safety are prompted by fears that airlines will cut back on maintenance expenditures as marketplace competition rises, that new airlines will be less safe than established carriers, and that the air travel infrastructure will be inadequate to meet the needs of new passengers attracted by lower fares. To date, however, there is no evidence that these fears have been justified.

Critics of airline deregulation point out that the airline industry has become more concentrated in the years since deregulation. In 1988, the top eight carriers controlled 94 percent of the domestic passenger market, and an increasing number of communities are being served by only one or two carriers.[34] Mergers and consolidations have had a devastating effect on workers who have lost their jobs and communities that have lost all service. Furthermore, fares will inevitably rise in the years ahead, the critics argue, as the anticompetitive consequences of consolidation take their toll.

SUMMARY

Government regulations are rules that restrict business operations to accomplish government purposes. Regulations constitute an elaborate network of restrictions that affect every facet of business activity.

Economic regulation was designed to provide the benefits of competition in industries where genuine competition was not possible, such as railroads and public utilities. Social regulation seeks to achieve social objectives by specifying how business operates in specific situations. Regulation is often regarded as a device to achieve public purposes, but there is increasing evidence that it is used by business and public officials to advance their private objectives.

In the 1970s, most academic commentators concluded that independent regulatory commissions were impeding rather than assisting the performance of firms in the industries they were created to oversee. Other critics argued that the goals of social regulation were too costly and that the performance of social regulatory agencies was arbitrary. These criticisms were carried into the political arena and became the basis for the decade's contest between those who sought to deregulate various areas of social and economic life and others who strived to make regulation less burdensome and more effective.

Selected Readings

George C. Eads and Michael Fix, *Relief for Reform? Reagan's Regulatory Dilemma* (Washington, D.C.: Urban Institute Press, 1984).

Larry N. Gerston, Cynthia Fraleigh, and Robert Schwab, *The Deregulated Society* (Pacific Grove, Calif.: Brooks/Cole, 1988).

Edward J. Kane, *The S&L Insurance Mess: How Did It Happen?* (Washington, D.C.: Urban Institute Press, 1989).

Roger E. Meiners and Bruce Yandle (eds.), *Regulation and the Reagan Era: Politics, Bureaucracy and the Public Interest* (New York: Holmes & Meier, 1989).

Leon N. Moses and Ian Savage (eds.), *Transportation Safety in an Age of Deregulation* (New York: Oxford University Press, 1989).

Notes

1. Ned Eichler, *The Thrift Debacle* (Berkeley: University of California Press, 1989), p. vii.
2. This account relies on James Ring Adams, *The Big Fix: Inside the S&L Scandal: How an Unholy Alliance of Politics and Money Destroyed America's Banking System* (New York: Wiley, 1990), pp. 23–54.
3. The Senators deny any illegality or that Gray was asked to withdraw the regulation. See James Ring Adams, *The Big Fix*, p. 245.
4. David J. Jefferson, "Keating of American Continental Corp. Comes Out Fighting," *Wall Street Journal*, April 18, 1989, quoted in Adams, *The Big Fix*, p. 254.
5. Eichler, *The Thrift Debacle*, p. 104.
6. These paragraphs rest on Edward J. Kane, *The S&L Insurance Mess: How Did It Happen?* (Washington, D.C.: Urban Institute Press, 1989).
7. Eichler, *The Thrift Debacle*, p. 101.
8. Louis Galambos and Joseph Pratt, *The Rise of the Corporate Commonwealth: United States Business and Public Policy in the 20th Century* (New York: Basic Books, 1988), p. 56.
9. Barry M. Mitnick, *The Political Economy of Regulation: Creating, Designing, and Removing Regulatory Forms* (New York: Columbia University Press, 1980), Chapter 3.
10. Marver H. Bernstein, *Regulating Business by Independent Commission* (Princeton: Princeton University Press, 1955).
11. Thomas K. McCraw, *Prophets of Regulation* (Cambridge, Mass.: Harvard University Press, 1984).
12. The viewpoint is also called the *public choice* perspective.
13. This discussion is based on Sam Peltzman, "Toward a More General Theory of Regulation," *Journal of Law and Economics* (August 1976); Robert E. McCormick, "A Review of the Economics of Regulation: the Political Process," in Roger E. Meiners and Bruce Yandle (eds.), *Regulation and the Reagan Era: Politics, Bureaucracy and the Public Interest* (New York: Holmes & Meier, 1989), pp. 16–37; and William F. Shughart, *Antitrust Policy and Interest Group Politics* (New York: Quorum Books, 1990), Chapters 1-2.
14. Bruce M. Owen and Ronald Braeutigam, *The Regulation Game: Strategic Use of the Administrative Process* (Cambridge, Mass.: Ballinger, 1978).
15. This idea is derived from the concept of the antitrust pork barrel outlined in Richard A. Posner, "The Federal Trade Commission," *University of Chicago Law Review*, 37 (1969), pp. 47–89.
16. William A. Niskanen, *Bureaucracy and Representative Government* (Chicago: Aldine, 1971); James Q. Wilson, "The Politics of Regulation," in James W. McKie (ed.), *Social Responsibility and the Business Predicament* (Washington, D.C.: Brookings Institution, 1974), pp. 135–68.
17. Roger C. Noll and Bruce M. Owen, *The Political Economy of Deregulation: Interest Groups in the Regulatory Process* (Washington, D.C.: American Enterprise Institute, 1983).
18. 94 U.S. 113, 1877.
19. Kermit H. Hall, *The Magic Mirror: Law in American History* (New York: Oxford University Press, 1989), pp. 234–36.
20. 118 U.S. 557, 1886.
21. For a well-presented review of the ICC's development, see Damodar Gujarati, *Government and Business* (New York: McGraw-Hill, 1984), pp. 251–59.
22. This theme was expressed in the Railroad Revitalization and Regulation Act of 1976 and the Staggers Rail Act of 1980. The Motor Carrier Act of 1980 relaxed the ICC's regulation of the trucking industry.
23. Marver Bernstein, "The Regulatory Process: A Framework for Analysis," *Law and Contemporary Problems*, 26 (Spring 1961), 329-46; and Roger C. Cramton, "Regulatory Structure and Regulatory Performance: A Critique of the Ash Council Report," *Public Administration Review*, vol. 32, no. 4 July 1972), 284–93.

24. Eugene Bardach, "Social Regulation as a Generic Policy Instrument," in Lester M. Salamon (ed.), *Beyond Privatization: The Tools of Government Action* (Washington, D.C.: Urban Institute Press, 1989), pp. 197–229.

25. Bruce A. Ackerman and William T. Hassler, *Clean Coal Dirty Air* (New Haven: Yale University Press, 1981).

26. James Q. Wilson (ed.), *The Politics of Regulation* (New York: Basic Books, 1980).

27. American Bar Association, Commission on Law and the Economy, *Federal Regulation: Roads to Reform* (No site: American Bar Association, 1979); Michael S. Baram, *Alternatives to Regulation: Managing Risks to Health, Safety and the Environment* (Lexington, Mass.: Lexington Books, 1982); Leonard W. Weiss and Michael W. Klass, (eds.), *Case Studies in Regulation: Revolution and Reform* (Boston: Little, Brown, 1981); and Lawrence J. White, *Reforming Regulation: Processes and Problems* (Englewood Cliffs, N.J.: Prentice-Hall, 1981).

28. White, *Reforming Regulation*, p. 225.

29. Larry E. Ruff, "Federal Environmental Regulation," in Weiss and Klass (eds.), *Case Studies in Regulation*, pp. 235–61; and Robert E. Litan and William D. Nordhaus, *Reforming Federal Regulation* (New Haven: Yale University Press, 1983), pp. 89–99.

30. George C. Eads and Michael Fix, *Relief or Reform? Reagan's Regulatory Dilemma* (Washington, D.C.: Urban Institute Press, 1984).

31. This discussion is based on Jonathan D. Ogur, Curtis L. Wagner, and Michael V. Vita, *The Deregulated Airline Industry: A Review of the Evidence* (Washington, D.C.: Federal Trade Commission, 1988); Paul Stephen Dempsey, *The Social and Economic Consequences of Deregulation: The Transportation Industry in Transition* (New York: Quorum Books, 1989); and Leon N. Moses and Ian Savage (eds.), *Transportation Safety in an Age of Deregulation* (New York: Oxford University Press, 1989).

32. Leon N. Moses and Ian Savage, "Introduction," in Leon N. Moses and Ian Savage (eds.), *Transportation Safety in an Age of Deregulation*, p. 4.

33. Moses and Savage, "Summary and Policy Implications," in Moses and Savage (eds.), *Transportation Safety in an Age of Deregulation*, pp. 308–31.

34. Dempsey, *The Social and Economic Consequences of Deregulation*.

Privatization Revisited

WILLIAM T. GORMLEY JR.

Privatization—like regulation, subsidies, and loans—is a tool of government. As Butler (1991, p. 17) defines it, "Privatization is the shifting of a function, either in whole or in part, from the public sector to the private sector."[1] Privatization is often justified as an effort to reduce the costs of government. In some instances, it seeks to reduce the size and scope of government. In other instances, it seeks to improve the performance and effectiveness of government.

Privatization is not a new phenomenon. Contracting out, for example, has been with us since the early days of our Republic (Kettl, 1993). However, privatization attracted considerable interest and attention during the 1980s, thanks to strong support from President Ronald Reagan's administration in the United States and Prime Minister Margaret Thatcher's administration in the United Kingdom. During the 1990s, it has reemerged as an important issue in the U.S. as various governments seek to "reinvent" themselves and after the Republican Party regained control of both houses of Congress.

In this paper, I develop what has been called a "pragmatic" approach to privatization (Feigenbaum and Henig, 1994). Instead of treating privatization in ideological terms, I ask: When should we privatize? How should we privatize? To whom should we privatize? I distill some criteria from the literature and introduce some of my own. I treat privatization as a legitimate tool of government, but not the right tool for all occasions.

THE MANY FACES OF PRIVATIZATION

Privatization is a multifaceted phenomenon. It includes activities as routine as a local government's decision to contract out food or computer services provided in city hall and activities as momentous as a proposal that the federal government sell Amtrak or the Tennessee Valley Authority. It includes activities as innocuous as a decision to allow food stamp recipients to purchase food at the grocery store of their choice; activities as controversial as a proposal to permit parents to send a child to the private school of their choice.

Although privatization assumes many forms, four types of privatization have received the most attention: contracting out, vouchers, asset sales, and "load-shedding." The last two are of particular interest in western and eastern Europe and in the former Soviet Union. The first two are of particular interest in the U.S.

Contracting out is the most common form of privatization in the United States. Numerous examples can be cited at all levels of government. In fiscal year 1991, the federal government spent more than $210 billion through contracts (Kettl, 1993, p. 13). According to a Touche Ross survey (1987), 99 percent of all local governments had contracted out services over the previous five years; 96 percent expected to contract out services over the following two years. Contracts are also quite common at the state level. In New Jersey, for example, building maintenance, data management, advertising, drug treatment, educational testing, and other services are contracted out (Van Horn, 1991).

Vouchers are less common in the U.S. and elsewhere, but they are receiving growing attention. In Milwaukee, Wisconsin, an experiment is underway in which 1,000 families receive vouchers from the state government to purchase schooling from nonsectarian private schools that agree to participate in the program (Witte and Rigdon, 1992). Experiments sponsored by the federal Department of Housing and Urban Development have resulted in growing emphasis on housing vouchers and certificates (Kingsley, 1991). The Child Care and Development Block Grant program, established by Congress in 1990, mandates that states establish voucher programs for the distribution of certain child care subsidies if they wish to retain federal funding (U.S. House of Representatives, 1990, p. 251).

The sale of assets is exemplified by Germany's *Treuhandanstalt,* which systematically liquidated the assets of the German Democratic Republic. Efforts by Margaret Thatcher and Boris Yeltsin to privatize many of their respective countries' assets illustrate the same phenomenon.[2] In the U.S., asset sales are more unusual. According to Touche Ross (1987), only 24 percent of local governments sold some government assets over the previous five years and only 21 percent expected to do so over the next two years. At the federal level, the Reagan administration sold Conrail and several loan portfolios but was unable to generate support for proposals to sell Amtrak and the Naval Petroleum Reserves.

"Load-shedding" refers to systematic efforts to cut back on government functions or government financial support. During the Reagan years, the welfare state was under attack. Support for a variety of social programs was reduced, and "cutback management" became a familiar refrain. At the state level, governors and state legislatures have reduced government funding for general public assistance and other redistributive programs. Nevertheless, federal government spending as a percentage of gross national product has not diminished.[3] While shedding some loads, federal, state, and local governments have watched others grow.

In thinking about different forms of privatization, analysts have often focused on financing and performance. Thus Donahue (1989, p. 7) asks whether a particular form of privatization involves collective or individual payment (financing), and public or private service delivery (performance).[4] This yields a convenient four-fold typology that may be used to classify different forms of privatization. For example, contracting out in the defense industry involves collective payment for private service delivery; in contrast, moonlighting by police officers involves individual payment for public service delivery.

Although useful, Donahue's typology ignores a third important dimension of privatization—decision-making. Some forms of privatization, for better or worse, transfer considerable decision-making discretion to the private sector (individuals or organizations). Financing remains in government hands; the mix of service providers does not necessarily change; yet the relationship between the public and private sectors does change.

That, for example, is an apt description of vouchers. The government continues to pay for services, but the payments are routed through parents or tenants or consumers. The actual mix of service providers (schools, landlords, hospitals, etc.) may or may not change. What does change, by definition, is the locus of decision-making. The choice of which organization shall provide services to a particular client is made not by government officials but by the clients themselves.

The introduction of this third dimension makes it easier to distinguish between different forms of privatization, such as contracts and vouchers. Under contracting, the government decides who shall provide certain services, while the private sector actually delivers those services. Under vouchers, private individuals choose from a menu of service deliverers. To be sure, each dimension may have implications for other dimensions. Thus, contracting out may result in a diminution of government decision-making power if government officials ignore the need for careful contract management. By the same token, vouchers may result in a reconfiguration of the service delivery apparatus if clients make decisions that government officials would not have made. Regardless of these spillover effects, the third dimension of privatization warrants close and careful examination.

Another weakness of existing approaches to privatization is that they focus almost exclusively on the four techniques discussed above: contracting, vouchers, asset sales, and load-shedding. In fact, privatization takes other forms as well. Consider, for example, the phenomenon of "bounty-hunting" or third-party enforcement (Weimer, 1992; Greve, 1989). Under citizen suit provisions of the Clean Water Act, private parties (either individuals or organizations) are authorized to file suit against polluters. Many environmental groups have done so. If they win, they recover attorneys' fees and court costs. In principle, fines are to be paid to the U.S. Treasury. In practice, however, environmental groups have usually convinced private firms to allocate funds to environmental causes as part of a settlement process that both parties prefer to judicial resolution. Lured by such rewards, environmental groups have become significant enforcers of the Clean Water Act.

Nor is this an isolated phenomenon. With only one exception, all federal environmental statutes contain provisions allowing private parties to sue firms or municipalities for noncompliance (Greve, 1989, p. 15). Moreover, the phenomenon of third-party enforcement is not unique to environmental protection. Under the False Claims Act of 1986, Congress authorized anyone who discovers someone defrauding the government to sue the wrongdoer. If they win, claimants can recover attorneys' fees and court costs, plus from 15 percent to 25 percent of the total penalties awarded (Thompson, 1992-93, p. 729). This opens up numerous opportunities for private citizens to reduce waste in defense procurement and other areas.

As Table 9-4 suggests, other forms of privatization have also been proposed or tried. Rose-Ackerman (1992) recommends "proxy shopping" as a technique for remedying some of the weaknesses of vouchers in markets where consumers are poorly informed (e.g., nursing homes). Under proxy shopping, the government pays firms with both subsidized and non-subsidized customers based on the decisions made by the non-subsidized customers, who are presumably better informed. This technique has considerable potential in the health services area or in any area where strong information asymmetries exist.

Table 9-4
Three Dimensions of Privatization:
What Is Being Privatized?

Form of Privatization	Private Payment	Private Delivery	Private Decision
Asset sales (transportation)	X	X	X
Contracting (refuse collection)		X	
Load-shedding (welfare)	X	X	X
Vouchers (education)			X
Bounty hunting (environmental protection)		X	
Offeror process (consumer protection)			X
Private inspections (child care)		X	
Proxy shopping (health care)			X
Tenant management (housing)		X	X

A short-lived experiment at the Consumer Product Safety Commission illustrates a rather different form of privatization. Under the so-called "offeror" process, the CPSC invited private citizens and groups to draft safety standards for particular consumer products. In effect, private groups were authorized to write regulatory standards (Johnson, 1990, pp. 76-77). The CPSC's offeror process was repealed by Congress in 1981 after numerous difficulties developed (Harter, 1982, pp. 61-63). However, the CPSC's offeror process is an extreme and unsuccessful example of a more widespread phenomenon: Government turning to the private sector to develop rules and standards for building construction, securities transactions, and other areas (Harter, 1982, p. 26). These are useful reminders of the many forms that privatization takes.

WHEN TO PRIVATIZE

We have accumulated considerable evidence on the effects of privatization—in transportation, employment and training, environmental protection, even law enforcement. From these studies, analysts have distilled general principles applicable to a wide range of privatization decisions. Two of the more useful sets of principles have been developed by Donahue (1989) and Kettl (1993), both of whom believe that privatization is more appropriate in some settings than in others.

Donahue, who focused in particular on contracting out, offers three general guidelines:

1. Privatization is more promising if a task can be specified precisely in advance and if its performance can be evaluated after the fact.
2. Privatization is more promising if it is relatively easy to replace contractors whose performance is disappointing or unacceptable.
3. Privatization is more promising if the government is more concerned about ends (results) than means (procedures).

More broadly, Donahue argues that privatization is more likely to succeed if the conditions for meaningful competition are present or can be replicated. In Donahue's words (1989, p. 218), "Most of the kick in privatization comes in the greater scope for rivalry when functions are contracted out, not from private provision per se."

These guidelines suggest that physical services (or hard services) are natural candidates for privatization, as Savas (1987, p. 279) has pointed out. Food services, laundry services, trash pickup, and street cleaning can easily be privatized because tasks can be specified in advance (i.e., you shall serve three meals a day, with the three basic food groups represented); because unsatisfactory contractors can be replaced (i.e., if you return jackets with holes in the elbows, you're out of work); and because ends matter more than means (i.e., you can drive east to west or west to east, but make sure all the trash is picked up).

Donahue's guidelines also help to pinpoint problematic areas. Diplomacy is not easily privatized, because it's difficult to imagine a contract that would take all relevant contingencies into account.[5] The community water supply is not easily privatized, because the danger posed by interrupted service is so serious (Starr, 1990, p. 43). Likewise, law enforcement is not easily privatized because we are concerned about both crime reduction and the rights of criminal suspects.[6]

Like Donahue, Kettl (1993) focuses primarily on contracting out. He shares Donahue's emphasis on the need to replicate well-functioning markets. More so than Donahue, however, Kettl treats the government as a flawed participant in marketplace transactions by drawing our attention to both market failures and government failures and explaining how the two interact. Three of Kettl's principles may be summarized as:

1. Privatization is more promising when the government knows what it is buying.
2. Privatization is more promising when the government knows who can deliver what it wants to buy.
3. Privatization is more promising when the government knows how to judge what it wants to buy.

These principles, like Donahue's canons, make a stronger prima facie case for privatization when physical services are involved. Kettl (1993, ch. 4), however, documents problems that may arise even with hard services, such as telecommunications and data processing. In awarding contracts under the federal government's new FTS system, the General Services Administration found itself plagued by diminishing competition, precarious corporate alliances, inadequate in-house expertise, and congressional interference. Both "supply-side" (corporate) and "demand-side" (governmental) problems contributed to sub optimal contract award and management decisions.

Kettl also warns that robust competition is not enough to guarantee successful privatization. In the case of Superfund, for example, the absence of technical expertise within the Environmental Protection Agency made it difficult for it to monitor and evaluate the performance of Superfund contractors. Thus, the agency found itself relying upon contractors to evaluate contractors—a practice fraught with difficulties (Kettl, 1993, ch. 5).

Most of the cases studied in depth by Donahue and Kettl involve government purchases of goods or services. Their principles are especially applicable to such decisions. But what about regulatory functions such as enforcement? Dane County, Wisconsin, contracts a nonprofit organization, Community Coordinated Child Care, to conduct inspections (known euphemistically as home visits) of family day care homes that care for between one and three children. The process, known as registration, is voluntary. Is this form of privatization appropriate or does it reduce the legitimacy of the certification process? Does it consider the use of third parties to enforce environmental statutes, as discussed earlier? Is this form of privatization appropriate or does it vest too much power in private hands?

To answer these questions, it is necessary to take a closer look at the nuances of regulatory enforcement in both instances. It is also necessary to introduce additional criteria for choice.

The Dane County case has certain characteristics that lessen concerns over private regulatory enforcement. First, task complexity is relatively low. The rules and regulations that apply to family day care homes that care for only one to three children are simpler and easier to apply than those that pertain to other child care settings.[7] Second, the trustworthiness of the Community Coordinated Child Care (also known as 4C) program is very high, thanks to considerable experience, able leadership, and the provision of a variety of services that clearly benefit family day care providers (resource and referral services, the Child and Adult Care Food Program, etc.). Third, the acceptability of the 4C program to providers is also very high. Indeed, a "visitor" from the 4C program is probably less threatening than an "inspector" from the state bureaucracy.

Third-party enforcement in environmental protection also has some noteworthy characteristics. First, redundancy is built into the system. Citizen suits do not displace government suits; rather, they supplement them. If citizens fail to come forward to pursue a violation of environmental statutes, government officials are free to prosecute the case themselves. Second, environmental groups, whose goals make them natural candidates to sue polluters, already exist in ample numbers. Thus, the interest group environment is conducive to third-party enforcement. Third, regulatory functions offer potential rewards to environmental groups, including financial rewards. These funds help to sustain other worthwhile environmental protection efforts undertaken by such groups.

These examples suggest the need for additional criteria:

1. Privatization is more promising when the private organization enjoys considerable experience in the policy area and considerable respect in the policy community.
2. Privatization is more promising when the government is free to intervene should private intervention prove wanting.
3. Privatization is more promising when the private organization provides other useful public services.

HOW TO PRIVATIZE

In general, analysts agree more on how to privatize than on how often to privatize. Privatization itself continues to generate considerable controversy, especially outside the hard services area. When it comes to managing contracts, there is greater agreement (see Table 9-5). Disagreements on the management of privatization concern the feasibility of achieving good management practices more than the specification of good management practices in the first place.

Over the past two decades, much has been learned about the management of contracts. Despite all the complexities, several general principles have begun to emerge.

First, it is important to secure genuine competition in the bidding process, so that the government can make real choices in awarding contracts. If the advantages of privatization are to be fully captured, then market forces must be given an opportunity to work through competitive bidding. As Pack (1991, p. 301) has demonstrated, there is a positive relationship between meaningful competition and long-run savings. Studies show, however, that the mere establishment of a competitive bidding process does not guarantee that real competition will occur.

For example, Schlesinger et al. (1986), in a study of contracting for mental health services in Massachusetts, found that only 20 percent of the state's mental health contracts were competitively bid. Furthermore, almost two-thirds of the competitively bid contracts had responses from only one vendor. Another source of concern is that the goal of competition often conflicts with the goal of continuity of care, which can be very important in mental health care, child care, and other areas. Schlesinger et al. (1986, p. 253) put it this way: "Competitive bidding and the purchase of mental health care services from private providers has not proven as simple or as beneficial as was once expected."

If competition is thought to be more illusory than real, there is much to be said for the government's remaining a supplier of services, if only a partial supplier of services. Thus, in Phoenix, the Department of Public Works established a competitive bidding process for trash collection in which both the public and private sectors could compete (Jensen, 1988). Planners carved up the city into districts where, in principle, either public or private vendors might pick up trash. Under such circumstances, if the private market for garbage pickup collapses or deteriorates, the public sector is better able to take up the slack. According to Savas (1987, p. 264), the Phoenix approach—sometimes referred to as "contracting in"—has been successfully employed in other cities as well.[8]

Table 9-5
Contracting Options

Contract Awards	Sole-source contracting is dangerous but may be unavoidable in some instances.	Competitive bidding is superior, though it does not guarantee meaningful competition.
Contract Design	Ambiguity can result in cream-skimming but may be necessary for "coping" agencies.	Specificity is desirable but can result in problems should circumstances change suddenly.
Contract Implementation	Loose monitoring can lead to cost overruns and mismanaged programs.	Tight monitoring is recommended but can degenerate into micromanagement, beancounting.

Second, contracts need to be written with considerable care, so that the government's expectations are clear. Obviously, this will be more difficult in human services than in hard services areas. But human services contracts must also state with specificity what services are to be delivered, to which recipients, and with what results. Otherwise, contracts can quickly degenerate into opportunities for private entrepreneurs to disregard legislative intent.

Donahue (1989) cites a good example of contracts gone awry, in his discussion of the Job Training Partnership Act. Contracts awarded under this act failed to specify the importance of targeting the hard-core unemployed. As a result, many job-training programs engaged in "cream-skimming," selecting those persons who were most likely to find employment rather than those persons who were most likely to benefit from employment training. Cream-skimming has been a problem in other employment and training programs as well (Baumer and Van Horn, 1985, pp. 89–123).

Third, contracts, once awarded, need to be monitored closely to be sure that contract terms are implemented. The faithful implementation of government programs by private individuals is no more automatic than the faithful implementation of government programs by government officials. Both require considerable vigilance and follow-up. Accountability is essential if contracting is utilized. Yet accountability continues to be the Achilles heel of many contracts.

For example, DeHoog (1984, pp. 101–112) describes the implementation of Title XX contracts by the Michigan Department of Social Services. Performance reviews, she found, were infrequent and ineffective. Due to staff shortages, the Department of Social Services relied primarily on information compiled by contractors themselves. Clients were not contacted for their views or experiences. Attention shifted quickly from performance to contract compliance, narrowly defined. A study of social service delivery in Massachusetts reached similar conclusions. According to Gurin (1989, p. 200), who helped to conduct the study, quality controls were rapidly overwhelmed by fiscal controls. On a more positive note, however, some rudimentary quality control was achieved through inquiries into client satisfaction.

In thinking about these issues, Kettl (1993) has emphasized the indispensability of in-house expertise. He recommends that government agencies hire (and reward) front-line bureaucrats trained to manage contracts. He also recommends that mid-level bureaucrats be retrained to understand the complexities of contract management. Yet this does not appear to be happening. As Smith and Lipsky (1992, p. 246) note, the growth of contracting has not been matched by a parallel growth in government auditing staffs. Moreover, audits, when conducted, tend to focus more on outputs than on outcomes (Gormley, 1989, pp. 159–164).

The management of voucher programs has generated less scholarly attention than the management of contracts, perhaps because vouchers are far less common. At the local level, for example, between 3.8 percent and 7.6 percent of cities used vouchers for a variety of services in 1988; in contrast, between 15.4 percent and 36.9 percent of cities used contracts for the same types of services (Stein, 1993, p. 29). Thus, we have accumulated less evidence on how vouchers work than on how contracts work. Nevertheless, some general observations may be offered.

First, information is absolutely essential if voucher programs are to succeed. Without well-informed consumers, voucher programs run the risk of failure. Parents cannot choose child care facilities unless they know what constitutes high-quality child care. Parents cannot choose schools unless they know which schools are more successful than others. Tenants cannot choose homes unless they know the difference between a good buy and a bad one. Just as the market depends on well-informed consumers, so too do vouchers, as market-like mechanisms, depend on well-informed clients.

Yet information is often lacking. In child care, for example, resource and referral agencies have proliferated in recent years, but only 10 percent of all parents use them (Wilier et al., 1991, p. 24). The problem is particularly serious for poor parents, many of whom are now required to place young children in child care under the Family Support Act of 1988. As Mitchell, Cooperstein, and Lamer (1992) discovered, many poor parents are poorly informed about the menu of child care choices available to them and the relative merits of each option. This results in sub optimal decisions, disruptions in service, and frustration with job training programs that encompass the "free" child care services.

The same problems are likely to bedevil any school choice program. In developing a blueprint for a school choice system, Chubb and Moe (1990, p. 221) propose the creation of a Parent Information Center within each school district. The Parent Information Center would collect and dispense information on each school within the district.[9] To ensure some modicum of informed judgment, Chubb and Moe would require parents to visit the center at least once. In practice, however, significant information disparities are likely to persist between advantaged and disadvantaged parents. Heroic efforts to improve information resources can narrow these disparities but cannot eliminate them.

Second, subsidies must be generous enough to permit the purchase of high-quality services. The ability to discern the difference between a good program and a bad program does consumers little good if they cannot opt for the good program. This same principle applies to voucher programs for housing, schools, and child care facilities.

It is difficult to know for sure whether subsidies are high enough in a particular case. For example, under the Child Care and Development Block Grant program, established in 1990, subsidies are set so that eligible parents could purchase care from 75 percent of the child care providers in their community. Obviously, this means that relatively expensive programs (the upper 25 percent) are out of reach. In some instances, this will work a hardship on parents. Also, the lower the subsides, the smaller the stimulus to child care providers, who are among the poorest paid workers in America.[10]

School choice proposals suffer from the same affliction. Unless subsidies are set at relatively high levels, poor parents will not be able to purchase the same educational services available to wealthier parents. On the other hand, every social program involves trade-offs between larger subsidies for a smaller group of eligibles, smaller subsidies for a larger group of eligibles. These trade-offs can be evaded only if other government programs are cut, if additional taxes are raised, or if budget deficits are allowed to grow.

Third, fairness must be built into voucher programs if they are to command popular support. The ever-present danger of racial discrimination must be addressed. If subsidies are to be limited to a subgroup of individuals, the criteria for including some persons and excluding others must be clear and defensible. Also, mechanisms must be institutionalized for detecting—and correcting—both errors of inclusion and errors of exclusion.

These general principles are useful guidelines, but they do not resolve all of the specific questions that arise in managing a particular voucher program. In many instances (school vouchers, child care vouchers, etc.), church-state questions must be addressed. In other instances, client participation must be monitored (e.g., through attendance checks) to avoid absenteeism or outright fraud. And many logistical problems must be circumvented, if programs are to run smoothly.[11]

CHOOSING BETWEEN SECTORS

If privatization seems appropriate, and contracting also seems appropriate, other questions still remain. Most importantly, government officials must decide whether to contract out to a for-profit firm or a nonprofit organization. They must choose between the second and third sectors, as they are sometimes called.

In *Reinventing Government*, Osborne and Gaebler (1992) argue persuasively that different sectors are better suited for different tasks. They then proceed to specify the tasks at which the private (for-profit) sector excels:

When tasks are economic in nature or when they require an investment orientation, the private (for-profit) sector is far more effective than either the public or third sector. It is also far better at replicating successful experiments, because the profit motive attracts investors and drives private companies to imitate their successful competitors (Osborne and Gaebler, 1992, p. 345).

In contrast, the nonprofit sector excels at tasks that:

- generate little or no profit margin; require compassion and commitment to other humans;

- require a comprehensive, holistic approach;
- require extensive trust on the part of customers or clients;
- require volunteer labor;
- and require hands-on, personal attention such as day care, counseling, and services to the handicapped or ill (Osborne and Gaebler, 1992, p. 346)

At first glance, these criteria seem eminently reasonable. Where efficiency is the sole or primary goal, they imply a strong role for the for-profit sector. Where other considerations are paramount (equity, sensitivity, responsiveness), they imply a strong role for the nonprofit sector. Yet, if Osborne and Gaebler are correct, numerous government officials in the U.S. have made some very bad contracting decisions over the years.

The fact of the matter is that many social services that call for compassion, trustworthiness, and the ability to reach diverse populations are routinely provided by for-profit firms. Table 9-6 illustrates this by focusing on four big industries: hospitals, nursing homes, higher education, and social services. In only one of these industries, higher education, is the role of the for-profit sector negligible. In two of the industries, hospitals and social services, the role of the for-profit sector is significant. In the nursing home industry, the for-profit sector is dominant.

A closer look at the social services sector reveals a very high profile for the for-profit sector in at least two areas: child care and residential care (Salamon, 1992, p. 85). Furthermore, the role of the for-profit sector appears to be growing in several important areas. During the 1980s, the role of the for-profit sector increased more rapidly than that of the government or the nonprofit sector in hospital care, outpatient clinic and home health care, social services, and higher education (Salamon, 1992, 1993). The role of the for-profit sector in nursing home care slipped, but for-profit firms remain the leaders in this field.

Should we be concerned about the growth of the for-profit sector in these areas? That depends in part on whether Osborne and Gaebler's generalizations are true. Is the for-profit sector so obsessed with "the bottom line" that quality suffers? Does the for-profit sector demonstrate less caring behavior

---

Table 9-6
The Mix of Service Providers in Four Industries

Industry	For-Profit	Nonprofit	Government
Nursing homes	67 percent	27 percent	6 percent
Social services	17 percent	74 percent	9 percent
Hospitals	10 percent	65 percent	25 percent
Higher education	2 percent	34 percent	64 percent

Note: The figures refer to the percentage of revenues (social services, nursing homes) or expenditures (higher education, hospitals) attributable to each sector. The data are from 1986 (nursing homes), 1987 (social services), 1988 (higher education), and 1989 (hospitals).

Source: Lester Salamon, *America's New-Profit Sector: A Primer* (New York: The Foundation Center, 1992).

than the non-profit sector? Does the for-profit sector have difficulty dealing with diverse populations?

In two areas—nursing home care and child care—it is possible to begin to answer these questions. According to Weisbrod (1988, pp. 146–159), nonprofit nursing homes perform better than for-profit homes. Relatives of patients at the nonprofit homes were more satisfied with the buildings and grounds, treatment services, relations with staff, and social activities. In addition, nonprofit homes were far less likely to administer sedatives to patients—a practice that could be construed as a cost-cutting device. According to a variety of measures, the performance of nonprofit facilities for the care of the mentally handicapped was also superior. The findings on facilities for psychiatric care were mixed.

The evidence on child care is even more compelling. A nationwide survey of 2,089 group day care centers, conducted in 1990, reveals significant differences between for-profit and nonprofit providers (Wilier et al., 1991, pp. 18–19). At for-profit centers, the teachers receive lower wages and turnover is higher. At for-profit centers, child/staff ratios are higher and staff credentials are less impressive. For-profit centers are also less likely to care for disadvantaged children. This is not surprising, since for-profit providers have been reluctant to locate in low-income neighborhoods (Kamerman and Kahn, 1989, p. 248).

This seems to confirm the suspicions voiced by Osborne and Gaebler. It also suggests the need to reverse course and reduce the role played by for-profit firms in providing health care, child care, and similar services. Yet, before taking these steps, government officials need good answers to the following questions:

- How would for-profit firms perform if they received the same tax benefits that nonprofit organizations enjoy?
- How would for-profit firms fare if they were eligible to participate in various government programs on the same footing as nonprofit organizations?
- How would for-profit firms do if they received the same supply of volunteers that nonprofit organizations enjoy?
- What would happen to a given industry if for-profit providers were to disappear?

Differences between the for-profit and nonprofit sectors may reflect different priorities and goals. But they may also reflect different levels of external support. Also, in certain industries, such as child care, we may need all the responsible providers we can get.

It is also important to stress that nonprofit organizations are not equally virtuous. In particular, religious organizations seem quite distinctive. Interestingly enough, their distinctiveness has different implications in different areas. In his study of nursing homes, Weisbrod (1988) found that religious nonprofits applied an extra measure of devotion to caring and healing tasks. In contrast, religious day care centers may be weaker in some respects than other day care centers. For example, religious day care centers are less likely than other nonprofits to care for disadvantaged children. Indeed, religious day care centers are somewhat less likely than for-profit firms to care for disadvantaged children. (Wilier et al., 1991, pp. 18–19).

Overall, it may well be that the nonprofit sector has advantages over the for-profit sector in delivering health, education, and welfare services. The nonprofit sector may be somewhat more likely to experiment and to offer diverse services (Rose-Ackerman, 1992, p. 180). The nonprofit sector may be somewhat more willing to assist the needy and to serve diverse populations (Salamon, 1993, p. 37). Clearly, however, we need to test these (and other) hypotheses before dismissing for-profit firms as ill-suited to these policy areas.

CONCLUSION

In thinking about privatization, it is customary to begin—and sometimes end—with the goal of efficiency. Undoubtedly, we need more efficiency both inside and outside government. But it is impossible to discuss privatization fairly without considering other important goals as well. Effectiveness, equity, accountability, legitimacy, quality, reliability, empowerment, and choice are among the other goals that need to be considered (Gormley, 1991, pp. 7–8).

In evaluating privatization options, we often distinguish between contracts and vouchers, for-profit firms and nonprofit organizations. These distinctions are eminently useful, but they do not cover the waterfront. Competitive bidding and sole-source contracting have radically different implications for long-term efficiency. Vouchers that include or exclude religious organizations as potential vendors have significantly different implications for equity, quality, and choice. Corrections services provided by for-profit firms raise questions of legitimacy only if those services require judgments that could undermine a person's legal or constitutional rights. In these and other cases, a fine-grained analysis is needed.

It is also important to make explicit comparisons between public and private alternatives. Institutional hybrids are also worthy of consideration, such as public-private partnerships, public-private competition, and the extensive use of volunteers by public agencies. In a number of policy arenas, institutional hybrids have proven successful. Tenant management of public housing projects and moonlighting by public police officers are two examples. The first combines public facilities with private personnel; the second combines private facilities with public personnel. There is much to be said for such experiments.

There is also considerable evidence that the public sector has learned from the privatization debate. Purely public alternatives are now more interesting because the public sector has been challenged by the private sector. Open enrollment programs within the public school system and community-oriented policing illustrate privatization logic without privatization. In the first instance, parental choice has been stressed without weakening public schools; in the second instance, responsiveness has been emphasized without diminishing the authority or discretion of police officers. Both initiatives have been successful in the right setting (Elmore, 1991; Skogan, 1990).

In the future, privatization will continue to be an important tool in the tool kit that government officials employ. In order to decide when and how to use that tool, government officials should ask the questions that have been raised in this paper. More broadly, they should recognize that privatization debates require certain intellectual tasks:

- matching, to link good candidates for privatization with appropriate alternatives
- combining, to incorporate public and private sector solutions in creative ways
- monitoring, to avoid unfettered discretion
- evaluating, to ensure that programs actually produce desired results

If public officials think strategically about privatization, it can be a useful tool in the tool kit. But they must be careful not to select a hammer when they really need a wrench.

Notes

1. Other definitions are less satisfactory. For example, Donahue (1989, p. 3) defines privatization as "the practice of delegating public duties to private organizations." Yet several prominent forms of privatization (e.g., vouchers) transfer power to private individuals, not private organizations. Moreover, the concept of public duties implies a greater consensus concerning governmental responsibilities than may exist.
2. Starr (1990, p. 30), however, does draw a useful distinction between privatization as institution-building (Russia) and privatization as balance-shifting (Great Britain).
3. When Ronald Reagan was first elected President, in 1980, federal expenditures constituted 22.5 percent of GNP. Eight years later, in 1988, federal expenditures constituted 22.9 percent of GNP (U.S. Advisory Commission on Intergovernmental Relations, 1992, p. 52). Margaret Thatcher was equally unsuccessful in reducing central government spending as a percentage of GNP in Great Britain (Starr, 1990, p. 25).
4. An earlier conceptual framework introduced by Kolderie (1986) is similar but muddier. Kolderie distinguishes between production (roughly analogous to Donahue's service delivery category) and provision (a multidimensional category that is difficult to operationalize). An additional weakness of Kolderie's conceptual scheme is that the word "provision" is commonly used to refer to service delivery (who provides the services?), which inadvertently blurs the distinction between Kolderie's two categories.
5. Wilson (1989, p. 358) puts this elegantly: "Diplomacy is a process of suggesting, testing, considering and reconsidering proposals and counterproposals. It would be difficult if not impossible to write a contract that specified in advance what the firm (Diplomats, Inc.) should do in each case, in large part because the government itself does not know; its preferences are formed by the process of negotiation."
6. Law enforcement is not the only area where procedural fairness matters. For example, Donahue (1989, p. 83) cites a case where the Veterans Administration offered bonuses linked to rapid performance. When some officials disposed of cases in less than 10 minutes, the VA began to rethink the wisdom of its policy. Although privatization was technically not involved in this instance, one can imagine the same dynamics and the same dilemmas if VA or Social Security Administration decisions were routinely contracted out.
7. As a rough barometer, the rules pertaining to "certified" family day care homes occupy 13 pages; the rules pertaining to "licensed" family day care homes occupy 27 pages; and the rules pertaining to licensed group day care centers occupy 38 pages.
8. Saves (1987) cites Montreal, Minneapolis, New Orleans, Kansas City, Newark, and Oklahoma City as examples.

9. Under Chubb and Moe's proposal, private schools, including religious schools, would be eligible to participate, "as long as their sectarian functions can be kept separate from their educational functions" (Chubb and Moe, 1990, p. 219).

10. The average annual wage for a full-time teacher at a group day care center is $11,000. Family day care providers, who care for children at home, are paid even less. Overall, among all occupational groups in the U.S., only the clergy are paid less than child care workers. And the clergy receive other forms of compensation.

11. For example, Chi et al. (1989, p. 80) report that a Lehigh County, Pennsylvania child care voucher program ran into difficulties when voucher books proved unwieldy and inefficient. An authorization card system improved the situation.

References

Baumer, D. and Van Horn, C. (1985). *The politics of unemployment.* Washington, DC: Congressional Quarterly Press.

Butler, S. (1991). *Privatization for public purposes.* In W. T. Gormley, Jr. (Ed.), Privatization and its Alternatives (pp. 17–24). Madison, WI: University of Wisconsin Press.

Chi, Keon et al. (1989). Use of the private sector in the delivery of human services. In J. Allen et al. (Ed.), *The private sector in state service delivery* (pp. 75–102). Washington, DC: Urban Institute Press.

Chubb, J. and Moe, T. (1990). *Politics, markets, and America's schools.* Washington, DC: Brookings Institution.

DeHoog, R. (1984). *Contracting out for human services.* Albany, NY: State University of New York Press.

Donahue, J. (1989). *The privatization decision: Public ends, private means.* New York: Basic Books.

Elmore, R. (1991). *Public school choice as a policy issue.* In W. T. Gormley, Jr. (Ed.), *Privatization and its alternatives* (pp. 55–78). Madison, WI: University of Wisconsin Press.

Feigenbaum, H. and Henig, J. (1994). The political underpinnings of privatization: A typology. *World Politics, 46*(2), 185–208.

Gormley Jr., W. T. (1991). The privatization controversy. In W. T. Gormley, Jr. (Ed.), *Privatization and its alternatives* (pp. 3–16). Madison, WI: University of Wisconsin Press.

Gormley Jr., W. T. (1989). *Taming the bureaucracy: Muscles, prayers, and other strategies.* Princeton, NJ: Princeton University Press.

Greve, M. (1989). Environmentalism and bounty hunting. *The Public Interest, 97*(11), 15–29.

Gurin, A. (1989). Governmental responsibility and privatization: Examples from four social services. In S. Kamerman and A. Kahn (Eds.), *Privatization and the welfare state* (pp. 179–205). Princeton, NJ: Princeton University Press.

Harter, P. (1982). Negotiating regulations: A cure for malaise. *Georgetown Law Journal, 71*(1), 1–118.

Jensen, R. (1988). *Public-private competition: The Phoenix approach to privatization.* Madison, WI: Robert M. La Follette Institute of Public Affairs.

Johnson C. (1990). New wine in new bottles: The case of the CPSC. *Public Administration Review, 50*(1), 74–81.

Kamerman, S. and Kahn, A. (1989). Child care and privatization under Reagan. In S. Kamerman and A. Kahn (Eds.), *Privatization and the welfare state* (pp. 235–259). Princeton, NJ: Princeton University Press.

Kettl, D. (1993). *Sharing power: Public governance and private markets.* Washington, DC: Brookings Institution.

Kingsley, G. T. (1991). *Housing vouchers and America's changing housing problems.* Madison, WI: University of Wisconsin Press.

Kolderie, T. (1986). The two different concepts of privatization. *Public Administration Review, 46*(3), 285–291.

Mitchell, A., Cooperstein, E., and Lamer, M. (1992). *Child care choices, consumer education, and low-income families.* New York: National Center for Children in Poverty, 1992.

Osborne, D. and Gaebler, T. (1992). *Reinventing government.* Reading, MA: Addison-Wesley Publishing.

Pack, J. (1991). The opportunities and constraints of privatization. In W. T. Gormley,Jr. (Ed.), *Privatization and its alternatives* (pp. 281–396). Madison, WI: University of Wisconsin Press.

Rose-Ackerman, S. (1992). *Rethinking the progressive agenda: The reform of the American regulatory state.* New York: Free Press.

Salamon, L. (1992). *America's nonprofit sector: A primer.* New York: Foundation Center.

Salamon, L. (1993). The marketization of welfare: Changing nonprofit and for-profit roles in the American welfare state. *Social Service Review, 67*(1), 16–39.

Savas, E. S. (1987). *Privatization: The key to better government.* Chatham, NJ: Chatham House.

Schlesinger, Mark et al. (1986). Competitive bidding and states' purchase of services. *Journal of Policy Analysis and Public Management, 5*(2), 245–263.

Skogan, W. (1990). *Disorder and decline.* New York: Free Press.

Smith, S. R. and Lipsky, M. (1992). Privatization in Health and Human Services: A critique. *Journal of Health Politics, Policy and Law, 17*(2), 233–253.

Starr, P. (1990). The new life of the liberal state: Privatization and the restructuring of state-society relations. In E. Suleiman and J. Waterbury (Eds.), *The political economy of public sector reform and privatization* (pp. 320–339). Boulder, CO: Westview Press.

Stein, R. (1993). Alternative means of delivering municipal services: 1982-1988. *Intergovernmental Perspective, 19*(1), 27–30.

Thompson, F. (1992-93). Deregulating defense acquisition. *Political Science Quarterly, 107*(4), 727–750.

Touche Ross. (1987). *Privatization in America.* Washington, DC: Author.

U.S. Advisory Commission on Intergovernmental Relations. (1992). *Significant features of fiscal federalism* (vol. 2). Washington, DC: U.S. Government Printing Office.

U.S. House of Representatives. (1990). *Omnibus Budget Reconciliation Act of 1990: Conference report to accompany H.R. 5835.* Washington, DC: U.S. Government Printing Office.

Van Horn, C. (1991). The myths and realities of privatization. In W. T. Gormley, Jr. (Ed.), *Privatization and its alternatives* (pp. 261–280). Madison, WI: University of Wisconsin Press.

Weimer, D. (1992). Claiming races, broiler contracts, heresthetics, and habits: Ten concepts for policy design. *Policy Sciences, 25*(2), 135–160.

Weisbrod, B. (1988). *The nonprofit economy.* Cambridge, MA: Harvard University Press.

Willer, B. et al. (1991). *The demand and supply of child care in 1990.* Washington, DC: National Association for the Education of Young Children.

Wilson, J. Q. (1989). *Bureaucracy: What government agencies do and why they do it.* New York: Basic Books.

Witte, J. F. and Rigdon, M. E. (1993). Education choice reforms: Will they change American schools? *Publius, 23*(3), 95–115.

Public-Private Partnerships
in the Twenty-First Century

GRAHAM FINNEY
DAVID A. GROSSMAN

In this paper, we have tried to look at the some possible future developments in one of the most interesting new concepts in public administration: the public-private partnership. First, we describe how the partnership idea has grown as a means for government to cope with the reality of scarcer resources by enlisting the participation of diverse private interests. Next, we indicate the broad range of forms the partnership concept has taken. Finally, we suggest some alternative scenarios for the ways in which public and private roles may develop in the coming century.

From its earliest days, the United States has displayed a highly flexible attitude toward the appropriate roles of public and private organizations in the provision of common services and goods. For example, education has been a primarily public function since Colonial days, especially at the elementary and secondary levels, but there have always been significant private and religious schools and much pre-school care is private as well. Human and health services agencies largely began as private charities, but are now largely financed by public payments. Most business activities have been considered private sector prerogatives. This extended even to natural monopolies such as electricity and gas distribution. However, there has been little uniformity. For example, while electric and gas utilities are usually private companies, other utilities, such as water supply and waste water treatment services, are generally public sector operations. Mass transportation, originally private, became largely a public function as costs rose higher than fares could finance. One can find examples, somewhere in the United States, where almost any imaginable common service function is directly provided by government and others where the same function is provided by a private firm.

This mixed American tradition continues in force today. There are, however, three developments that seem to be new in recent decades. For one thing, there is a more conscious appreciation of the choices available, especially to the public sector, in how to accomplish its principal tasks. For another, growing cost pressures on the public sector, especially as it has accepted broader responsibility in areas such as public health and welfare, have led it to seek ways of sharing the burden. In addition, there appears to be a growing desire on the part of the private sector, and especially its nonprofit component, to become a principal provider of common goods and services, financed where feasible by public funds.

A new concept has also emerged: the public-private partnership. This term has come to be used to describe a broad variety of activities and relationships. Examples include: the use of public powers such as eminent domain and public financing subsidies such as tax-exempt bonds to stimulate private capital investment; contracting by government with groups of non-profits to deliver human services such as home care; contracting with business firms to deliver public services, such as solid waste collection, more cost-effectively; and even creating business improvement districts where private firms agree to levy a tax on themselves, collected by government, to finance a higher level of services than the public sector alone can afford.

The term "public-private partnership" has even been used to describe quite different sets of relationships, such as consultation by public agencies with private businesses or community groups or arrangements such as the "load-shedding" of public functions to the private sector, as, for example, when businesses are made responsible for their own refuse collection. Just as there are many forms of partnership in the commercial world, so there are in the inter-sector world as well.

There are some discernible differences between the two major kinds of public-private partnership: those between government and the for-profit business sector on the one hand and those between government and the growing nonprofit "voluntary" sector on the other. But whatever the type, the basic components of an inter-sector partnership seem to come down to three factors: voluntary willingness to collaborate (neither party should be acting under compulsion, even if they are not equal partners); a truly public purpose (not simply a desire to enhance private return at public expense); and the ability of the partners to accomplish something collectively that they could not do as well, or perhaps even at all, separately.

RECENT EXPERIENCE WITH PARTNERSHIPS

The current widespread use of public-private partnerships dates to the Carter Administration, when it was first widely recognized that government resources and powers could not alone resolve many complex domestic issues. Public-private partnerships were seen as a means to make creative use of a time of governmental austerity by bringing to bear the complementary powers of both sectors. To pursue this objective, a special partnership promotion unit was established in the Department of Housing and Urban Development. Subsequently, in the Reagan Administration, the concept gathered strength. An Office of Private Sector Initiatives was established in the White House to publicize inter-sector cooperation and disseminate information about exemplary programs around the nation. Private corporations were urged to enlarge their community presence as government resources were being cut back. President Bush's Points of Light program continued the thrust, with an emphasis upon renewed voluntarism and the value of the nonprofit sector. One outgrowth was America: 2000, a program for educational reform that enlisted corporations to invest in the design of new models of elementary and secondary education. Today, in the Clinton Administration, with budgetary constraints still severe, Federal support for public-private partnerships remains strong.

Edmund Muskie once observed that in the postwar years of expansive public initiative, intergovernmental relations became "almost a fourth branch of government." Now, in the austere decade of the 1990s, intersector relations are receiving comparable recognition, as confirmed by a growing number of public-private partnerships functioning in communities across the nation. Examples can readily be identified in many fields:

- *Elementary and Secondary Education.* Partnerships here range from adopt-a-school programs and other forms of business-school collaboration range to mentoring programs in individual schools and school systems to far-reaching joint efforts to modify curriculum, introduce new technology, and restructure financial and management systems. Alternative and magnet schools, often with a job training emphasis, now complement conventional school structures in many cities. These partnerships are usually based upon a sense of corporate social responsibility and are supported by private charitable contributions. More recent arrangements, in cities like Baltimore and Hartford, involve contracting out the operation of individual schools or even the entire educational function to private management.

- *Higher Education.* Partnerships have also become common in higher education where both public and private institutions have joined forces with private firms to explore the mutually profitable development of new inventions and discoveries in fields like biomedicine and electronics.

- *Employment and Training.* The job training and placement field provides numerous examples of combined public-private efforts to upgrade the skills and competencies of both adults and youth. Private Industry Councils, formed under the Joint Training Partnership Act, require that private sector leadership, working closely with manpower and education officials, oversee the investment of public training dollars at the local level. Two research and demonstration organizations, the Manpower Development and Research Corporation (MDRC) and Public/Private Ventures (P/PV) combine public and philanthropic resources to determine more cost-effective ways to bridge school- and welfare-to-work connections. Both MDRC and P/PV are often called intermediaries, a special form of partnership formed to address a previously unattended issue or opportunity. Other examples of intermediaries are the Drug Abuse Council, formed to develop preventative and rehabilitative techniques to combat drug use, and SEEDCO, which attempts to build closer relationships between major educational and health care institutions and their surrounding neighborhoods through jointly sponsored housing and economic efforts.

- *Community Development.* Partnerships have grown rapidly in this field, in communities large and small, over the past two decades. They are usually launched with public and philanthropic dollars in order to cope with disinvestment, abandonment and the impact of aging physical plant. The private sector becomes involved as the essential source of investment dollars, technical assistance and training for local leadership, and in advocacy of constructive change. From their origins in such neighborhoods as Brooklyn's Bedford-Stuyvesant and the Woodlawn section of Chicago, nonprofit community development corporations have become smart and powerful forces in local communities. Their success has been strengthened through nonprofit quasi-banking groups such as the Local Initiatives Support Corporation (LISC), a national organization which has raised millions of dollars from corporate America to underwrite neighborhood-based housing and economic development. One such community development partnership has, through the years, become a national organization. The Neighborhood Reinvestment Corporation's formula is a mutually reinforcing combination of stepped-up city services, foundation assistance in the assembly and rehabilitation of difficult properties and action by local banks which agree to make mortgage money available in previously redlined areas.

- *Economic Development.* Inter-sector ties are even closer in the maze of city-wide and regional economic development activities designed to retain and attract taxpaying business interests. Industrial development corporations, with private and public sector members on their boards, offer low interest loans, as well as grants and other carrots, in order to foster growth. Municipalities have extended the use of their tax exempt bonding privilege to private firms in another type of partnership or have established "enterprise zones" with tax reductions offered to stimulate economic growth.

- *Policy Participation.* Another important field of inter-sector cooperation has been the growth of policy and planning partnerships in urban centers and metropolitan regions. Usually, these are under corporate leadership, but there are increasing efforts to engage minority, women, labor, neighborhood and other constituencies. Typically, these groups seek to develop close working ties with elected officials on matters of common concern, such as achieving public fiscal stability, stemming job losses, educational restructuring and a range of environmental issues. Notable examples include the Pittsburgh area's Allegheny Conference, Greater Philadelphia First and comparable groups in Cleveland and Los Angeles. More and more, these policy partnerships also seek to address the mutual needs of central city and suburbs.

SOME LESSONS LEARNED ABOUT PARTNERSHIPS

Despite their proliferation, public-private partnerships have remained undervalued, loosely defined organizational forms, generally not yet subject to serious examination. The following observations can be made, however, based upon the authors' review of the available literature and their personal experience.

- Extreme care must be taken early on to spell out the respective roles and responsibilities in a partnership. In all too many cases, *ad hoc* or casual relationships are mistakenly felt to suffice. Formed with great fanfare or to meet a crisis, many partnerships soon crumble for lack of clear answers to questions about roles and expectations. For example, neighborhood groups frequently complain that, once a partnership is forged, theirs becomes a clearly secondary, even passive role compared to the dominant position of political or business interests. To guard against such reactions, a carefully drafted compact or contract should be adopted at the outset, together with an agreed-on mechanism for revisiting its terms periodically.

- By their very nature, partnerships raise novel legal, accounting, personnel and other issues for their boards, staffs, funders and constituents. What financial reports, marketing methods and evaluation procedures should be developed? How much delegation of responsibility can be allowed in the use of public funds? In many cases, a new nonprofit entity may have to be created as the structural form of the partnership. In most cases, how best to combine the strengths brought from each sector (for example, how to link private sector marketing acumen and financial incentives with regulatory and political support from the public sector) will be a key issue to be resolved before successful operations can begin.

- Both the formal and informal aspects of the partnership need to be carefully considered. In most cases, the parties will bring very different experiences and outlooks to the task at hand. Strange bedfellows must learn to recognize each others' strengths and weaknesses. Culture clashes should be anticipated. It is only natural that a corporate executive may find it difficult to treat angry parents or teachers as co-equals. Race, gender and professional factors must also be addressed. Stereotypes about lazy, plodding public servants and greedy businessmen must both be laid to rest if the public-private connection is to provide a firm base for progress.

- If partnerships are to play a significant role in future years, a strong public sector must be sustained even if certain of its functions are reduced or eliminated. The public sector cannot be perceived to be weak or dependent, or lack sufficient credibility to take on its share of a vital project. In a leaner public environment, public managers will need to be more skilled, experienced and knowledgeable about the workings of the private sector than in the past.

- Special issues affecting partnerships will often arise as by-products of contracting out and privatization. Once a function is privatized, the same audience or clientele may not be served in the same way. This is especially the case for poorer and less accessible citizen-consumers. Examples in health care and transit, in cases where private operations have replaced formerly public services, give credence to this concern.

Partnership as a strategy of public policy seeks to achieve the greatest possible benefits from combining the public sector's access to resources, its authority to legislate and regulate, and its solemn obligation to sustain the public interest with the private sector's capacity for risk taking, innovation, marketing and for tapping a variety of financial resources. Proponents of partnership argue that blending the best of both worlds offers the greatest current hope for treating many intractable urban issues.

There is some evidence that inter-sector relationships do indeed show the promise set forth by their proponents. But the evidence to date is largely anecdotal. The field of partnering remains inchoate and poorly researched, to the detriment of scholars and practitioners alike. It is fitting that Baruch College at this conference, commemorating the launching of its new School of Public Affairs, should choose to examine the subject. We urge it to continue to do so as an element of its research agenda and curriculum.

SOME ALTERNATIVE SCENARIOS

The remainder of this paper considers the likely future for inter-sector partnerships. Recognizing that public functions and services are likely to change
over the coming century in ways that we can now only vaguely imagine, here
are some alternative scenarios that might develop in the twenty-first century.

A PRIVATE SECTOR DOMINANT SCENARIO

As we approach the end of the current century, the too common view of the
public sector is dismal and disapproving. Despite great strides in government
administration, the competence, even-handedness and other virtues of
today's public service go unrecognized. Instead, the too-widespread image is
of a public sector dominated by time-serving union members, tax-loving
elected officials and greedy lobbyists, driven by profligate policies that most
reward the least deserving segments of society.

The United States Congress currently has the worst image of all. But any
recent President who has tried to do more than campaign against his own
Administration has also been quick to incur public disapproval. The situation
is little better at the local level. Mayors and other local executives may enjoy
periods of popular support—usually shortly after their election—but the
experienced ones know that there is only a small slip between praise and con-
demnation.

In marked distinction, the private sector now enjoys a broad level of popular support. With occasional exceptions, both the for-profit business world
and, to a lesser extent, the nonprofit charitable sector receive higher marks for
their efficiency and effectiveness. With regard to the private business sector,
earlier cynicism about the profit motive and fears of corrupting influence
seem to have given way to a near-mystical belief in the magic of the market.
The nonprofit sector has also been able to maintain its noble-spirited charitable image even while becoming a major beneficiary of the public purse—
despite the occasional scandal of high living or incompetence that the sector
has endured.

Given these trends, the next century might well find the private sector
playing an even broader role in what has been the domain of government. The
precedents for such a development already exist. Somewhere in the United
States, almost every conceivable governmental function is being performed by
private organizations, whether as contractors paid by government or on their
own. Private schools are an old story; a newer approach is to contract out the
operation of public schools to private companies. In health and human service
delivery, privatization has long been a familiar pattern. Refuse collection is
contracted out to private firms or made a private responsibility so that there is
no government role at all except perhaps for limited monitoring. Small town
fire departments have long been the province of volunteers and some municipalities already contract with private firms of fire-fighters. Prison guards and
even whole prisons have been privatized in the rush to combat crime. There
are already more private security guards than public police.

Other options for expanding the private sector's role remain to be fully
explored. The imagination can easily conceive new privatized approaches,

such as franchises: a MacDonald's for home care or a RotoRooter for refuse composting. The "gated communities" now spreading across suburban America offer yet another, far more disturbing, image of a privatized future.

Are there any unquestionably public functions? Thus far, the principal exclusive holdouts of the government sector have been central policy functions such as budgeting and revenue-raising, regulation, and the award and monitoring of contracts. Some cities are even experimenting with the privatization of these functions. For example, in the case of business improvement districts, essentially private special districts that levy taxes and make service delivery decisions under conditions where fees can be charged that cover the cost of services such as sanitation and security.

There are some undeniable advantages to public bodies getting out of the business of direct service delivery, leaving service levels and types to be driven more clearly by market forces. Among them: no more collective bargaining with powerful public employee unions, fewer commitments to costly fringe benefits and pensions, and ease of avoidance of government's own strangling regulations. The countervailing negative effects could, however, prove exceedingly costly to a democratic society. Private firms may well be favored by those who can afford the fees they would have to charge for service. For the less well off segments of society, however, privatization may mean exclusion or even poorer services. Of course, this need not be the case. Techniques such as the use of either explicit or internal subsidies could assure that the poor are not entirely overlooked. Services at minimal cost could be mandated in any license agreement for privatization. Unfortunately, it is also possible that only the most profitable parts of the public service system would be hived off, leaving those unable to pay to suffer in what remains of the public sector. Years of such dominance could easily become years of growing disparity and inequity, and, in time, instability.

A PUBLIC SECTOR DOMINANT SCENARIO

A new century might, however, produce exactly opposite trends. There is nothing inherently impossible in projecting a golden age of civic responsibility and the re-emergence of a competent, respected public sector. Such an era might come about either because privatization fails to live up to its promise, because efforts to "re-invent" government fully succeed, or because both happen at the same time.

For much of the modern history of the United States, democratic local and national government has been not only accepted but widely praised as a public sector that works for the benefit of all. Even today, when American governmental performance is in generally low repute at home, it is the marvel and envy of most Third World countries where corruption and incompetence are suffered to a degree that would give rise to a second American revolution. Even when compared with the advanced industrial worlds of Western Europe and Japan, there are notable strengths in this nation's capacity to govern.

What would it take to restore and re-invigorate public sector dominance in service delivery? Three concurrent changes come to mind. First, there would have to be widespread adoption of improved systems of management that would put government operations on a par with those of the best private businesses. Second, we would need an upgrading of governmental personnel sufficient to re-establish confidence and competence in the civil service. Third, we would need to see political change that would return of government to the position of credibility and public acceptance that it held in times past.

With regard to improved management systems, a marked upgrading of government performance seems difficult but far from impossible. The single most important factor that makes quantum improvements feasible in government—as it has been in successful private firms—is the computer-centered revolution in communication and control. While neither local, state nor national government agencies have been conspicuously successful in adopting such management and operating systems, this is a field still in its infancy. Partnerships between government and those private corporations which have already made major strides in systems improvement may help speed the transition for the public sector.

Improving the actual and perceived capability of the civil service involves more than upgrading the personal skills, morale and integrity of the men and women who work for government. Equally important is strengthening the organizational framework within which they work so that it is equal to the challenging tasks the public sector must confront and provides greater incentives for performance. Today, government jobs, especially at the managerial level, are generally less attractive than those in the private sector. At the same time, the growth of "red tape," virtuously intended to preclude undesirable outcomes, has made public sector management an almost impossibly complex task. Inability to muster the competent personnel and supporting resources such as space, computers and communications often lies at the base of decisions to contract out or privatize. To change this will require action both from within and beyond government. Perhaps the single greatest challenge for schools of public administration will be to identify the changes that are needed and to help strengthen the capacity of public servants to choose wisely.

The third change that is needed to usher in a century of restored pride and confidence in government is the most subtle and difficult to influence. It may require nothing less than a paradigm shift in the way Americans view the public sector. We need to see government as a mechanism for expressing the general democratic will, never ideally efficient or responsive but still, in Winston Churchill's telling phrase, "better than any other system known."

What could possibly cause such a change? Looking back, it is possible to describe some of the conditions that have given rise to periods of higher regard for government's role in society. Great crises, such as war, economic catastrophes like the Great Depression and national disasters have done so in the past. On a smaller scale, there are times when we have elected dedicated and clear-sighted executives and supported them with legislators who viewed the public service as having the potential to improve the quality of life. Such events, whether on a grand or local scale, can have long-lasting consequences that spread through many aspects of society. As we enter the twenty-first century, there will no doubt be such periods again that result in a shift in the balance toward a revitalized public sector.

If this were to happen, it is possible to envision situations in which public enterprises take on some of the incentive-motivated characteristics of market-oriented private funds as well as some of the client-oriented features of community-based nonprofits. Public enterprise could then become as well-received a description as private enterprise, with the added sense of disinterested public service. In such a context, there would be little need for government to shed the responsibilities of common goods provision. Fee structures could be used to motivate appropriately conservative consumption of scarce resources by all, rather than to maximize profit for the firm. Partnerships with the private sector could be sought to improve the quality of life, not merely to evade the impact of austerity.

A PARTNERSHIP SCENARIO

Neither of the previous scenarios seems very likely to occur, at least in pure form. Rather, the most likely outcome appears to be a continuation of current trends which are in the best tradition of American pragmatism.

As we enter the next century, basic public service delivery systems are most likely to remain public responsibilities, but with wide variations from place to place and among service functions in how they are delivered and even how they are financed. For example, it is hard to foresee a shift back to public works agencies that are directly responsible for the design and implementation of all governmental construction or to health agencies that run a purely public health and hospital system. The advantages that come from both governmental and private involvement in planning, financing and monitoring these costly and universally-needed service systems will continue to give rise to public-private partnerships.

The many attractions of inter-sector partnership for government will persist: avoidance of legislated rigidities; leveraging of non-public resources, and access to special expertise. For the nonprofit sector, the concept of partnership should become ever more attractive in a period in which it seems likely that charitable funding will become a smaller part of the sector's financing. To private for-profit business, partnerships should also continue to present numerous advantages, enabling business leaders to play influential policy roles in places where they don't vote, allowing firms to benefit from public powers and financial aid to carry out their own investment projects and viewing government as a vital part of the demand side of the private market.

In summary, it seems to us that the nation's already thoroughly mixed economy will become even more so as in the new century. No purist prescriptions will overcome our strong tendency to pursue realistic short-term strategies. The partnership model is entirely consistent with such an outlook, offering as it does an opportunity for creative use of the sectors in a changing array of mix and match responses that neither of the other two scenarios can surpass. If this is true, then schools of public administration and policy will do well to highlight the possible worlds of inter-sector relationships as they prepare the next generations of public servants.

10 Public Administration in the Twenty-First Century

No "real world" activity or academic field can stand still even if you want it to. Events—"real world" *and* intellectual—continue, and society changes.

Change is increasingly rapid in American life. If public administration and public administrators are to retain their vitality, they must constantly be in the process of adaptation.

It is clear that for many in American society—outside and inside government—the time has arrived for the reform of government. No federal institution has been free of criticism: the Congress, the President, the courts, and the administrative agencies. States and localities feel similar pressures.

For public administration, reform is already on the way. The first article in Chapter 10 is by David Osborne and Ted Gaebler, and is drawn from their already well-known book, *Reinventing Government*. Osborne and Gaebler seek movement from Weberian, centralized, hierarchical bureaucracies to decentralized, mission-driven, entrepreneurial organizations. They seek new approaches to public service, new methods of serving the public interest.

In what some observers see as continuous reinvention, a variety of efforts are underway to "reinvent" the way the administrative arm of government does business. At the federal level, reinventing government is led by Vice President Al Gore and the National Performance Review. The stated goal is more performance-based administration in the federal government, a government that "works better and costs less."

In the second article here, Patricia Ingraham provides an early assessment of the National Performance Review and its approach to administrative reform. Ingraham finds three different levels of reinvention, with decentralized reinvention laboratories throughout the federal government. She finds uneven progress and a failure to ask some important questions, but Ingraham also seems hopeful about long-term change at the federal level as long as political support and staff commitment can be sustained.

In the third article in this chapter, Gerald Caiden and Jeffrey Luke make clear just how important a global society is, not just to State Department diplomats but to state and local administrators as well. The authors point out changes to which we all will have to adapt.

In the final article in this collection, James Q. Wilson continues the theme of change for a new century. In a period of declining trust in government, he makes what some might see as a radical proposal, "To do better we have to deregulate the government." A longtime observer of public bureaucracies, this prominent political scientist provides his own prescription for change.

April 19, 1995, is an important and shocking date in the history of American public administration. For two decades the anti-government, anti-bureaucrat sentiment had been building, often mindlessly. On that morning, 168 men, women, and children were killed by a powerful explosion as they prepared for the work day to begin in the Murrah Federal Building in Oklahoma City.

Most initially thought that this was terrorism originating from outside the United States. It was not. At the dawn of a new century, in an organizational society where the institutions of government inevitably will play a central role, the Oklahoma City bombing is a reminder of the human challenges ahead.

Chapter 10 deals with public administration at the edge of the twenty-first century:

- What kinds of changes do Osborne and Gaebler, and Wilson, seek in American public administration?
- Judging by the federal government's efforts at reinvention, is the federal administrative apparatus improving?
- How does the new global environment affect public administration at home?
- Based on reading this book, what kind of changes would you like to see—in the federal government, in your state, in your city—in the next century?

Reinventing Government

DAVID OSBORNE
TED GAEBLER

Our thesis is simple: The kinds of governments that developed during the industrial era, with their sluggish centralized bureaucracies, their preoccupation with rules and regulations, and their hierarchical chains of command, no longer work very well. They accomplished great things in their time, but somewhere along the line they got away from us. They became bloated, wasteful, ineffective. And when the world began to change, they failed to change with it. Hierarchical, centralized bureaucracies designed in the 1930s or 1940s simply do not function well in the rapidly changing, information-rich, knowledge-intensive society and economy of the 1990s. They are like luxury ocean liners in the age of supersonic jets: big, cumbersome, expensive, and extremely difficult to turn around. Gradually, new kinds of public institutions are taking their place.

Government is hardly leading the parade; similar transformations are taking place throughout American society. American corporations have spent the last decade making revolutionary changes: decentralizing authority, flattening hierarchies, focusing on quality, getting close to their customers—all in an effort to remain competitive in the new global marketplace. Our voluntary, nonprofit institutions are alive with new initiatives. New "partnerships" blossom overnight—between business and education, between for-profits and nonprofits, between public sector and private. It is as if all institutions in American life were struggling to adapt to some massive sea change—striving to become more flexible, more innovative and more entrepreneurial.

Most of our leaders still tell us that there are only two ways out of our repeated public crises: we can raise taxes, or we can cut spending. For almost two decades, we have asked for a third choice. We do not want less education, fewer roads, less health care. Nor do we want higher taxes. We want better education, better roads, and better health care, for the same tax dollar.

Unfortunately, we do not know how to get what we want. Ronald Reagan talked as if we could simply go into the bureaucracy with a scalpel and cut out the pockets of waste, fraud, and abuse.

But waste in government does not come tied up in neat packages. It is marbled throughout our bureaucracies. It is embedded in the very way we do business. It is employees on idle, working at half speed—or barely working at all. It is people working hard at tasks that aren't worth doing, following regulations that should never have been written, filling out forms that should never have been invented.

Waste in government is staggering, but we cannot get at it by wading through budgets cutting line items. As one observer put it, our governments are like fat people who must lose weight. We need to get them eating less and exercising more; instead we cut off a few fingers and toes.

To melt the fat, we must change the basic incentives that drive our governments. Our more entrepreneurial governments have shown us the way; the lessons are there. Yet few of our leaders are listening. Too busy climbing the rungs to their next office, they don't have time to stop and look anew. So they remain trapped in old ways of looking at our problems, blind to solutions that lie right in front of them. As the great economist John Maynard Keynes once noted, the difficulty lies not so much in developing new ideas as escaping from old ones.

(Osborne and Gaebler offer ten principles of entrepreneurial government. What follows is the essence of these principles. —Ed.)

1. CATALYTIC GOVERNMENT: STEERING RATHER THAN ROWING

During the mid '80s, mayors and governors and legislators chained themselves to the wagon of taxes and services. This was fine as long as tax revenues were rising 5.3 percent a year, as they did from 1902 through 1970. But when economic growth slowed and fiscal crisis hit, the equation changed. Now when problems appeared and voters demanded solutions, public leaders had only two choices. They could raise taxes, or they could say no. For officials who wanted to be reelected, this was no choice at all.

In Washington, our leaders escaped the dilemma by borrowing money. But in state and local government, where budgets have to balance, they began to look for answers that lay somewhere between the traditional yes and no. They learned how to bring community groups and foundations together to build low-income housing; how to bring business, labor, and academia together to stimulate economic innovation and job creation; how to bring neighborhood groups and police departments together to solve the problems that underlay crime. In other words, they learned how to facilitate problem solving by catalyzing action throughout the community—how to steer rather than row.

Most people have been taught that public and private sectors occupy distinct worlds; that government should not interfere with business, and that business should have no truck with government. This was a central tenet of the bureaucratic model. But as we have seen, governments today—under intense pressure to solve problems without spending new money—look for the best method they can find, regardless of which sector it involves. There are very few services traditionally provided by the public sector that are not today provided somewhere by the private sector—and vice versa. Businesses are running public schools and fire departments. Governments are operating professional sports teams and running venture capital funds. And nonprofits are rehabilitating convicts, running banks, and developing real estate. Those who still believe government and business should be separate tend to oppose these innovations, whether or not they work. But the world has changed too much to allow an outdated mind-set to stifle us in this way. "We would do well" as Harlan Cleveland writes in *The Knowledge Executive,* "to glory in the blurring of public and private and not keep trying to draw a disappearing line in the water."

2. COMMUNITY-OWNED GOVERNMENT: EMPOWERING RATHER THAN SERVING

George Latimer, former mayor of St. Paul, likes to quote Tom Dewar, of the University of Minnesota's Humphrey Institute, about the dangers of "clienthood":

> Clients are people who are dependent upon and controlled by their helpers and leaders. Clients are people who understand themselves in terms of their deficiencies and people who wait for others to act on their behalf. Citizens, on the other hand, are people who understand their own problems in their own terms. Citizens perceive their relationship to one another and they believe in their capacity to act. Good clients make bad citizens. Good citizens make strong communities.

Clienthood is a problem that emerged only as our industrial economy matured. Before 1900, what little control existed over neighborhoods, health, education, and the like lay primarily with local communities, because so many products and services, whether public or private, were produced and sold locally. It was only with the emergence of an industrial economy of mass production that we began to hire professionals and bureaucrats to do what families, neighborhoods, churches, and voluntary associations had done.

We started with the best intentions, to heal the new wounds of an industrial, urban society. We moved ahead rapidly when the economic collapse of the Depression strained the capacities of families and communities to the breaking point. And we continued on after the depression, as prosperity and mobility loosened the old bonds of geographic community, leaving the elderly far from their children, the employed uninvolved in their neighborhoods, and the churches increasingly empty. But along the way we lost something precious. The progressive confidence in "neutral administrators" and "professionalism" blinded us to the consequences of taking control out of the hands of families and communities.

AIDS catalyzed perhaps the most profound shift from the old model to the new. "The San Francisco gay and lesbian community adopted the hospice model," explains David Schulman, who runs the Los Angeles City Attorney AIDS/HIV Discrimination Unit. "They got teams of friends and volunteers together to care for people with AIDS at home—at a fraction of the cost of hospital care. It not only works better, it helped San Francisco cope with a problem that could have bankrupted it."

In a powerful article in the *Washington Monthly,* Katherine Boo described the process. It began when a gay nurse at San Francisco General Hospital, Cliff Morrison, convinced his superiors to let him suspend the normal hierarchical, bureaucratic rules on the AIDS ward. He let patients set visiting rules, recruited hundreds of volunteers to help AIDS patients—often just to sit with them—and set up a special kitchen and other facilities.

But "a comfortable hospital is still a hospital," as Boo put it. So Morrison and his staff "began suturing together a network of local clinics, hospices, welfare offices, and volunteers that would get patients out of the ward and back into the community." For two years Morrison spent much of his time "battling the higher-ups." But when San Francisco's average cost of AIDS treatment dropped to 40 percent the national average, they finally understood.

3. COMPETITIVE GOVERNMENT: INJECTING COMPETITION INTO SERVICE DELIVERY

Phoenix has used competition not only in garbage collection but in landfill operation, custodial services, parking lot management, golf course management, street sweeping, street repair, food and beverage concessions, printing, and security. Between 1981 and 1984, it moved from 53 major private contracts to 179. The city eventually decided that ambulance service, street sweeping, and maintenance of median strips were better handled by public employees. But overall, the city auditor estimates savings of $20 million over the first decade, just in the difference between the bids the city accepted and the next lowest bid. Since competition has forced all bid levels down, this is but a fraction of the real savings.

City Auditor Jim Flanagan has overseen the process from the beginning. There is no truth to the old saw that business is always more efficient than government, he has learned. The important distinction is not public versus private, it is monopoly versus competition: "Where there's competition you get better results, more cost-consciousness, and superior service delivery."

In government, of course, monopoly is the American way. When the Progressives embraced service delivery by administrative bureaucracies, they embraced monopoly. To this day we deride competition within government as "waste and duplication." We assume that each neighborhood should have one school, each city should have one organization driving its buses and operating its commuter trains. When costs have to be cut, we eliminate anything that smacks of duplication—assuming that consolidation will save money. Yet we know that monopoly in the private sector protects inefficiency and inhibits change. It is one of the enduring paradoxes of American ideology that we attack private monopolies so fervently but embrace public monopolies so warmly.

Competition is here to stay, regardless of what our governments do. In today's fast-moving marketplace, the private sector is rapidly taking market share away from public organizations. Public schools are losing ground to private schools. The Postal Service is losing ground to Federal Express and UPS. Public police forces are losing ground to private security firms, which now employ two out of every three security personnel in the nation.

We can ignore this trend and continue with business as usual, watching fewer and fewer people use public institutions. We can sit idly by as a vicious cycle unwinds in which the less people depend on government the less they are willing to finance it, the less they finance it the worse it gets, and the worse it gets the less they depend on it. Or we can wake up—as entrepreneurial leaders from Phoenix to East Harlem to Minnesota have—and embrace competition as a tool to revitalize our public institutions.

The choice is not quite as stark as it would be in a competitive marketplace: compete or die. But it is stark enough. Our public sector can learn to compete, or it can stagnate and shrink until the only customers who use public services are those who cannot afford an alternative.

4. MISSION-DRIVEN GOVERNMENT: TRANSFORMING RULE DRIVEN ORGANIZATIONS

Missions do not respect turf lines. In his book *Neighborhood Services,* John Mudd, a former New York City official, put it this way: "If a rat is found in an apartment, it is a housing inspection responsibility; if it runs into a restaurant, the health department has jurisdiction; if it goes outside and dies in an alley, public works takes over." Similarly, if a poor woman needs health care, she must sign up with Medicaid; if she needs money, she must visit the welfare department; if she needs a job, she must find her way through a maze of training and placement programs; if she needs housing, she must negotiate a similar maze. Improving the lives of the poor is the core mission of none of these agencies or programs. Each simply provides a discrete service.

Organizations built around turf rather than mission tend to be schizophrenic. Commerce departments that handle matters related to business—rather than to a particular mission—must simultaneously regulate existing businesses and try to recruit new businesses. Welfare departments that handle the welfare turf—rather than a mission of helping the poor—often urge people to get jobs with one hand, while stripping those who succeed of their health coverage with the other.

The solution is to reorganize around mission, not turf. When George Latimer became mayor of St. Paul, five organizations dealt with planning and development: the Port Authority, the Housing and Redevelopment Authority, the Office of City Planning, the Community Development Office, and the Planning Commission. All five charged off in different directions. Latimer pushed through a reorganization that left three agencies, each focused on a specific mission and each extraordinarily effective in pursuing that mission.

5. RESULTS-ORIENTED GOVERNMENT: FUNDING OUTCOMES NOT INPUTS

Rewarding success may be common sense, but that doesn't make it common practice. In education, we normally reward failure. "If you're failing, you qualify for aid," explains East Harlem's Sy Fliegel. "If you're doing well, then you lose the aid." In public safety, we also reward failure: when the crime rate rises, we give the police more money. If they continue to fail, we give them even more. In public housing, we reward failure: Under federal funding formulas, the better a local housing authority performs, the less money it gets from HUD.

Rewarding failure creates bizarre incentives. It encourages school principals to accept the status quo. It encourages police departments to ignore the root causes of crime and simply chase criminals. It discourages housing authorities from working to improve their operations.

Our tendency to reward failure has literally crippled our efforts to help the poor. Most of the money we spend on the poor—welfare, food stamps, Medicaid, public housing, housing vouchers, child care vouchers—rewards failure, because it goes only to those who remain poor.

If a welfare recipient saves enough to buy a car so she can look for work, her grant is reduced. If she finds a job, she not only loses her welfare check, she loses her Medicaid coverage (after a year), her food stamps are reduced, and if she lives in public housing, her rent often triples. One study, done in Louisville, showed that a public housing resident with two preschool children had to earn $9 an hour in 1989 just to break even with the total welfare package. And Louisville is not an expensive place to live; elsewhere the figure would be higher.

Under these circumstances, why would a single mother with two or three children ever leave welfare? This explains why even our most effective efforts to move people into jobs seem never to shrink the welfare rolls.

Not only do we punish those who get off welfare, we require little of those who stay on. In fact, we call programs like welfare "entitlements" precisely because people are "entitled" to them, regardless of how they behave. The combination of rewarding failure and expecting nothing in return for benefits breeds dependency—undermining people's motivation to improve their lives.

Healthy relationships are built on mutual obligations. If we expect nothing from people, we usually get it. But if we expect effort in return for what we give, we usually get that. Louisville Housing Services is extremely strict about mortgage payments from the former public housing tenants who buy its condominiums. "If you raise the expectations," says Director David Fleischaker, "people will jump through the hoops."

Increasingly, governments are beginning to build demands for performance into their poverty programs. The federal Family Support Act in 1988 required many welfare recipients to participate in education, training, or work. Minnesota's Learnfare initiative requires teenage mothers of school age to attend school if they want welfare. Wisconsin's Learnfare program penalizes welfare families when their teenage children miss three days of school without a written excuse. Arkansas requires the social security numbers of both parents when birth certificates are issued, then uses that information to track down absent fathers and demand parental support for welfare children.

6. CUSTOMER-DRIVEN GOVERNMENT: MEETING THE NEEDS OF THE CUSTOMER, NOT THE BUREAUCRACY

As we become a society dominated by knowledge workers, we are also breaking into subcultures—each with its own values and life-style, each watching different things on television, each shopping at different kinds of stores, each driving different kinds of cars. We have been transformed from a mass society with a broad and fairly homogeneous middle class to a mosaic society with great cultural diversity, even within the middle class. We have come to expect products and services customized to our own styles and tastes, from television networks to restaurants to beer.

And yet traditional public institutions still offer one-size-fits-all services. Traditional education systems still deliver a "brand X" education. Traditional housing authorities still offer an identical apartment in a cluster of identical high-rises. Traditional public libraries still offer only books, newspapers, and magazines. When consumers accustomed to choices confront public institutions that offer standardized services, they increasingly go elsewhere.

To cope with these massive changes, entrepreneurial governments have begun to transform themselves. They have begun to listen carefully to their customers, through customer surveys, focus groups, and a wide variety of other methods. They have begun to offer their customers choices—of schools, of recreation facilities, even of police services. And they have begun to put their customers in the driver's seat, by putting resources directly in their hands and letting them choose their service providers.

This takes competition a step further: rather than government managers choosing service providers in a competitive bidding process, it lets each *citizen* choose his or her service provider. It establishes accountability to customers. "I can't think of a better mechanism for accountability than parental choice," says Sy Fliegel, of East Harlem's District 4. "If you begin to see that youngsters are not coming to your school, that is the highest form of evaluation."

To make their public institutions as customer-driven as businesses, in other words, entrepreneurial governments have learned to finance them like businesses. If schools lose money every time a student departs—as in Minnesota—do teachers and administration act differently? Of course. If motor vehicle offices were paid only when they processed driver's licenses or registrations—so the more they processed, the more money they received—would their employees act differently? You bet. With the consequences of attracting customers so clear, the scramble to cut waiting times would be intense. We might even find offices staying open evenings and Saturdays, operating drive-by windows, and advertising the shortest waiting lines in town!

7. ENTERPRISING GOVERNMENT: EARNING RATHER THAN SPENDING

Our budget systems drive people to spend money, not to make it. And our employees oblige. We have 15 million trained spenders in American government, but few people who are trained to make money. In most governments few people outside of the finance and revenue departments even think about revenues. No one thinks about *profits*. Can you imagine the creativity our public employees would turn loose if they thought as much about how to *make* money as they do about how to *spend* it?

Many readers remember the 1984 Olympics. Eight years before, in Montreal, the Olympics had rolled up a $1 billion public debt—a debt Canadians will still be paying off in the year 2000. But the Los Angeles Olympic Organizing Committee, formed about the time Proposition 13 passed in California, understood that the citizens of Los Angeles were not about to pay $1 billion to subsidize the Olympics. So they spent three years convincing the International Olympic Committee that they could break the pattern of 85 years and finance the Olympics without public money.

The Olympic Committee finally agreed, and the organizers went to work. They recycled old facilities. They drummed up corporate sponsors. They recruited 50,000 volunteers—not just to park cars, but to organize transportation, to feed thousands of people from 118 countries, and to help with a sophisticated antiterrorist system. The organizing committee, led by civic entrepreneur Peter Ueberroth, painted a vision that included not only spending money but making money. And the 1984 Olympics turned a profit of $225 million.

Pressed hard by the tax revolts of the 1970s and the 1980s and the fiscal crisis of the early 1990s, entrepreneurial governments are increasingly following Ueberroth's example. They are searching for nontax revenues. They are measuring their return on investment. They are recycling their money, finding the 15 or 20 percent that can be redirected. Some are even running for-profit enterprises.

8. ANTICIPATORY GOVERNMENT: PREVENTION RATHER THAN CURE

In an age when change comes with frightening rapidity, future-blindness is a deadly flaw. "We've all seen companies that were exceptionally well run or cities that were well run—that did everything just right—and suddenly the environment changed around them and they fell apart," says Bill Donaldson, a city manager renowned for his entrepreneurial leadership in Scottsdale, Arizona; Tacoma, Washington; and Cincinnati, Ohio.

In today's global village, events in Japan or Kuwait can suddenly turn our world upside down. Ask the Rust Belt states, which saw entire industries die in the early 1980s. Or ask the oil states, which saw their tax revenues drop through the floor when the price of oil collapsed. "For a long time, government could be somnolent," says political scientist John Bryson. "But now we're sleeping on waterbeds—and we're not alone in the bed. When anybody moves in the bed, we wake up."

Fortunately, the pendulum appears finally to be swinging the other way. New governors in three of our largest states—California, Florida, and Illinois—have made prevention a central theme of their administrations. States, cities, and counties are increasingly banning the sale of unnecessary pollutants: ozone-depleting chemicals, polystyrene foam cups, nonrecyclable plastic packaging. States are shifting dollars from high-technology medicine designed to prolong life for the already feeble to preventive medicine designed to give newborns a healthy start.

"How much better to provide prenatal care to assure 50 or 60 healthy newborns than to pay for neonatal care for one unhealthy baby," says Governor Pete Wilson of California. "How much better to prevent pregnant women from using drugs, than to suffer an epidemic of drug babies."

Anticipatory governments do two fundamental things: they use an ounce of prevention, rather than a pound of cure; and they do everything possible to build foresight into their decision making.

In a political environment, in which interest groups are constantly pressing public leaders to make short-term decisions, neither is easy. Hence anticipatory governments have been forced to change the incentives that drive their leaders. They have developed budget systems that force politicians to look at the 10-year implications of all spending decisions. They have developed accounting methods that force politicians to maintain the programs and infrastructure they build. And they have begun to attack the electoral process—with its political action committees, campaign contributions, and 30-second sound bites—that produces future-blind politicians.

9. DECENTRALIZED GOVERNMENT: FROM HIERARCHY TO PARTICIPATION AND TEAMWORK

Today information is virtually limitless, communication between remote locations is instantaneous, many public employees are well educated, and conditions change with blinding speed. There is no time to wait for information to go up the chain of command and decisions to come down. Consider the school principal who discovers students wearing beepers to stay in contact with their superiors in the drug trade. In a centralized system, the principal asks the school board to promulgate a regulation about beepers. By the time a decision comes down, six months later, the students are carrying mobile phones—if not guns.

In today's world, things simply work better if those working in public organizations—schools, public housing developments, parks, training programs—have the authority to make their own decisions.

In the information age, "the pressure for accelerated decision-making slams up against the increased complexity and unfamiliarity of the environment about which the decisions must be made," Alvin Toffler wrote in *Anticipatory Democracy.* The result is "crushing political overload—in short, political future shock."

Many public managers believe that unions are the greatest obstacle standing in the way of entrepreneurial government. Certainly unions resist changes that threaten their members' jobs—as any rational organization would. But most entrepreneurial managers tell us that unions have not been their primary obstacle. The real issue, they believe, is the quality of management. "Labor management problems are simply a symptom of bad management," says John Cleveland, who ran the Michigan Modernization Service. "The issue in all organizations is the quality of top managers. And traditionally, in political environments, the top appointees have no management experience. They don't stay around very long, and they don't pay much attention to management."

When the consulting firm Coopers & Lybrand conducted its Survey on Public Entrepreneurship, it found that local government executives said "governmental regulations," "institutional opposition," and "political opposition" were the greatest barriers to productivity improvements. "Organized labor opposition" ranked fourth out of six choices.

The rank and file are "anxious to help make changes," says Rob McGarrah of the American Federation of State, County and Municipal Employees (AFSCME). They understand what a poor job many public institutions do. If change means losing pay or giving up collective bargaining, they're not interested. "But if it's a question of new opportunities, our people are hungry for new opportunities."

Public sector unions are in much the same position as their private sector counterparts were when foreign competition decimated so many American industries. They can resist change and watch their industry decline. Or they can work with management to restructure their organizations and regain the trust of their customers—the taxpaying public.

10. MARKET-ORIENTED GOVERNMENT: LEVERAGING CHANGE THROUGH THE MARKET

If you had to set out to buy a home in 1930, you would have saved up 50 percent of the purchase price for a down payment and applied at your local bank for a five-year mortgage. That was how people bought houses in 1930, because that was how banks did business. During the New Deal, Franklin Roosevelt's Federal Housing Administration (FHA) pioneered a new form of mortgage, which required only 20 percent down and let the borrower repay over 30 years. Other government corporations created a secondary market, so banks could resell these new loans. And the banking industry converted. Today we take our 30-year, 20 percent down payment mortgages for granted, because the federal government changed the marketplace. Ask yourself: would we be better off if FDR had created half a dozen low- and moderate-income housing programs?

American governments have always used market mechanisms to achieve their goals to one degree or another. We have long used tax incentives to influence individual and corporate spending. We have long used zoning to shape the growth of our communities. We have always set the rules of the marketplace—and often changed them when we wanted different outcomes.

But when confronted with a problem, most people in government instinctively reach for an administrative program. They believe their job is to "run things"—not to structure a marketplace. They share an unspoken assumption with a deputy mayor of Moscow described to us by E.S. Savas. An old guard Communist, he listened skeptically as Savas discussed the need for a variety of service delivery strategies in America's diverse and complex cities. Finally he announced, with great finality: "You cannot have each station master making up the railroad schedule! It's got to be centralized; somebody's got to control it."

In reality, of course, cities are not much like railroads. They don't have master schedules. They don't operate on one set of rails. They don't have one task. Cities are much more like markets: vast, complex aggregations of people and institutions, each constantly making decisions and each adjusting to the other's behavior based on the incentives and information available to them.

In a city, or state, or nation, managers cannot make up "the schedule" or "control" the decisions. They can manage administrative programs, which control specific activities. They could even manage a railroad. But to manage the entire polity, they must learn how to steer.... And perhaps the most powerful method of steering is structuring the marketplace: creating incentives that move people in the direction the community wants to go, while letting them make most of the decisions themselves.

Much of what we have discussed ... could be summed up under the rubric of market-oriented government: not only systems change, but competition, customer choice, accountability for results, and of course, public enterprise. But market mechanisms are only half the equation. Markets are impersonal. Markets are unforgiving. Even the most carefully structured markets tend to create inequitable outcomes. That is why we have stressed the other half of the equation: the empowerment of communities. To complement the efficiency and effectiveness of market mechanisms, we need the warmth and caring of families and neighborhoods and communities. As entrepreneurial governments move away from administrative bureaucracies, they need to embrace both markets and community. In Washington, this would be called moving right and left at the same time. The political media are quick to label "conservative" those who embrace markets and "liberal" those who empower communities. But these ideas have little to do with traditional notions of liberalism or conservatism. They do not address the goals of government, they address its methods. They can be used to implement any agenda. They can help a community or nation wage war on poverty, if that is its priority, or lower taxes and cut spending, if that is its priority. *Reinventing Government* addresses how governments work, not what governments do. And regardless of what we want them to do, don't we deserve governments that work again?

PUTTING IT ALL TOGETHER

Our map is complete. It is now yours to use. We hope that you find it a helpful guide in the process of changing your governments. Used almost as a check list, the ten principles offer a powerful conceptual tool. One can run any public organization or system—or any of society's problems—through the list, and the process will suggest a radically different approach from that which government would traditionally take. This is the checklist's ultimate value: the power to unleash new ways of thinking—and acting.

Reinventing the American Federal Government: Reform Redux or Real Change?

PATRICIA W. INGRAHAM

To fully understand the effort to reinvent government in the United States, it is necessary to analyze it from several perspectives. At a minimum, these perspectives include that of presidential politics, that of the organizations in which many of the changes are taking place, and that of the larger systems and institutions which must be changed if reinvention is to have a long-term impact. Most of the targets of reinvention are not easily reshaped; they have successfully resisted most past efforts at reform. If the current endeavor is to succeed, the glue of politics and political will must hold it together, and therein lies a major part of the story.

Equally significant, however, are the efforts made inside the bureaucracy to change rule-bound processes and to focus on quality, rather than procedure. This is the much quieter side of reinvention, but it deserves equal billing. The final perspective, that of large-scale system change, is significant because it mandates legislation to eliminate programs and to remove existing statutory constraints on public organizations and their managers; that, in turn, mandates congressional buy-in and action. Despite the furor over the 1994 congressional elections, this buy-in is currently the least clear part of the equation.

Reinvention is only the latest initiative in the enduring cycle of reform in the United States. The Clinton Administration's "reinventing government" effort, spearheaded by Vice-President Al Gore and his National Performance Review, has two firm, but different, foundations. The first is a clear political mandate for change—any change. President Clinton's election was premised on change; his announced intent for the National Performance Review was to fix a government that was "broke and broken." The 1994 congressional elections underscored the importance of that foundation.

The second foundation is the Osborne and Gaebler (1992) argument for smaller, flatter, more entrepreneurial, and more responsive government. David Osborne was a leading figure in the activities of the National Performance Review; he played a key role in its report. He recently wrote that reinvention is floundering because President Clinton has strayed from its intent, permitting White House advisors to derail important initiatives and settling for modest, inconsequential changes (Osborne 1995).

Nonetheless, reinvention activities are now present in every major federal agency. Responses to reinventing have varied widely: there are different levels of enthusiasm, different levels of conviction that change is necessary, different levels of confidence that the Clinton Administration is serious about the changes, different levels of political executive commitment inside the agencies, and different problems being addressed.

Some observers of these efforts have argued that the Clinton Administration dropped the ball when they did not follow through on NPR (National Performance Review) recommendations more aggressively; to be sure, the Clinton Administration had what can euphemistically be called a very modest implementation plan. Others argue that in the months since the report was released, a "beachhead" has been established, and the "NPR invasion cannot be allowed to fail" (Kettle 1994 p. 4). Still other observers are not so sanguine about either the effort itself or the progress it has made, arguing that reinventing government misinterprets the problem, or, more resoundingly, flat-out condemning the efforts (Moe 1994).

The political mandate that was perceived to have emerged from the 1994 elections gave the Administration's plan new vigor and sparked discussion of a second National Performance Review: whether reinvention *per se* is a part of the Republicans' "contract with America" strategy is not yet clear. Quite clearly, however, there is congruence between the intent of reinvention and the electorate's demand for change. Further, reinvention proposed to reduce the size of government substantially; that, too is part of the perceived new mandate.

At the same time, the political demands and the reinvention proposals contain some of the tensions present in Europe's managerialist reforms in the 1980s: smaller, more flexible, decentralized agencies and managers with more discretion may be desirable on one level, but the issue of continued political direction—and, in fact, control—lurks behind each trade-off. That is why it is important to compare the political rhetoric of reinvention to the reality of legislative change.

REINVENTION AND THE REPORT
OF THE NATIONAL PERFORMANCE REVIEW

Shortly after assuming office, President Clinton appointed Vice-President Gore to head the National Performance Review. The NPR was staffed largely by career civil servants on leave from their agencies; the Vice-President's Office closely monitored and directed the activities. David Osborne served as consultant to the effort. The staff examined every cabinet department and ten agencies. Public hearings were held and expert testimony from a variety of sources was solicited. In addition, reinvention teams were created in each department and agency and cabinet secretaries were asked to establish reinvention laboratories—limited agency-specific initiatives which were to solve problems identified *by the agencies* in more flexible and creative ways.

The report proceeded from five principles, taken directly from Osborne and Gaebler:

- cutting unnecessary spending;
- serving customers;
- empowering employees;
- helping communities solve their own problems, and
- fostering excellence.

The report argued that government would change by:

- creating a clear sense of mission;
- steering more, rowing less;
- delegating authority and responsibility;
- replacing regulations with incentives;
- developing budgets based on outcomes;
- exposing federal operations to competition;
- searching for market, not administrative solutions, and
- measuring success by customer satisfaction.

The report contained 384 major recommendations, covering 27 federal agencies and 14 systems (such as procurement, personnel and budgeting). It recommended cutting the federal workforce by 12 percent, or 252,000 positions over five years. The report estimated that $108 billion could be saved over the same period, noting that $22 billion could be saved by reforming the procurement system alone (NPR 1993, p. iv).

The recommendations emphasized cutting red tape—streamlining budget processes, decentralizing personnel policies, redesigning the procurement system, and eliminating regulation whenever possible. The authors of the report argued, for example, that the entire 8,000 page Federal Personnel Manual should be abolished. Oversight functions and positions in budget, personnel finance and other areas were to be eliminated or drastically reduced.

In combination with decentralization and delegation of authorities to the agency level, the report included many recommendations related to customer choice and satisfaction. It recommended setting customer service standards, surveying customers to determine quality of service delivered, and reducing paperwork whenever possible. The report argued that the standard for customer service in the federal government ought to be "equal to the best in business" (NPR 1993, p. 44).

Finally, in a chapter entitled "Cutting Back to Basics," the report recommended closing facilities and eliminating programs that were duplicative or unnecessary, streamlining regional and field office systems, and collecting more user fees and other revenues from federal facilities and services. The chapter concludes in the following way: "We have not simply offered a list of cuts in this report. Instead, we have offered a new process—a process of incentives that will imbue government with a new accountability to customers and a new respect for the public's money" (NPR 1993, p. 120).

REINVENTION AT THE DEPARTMENT AND AGENCY LEVEL

A frequently overlooked component of NPR'S recommendations was the creation of reinvention teams and laboratories in departments and agencies. This component of reinvention was completely decentralized; while the NPR team drew on some agency specific analysis for their recommendations, activities and structures inside each agency were at the agency's prerogative and were not centrally monitored. Indeed, only a "virtual organization" created on the Internet provided a central repository of information about specific initiatives and who had responsibilities for them.

The initiatives that federal agencies themselves have chosen are the stuff of dreams for professors of public administration; they are undoubtedly less tantalizing for others. Very real and fundamental changes have occurred in many places, however, and these changes are important. Members of the public service are keenly aware that the culture of government is changing and that it will not return to the "bureaucratic Garden of Eden" (Peters 1994). In all of the agencies studied and reported on here, career members of the public service are well aware that they are taking risks—sometimes enormous risks—in the name of reinvention. While the framers of NPR and reinvention have relied on lofty rhetoric—often based on what Kettl terms "mushy thinking" (1994, p. 30)—members of the public service inside the organizations are left to actually manage the change and to deal with its implications and consequences in human, organizational and programmatic terms. Those implications include a decreased—and still undefined—new role for middle managers, a need to "streamline" the agency while also reinventing, and a need to maintain performance and productivity in the face of these shifts. The pain of managers and executives struggling to balance all of these at one time is palpable.

The following brief descriptions of agency activities are based on interviews conducted by the author and research associates from the Maxwell School; given the absence of a central data source, the summary cannot be considered systematic, but it does provide a representative cross-section of experience.[1]

The nature of reinvention laboratory initiatives has varied widely. The location of responsibility for reinvention inside the organization has varied as well. In some organizations, such as the Department of Defense and the Internal Revenue Service (IRS), reinvention changes built on, or were added to, other very significant organizational change efforts already underway. In other agencies, such as Education (a department under serious external assault), the opportunities provided by reinvention were seized upon as a way to discard much of the past and begin anew. The director of reinvention in that department noted that NPR recommendations and "daily activities" were integrated, adding that

> You will not find another agency that has reinventing government as central to its operations as the Department of Education. We view NPR as an opportunity for the department. The fact that we had big problems was very good in a sense because we got a lot of motivation to use NPR (Jones and Thompson 1994, p. 12).

In Education, formal responsibility for reinvention resides with the Deputy Secretary, the second highest political appointee in the agency, who chairs the Reinvention Co-ordination Council. As in many other organizations, a good part of the change emphasis at Education is on human resource management systems. Other foci for laboratory efforts at Education are management of grants and contracts and longer term strategic change (Goals 2000).

The Department of Agriculture also represents an aggressive use of reinvention tools and rhetoric. The NPR team in Agriculture began its operations very shortly after the initiative was announced; over a five-month period the team analyzed six broad issue areas. Rules and regulations, human resource management, information management, service delivery, budget and fiscal processes and organizational structure were addressed. This last analysis resulted in a proposal to restructure the department along six mission lines, to reduce the number of agencies in the central office, and to consolidate central support staffs (Jones and Thompson 1994, p. 26).

The NPR recommended that Agriculture eliminate 1,200 field offices; Agricultural itself recommended that the number be slightly higher and that the total employee reduction be increased as well. Reinvention at Agriculture, while still in early implementation, has been dramatic. After Congress passed legislation permitting a major reorganization in late 1994, the Secretary announced his intention to restructure the central office, eliminating 14 of the 43 departmental agencies and eliminating 10 of the 17 administrative units in Washington. If this restructuring and the field office closures proceeds as planned, the department anticipates elimination of 11,000 jobs and a savings of $3.6 billion over a five-year period (Shoop 1995, p. 25). Reinvention activities are being pursued so aggressively at Agriculture that one observer used General George Patton's dash across Europe in the Second World War as a comparison: managers in Agriculture, he said are "managing off the map" (Kettl 1994).

Another dramatic reinvention and streamlining example is provided by the Department of Interior's Bureau of Reclamation. The NPR Status Report described the Bureau as 'one of the five agencies at the forefront of reinvention' (Kettl 1994, p. 24). The changes now being implemented are fundamental: the agency's core mission is being reevaluated and changed from that of a water resource development and dam construction organization to one that focuses on water resources management. The Bureau's central office is being substantially downsized (by 20 percent); both Senior Executive Service (SES) and middle management positions are being eliminated; and a great deal of decision-making authority is being decentralized to field offices.

Research now underway at the Bureau of Reclamation demonstrates the challenges of managing this level of change. "The jury is out", noted one manager, "on whether or not we will be able to gain the level of efficiency that we need to." Said another, "We have concerns about people's well-being in terms of pressure and stress … in many cases, employees feel that we don't have a clue as to what we are trying to do" (Jones 1995). For middle managers particularly, the daily job has become much more demanding and stressful; at the same time, their long-term futures are in serious jeopardy.

At other federal agencies, the changes have not been so broad. The Department of Health and Human Services (HHS), for example, has created a "Continuous Improvement Program" (CIP), headed by the Deputy Secretary, which serves as the reinvention vehicle. Six career working groups report to the CIP Advisory Committee. All HHS employees were asked to contribute suggestions for improvement of HHS programs and services; about 3,500 suggestions were received. In addition, an external group of experts prepared a plan for the Deputy Secretary and Secretary's consideration which proposed a major overhaul of the department, with particular attention focused on coordination at its highest levels. No formal action plans have yet emerged, however.

In the meantime, one former HHS agency, the Social Security Administration (SSA), has undertaken its own reinvention initiatives. At SSA, these efforts have emphasized improving customer service. Customer satisfaction surveys indicated dissatisfaction with timeliness of benefits delivery; SSA subsequently committed to shorter turnaround times and more simple procedures. Other quality improvement techniques are also included in reinvention activities at the Social Security Administration.

A somewhat similar process is underway at the Department of Housing and Urban Development, but with fewer obvious results. Retreats involving all employees produced nearly 15,000 recommendations for improvement. After winnowing that number to 2,500, the Secretary, Henry Cisneros, and other political appointees assigned the recommendations to program offices for action. The reinvention team has been disbanded, however, and monitoring of implementation is not occurring in any systematic way. Indeed, in the Clinton Administration's response to the 1994 elections, HUD was one agency identified as potentially liable to complete elimination.

The cases in which reinvention was "layered" onto other major changes is also worth noting. The Internal Revenue Service, an established leader in management innovation among federal agencies, had two other very substantial change efforts underway when reinventing began. A Total Quality Initiative to modernize tax systems had been established two years before. Total quality teams were examining issues such as customer satisfaction and improved service delivery well before NPR advocated them. Information processing and management systems were redesigned; implementation of the new processes which were created preceded reinvention.

In addition to these activities, IRS was engaged in the process of "business system reengineering" (Hammer and Champy 1993). The organization was moving from a structure and delivery system based on function to one based on integrated processes and systems. That meant, among other things, that the number of top level executive staff (Assistant Commissioners) would be reduced by more than half, that the field structure would be dramatically altered, and that a general downsizing was probably likely (Thompson and Ingraham 1993).

For all practical purposes, most of the changes proposed by reinvention were modest compared to those already underway at the IRS. IRS does, however, have a separate set of reinvention initiatives; its parent department, Treasury, also had adopted an extensive reinvention strategy. Most of the components of these activities are targeted to reduce overhead rules and regulations and to simplify internal processes.

The Department of Defense (DOD), another long-time leader in management innovations, was also undergoing major changes unrelated to reinvention. The end of the Cold War and the very significant reduction in both military and civilian personnel that it permitted had caused DOD to begin the change planning process several years ago. Dramatic downsizing, internal restructuring, consolidation of personnel functions, improved information management and other changes were already underway at DOD. Reinventing became another tool in the overall activity, but only one of many.

This brief summary illustrates several points. While there are commonalities in changes pursued under the banner of NPR (human resource management systems and reduction of rules and regulations are frequent targets), there is also great diversity in both the scope of proposed change and the manner in which the changes will be implemented and monitored. Second, in some—and possibly many—federal agencies, reinvention is only one part of very significant and multi-levelled change processes. In that respect, many agencies and departments were well ahead of the NPR in identifying and acting upon the need for organizational redesign, improved service delivery, and better responsiveness to both citizens and elected officials.

An important commonality is that, in every case examined except the Department of Defense and the IRS, the primary responsibility for reinvention activities is with a political appointee. In most agencies, that political appointee is high ranking; in others, such as the Department of Labor, the reinvention "chief" is a lower level political appointee. In Labor, however, other politicals—particularly Assistant Secretaries—have taken lead responsibility within their bureaus. One Assistant Secretary at Labor described that responsibility as "leading the department into a brave new world." Conversely, at the Department of Defense where political appointees are keeping a comparatively low profile in reinvention, one Deputy Assistant Secretary dismissed the efforts as "the latest round of rhetoric."

Even with general reliance on political leadership, however, career employees have played a very significant role in both the National Performance Review and in the individual agency analyzes and plans. In addition to extensive career participation on formal reinvention teams, virtually every department had made an effort to include as many career employees as possible in problem definition. Forums for this involvement have included town meetings, formal retreats for all employees, and focus groups. This involvement and buy-in is critical if the reinvention efforts are to be ultimately successful.

REINVENTION AND THE CLINTON ADMINISTRATION

The relationship between the Clinton Administration and reinventing government is more complicated than would be anticipated from the Administration's strong early emphasis on the reform. Two points are significant: first, reinventing was—and is—quite clearly a political initiative and was intended to serve a political purpose. The organizational changes described in the previous section are important, but they are also subdued and, in some ways, boringly bureaucratic. Reinventing government as a political symbol is much more flamboyant and dramatic. It is significant that, when the NPR report was released, both NPR and White House staff concluded that the rhetoric had to emphasize cutback and reduction; David Osborne noted later that such an emphasis was necessary if reinvention was to pass the "smell test" (Osborne 1995, p. 15). That strategy attracted substantial media attention. Congress also found the cutbacks, and the $23 million they were promised to save, compelling (and promptly committed the proposed savings to funding a crime bill).

Initial administration follow through was also dramatic and very political. The President's Management Council (PMC) and the National Partnership Council (NPC) were created by President Clinton. The former was to oversee management system improvement and coordination throughout government; Kettl (1994, p. 2) argues that the PMC has proved to be a "valuable weapon" in selling the reinvention message to federal agencies, but also has focused attention on management issues generally and has assisted in organizing political support for key legislation. The legislation to which Kettl refers is the buyout bill, which gave agencies and departments authority to encourage early retirement by buying out remaining years of employment or providing other retirement incentives. There are, however, differing views on the extent to which the administration has provided effective legislative support for reinvention; given the promise of the rhetoric, the actual record is quite slim.

The objective of the National Partnership Council was to reinvent the contentious labor/management relations in the federal government; in many ways, this was presumed to be a payoff from a democratic administration for its traditionally strong support from labor. The NPC report confirmed many such suspicions. The NPC was to present its final report on the reinvention of labor/management relations to Vice-President Gore by 31 January 1994. This was a demanding schedule and one which essentially guaranteed that fundamental issues could not be addressed. The effort was further complicated by the composition of the Council—top political executives of agencies with large numbers of unionized employees, such as Defense and the IRS and leaders of the major public employee unions. Career executives with experience in collective bargaining played a modest and very tangential role.

Although the proceedings of the NPC were not well publicized, they were frequently "business as usual," in the words of one participant. The final report includes many concessions to the unions, which, if implemented, will genuinely reinvent the relationship between labor and management in federal agencies and significantly abrogate management authority. Major management prerogatives (responsibility for performance management systems, for example) would be ceded to new teams in which labor would be an active—

and perhaps a dominant—participant. Most of these recommendations have not received formal action. They are not likely to receive strong support in the new Congress, but some are included in the Clinton Administration's draft civil service reform legislation.

The second major point that must be considered in the assessment of the Clinton Administration's commitment to reinvention is that, after the initial fanfare, follow through was low key and proceeded with very limited resources. The NPR continued to exist, but with an unclear mission and an essentially undefined implementation strategy. The NPR staff was greatly reduced; most career personnel who had been seconded from their agencies returned to them. Top level political staff also moved on to other White House assignments or ended their temporary appointments. Computer networks were created to exchange information, but have been only modestly successful in producing systematic information. The decentralized and unmonitored implementation of the agency and department activities has not permitted comprehensive description of reinvention efforts, much less analysis or evaluation of these efforts.

If the NPR staff played a limited role in implementation, did another group accept the task? Initially there were at least three possibilities. One was the Office of Personnel Management (OPM), which, as the federal human resource management specialist, should have had a keen and vested interest in the outcomes of reinvention as they related to human resource systems. The second possibility was the Office of Management and Budget's (OMB) management branch, which also should have had an interest in reinvention outcomes and whose leader in early implementation had close ties to the president. The third possibility was the newly created President's Management Council. The PMC was, and continues to be, a rather unknown quantity. Composed entirely of political appointees and with borrowed staff, it has little familiarity with public sector reform and change and less analytical or policy advising capability. It is, however, currently the group with implementation responsibility for reinventing government, largely because neither of the other two possible contenders was able to assume the task.

OPM has been a nonplayer in the reform effort. It has suffered from weak leadership in the Clinton Administration; the organization is currently undergoing a substantial reorganization and reduction in force and is viewed by many as unstable and seriously weakened. While it has had some symbolic significance in reinvention—the director of OPM received substantial press attention for dumping the entire Federal Personnel Manual from a wheelbarrow onto the White House lawn—the overall capability of the organization has been seriously diminished. Indeed, its complete elimination has been discussed.

The Office of Management and Budget implemented a major reorganization of its own during this critical period for reinvention. OMB's changes are based on recommendations from *OMB 2000*, a document that outlines the need to eliminate the *M* position in OMB and combine management and analysis in all of the agency's units. Moe argues that this move "... represents the final act in subservice of management to budgetary priorities" (in the federal government) (Moe 1994, p. 131). Whatever else it did, the move diminished OMB's influence in reinvention implementation.

OMB has, however, played a major role in the implementation of pilot programs under the provisions of the Government Performance and Review

Act (GPRA), which reinforces reinvention in important ways. That legislation, passed in 1993, is intended to create monitoring and evaluation systems that permit analysis of the relationship between costs of programs—and organizations—and the benefits they provide. OMB is only beginning this project; the role of GPRA will play in a more hostile congressional environment is not clear.

SO WHAT?

The early Clinton Administration approach to implementation can be interpreted in two ways. First, the lack of a central directing and monitoring capacity is congruent with the entrepreneurial management and empowerment of lower level managers and employees advocated by Osborne and Gaebler and by the report of the National Performance Review. In that sense, assuming that the main recommendations have the cohesion to be delegated and carried out at the agency level is in line with the report's major emphases.

On the other hand, given the many different kinds of recommendations contained in the report and the different priorities and activities they represent, lack of a central strategy can be seen either as naive or as indicative of a lack of commitment to serious reinvention. Some recommendations, for example, required legislation to remove obstacles to their full implementation. For many of the discretionary powers necessary to reinvention, large system changes are necessary. Changes in classification and pay are leading examples. Federal classification law was last comprehensively reformed in 1949; if the classification system is to help, rather than hinder reinvention efforts, a significant overhaul of existing laws and regulations is necessary.

Pay is equally important. Broad banding and other flexibilities were strongly recommended by the NPR report; many agencies and departments have included pay and classification changes in their own reinvention strategies. The administration's early failure to write and introduce legislation, therefore, can be seen as lack of commitment to full implementation of reinvention, but also failure to provide a safety net to those organizations and employees that chose to begin their own initiatives.

Legislation that the administration introduced in 1995 proposed to create some necessary flexibilities; organizations that have demonstrated commitment to change and success in managing it would clearly be the winners if such legislation were approved. The Clinton Administration's proposal did not fare well in the Republican Congress, however.

The Administration's own commitment to these system changes may also be questioned again. In December 1994, the *Washington Post* reported that the Clinton Administration had "new enthusiasm" for the reinvention effort, and quoted a White House official: "Some people (inside the Administration) didn't see how you could make big words like reinventing government become real to ordinary people. It's now very clear that the American people know exactly what these words mean" (*Washington Post,* 12 December 1994). Elaine Kamarck, Gore's former Senate chief-of-staff and one of the highest ranking politicals involved with NPR, echoed that, noting that there had been a "shift in emphasis. Instead of focusing on how to improve the way government works," she said, "now the administration will ask 'What is government doing that it shouldn't be doing anymore?'" (*Washington Post*, 12 December 1994).

All of this suggests that the Administration will pursue reinvention more vigorously in the next two years. A second National Performance Review, most observers agree, will focus much more strongly on cutting back and eliminating than did the first. David Osborne's admonition to the President that he must be willing to "throw obsolete programs overboard" (*Washington Post*, 8 January 1995, p. 16) contains the tone that is likely in a new NPR and in the recommendations that would flow from it.

WHAT OF CONGRESS?

If sweeping change is necessary and new legislation must support it, where does Congress stand and what role is it likely to play? Quite clearly, some of reinvention's objectives fit neatly with those of the new Congress and with the Republicans' stated intent for change. Generally, however, the recommendations of the first NPR did not go nearly far enough to meet current Republican plans. Further, because Congress was not an active player in the deliberations of the first NPR, they came to the game late and with limited enthusiasm for the endeavor.

Members of Congress saw the report at the same time it was released to the public. Kettl observes that the NPR report received "grudging support" on Capitol Hill (1994, p. 49). Members of Congress did not, as NPR staff and the Administration hoped, buy into the reform simply because it made so much sense. Instead, they selectively supported downsizing and other more limited components of the proposed reforms. This immediately undercut a critical part of the logic of reinvention: performance would improve and savings would be achieved if basic systems—personnel, budget, procurement—were reformed first, so that other components of the reform could build on this base.

Congress, however, was interested in the savings, not in the more basic changes. This is a long-standing problem. Again, Kettl provides an apt summary:

> Congress as an institution works on the input side. The NPR focuses on the output side. Congress has little incentive to worry about results and, in fact, has long indulged itself in a separation-of-powers fantasy that absolves it from any complicity in the executive branch's performance problems (1994, p. 49).

Foreman is somewhat kinder, but reaches essentially the same conclusion, observing that "efficiency is rarely a legislative passion," and that the institution is slow "to grapple effectively with even the most manifest administrative problems" (1995a, p. 35).

Nonetheless, Congress has passed two pieces of legislation that are important to reinvention and many more that have tangential relevance. The Federal Workforce Restructuring Act, intended to facilitate the downsizing of government is commonly referred to as the "Buyout Bill." It is based on the Department of Defense's experience in achieving the enormous workforce reductions that the end of the Cold War demanded. Provisions of the buyout legislation allow federal agencies to offer early retirement incentives of up to $25,000. The bill also raised the total numbers of federal employees to be cut to 272,900 (Foreman 1995a, p. 36).

The second major piece of legislation, the Federal Acquisition Streamlining Act, reformed the archaic and overregulated procurement system. The flexibilities created in the new procurement system are similar to those necessary for the other basic systems identified earlier: greater simplicity, more common sense, and an emphasis on reduced cost. Although there was strong congressional support for the bill's intent, the final product did not completely exclude the other objectives Congress has traditionally tacked onto procurement; affirmative action, for example, remains part of the new system's goals.

The NPR argues that these bills must be considered in conjunction with the nearly thirty others that touch on some aspect of reinvention. In truth, however, the connection is often apparent only to a rabid reinventor, and, as noted earlier, major legislation to reform other fundamental systems—personnel and budget—has not been passed. Again, it must be emphasized that this problem cannot be placed only at the feet of Congress. The Clinton Administration is still in the drafting stages of civil service reform legislation, for example, and has been unenthusiastic about tentative congressional musings on budget system reform. Further, the administration rejected overtures from the Senate Governmental Affairs Committee to create a bipartisan reinventing government commission. That body, much like the earlier military base closing mission, would have assembled sets of NPR recommendations for a straight up-or-down vote.

The new Republican Congress poses particular challenges to reinvention. While Christopher Foreman argues that reinvention allows the Republicans the opportunity to claim that they "... have tamed, if not slain, the bureaucratic dragon" (1995b, p.165), the first meeting of the Senate subcommittee responsible for federal personnel heard testimony critical of reinvention. The meeting also included, however, a promise by the chair to ask "provocative" questions about a personnel system that "needs repair" (*Washington Post,* 19 January 1995, p. A23).

WHERE NEXT? DOES ANY OF THIS MAKE SENSE?

Will this reform be any more successful than those that preceded it? The answer is both "yes" and "no." There are obvious problems. The arguments for reform contained in Osborne and Gaebler and the National Performance Review report, for example, have been frequently challenged by academic and other observers (Rosenbloom 1993; Moe 1994; National Academy of Public Administration (NAPA) 1993; DiIulio, Garvey and Kettl 1993). The basic challenge rests upon two points: first, many of the "principles" of reinvention conflict with the traditional view of the legitimate executive and policy roles of members of the federal civil service.

The most frequently cited example is the exhortation to "Steer more; row less." Translated to the real world of public management, this innocuous sounding principle means that members of the career service would become more proactive planners and policy shapers; they would exercise much greater discretion in decision making. This role conflicts sharply with that created for federal managers and executives by civil service laws and regulations, by political management efforts, and by congressional oversight and direction (NAPA 1983; Ingraham 1987; Light 1994; Ingraham and Romzek 1994). This fundamental point—that the multiple accountability mechanisms now in place to direct and control federal managers preclude the kinds of discretion advocated, indeed, assumed, by reinvention—cannot be overlooked (Romzek and Dubnick 1994).

Similarly, the emphasis on customer satisfaction and accountability to customers is in direct conflict with the hierarchical control mechanisms still so prevalent in public management, in political management strategies and in congressional micro-management (Ingraham 1994). The reality of a public bureaucracy more responsive to citizens than to Members of Congress and congressional staff has not been confronted.

To complicate matters further, the view of government contained in the reinvention "vision" is, at best, a composite of different priorities. Peters (1994) has argued persuasively that reinvention and other current reform efforts build on and incorporate at least four views of government and governance. Peters' four "visions" of government include the "Market Model," the "Parliamentary State Model," the "Flexible Government Model," and the "Deregulated Government Model" (Peters 1994). Each of these models assumes a somewhat different role for the public service, both in terms of policy and requisite management skills and flexibilities.

The Market Model, prevalent in the managerialist reform schemes found in the Thatcher regime in the UK, the Mulroney regime in Canada, and the Reagan Presidency in the US, advocates both greater decentralization and greater responsiveness to central political direction (Savoie 1994). The Parliamentary State Model, on the other hand, assumes greater delegation of authority down through the organization and greater responsiveness to citizen demands and satisfaction. There are clear and obvious tensions both within and between these models. When the models are combined in a reform agenda, these tensions become real, practical, and confounding to implementation.

Jones and Thompson argue that reinvention and the National Performance Review do, in fact, incorporate elements not only of one or two, but of all of Peters' models (1994). Although such lack of coherence is fairly common in reform efforts, Jones and Thompson observe that the "... NPR appears to be unusual in its lack not only of any theoretical coherence, but of an ideological foundation" (1994, p. 4). The foundation of NPR may provide, therefore, a very shaky base from which to proceed with decentralized implementation, particularly if Congress does not become a full partner in reinvention. The combination of reinvention with streamlining and downsizing seriously exacerbates this problem. While the federal government in the United States does appear to be moving away from a bureaucratic service delivery model, it is not clear what it is moving toward.

THE ROLE OF POLITICS AND POLITICAL MANAGEMENT

The second major difficulty with the implementation activities to date has two components: the role of political appointees as leaders of the change and the role of the larger political environment and Congress in implementation. The first of these issues had been addressed in many analyzes of presidential management strategies (Pfiffner 1990; Ingraham, Thompson and Eisenberg,

1995). Two problems with the use of political appointees as change managers emerge from the analyzes. Change in large organizations is a long-term process and one that cannot be effectively shortened (Moss-Kantor 1987). Further, it requires strong and committed leadership for the duration of the process. This implies excellent executive skills as well as a thorough and sound understanding of the organization and its employees.

Most political executives are not likely to meet these criteria. Tenure in position has been a consistent problem in American political management strategies; even with an average tenure of about two years for upper level appointees, the issue of their ability to act as effective change managers exists (Ingraham 1987). Further, because as the total numbers of appointees increase, the presidential staff's ability to screen and match skills with placement decreases, the likelihood of putting the right appointee in the right place is rather slim. To the extent that the White House is unable to get appointees—any appointees—into place (as has been the case for many departments and agencies in the first years of the Clinton Administration) the problem is somewhat different, but the implications for leading and managing change are similar.

The larger numbers of political appointees, particularly in lower level positions, such as those filled by Schedule C authority, also appear to be leading to a practice more closely related to simple patronage than to any management considerations (Ingraham, Thompson and Eisenberg 1995). Rather than improving public management, the use of more political appointees has contributed to what Paul Light terms the "thickening of government"(1995). Additional numbers of politicals at the top levels of the organization create additional management levels; this not only causes the organization to be more unwieldy, but directly contradicts the NPR plea for "streamlined government."

Finally, the emphasis on the role of presidential staff in creating and overseeing change again raises the issue of the balance between the President and the Congress in relation to permanent bureaucracy. This has been a consistent point of contention in relation to presidential management strategies; it is no less significant in relation to reinvention. Christopher Foreman notes "The Reagan-Bush era ought to have shown that high-profile domestic policy initiatives by executives invite political struggle, and that neither the president nor the judiciary can keep Congress at bay with high-minded admonitions to know its place and stay there" (1995b, p. 166).

CONCLUSION

There is no doubt that reinvention and the National Performance Review recommendations will make a difference in the federal government. In a very basic sense, it almost does not matter whether reinvention is the right reform with the right answers. After reviewing two scathing academic attacks on NPR and reinvention, a well-respected syndicated columnist concluded that, while the arguments contained some valid points, they missed the main one: there is so much dissatisfaction with government that change *must* occur. Reinvention will be pursued for that reason alone; if it is not the right solution in its current guise, it will reemerge in another.

Further, given the breadth of the changes being advocated and attempted by reinvention, some will take hold. Many organizations have taken bold steps toward change. Those organizations willing to take risks and to break old molds find ample reason for doing so in the analysis and rhetoric of the National Performance Review. Agencies less inclined to dramatic change have the option of focusing on more limited, agency specific reinvention laboratories. Downsizing, whether or not considered a formal part of reinvention, is also driving change in many organizations. Change is, therefore, a reality on many levels.

The question is, what will be the depth, the longevity, and the consequences of the changes? Will government be reinvented or reattacked? The United States and many other modern nations now have a long history of reform. Policy learning from these reforms has been remarkably limited, given the extensiveness of the opportunities (Ingraham 1995b). Neither analysts nor elected officials have successfully identified "principles" for effective change or components of effective implementation change. Public employees and managers, however, have continued to endure multidimensional and complex changes and have been the target of considerable negative rhetoric for failure to succeed in any of them.

With reinvention, as with previous reforms, success will be hard to recognize because criteria for success have been very loosely defined. Will success be the series of small—but important—agency level changes that are likely to occur? Or will success only be achieved if more dramatic systemic changes take place? Will it be elimination of entire agencies and government functions? How will these broader changes fit with the downsizing that will so clearly be a part of reinvention and may well be the primary focus of a second National Performance Review?

Of equal significance, will the career civil servants who played such a key role in reinvention activities to date—and must continue to do so—be allowed the freedom to experiment and even to fail and be spared the punitive rhetoric that has accompanied public reforms in the past? Will the reforms and other changes bring new accountability mechanisms to replace the overhead rules and regulations whose elimination is advocated? Or will the reformed organizations be thwarted by old accountability structures?

It is clear at this early point of reinvention experience that both the White House and the Congress have backed away from their role in creating some of the conditions necessary for success. Further, they have neither asked nor answered key questions: What is the view of government that underpins reform efforts? Will political reality permit the transfer of necessary authority to the public service and allow the creation of new accountability processes? Are public managers part of the problem or part of the solution?

These are the issues. There are important questions to be asked, lessons to be learned, and legislation to be passed. If the Congress and the Administration back away from these parts of the change and reform process, reinvention may be better called *déjà vu*.

Note

1. This absence of a central information source is now being remedied; in December 1994, the NPR staff released a list of all reinvention laboratories and contact persons for them. That list is now the basis of more systematic research, but data from such research is not yet available.

References

DiIulio, John, Gerald Garvey, Donald Kettl. 1993. *Improving government performance: An owner's manual.* Washington, DC: The Brookings Institution.

Foreman, Christopher H., Jr. 1995a. "Reinventing Capitol Hill," *The Brookings Review* (winter) 34–38.

———. 1995b. "Reinventing politics: the NPR meets Congress," in Donald F. Kettl and John J. DiIulio, Jr. (eds.), *Inside the reinvention machine: Appraising governmental reform.* Washington, DC: The Brookings Institution.

Hammer, Michael and James Champy. 1993. *Re-engineering the corporation.* New York: HarperCollins.

Ingraham, Patricia W. 1987. "Building bridges or burning them? The president, the appointees and the bureaucracy," *Public Administration Review* 47, (Sept./Oct.).

———. 1995a. "Quality management in public organizations: Prospects and dilemmas," in B. Guy Peters and Donald Savoie (eds.), *Governance in a changing environment.* Ottawa: McGill-Queens University Press.

———. 1995b. *The foundation of merit: Public service in American democracy.* Baltimore: The John Hopkins. University Press.

Ingraham, Patricia W. and Barbara S. Romzek (eds.). 1994. *New paradigms for government: Issues for the changing public service.* San Francisco: Jossey Bass.

Ingraham, Patricia W., James Thompson and Elliot Eisenberg. 1995. "Political career relationships in the federal bureaucracy: Where are we now?" *Public Administration Review* 55 (May/June).

Jones, Vernon Dale. 1995. *Management strategies for reinvention and downsizing in the federal government.* Unpublished PhD. Dissertation: The Maxwell School, Syracuse University.

Jones, Vernon Dale and James Thompson. 1994. "A closer look at reinventing government." Paper prepared for the Annual Meeting, Midwest Political Science Association, Chicago, IL.

Kettl, Donald, F. 1994. *Rethinking government: Appraising the national performance review.* Washington, DC: The Brookings Institution.

Light, Paul C. 1994. "Innovation producing governments," in P. Ingraham and B. Romzek (eds.), *New paradigms for the changing public service* (see above).

———. 1995. *The thickening of government.* Washington, DC: The Brookings Institute.

Moe, Ronald C. 1994. "The 'reinventing government' exercise: misinterpreting the problem, misjudging the consequences ," *Public Administration Review* (June/July).

Moss-Kantor, Rosabeth. 1983. *The change masters.* New York: Simon and Shuster.

National Academy of Public Administration. 1983. *Revitalizing federal management: Managers and their overburdened systems.* Washington, DC: NAPA.

National Performance Review. 1993. *Creating a government that works better and costs less.* Washington, DC: Government Printing Office.

Osborne, David. 1995. "Resurrecting government," *The Washington Post Magazine* 8 Jan., pp. 13–17, 28–32.

Osborne, David and Ted Gaebler. 1992. *Reinventing government: How the entrepreneurial spirit is transforming the public sector.* Reading, MA: Addison-Wesley.

Peters, B. Guy. 1994. "Government reform and visions of governance," in P. Ingraham and B. Romzek (eds.) (see above).

Pfiffner, James (ed.). 1990. *The managerial presidency.* Chicago: Dorsey.

Romzak, Barbara and Mel Dubnick. 1994. "Changing paradigms and public service accountability," in P. Ingraham and B. Romzek (eds.) (see above).

Rosenbloom, David. 1993. "Editorial: Have an administrative Rx? Don't forget politics!" *Public Administration Review* 53 (Nov./Dec.).

Savoie, Donald. 1994. *Reagan, Thatcher and Mulroney.* Pittsburgh: University of Pittsburgh Press.

Shoop, Tom. 1995. "Season for streamlining," *Government Executive* (Feb.) pp. 25–31.

Thompson, James and Patricia Ingraham. 1995. "Change in public organizations:

theory and reality," in Donald F. Kettl and H. Brinton Milward (eds.), *The public management research agenda.* Baltimore. The John Hopkins University Press.
US General Accounting Office. 1993. "Comments on the Report of the National Performance Review," 3 Dec. Washington, DC: GAO.
Washington Post. 1994. "Sizing up new climate on Hill, Clinton chose downsizing," 12 Dec.
———. 1995. (by David Osborne) 8 Jan.
———. 1995. 19 Jan.

Coping with Global Interdependence

JEFFREY S. LUKE
GERALD A. CAIDEN

In the last twenty years, public administration has been transformed by an increasingly complex globalized environment. Characteristic of this new international order are spreading networks of subtle and direct interconnection and interdependence that enmesh public officials at all levels of government, from one part of the planet to another. Such networks have always existed, although for the most part they have been weak, temporary, and insignificant. But since World War II, and particularly in recent years, global interdependence has gained strength, permanence, and significance.

Historically separate and autonomous jurisdictions are now closely linked in elaborate overlays of formal and informal arrangements. Global, regional, and local interdependence is connecting the political and economic fortunes of city, county, and state governments more closely than ever before. Modern self-governance has now become a process of managing global and local interdependence. Consequently, a major function of public executives—both elected and appointed officials—is to manage this increasing interdependence.

Increasing interdependence among formally separate and distinct jurisdictions creates both problems and opportunities. On the one hand, it adds new constraints on self-governance and administrative performance. It seriously challenges the viability of traditional political boundaries and administrative accountability and diminishes the relevance of many traditional approaches to public administration. On the other hand, global interdependence generates possibilities for new opportunities. To take advantage of these new opportunities, the public interest now demands administration that emphasizes a broader strategic vision, a capacity for integrative thinking, a catalytic style of leadership, an interest in multicultural learning, and a more fundamental change in ideology from separation to interconnectedness.

GLOBAL INTERDEPENDENCE

Globalization—the internationalization of trade, finance, and technology transfer—has been progressing for several decades. Compared to other Western countries, American citizens were late in recognizing global interdependence because of our emergence from World War II in a position of economic dominance (Kline, 1984). Awareness among American public administrators of expanding global interdependence began in the early 1970s as a result of a series of economic shocks stemming from the world energy crisis in 1973, followed by a world recession and by the emergence in the 1980s of recurrent and record export trade deficits. Separation and isolation are no more; they have been replaced by intricate networks of interdependence, first noted in the economic sphere and now spreading to a wide variety of other public policy areas, such as immigration, law enforcement, energy consumption, and public health. This "passing of remoteness" (Cleveland, 1985) forces public administrators to look outside their organizations more, and inward less.

Essentially, interdependence means interactions characterized by reciprocal effects among public administrators and involves "mutual dependence," where actions of one individual or agency both influence and are constrained by actions of another. Interdependence—high-cost, very important mutual dependence—can be further distinguished from interconnectedness (that is, low-cost, relatively unimportant mutual dependence) (Keohane and Nye, 1977). Although interdependence has evolved since the 1950s, fundamental changes have recently occurred in three particular areas: communications, economics, and natural resources.

Global "Infostructure." International space has shrunk; technology has dramatically lessened geographical and social distance. The world is being rendered smaller and smaller, making the interaction of international, national, and local systems more pervasive and intense (Rosenau, 1980). Recent advances in communications, transportation, and information processing have linked countries in such an interlocking system that actions in one country can have both immediate and delayed effects on American states and communities. And there can be no reversal. With satellite communications, jet transport, and personal computers, every part of the world is accessible and potentially visible to every other part. Distance has been rendered less relevant as the new "infostructure" makes it possible to reach anywhere electronically. Portable dishes now fit into small packing crates and are assembled like petals of a flower to receive pictures and data transmitted by satellites. Any organization can broadcast or receive video information from remote disaster areas and the most isolated hamlets. The result is a quantum jump in ability to identify, sort, retrieve, transmit, create, and apply information (Clarke, 1986). States, counties, and cities now easily interact with provinces and communities around the globe. Another result is expansion of the political arena, drawing in new participants and multiplying potentially influential actors in policymaking.

Global Economy. Perhaps the most important impact of the new global infostructure is that it has ushered in a truly global economy that goes well beyond mere international trade. All countries in recent years—including some, like Albania and Burma, that tried to cut themselves off—have experienced an escalation of economic and resource interdependence. The global economy is now characterized by an increasing reliance on foreign trade for the sale of domestic products, the acceleration of financial flows and capital movement across national boundaries, the growth of labor migration from one country to another, and the expansion of multinational corporations that globally link branch offices through electronic networks.

There has been a progression from local to regional markets, and from regional to national and then to international markets. There are more foreign companies competing in the United States, and more American companies are exporting or operating abroad. Currently in the United States, nearly 80 percent of new manufacturing jobs are related to exports. International trade, in terms of gross national product, has almost doubled over the past decade, despite a decline in the U.S. share of world manufacturing exports from 25 percent in 1960 to about 17 percent (Shelp, 1985). Where once national economies may have been relatively insulated from one another, there now exists one global interdependent economy, which forces openness, erodes national independence, and forces state and local government executives to think in global terms.

Natural Resources. Every government—local, regional, or national— now functions in a situation of resource scarcity. No jurisdiction is immune; none is self-sufficient and insulated from the outside world. National and local self-sufficiency is no longer possible in the production and consumption of natural resources. Furthermore, there is a growing awareness of interdependence among natural resources, particularly of the interconnectedness of natural life-support systems on the planet, and of the need to protect the ozone layer, the equatorial forests, and phytoplankton in the oceans. The concept ecosystems captures the essence of this interdependence among various levels of our biological and environmental systems.

IMPACTS ON PUBLIC POLICY

The global "infostructure," the international economic fabric, and the biological ecosystems create a web of overlapping interconnections and reduce separateness. Few problems can be isolated. Local unemployment, for example, cannot be resolved without reference to world trade problems and the relative strength of currencies. The substance of foreign policy is increasingly related to internal domestic issues, rather than just to international affairs. Foreign policies influence domestic policies; domestic variables shape and determine foreign policies. All national actions in foreign policy thus have state and local consequences.

The emerging links between international issues (usually considered foreign policy) and local problems (traditionally considered domestic policy) are expanding the arenas necessary for self-governance. Increasing numbers of critical policy issues facing local and state governments—such as job creation and environmental protection—are simultaneously and inseparably both domestic and international. Simple and local problems that were once isolated now tend to be replaced by interrelated problems that are more complex, are broader in scope, and require a multiplicity of corporate and public executives to share responsibility for corrective action. Critical policy problems can no longer be handled as if they were primarily domestic issues. Similarly, foreign policy directly affects the capacity for self-governance at the state and local levels. As a result, cities and states are now making their own foreign policies.

One pragmatic outcome of the new interdependence is that public administrators are forced to react not only to local, regional, and national events but also to international events and to initiate contacts with counterparts abroad. In the United States, the once-exclusive control of foreign affairs by the federal government has been broken by state and local governments (Elazar, 1984); States and cities are asserting their local interests in the global arena and are shaping their own foreign policies by pursuing three strategies. First, they and their umbrella organizations, such as the National Governors' Association and the National League of Cities, are learning how to successfully lobby federal government agencies on such issues as the trade barriers that directly affect their own jurisdictions and interests (Kincaid, 1984; Kline, 1984). Second, they are conducting their own independent transborder policies (Duchachek, 1984), crossing national borders to negotiate with their counterparts in Canada and Mexico over matters of mutual concern. The northern border states, for example, have signed over six hundred protocols with Canadian provinces on fire protection, international bridges and highways, and seaways and commerce, while the southern border states have negotiated agreements with Mexican authorities concerning industrial development, agriculture, undocumented workers, and cultural exchanges (Kincaid, 1984). Third, state and local administrators can be found in larger numbers conducting constituent diplomacy around the world—foreign diplomacy over the unique interests of their local constituents (Kincaid, 1988). They maintain permanent liaison offices in foreign countries, they organize missions to promote foreign investment, trade, and tourism, and they schedule trade and investment shows overseas.

International Economic Development. Many of these initiatives in domestic lobbying, transborder relations, and constituent diplomacy have been prompted by the need to stimulate state and local economic development. It is estimated that the United States lost as many as two and a half million jobs in the first half of the 1980s as a result of foreign competition, foreign capture of domestic markets, and the relocation of investment and employment by multinational corporations to Third World countries. The globalization of the economy, as well as the need to export, have stimulated firms and industries to look to state and local governments for assistance (Luke, Ventriss, Reed, and Reed, 1988).

In response, public administrators have encouraged local exports and sought foreign investment and tourism in order to foster economic development. Cities, counties, and states have developed a wide variety of international trade initiatives. Many programs involve nothing more than providing counseling, information, and technical assistance to business enterprises willing to try exporting. Most states now provide export information and conferences, trade missions, sales promotion, export consulting, trade shows, and international market studies and newsletters (Luke, Ventriss, Reed, and Reed, 1988). The second approach by state and local governments to stimulating international trade is the creation of export finance mechanisms. By 1988, twenty-three states were helping to finance local exports by providing loan guarantees, credit insurance, and direct subsidies (Sylvester, 1988). Promotion of exports by states, although there is considerable diversity of approaches, appears to have a positive impact on job creation (Coughlin and Cartwright, 1987).

International Public Finance. The globalization of the economy has created a second international arena for public administrators: international public finance. First, as financial markets become more interconnected and the U.S. tax-exempt bond market shrinks, state and local finance officers are turning to offshore capital markets as potential sources of funds for infrastructure and capital projects. Foreign debt is increasingly attractive because it can be a source of lower-cost financing, it is a new pool of debt financing for most municipal borrowers, and there are financing structures available in overseas capital markets that may not be available in the United States (McCarthy, 1988).

In addition to selling debt, public administrators are engaging in international investing. Overseas investments by pension plans of cities, special districts, and states have increased dramatically. In 1983, the total invested by these public agencies overseas was $144 million. This jumped 1,000 percent, to $1.4 billion in 1984, and by 1986 had reached $6 billion. States as varied as North Dakota and Massachusetts invest 10 percent of their pension funds in international markets (Emken, 1988). Moreover, the percentage of all public pension assets invested abroad is expected to increase, highlighting the increased global financial interdependence of state and local governments.

Other Emerging Policy Issues. Although fiscal issues have propelled public administrators into the global arena, the internationalization of state and local policy issues now includes a wider variety of social and environmental questions that demand attention, particularly immigration, law enforcement, environmental pollution, and education. Illegal immigration is of critical concern to border states and cities that have to provide public services for a swollen population and for a permanent underclass of economically marginal families. Environmental pollution, often bitterly contested across the borders, is a perennial problem, one that can become a strong local issue. For instance, Oregon billed the Soviet Union for costs incurred by state agencies as a result of radioactive contamination from the Chernobyl fallout. These are only a few examples of the expansion of social and political arenas that has created a truly interconnected intergovernmental and intersectoral web, which challenges the traditions of self-governance, local autonomy, and independent action.

IDEOLOGICAL SWITCH

Every generation inherits intellectual "baggage" that contains outdated or increasingly outmoded patterns of believing and behaving. Customary beliefs run counter to contemporary experience. Increasing interdependence in the realm of public business now requires a switch in the thinking of public administrators, from separation to interconnectedness. This ideological switch will not be easy to make. The idea of separation is strong in the American tradition. It predates the War of Independence and goes back to English legal theory, to the philosophies of Locke and Montesquieu, to the concept of town government in New England, to frontier individualism, and to the vision of a land with abundant room for all and an open door to all comers who wished to preserve their separate identities. It is embedded in the theory and application of the Constitution, in free competition and laissez-faire capitalism, and in political parochialism.

But the idea of separation is rooted in a past that is no more and cannot be recreated. The future belongs to interconnectedness. Effective public administration must implicitly assume the existence of global interdependence. Government jurisdictions and private bodies certainly have their own separate identities and their own unique internal governance or management systems. They are also legally separate entities; but they are no longer independent. The notion of separation is no longer even a useful fiction. Government jurisdictions are no longer autonomous self-reliant entities, separate from one another, separate from the private sector, or separate from global dynamics. The crystallization of global interdependence demands the replacement of the idea of separation with that of interconnectedness. Such an ideological shift entails changes in perceptions, values, and priorities. In addition, new policy approaches and managerial responses are required.

POLICY IMPLICATIONS

The new interdependence arising from increasing interconnectedness is eroding conventional public administration and management. The experience and past working knowledge of public administrators are increasingly outdated and can even be detrimental. The new environment is significantly different from yesteryear's, where independence and self-sufficiency (that is, separation) guided politics and administration. The new constraints are real and compelling. Public action occurs in expanding and crowded policy arenas where power is dispersed and shared by multiple overlapping publics and policy actors. The capacity for any one jurisdiction or policy actor to act unilaterally is significantly reduced. Public administrators are increasingly vulnerable to outside influences, and they are increasingly dependent on others beyond their view. Policy choices and public actions often have unforeseen, unintended, undesirable, and indirect consequences beyond the normal externalities.

New public policies, based on the existence of global interdependence, are needed. They must now be formulated from larger frames of reference that assume an expanded set of interrelated variables to produce successful outcomes. American economic policy has failed to recognize adequately the profound changes that have taken place in the global economy (Thurow, 1980). Basic assumptions governing monetary policy, for example, are now quite misleading and certainly inaccurate (Bryant, 1980).

In an environmental context of interconnectedness, each problem becomes linked to every other problem, interweaving and causing unpredicted new problems. Each new public policy typically interacts with other policies, greatly increasing the probability of unanticipated outcomes. Thus, policies can easily create more problems that they solve, generating ripple effects that unpredictably extend far into the future (the temporal dimension), cross jurisdictional boundaries (the spatial dimension), and interfere with other governmental functions and policies (the functional dimension).

More appropriate policy strategies now require more modest programs and policy initiatives, which are based on longer-term goals or visions pursued collaboratively by intergovernmental and intersectoral stakeholders who inhabit particular policy domains. Such a collaborative strategy entails mobilizing interorganizational resources and formulating appropriate action for governmental and nongovernmental agencies. It requires a systematic response by policy actors, based on a shared interest in certain outcomes. New government policymaking strategies should be devised that can more effectively guide public action in an interconnected environment. They should be based on enlarged frameworks and models that assume interdependent relationships among increasing numbers of variables, be smaller in scope—incremental and experimental—yet sustained by some larger vision of policy goals, and be collective, collaborative efforts that mobilize a variety of interorganizational actors in the public, private, and nonprofit sectors.

MANAGERIAL RESPONSES

Increasing global interdependence dissolves jurisdictional boundaries and weakens capacities for traditional self-governance. Public administrators concerned with organizational performance are now forced to pay increasing attention to the external dynamics of organizational environment and less attention to internal operations and productivity. In an interconnected context, public administrators are impelled to bring to their work an understanding of sectoral and governmental interdependence. More important, successful public administrators will have developed and will continue to refine skills in three specific areas: strategic thinking, catalytic leadership, and multicultural learning.

Strategic Thinking. The artful public administrator now becomes a "weaver" who sees patterns and connections in the global environment and threads them into effective networks capable of local public action. The public interest requires skills in strategic thinking: being able to think globally and act locally. At the administrative level, it involves moving incrementally and opportunistically toward strategic, longer-term goals. Strategic thinking also includes the following elements (Botkin and others, 1979; Luke, 1986; Mitroff and Kilmann, 1984):

- Stimulating the formulation of an overarching macropurpose from several different micropurposes
- Thinking about a web of local and global strategies that can be constantly updated and refined
- Considering the broadest possible set of local, national, and international stakeholders
- Detecting local-global interrelationships and assessing the importance of their linkages
- Anticipating what the future will demand of the public agency in order to shorten response time to problems

- Thinking systematically—that is, seeing multiple, rather than single, causes and effects

Catalytic Leadership. Strategic thinking alone will not suffice. It must also be joined by an ability to interact with policy actors and groups outside one's agency and to manage organizational interfaces. A leader in an interconnected environment must be skillful in stimulating action by a variety of stakeholders toward a particular goal or vision. This requires building coalitions and collaborating in situations where multiple stakeholders need to agree on goals and strategies. At the practical level, it requires more telephone calls, attendance at more meetings, and more travel outside the office.

More specifically, this interpersonal skill can be characterized as *catalytic leadership*—the ability to coalesce key public and private stakeholders around a critical global-local issue, such as acid rain, immigration, or economic diversification. A catalytic leader stimulates the development of a critical mass of diverse policy actors motivated by a goal or vision created collectively among them. Only such facilitators are able to move the interdependent web of government and corporate actors. A charismatic leader, with his or her individual vision, is seldom able to move the web of government and corporate actors in a particular policy direction.

Whereas most traditionally oriented public executives view environmental constraints created by the various webs of interdependence as a source of substantial grief, catalytic leaders understand that interconnectedness generates possibilities for new and as yet undiscovered opportunities. Emerging interdependence provides new opportunities for public action and an equally new set of available resources. The opening of international capital markets for financing local government bonds provides a good example. Interdependence and interconnectedness provide new resources and new patterns for initiating action in arenas previously thought separate and insulated. This increases the number of potential access points and creates new avenues for catalytic action to initiate particular policies.

Multicultural Learning. There is an increasing need for multicultural, international skills. First, an international perspective is required that reflects the current interdependent global economy, as well as an expanded knowledge of values, viewpoints, capital markets, and government structures in other nations. Second, increased skills in international communications and foreign languages will enable public administrators to observe, think, and act in an interdependent world.

The globalization of the economy, in particular, creates a need for heightened understanding of the cultures, markets, and languages of other countries. Public administrators must learn, for example, how to discuss exports, deal with foreign officials, and develop understanding of investment opportunities abroad that affect the vitality of a state's or a community's economy.

SUMMARY

Public administrators are discovering that there is much that can be learned from the new interdependence. Their problems are shared by many, and possible solutions are already being implemented elsewhere. To be effective, public administrators will need a lively intellectual curiosity. They are going to have to read more, inform themselves about the international and national scenes, travel more, spend more of their time reflecting on world events and working out their real implications, mix more with foreign counterparts, negotiate more border crossings, and facilitate more combined operations and cooperative ventures.

Strategic thinking is also required. It involves an awareness of global interconnectedness and the ability to assess the international ripples that emanate from different directions at the same time and are occasionally obscured by the shock waves sent out from exceptional events. Sooner or later, external influences will affect local situations, and it is better to have anticipated such influences than to have to react hastily and improvise.

One clear implication is that any distinction that may still exist between politics and management in the conduct of public business is fast disappearing. Elected and appointed officials have to master the identical challenge of managing global interdependence. To do this, elected officials must comprehend the new realities of the much-enlarged managerial world, while appointed officials must think in broader political, economic, social, and cultural terms. Together, they may realize that while effective action may have become more difficult, the internationalization of public business and the enlargement of personal networks have made their jobs easier. No longer do they have to be so original. They can now borrow more from better practice elsewhere, with greater certainty that such practice will probably work better locally, too. Improving the performance of public organizations depends on understanding the new interconnected environment of public administration and mastering the new interdependence.

Note: The authors wish to thank John Kincaid and Curt Ventriss for their comments on earlier drafts.

References

Botkin, J. W., and others. *No Limits to Learning: Bridging the Human Gap.* Elmsford, N.Y.: Pergamon Press, 1979.

Bryant, R. *Money and Monetary Policy in Interdependent Nations.* Washington, D.C.: Brookings Institution, 1980.

Clarke, M. *Revitalizing State Economies.* Washington, D.C.: National Governors' Association, 1986.

Cleveland, H. *The Knowledge Executive: Leadership in an Information Society.* New York: Dutton, 1985.

Coughlin, C. C., and Cartwright, P. A. "An Examination of State Foreign Exports and Manufacturing Employment. " *Economic Development Quarterly,* 1987, *1* (3), 257–267.

Duchachek, I. D. "The International Dimension of Subnational Self-Government." *Publius,* 1984, *14* (4), 5–31.

Elazar, D. "Introduction: Symposium on Federated States and International Relations." *Publius,* 1984, *14* (4), 1–4.

Emken, A. R. "International Investing in State and Local Governments." *Government Finance Review,* 1988, *4* (1), 33–42 (special supplement).

Keohane, R., and Nye, J. S. *Power and Independence.* Boston: Little, Brown, 1977.

Kincaid, J. "The American Governors in International Affairs." *Publius,* 1984, *14* (4), 95–114.

Kincaid, J. "Implications of Constituent Diplomacy for the Nature and Future of the Nation State. "In H. J. Michelmann and P. Soldators (eds.), *Federalism and*

International Relations: The Role of Subnational Units. Oxford, England: Oxford University Press, 1988.

Kline, J. "The International Economic Interests of U.S. States." *Publius,* 1984, *14* (4), 81–94.

Luke, J. S. "Finishing the Decade: Local Government to the 1990s. " *State and Local Government Review,* 1986, *18* (3), 132–137.

Luke, J. S., Ventriss, C., Reed, B. J., and Reed, C. *Managing Economic Development: A Guide to State and Local Strategies.* San Francisco: Jossey-Bass, 1988.

McCarthy, C. "Offshore Financing and State/Local Government Capital Financing Needs." *Government Finance Review,* 1988, *4* (1), 25–32 (special supplement).

Mitroff, I., and Kilmann, R. *Corporate Tragedies.* New York: Praeger, 1984.

Rosenau, J. *The Study of Global Interdependence: Essays on the Transnationalization of World Affairs.* New York: Nicholas, 1980.

Shelp, R. K. "A New Strategy for Economic Revitalization." *Economic Development Review,* 1985, *3* (3), 24–31.

Sylvester, K. "Exporting Made Easy." *Governing,* 1988, *1* (4), 36–42.

Thurow, L. *The Zero-Sum Society: Distribution and the Possibilities for Economic Change.* New York: Basic Books, 1980.

A Few Modest Suggestions
That May Make a Small Difference

JAMES Q. WILSON

To do better we have to deregulate the government.* If deregulation of a market makes sense because it liberates the entrepreneurial energies of its members, then it is possible that deregulating the public sector also may help energize it. The difference, of course, is that both the price system and the profit motive provide a discipline in markets that is absent in non-markets. Whether any useful substitutes for this discipline can be found for public-sector workers is not clear, though I will offer some suggestions. But even if we cannot expect the same results from deregulation in the two sectors we can agree at a minimum that detailed regulation, even of public employees, rarely is compatible with energy, pride in workmanship, and the exercise of initiative. The best evidence for this proposition, if any is needed, is that most people do not like working in an environment in which every action is second-guessed, every initiative viewed with suspicion, and every controversial decision denounced as malfeasance.

---

* I first saw this phrase in an essay by Constance Horner, then director of the federal Office of Personnel Management: "Beyond Mr. Gradgrind: The Case for Deregulating the Public Sector," *Policy Review* 44 (Spring 1988): 34–38. It also appears in Gary C. Bryner, *Bureaucratic Discretion* (New York: Pergamon Press, 1987), 215.

James Colvard, for many years a senior civilian manager in the navy, suggests that the government needs to emulate methods that work in the better parts of the private sector: "a bias toward action, small staffs, and a high level of delegation which is based on trust."[1] A panel of the National Academy of Public Administration (NAPA), consisting of sixteen senior government executives holding the rank of assistant secretary, issued a report making the same point:

> Over many years, government has become entwined in elaborate management control systems and the accretion of progressively more detailed administrative procedures. This development has not produced superior management. Instead, it has produced managerial overburden.... Procedures overwhelm substance. Organizations become discredited, along with their employees.... The critical elements of leadership in management appear to wither in the face of a preoccupation with process. The tools are endlessly "perfected"; the manager who is expected to use these tools believes himself to be ignored.... Management systems are not management.... The attitude of those who design and administer the rules ... must be reoriented from a "control mentality" to one of "how can I help get the mission of this agency accomplished."[2]

But how can government "delegate" and "trust" and still maintain accountability? If it is a mistake to foster an ethos that encourages every bureaucrat to "go by the book," is it not an equally serious problem to allow zealots to engage in "mission madness," charging off to implement their private versions of some ambiguous public goal? (Steven Emerson has written a useful account of mission madness in some highly secret military intelligence and covert-action agencies.[3]) Given everything we know about the bureaucratic desire for autonomy and the political rewards of rule making, is there any reason to suppose that anybody will find it in his or her interest to abandon the "control mentality" and adopt the "mission accomplishment" mentality?

Possibly not. But it may be worth thinking about what a modestly deregulated government might look like. It might look as it once did, when some of the better federal agencies were created. At the time the Corps of Engineers, the Forest Service, and the FBI were founded much of the federal government was awash in political patronage, petty cabals, and episodic corruption. Organizing an elite service in those days may have been easier than doing so today, when the problems are less patronage and corruption than they are officiousness and complexity. But the keys to organizational success have not changed. The agencies were started by strong leaders who were able to command personal loyalty, define and instill a clear and powerful sense of mission, attract talented workers who believed they were joining something special, and make exacting demands on subordinates.

Today there is not much chance to create a new agency; almost every agency one can imagine already has been created. Even so, the lessons one learns from changing agencies confirm what can be inferred from studying their founding.

First: Executives should understand the culture of their organizations—that is, what their subordinates believe constitute the core tasks of the agency—and the strengths and limitations of that culture. If members widely share and warmly endorse that culture the agency has a sense of mission. This permits the executive to economize on scarce incentives (people want to do certain tasks even when there are no special rewards for doing it); to state general objectives confident that subordinates will understand the appropriate ways of achieving them; and to delegate responsibility knowing that lower-level decisions probably will conform to higher-level expectations.

A good executive realizes that workers can make subtle, precise, and realistic judgments, but only if those judgments refer to a related, coherent set of behaviors. People cannot easily keep in mind many quite different things or strike reasonable balances among competing tasks. People want to know what is expected of them; they do not want to be told, in answer to this question, that "on the one hand this, but on the other hand that."

In defining a core mission and sorting out tasks that either fit or do not fit with this mission, executives must be aware of their many rivals for the right to define it. Operators with professional backgrounds will bring to the agency their skills but also their biases: Lawyers, economists, and engineers see the world in very different ways. You cannot hire them as if they were tools that in your skilled hands will perform exactly the task you set for them. Black and Decker may make tools like that, but Harvard and MIT do not. Worker peer groups also set expectations to which operators conform, especially when the operators work in a threatening, unpredictable, or confrontational environment. You may design the ideal patrol officer or schoolteacher, but unless you understand the demands made by the street and the classroom, your design will remain an artistic expression destined for the walls of some organizational museum.

These advantages of infusing an agency with a sense of mission are purchased at a price. An agency with a strong mission will give perfunctory attention, if any at all, to tasks that are not central to that mission. Diplomats in the State Department will have little interest in embassy security; intelligence officers in the CIA will not worry as much as they should about counterintelligence; narcotics agents in the DEA will minimize the importance of improper prescriptions written by physicians; power engineers in the TVA will not think as hard about environmental protection or conservation as about maximizing the efficiency of generating units; fighter pilots in the USAF will look at air transport as a homely stepchild; and navy admirals who earned their flag serving on aircraft carriers will not press zealously to expand the role of minesweepers.

If the organization must perform a diverse set of tasks, those tasks that are not part of the core mission will need special protection. This requires giving autonomy to the subordinate tasks subunit (for example, by providing for them a special organizational niche) and creating a career track so that talented people performing non-mission tasks can rise to high rank in the agency. No single organization, however, can perform well a wide variety of tasks; inevitably some will be neglected. In this case, the wise executive will arrange to devolve the slighted tasks onto another agency, or to a wholly new organization created for the purpose. Running multitask conglomerates is as risky in the public as in the private sector. There are limits to the number of different jobs managers can manage. Moreover, conglomerate agencies rarely can develop a sense of mission; the cost of trying to do everything is that few things are done well. The turf-conscious executive who stoutly refuses to surrender any tasks, no matter how neglected, to another agency is courting disaster; in time the failure of his or her agency to perform some orphan task will lead to a political or organizational crisis. Long ago the State Department should have gone out of the business of building embassies. Diplomats are good at many things, but supervising carpenters and plumbers is not one of them. Let agencies whose mission is construction—the Army Corps of Engineers or the navy's Seabees—build buildings.

Second: Negotiate with one's political superiors to get some agreement as to which are the *essential* constraints that must be observed by your agency and which the marginal constraints. This, frankly, may be impossible. The decentralization of authority in Congress (and in some state legislatures) and the unreliability of most expressions of presidential or gubernatorial backing are such that in most cases you will discover, by experience if not by precept, that all constraints are essential all of the time. But perhaps with effort some maneuvering room may be won. A few agencies obtained the right to use more flexible, less cumbersome personnel systems modeled on the China Lake experiment, and Congress has the power to broaden those opportunities. Perhaps some enlightened member of Congress will be able to get statutory authority for the equivalent of China Lake with respect to procurement regulations. An executive is well advised to spend time showing that member how to do it.

Third: Match the distribution of authority and the control over resources to the tasks your organization is performing. In general, authority should be placed at the lowest level at which all essential elements of information are available. Bureaucracies will differ greatly in what level that may be. At one extreme are agencies such as the Internal Revenue Service or maximum-security prisons, in which uniformity of treatment and precision of control are so important as to make it necessary for there to be exacting, centrally determined rules for most tasks. At the other extreme are public schools, police departments, and armies, organizations in which operational uncertainties are so great that discretion must be given to (or if not given will be taken by) lower-level workers.

A good place in which to think through these matters is the area of weapons procurement. The overcentralization of design control is one of the many criticisms of such procurement on which all commentators seem agreed. Buying a new aircraft may be likened to remodeling one's home: You never know how much it will cost until you are done; you quickly find out that changing your mind midway through the work costs a lot of money; and you soon realize that decisions have to be made by people on the spot who can look at the pipes, wires, and joists. The Pentagon procures aircraft as if none of its members had ever built or remodeled a house. It does so because both it and its legislative superiors refuse to allow authority to flow down to the point where decisions rationally can be made.

The same analysis can be applied to public schools. As John Chubb and Terry Moe have shown, public and private schools differ in the locus of effective control.[4] At least in big cities, decisions in private schools that are made by headmasters or in Catholic schools that are made by small archdiocesan staffs are made in public schools by massive, cumbersome headquarters bureaucracies. Of course, there are perfectly understandable political reasons for this difference, but not very many good reasons for it. Many sympathetic critics of the public schools believe that the single most useful organizational change that could be made would be to have educational management decisions—on personnel, scheduling, and instructional matters—made at the school level.[5]

Fourth: Judge organizations by results. This book has made it clear that what constitutes a valued result in government usually is a matter of dispute. But even when fairly clear performance standards exist, legislatures and executives often ignore them with unhappy results. William E. Turcotte compared how two state governments oversaw their state liquor monopolies. The state that applied clear standards to its liquor bureaucrats produced significantly more profit and lower administrative costs than did the state with unclear or conflicting standards.[6]

Even when results are hard to assess more can be done than is often the case. If someone set out to evaluate the output of a private school, hospital, or security service, he or she would have at least as much trouble as would someone trying to measure the output of a public school, hospital, or police department. Governments are not the only institutions with ambiguous products.

There are two ways to cope with the problem in government. One (discussed in the preceding chapter) is to supply the service or product in a marketlike environment. Shift the burden of evaluation off the shoulders of professional evaluators and onto the shoulders of clients and customers, and let the latter vote with their feet. The "client" in these cases can be individual citizens or government agencies; what is important is that the client be able to choose from among rival suppliers.

But some public services cannot be supplied, or are never going to be supplied, by a market. We can imagine allowing parents to choose among schools but we cannot imagine letting them choose (at least for most purposes) among police departments or armies. In that case one should adopt the second way of evaluating a public service: carry out a demonstration project or conduct a field experiment. (I will use the two ideas interchangeably, though some scholars distinguish between them.[7]) An experiment is a planned alteration in a state of affairs designed to measure the effect of the intervention. It involves asking the question, "If I change X, what will happen to Y, having first made certain that everything else stays the same?" It sounds easy, but it is not.

A good experiment (bad ones are worse than no experiment at all) requires that one do the following: First, identify a course of action to be tested; call it the treatment. A "treatment" can be a police tactic, a school curriculum, or a welfare program. Second, decide what impact the treatment is intended to have; call this the outcome. The outcome can be a crime rate, an achievement score, a work effort, a housing condition, or an income level. Third, give the treatment to one group (the experimental group) and withhold it from another (the control group). A group might be a police precinct, a class of students, the tenants in a housing project, or people who meet some eligibility requirement (say, having low incomes). It is quite important how the membership in these groups is determined. It should be done randomly; that is, all eligible precincts, schools, tenants, or people should be randomly sorted into experimental and control groups. Random assignment means that all the characteristics of the members of the experimental and control groups are likely to be identical. Fourth, assess the condition of each group before and after the treatment. The first assessment describes the baseline condition, the second the outcome condition. This outcome assessment should continue for some time after the end of the treatment, because experience has shown that many treatments seem to have a short-term effect that quickly disappears. Fifth, make certain that the evaluation is done by people other than those providing the treatment. People like to believe that their efforts are worthwhile, so much so that perhaps unwittingly they will gather data in ways that make it look like the treatment worked even when it did not.†

The object of all this is to find out what works. Using this method we have discovered that tripling the number of patrol cars on a beat does not lower the crime rate; that foot patrol reduces the fear of crime but not (ordinarily) its incidence; and that arresting spouse-beaters reduces (for a while) future assaults more than does counseling the assaulters.[8] We have learned that giving people an income supplement (akin to the negative income tax) reduces work effort and in some cases encourages families to break up.[9] We have learned that giving special job training and support to welfare mothers, ex-offenders, and school drop-outs produces sizable gains in the employment records of the welfare recipients but no gain for the ex-offenders and school drop-outs.[10] We have learned that a housing allowance program increases the welfare of poor families even though it does not improve the stock of housing.[11] We have learned that more flexible pay and classification systems greatly benefit the managers of navy research centers and improve the work atmosphere at the centers.[12]

There also have been many failed or flawed management experiments. In the 1930s, Herbert Simon carried out what may have been the first serious such experiment when he tried to find out how to improve the performance of welfare workers in the California State Relief Administration. Though elegantly designed, the experimental changes proved so controversial and the political environment of the agency so unstable that it is not clear that any useful inferences can be drawn from the project.[13] The attempt to evaluate educational vouchers at Alum Rock was undercut by the political need to restrict participation by private schools.... There are countless other "studies" that are evaluations in name only; in reality they are self-congratulatory conclusions written by program administrators. The administrative world is a political world, not a scientific laboratory, and evaluators of administration must come to terms with that fact. Often there are no mutually acceptable terms. But where reasonable terms can be struck it is possible to learn more than untutored experience can tell us about what works.

Such dry and dusty research projects probably seem thin fare to people who want Big Answers to Big Questions such as "How can we curb rampant bureaucracy?" or "How can we unleash the creative talents of our dedicated public servants?" But public management is not an arena in which to find Big Answers; it is a world of settled institutions designed to allow imperfect people to use flawed procedures to cope with insoluble problems.

The fifth and final bit of advice flows directly from the limits on judging agencies by their results. All organizations seek the stability and comfort that

---

† Matters are, of course, a bit more complicated than this summary might suggest. There is a small library of books on evaluative research that go into these matters in more detail; a good place to begin is Richard P. Nathan, *Social Science in Government* (New York: Basic Books, 1988). On the political aspects of evaluation, see Henry J. Aaron, *Politics and the Professors* (Washington, D.C.: The Brookings Institution, 1978). On the technical side see Thomas D. Cook and Donald T. Campbell, *Quasi-Experimentation* (Chicago: Rand McNally 1979). There is even a journal, *Evaluation Review,* specializing in these issues.

comes from relying on standard operating procedures—"SOPs." When results are unknown or equivocal, bureaus will have no incentive to alter those SOPs so as better to achieve their goals, only an incentive to modify them to conform to externally imposed constraints. The SOPs will represent an internally defined equilibrium that reconciles the situational imperatives, professional norms, bureaucratic ideologies, peer-group expectations, and (if present) leadership demands unique to that agency. The only way to minimize the adverse effect of allowing human affairs to be managed by organizations driven by their autonomous SOPs is to keep the number, size, and authority of such organizations as small as possible. If none of the four preceding bits of advice work, the reader must confront the realization that there are no solutions for the bureaucracy problem that are not also "solutions" to the government problem. More precisely: All complex organizations display bureaucratic problems of confusion, red tape, and the avoidance of responsibility. Those problems are much greater in government bureaucracies because government itself is the institutionalization of confusion (arising out of the need to moderate competing demands); of red tape (arising out of the need to satisfy demands that cannot be moderated); and of avoided responsibility (arising out of the desire to retain power by minimizing criticism).

In short, you can have less bureaucracy only if you have less government. Many, if not most, of the difficulties we experience in dealing with, government agencies arise from the agencies being part of a fragmented and open political system. If an agency is to have a sense of mission, if constraints are to be minimized, if authority is to be decentralized, if officials are to be judged on the basis of the outputs they produce rather than the inputs they consume, then legislators, judges, and lobbyists will have to act against their own interests. They will have to say "no" to influential constituents, forgo the opportunity to expand their own influence, and take seriously the task of judging the organizational feasibility as well as the political popularity of a proposed new program. It is hard to imagine this happening, partly because politicians and judges have no incentive to make it happen and partly because there are certain tasks a democratic government must undertake even if they cannot be performed efficiently. The greatest mistake citizens can make when they complain of "the bureaucracy" is to suppose that their frustrations arise simply out of management problems; they do not—they arise out of governance problems.

BUREAUCRACY AND THE AMERICAN REGIME

The central feature of the American constitutional system—the separation of powers—exacerbates many of these problems. The governments of the United States were not designed to be efficient or powerful, but to be tolerable and malleable. Those who devised these arrangements always assumed that the federal government would exercise few and limited powers. As long as that assumption was correct (which it was for a century and a half) the quality of public administration was not a serious problem except in the minds of those reformers (Woodrow Wilson was probably the first) who desired to rationalize government in order to rationalize society. The founders knew that the separation of powers would make it so difficult to start a new program or to create a new agency that it was hardly necessary to think about how those agencies would be administered. As a result, the Constitution is virtually silent on what kind of administration we should have. At least until the Civil War thrust the problem on us, scarcely anyone in the country would have known what you were talking about if you spoke of the "problem of administration."

Matters were very different in much of Europe. Kings and princes long had ruled; when their authority was captured by parliaments, the tradition of ruling was already well established. From the first the ministers of the parliamentary regimes thought about the problems of administration because in those countries there was something to administer. The centralization of executive authority in the hands of a prime minister and the exclusion (by and large) of parliament from much say in executive affairs facilitated the process of controlling the administrative agencies and bending them to some central will. The constitutions of many European states easily could have been written by a school of management.

Today, the United States at every level has big and active governments. Some people worry that a constitutional system well-designed to preserve liberty when governments were small is poorly designed to implement policy now that governments are large. The contrast between how the United States and the nations of Western Europe manage environmental and industrial regulation ... is illuminating: Here the separation of powers insures, if not causes, clumsy and adversarial regulation; there the unification of powers permits, if not causes, smooth and consensual regulation.

I am not convinced that the choice is that simple, however. It would take another book to judge the advantages and disadvantages of the separation of powers. The balance sheet on both sides of the ledger would contain many more entries than those that derive from a discussion of public administration. But even confining our attention to administration, there is more to be said for the American system than many of its critics admit.

America has a paradoxical bureaucracy unlike that found in almost any other advanced nation. The paradox is the existence in one set of institutions of two qualities ordinarily quite separate: the multiplication of rules and the opportunity for access. We have a system laden with rules; elsewhere that is a sure sign that the bureaucracy is aloof from the people, distant from their concerns, and preoccupied with the power and privileges of the bureaucrats—an elaborate, grinding machine that can crush the spirit of any who dare oppose it. We also have a system suffused with participation: advisory boards, citizen groups, neighborhood councils, congressional investigators, crusading journalists, and lawyers seeing writs; elsewhere this popular involvement would be taken as evidence that the administrative system is no system at all, but a bungling, jerry-built contraption wallowing in inefficiency and shot through with corruption and favoritism.

That these two traits, rules and openness, could coexist would have astonished Max Weber and continues to astonish (or elude) many contemporary students of the subject. Public bureaucracy in this country is neither as rational and predictable as Weber hoped nor as crushing and mechanistic as he feared. It is rule-bound without being overpowering, participatory without being corrupt. This paradox exists partly because of the character and mores of the American people: They are too informal, spontaneous, and other-directed to be either neutral arbiters or passionless Gradgrinds. And partly it exists because of the nature of the regime: Our constitutional system, and above all the exceptional power enjoyed by the legislative branch, makes it impossible for us to have anything like a government by appointed experts but easy for individual citizens to obtain redress from the abuses of power. Anyone who wishes it otherwise would have to produce a wholly different regime, and curing the mischiefs of bureaucracy seems an inadequate reason for that. Parliamentary regimes that supply more consistent direction to their bureaucracies also supply more bureaucracy to their citizens. The fragmented American regime may produce chaotic government, but the coherent European regimes produce bigger governments.

In the meantime we live in a country that despite its baffling array of rules and regulations and the insatiable desire of some people to use government to rationalize society still makes it possible to get drinkable water instantly, put through a telephone call in seconds, deliver a letter in a day, and obtain a passport in a week. Our Social Security checks arrive on time. Some state prisons, and most of the federal ones, are reasonably decent and humane institutions. The great majority of Americans, cursing all the while, pay their taxes. One can stand on the deck of an aircraft carrier during night flight operations and watch two thousand nineteen-year-old boys faultlessly operate one of the most complex organizational systems ever created. There are not many places where all this happens. It is astonishing it can be made to happen at all.

Notes

1. James Colvard, "Procurement: What Price Mistrust?" *Government Executive* (March 1985): 21.
2. NAPA, *Revitalizing Federal Management: Managers and Their Overburdened Systems* (Washington, D.C.: National Academy of Public Administration, November 1983), vii, viii, 8.
3. Steven Emerson, *Secret Warriors* (New York: G. P. Putnam's Sons, 1988).
4. John E. Chubb and Terry M. Moe, "Politics, Markets, and the Organization of Schools," *American Political Science Review* 82 (1988): 1065–87.
5. Chester E. Finn, Jr., "Decentralize, Deregulate, Empower," *Policy Review* (Summer 1986): 60; Edward A. Wynne, *A Year in the Life of a School* (forthcoming).
6. William E. Turcotte, "Control Systems, Performance, and Satisfaction in Two State Agencies," *Administrative Science Quarterly* 19 (1974): 60–73.
7. Richard P. Nathan, *Social Science in Government: Uses and Misuses* (New York: Basic Books, 1988), chap. 3.
8. These projects were all done by the Police Foundation and are described in James Q. Wilson, *Thinking about Crime*, rev. ed. (New York: Basic Books, 1983).
9. See Joseph A. Pechman and P. Michael Timpane, eds., *Work Incentives and Income Guarantees* (Washington, D.C.: Brookings Institution, 1975); and R. Thayne Robson, ed., *Employment and Training R&D* (Kalamazoo, Mich.: Upjohn Institute for Employment Research, 1984).
10. Nathan, *Social Science*, chap. 5; and Manpower Demonstration Research Corporation, *Summary and Findings of the National Supported Work Demonstration* (Cambridge, Mass.: Ballinger, 1980).
11. See studies cited in chapter 19 of James Q. Wilson, *Bureaucracy: What Government Agencies Do and Why They Do It* (New York: Basic Books, 1989).

12. See references to China Lake research cited in chapter 8 of James Q. Wilson, *Bureaucracy: What Government Agencies Do and Why They Do It* (New York: Basic Books, 1989).

13. Clarence E. Ridley and Herbert A. Simon, *Measuring Municipal Activities* (Chicago: International City Managers' Association, 1938).

Current Cases in Public Administration

● ●

Case studies in public administration help students to focus on the real-life administrative process. Four case studies were selected for inclusion in this volume to illustrate the dynamics of change taking place around the country at the beginning of a new century. The authors of the cases vary, from a journalist to nationally-recognized experts to actual participants in the situation described.

In analyzing case studies, students should look for possible broader lessons to learn, for new perspectives and approaches to administrative situations, for linkages to the readings in this collection. Three of the cases are about local government and one case deals with a federal agency.

In analyzing case studies, students might want to keep the following framework in mind:*

(1) *The Setting:* Social, economic, historical, and especially political aspects of the environment in which the case took place.

(2) *Participants:* Include interested individuals and organizations, the actors who are involved.

(3) *Issues:* Identify and describe the main issues and problems raised in each case study.

(4) *Key Decisions:* List the key decisions made, who made them, and how they were made. Was timing important? What alternative courses of action were passed by?

(5) *Results:* Analyze the key decision or series of decisions and actions that took place. Why were these particular choices made? What was the impact on the participants and on citizens?

(6) *Generalizations:* What lessons can be learned from the case? How do they illustrate public administrative behavior?

*The earlier contributions of Professors Daniel Henning and Robert T. Golembiewski and of the late Professor Roscoe C. Martin are hereby acknowledged.

The FEMA Phoenix: How One Federal Agency Rose from the Ashes to Become a Symbol of What Government Can Do

Daniel Franklin
(Research assistance provided by Nicholas Kulish)

Rarely had the failure of the federal government been so apparent and so acute. On August 24, 1992, Hurricane Andrew leveled a 50-mile swath across southern Florida, leaving nearly 200,000 residents homeless and 1.3 million without electricity. Food, clean water, shelter, and medical assistance were scarce. Yet, for the first three days, the Federal Emergency Management Agency (FEMA), which is responsible for coordinating federal disaster relief, was nowhere to be found. And when FEMA did finally arrive, its incompetence further delayed relief efforts. Food and water distribution centers couldn't meet the overwhelming need; lines literally stretched for miles. Mobile hospitals arrived late. In everything it did, FEMA appeared to live up to the description once given to it by South Carolina Senator Ernest Hollings: "the sorriest bunch of bureaucratic jackasses I've ever known."

Fast forward one year to the summer of 1993: Weeks of unrelenting rainfall had driven the level of the Mississippi River and its tributaries far beyond the previous records. Every county in the state of Iowa was declared a federal disaster area, as were portions of eight other states in the river basin. But this time, FEMA's response earned nothing but praise. The agency met the needs of the flood victims quickly and with few of its trademark bureaucratic tangles. Said Congressman Norman Mineta, then chair of the committee that oversees the agency, "FEMA has delivered finally on its promise to stand with the American people when floods or hurricanes or earthquakes devastate their communities."

How FEMA transformed itself from what many considered to be the worst federal agency (no small distinction) to among the best is the most dramatic success story of the federal government in recent years. Not only does it provide further evidence that the government can work, it offers a blueprint for what it takes: strong leadership, energetic oversight, and, most importantly, a total reevaluation of its mission.

With a budget of less than $1 billion and only 2,800 employees, the relatively small agency has an enormous and vital role. Few areas provide such a clear case for federal involvement as does disaster relief. State and local governments simply do not have the resources to cope with natural catastrophes like the flood of 1993 or Hurricane Andrew.

But after a string of natural catastrophes to which FEMA's response was, well, catastrophic, people began to wonder whether the feds really did have a role in disaster response. When FEMA bungled its relief efforts after the 1990 Loma Prieta, California earthquake, Congressman Mineta concluded that FEMA "could screw up a two-car parade." In the wake of Hurricane Andrew, the criticisms were even more pointed. *The Wall Street Journal* ran a front page article that quoted a range of disaster specialists who thought that the agency was more trouble than it was worth; it would be better, they maintained, to dissolve the agency entirely than to try to reform it.

One of the most maddening problems with FEMA, the critics said, was the constant bureaucratic delay. FEMA workers would routinely hold up vital aid requests because the proper forms were not filled out or certain signatures had not been included. "If we had asked for a certain resource this way we could have gotten it," said Kate Hale, director of the Dade County Emergency Services of her experience after Hurricane Andrew, "but FEMA would say that we hadn't framed the question properly.... FEMA's employees appeared to be terrified at making a mistake, so they'd rather do nothing than make a mistake because a mistake could cost them their career."

It was a problem that had long dogged FEMA. In 1990, as Hurricane Hugo hurtled towards Puerto Rico with winds of 120 miles per hour, Governor Rafael Hernandez-Colon sent the proper federal aid request forms to FEMA headquarters in Washington. One scrupulous bureaucrat, however, noticed that the governor had failed to check one section of the form. Dutifully, the FEMA worker sent the request back—via the U.S. mail. The returned forms did not reach the governor until after Hugo hit. As Puerto Ricans were cleaning up the mess left by their worst hurricane this century, Governor Hernandez-Colon was forced to refile the request forms and send them, once again, through the mail. Federal aid was held up for days.

The red tape was aggravated by old-fashioned incompetence. FEMA was, in the words of former advisory board member and defense analyst Lawrence Korb, a "political dumping ground," a backwater reserved for political contributors or friends with no experience in emergency management. President Bush, for example, appointed Wallace Stickney, head of New Hampshire's Department of Transportation, to lead FEMA. Stickney's only apparent qualification for the post was that he was a close friend and former next door neighbor of Bush Chief of Staff John Sununu. Throughout his time there, Stickney was nearly invisible, except for regular trips to Capitol Hill to defend the agency against its many critics.

Because FEMA had 10 times the proportion of political appointees of most other government agencies, the poorly chosen Bush appointees had a profound effect on the performance of the agency. Sam Jones, the mayor of Franklin, Louisiana, says he was shocked to find that the damage assessors sent to his town a week after Hurricane Andrew had no disaster experience whatsoever. "They were political appointees, members of county Republican parties hired on an as-needed basis.... They were terribly inexperienced."

FEMA's most serious problem, though, was even more basic: Its mission was misdirected. First, FEMA was still spending nearly half of its budget on the mission it had been created in 1979 to perform: to prepare for a massive nuclear attack. The more immediate mission of natural disaster response was handicapped by the drain this operation put on the agency's resources.

But even in responding to natural disasters its mission was muddled. FEMA saw its main responsibility as distributing federal loans and grants to help rebuild an area after a disaster. It would not issue direct aid to a state—

or even prepare to deliver aid—until it was given a specific request by the governor. That may seem reasonable—why give help that isn't asked for?—but, as Hurricane Andrew made clear, this wholly reactive interpretation of the agency's role was at the root of many of its difficulties.

In Florida, the hurricane so overwhelmed state officials that they didn't even know what had happened, let alone what help they needed. Initially, Andrew was expected to hit Miami. But when the hurricane hit 20 miles south of the city the morning of August 24, most Floridians breathed a sigh of relief. "The storm surges were not as bad as anticipated," said one spokesperson for Governor Lawton Chiles. One National Guard major issued this report the day after the hurricane: "Florida has not requested any support from other states or federal agencies, nor do we project a need."

Florida was slow to realize its own dire straits because many of its emergency workers were among the storm's victims. Half of the members of the Dade County Police and Fire Departments had lost their homes. Most of the area's fire and police stations were destroyed. Like their fellow southern Floridians, disaster management workers were looking for food, water, shelter, and medical care. The state was unable to issue specific requests for aid because it had no one available to assess the damage.

Finally, as the full extent of the damage—and the lack of federal action—prompted heavy criticism, President Bush circumvented FEMA and formed a hurricane task force led by Secretary of Transportation Andrew Card. Card and the task force flew down to Florida to assess the damage. As the Department of Transportation airplane passed over southern Florida, the members of the task force were stunned by the extent of the damage. "This eerie silence came over the plane as we flew over mile after mile of pure devastation," remembers Shelley Longmuir, the task force's chief of staff. "You got the feeling that you were no longer in the United States, but in some far away, mystical place because there were none of the reference points of civilization. . . . It looked like Beirut."

FEMA would have seen as much—had it bothered to look. Because of its reactive posture, it had never sent a team of damage assessors to survey the wreckage. Not until Card and the task force flew to Florida did the federal government have a true sense of the storm's impact.

Upon landing, Card met Chiles in the Miami airport to offer federal aid. Chiles initially declined, saying that Florida could handle the emergency. It is more likely that the governor did not want to have to pay the required 10 percent of the recovery costs. Unlike the FEMA officials who took Chiles at his word, Card insisted that the damage was beyond Florida's response capabilities, and pressed Chiles to accept massive federal aid to be delivered by a large U.S. Army presence.

After some pushing, Chiles eventually agreed. That day, Bush signed the order to send in Army troops to build shelters and provide food and medical care to the victims of the storm. The next day 3,500 troops were in southern Florida, the first of 17,000 that would eventually serve. Almost immediately, Hale says, the situation changed. "The first thing that happened was the morale improved the minute that people felt they weren't alone, they weren't abandoned. . . . You could just see people find the strength to go one more day when they were at the point of collapse."

As life in southern Florida began its long march back to normalcy, Congress began to consider what should be done with FEMA. It was clear to many on Capitol Hill that it was time to either fix FEMA or do away with it altogether. In the fall of 1992, Senator Barbara Mikulski, then the chairman of the appropriations subcommittee with jurisdiction over FEMA's budget, told the General Accounting Office (GAO) that it had to suggest real improvements for FEMA or else the GAO itself would see its budget slashed. Officials took the threat from Mikulski, whose subcommittee had jurisdiction over the GAO's budget as well, very seriously. "This isn't a member of Congress we were eager to upset," says GAO administrator Stan Czerwinski. "She wanted this fixed and she's a very key player in Congress for us, and we were there to help her."

With uncommon motivation, the GAO took a tack not often found in government audits. Rather than looking at whether FEMA lived up to its own expectations, as previous studies on the agency had done, the GAO asked what the most effective and efficient role for the federal government would be in a large disaster, and how FEMA could fill that role. This common-sense shift had a profound impact. When agencies and departments pause to self-reflect, they usually ask themselves how to improve their performance in what they are already doing. Rarely do they ask, "What should we be doing in the first place?"

With this question in mind, says Jeffrey Itell, the GAO project manager who conducted the study, the answer was "a no-brainer." FEMA's enabling legislation, the Stafford Act, provided FEMA officials with powers that the bureaucrats didn't exercise. "We found that without state requests, FEMA could assess the catastrophic area, assess what assistance the state needed, start mobilizing that relief, present its recommendations to the governor, and, if necessary—as Andrew Card did—get in the governor's face to force the issue of accepting federal help. Before Hurricane Andrew, FEMA officials took almost none of these steps. Consequently, when a disaster occurred, FEMA's relief efforts were inevitably too little, too late."

The GAO's final report recommended that FEMA develop a more proactive sense of its mission. The report caught a bit of luck in November 1992 with the election of Bill Clinton. The model for FEMA fit nicely with the new president's notion of an activist federal government. To implement this change in mission, the President appointed James Lee Witt as the agency's director. An unassuming and direct man, Witt was a former construction company owner and county judge who had worked with Clinton in Arkansas as the director of the state Office of Emergency Services. As state director, he had earned high marks for the successful management of three presidential disaster declarations, including two major floods in 1990 and 1991.

Witt's first challenge was to assemble a staff to direct the new FEMA. Much criticism had been leveled at the high number of political appointees in the agency. More than one member of Congress, including Senator Mikulski, had called for FEMA to be reorganized along the lines of most federal agencies, to be "professionalized." In other words, only the highest positions would be appointed by the president, while all other positions would be staffed by career civil servants. Only then, these critics suggested, could FEMA properly respond to catastrophes.

But Clinton and Witt demonstrated an understanding of the virtues of the patronage system. The high number of political appointees allowed the new administration to free itself of the incompetents and replace them with talented new people. Clinton agreed to let Witt interview all potential appointees to ensure that they were qualified for the jobs. As a result, the resumes of the team they assembled are formidable. Elaine McReynolds, head of the Feder-al Insurance Administration served as the insurance commissioner of Tennessee for over seven years. Richard Moore, a former state legislator from Massachusetts, was appointed to help make state and local governments better prepared for disasters. Carrye Brown, head of the Fire Administration, had worked on Capitol Hill for 18 years where she was a specialist in disaster and fire legislation.

With a new mandate and the staff to go with it, Witt conducted a top-to-bottom review of FEMA's mission, its personnel, and its resources. The review brought swift changes. In its first two years, the agency shut down several unneeded field offices. It reduced internal regulations by 12 percent and drafted a plan to reduce them by 50 percent by the end of 1995. It strengthened programs that prepared states for natural disasters. And, so it could better inform state directors what aid was available, FEMA conducted the first comprehensive inventory in the agency history.

Recognizing the unlikelihood of a massive nuclear attack, Witt also moved the agency out of the nuclear war business, making available to natural disaster responses many of the resource the agency had accumulated in preparation for Soviet attack. One hundred FEMA disaster specialists were freed up to deal with natural catastrophes.

Virtually overnight, the agency has developed a new reputation for quickness and efficiency Gone are the bureaucratic swamps that the old FEMA had made its hallmark. It is telling that when state disaster officials talk about FEMA's response time, they no longer speak in days or weeks, but in hours. They speak of phone calls, not of forms dropped in the mail.

Consider the Oklahoma City bombing. Tom Feuerbome, director of Oklahoma's Civil Emergency Management Department, can cite the events of April 19, 1995 almost down to the minute. It was 9:02 a.m. when a truck bomb ripped through the Alfred P. Murrah Federal Office Building in downtown Oklahoma City. At 9:30, Feuerborne placed a phone call to FEMA's headquarters in Washington. At 2:05, FEMA's advance team arrived, complete with damage assessors and members of Witt's staff. Six hours later, at 8:10 that evening, Witt himself arrived to be briefed on the situation. By 2:30 a.m. April 20, the first of FEMA's search and rescue teams had arrived to supplement the efforts of the Oklahoma City fire department. Says Feuerborne, "My office is *very* happy with the quick response of FEMA."

Ellen Gordon, administrator of Iowa's Emergency Management Division, has a similarly uncanny memory when it comes to FEMA's response to the Midwestern floods of 1993. Shortly after midnight on Sunday, July 11, she received a call from L.D. McMullen, the general manager of the Des Moines Water Works. Their operation was at the point of collapse, he said. The 250,000 citizens of Des Moines would soon lose all of their water.

One year earlier, Gordon would have mailed federal relief request forms to Washington, where, as Puerto Rico's Governor Hernandez-Colon discovered, they may have received a less-than-speedy response. But all Gordon had to do was place a phone call to the FEMA disaster field office located in Davenport. Early Sunday morning, FEMA officials arrived in Des Moines, and, by 11:30 a.m., they had determined a plan of action. By that evening, 29 water distribution centers had been established. The next morning, the first of 30 self-contained water purification machines arrived. For the next two-and-a-half weeks, the Des Moines Water Works was inoperable, but the city had all the water it needed. "Nothing sticks out in our minds that we had to haggle over or justify," says Gordon. "Whenever we asked for assistance it was there."

It is a sentiment shared by virtually all those involved with the response to the midwestern floods. At a Congressional hearing in October 1993 to appraise FEMA's performance, congressmen and state disaster officials who testified praised FEMA's efforts and marveled at the turnaround Witt had engineered. Missouri State Emergency Management Director Jerry Uhlmann said that, "this flood showcased FEMA's new commitment and successful efforts in disaster response to catastrophic events." And, as disasters are bipartisan, the response to FEMA's success has been as well. "I haven't spent a lot of time complimenting the President on his appointments," said Oklahoma Republican Daniel Inhofe, "but I sure did on this one."

The true judge of FEMA's success lies not in the praise of Congress, though, but in the minds of the victims of natural disasters. Last year, FEMA sent 5,000 surveys to victims to ask them about the agency's performance. More than 80 percent of the respondents approved of the way the agency was doing its job—a percentage that would have been unthinkable in the dark days following Hurricane Andrew just one year before.

To be sure, Witt deserves ample praise, but do not miss the lesson of FEMA's rebirth. The change he brought to FEMA is to varying degrees within the capabilities of any government agency or department with strong leadership. "It is absolutely critical that you look ... at your role and mission," he says, "and redefine that role and mission to what you feel is important for that agency to be responsible for." In other words, you can't expect to do a good job unless you know what job you're trying to do.

How to Run a Police Department

GEORGE L. KELLING

From Plato in Athens to Police Commissioner William Bratton in New York, experts on public order have ceaselessly worried over one key problem: how to control the police who maintain that order. Truly, it's a conundrum. The police, unlike almost everyone else in American society, are commissioned to use force, even deadly force. But unlike other groups licensed to use force— prison guards, say, or soldiers—they are not sequestered in prisons or on bases. They don't operate in groups under close command. They are dispersed throughout society. And as they patrol the streets unsupervised, singly or in pairs, their power exposes them to mighty temptations.

Citizens and politicians constantly urge them to "do something, *now*," about drugs, crime, and violence. Hampered by constricting criminal procedures, and at times by the lack of authority or resources, officers feel pressure (even from the administrators of their own departments) to do "what has to be done"—that is, to abuse their authority by settling matters with their own version of street justice. In addition, police become enmeshed with society's most troubled and most needy, as well as with its most vicious and most depraved. Their immersion in the world of vice and misery can breed cynicism and contempt for those around them and can tempt them to commit crimes like accepting payoffs not to enforce the law or even shaking down drug dealers.

Recently, Commissioner Bratton has had more reason than ever to ponder this problem: even as his aggressive anti-crime push has dramatically cut the city's crime rate—with murder down an astonishing 32 percent and robbery down 22 percent—the NYPD's well-publicized instances of lawlessness and corruption in the 30th Precinct along with officers' unwillingness to finger their colleagues who made a drunken shambles out of a Washington police convention, have dramatized just how hard it is even for a successful top cop to keep his troops in line. The solution Bratton brings to that problem is as innovative and promising as his crime-busting strategies.

In fact it is, at bottom, the same strategy. If you can devise ways of reducing crime that work dramatically, most police officers will find success so gratifying that their own self-image, their pride in being part of a winning organization, will serve as an internal bar to misbehavior. If you set up a managerial structure that keeps everyone focused on the department's core crime-reducing mission, that in itself will go far to controlling officers. And if you make sure officers have the legal tools to do the job properly, they won't feel pressure to exceed their authority, and they won't develop the cynicism that comes from trying to do a job whose requirements are in irreconcilable conflict.

But here's the rub: this winning strategy is so far in advance of the conventional wisdom that New York State's legislators and judges don't begin to understand it. In June the State Legislature, pushed by the state's judiciary, blunderingly passed a little-noticed amendment to the budget that inadvertently stripped New York cops of the legal authority they need to police in Bratton's twenty-first-century style. New York City officials are scrambling to undo the Legislature's blunder, which threatens to subvert the city government's biggest success in years. As Bratton told me, "If this is not corrected, it has the potential to undermine the whole effort."

Bratton's solution to the problem of control flies in the face of an orthodoxy that goes at least as far back as the early twentieth century. Since then, the effort to prevent corruption and control officers has shaped virtually every aspect of police organization, administration, and tactics. By mid-century, police and political leaders throughout the United States had established a rigidly hierarchical command structure designed for this purpose, a structure that remains in place today.

Rules and regulations cover every conceivable aspect of organizational life. Extensive training socializes not just recruits but also seasoned personnel. Until recently, departments kept officers in cars to prevent "contamination" by citizen contact, and regulations prohibited cops from making drug arrests, so as to forestall seduction by the mountains of money involved in drug dealing. A central 911 emergency call system screens requests for police service to ensure that individual officers aren't asked to do improper things. A powerful, secretive internal affairs bureau penetrates every nook and cranny to guard against corruption. And police administrators have tried to restrict cops to dealing with only the most serious crimes, since enforcement of laws against minor crimes like panhandling and disorderly conduct plunges patrol officers into ambiguity and requires them to exercise considerable discretionary judgment.

Given all these tools of control and socialization, managers should be able to shape a powerful, unified culture that would dominate their departments and prevent corruption. But no. Instead, police departments—the NYPD included—have two separate cultures: the cop culture and the management culture. The cop culture's most visible manifestation is the blue curtain—the protective allegiance of cops to one another, their in-the-trenches loyalty that places a higher value on solidarity and protecting comrades than on professional standards of conduct. But the cop culture, as researcher Elizabeth Reuss-Ianni has shown, is more than that. Penetrating deep into police departments, it shapes how cops view citizens, police managers, and their work. Line officers believe that managers' only concern is getting ahead, and that they have "sold out" to politicians, the media, civilians, and others who don't understand "real" police work, with its constant ambiguity and relentless pressure to "do something, now." Officers believe they are on their own, forced to do society's dirty work with little understanding from the public and little support from their leaders.

Recent internal surveys in the NYPD confirm the deep-rootedness of this culture: 91 percent of patrol officers believe the public has little understanding of police problems; 75 percent disagree with the statement that the police and the community have a good relationship; 81 percent agree with the statement that the public believes that police use too much force; and 72 percent disagree with the statement that the Internal Affairs Bureau is fair to police officers and exonerates them when they're innocent.

How do such cynical views perpetuate themselves? Why do so many of the idealistic young men and women who enter policing turn against their organizations and citizens and tolerate corruption and brutality?

We can begin to answer these questions by looking more carefully at officers' experiences as they do their jobs. Take a concrete scenario: a police officer sees a cabdriver and a patron in a dispute. It is vehement and might erupt into violence. A good officer will step in and resolve the dispute. That's the end of it. No crime has occurred; no arrests. Officially, nothing has happened. Although the event does not exist officially, it is typical of routine police work: relatively unremarkable events that have the potential for mayhem but that the officer exercising skill and good judgment can resolve without fanfare.

Now change the scenario slightly. Suppose the officer ignores the dispute, and it turns violent. *Then* the officer moves in and makes an arrest or two. Something official has now occurred. According to the traditional law-enforcement view, the officer has achieved a valued outcome by arresting someone—never mind that the officer ignored his responsibility to keep the peace. The officer who does his job well goes unrecognized, because nothing has happened officially, while the negligent officer gets credit for an arrest.

Change the scenario again, and it becomes apparent that the officer's incentives are even more perverse. Suppose the officer intervenes in a potential conflict, and something untoward happens—the officer makes a mistake, or one of the disputants is dead-set to cause trouble. One of the disputants files a complaint against the officer. Then too the event becomes official, at considerable risk to the officer's career. We begin to see the officer's dilemma: not only is the vast majority of his work unofficial, unrecognized, and unrewardable, but the official outcome of much of his work can only be trouble.

The patrol officer's dilemma goes deeper still. Many police believe that managers exploit them by sending double messages. Thus—to use an example well-known in policing—when the message comes down to cops from on high, "Bums are bothering secretaries in the park; don't do anything illegal, but get them outta there," officers nod and smile ruefully. They understand the real message: "Do what you gotta do and cover your ass." Doing "what you gotta do"—whether dealing with vagrants, drug dealers, squeegee men, or whoever—is tacitly understood in policing as an underhanded deal in which police use illegal means to accomplish what may be a desirable goal. This dilemma has progressively deepened since the 1960s, as the courts, under militant pressure from groups like the New York Civil Liberties Union, have outlawed many traditional and appropriate techniques of maintaining order.

More than anything else, the disparities between "official" police work and actual police work are what breed frustration, cynicism, stress, and a wary, isolated culture among officers. When officers say that "citizens don't understand" or "you had to be there to understand," when they view citizens as actual or potential enemies, they are expressing their deep frustration at a system in which success or humiliation can so often be based on random luck, departmental politics, or wildly unpredictable encounters with citizens.

A recent example from New York City illustrates the kind of administrative action that breeds rank-and-file cynicism. In 1989, Robert Kiley, then chairman of the Metropolitan Transportation Authority, asked transit police management to develop plans to deal with the "homeless" problem in the subways. (This was a misnomer: the problem was the illegal disorderly behavior of individuals who mostly were not homeless.) After fussing about what they couldn't do, police managers proposed that maintenance crews should go into subways with high-power hoses to "clean" the areas in which the "homeless" congregated. Police, in support of "cleaning" operations, would eject the "homeless." This, of course, was a transparent ruse designed to evade serious constitutional, moral, and practical concerns. Officers were keenly aware of the duplicity and the risk for them. When things went wrong, the "white shirts," as officers called managers, would either be closeted in their offices or nicely home in bed, while line officers would face the glare of cameras and the wrath of advocates. Officers could hardly look to management for support and protection. Instead, they would do what they had to and pull the blue curtain around their activities. Happily, Kiley rejected the idea.

Police pundits have argued that the self-protective culture of line officers persists because police managers don't carry out their control strategy very well. Managers, for their part, blame police unions—though the blue curtain long predated unionization. But in fact the cop culture is an understandable though troubling response to the simple reality that the management practices that have dominated policing for most of the twentieth century don't work.

As Bratton understands, the control strategy is fundamentally flawed. And for a simple reason: most police activities are not under the control of central administrators at all. To be sure, the command-and-control paradigm of management has an impeccable pedigree. From Adam Smith through

Frederick Taylor to General Motors, the principles of task routinization and simplification, the assembly line, and bureaucratic notions such as layers of control, span of control, and extensive rules and regulations were at the forefront of organizational thinking. Yet however well this model once worked in factories, it has never worked well in police departments.

After all, police work cannot be broken into simple tasks. Police deal with extraordinarily complex human interactions. Furthermore, police work cannot be scrutinized by overseers. Most police work is performed either by an officer alone or with a partner. The nature of their work requires officers to make fine judgments, often in dangerous and confusing circumstances, usually by relying on their internalized values, knowledge, and skills rather than on direct oversight.

In ignoring these factors, police leaders have constructed control systems that leave the vast majority of police work uncontrolled. Departmental regulations are the most obvious example. Up to 80 percent of rules cover the internal manners and mores of the organization: issues like wearing uniforms, filling out forms, saluting, and handling property. The rest deal with very important but rare events: use of force, hot pursuit, and processing arrests. When sociologist Egon Bittner asks indignantly, "What has all of this to do with *policing?*" he is only slightly exaggerating, since actual police work consists primarily of helping people manage crises and conflicts. Most police officers, for their part, would give a cynical answer to Bittner's question: "What all these rules and regulations have to do with police work is that they can be used to 'get' officers when they make a mistake or when things go wrong it gets publicity."

Nonetheless, in the 1960s and 1970s a conventional wisdom developed not only among police managers and policy makers but also within the elites and the press. The reflexive solution to every police problem was more centralization and stronger controls. Even chiefs who wish to move away from the command-and-control paradigm can't, for fear that they'll be labeled "soft" on corruption. In New York City's current public debate about how to deal with corruption, this centralizing impulse goes largely unchallenged. The only question is how to do it: one side of the debate favors strengthening the Internal Affairs Bureau; the other, instituting a system of external review.

We can't solve the problem, however, merely by pointing out that traditional control measures don't work. Somehow, line police must be controlled. Although the forces that corrupt police may change over time—machine politics yesterday, drug money today—they are always powerful. But paradoxically, the only way to control police effectively is not to focus primarily on controlling them. Instead, police departments must concentrate with utter dedication on their principal mission: preventing crime and keeping order. If managers win officers' commitment to that primary goal, cops' own internal values will make them resist corruption as inconsistent with the kind of officer they are dedicated to being.

Evidence is accumulating that Commissioner Bratton's new solutions to the problem, based on this principle, are beginning to work. As Harvard criminologist Mark H. Moore describes it, the trick for any leader trying to change an organization radically—to transform its culture so completely that employees feel a profoundly changed relation to the whole enterprise—is to find methods of change that will shake the organization it to its core. Bratton has done this in two ways: by sending a powerful message to his officers about their work, and by devolving authority down so as to encourage creativity, while establishing a process to hold key staff accountable. In important instances, he uses the same technique to achieve both goals.

First, the message. Bratton has made sure that everyone understands the business of the NYPD: to reduce crime—not just a little, a lot. ("Think bold," he said shortly after taking office. "I don't want a 2 to 3 percent reduction in crime this year—I want 15 to 25 percent." And he got it.) Police can reduce crime now, within constraints—they needn't wait for new cars or computers, more cops, bigger budgets, or more overtime. But meanwhile, of course cops should have semiautomatic weapons, because they deserve the best equipment and, with training, they can be trusted to use it properly. Cops deserve smart-looking uniforms—and should wear them smartly—because they represent both the city and the profession. When cops come under criticism for doing their job properly, as they do on occasion, they deserve wholehearted support.

Bratton also sends strong messages about his disgust with corrupt police. When cops are corrupt, the commissioner goes out to arrest and publicly shame them—taking their shields, symbolic of their oaths, from them personally. Reinforcing the message, Deputy Commissioner Jack Maple reminds police over and over: "Do not lie to get an arrest." If an officer inadvertently conducts an illegal search, he should admit it. "Don't start making things worse by inventing stories like: 'The bag of white powder was sitting on the front seat alongside the driver when I made the traffic stop.' Don't ruin your career by escalating a simple mistake into perjury."

Bratton's most powerful message is about the seamless web that connects disorder, fear, serious crime, and urban decay. He makes the Broken Windows argument that James Q. Wilson and I developed: disorder and petty crimes, left untended, signal that no one cares, and lead to fear, serious crime, and urban decay.

Broken Windows flies in the face of the assumption that serious crime is the only proper business of the police, an assumption that unites two utterly opposite ideologies: the traditional law-enforcement view of the police as crime solvers and felon catchers, and the radical individualism of the sixties that tolerated all forms of nonviolent deviance, lawful or not. The Broken Windows theory emphasizes instead that the best way to prevent major crimes and urban decay is to target minor crimes—panhandling, youths taking over parks, prostitution, public drinking, and public urination. Bratton's message goes something like this: People should not urinate publicly (or drink in public, or engage in prostitution, and so on). If they do, cite them. If they do it again, arrest them. If they appear to be carrying a weapon, search them; and, in any case, question them about other neighborhood problems. (Police ask suspects questions like: Do you know where to get a gun? Do you know where to buy drugs?) If information about other problems surfaces, relentlessly pursue it.

For many officers, steeped in the traditional police culture, this is a hard sell. In their minds, they are so busy dealing with "important" problems that they can't be bothered with trivial offenses, regardless of how bothersome they are to citizens. Real policing is arresting felons.

But now the NYPD troops are buying Bratton's message. Anecdotes about how well the policy works abound in the department, passed on from cop to cop with the same enthusiasm that transit police felt five years ago when they started arresting fare-beaters at the orders of their then-boss, Bratton, and discovered that these seemingly inconsequential lawbreakers often turned out to be carrying illegal weapons. In the 9th Precinct, a man arrested for public urination provided information about a neighbor who was handling stolen property, especially guns. Police arrested the man and recovered a stash of weapons.

What makes these experiences in the NYPD so convincing, even in advance of formal research, is that the department itself has called the shots. It publicly declared it would improve the quality of life in New York, and it is doing so—the virtual elimination of the squeegee nuisance is just one example. It said it would take guns off the streets, and preliminary evidence suggests that it is doing so: in August 1995, for instance, the proportion of arrested suspects who were carrying guns was 39 percent lower than two years earlier. The department has said that taking guns off the streets would reduce violent crime, and statistics show that it has. Because its successes are not random, it's hard to attribute them to luck or to anonymous "larger forces," such as demographics.

One place where the NYPD calls its shots is in its published anti-crime strategies. Distributed to everyone in the department from sergeants and up, political leaders, journalists, and interested members of the public, the strategies target specific issues: illegal guns, youth violence, domestic violence, quality-of-life crimes, and police corruption. "Police Strategy No. 5: Reclaiming the Public Spaces of New York" puts forward the underlying premise of New York's anti-crime strategy: "By working systematically and assertively to reduce the level of disorder in the city, the NYPD will act to undercut the ground on which more serious crimes seem possible and even permissible." It then goes on to document particulars: precinct commanders will have the authority to maintain order and will be free to conduct their own operations against prostitution, "boom box cars," sales of liquor to minors, and other forms of disorder. It's crucial that the department is enhancing individual officers' authority to control such problems, first, by allowing them to arrest persistent offenders; second, by seeking new legal tools, such as anti-panhandling ordinances; and third, by training officers in the use of civil procedures, like injunctions and nuisance-abatement laws (for which the thresholds of evidence are different from those of criminal laws), to deal with problems such as crack houses and prostitution.

These published strategies amount to a contract between the NYPD's leadership, its officers, and the citizens of New York. They expose citizens to departmental thinking while communicating directly to patrol officers what the department expects of them and what steps the department will take to achieve its goals—steps that can be monitored by those who will be accountable for success or failure. They commit the department to report publicly on the results of its efforts.

Police officers may be buying Bratton's strategy, but neither the Legislature nor New York's judges seem to have any idea what lies behind the city's amazing drop in crime on Bratton's watch. In the name of cost reduction they have pulled the rug out from under Bratton's winning methods. Judges persuaded legislators that having the criminal courts deal with minor offenses against public order is costly and inefficient. The courts, they claimed, could save $1 million a year by moving such offenses to administrative rather than criminal jurisdiction. The more likely reason is that judges feel as reluctant to deal with such seemingly trivial dirty work as cops were before Bratton won them over. In any event, legislators bought the argument and made the change, which took effect October 1.

The result: New York's cops have lost their principal tool for order keeping. Until October 1, officers could control public drunkenness or public urination or squeegeeing because they could arrest people who failed to answer summonses for such offenses. They could require people they stopped for such offenses to identify themselves and could then check if they had any warrants outstanding. But with these offenses moved to administrative jurisdiction, cops have lost the authority to make arrests. They can hand out tickets, but if offenders don't answer them, as most don't, police can do ... nothing. Nor can officers compel offenders to identify themselves. As a practical matter, the Legislature has made the laws against such offenses unenforceable.

New York City officials are desperately trying to repair this incalculable damage. The NYPD's legal staff is scrambling to identify other sources of authority to arrest people for some of these offenses: public urination, for instance, may qualify as a misdemeanor violation of the health code. Officials persuaded the City Council to restore some offenses to criminal jurisdiction by elevating them from administrative offenses to misdemeanors. But the Council refused to recriminalize the most important offenses to the Bratton strategy—such as public urination, drunkenness, and squeegeeing. Officials have asked the Legislature to reconsider the change, and meanwhile they have asked the courts to stay the new arrangement. If nothing is done, the Legislature will have committed its biggest offense against the public interest in many years. "It's obvious," Bratton says, "that judges and legislators haven't gotten the message from citizens that police departments have."

Drawing upon the re-engineering experience of private industry, Bratton has made changes in the department's management structure that aim to do much more than merely cure bureaucratic paralysis and organizational bloat. The crucial goal is to create a unified police culture that both empowers officers to do police work and ensures that they will do it properly—reflexively, out of habit. Bratton's most important move has been to push decision making downward, under the assumption that the closer to the ground the decision makers are, the more likely that they will be focused on and responsive to neighborhood needs. The most natural level of decision making seems to be the precincts, geographical entities with histories and traditions. With 200 to 400 employees, they are small enough that commanders can wrap their minds around them.

Consequently, Bratton has moved aggressively to devolve authority to precincts. Early in his tenure he sent the message that the NYPD's most capable mid-managers would head precincts. The transfer of power from the department's 55 chiefs to these new precinct commanders has been real. Frank Hartmann, director of Harvard's Criminal Justice Program, has conducted focus groups with precinct commanders to help Bratton understand their problems. Hartmann has described to me the heady, almost giddy experience that young and highly motivated commanders are having with their newly acquired power to administer their districts. In response to concerns commanders have voiced in these focus groups—lack of some basic equipment, uncertain authority, staff scheduling problems, lack of support from specialized police units—chiefs, the commanders' superiors, now *guarantee* that legitimate needs will be met in a specified way, by a specified date, and in ways that satisfy the precinct commanders. This idea, picked up from business, is another revolution in police thinking.

How will police leaders ensure that precinct captains' new authority will be used to implement Bratton's strategy to prevent crime and keep cops clean? In the NYPD, a powerful new management tool—crime control strategy meetings—has become the primary means of translating Bratton's vision of policing into action and of holding precinct commanders, as well as other personnel, accountable. These dramatic meetings have not only captured the imagination of the NYPD; they have attracted attention around the world. Mayors, police chiefs, and scholars from San Diego to Singapore to Saudi Arabia have come crowding into the NYPD's meeting room to learn firsthand how this new technique works.

Participation in the three-hour, twice-weekly meetings is mandatory for all 76 precinct commanders, super-chiefs, deputy commissioners, and borough chiefs. In the department's high-tech command and control center, the operational "guts" of the NYPD during riots or other calamities, a lectern beneath a huge projection screen looks out over tables arranged in a U. A placard to the left of the screen lists the "4 Steps to Crime Reduction" in bold print: "Accurate & Timely Intelligence; Rapid Deployment; Effective Tactics; Relentless Follow-Up & Assessment." To the right hangs the slogan, "We're not just report takers; we're the police." Along the sides of the U sit a dozen or so precinct commanders and the detective lieutenants from the borough that will be the focus of this particular meeting. At the end of the U, Chief of Detectives Charles Reuther, Chief of Patrol Louis Anemone, Chief of Narcotics Patrick Harrnett, Chief of Organized Crime Control Martin O'Boyle, and Deputy Commissioner Maple (specially appointed by Bratton and known by everyone to be one of his closest and most loyal sidekicks) face the speaker at the lectern. Around the sides of the room sit or stand representatives of schools, district attorneys' offices, and the parole department, along with heads of NYPD special units and support staff. Outside observers fill out the standing-room-only space. Maple runs the meetings: whether he is sick, hoarse, or simply exhausted from being called out in the middle of the night, the show will go on.

Steaming coffee cups in hand, people flow into the room to typical cop talk: aggressive humor, teasing. Maple calls the meeting to order—on time. The banter stops. The first of the five or so precinct commanders to speak on any given day takes the lectern. On the screen above appears every conceivable bit of information about the commander's precinct: the crime rate over time as reflected by index crimes (murder, rape, robbery, aggravated assault, larceny, and car theft); arrest data; shooting victims and incidents; lists of precinct residents who are on parole or have felony or parole warrants outstanding; and data on summonses for quality-of-life violations like public drinking and public urination. A map of the precinct displays the geographical distribution and clustering of crimes. Meeting participants receive printouts that include data about precinct citizen complaints, overtime, and the proportion of calls for service that prove unfounded (if too large, it's a signal that the precinct commander may be cooking the books to make the crime rate appear lower than it is). A picture of the precinct commander, along with background information about him, appears in the upper-right corner of the printout, making clear who is in charge and has to answer for what's happening in the precinct.

A few minutes into the commander's presentation, Maple begins to probe: "Your commercial robberies are up. How many of the robberies are kids stealing cupcakes? How many are guys walking in with Uzis?" The commander begins to unpack the robberies, describing them in detail. He tries to get back to the formal presentation, but Maple continues to scrutinize the data. "What about household burglaries? They're down." The commander shoots back: "Yeah, we got wind of about four really active burglars, so we targeted on them." He provides details about how the police recognized the pattern, gathered information, devised a plan, and made arrests. The commander's peers break into applause.

Another commander steps up to the podium. "You had eight rapes this month, four above last year," Maple says. "What's going on?" The commander begins disaggregating: "Four rapes involved friends and family, one was a date rape, and three were stranger rapes. Two of those appear to be the work of one person." Maple turns to the detective lieutenant assigned to the precinct and standing beside the commander. "Tell me about the investigation." The lieutenant moves to the podium and describes the investigation. Maple interrupts and addresses another precinct commander seated at the table: "You had a similar problem a couple of months ago, didn't you? How did you handle it?" Later in the presentation, while discussing auto theft, the commander asks if it's legal to stop tow trucks towing cars (a common method of theft). Several people call out a jumble of opinions. Maple cuts them off. Nodding to the head of the legal department, he guarantees the captain a quick response: "We're not sure. Legal will get back to you with an answer by the end of the day." Finally, after half an hour or so, Maple allows the commander to wrap up his presentation.

Before he steps down, though, the commander recognizes two patrol officers: "I would like to introduce officers Jacques Guillois and John Bakke. Recently we were having particularly vicious robberies in Queens and Brooklyn. Crime analysis identified that robbery pattern, 27 in Queens and 40 in Brooklyn were virtually identical. [The NYPD assigns a number to every robbery pattern—mode of operation, number of offenders, descriptions, and so on.] There were also similar robberies in Nassau County. The violence was worsening with each robbery: it was only a matter of time until someone was killed. We convened a special crime control strategy meeting [of super-chiefs, borough chiefs, precinct commanders, heads of special units, and Nassau police]. We shared information and developed a coordinated response. We alerted units in Brooklyn, Queens, and Nassau County. Officers Guillois and Bakke, while patrolling in an unmarked car, recognized the license number [which had been identified in the robbery patterns], stopped the car, and arrested two persons—the driver for being unlicensed and the passenger for having three bags of marijuana. Guillois and Bakke arranged for a lineup—so that a victim could make a positive identification. The pair was identified as the robbers we were looking for by a Burger King employee. Officers Guillois and Bakke, please stand up."

Along with the rest of the participants and the audience, chiefs, *super-chiefs*, rise and applaud—applaud patrol officers. The officers have been assigned to a month of special duty in the detective unit, a career-enhancing honor.

In another case, participants in a meeting were perplexed by a burglary pattern in Washington Heights: burglars were concentrating on cable TV boxes. Maple and Anemone pushed the issue, instructing the commander of the 34th Precinct to find out where the boxes were going and report back at the next meeting. Back in the precinct, the commander assembled a team of officers who put together a plan: youthful officers posing as burglars worked the street trying to sell "hot" cable boxes actually supplied by the cable company. Finally they found someone willing to buy them. They obtained a warrant and searched the buyer's residence, where they found a cache of stolen boxes that he planned to resell. At the next meeting the precinct commander proudly announced that the problem was solved: by arresting the suspect, police had shut down the market for the stolen boxes. He introduced the team of officers, who received a hearty round of applause.

The crime control strategy meetings have captured the imagination of the New York City Police Department and have riveted the attention of everyone in the department on neighborhood problems. Those familiar with contemporary management theory will recognize the meetings as the NYPD's version of what Robert Simons of the Harvard Business School calls an "interactive control system." In an elegant and simple way, the meetings portray the devolution of authority to precinct commanders and the corresponding increase in their accountability. They dramatize the department's new processes for extending services to communities; they give immediacy and urgency to crime control (not "Send your request to legal," but "We'll have an answer for you"); and they reinforce Bratton's vision of policing as central to controlling disorder, fear, and crime in the city's neighborhoods.

These changes will permanently alter the police culture if the Legislature restores the legal authority the department needs. Indeed, the culture is different already. Anyone familiar with policing can feel the re-invigoration of officers. Like the transit police before them, officers throughout the NYPD have had the experience of successfully restoring order and preventing crime. Some have heard their efforts applauded at One Police Plaza; many others have received applause from the citizens they serve. The lesson is overpowering: deal with the little stuff, and the big stuff will follow.

Nothing will change cop culture so fast as adopting a management culture that understands and affirms the true nature of police work. Managers, or "white shirts," are now preoccupied with what is happening on the ground. Woe to the commander whose attention is not riveted on precinct crime and problem patterns. Moreover, woe to the commander who is not scanning the entire city to see if similar patterns are developing elsewhere, and quickly working to coordinate efforts if they are.

As the NYPD devolves authority to precinct commanders and below, how will it prevent corruption? Police leaders are striving to ensure that the new police culture will be a culture of integrity. The message to officers is: management will not subtly ask you to make dirty deals and be duplicitous. If the department doesn't have the authority to deal with a problem, it will not ask you to "do what you have to do." Instead, it will seek legitimate authority—by, for example, proposing new laws to deal with panhandling, as the department is now doing. There's no reason for you to worry if you've made an honest mistake. If the NYPD itself is scrupulously honest, Bratton believes, officers will be less prone to, and tolerant of, corrupt behavior.

Moreover, precinct managers have also been made directly responsible for keeping their personnel clean. Each precinct has an integrity control officer; both he and the commander have the power to launch a corruption investigation. Just as they are learning to scan for neighborhood problems and street crime, managers are now learning to scan complaints against officers for patterns that may indicate corruption.

Bratton's message has inspired officers, and the processes he has established have changed the accountability structure of the NYPD. Even if the Legislature acts responsibly, could these changes be wiped out by a new police administration? Certainly, for Bratton's effort to change the department remains incomplete; the final step will be for precinct leaders to come up with ways of devolving authority to their staffs, especially to patrol officers, to win them over irrevocably to the new culture and the new mission. Yet it is hard to overturn dramatic success. Recall that since Bratton reoriented the transit police in 1990, not only has order been re-established in the subway, but felonies are down 75 percent in four years. This pattern now is repeating itself on the city's streets and in its neighborhoods. Cops truly aren't just report takers—they're the police. And proud of it.

Editor's Note: This case tells the story of one police department and one city; the story continues even now. The Mayor of New York City eventually pushed out the Police Commissioner, and New York City's crime rate generally continues to decline, at least at the point this volume goes to press. William Bratton's advice is still widely sought by cities across the country.

For the 1995, 1996, and 1997 fiscal years, over 2,000 claims of brutality were filed annually against the City of New York Police Department. Settlements of these claims by the City, typically without admission of guilt, averaged over $20 million a year. On August 9, 1997, a Haitian immigrant apparently was brutalized in the bathroom of the 70th Precinct station house in Brooklyn. That case continues to echo in New York. — FSL.

A Lesson in Reinvention

DAVID OSBORNE
PETER PLASTRIK

City employees in Hampton, Virginia, didn't always do their jobs last year.

Instead of tending to her desk work as assistant city manager, Mary Bunting dug ditches with a city sewer crew.

The heavy construction team in the Public Works Department spent weeks developing a new city park for another agency.

Donald Gurley, the chief housing inspector, put in time to organize an exhibition about city services for the Neighborhood College, the city's training program for residents.

Kevin Gallagher, who runs the city's recycling programs, helped street crews clear away snow and ice.

Most of the city's 1,300 employees participated in one or more of its 115 task forces, advisory groups, self-directed teams, committees and councils—doing work that was not their job.

Why did Hampton's employees behave in these ways? In part it was because Bob O'Neil, the city manager, wanted his assistants to know more about how various agencies really worked. Bunting says the field work changed her assumptions about city sewer employees. They were much more skilled and flexible about taking on new responsibilities than she had expected. The job rotation experience also helped prepare her to run the agency temporarily when Ed Panzer, the public works director, retires.

Motivation was different for the heavy construction team. Under Ed Panzer's stewardship, they took on the park development project when the parks director asked for help. Panzer knew the park was a community priority.

Donald Gurley ran the exhibit for the Neighborhood College because, as he put it, "I opened my big mouth." Two years earlier, he had attended a Neighborhood College session in which department heads made speeches to attendees. "It didn't keep their attention," Gurley says. "I suggested we do something like a career day, letting people rotate around to work stations for each department." People seemed to like the idea. Gurley volunteered to make it happen.

Kevin Gallagher turned up during snowstorms to help clear the streets for the simple reason that it needed to be done. "My job description is recycling manager, but my duty is customer service for the citizens of Hampton," he says. Gallagher enjoys working on teams because it connects him to other employees. "It lets me know who's who in the organization. I invite people into my world, and I dabble in theirs."

Hundreds of employees seized the chance to work elsewhere within the city. The informal networking and connecting with people "means we're more than just organization charts and boxes," says Tharon Greene, director of human resources. "A lot of us feel that by working this way we have a voice in where the organization is going."

In short, an extraordinary number of Hampton employees collaborated avidly with one another and routinely went the extra mile for citizens because they wanted to.

Hampton employees weren't always so flexible. City government used to be a standard issue bureaucracy: The city manager was the boss. Assistant city managers told department heads what to do. The department heads protected their turf, hoarding decisions and information. They commanded middle managers and supervisors, who controlled the day-to-day work of employees.

Managers and employees focused on complying with detailed operational procedures. Communications followed the chain of command: up, over and down. Most people stayed in their institutional boxes and worried about pleasing their bosses. They waited for orders or permission to act. The organization prized loyalty, stability, certainty and control.

Things began to change in 1984, when the mayor and council reviewed the city's condition. Its population was stagnant at 130,000. Taxes were among Virginia's highest. Home values and per-capita income were the lowest in the region. The budget was strained by debt repayments. The city was losing business to nearby communities.

"The statistics scared us," says Mayor James Eason. Hampton was dying in slow motion.

When this realization sunk in, the politicians developed an aggressive economic development agenda, including the acquisition and development of land, improvements in the city's physical appearance and tax cuts. To implement it, they needed a city government that was more responsive to the community's needs, innovative, flexible and action-oriented.

When the city manager retired, Eason and the council went looking for a successor who would change things. They found someone right in town. Bob O'Neill knew the bureaucracy from the inside. A dozen years earlier, he had begun working for the city as a young intern and risen quickly to the post of assistant city manager. But he was also an outsider: In 1979, he had left government to work as a business consultant.

Although many people in city government knew O'Neill, they weren't sure what to expect from him. The council wrote him a performance contract that spelled out specific goals for city government. It emphasized what Eason calls "the Noah Principle" of management: "No more prizes for predicting rain; only prizes for building the ark."

O'Neill didn't have a blueprint for the ark he was supposed to build. The only grand plan he had was a belief that city government had to anticipate and adapt to future changes. "The issue is whether one can be excellent over time, not whether you can do it one time," he says.

To make the organization more adaptable, O'Neill would have to find the levers that would fundamentally change city government's bureaucratic behaviors and instincts.

O'Neill began with what we call the "control" strategy. He told his assistant city managers to stop micromanaging their departments and to work instead on long-term strategic issues, such as the city's relationship with the local schools. He gave directors full control over their agencies.

Then O'Neill created a handful of interdepartmental task forces to focus on major common functions, such as physical infrastructure, public safety and citizen services. He told his directors to build cooperative relationships with those who could support their department's mission. Department heads decided who should participate in the groups and chaired them. The task forces had the power to allocate resources across departmental lines.

For a while, employees weren't sure what to do in the task forces. When O'Neill told department heads that they could structure the task forces any way they wanted, they hesitated "They said, 'What's the answer? Tell us what you *really* want,'" O'Neill recalls. His answer was to assign Assistant City Manager Mike Monteith to help the new groups but not to tell them what to do.

Eventually, the task forces evolved into problem-solving groups. "Someone would say, 'I've got a problem,' and the group dealt with it," O'Neill says.

The change in atmosphere vas noticeable. When Walt Credle joined city government as social services director in 1990, he found that the task forces had fostered a great deal of work across departmental lines and created an environment that was like nothing he had seen before. "There's no sense of competition, of hidden agendas, of politics," he says.

For Don Gurley, the change in control was inspiring. "Information was filtering down to my section," he says. "They wanted my input. That wasn't done before. I was becoming more involved with the process because I was being consulted on different things."

The city government also began pushing control out into the community. When city officials became worried about the number of Hampton youths who were not succeeding in school, they asked the community what should be done. The answers surprised them. "We ended up with a conversation about how the whole community was part of raising a child," says Monteith.

"It was all about the importance of neighborhoods and family." The city organized a community-wide coalition of parents, businesses, community groups, youth advocates and teenagers. More than 5,000 people helped develop recommendations that became part of the city's strategic plan.

Again, when city leaders worried about the health of Hampton's neighborhoods, they shared control of the city's planning process with neighborhood groups. The planning agency also required developers to meet with neighborhood groups before they requested zoning changes and use permits. Then the city created a Department of Neighborhood Services, as recommended by the community coalition, to meet the unique needs of each neighborhood. It provided small grants for neighborhood development, launched an institute to train neighborhood leaders, helped develop neighborhood groups, linked neighborhoods to each other so they could exchange services, and leaned on other city agencies to support neighborhoods.

O'Neill also worked with the city council to set clear goals. This is what we call the "core" strategy. He put department heads on performance contracts that spelled out the results they were expected to produce, then tied their bonuses to their achievements, using the "consequences" strategy.

These efforts began to change the culture. But O'Neill, Mayor Eason and the city council decided that employees also needed what the mayor calls "a compelling vision of a desired state of affairs." Since Eason deems vision "the link between dream and action," he wanted Hampton's elected officials, city managers and public employees to share the same mental picture of the organization's purpose.

O'Neill, the council and hundreds of city employees worked together to develop vision and mission statements that described the purpose and role of city government. The final vision statement pledged that Hampton would become "the most livable city in Virginia." The new mission statement said the city would "bring together the resources of businesses, neighborhoods, community groups and government" in order to realize that vision. The mission embodied the council's view that government should become a broker of the community's resources, not just a provider of services and regulations. The council embraced both statements, and O'Neill used them to develop measurable objectives and action plans for the departments.

" 'The most livable city in Virginia'—everybody knows those words," says Kevin Gallagher. They were hard to miss when he started his first city job. Not only were the words plastered in all city offices, they were "even on our paycheck stubs."

The mission and vision statements were the opening shots in O'Neill's application of the "culture" strategy. The statements began to reshape employees' thinking about how to get their jobs done. For example, the city was under pressure to create community centers in several neighborhoods. But instead of building and operating new centers (the old service role), the city brokered two centers into existence. In one case, officials enticed the YMCA to establish a branch in the wing of a closed high school. The YMCA rehabilitated two gyms and the outside athletic fields, then began raising money to build an extension with an indoor swimming pool. In a second neighborhood, the city renovated a facility, then turned it over to the neighborhood to operate.

The overhauls throughout city government created both anxiety and enthusiasm among employees. Many were unsettled by the new emphasis on performance, autonomy, accountability and change. "For a long time there would be lines of people outside my door who wanted to come in and say, 'Is it OK if we do this?'" recalls Human Resources Director Tharon Greene. Others, including a few top managers, couldn't survive in the new environment.

Most employees liked the changes, though. A majority, O'Neill reports, feel like they have been freed of constraints and can finally do their jobs the way they've always dreamed of doing them.

Nonetheless, as O'Neill's efforts took hold, employees raised all kinds of issues. They were, in effect, testing whether the city was going to be consistent about building a new culture. Some complained, for instance, that there was no way of recognizing people who did extraordinary work over time. The city reacted by creating a program that allowed each department to develop awards for employee innovations and productivity improvements. The agencies shared 10 percent of annual savings with employees and provided awards such as office equipment, dinners and premium parking spaces.

Employees also complained that their compensation did not reward them for customer service. That's when O'Neill instituted an annual bonus based on citizen satisfactory surveys—a version of the "customer" strategy.

Each challenge employees threw at him O'Neill saw as an opportunity to reinforce the culture he was trying to develop "Once you pass these tests enough times and people see things happening differently, they build a commitment to the new culture. The way they think about things and the way they behave changes dramatically."

By the mid-1990s, Hampton was a big success story. The city's financial indicators remained strong even during the recession of the early 1990s. Downtown development had leaped forward. Property taxes, once high, were now among the lowest in Virginia. Debt payments had been cut in half. Mayor Eason had been reelected three times, and his allies on the council had also worn well with voters. Citizen satisfaction with city government hovered around 90 percent. Employee morale, measured annually, was consistently good. Many employees believed a new culture had emerged.

The drive to perform had, however, left the organization exhausted. People were getting tired of change. "People were feeling wrung out," says Tharon Greene. "We'd been doing more with less for years."

In 1995, O'Neill met with his department directors to talk about the problem and to rally the troops. He told them he was just as worn out as they were and wouldn't mind taking a break either. But their world was changing rapidly. If the city wasn't prepared to stay in front of the curve, it would lose its edge. "As much as we'd like to take a break," he told them, "it's not doable."

Then he launched a new wave of changes.

O'Neill had his eye on two challenges. One was problems the city faced that could not be solved within its perimeters. A whole range of issues, such as air quality standards and employment, for instance, transcended city boundaries. The other challenge was that Hampton's citizens still didn't think city government was responding adequately to their neighborhoods' needs.

The city was not well prepared to deal with either challenge. It didn't have strong connections with other entities in the region, and its departmental structure got in the way of creating healthy neighborhoods. "We had trouble getting department heads to buy in to the fact that [neighborhood service] was their priority," says Joan Kennedy, who ran the fledgling unit created to help neighborhoods. "They viewed it as an add-on to the regular job." As a result, she spent most of her time "jumping organizational hurdles."

The Five C's: Strategies for Reinventing Your Government

Underneath the complexity of government systems there are a few fundamental levers that make public institutions work the way they do. Changing the levers triggers shifts that cascade throughout the system.

Here are five powerful strategies to transform the basic levers that shape a government organization or system: its purpose, incentives, accountability systems, power structure and organizational culture.

1. THE CORE STRATEGY: CREATING CLARITY OF PURPOSE

If an organization is unclear about its purpose—or has been given multiple and conflicting purposes—it cannot achieve high performance. The core strategy deals with the essential function of government: steering. It does so by creating new mechanisms to define goals and strategies, and it eliminates functions that no longer contribute to those goals. It uncouples steering from rowing and service delivery from compliance functions, so each organization can focus on one clear purpose.

2. THE CONSEQUENCES STRATEGY: CREATING CONSEQUENCES FOR PERFORMANCE

The usual bureaucratic setup gives employees powerful reasons to follow the rules and keep their heads down—but not much motivation to improve results. This can be changed by creating consequences for producing results. When appropriate, public organizations can be pushed into a competitive marketplace where they have to earn their revenues from their customers. When that is not appropriate, contracting can be used to create competition between public and private organizations (or public and public organizations). When neither is appropriate, performance can be measured to create both positive and negative consequences, such as pay-for-performance, recognition awards or gainsharing bonuses.

3. THE CUSTOMER STRATEGY: PUTTING THE CUSTOMER IN THE DRIVER'S SEAT

Government managers and employees are normally held accountable for following rules and spending their funds as appropriated by elected officials. But public leaders can also hold employees accountable for pleasing their customers by letting those customers choose their service-delivery organizations and setting customer service standards those organizations must meet.

4. THE CONTROL STRATEGY: SHIFTING CONTROL AWAY FROM THE TOP AND CENTER

In bureaucratic systems, most power remains near the top of the hierarchy. Central administrators rule through the use of detailed budget instructions, personnel rules, purchasing procedures and auditing practices. With a control strategy, organizations loosen the grip of the central administrative agencies, then give employees with front-line knowledge the authority to make decisions, respond to customers and solve problems. Sometimes the strategy calls for shifting control all the way out to the community.

5. THE CULTURE STRATEGY: CREATING AND ENTREPRENEURIAL CULTURE

An organization's culture is powerfully shaped by its purpose, incentives, accountability system and power structure. When you change these, the culture changes. But it's not always the kind of transformation leaders were hoping for. At times the metamorphosis tends toward resistance and resentment. Or the change may come too slowly to satisfy customers and policy makers. Hence, virtually every organization that has used the other strategies has eventually decided it needed a deliberate campaign to reshape the habits, hearts and minds of its employees.

In response to these concerns, O'Neill asked his department heads to figure out the make-or-break issues the city faced. They came up with five major challenges: creating healthy families, healthy neighborhoods, healthy businesses, a prospering region and delighted customers. They recommended permanently dismantling the remaining walls between departments and shifting resources to these strategic goals. "We're talking about department boundaries disappearing within a year," says Greene.

No one knows where the process will lead. But in Hampton, this is not unusual. "It's just the next big change," says Assistant City Manager Montieth. "Given that we are continually looking for the better way to make things happen, this organization is going to keep on changing."

Rightsizing in Charlotte

O. WENDELL WHITE
PAM SYFERT
DAVID COOKE

The March 1993 meeting where months of hard and often painful work were laid before the city council marked a significant moment for Charlotte, North Carolina. Detailed for the city council were the following accomplishments of the city organization in response to rightsizing:

- reduction of 272 positions from the city's work force with no layoffs,
- innovations from city employees resulting in $2.8 million in cost savings,
- reductions in layers of management in 12 city departments,
- employees working in teams to accommodate a smaller work force and improve service delivery,
- establishment of the Customer Service Center,
- a planned city-wide reorganization focusing on nine "key businesses" and
- prioritization of city services resulting from a services assessment process.

RIGHTSIZING VS. DOWNSIZING

The City of Charlotte clearly delineates the difference between rightsizing and downsizing, as an analysis of the above accomplishments reveals. Critics of rightsizing had argued that significant change could not occur in the city organization without across-the-board reductions or layoffs. The city demonstrated, however, that through rightsizing—the reallocation of resources and positions from lower to higher priority areas—the government could be run more efficiently.

As the total general fund-supported work force declined by approximately 8 percent from July 1991 to March 1993, the changes by departments and composition of the work force were more dramatic. As shown in Exhibit 1, six departments reduced total positions by more than 20 percent, 11 departments realized reductions ranging from 10 percent to 19 percent, and seven departments increased in size. Some employee groups were affected more than others: proportionally more management, clerical, administrative and other exempt (professional) positions were eliminated than were labor/trade and public safety positions. The resultant composition of the work force is shown in Exhibit 2. These are the results of rightsizing, not downsizing.

How did the city accomplish these things? The story begins in January 1992 when the city manager, faced with the financial realities of the 1990s and the need to embark on a long-term organizational change process, presented the concept of rightsizing at the city council's annual retreat. This article presents a case study of how the leadership and management efforts to rightsize Charlotte's government paid off in a leaner, more effective government. The case study does not detail why the City of Charlotte had to rightsize government, except that the city's revenues could not and would not keep pace with expenditures and Charlotte's city council stands fast against property tax increases.

The premise of rightsizing was to ask the city organization, "If we were to design city services anew today, what would they look like?" The city's approach was to seek answers to four basic questions:

- What services should city government provide?
- How should these services be financed?
- How should resources be organized to deliver services effectively?
- What is the most efficient method of providing city services?

The city's philosophy and intent for rightsizing and the principles and guidelines that would govern the rightsizing process were spelled out in a document called *Rightsizing Public Service: A Process for Managing Change in the '90s.* The principles and guidelines were built around the city's mission statement, *Public Service Is Our Business,* and six core values: quality and excellence, accountability, openness, productivity, teamwork and people development. The [graph on page 421] lists some of the principles and guidelines that governed the rightsizing process. City council approved the rightsizing plan and instructed the city manager to bring results back to council within 12 months.

Charlotte's Blueprint for Rightsizing

- Hiring freeze and job bank
- Retirement incentive program
- Guidelines for layers of management
- A services assessment process
- Citywide workforce teams
- Training as a strategic resource
- Investment in technology
- A customer service center

Exhibit 1

Full-Time Position Changes
July 1991 through February 1993

Departments with reductions of 20 percent or greater

Economic development
Human resources
Manager and mayor
Neighborhood services
Planning
Public service and information

Departments with reductions of 10 percent to 19 percent

Animal control
Budget and evaluation
City attorney
Communications and information services
Community development
Engineering and stormwater
Finance and division of insurance and risk management
General services
Purchasing
Solid waste services
Transportation

Departments with increases

Aviation
City clerk
Community relations
Employment and training
Fire
Police
Utilities

Position reductions by function and area

Management	9.8 percent
Exempt	9.1 percent
Public safety	less than 1 percent
General	
Clerical/admin.	14.5 percent
Labor/trade	6.7 percent

BLUEPRINT FOR RIGHTSIZING

With city council's approval of rightsizing, the city manager had to prepare and mobilize the 5,000-member work force to adopt rightsizing as an organizationwide effort and move the city toward achieving the goals of rightsizing. How does one get 5,000 employees to understand what rightsizing means? How should the effort be organized and started? What would departments and employees be expected to do?

To answer some of those questions, the city manager prepared an internal document titled *Blueprint for Rightsizing,* which described what the organization should look like one year hence, the strategies that would be put into

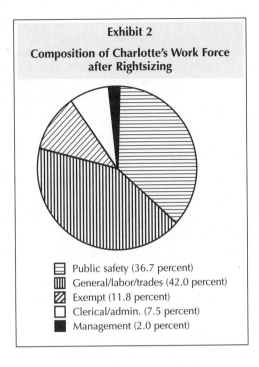

Exhibit 2

Composition of Charlotte's Work Force after Rightsizing

- Public safety (36.7 percent)
- General/labor/trades (42.0 percent)
- Exempt (11.8 percent)
- Clerical/admin. (7.5 percent)
- Management (2.0 percent)

practice to begin the effort, how the strategies would be implemented, and how the progress and achievements of rightsizing would be monitored. The blueprint also outlined the key characteristics and principles the city manager wanted the organization to strive for throughout the rightsizing process. Emphasis would be on leadership, as opposed to supervision, and on decisions made by self-managed work teams. The city organization would aim to be customer focused; decentralized; competitive with private services; able to respond quickly to innovation and technology, new programs or changes in service delivery; innovative and results oriented; and flexible in dealing with citizens.

Eight strategies were used by the city to achieve the objectives of rightsizing: a hiring freeze and job bank, a retirement incentive program, guidelines concerning layers of management, a process for assessing city services, citywide teams, training enhancements, technology investments and a customer service center. Described in the following sections, these strategies were especially significant in view of the city manager's "no layoff" policy.

Hiring Freeze and Job Bank

Prior to and throughout the rightsizing effort, the city had a hiring freeze in effect. Once a job became vacant, it was frozen and placed into the job bank. The job bank concept was used so that critical jobs would still be filled but other vacancies would be banked and evaluated for elimination or transfer to a higher priority city need. Departments could still request to fill vacant positions. These requests were reviewed by a placement committee whose job was to ensure that high priority vacancies were filled, while maintaining the job bank at a designated level during rightsizing.

The hiring freeze and critical review prior to filling positions were based on the premise that each vacancy is an opportunity for change: once a vacancy is created, an adjustment in the organization must take place. The adjustment may be temporary if the vacancy is subsequently filled or may be permanent if the position is eliminated. Each vacancy that was approved to be filled could only be filled, with very few exceptions, by another city employee. As a result, each vacancy being filled created another vacancy that would go through the same review process.

Retirement Incentive Program

The purpose of the retirement incentive program, similar to that of the vacancy freeze, was to create opportunities for change. The program was offered to all employees eligible for full or early retirement in accordance with guidelines of the State of North Carolina's retirement system.

Each eligible employee was offered 26 weeks of his/her salary or $15,000, whichever was greater; those accepting were required to retire between July 1, 1992, and December 31, 1992. In order to fund the retirement incentive program during FY93, all vacancies created through retirements were subject to the freeze and job bank process.

Layers-of-Management Guidelines

Perhaps the most controversial strategy was the guideline related to layers of management. The blueprint stated:

By June 1, 1992, each department will have a plan for reducing layers of management. Those departments with more than 125 employees will have a goal of five layers or less; 50 to 125 employees, three or less; less than 50 employees, two or less.

These arbitrary guidelines were chosen because they would require most (but not all) departments to review their structure for change. Departments were allowed to request an exemption from the guidelines, but the burden of proof was on the department to justify why the desired number of management layers was necessary. During the process some exemptions were requested, but no exemptions were granted.

Services Assessment Process

A services assessment process was used to answer the question, "What services should Charlotte's city government provide?" This process, which involved the city council throughout, included inventorying all city services, identifying their costs and prioritizing the services.

The methodology adopted called for categorizing city services into 41 service profiles (police patrol, residential garbage collection, firefighting and rescue, housing preservation, landscape maintenance, crime prevention, etc.) and using "paired comparisons" to assess services along two dimensions: the relative importance and the relative effectiveness of the service.

Participating in the assessment of services were the mayor and city council, a city-management group and a 44-member citizens' assessment panel. Each person who participated in the assessment process was provided a written description of the 41 service categories and, using a personal computer, made 1,640 individual selections (each of the 41 service categories compared with one another) responding to the question: "In your opinion, which of the following two services is of more importance and value to the community of Charlotte?" Exhibit 3 lists the top 10 services ranked by their relative importance. Another 1,640 individual selections were made responding to the question, "From the customer's point of view, which of these two services is being provided better?" The results of the assessments were then plotted on a matrix with the horizontal axis representing the relative importance of the service and the vertical axis representing the relative effectiveness of the service.

Participation from the Work Force in Citywide Teams

The rightsizing effort involved a citywide organization team, innovations team and communications team. Each team included employees from all levels of the organization and from the various departments.

The organization team's objective was to assist in developing a new organizational model emphasizing the principles described in the blueprint. The product of their work was a document entitled "Model and Principles for Organizational Change," which included a set of tools to assist departments in evaluating their organizations.

The innovations team was charged with challenging any of the practices, policies and procedures of the city and recommending changes. The $2.8 million in savings that this team identified in one year included such actions as:

- implementing a computerized sign-in/sign-out board, which realized $23,000 in staff savings;
- bringing the task of construction inspection in-house using temporary construction inspectors rather than consultants, which created savings of $30,000; and
- negotiating a new contract for long-distance telephone rates, which reduced these costs by 30 percent.

The goal of the communications team was to communicate the efforts, challenges, achievements and status of the various rightsizing initiatives. This

Exhibit 3
Overall Rankings:
Relative Importance of Service

Rank	Service
1	Police patrol
2	Firefighting/rescue
3	Criminal investigations
4	Police street drug interdiction
5	Pick-up household waste/recyclables
6	Crime lab
7	Crime prevention
8	Transit system
9	Youth services (police)
10	Move traffic

team's many methods of communicating with employees included a biweekly "Rightsizing Update" distributed with each employee's paycheck, brown-bag lunch meetings, a rightsizing hotline for employees to call with questions, and monthly business meetings conducted by the city manager which were televised on the city's training channel so employees in outlying locations—fire stations, water treatment plants, etc.—could participate in the meeting. A feature of these monthly meetings consisted of the city manager responding to anonymous questions from the audience. Many of these communications tools continue to be used today.

Training as a Strategic Resource

During a large-scale organizational change, training is a key factor for success. Charlotte's training team, which had been part of the human resources department, began reporting directly to the city manager's office, and additional city staff were temporarily transferred to the team. Training was offered to all city employees in the areas of stress and change management, customer service, working in teams, etc. Retraining was also a critical need during rightsizing, as the city is committed to training and retraining employees who are transferred into new positions.

Investment in Technology

The city committed funds for technology improvements to help realize the goals of rightsizing. The intent was to use technology to enable employees to work in teams, flatten layers of management, reduce clerical and administrative positions, and improve internal and external communication and customer service. Control policies were loosened, lifting restrictions that had prevented departments from acquiring cellular phones, personal computers, pagers, etc. These and other investments— in phone mail equipment, local and wide area networks, electronic bulletin boards, etc.—highlighted all of the above changes.

Customer Service Center

The city is committed to delivering outstanding customer service. By establishing the Customer Service Center during rightsizing, the city achieved two goals: 1) it improved service to citizens/customers by providing one phone number to call to get questions answered or problems resolved and 2) it focused the organization on one of the keys to success—customer service.

WHAT WORKED WELL?

Hindsight is 20/20. It is easy to look back now and see what went well, what did not go well and what made it difficult to succeed. Observations on what went well, what made rightsizing work, are presented below.

Consistent and Committed Leadership

The leaders made it clear from the start that this was to be a serious, long-term effort; they did not waiver when there were few answers to many questions; they did not quit when the going got tough. Consistency is key in overcoming the "This is just another management initiative" attitude.

RIGHTSIZING IN CHARLOTTE: PRINCIPLES AND GUIDELINES

Accountability

- The city council will be responsible for assessing the need for city services and how they should be financed.
- The city manager will be responsible for organizing resources for effective and efficient service delivery.
- Each city employee is accountable for doing his/her job as productively as possible. Employees will be empowered to make decisions at the lowest appropriate level.

Quality and Excellence

- City services will be determined by the values and priorities of the community, not the organization.
- The highest priority will be given to those services that serve customers directly.
- Our goal is to achieve 100 percent of established customer service objectives.

Productivity

- We will continue to use a managed vacancy program for reassigning employees. Under rightsizing, any filled positions identified for elimination will be handled by offering these employees retraining and reassignment to positions in high priority service areas. There will be no layoffs as a result of rightsizing.
- We want our employees to be motivated, well-trained and compensated fairly in order to provide the highest level of service to the public.
- We are open to and use a variety of ways to streamline services and reduce costs. Strategies include ongoing analyses of operations, consolidation, privatization and application of latest technologies.

Teamwork

- We value and emphasize teamwork. We encourage employee communications up, down and across organizational lines.
- We expect the team concept to result in a flatter organizational structure, inverting the traditional hierarchy and emphasizing bottom-up communication.

Openness

- We desire and expect all employees to challenge the traditional ways of providing service in an open, nonthreatening environment.
- We will keep all employees fully informed of the progress and decisions made on rightsizing.

Communication with Employees

City staff learned to communicate in ways they never did before. Over-communication is impossible during organizational change.

Participation from Employees

Rightsizing cannot be done without the involvement of many because, first, employees providing a service are the best source of ideas when an organization is looking for ways to improve and, secondly, most people want to participate in events that will impact and shape their jobs and their careers.

Involvement of City Council

City council's role in rightsizing centered around the question: What services should the city government provide and at what level? Their role in the services assessment process included participating in the selection of the assessment process, preparing the request for proposals, interviewing and selecting consultants, and participating in the assessments. City council owned a part of the process and participated in its success.

A Variety of Strategies

Not all strategies worked as well as planned, while others exceeded expectations. Trying several strategies increased the chances of success

An Overall Plan

The *Blueprint for Rightsizing* became the focal point for the entire organization. It laid out the plan for the city to follow.

Willingness to Change

The city was willing to change its systems. Early in the process the leaders realized that the city's current pay and classification system did not support the organization that it was trying to become. The city scrapped the old one (without having a new one) and set out to design one anew.

WHAT WERE THE OBSTACLES?

The main obstacles that made rightsizing difficult were mostly related to employees' reaction to change.

The Power of Tradition

Many of the city's departments were known for being among the most progressive and emulated in the nation. Employees were hard pressed to understand why change was needed when one's reputation was already strong. "If it ain't broke, don't fix it" was a common phrase heard early during rightsizing. Few were willing to adopt the attitude of "If it ain't broke, break it!"

although that is what had to be done in many cases. City government tradition was difficult to overcome, and the leaders had to remain committed to change.

Lack of Incentives for Change

Other than the promise that no one would be laid off, and that rightsizing could help the city succeed for the benefit of the community, there were no incentives for change. If the city were to rewrite the blueprint, it certainly would include an incentive strategy as well.

Employee Morale

No matter how well the leaders communicate and how they try to reduce negative impacts, morale still suffers during organizational change. The bottom line is: employees do not like uncertainty, which is an inevitable element during any change process.

Variable Rates of Change

Once the blueprint was introduced, departments and employees responded differently and at different paces. Some departments took off—developed their own internal blueprint, established teams, organized to meet the objective of rightsizing, etc. Some departments took smaller, more careful and less radical steps. Some departments did not do anything and waited to see if rightsizing was real. This situation requires tracking the progress and achievements of the various departments and devising follow-up strategies to address individual situations.

MOVING FORWARD

Two years after first presenting rightsizing to city council, the City of Charlotte is still moving forward with initiatives that were started during rightsizing:

- a city-wide reorganization around nine key businesses took place in September 1993;
- a new pay and classification system, called broadbanding, was initiated in August 1993;
- the city is beginning to learn what it means to compete with the private sector and has competitively bid some services;
- the city implemented incentive pay programs beginning in fiscal year 1994.

Rightsizing allows employees to realize how successful they can be when they collectively participate in change and that they can adapt strategies into their everyday work environment to achieve the ingredients for continuous improvement. If that happens, the city will never again have to write a blueprint for rightsizing.

Acknowledgments (continued from page ii)

"Why Study Bureaucracy?" by Peter M. Blau and Marshall W. Meyer. From Peter M. Blau and Marshall W. Meyer, *Bureaucracy in Modern Society,* Third Edition, pp. 3-14, 18-25. Copyright © 1987 by Random House. Used by permission of McGraw-Hill, Inc.

"Public and Private Management: Are They Fundamentally Alike in All Unimportant Respects?" by Graham T. Allison, Jr. This article was presented as part of the Public Management Research Conference, Brookings Institution, Washington, D.C., November 1979. Used by permission of the author.

"Working for the Government Is Cool" by Garth Cook. From *The Washington Monthly.* Copyright by The Washington Monthly Company, 1611 Connecticut Avenue, N.W., Washington, D.C. 20009. Reprinted with permission.

"The Rise of the Bureaucratic State" by James Q. Wilson. From *The Public Interest,* No. 41 (Fall 1975). Used by permission of the author.

"American Bureaucracy in a Changing Political Setting" by Francis E. Rourke. From *Journal of Public Administration Research and Theory,* I, No. 2 (April 1991), pp. 111-129. Reprinted by permission.

"The Evolution of American Federalism" by Alice M. Rivlin. From *Reviving the American Dream.* Copyright © 1992. Reprinted by permission of the Brookings Institution.

"Fine Print: The Contract with America, Devolution, and the Administrative Realities of American Federalism" by John J. DiIulio, Jr., and Donald F. Kettl. From *Brookings' Center for Public Management Report* CPM 95-1 (March 1, 1995). Reprinted by permission of the Brookings Institution Press.

"Two Roads to Serfdom: Liberalism, Conservatism, and Administrative Power" by Theodore J. Lowi. From *American University Law Review,* 36, no. 2 (1987), pp. 295-322, as it was modified to appear in *A New Constitutionalism,* edited by Stephen L. Elkin and Karol Edward Solton, 1993. Reprinted with permission.

"Accountability Battles in State Administration" by William T. Gormley, Jr. From *The State of the States,* Second Edition, Carl E. Van Horn, ed., pp. 171-191. Used by permission of Congressional Quarterly Press.

"Public Administration and Ethics" by Dwight Waldo. Reprinted by permission of the publisher. From *The Enterprise of Public Administration: A Summary View* by Dwight Waldo. Copyright © 1980 by Chandler & Sharp Publishers, Inc. All rights reserved.

"The Evolution of Work in Public and Private Bureaucracies" by Russell M. Linden. From *Seamless Government: A Practical Guide to Re-engineering in the Public Sector.* Copyright © 1994 Jossey-Bass Inc., Publishers. Reprinted with permission.

"Reframing Organizational Leadership" by Lee G. Bolman and Terrence E. Deal. Used by permission from the authors.

"The Implications of Changing Technology" by James L. Perry and Kenneth L. Kraemer. From *Revitalizing State and Local Public Service,* edited by Frank J. Thompson. Copyright © 1993 Jossey-Bass Inc., Publishers. Reprinted with permission.

"The State of Merit in the Federal Government" by Patricia W. Ingraham and David H. Rosenbloom. From *Agenda for Excellence: Public Service in America,* edited by Patricia Ingraham and Donald F. Kettl. Copyright © 1992. Used by permission of Chatham House Publishers.

"Realizing the Promise of Diversity" by Sonia M. Ospina. From *Handbook of Public Administration,* Second Edition, edited by James L. Perry. Copyright © 1996 Jossey-Bass Inc., Publishers. Reprinted with permission.

"Mapping the Federal Budget Process" by Allen Schick, from his book *The Federal Budget* (Brookings, 1995). Reprinted by permission of the Brookings Institution Press.

"Sense and Nonsense about Budget Deficits" by Robert Eisner. From *Harvard Business Review* (May-June 1993), pp. 99-111. Copyright © 1993 by the President and Fellows of Harvard College. All rights reserved.

"Policy Analysis" by Laurence E. Lynn, Jr. From *Managing Public Policy*, pp. 170-180 (Exclusive of Figure 8-1 on page 279). Copyright © 1987 by Laurence E. Lynn, Jr. Reprinted by permission of HarperCollins Publishers, Inc. Excerpt (p. 277) from the case "Joan Claybrook and NHTSA (C) (385.0)," written by David Whitman under the supervision of Professor Mark H. Moore for use at the John F. Kennedy School of Government, Harvard University. Copyright © 1981 by the President and Fellows of Harvard College. Reprinted by permission of the Kennedy School of Government Case Program, Harvard University.

"Two Decades of Implementation Research: From Control to Guidance and Learning" by Paul A. Sabatier. Reprinted with the permission of Paul A. Sabatier, copyright holder.

"Performance Measurement in Local Government" by David N. Ammons. From *Accountability for Performance* (ICMA, 1995), adapted from "Performance Measurement and Benchmarking" in *Municipal Benchmarks* (Sage Publications, 1996). Copyright © 1996 by Sage Publications, Inc.

"Understanding Government Regulation" by Richard Lehne. From *Industry and Politics* by Richard Lehne. Copyright © 1993. Reprinted by permission of Prentice-Hall, Inc., Upper Saddle River, NJ.

"Privatization Revisited" by William T. Gormley, Jr. From *Policy Studies Review* (Autumn/Winter 1994), pp. 214-234. Permission granted by The Public Studies Organization, University of Illinois at Urbana-Champaign, Urbana, Illinois 61801.

"Public-Private Partnerships in the Twenty-First Century" by Graham Finney and David A. Grossman. Copyright © 1998 by Graham Finney and David A. Grossman. Used with permission from the authors.

"Reinventing Government" Copyright © 1992 by David Osborne and Ted Gaebler. Reprinted by permission of Perseus Books Publishers, a member of Perseus Books, L.L.C.

"Reinventing the American Federal Government: Reform Redux or Real Change?" by Patricia W. Ingraham. From *Public Administration*, Vol. 74 (Autumn 1996), pp. 453-475. Permission granted by Blackwell Publishers.

"Coping with Global Interdependence" by Jeffrey S. Luke and Gerald A. Caiden. From *Handbook of Public Administration*, edited by James L. Perry. Copyright © 1989 Jossey-Bass Inc., Publishers. Reprinted by permission.

"A Few Modest Suggestions That May Make a Small Difference" by James Q. Wilson. From *Bureaucracy: What Government Agencies Do and Why They Do It.* Copyright © 1989 by Basic Books, Inc. Reprinted by permission of Basic Books, a subsidiary of Perseus Books Group, L.L.C.

"The FEMA Phoenix: How One Federal Agency Rose from the Ashes to Become a Symbol of What Government Can Do" by Daniel Franklin. Reprinted with permission from *The Washington Monthly.* Copyright by The Washington Monthly Company, 1611 Connecticut Avenue, N.W., Washington, D.C. 20009.

"How to Run a Police Department" by George L. Kelling. This article first appeared in the Autumn 1995 issue of *City Journal,* a publication of the Manhattan Institute for Policy Research. Used with permission.

"A Lesson in Reinvention" by David Osborne and Peter Plastrik. Copyright © 1997 by David Osborne and Peter Plastrik. Reprinted by permission of Perseus Books Publishers, a member of Perseus Books, L.L.C.

"Rightsizing in Charlotte" by O. Wendell White, Pam Syfert, and David Cooke. From *Government Finance Review* (December 1994), pp. 7-10. Reprinted with permission from the Government Finance Officers Association, Washington, D.C.

Figure 8-1 (p. 279): "Classification of Policy Analysts" from *Policy Analysts in the Bureaucracy* by Arnold Meltsner. Copyright © 1976 The Regents of the University of California. Reprinted with permission of University of California Press. Appeared in *Managing Public Policy* by Laurence E. Lynn, Jr., Fig. 7-1, p. 179.

Excerpt (p. 302): Reprinted with permission from the September 1991 issue of *Public Management* magazine *(PM)*, published by the International City/County Management Association (ICMA), Washington, D.C.

About the Authors

Students are often curious about the authors of the articles they are reading. For that reason, a brief note about each contributor to this anthology is included below.

Graham T. Allison Jr. is Douglas Dillon Professor of Government and former dean of the John F. Kennedy School of Government at Harvard University; he is also the author of *Essence of Decision: Explaining the Cuban Missile Crisis.*

David N. Ammons is an associate professor in the Institute of Government at the University of North Carolina, Chapel Hill, and author of *Municipal Benchmarks: Assessing Local Performance and Establishing Community Standards.*

Peter M. Blau is Robert Broughton Distinguished Research Professor of Sociology at the University of North Carolina, Chapel Hill.

Garth Cook is an editor of the *Washington Monthly* magazine.

Lee G. Bolman is Marion Bloch Professor of Leadership at the Bloch School of Business and Public Administration, University of Missouri, Kansas City.

Gerald A. Caiden is Professor of Public Administration in the School of Public Administration, University of Southern California, in Los Angeles.

David Cooke is Director of Business Support Services for the City of Charlotte, North Carolina.

Terrence E. Deal is Professor of Education at Peabody College of Vanderbilt University in Nashville, Tennessee, and coauthor (with Lee G. Bolman) of *Reframing Organizations: Artistry, Choice, and Leadership,* second edition.

John J. DiIulio Jr. is Professor of Politics and Public Affairs at Princeton University, and director of the Partnership for Research on Religion and At-Risk Youth, based in Philadelphia.

A past president of the American Economic Association, **Robert Eisner** is William R. Kenan Professor of Economics at Northwestern University, Evanston, Illinois.

Formerly a founder of Public-Private Ventures and a principal with the Conservation Company, **Graham Finney** is a Philadelphia-based consultant to public and nonprofit organizations.

Daniel Franklin writes for the *Washington Monthly* and other publications.

Formerly a City Manager in Ohio and California, **Ted Gaebler** is president of the Gaebler Group, a public-sector management consulting firm in San Rafael, California.

William T. Gormley Jr. teaches political science, public policy, and public administration at Georgetown University, Washington, D.C.

A former New York City Budget Director, **David A. Grossman** is the president of Nova Institute, Inc., a New York City-based, nonprofit management consulting and policy analysis organization.

Patricia W. Ingraham is Professor of Public Administration and Political Science at the Maxwell School of Citizenship and Public Affairs, Syracuse University, Syracuse, New York.

George L. Kelling is a criminologist who teaches at Northeastern University, Boston, Massachusetts, and is a consultant to police departments across the country.

Donald F. Kettl is a professor in the Department of Political Science and Director of the Robert M. La Follette Institute of Public Affairs at the University of Wisconsin, Madison, Wisconsin.

Kenneth L. Kraemer is a professor in the Graduate School of Management at the University of California, Irvine.

Frederick S. Lane is a professor in the School of Public Affairs, Bernard M. Baruch College, City University of New York.

Richard Lehne teaches political science at Rutgers University, New Brunswick, New Jersey.

Russell M. Linden is a management consultant based in northern Virginia; he is also the author of *Seamless Government: A Practical Guide to Re-engineering in the Public Sector.*

One of America's most prominent political scientists, **Theodore J. Lowi** is John L. Senior Professor of American Institutions at Cornell University, Ithaca, New York.

Jeffrey S. Luke is a faculty member in the Department of Planning, Public Policy, and Management and is Director of the Bureau of Governmental Research and Service at the University of Oregon, Eugene, Oregon.

Laurence E. Lynn Jr. is Professor of Public Policy Studies and of Social Service Administration at the University of Chicago; he has held a number of high-level positions in the federal government, including assistant secretary (planning and evaluation) of the Department of Health, Education, and Welfare, and assistant secretary (program development and budget) of the Department of the Interior.

Marshall W. Meyer is a faculty member at the Wharton School of the University of Pennsylvania in Philadelphia.

A Boston-based consultant to governments, **David Osborne** is the coauthor (with Ted Gaebler) of *Reinventing Government: How the Entrepreneurial Spirit Is Transforming the Public Sector.*

Sonia M. Ospina teaches public administration at the Robert F. Wagner School of Public Service, New York University.

James L. Perry is a professor in the School of Public and Environmental Affairs, Indiana University, Bloomington, Indiana.

A former executive in the Michigan State Department of Commerce, **Peter Plastrik** is coauthor (with David Osborne) of *Banishing Bureaucracy: The Five Strategies for Reinventing Government.*

An economist, **Alice M. Rivlin** is Vice Chairman of the Board of Governors of the Federal Reserve System; she was formerly director of the U. S. Office of Management and Budget and the first director of the Congressional Budget Office.

David H. Rosenbloom is Distinguished Professor of Public Administration at American University in Washington, D.C.

Francis E. Rourke is Benjamin H. Griswold III Professor of Public Policy Studies at Johns Hopkins University in Baltimore, Maryland.

Paul A. Sabatier is a professor in the Division of Environmental Studies, University of California, Davis.

Allen Schick is Professor of Public Policy at George Mason University, Fairfax, Virginia.

Pam Syfert is the deputy city manager of the City of Charlotte, North Carolina.

Dwight Waldo is Professor Emeritus of Public Administration at the Maxwell School of Citizenship and Public Affairs, Syracuse University, where he held the Schweitzer Chair in the Humanities.

O. Wendell White is the city manager of Charlotte, North Carolina.

A political scientist, **James Q. Wilson** is James Collins Professor of Management in the John E. Anderson Graduate School of Management, University of California, Los Angeles, and author of *Bureaucracy: What Government Agencies Do and Why They Do It.*